The Restaurants of New York
1978-1979 Edition

THE
RESTAURANTS
of NewYork
1978-1979 Edition

SEYMOUR BRITCHky

RANDOM HOUSE NEW YORK

All of the reviews in the book originally appeared, in somewhat different form, in *The Restaurant Reporter,* except the following, which appeared in *New York* magazine: Auberge Suisse, Brasserie, Café Loup, Hermitage, Hungaria, Market Dining Rooms & Bar, La Métairie, Mon Paris, René Pujol, Russian Tea Room, United States Steakhouse Co. and Le Veau d'Or.

Library of Congress Cataloging in Publication Data

Britchky, Seymour.
The restaurants of New York, 1978–1979 Edition.

Edition for 1977–1978 published under title:
Seymour Britchky's Restaurants of New York.
1. New York (City)—Restaurants, lunch rooms, etc. I. Title.
TX909.B74 1978   647'.957471   78–57105
ISBN 0–394–73480–7

Manufactured in the United States of America
2 4 6 8 9 7 5 3
First Edition

CONTENTS

Introduction

On an average night in New York there are more people eating out in restaurants than there are in all the concert halls, at all the ballet performances or in all the Broadway theaters. Second-rate restaurants have more patrons than first-run movie houses. The museums of art by day never draw as well as the restaurants of Chinatown by night. Attendance at an Italian opera at the Metropolitan Opera House is easily surpassed by the number of pasta eaters eating out in Little Italy and Greenwich Village during the same hours. Yet fans of music and dance, theater and art can read in the local press the essays of first- to fifth-string critics who note for all time everything from doomed debuts and hopeless opening nights to has-been farewell performances; while citizens who prefer to spend their hours and paychecks in this city's restaurants are served in New York's press by a pathetic string of primitive and sophomoric critical mentalities. Their coverage of the field is shallow, cute, exhibitionistic, pedantic, preachy—little people wallowing up to their toenails in the dizzying power of public judgment.

It will be argued that restaurants are inherently less noble than art, that the tawdry attention they are given is what they merit. Even if we accept the notion that *Annie* is more uplifting than a perfect soufflé, there is no excuse for suspending the principles of critical appraisal when the subjects are merely restaurants. Yet most of the people who write about eating places seem to think they have fulfilled their responsibilities when they have revealed their preferences or passed judgments of "right" or "wrong."

Nothing is more irrelevant to a critic's work than his likes and dislikes, and nothing is more destructive to his subject than the handy collection of rules he carries around in his head where his open mind belongs. It is not a critic's job to love or loathe; it is his job to evaluate, and the standards of evaluation vary from subject to subject—they inhere in the pretensions and objectives of the subjects themselves. We do not criticize *Die Fledermaus* for failing to be *Fidelio,* or a meat loaf because it is not a pâté en croûte. Either of either pair is capable of succeeding or failing on its own terms, and no other standards are anything more than tangential.

There was a restaurant critic who, when asked his opinion of certain Italian wines, answered that he drank only French wines. We may as well have restaurant writers who are vegetarians, or who eat only kosher food, or who cannot be bothered with fish because of the bones.

And when our critics are not averting their noses from what they did not learn to like at their mothers' knees or on the grand tour, they reserve judgment on what they eat until they have looked it up to see if it was made according to Hoyle. It is something of a burden to New Yorkers in search of a hot meal and a good time to be stuck with critics who cannot enjoy themselves without consulting authority. Some of these critics have never lost touch with their earliest educations, when the correct answers were in the back of the book. Many good restaurants are dismissed by them because their virtues are not in the back of the book. The principal danger of the grammar-school school of critics is their love of joyless restaurants that score high on standard tests—the Coach House is the kind of place they are always pushing.

It is the restaurant critic's responsibility to have a capacity for pleasure that encompasses a motley scene. But the first function of a critic—literary critic, music critic, any kind of critic—is to describe, so that the reader learns about the subject rather than the critic. When restaurant critics tell us that this or that is "mouth-watering," which they do tediously often, all we have learned is that they salivate. The purpose of this book—invective, derisions and lyricisms notwithstanding—is to make the places described seem real to the reader. The author's opinions, clearly as they may show through, are secondary.

Nevertheless, for those who demand it, the sums of these opinions are abbreviated, as follows:

★★★★	Excellent
★★★	Very good
★★	Good
★	Good (but not *as* good)
●	Acceptable
○	Unacceptable

It is hoped and intended that readers will give more attention to the text than to the stars and circles.

Withal, and despite the fact that this edition of *The Restaurants of New York* includes more reviews than previous ones, we have included, on pages xxvii–

xxviii, a Supplementary List of 170 restaurants with star and circle ratings only. Complete reviews of most of these restaurants appeared in earlier editions. Space limitations make it impossible to include full reviews of them in this one. These places are, by and large, of less interest than those that are reviewed fully in this volume, though many of them are more than decent. This Supplementary List is intended mainly to confirm, or protect you from, advice from other sources.

TEN SENSIBLE RULES ABOUT GOING TO, EATING IN, PAYING AT AND DEPARTING FROM NEW YORK RESTAURANTS

1. RESERVATIONS. Before going to a New York restaurant, telephone to make a reservation. True, reservations are often not accepted, but this is sometimes because the restaurant no longer exists. By telephoning you determine whether the place is still in business, and if so, whether you can get a table when you want one.

2. NO RESERVATIONS. If a restaurant does not accept reservations, it is probably because it is so busy that it can get away without offering the convenience. Ask if the place is likely to be crowded when you want to go. Sometimes you will get a helpful answer, sometimes an honest one, sometimes both.

3. COMPLAINTS. It's no fun to complain throughout your meal. After all, you go to a restaurant to enjoy yourself, your food and your companions. But it's a good idea to complain about *something* early on. People who complain are people who seem to know what they want and what they are about, and they get better treatment than the timid or unsure. If you are shy or diffident, or don't know what you want, that's too bad, but it need not be a guarantee that you will not enjoy eating in New York restaurants.

4. SENDING BACK. If you don't like something you ordered, tell the waiter it tastes terrible and send it back. Do the same thing if what should be hot food is cold or if there is anything else clearly wrong with what is brought to you.

5. WINE. If you like wine but don't know much about it, order an inexpensive bottle. Modestly priced wines are the most reliable ones in restaurants. They are what they are. Restaurants are not the places to give yourself a wine education; it is much too expensive and unreliable. Expensive wines in restaurants may be too young or too old, or damaged from poor storage, and if you're unsure of yourself, you may not know why you don't like what you get and whether you really ought to return it. If there is a sommelier (the man with the chain around his neck), his business is to sell you wine (after suitable discussion), pour your first glass, and generally convert the purchase and consumption of a bottle of mild booze into an important event. Few New York restaurants have sommeliers any more, but those that do generally have pretty good wine stocks. If the sommelier seems like a decent sort and if you want to spring for a fancy bottle, tell him how much you are willing to spend, and he will recommend a bottle at the price, and probably a good one.

6. EMERGENCIES. If you need service at once and are unable to catch your waiter's or captain's eye, the best system is to rise from your chair and approach the nearest responsible member of the staff. The late English conductor Sir Thomas Beecham used to brush dishes to the floor to get attention, but as most dining-room floors in New York restaurants are carpeted, this ploy might go unnoticed. Flinging dishes against the walls or ceiling, however, is a sure-fire way to bring the help.

7. YOUR CHECK. Review it. It's wrong about one time in ten; in your favor

about one time in a hundred. Ask for a menu to check the prices if you think you have been overcharged or charged for a more expensive item than the one you ordered. Check the addition. Of course you may have had a few drinks and a bottle of wine, while the waiter is probably sober, so he may be right, and you may be wrong.

8. TIPPING—HOW. Don't leave your tip under a plate. It simply is not done. If you want to give someone a tip, hand it to him. If you don't spot him, leave the money out in the open where it is easy to see. If you're tipping on a credit card voucher, write in the tip *and write in the grand total.* If you do not, an emendation may be made favoring the waiter and penalizing you. This is so common that the credit-card companies have a name for it; they call it an "override."

9. TIPPING—HOW MUCH. Par is 15 percent of the before-tax food total, plus some lesser percentage of the liquor and wine. If you are served by both a waiter and a captain, 20 percent is fair, most of it to the waiter, the exact proportion depending on whether the captain did no more than cursorily take your order or if, at the other extreme, he thoroughly explained the menu, prepared sauces and desserts, and helped with the selection of wine.

Reasons for tipping more: You ate the least expensive items on the menu and occupied the table for three hours; the service was terrific; you are feeling expansive.

Reasons for tipping less: The reverse of the above, except that waiters should not be penalized for your depression unless it is their fault.

Sommeliers should be tipped $2 per bottle, but no less than $3 in total if they have been really helpful.

10. DEPARTURE. Leave when you are good and ready. It is your right to eat at your own pace, including lingering over a second cup of coffee. Enjoy possession of a table that others are waiting in line for. Later they will.

A NOTE ON PRICES

The restaurants in this book have been classified as "inexpensive," "medium-priced," "expensive" or "very expensive."

When the book went to press, these categorizations were roughly defined as follows, for complete dinners for two, with wine or some other suitable beverage, tax and tip included:

> Inexpensive: $30 or less
> Medium-priced: $30 to $45
> Expensive: $45 to $55
> Very expensive: More than $55

By the time the book is printed, bound, distributed and purchased by you, these definitions, in many instances, will no longer be accurate. First, prices in all restaurants seem to go up steadily—that is inflation. Second, if an inexpensive or medium-priced restaurant is doing very well, it may shift from one category to the next—that is the profit motive. A press-time $30 dinner may run to $45 by the time you eat it.

In some few instances specific prices of dishes or drinks or wines are referred to in the text. They are meant to give an impression of the restaurant's pricing policy. The information was correct when written, and the impression is probably still correct, even if the exact price has changed.

Listings of Restaurants

BY TYPE OF FOOD

AMERICAN

xiv

BY RATING

★ GOOD (but not *as* good)

● ACCEPTABLE

○ UNACCEPTABLE

BY NEIGHBORHOOD

OPEN ON SUNDAY

OPEN LATE (until midnight, or later, each night that the restaurant is open for business)

SUITABLE (by reason of economy/menu/accommodations) FOR LARGE FAMILY GROUPS

Beansprout **19**
Benihana of Tokyo **21**
Brasserie **32**
Cedars of Lebanon **50**
Gage & Tollner **107**
Ho's Pavilion **135**
Lüchow's **152**
Lundy's **153**
Mamma Leone's **161**
Marchi's **162**
Oh-Ho-So **188**

Oscar's Salt of the Sea **198**
Oyster Bar & Restaurant **199**
Rusty's **251**
Shun Lee Palace **268**
Silver Palace **271**
Sun Hop Kee **277**
Szechuan **283**
Tavern on the Green **284**
Trattoria **296**
Ukrainian Restaurant **299**
Uncle Tai's Hunan Yuan **300**

OUTDOOR DINING AND ENCLOSED GARDENS

Barbetta **18**
La Cocotte **70**
DaSilvano **84**
David K's Chung Kuo Yuan **85**
Italian Pavilion **141**

Lutèce **154**
L'Olivier **192**
Paris Bistro **208**
Ruc **248**
Tavern on the Green **284**

ENCLOSED SIDEWALK CAFÉS

Beansprout **19**
Ginger Man **116**
Maxwell's Plum **167**
O. Henry's Steak House **187**

O'Neals' Baloon **194**
Victor's Café **308**
Vivolo **311**

BRING YOUR OWN WINE (or whatever)

Caffè da Alfredo **43**
Casa Brasil **48**
Cuisine of Szechuan **78**
East-West Cookery **91**
India Pavilion **139**
Le Petit Pré **221**
Phoenix Garden **222**

Sabor **252**
Sakura Chaya **254**
Silver Palace **271**
Sloppy Louie's **272**
Sun Hop Kee **277**
El Tenampa **289**

SUPPLEMENTARY LIST . . . 170 Manhattan
restaurants rated without comment

- Adam's Rib
- L'Aiglon
- À la Fourchette
○ Allen's Catch of the Sea
- Antolotti's
★ Aperitivo
○ Artists and Writers
○ Ashley's
★ Assembly Steak House
- Aunt Fish
- Ballroom
- Il Bambino
★ Le Beau Père
★ Le Bec Fin
- Berry's
- La Bibliothèque
- Bistro Montmarte
- Bo-Bo
★ Le Boeuf à la Mode
- Bondini's
★ Brazilian Coffee
- Bristol
★ Brittany du Soir
○ Bull & Bear
★ Cabana Carioca
- Café Argenteuil
★ Café de France
○ Café du Soir
○ Café Nicholson
- Caliban
★ Capriccio
- Captain's Table
○ Cattleman
- La Cave Henri IV
★ Le Chambertin
★ Le Chanteclair
- Charlie & Kelly
★ La Chaumière
- Chef Ma's
○ Chelsea Place
★ Le Cheval Blanc
○ Le Chevalier
★ Chez Vous

★ Chi Mer
- Christo's
○ Christy's Skylite Gardens
★ Chun Cha Fu
○ Company
- Coriander
★ El Cortijo
★ Csarda
- D'Angelo's
○ Di Anni
○ Dubrovnik
★ L'Esterel
○ Farnie's 2nd Ave. Steak Parlour
- El Faro 72
- Fiorello's
- 411 Bleecker Street
- Four Five Six
★ French Shack
- Gaetano
★ Il Gattopardo
- Gavroche
- Genghiz Khan's Bicycle
- Georges Rey
- Gingko Tree
- Gino's
○ Giordano
★ Giovanni
★ Grand Ticino
○ Great Aunt Fanny's
○ La Griglia
★ La Grillade
- La Groceria
★ Ground Floor
- Harvey's Seafood House
★ Havana East
- Hopper's
- Horn of Plenty
- Hunan Balcony
- Hungarian Rendezvous
★ Inagiku
- Inca
○ Isle of Capri
★ Jacques' Tik Tak

- Jimmy's La Grange
- ★ John's
- Katja
- ★ Kenny's Steak Pub
- Kleine Konditorei
- Knickerbocker Steak House
- Landmark Tavern
- Larré's
- Laurent
- Leopard
- Livorno
- ○ Lou G. Siegel
- ★ Maharaja India
- ★ Malaga
- ★ Le Manoir
- Marty's Bum Steer
- Mary's
- ★ McCarthy's
- ★ Meson Botin
- Le Moal
- Monastery
- ★ Monte Carmela
- Monte's
- Mr. Lee's
- Mr. Mike's
- ○ Mrs. J's Sacred Cow
- Museum Café
- ★ New Port Alba
- Nickels
- ★ Nippon
- ○ Oak Room (at the Plaza)
- Oggi
- Olé
- Once Upon a Stove
- O'Neal Brothers
- ○ One-Fifth
- One if by Land, Two if by Sea
- Paolucci's
- ★ Patsy's
- ★ Paul & Jimmy's Place
- Pen & Pencil
- Penguin

- ★ Per Bacco
- Peter's Backyard
- ○ Pete's Tavern
- Piccolo Mondo
- ★ Piro's
- ★ Les Pleiades
- ○ Ponte's
- Portofino
- ★ Promenade Café
- ○ Proof of the Pudding
- ★ Le Provençal
- ★ El Quijote
- Le Rabelais
- ★ Raffaella's
- The Ravelled Sleave
- ○ Recovery Room
- Red Baron
- ★ Residence
- ★ Il Rigoletto
- Rocco
- ★ Romeo Salta
- Ruskay's
- ★ Saito
- Sal Anthony's
- San Remo
- ★ San Remo East
- ★ Say Eng Look
- Scoop
- ○ Sea Venture
- ★ La Strada East
- Sumptuary
- ★ Szechuan East
- ★ Szechuan Taste
- Teachers
- ★ La Toque Blanche
- ○ Trader Vic's
- ★ Trattoria da Alfredo
- Under the Stairs
- Il Vagabondo
- ★ Wally's
- ★ Wo Ping
- Z

The Restaurants of New York
1978–1979 Edition

★★ ALFREDO

240 Central Park South
LUNCH, MONDAY TO FRIDAY; DINNER, MONDAY TO SATURDAY. CLOSED SUNDAY.
Reservations, 246–7050.
Credit cards: AE, DC, MC.
Expensive.

Gold-on-gold wallpaper, golden draperies, mirrored pillars, fresh flowers, pale, starched lemon-yellow linen, carpeting, an interior portico leading to an ornate cocktail lounge—just what you think of when you think of Central Park South, except for the view of the park. The customers will not surprise you. They are prosperous and well-fed, bejeweled and besilked, cuff-linked and starched. Only the opera singers who frequent this place flash a little style.

Though tastelessly posh, the place is comfortable; the service is polished; and the portly tenors and sopranos have found that the food is eminently good enough to preserve their figures, and the short walk to Lincoln Center a painless gesture to the health of the lung.

To stretch the skin you might begin with Spiedino alla Romana—layers of bread and mozzarella cheese, fried to a nice brown exterior, in a sauce of wine, lemon juice, capers and anchovies. It is at once solid and stimulating, but when you think of this familiar dish, you think of anchovies; lots of people do not like anchovies, and there are only traces of the salty fish in this version. Pass up the Scampi alla Griglia—the menu provides the clue: "Broiled Jumbo Shrimps—Barbecue Sauce." Barbecue sauce? In an Italian restaurant? Sure enough, the three large shrimp are served in a plain tomato sauce that is barbecue-ized with Worcestershire and Italianized with oregano—an international error. The menu lists Cozze alla Posillipo, but if mussels are not available, or simply if you prefer, you may have Vongole (clams) instead. In either event, you get a good, briny tomato sauce, flavored with parsley and lots of red pepper, and the mollusks are fresh. The Zuppa Celestina is far from celestial, which does not mean that it is far from good—its goodness, however, is quite earthy, deriving, as it does, from a strong chicken broth in which there is plenty of chicken fat, and slices of a simple, breadlike, lightly browned omelette, made with lots of parsley.

Of course there is pasta, including a number of interesting preparations. Chicce alla Bergonzi, for example—a green pasta in the shape of short lengths of string bean, but with a very discernible flavor of spinach. The sauce is a creamy tomato mixture, with aggressive doses of black pepper and grated cheese. If that color scheme offends, there is Tortelli Fatti (fat tortellini, presumably)—little donut-shaped pasta dumplings filled with meat and cheese, flavored with rosemary and parsley (lots of it, the filling is quite green), sprinkled with cheese and browned. Both of these dishes are exceptional.

If you are a purist and don't wish to have your salad at what is sometimes called this point in time, betray your inside knowledge of the place by asking for some marinated zucchini to dawdle over. It is not listed on the menu, but it is usually available, and the captains suggest it to the people they feel like suggesting it to. It consists of very thin slices of zucchini, cut the long way, each slice the shape of a wide tongue depressor. This, however, you swallow, and *then* say "Ah." The vegetable is roasted with garlic until its edges are blackened, and is then marinated in oil; the flavors

3

of the blackened skin and the garlic, the texture of crinkly seeds, and the smoothness of the oil combine into a singular dish.

If you are wild about brains, and under no other circumstances, try the Cervella Dorate. The dish consists of brains that have been deep-fried in an egg batter, and a couple of slices of lemon which you may squeeze on. The brains are perfectly cleaned and poached before they are put through the final preparation, and they are rich and oily—all very pure. The Steak Pizzaiola is good, though the sauce is milder than what goes by this name in restaurants that are frankly Neapolitan; the steak itself is of good beef, accurately grilled. There are several familiar veal dishes, and also one called Involtini alla Partenopea—thin veal slices rolled around a stuffing of bread crumbs, chives, parsley and oregano, served with a strong, winy mushroom sauce that is flavored with rosemary—a nice, solid dish. Suprema di Polla Veronica is a boned breast of chicken (one bone is left in, and the dish arrives with the bone standing up, as a decoration) served with a thick cream sauce and grapes. The whole thing is browned before the dish is served, and it is not bad. There are pretty good à la carte vegetables at $2 to $3. This restaurant is not above serving a salad, on occasion, that is of old greens.

Mostly simple desserts: an excellent caramel custard; a chocolate rum cake that manages to seem a little sinful despite the use, or at least the taste, of artificial rum; good zabaglione. The big dessert deal here is Sorpresa alla Colzani, a rum-and-pineapple creation that belongs in Trader Vic's, at the other corner of the park.

• ALGONQUIN HOTEL

59 West 44th Street
LUNCH AND DINNER. CLOSED SUNDAY NIGHT.
Reservations, 687–4400.
Credit cards: AE, CB, DC, V.
Medium-priced.

You arrive for late supper and you are instructed to check your coat. Fine. But the hatcheck hag informs you that she's going home at midnight and she's not hanging around for one or two coats, so if you want to check it, OK, but ya better be ready to pick it up at midnight or she won't be responsible, in fact she'll just hang it here outside the hatcheck room and you can get it when you want it. You point out that you have been *instructed* to check it, that outside the hatcheck room the coat is insufficiently protected from unprincipled coat collectors, and that you insist on either keeping the coat with you or putting it in the safekeeping of the Algonquin staff. She moans, groans, accepts the coat, and informs you that she will deliver it to your table at midnight, and you do not enter into a discussion with her of the idiocy of compulsory checking of coats to assure neatness of the dining room if neatness does not count after midnight.

Try lunch, and try informing your waiter that you want your salad after your main course, and he places the already dressed salad on the far corner of your table so that you can easily reach it later. If you actually settle for that cold supper, you will find that the waiter may politely ask whether you want cole slaw or potato salad with your

Assorted Cold Meats, apparently for the purpose of bringing the one you did not want; that to get the Apple, Walnut and Raisin Salad that ostensibly accompanies the Tongue and Swiss Cheese platter you simply have to get lucky; and to get mustard with any of these things, you must stand and wave your arms.

Whatever you try, your check arrives unrequested. And if that is not enough to unseat you, there is always plenty of closing-up activity at the end of lunch or supper to make the idea of a brandy and coffee unthinkable—the lights are turned up, tables are stripped, yawning waiters bid each other goodbye.

This is the famous Hotel Algonquin, with its handsome wood-paneled Oak Room, much like the dining room of an ancient men's club, where the lunchtime talk is business, business, business, where half the customers are known by name, and where the peculiar eating habits of many are catered to without so much as a double take (cornflakes and milk for this one, Melba toast and raw vegetables for that one). And there is the ornate, pillared pink Rose Room, where the gay after-theater crowd tumbles in at around ten o'clock to tipple and nibble. But most of all, of course, there is the literary lobby lounge, with its Victorian sofas and deep armchairs, to which one-half the editorial staff of *The New Yorker* repairs at four o'clock in the afternoon (three on Friday) to check up on who is leaving the office early, where the food is peanuts and the wine is whiskey, and where there are bells on the low cocktail tables to summon the waiter for another round.

Some of the food here is dreadful, some is good, and a few items are superb; and the inconsistency among items is almost matched by the inconstancy of any given dish. On one day, for example, your Steak Tartare, Garni, is made with far too much mustard, no oil, anchovies that are sliced in half, at best in thirds, rather than reduced to a paste, or left out and served as a garnish; on another day the balance is better. The meat is always good, apparently ground to order, but the waiters simply do not know the dish, and you should insist on mixing it yourself or not order it. Sometimes there is bouillabaisse, and since it is made to order, the fish is not overcooked. The ingredients are not the world's finest (mackerel, a few shrimp, and a recently frozen crayfish from another continent), but the broth is fairly well garlicked, there is actually saffron in the preparation, and the whole thing is a decent plate of food. The roast beef is thick, pink and tender, and the calf's liver is expertly grilled, so that the flavor is brought out without eliminating the moistness of the thin slices. There are decent steaks, French and Italian dishes that are available in better versions in French and Italian restaurants, good egg dishes, and good salads if you avoid those that are basically green salads. The Apple, Walnut and Raisin Salad, for example, is made with crisp apples, crunchy walnuts, fresh celery and soft black raisins, all in a thin mayonnaise, garnished with currant jelly.

The lunch and dinner menus are very much alike, and the supper menu is a simplification of those, eliminating all items that require a staff in the kitchen except for a couple of hot items that are kept in chafing dishes at the buffet setup at the back of the lounge. You order from the menu, and the waiter orders from the gent behind the buffet. Sometimes there is curried seafood, but it is made with canned crabmeat, scallops and packaged curry powder. Sometimes there is Beef Stroganoff, but it is not made with sour cream, if you can imagine such a thing. The best supper here is a cold supper, and if you must have something hot, the onion soup is not bad. The base is consommé rather than good, strong stock, but it is an acceptable bowl of hot soup. The cold cuts and cheese are in good condition, as are the cole slaw, potato salad, pickles and olives that are the usual garnishes.

The best food at the Algonquin is the desserts. The mocha mousse layer cake is vibrant with its strong flavor of fresh coffee; the so-called apricot tart is more than that, consisting as it does of a layer of cake that is a kind of date-nut bread on which apricot preserves are spread, all of which is then buried in whipped cream and almonds. Regular coffees and fancy coffees.

The Algonquin is one of those institutions which are not exactly run, but permitted to chug along. Some of the waiters are so incompetent that they arouse your sympathy before they outrage you. When the customers fill the place, their comfort in these familiar surroundings adds more to your feeling of well-being than anything the house undertakes.

★ LE ALPI

234 West 48th Street
LUNCH AND DINNER. CLOSED SUNDAY.
Reservations, JU 2–7792.
Credit cards: AE, DC, MC, V.
Medium-priced.

This rather spacious restaurant has been doing business in a respectable manner at this site for more than a decade, having built a little clientele all its own, not exactly of food freaks, but of those folk who find places they like and make them their own. So, some enchanted evening, make it *your* own, for without ever serving anything sensational, this establishment almost always satisfies.

The place could pass as nothing more than a Broadway bar, its dining room in the remote rear, for the dark and cavernous front room is very forbiddingly that kind of place where, one suspects, capers are planned, booty divided, where the *nostalgie* is *de la boue*—oh, those glorious days on the inside—and where the wistful dreams are of that day in the future when one has made enough to retire and go straight. The front room is dark and murky. A lengthy bar cuts diagonally across one corner, there is a big quiet piano, pictures of the great and famous (Frank Sinatra types) on the walls, little tables with red-and-white-checked cloths. What one sees seated at the bar are not so much people as forms. At the tables, pairs of men sit at adjacent sides so that they may whisper mouth to ear. A couple of innocents wander in, and the host's politesse is so studied that one suspects he is more accustomed to very casual greetings to regular customers.

But the dining room is of another cast, something quite else, homely and comic in its grotesque snatches of décor. One thinks of a certain kind of "hall" if one hears the expression "hired hall." Perhaps you will understand if you imagine the site of the annual "affair" of the Fraternal Order of South Brooklyn Accordionists. The walls of the large place are old beige; massive mirrored columns form a line of three along the axis of the room's length; brass chandeliers, each with eight little lampshades, hang from the high ceilings. There are picture-postcard paintings, and fresh flowers among plastic greenery in little lacquered vased on all the tables. The total effect is at once garish and plain, especially so with respect to the papier-mâché title role. "Le Alpi" refers to the Alps, and on a ledge high up on the back wall there is a—how you say? —construction or assemblage of green alps (snow-capped, of course), an assortment of mountain climbing and skiing gear (ropes and picks and poles), and, somehow, bottles of Italian wine. If you stare at the thing long enough you think you are having an odd dream.

The printed menu also sports eccentricities. It is mostly à la carte, but stapled to its corner is a little card whereon two prix-fixe dinners are listed—Pope John one is called, Toscanini the other.

But back to the beginning, when you are seated by your host, then greeted by your waiter, a gent whom you discover to be of sweetness and cordiality. You inquire of him as to the quality of the house wine. He places his hand on his breast as he tells you that it is good. You inquire as to its provenance, and he spreads his open hands before you, as if to show that he conceals nothing when he avers that it is from northern Italy, that being so great a recommendation. And he volunteers without prodding that the red is made of the Tokay grape (northeastern Italy is, after all, not far from Hungary). At $7 per giant carafe, this huge serving should hold two of you through dinner, and do not fear that it is sweet—the Tokay grape yields sweet wine only when it is permitted to rot a little before wine is made from it.

Going by noble order, we begin with Pope John, or, come to think of it, perhaps it is Toscanini, who begins with a scallop shell of shrimp in a Mornay sauce made with strong cheese—the shrimp are crisp and clear-tasting, the sauce solid. The other eminent begins with a cold antipasto consisting of a pleasant enough little garden salad of cool peas and carrots and so on in a creamy mayonnaise, slices of strong salami, smoky ham, loud cheese, olives, cold beets—all of it perfectly good, none of it exciting. It is either the cleric or the conductor who proceeds to Fettuccine Bolognese, eggy noodles aswim in a warm and gentle meat sauce, and either the musician or the pontiff who opts instead for the Gnocchi al Pomodoro, soft little potato dumplings in a slightly tart tomato sauce—a tender dish with a bit of an edge. It is probably the maestro, though it may well be the ecclesiastic, who then favors a combination dish—a delicate cutlet of veal surmounted by a slice of ham and some melted cheese, the asymmetrical sandwich adorned with a light tomato sauce; and a breaded and sautéed breast of chicken. Neither of these is dynamite, but they are perfectly nice. Meanwhile the divine (if it is not the music maker) is consuming another combo, a cutlet of beef in a mushroom sauce and a simple one of veal sautéed in butter, both of these moistened with simple pan sauces—not much dynamite on this side of the table either, but all quite acceptable. And at the end it is the erstwhile archbishop and the reformed cellist together at last for some solid cheese cake—thick, sweet, studded with moist candied fruits.

Those who eschew leadership of either kind may go their own à la carte way, beginning perhaps with Spiedino Alpigiano, a deep-fried brochette of chunks of ham, slabs of cheese, and hefty crusts of bread, the whole breaded and deep-fried and served in a very salty anchovy sauce—pungent. Or you may express your independence through Manicotti di Ricotta al Pomodoro, a massive but delicate dish in which envelopes made of pasta are filled with ricotta cheese and served in a light tomato sauce that is thickened with melted cheese—a warming dish of very pleasant food. You may continue on your own way via Calamari Fritti, not your usual Italian squid dish, but a deep-fried variant which consists of very delicately breaded little slivers of the ceph-alopod which have been so elegantly fried that you can detect nary a hint of grease—

do squeeze on that lemon. For yet another means of turning your back on direction, head for the Ossobuco con Risotto—not the tenderest meat falling off the bone, as the best ossobuco is, but a good dish, marrow in the bone, onions in the rice that is its accompaniment.

Not a dessert house—there is the aforementioned cheese cake, and the gentleman will make you a good zabaglione if you wish.

★★ ANGELO'S

146 Mulberry Street (near Grand Street)
LUNCH AND DINNER. CLOSED MONDAY.
Reservations, WO 6–1277.
Credit cards: AE, DC, MC, V.
Medium-priced.

Just inside the door is a hatcheck facility, the simple appearance of which is no clue to the turmoil that can develop around it. We have here an aisle, three feet wide, formed by the door and the wall opposite. Mounted on the wall are coat hooks—six feet of them, about fifty in all. About fifteen inches from the wall (we are still in the three-foot aisle) there is a Formica counter, long as the row of hooks, and six inches deep. The condition between the counter and the wall, when the coat hooks are all in use, is one of not enough space for anything more, certainly not for the plump young thing whose post is, technically, between the counter and the coats. (Conditions on the other side of the counter are equally dense when customers arrive in groups of more than two normal or one stout. And as customers not only arrive here but also leave, the scene is frequently one of direct confrontation, unalleviated by right-of-way guidelines.) What happens, of course, is that the attendant must contort herself wickedly to hang or retrieve a coat. As she stretches, her short sweater rises above her skirt, revealing a band of well-filled skin. This attracts the attention of the waiter at the front table, whose customers, in a moment, find themselves giving their order to empty air because the waiter has stuck his pencil behind his ear, to free his right hand to caress the revealed skin as he shares a whispered country thought with the harried soubrette. When things ease up she comes out from behind her counter and parks on a chair near the door—here she scratches herself a lot (perhaps she is allergic to coats) and pretends to read the *News*. The natty host (he constantly buttons and unbuttons his velvet jacket) keeps her company with suggestions about what they might undertake after work. She levels a look of transcendent boredom, then giggles and turns a page.

Farther inside is a restaurant. It is a comfortable if overdecorated place. There are three rooms, back to back, and a kitchen that is visible from the street through a steamy window. The front room is red-flocked; the second one is done in crazed mirrors and illuminated, framed beachscapes; and the back room is dominated by a hazy mural, the central feature of which is a mosque—it's hard to figure. The food is good, the service serviceable, and the price tolerable. The customers are expansive and well-fed.

Before you get to the pasta and main courses you may want to have something light —the Angelo Special Antipasto di Mare (served for two people at $4). It is light stuff, but you get a heavy amount of it—a foot-long platter of squid, conch, shrimp, scallops and celery cut into small pieces, dressed in garlicky oil and a little lemon, and sprinkled with coarsely chopped fresh parsley. The ingredients are fresh-tasting and the dish is stimulating, but you can't be sure that the conch will not be leathery—but for this occasional flaw, the salad is a wonderful and stimulating first course. If you don't wish to take a chance on tough conch, or if you want hot food right from the start, the hot first courses include Eggplant Provenzana (thoroughly sautéed eggplant, browned, soft and oily, in a tomato sauce flavored with garlic and herbs); there are also stuffed mushrooms—they are fresh, and the stuffing of bread crumbs, oil and chopped red peppers is tasty without overpowering the mushrooms; as part of the Home Made Hot Antipasto you also get a couple of whole bell peppers, sautéed in oil until there are little black spots here and there, which add a strong accent to the hot, limp and oily vegetable.

This place has something of a reputation for its linguine with clam sauce. It is served here with the clams still in their shells, the pasta dressed with oil and plenty of garlic. Theoretically this should be a wonderful dish—as the clams are steamed separately from the preparation of the sauce, they can be tender; and because they arrive still housed in and attached to their shells, you know they are fresh. But despite the advantages, the clams are sometimes tough, which makes the whole dish an absurdity. The linguine, however, is good and not overcooked, and the garlic has not been browned, so it has the strong flavor of the barely adulterated genuine article. There are also some quite eggy homemade noodles here, served in a variety of sauces, including a frankly southern mushroom sauce—a thick tomato sauce, very spicy, combined with plenty of sautéed fresh mushrooms. (About 90 percent of New York's Italian restaurants now call themselves "northern," no matter what kind of Italian food they serve —it's the fad. In Little Italy that fashion would be suicide, as the population down here, after lifetimes of powerful sauces, is largely unable to detect the flavor in anything that lacks garlic and/or hot red pepper.) For a noodle made with potatoes instead of flour, the Gnocchi di Casa alla Napoletana are pleasantly gummy and amorphous little morsels—the sauce is, of course, strong and red, with sautéed onions, and over the whole dish there is a layer of melted cheese. Hard to beat.

The Veal Pizzaiola is served in a hearty sauce that is made with lots of red peppers and oregano and mushrooms; but you can't be certain of getting tender veal in the scaloppine dishes. The fish, on the other hand, is reliable—fresh, moist and flaky—and the Bass Livornese, in its sauce of capers, olives, onions, tomatoes and, you guessed it, garlic, is a good choice if you have already had a couple of courses, because there is room for a light fish where a heavy meat will not fit. If you are not having that problem, then try the Calves' Brains Arreganata—the brains are white, rich, tender, lightly breaded and browned, and they are served with a sauce that includes *whole cloves* of garlic and an abundance of oregano.

Some of the vegetable dishes at Angelo's are well above average, and in the city-wide deep-fried-zucchini contest, the crisp and moist zucchini you get here maintains a respectable position. For an item you will not encounter all over town, try the Escarole alla Monachina—the strong green leafy vegetable is sautéed in oil with garlic, black olives, pine nuts, strong and salty anchovies, and sweet black raisins. The result is an amazingly well balanced dish, despite the unbelievable diversity of its elements.

The pastries come from Ferrara, of course, so if you have been to Ferrara, you know that the cheese cake is a compromise—the menu refers to it as Torta di Ricotta, and sure enough, there is a little ricotta cheese in it, but mostly cream cheese. The cake is fairly moist, studded with candied fruit and flavored slightly with lemon. The rum cake is a rum-moistened sponge cake with whipped cream on top—a meaningless item.

This is a spotty restaurant with a mixed clientele: families, with children; hirsute East Villagers on a spree; the gay; SoHo artists and hangers-on. It is just for a few hours, so they all get along.

★ ARARAT

4 East 36th Street
LUNCH, MONDAY TO SATURDAY; DINNER, DAILY.
Reservations, 686–4622.
Credit cards: AE, DC.
Medium-priced.

Much red upholstery, golden draperies, carved wooden partitions, crystal chandeliers, all very Eastern-posh and Hollywood-harem. There is a back room in blue and ivory—probably left over from another restaurant.

Armenian dried beef is very much an indelicate Armenian delicacy, but New York's Armenian restaurants rarely list it because its flavor, to the uninitiated palate, may seem rank. It is surely strong, tastes aged rather than cured, gamy rather than smoky. But it is good meat, cool, dark, fibrous and loud. A few slices and you will be a convert.

This is an inconsistent restaurant, and though you can get as good a dinner here as at The Dardanelles or The Balkan Armenian if you order the right items, the menu offers more opportunities for ordering the wrong ones. Two appetizers to avoid here are the midia dolma (baked stuffed mussels, served cold) and the enguinar (artichokes cooked in oil and lemon, with carrots and onions, also served cold). The trouble with the mussels is that they are greasy, the sweetness of the sweet spices excessive, the texture of the pine nuts lost. And the trouble with the artichoke is that the heart and stem have not been perfectly separated from the leaves, which seems to prevent the flavor of the other vegetables from permeating the artichoke. But Ararat seems to do best what its competitors will not do at all: chi kufta, superfluously described on the menu as "Armenian tartar steak," is then further described as "lean ground raw lamb and seasoned cracked wheat garnished with chopped fresh onion and parsley . . ." This is extremely rich stuff, the sharpness of the raw onion almost essential if you are going to finish the substantial serving. There are also good versions of cheese boreg (cheese, wrapped in pastry and served warm), and imam bayeldi (eggplant, baked in oil, with tomatoes and onions, served cold), and tarama (the paste of red fish roe, bread, garlic and lemon), but if you go out of your way to come to this out-of-the-way place, the things to start your dinner with are the dried beef and the raw lamb.

Of course there is moussaka, composed of a layer of eggplant, another of ground lamb, a top one of heavily cheesed white sauce, the whole thing oozing spicy red oil. And, equally of-course, there is shish kebab—tender blackened chunks of good lamb, skewered with slices of tomato and onion. But the real winner is boud skara, a marinated lamb steak, the meat lightly seasoned, seared and rare—this is a strong dish, partly because the lamb here is a little gamy, and partly because it has been made even louder by its marinade. That weird dish called harpoot kufta is also served here. This is the elaborate construction of hollow balls of cracked wheat, stuffed with seasoned ground lamb, and served in broth. At its best, each of the three elements of the dish is distinctive—the cracked wheat crusty, the lamb oily, spicy and succulent, the broth hot and clear. The version served here is perfectly good to eat, but the elements are somehow all blended together. Too bad.

To an Armenian, fruit compote is not something you put on menus for sick people. Armenians take fruit compote seriously. The one served here is made with prunes, dried apricots, apples and pears. The four fruits are cooked with lots of clove, and the final dish is strong, sweet, winy. Good nut pastries and puddings and bread cooked in syrup, all of them available with kaimak, the exceptional Armenian cream that is as sweet as ice cream and as rich and thick as butter, with which you will need a cup of the potent coffee served here—half coffee, half sediment.

★★ ARIRANG

28 West 56th Street
LUNCH, MONDAY TO FRIDAY; DINNER, MONDAY TO SATURDAY. CLOSED SUNDAY.
Reservations, LT 1–9698.
Credit cards: AE, CB, DC, MC, V.
Medium-priced.

This is a low-ceilinged, dark, clubby little restaurant, in what one takes to be an Oriental way. It is conceivable that much of New York's Korean community dines here, and it may well be a small community, for as they arrive and leave they chat with people at half the tables they pass. The dim, misty paintings that hang on the dark walls add to the murky effect of places not only far away, but lost somewhere back in time. But in other ways this is unmistakably a twentieth-century restaurant in an American city, for the barroom into which you enter could easily be that of a resort motel that has taken an Oriental motif upon itself, for lack of anything better to do—the Chosen Motor Inn is a likely name for the place—and it has been additionally decorated with bewitching examples of the Korean Young Female, half a dozen of whom, at any given time, are drifting through the place like shafts of light, in lengthy dresses of shimmering and vivid colors—turquoise, lilac, lemon, pale bronzed apricot, and deep navy blue, not to mention fire-engine red—on which are embroidered, down near the hem and at the ends of the sleeves and at the shoulders, fauna and flora and geometric patterns, all in glistening silk. The waitresses are placid and efficient, occasionally even smiling, not at all depressed by the drawn-out soulful Korean music in the background. Perhaps the tunes are cheery to accustomed ears.

This is one of those places that have appetizers on the menu as a method of converting reasonably priced main courses into overpriced dinners. Among the tidbits that must bear the burden of the conversion are Kujo Pan—atoms of marinated beef that are sautéed with fresh vegetables and wrapped in a noodle sheet, to form a sausage-shaped object. The sausage is cut into four inch-long discs and served up—lovely morsels, a dozen of which would hold you. Then there is Wanja, harmless deep-fried meatballs. And there is Mandu Tuikim, in which the ground meat is wrapped in a bit of noodle before it is deep-fried. You can sample the lot in the Combination, at no extra charge.

Much better to divvy up an order of Yauk Hae to begin—strands of raw beef, red, fresh and tender, bathed in sesame oil and served with slices of just-cut raw onion. You dip the beef in a thick and sour sauce and send for some more Kirin, the beer from Japan. If you prefer your beef with a bit of fire, there is Pulkoki, marinated beef that is charcoal-broiled and served awash in a thick sauce that is powerfully spiced and pleasantly sour. Proceed to Dak Tuikim—morsels of chicken deep-fried in a light batter. This crusting is not as feathery as some tempuras you have had, but what makes the dish is the meat within, for this is fresh chicken that tastes like a well-fed bird. Keep going with Saewu Tuikim, butterflied shrimp that have been similarly deep-fried in a light, eggy batter; and the shrimp, like the chicken, have the clear sweet taste of the never-frozen article. The deep-fried dishes are served with a dark winy sauce, which the batter soaks up like a sponge.

Marinated bean sprouts, marinated spinach and cool mashed turnips are served with all meals—they are bland but pleasant. There are other garnishes available, of which the best-known is probably Kimchi, a violently hot pickled cabbage which may require a quick mouthful of rice to tame. Kim is a dish of paper-thin, dry seaweed sheets that are served in a stack on a stick, like bills on a spike. It has the familiar oceanic flavor of seaweed, not much adorned, but its vague, cloudlike and airy quality may make it hard to identify as food for the yearning stomach—a serving could be compressed to approximately the size of a pencil eraser.

The melon that is sometimes available for dessert is not invariably ripe. The only other dessert, ice cream, is the local dish you know from your childhood.

It is notable that the food in this restaurant always arrives aglow; nothing seems to be warmed over or reheated or taken out of the icebox upon your order. You get unusual and interesting food, the condition of which is always reliable, and you can ask for little more than that.

○ ASTI

13 East 12th Street
DINNER. CLOSED MONDAYS AND JULY AND AUGUST.
Reservations, AL 5–9095.
Credit cards: AE, CB, DC, MC, V.
Medium-priced.

Asti would be worth a visit about once a decade if it had at least an element of professionalism in its management. There are times when an exuberant drunken evening, in deafening surroundings, is in order, such as your college roommate's fourth bachelor party. And Asti does provide some hilarious moments, a few of them intentional.

Asti is a barnlike place in which no effort has been spared to eliminate comfort, intimacy and charm. The giant room is dominated by a bar, at which middle-aged adolescents brandish their *joie de vivre,* starting at cocktail time, only to find it transformed into *Weltschmerz* at midnight. The principal competition for the bar comes from the bandstand, where waiters, hosts and customers bellow operatic familiarities in a spectrum running roughly from Gilbert & Sullivan to Verdi, all accompanied by a chubby pixie at an electric organ. The cigarette girl throws on a shawl to sing *Carmen* in French, supported by a chorus in Italian and English. The highlight of the evening is a five-minute production of *Il Trovatore,* featuring an Anvil Chorus, in which the bartender smashes out home runs on a chime installed near the Scotch; and a "Miserere," for which the lights are dimmed, as a busboy in a hooded cloak blesses the diners, while he leads a candle-carrying procession from the kitchen, through the dining room, to the telephone.

Apparently the waiters find this amusing night after night. They become enthralled and forget about their customers, which is just as well, because the food is not good enough to actually serve.

Asti does win a prize for pictures on the walls: floor to ceiling, front to back, Beniamino Gigli and Richard Tauber mingle with Marilyn Monroe and Count Fleet. There is still room for one or two postage stamps, but no encroachment will be permitted on the sacred parcel of rear wall allotted to an oil of Caruso during his mad period.

Half the people present wander around managerially, as if they owned the place. An actual proprietor (identified as such when he called a waiter "dopey") was observed eating a plate of Fettuccine Romana, so if you get stuck here, try that, it may be palatable.

In this crowd "You gotta have respeck" is the motto. And they do have respeck. They keep hands off Mozart.

★★★ AUBERGE SUISSE

153 East 53rd Street
LUNCH AND DINNER.
Reservations, 421–1420.
Credit cards: AE, CB, DC, MC, V.
Expensive.

Two small rooms—fewer than a dozen tables in each—and a short bar are the whole of Auberge Suisse. The look of Swiss modernity is neutrality and variations thereon. This rendition is silvery and sleek and just a little soft, with glinting walls of charcoal-gray glass, walls and banquettes of chestnut-colored suede, gray suede booths, modern bentwood chairs. The tables are set with beige linen and beige china. You walk on brown carpeting under a ceiling of metallic acoustical tiles—they reflect the room back with a somber glow. It is a perfect rendering of a cool style, it eschews ornament, and it can be forbidding. But when the restaurant is busy, the sight and sounds of people dress it up. And the vivid food this kitchen turns out is all the more dramatic, in look and taste, for its cool setting.

The sparkling food includes a refreshing salade de boeuf bouilli, strands of cool, rare beef and crisp vegetables in a tangy vinaigrette; fillets of boned smoked trout, cool, flaky and a little oily, served with a horseradish sauce that has the head-clearing pungency of the just-grated root—the sauce is cut with slivers of apple, but the fruit makes little impression in this fiery context; and viande de Grison et jambon cru, thin slices of mahogany-colored air-dried beef, chewy and a little gamy, and smoky ham, the pink meat rimmed with delicate white fat, served with slivered onions—just cut, strong and crisp—a vivid foil to the high-flavored meats.

This place makes snails in a version they call escargots "Café de Paris." This is a singular preparation, in which the plump and tender snails are baked in brandy and flavored butter. What they put in that butter is a mystery—your waiter questions the chef and returns with the dubious advice that the recipe calls for twenty herbs and spices—but sweeter spices and the perfume of green herbs dominate. The snails are served in shells in a little pot; just before serving, the entire production is lightly covered with good cheese and browned. A wondrous dish.

Good soups, mostly, including a hot, clear and profound oxtail broth that is livened with the sharpness of minced chives; and an item given as potage balois, a creamy beef soup that has a strong and earthy flavor of whole grain. There is a cold apricot soup as well, but it may strike you as little more than liquefied preserves.

More trout (Switzerland is sweet-water country), this one poached in wine, boned, skinned and served in a creamy white sauce that is dotted with fresh herbs—the fish is immaculately fresh, and the sauce has the smoothness and polish of a thing just made.

It is unlikely that you will get a better cheese fondue in New York than the one served here (for two people or more). It is brought to you in a broad ceramic pot, within which it is bubbling; on your table it is kept hot and active over a little burner; and as is the way with this dish at its best, its flavor deepens as it continues to bubble, darken and grow thick. There are wine, garlic and seasonings in this dish, but in such judicious dosages that they heighten the flavor of the melted Gruyère cheese without intruding their own. You are supplied with long forks and a copious mound of chunks of crusty bread. You pierce the bread with the forks, dip it into the seething cheese, and eat. If you are normal, you will frequently burn your lips and palate with the hot tines and molten cheese.

Emincé de veau Zurichoise is a wonderful veal dish in which slivers of delicate veal and chunks of fresh mushroom are served in a dark sauce. The veal is accompanied by rösti potatoes, the marvelous Swiss potato tart that has a crust of browned potatoes, a core that is soft and moist. The plat Bernoise is the low point of the place, a leaden collection of sausages, meats and sauerkraut. But the saucisse de veau grillé is fine— a substantial veal sausage, pale, smooth and rich, served under strands of onion that are sweet and dark from long braising. Sausages again, this time as a garnish to the elegant calf's liver that arrives with dark-brown grill marks on the outer surfaces of the pink meat—the accompanying little sausages are chippolatas, strong and charred, the dark, spicy meat filling heavily fatted, just about bursting from the crackling cases.

A complex steak production is served up here. It is styled tournedos cordon-rouge, and it is a stack of things—the steak, fois gras, ham, a big mushroom, Béarnaise sauce —and it is served with a gravy that is so winy it is purple. The fois gras is not first class, but everything else is okay, and the dark gravy is marvelously suited to the salty buttered noodles that accompany this dish. The production more than survives its overdesign.

If you did not scorch yourself on cheese fondue, you get a second chance with chocolate fondue, bubbling milk chocolate that is studded with nuts—you scoop it out of its pot on chunks of cake or pineapple, or on strawberries or grapes. There is a superb excess called coupe rouge et blanc, a mousse of white chocolate that is mingled with whipped cream and liquored strawberries—for all its richness it is light. And there is a good carrot cake, nutty and substantial and moist. The most elegant dessert is a sherbet item for some reason called "Le Colonel"—the lemon ice is soaked with pear brandy, and the dish has a strong sweetness that seems to glisten.

Swiss wines are perfectly decent, but not especially interesting if you are used to sampling the best of France and California. If you are curious, this place offers about a dozen that are perfectly drinkable.

★ BALKAN ARMENIAN

129 East 27th Street
LUNCH, MONDAY TO FRIDAY; DINNER, MONDAY TO SATURDAY. CLOSED SUNDAY.
Reservations, MU 9–7925.
Credit cards: AE, DC, MC, V.
Inexpensive.

This is a very satisfying little Armenian restaurant. The tables may be small, the service plodding, and the decorations a bit silly, what with Oriental rugs, and paintings that are not merely primitive but atavistic, on the dark walls. But it is a relaxed neighborhood restaurant, set in its ways, not trying to make a buck any faster than it made one in the past, and accordingly, one is treated simply as a hungry human rather than as an element in a financial program.

Watch out for the generalizations, but Armenians are generally very proud of their background. The intensity of this pride varies from, at one extreme, the belief that Armenians are the greatest race on earth to, at the other extreme, the conviction that Armenians are the greatest race on earth and that Armenia is the fount of all that is worth preserving in civilization. The menu here makes a modest contribution toward the defense of these propositions, itemizing, at no charge, "The Birth of a People," "A Few Famous Armenians," a short history of the Balkan Armenian restaurant itself (during Prohibition, shish kebab was 50 cents, and arrack was sold in demitasses), and a tabulation of the world distribution of Armenians, the upshot of which is that most Armenians live in Armenia.

The list of dishes does not hew slavishly to the Armenian line, making it possible to have tarama as a first course—the famous paste of roe and moistened bread, flavored with lemon. It is served here in a wonderfully well-balanced version, thick, but moist enough to spread, and heavily flavored of roe. The cold stuffed grape leaves, however, are overly oiled and dilled, which gives them a slightly sour taste, and the cold yogurt soup, with barley, is garnished with a level teaspoon of dried mint, like a spoonful of dust.

The main course of hot grape leaves (with meat in the stuffing, and quite another dish from the cold appetizer) is really delicious. The leaves have not been rendered limp and retain their slightly papery texture; and the filling, of rice and gamy ground lamb, is accented perfectly by the strong, tart, homemade yogurt served with them.

The shish kebab is of good meat, perfectly broiled; and the patlijan silkme—a heavy and extremely satisfying amalgam of sautéed eggplant and pot-roasted lamb—is powerfully flavored and rich. As in all Armenian restaurants, most of the main courses are based on lamb, and since the meat used here is tender and highly flavored, the main dishes are invariably satisfying, if never elegant. (The mushroom kebab is a standout exception—allegedly of fresh mushrooms, the dish is made with the canned variety, and it is a bore.)

The usual desserts of thin-layered pastry, walnuts and honey are available here in all the usual shapes—flat baklava, rolled checkme, etc. The pastry is crisp, the nuts crunchy, the honey thick and sweet, and what more can you ask? Avoid toulumba, which, the menu frankly admits, is a cruller, though it fails to point out that it tastes like the drugstore version.

There is a famous story of a lady seated on a park bench, babe in arms. "What a lovely child," remarks a passer-by. "You should see his pictures," says the lady.

"Ask to see our Kodachrome pictures of Armenian dishes," says the menu.

★ BALLATO

55 East Houston Street (near Mott Street)
LUNCH AND DINNER. CLOSED SUNDAY.
Reservations required at dinner, CA 6–9683.
No credit cards.
Beer and wine.
Medium-priced.

The proprietor claims that he opened this restaurant to prove a point—that location is nothing, that if you sell good food, people will seek you out. So he opened it, back in 1957, in a neighborhood that is not even a neighborhood. This is certainly not Greenwich Village, nor is it Little Italy, nor the East Village (the Lower East Side, as it was known then). It may qualify as SoHo, but we can't blame him for that, as there was no SoHo in those days.

The customers have certainly sought out Ballato, but whether it's because of good food or because of an indefinable quality that sometimes makes an improbable restaurant successful is debatable, since there are restaurants as good as this one and restaurants better than this one that would gladly sacrifice their locations for the loyal following that keeps Ballato going.

Which is not to say that this is not an honest place. Ballato consists of eleven tables in two rows, in a small, neat, oblong room. The walls are earth colors (earth, earth-green, earth-orange, earth-ochre), with a few prints and photographs. The problem of a swinging door between the kitchen and the customers has been eliminated by removal of the door, and the clean-looking kitchen is visible to almost all parts of the dining room through a large portal at the rear. The floor is staffed by the portly proprietor, looking like the help in a cotton jacket of the kind supplied by commercial laundries; a waiter in a formal, white dinner jacket, looking like the proprietor; and on busy nights, the fifth wheel, a hireling waiter who answers that the Bardolino is $7.50 (actual price: $5.50); that there is really no difference between the manicotti and the cannelloni; that, yes, you may have some celery (but you give up your olives in the process); and that, no, there isn't any cheese (the proprietor produces three varieties in good condition). It helps to know the ropes.

One of the ropes: ask for celery and olives when you sit down. The celery is green, crisp and clean, and the olives are black, flaccid and loud, having been marinated in oil, garlic, parsley and bay.

Another rope: the first courses are uninteresting. The stuffed things are either stuffed with a dull seasoned-veal mixture which, despite its blandness, reduces mushrooms, eggplant and zucchini to indistinguishable identity; or with an ordinary breading (in the mussels, clams and artichokes) which at least succeeds in permitting the flavor of the principal ingredient to predominate.

Begin, rather, with half portions of pasta: either firm green noodles in a thick sauce of cheese and cream, graced with a dollop of tomato sauce on top—a flawless dish, and you may prefer a full portion; linguine with white clam sauce, the sauce clear and briny, the clams fresh minced cherrystones, and lots of fresh parsley; or the Spaghetti Marinara, in which the tomato has been reduced to a strong, heavy paste, and the garlic sautéed until it tastes blackened.

Proceed to Home Made Sausage Pizzaiola with Peppers—crackling sausage skins, partially blackened, stuffed with a textured filling that includes hunks of meat as well as ground meat, all buried in a thick, garlicky tomato sauce with heavily oiled, sautéed green peppers and mushrooms. Or to Polpo Affogate—tender lengths of octopus in a creamy tomato sauce that tastes of strong meat stock, black pepper and herbs. Dishes that are not dominated by tomato sauces, however, are less successful. Chicken Ballato, of which one might, from the name, expect great things, is an uninspired combination of sautéed chicken, sautéed mushrooms and ham, in a bland wine sauce. The Veal Valdostana consists of a veal chop, a slice of boiled ham and bland cheese—a bit of tomato sauce redeems it.

The green salads are fresh, and the dressing is tart, garlicky and well flavored with oregano; chunks of bread, soaked in the delicious dressing, come buried under the arugula, watercress, lettuce or whatever. When there is cheese, it is at room temperature and fresh. The cheese cake is made with ricotta, not cream cheese; it is accented with candied fruit, and it is moist, almost wet.

Your host is a dignified, vandyked presence who enjoys very much his reputation of being quite a character. On occasion he will sit at your table to discuss the menu with you, but his instincts are sure and if you're not interested in camaraderie right now, thank you, he will not make a mistake. On a slow night he'll tell you of his Sicilian past back in the thirties when certain impotent groups entertained Utopian visions for the Europe of the future; and of his World War II days, when his earlier underground experiences provided priceless contacts and saved thousands of lives for the Allied forces. If you keep listening, you'll hear that the missus spends entirely too much time in church, but that that is her right; that the Church (and here his beady eyes become positively black, and he can barely remain in his seat) has been a force for regression in our lifetime; and that the help (what's this?) you get nowadays doesn't respect the value of the boss's dollar. Ballato is nonunion. He has his less passionate side, however —he kisses the hands of the new women customers and nuzzles the more familiar ones. He waddles behind a departing cashmered beauty, his beard in her ear. She takes note: "Ça va?"

A quite good restaurant if you stick to the pasta and the tomato-sauce dishes. The customers arrive in their large cars from some of the fanciest neighborhoods in town, and they wait patiently at the front (magazines are provided) for their tables. They make phone calls from the telephone in the kitchen. The comfort of the place cannot be denied.

★ BARBETTA

321 West 46th Street
LUNCH AND DINNER. CLOSED SUNDAY.
Reservations, CI 6–9171.
Credit cards: AE, CB, DC.
Expensive.

At one time Barbetta was just one of New York's innumerable Italian restaurants, like the others in the simplicity of its interior, better than many by a degree of superiority in cuisine, and unlike most in a clientele that included writers and artists who were attracted by the fair prices, good food and relaxed ambience.

The enterprise was so successful that the proprietors were able to send their young daughter to what are known as the finest schools—Brearley, Bryn Mawr, and all that—from which she emerged tainted by worldliness, which, in turn, when she took over management of the restaurant, tainted it. Now it is not only one of the most elaborately appointed eating places in town but also one which attracts some of the most elaborately appointed customers: gents in tailored shantung, accompanied by hard-coiffed ladies at night; suited matrons for the pre-Wednesday matinée lunch/fashion show (on this day the place is a field of hats through which lissome lovelies wander, displaying the current wares of this or that shop or house).

Within, there is silk wallpaper, a bar of *green onyx,* a terrazzo floor, giant crystal chandeliers in the main room, arched windows with silk shades, large and well-spaced tables, and brocade upholstery on the comfortable chairs—all very splendid. Without, in the garden, there is a pool with statuary of spouting fish, cherubs astride; overhanging shade trees and smaller, decorative ones near the brick or stucco walls; inset arches, with roses here, a Roman goddess there.

The prices are what you would expect in such grand surroundings, though lunch offers some reasonable possibilities. The food is not invariably what you hope for. And the service is the kind of service that is sometimes called Italian: an almost unbelievably unctuous host who wears an expression of such focused seductiveness that the matinée ladies, when it is turned on them, seem to shudder; a Franco Corelli captain who gestures grandly with his arms simply to accompany a "Very good," as he betrays no annoyance at your selection of a French wine for your Italian dinner; businesslike waiters who divide people into two categories—those who are going to the theater and must be served at once, and those who are perfectly happy to sit around long enough to see the theatergoers return for dessert (you may, if you wish—house policy).

Lots of eel served here, including, at lunch, a delicious Eel Carpione—discs of breaded and fried eel, marinated in vinegar and seasonings, and served cold. The prosciutto and melon is excellent, but such items as "Grande Antipasto Piemontese—served from the wagons," which is printed in red on the menu to indicate it is one of the "Specialties of Piemonte," is all in all one of the most misleading menu items in print. It is a disgrace consisting of Progresso caponata, a canned artichoke heart, a Portuguese sardine, and several items from several other packages, with the exception that the zucchini is probably boiled in the kitchen. Perhaps this mess is "served from the wagons" but the service takes place out of sight, and one's selection is made by one's waiter.

The Bagna Cauda here (also in red) consists of a plate of raw vegetables (plus a canned pimento) and a pot of hot oil-and-anchovy mix, over a candle. One dips the vegetable into the mix and eats. Very good.

The Fritto Misto is described as "a variety of fried meats and sweets," so you shouldn't be surprised when it consists mostly of vegetables and variety meats, largely sweetbreads, which is perhaps what is meant by "sweets" (self-starter etymology on 46th Street?). The mislabeling aside, it is delicious; the frying perfectly timed so that the different items—zucchini, mushrooms, liver, veal and sweetbreads—are all at their best.

The veal dishes are generally good, made with tender, white veal. There are such standards as veal Marsala—very sweet, lots of wine; and at lunch there is a really unusual and fabulous dish of raw Veal Steak Tartare alla Piemontese—a huge pancake of cross-hatched ground veal covered with lemon juice and olive oil, and served with a mound of sliced raw mushrooms, a smaller mound of minced fresh garlic and a pepper mill. There are many vegetables on the menu, including an outstanding asparagus— the stalks are peeled, poached just a little, sprinkled with butter and Parmesan cheese, and briefly broiled and browned. There are very good salads, and when they are available, a salad of arugula and raw mushrooms, moistened with a rather strong wine-vinegar-and-oil dressing, is really something.

The pasta dishes are very good, but at the dinner hour, cheapskates who want pasta as their main course must pay extra for their preference, which, when added to the cover charge (smallest typeface on the menu) can really put you in the position of paying something for nothing.

The desserts are not bad—the Zuppa Inglese is an ordinary sponge cake moistened with rum and covered with very fresh whipped cream. Many cooked fruits, including an orange served in a caramel sauce that has been thinned with orange juice, and garnished with strips of tart orange rind.

A wonderful restaurant in many ways, with a unique feel to it, but its occasional failings are cataclysmic.

★ BEANSPROUT

37 Barrow Street (at Seventh Avenue South)
LUNCH AND DINNER.
Reservations, 255–3066.
Credit cards: AE, MC.
Inexpensive.

There is a hint of healthfood in this multiprovince Chinese restaurant—brown rock-sugar in the bowls, an ode to the beansprout on the menu—but they make no claims for organic purity, and it seems that these signs of the times are simply commercial shrewdness with no promises, aimed at the myriad young Greenwich Villagers who seek the unsullied in what they eat. They may not be getting that here, but they are getting a lot of tasty food, and they are surrounded by their own kind, right down to the waiters—young Orientals with long hair, smiles, T-shirts emblazoned with the Beansprout logo and telephone number.

You enter to a tiny bar with the coatrack almost no one uses, for in the dining room proper—built out on the sidewalk—almost all of the tables accommodate two or three chairs of people and one or two chairs of their coats and hats and scarves and handbags and portfolios and notebooks. No dogs allowed. No, the place is not messy, but it is about as far as you can take casual. In fact, if there was no one here, it would be neat —hanging plants that make up an overhead jungle, simple tables of clear wood, glowing tanks of tropical fish swimming happily in their carefully controlled environments, much brick, and through the glass outer walls, a spectacular view of Seventh Avenue, carrying traffic to all points south.

Begin with the Noodles with Sesame Paste, a substantial mound of firm strands of cool pasta under a heavy ladling-on of a hot sauce in which the principal flavors are of sesame and peanut. With your chopsticks—you don't have to ask for them—you deftly rearrange the noodles until each of them is equally doused with the pungent sauce. This odd dish—it is at once gentle, cool and fiery—is best consumed with a couple of bottles of beer. You proceed to Hot and Spicy Shrimp, a grand platter of shrimp in a viscous, mahogany-colored sauce that is laced with about a quarter of a mile of scallion greens cut to quarter-inch lengths. The shrimp themselves are abundant, crisp and fresh-tasting, and the sauce, flavored with fresh ginger, is thick and strong. Proceed, while you are on your shellfish kick, to one of the best items in the place, Live Lobster in Black Bean Sauce. Most important, the lobster really does have the clean bite and firm but tender texture of the just-killed article. The thickened sauce it is served in seems at first glance like dozens of bland Cantonese sauces, with water chestnuts and bean sprouts, but those little nuggets of black bean here and there are startling counterpoint, unexpected even though they are right there in the title.

Beware, the lobster is in its shell in sauce and if you are not up to the messy work, try instead, and be a little disappointed by Chef's Special Beef—strands of beef and strands of tangerine rind bound together in a sauce that is flavored principally with hot pepper. This is an elemental dish, those three simple ingredients, and one wishes the beef were from a tastier, less coarse cut of meat. It is eminently well garnished with broccoli that has been barely steamed—it is crisp—and lightly moistened with sesame oil.

Oddly, for a restaurant that suggests itself as home for the pure-food enthusiasts, the vegetable dishes here can be uninspired. The Sautéed Eggplant arrives as small bricks of perfectly tender eggplant that have been battered and deep-fried—you dip these chunks into a black liquid that is studded with chopped scallions and peppers. It seems perfectly done but to no end.

○ BENIHANA OF TOKYO

47 West 56th Street
LUNCH, MONDAY TO SATURDAY; DINNER, DAILY.
Reservations, LT 1–0930.
Credit cards: AE, CB, DC, MC, V.
Medium-priced.

Except for an interlude in the forties, in this country the Japanese have always enjoyed a reputation for graciousness and hospitality. To erase this stigma, and to demonstrate at the same time that the Japanese can play the American game of creating an offensive restaurant gimmick to be duplicated all over the country (this country), a chain of eateries—Benihana This, Benihana That—has been strung from Puerto Rico to Honolulu.

To begin with, your protein-nourished six-foot American football star is expected to consume his lunch or dinner ensconced in (on) a chair that would be perfect in a Japanese kindergarten. These seats, in turn, are tightly assembled at the famous Benihana table—a twelve-inch wooden ledge around a gas-heated grill (which competes, victoriously, with the air conditioning in the summertime, and which supplements, and renders superfluous, the heating in wintertime), at which a trained juggler/"chef" prepares most of your dinner before (the menu points out) "your very eyes." As this system is most efficient (for the management) when a single chef cooks for a large group, the tables are designed for six or eight persons, and smaller groups are seated with perfect (or imperfect) strangers. If this is not enough to inhibit personal or confidential, not to mention intimate, conversation, the pace of the meal is determined not by your appestat, but by the availability of customers to fill out the tables, and of the chefs to put on their performances.

The complete dinner at these places consists of three set first courses, a choice of five main courses (four of which are steaks prepared in the same way), and those most traditional of Japanese desserts—ice cream or sherbet.

Waitresses serve drinks, soup and salad, one right after the other, and these items promptly overoccupy one's allotted ledge space. The soup (called "Onion au Gratin ala Japanese") is a harmless broth, cheeseless as well, in which a few scallion and mushroom slivers meander about. The "salad" is a batch of health food, with a touch of ginger in the dressing to prove it is Oriental.

Then the performing chef arrives, pushing his nurse's cart, and bangs the sauce dishes together with loud clacks to focus your attention on himself, and away from your companions. He oils the grill (still garnished with traces of the previously served meals) and proceeds to sauté the next course—shrimp (shells, and flavor, removed)—deftly, rapidly, and unnecessarily dissecting and de-tailing them in a series of rapid slices and shoves, tossing the tails, more or less accurately, into a refuse bowl deliberately placed two feet from the action, with a flick of the spatula, to oohs and aahs. He adds lemon, cooks a little further, then distributes these on the dinner plates in front of each diner, and you better eat 'em up now because already he is sautéeing the onions and zucchini which are part of the next course and—get this—flavors them with sesame seeds, yes, but how? By throwing the sesame seeds where? Right! Into the air! And where do they land? Right! *On the onions and zucchini!* Flip, flip, flip, flip, flip, flip, flip, flip, and eight people have sautéed onions and zucchini on their plates. Believe it or not, the steaks are this very moment being cut into bite-size (chopstick-size) pieces, to be cooked with the mushrooms. And how do you like your steak, sir? Rare? Bang! You got it (with raw mushrooms). Medium? Bang, bang! You got it (with medium mushrooms). Well-done? Bang, bang, bang! You got it (with tired mushrooms). A pile of bean sprouts is then prepared exactly like the shrimp, onions, zucchini, steak (or chicken) and mushrooms (with soy sauce, sesame, salt and pepper), the clown departs and you get your first moment's peace.

Your own early departure is clearly suggested when your check arrives with your ice cream. If you don't leave promptly, the table is set up for the next victims while you are still at it.

The steaks are good. Wine is out of the question. Warm sake is available, or the excellent Kirin beer from Japan. But the whole scene is an insult—to Americans, to the Japanese and to the digestion. There are other Benihanas in New York, at one of which—Benihana Palace—the hospitality is especially welcoming: in the cocktail lounge drinks are served on the floor.

Convenient for families of six or eight.

★★BENITO'S II

163 Mulberry Street (near Grand Street)
LUNCH AND DINNER. CLOSED SUNDAY.
No reservations (226–9012).
No credit cards.
Beer and wine.
Inexpensive.

Though clearly a slave to the garish, Papa Benito's taste in interiors is no narrower than just that. This half-again-as-large offspring of the original, tiny Benito's, half a block away, is hideous to look upon in a manner totally unreminiscent of its gewgawed, sherbet-yellow progenitor. Here we have a cubical room of glazed brick, grainy wood and a patterned-tile floor that seems to writhe beneath your feet. So you shouldn't miss a thing, the illumination is brassy and brilliant. And you get the kitchen, too: through an interior window in the back wall, a full view of the shining white and stainless-steel cookery, a handful of diligent men therein, all wearing BENITO'S II T-shirts—the house colors are navy blue on white.

Benito's the First was the best restaurant in Little Italy right up to the time it was reborn as its own big brother, and though the greater demands this place makes on its kitchen has increased the frequency of culinary fumbles a mite, the title has not been lost. Benito's II is the only restaurant down here where spectacular food, though not an every-course occurrence, is never a surprise. That, taken together with the indulgent prices, means there is often a wait for the unreservable tables at prime time. But this young crowd eats with dispatch—they pay their checks while they gulp their coffee—so the hold is usually short.

The sill of that window to the kitchen is adorned with platters of appetizers, the most eye-catching of which are the Stuffed Peppers, for they are bright-red, glistening with oil. They are heated up to your order, arrive steaming; and the plump, sweet vegetables turn out to be filled with a rich caponata of sautéed eggplant, celery, olives and big capers, all bound together by a thickened, spicy oil. Wonderful food. Benito's is a distinctly Sicilian establishment, which means that capers turn up almost everywhere —for instance, in among the leaves of the Stuffed Artichoke, tiny black olives as well, both in an oily herbed breading, the leaves and heart of the artichoke itself firm and salty. The eggplant is baked until it is limp and saturated with oil; then it is converted to Eggplant Parmigiana by the addition of a thick tomato sauce and strong cheese that is browned and pully. The Stuffed Mushrooms are filled with the minced stems and bits of hot red pepper, and they are served in a pool of butter that has been heavily dosed with coarsely chopped parsley, all of which is fine, except that the dish is heated once too often, and the mushrooms have lost much of their flavor and firmness.

The primitive pasta dishes are the best, including firm spaghetti in hot oil and an abundance of lightly browned garlic: linguine in a thick marinara sauce that is gamy if not profound—a last-minute sprinkling of parsley adds a sweet fragrance to to the otherwise pungent sauce; and gnocchi, rather too, too solid these little potato dumplings, but that quality is offset by the sharp and sour clarity of their simple, Piedmont-style tomato sauce.

Have your mother cut up your Octopus Sicilian Style, for the little beast arrives intact, his many arms just about waving, his flavor bristling with the murderous thoughts he entertained at the moment of his capture, his texture still firm from the instant when he braced himself—in these, his final moments, he is buried in a red sauce that is thick with capers, black olives and strands of sautéed onion—a briny dish of much character, best consumed by beginners only after a serious alcoholic indiscretion. Splendid Chicken Scarpariello, the skin crisped until it is noisy to the touch, the meat tender and moist, the abundant platter of chicken oily, redolent of garlic and livened with the flavor of southern herbs. The Rollatine Sicilian Style consists of cutlets of veal filled with cheese and minced ham, bread-crumbed and sautéed until the cheese within is melted and fragrant, the ham hot and moist, the veal crisped but still tender; it is served with freshly sautéed mushrooms that are mingled with onions and crushed garlic cloves. A superb dish that goes very well with the Escarole in Garlic and Oil, the sturdy leaves of the green marvelously sodden, more of those garlic cloves concealed within them.

The provolone cheese is the genuine Italian article and not bad. You can have good strawberries served in cannoli cream, the thick custard of the famous tubular dessert, here studded with bits of chocolate.

Very drinkable cheap Sicilian wine is available in carafes and in magnum bottles, and even the red is served cold.

★★ LE BIARRITZ

325 West 57th Street
LUNCH AND DINNER. CLOSED SUNDAY.
Reservations, 245–9467.
Credit cards: AE, DC, V.
Medium-priced.

As the cost of rental living escalates along Central Park South, it becomes necessary to offset. You descend from your penthouse as grandly as ever, smiling benignly to the elevator operator as he delivers you gently to the mirror-and-marble lobby at Main, you favor the doorman with a pleasantry, automatically wondering, at the same time, if you can possibly give him no more for Christmas this year than you gave him last, and you slink down to a place like this for a little prix fixe, vowing to eschew the extras, but a moment later rationalizing that the saving on cab fare would take care of half a dozen snails and that the whiskeys-and-soda you had at home instead of at Le Biarritz would permit your roommate (doing her best, the darling, to *enjoy* the *convenience* of washing her own hair) the luxury of some Bayonne ham.

You have begun to discover a whole new world of nether vogue. For example, many of the customers at Le Biarritz speak French; and this is a French restaurant. Now, there is a romance somewhere in there; something about something called *authenticity.* It seems, you have heard, that if people from a foreign country frequent a restaurant that serves food from that country, it suggests that the restaurant prepares the food *correctly* (whatever *that* means), and this is somehow *good.* Very interesting. And apparently this interior, looking much like what the old homestead in the Bronx would have looked like if Pa had let Ma let that skinny decorator have his head, is *charming.* Something about all this shiny copper and pottery and gilded chandeliers and flowers and plants and carpeting being, somehow, *innocent.* Very confusing.

Meanwhile, soak in some of these hors d'oeuvres. There is salami, thin slices of the redolent and oily stuff; a livery pâté that seems to be freshly made; crunchy celery rémoulade. For that little extra payment you can have silky ham rimmed with pure white fat, all nice and smoky, served over slices of ripe melon. For a cold night there is, when it is the soup of the day, a lobster bisque that is actually made with plenty of lobster—it is dark, thick, strong, sweet and winy.

The main courses are the usual West Side items, but they are all well-prepared. The Gigot aux Flageolets is rare, and your plate is quite covered with thin slices of the pink meat immersed in a thin, dark, bloody gravy; at the other end of the platter a mound of firm beans, a warm and juicy grilled tomato, and a cluster of crisp watercress. Terrific sweetbreads—thick slices of them, sautéed until they are crackling, the insides still oily and soft, served with mushrooms that have been sautéed until they are chocolate-brown, little onions that have been cooked with sugar, and roasted potatoes, all in a meaty sauce. There is duck in a cherry sauce that looks like chocolate syrup and tastes like a powerful stock that has just been lightly sweetened and brandied. The bird itself is carefully roasted, and you get a crisp skin around the moist, pleasantly oily meat. The salad is fresh, and it is served in a clear oily dressing.

The cheeses are in the refrigerator, the St. Honoré has been recently, and the Crêpes Suzette, though well-made, are overpriced at $7 for two. Stick to the mousse au chocolat, a gigantic dollop of the airy stuff, and the decent fruit tarts.

★ BILLY'S

948 First Avenue (near 52nd Street)
LUNCH, MONDAY TO SATURDAY; DINNER, DAILY.
Reservations, 355–8920.
Credit cards: AE, CB, DC, MC.
Medium-priced.

Billy's is like P. J. Clarke's, but without the drunks. Also without the juke box, preserved decay, bouncer and ice blocks in the urinals, for which blessings you pay through the trunk, for the prices here are an object lesson to P. J.'s of what you can get away with if you don't have to fill three large rooms to pay the real estate taxes.

You come here for your shrimp cocktail, for your sirloin steak, for your hamburger steak for the lady, for your lamb chops, for your Irish coffee. And you eat and drink these ingestibles amid furnishings and fixtures that graced Billy's at the old spot four blocks from here, for doth not the sign read "Established by Michael Condron Way Back in 1870," and is that not Michael's bar, the same one as was in the old place, and are not these the old gas lamps wired up for electric, and don't the wooden doors and panels with the brass knobs and hinges seem to be the same ones as Michael knew? Sure. And isn't there a bottle of ketchup on the red-checkered tablecloth, same as in the old place? Sure. And isn't that Michael's own begotten son, Billy, behind the bar? You bet it is. And even if the place does look like a saloon, the waiters wear those little long-sleeved vests so you can tell them from the customers, and the only loud talking is from the kiddies some folks don't mind bringing here because this is a family-type restaurant, even if it did forget to close during Prohibition.

The menu is painted on a slate, and occasional daily specials are indicated by little signs tacked on the wall. Tomato juice is half a dollar, the onion soup is pretty ordinary, and the shrimp cocktail consists of four carefully cooked shrimp and cocktail sauce (you can add horseradish).

Eschew the pork chops (cooked to the point where you not only will not get trichinosis, but anything else either). Pass up the lobster tails (either for political reasons—they are from South Africa—or for personal ones—they had a tough trip). Do not order the broiled filet of sole (it may be broiled, but it is gently broiled, so it tastes as if it has been stewed in butter; the coloration is paprika, not natural browning by fire). Whatever you order, do not order the sautéed onions. They are limp (as such onions should be), but they lack the accent of burnt grease that can make this dish a kind of sinful pleasure.

Do order the steak. It is thick, cooked exactly the way you ordered it, tender and tasty. Or order the chopped steak—large, made of freshly ground meat, and excellent with the steak sauce that is a companion to the ketchup on your table. Or order the steak tartare—the meat is freshly ground, and you can ask for the pepper mill or whatever if you want to adjust the seasoning. The broiled chicken seems to be of a fresh bird, and the lamb chops are as carefully made as the steaks. Fair French fries (they are the kind you put ketchup on, not the kind you put salt on), baked potatoes that seem to be made in a slow oven, so the skin, instead of being flaky and slightly blackened, is merely a tired container.

The apple pie is a fair commercial variety, but the cheese cake is dreadful.

★★LE BISTRO

827 Third Avenue (near 50th Street)
LUNCH, MONDAY TO FRIDAY; DINNER, MONDAY TO SATURDAY. CLOSED SUNDAY.
Reservations, 759–8439.
Credit cards: AE, MC, V.
Medium-priced.

The place is well-named, for this *is* very much a bistro, with its simple, square-room layout with a little bar at the front—tan walls, heavy hanging lamps, travel posters (behind glass!), a comfortable red banquette all around. The neatly set tables are covered with white linen, fringes of red gingham showing at the edges. Le Bistro is a cheerful place, everything about it is hearty, you enter and judge at once (correctly) that the food will be sturdy stuff. The surest clues are these waiters, barrel-chested, one and all, in aprons over shirt sleeves (the cuffs rolled up). They are gruffly polite, intelligent, on the job. They make suggestions. Take them.

Take, for example, the saucisson chaud. The sausages themselves are not the moist fatty ones that usually go by this name; they are, instead, rather dry and firm, but they are spicy almost to the point of hotness. They are served with superb warm potato salad —the potatoes are salty, they are covered with an oily dressing that is thick with mustard, and they are sprinkled with plenty of chopped fresh parsley. Or take the quiche—well above average, the custard light and fluffy, the bits of ham abundant, smoky and salty, the crust carefully made, so that it is crunchy and browned on the bottom as well as along the exposed edge.

You may get an undercooked artichoke here, hard-hearted, the leaves resistant to scraping by all but the sharpest teeth—good vinaigrette and all that, but too much work. You are better off with the mussels; do not be deceived by their not being in their shells—they are perfectly fresh, and the huge mound of them is in a good thick dressing that is highly flavored with bay.

Definitely a soup house. Sometimes there is a hot leek-and-potato soup; it is thick and slightly grainy, with lots of butter and sharp taste of boiled milk. And sometimes there is a cream of lentil soup, which is an elemental thing, thick, studded with discs of fairly uninteresting sausage, but the sum of it very satisfying. Of course there is onion soup—made with a good beefy stock and onions that have been cooked until they are dark-brown and sweet.

An oddity: Pieds de Porc Grillés—pig's feet, and very good, if not what the doctor ordered. You end up eating pig fat, cartilege, gelatine and an oily browned breading, which is all very succulent and sinful. You are left with a plate of glistening bones. The dish comes with some of the best French fries in town, crisp, thin, perfectly browned, tasty. This is one of the minority of French restaurants in New York where, when you order duck bigarade, you get duck *bigarade,* which is to say that the sauce is not a candied consommé but a flavored stock. This is not the best version of this dish in town, but it is the real thing—a good bird, with plenty of fat and moisture left behind in a judicious roasting, a more than decent sweet-and-tart sauce, and a nice garnish of sliced oranges.

On Fridays there is bouillabaisse—not a gargantuan bowl of it, which is surprising in this place, but the soup is thick and vibrant; the fish is flaky (albeit bony); and—surprise!—the lobster is fresh, you get a good bit of it, and it is cooked to the proper point.

The Boeuf Bordelaise is of good beef, accurately sautéed, but the sauce lacks balance—too strong a flavor of raw wine, which is not offset by the presence of good fresh mushrooms.

Some sturdy desserts, like Gâteau de Riz, a moist, heavy and extremely satisfying rice cake with a vanilla sauce. The chocolate mousse is intensely flavored of dark chocolate, fresh, and served with good whipped cream. Most restaurant parfaits are just ice cream and syrup, but the coffee parfait here is much better than that—the ice cream is of a strong coffee flavor, and the sauce is made with rum and caramel. Avoid the pears in wine—they taste as if they should be called pears in wine and water.

The place can be a mad scene at lunchtime, but in the evening it is neither packed nor deserted, which makes it a pleasant place for a pleasant dinner.

★ BOSPHORUS EAST

121 Lexington Avenue (near 28th Street)
LUNCH, MONDAY TO SATURDAY; DINNER, DAILY.
Reservations, 679–8370.
Credit cards: AE, DC, MC.
Medium-priced.

It is almost heretical for a Middle Eastern restaurant to eschew in its décor the warm end of the rainbow in favor of the kind of cool tones that are the colors of signs that read COMFORTABLY AIR-CONDITIONED (each letter capped with snow and weighed down with an icicle or two). This room is a jewel-like little box, of pale blue leather, mirrored walls and white linen set with cut-glass crystal. Along one side there are three intimate booths, giving onto the main room through onion-shaped peaked portals, within each a table, upon each of those a RESERVED sign, whether the table is reserved or not. These choice seats are set aside for choice customers, though unknown walk-ins can promote one by persuasion. Each romantic nook has its name painted over its archway, specifically TARABYA, BEBEK and ÜSKÜDAR, which, your waiter explains, are Turkish watering places like, that native Bronxer surmises, "Wildwood and Atlantic City." On the wall over the table in each of these escapist cubicles hangs a wraparound skirt (here un-wrapped around) of silken satin, matching bra and tiny briefs pinned thereto. It seems the proprietress was a belly dancer in her day, and these were the formals of her trade. A portrait of a tuxedoed Kemal Atatürk (president of Turkey 1923–38) glowers down on believers and heathens alike.

But it is only the appearances that are unconventional, for this restaurant's menu is very much the standard Turkish thing, including the customary dietary detours that are more Greek, Armenian or Lebanese than Turkish, and which are invariable exceptions to the rule.

You may begin with imam bayildi, the cool oil-soaked eggplant mash made with onions, tomatoes and Eastern spices. The one served here is served *too* cool, icebox cool, in fact, but the flavor and richness are all you expect from this familiar item. For something warmer and lighter, Bosphorus East's cheese boerek is among the flakiest and airiest in town. Arriving as six equilateral triangles set in a hexagon on a little plate, they may be dispatched in about two bites per triangle. Cheese boerek is often a fairly heavy first course, when the flaky pastry leaves are stuffed to plumpness with cheese, and those versions are solidly satisfying, whereas this one is handled as something of a delicacy. Then there are your regulars, your taramasalata (the paste of bread and red caviar, served here in a smooth, almost creamy version, albeit light on the roe), your midia dolma (that bizarre concoction, served cool in mussel shells, of mussels, nuts, onions and currants, always spiced, but in this version almost overwhelmed by cinnamon, and quite delicious anyway), and your yalanji yaprak (another cinnamoned wonder, this one what in English is usually called stuffed vine leaves, the moist and parchment-like leaves wrapped around sausage-shaped cakes of rice and currants). Oddly listed under "salads" is a refreshing yogurt dish in which the cool white cream is laced with chopped cucumbers, garlic and parsley—summer food. And for winter food there is a single hot soup on the menu, described as "yogurt soup with Armenian style wheat, garnished with mint . . ." What you receive, however, is something that fits the description only if you cannot distinguish wheat from rice. This is a satisfying hot soup, but disappointing if you were expecting the grainy flavor of wheat and end up with the bland one of overcooked rice.

At this point you remind your waiter that you ordered some red wine. He hastens away and returns with it, uncorks it and pours some in your glass. It tastes fine, but it is cold, and you point this out to him, whereupon your waiter wins, hands down, the Fast-on-the-Feet Hooey award by responding that "this coolness is all right, because it is the coolness of the cellar, not of the refrigerator."

To the accompaniment of your 40° red wine you sample the Bosphorus Special Shish Kebab, an estimable version of this standard dish, the lamb alternated on a skewer with lightly charred chunks of mushroom, green pepper, onion and tomato, the meat itself rather bloodless as a result of its marination, and gaining little flavor from that treatment, but charred and good anyway. Alternatively one may opt for Kouzou Dolma, a mound of what the menu refers to as "Bosphorus Fancy Pilaf," surmounted by baked lamb. That pilaf is a wonderful browned-rice mixture of the sweet-spiced grain, little peas, currants and pine nuts, but the meat that adorns it may be a little dry. For something reliably wet there is Kabak Dolma—hollowed-out zucchini tubes filled with a moist and meaty mixture of ground lamb, rice and onions, the entire device stewed in tomatoes, making a thick gravy.

The Cadillac of the desserts, if you judge by the cost, is Ashure, a heavily cinnamoned layer of chopped nuts over a pudding of apricots and raisins, the crunchy nuts an excellent foil for the sweetened and gooey fruits. Among other good sweets are Chekme, a tube of pastry filled with a mixture of chopped nuts, fruits and honey, and Ekmek Kadayif, a honeyed bread pudding served under that incredibly thick Middle Eastern cream called kaymak, which is made from several times its own volume of whole milk. Somehow, despite the cream's almost buttery quality, it is never insipid, even with this rich pudding.

★★★ BOX TREE

242 East 50th Street
LUNCH, MONDAY TO FRIDAY; DINNER, DAILY.
Reservations essential, PL 8–8320.
No credit cards.
Wine.
Very expensive.

Hardly more than a right turn and a left beyond the tiny vestibule, and you have seen the scene. The Box Tree is a little gem of a place, a tiny free-form bauble of dark glinting stones in which eight tables, twenty-one chairs and pretty things have been lovingly assembled, with an impeccable eye for ornament; it is a jewel bejeweled, the dabs of bright color here and there like high-class ice strewn on dusky velvet.

There are two small adjacent dining areas, the larger of the two holding four tables and thirteen chairs. The choice table is at the front window—not much to see through the lace curtain that filters your view of East 50th Street, so you turn your eyes to your immediate surroundings. The deep-green walls are spotted with small sconces, two tiny red lampshades per bracket. To supplement them, pale lamps of fluted glass hang from the high ceiling and glow weakly, white candles in turned copper candlesticks throw off one candlepower per table. The walls are adorned with polished pewter and framed prints, the tables carry brilliant arrays of fresh flowers in china vases. In the front room the period-piece tables are shown off without cloths, but in the back room things are different. It is hardly a room at all, rather a cubicle the size of a second-class stateroom on a second-class steamer. But the little area has been shrewdly exploited—four oblong tables arranged in the shape of a U, two as the base, one as each side; seating is on the colorful high-backed banquette that rims three sides of the room. Here the tables are linened, and one assumes that the need for furniture tailored snugly to the space precluded the use of antiques. This is intimate dining for eight people who know one another. By the evening's end, eight strangers will be at least acquainted. For privacy, specify a front-room table when you make your reservation.

One of the boys in white will keep you supplied with warm bread. If your bread-and-butter plate is bare, he will decorate it with a slice. You will want that bread and butter for the Terrine de Foie de Canard—a buttery and creamy mousse of duck liver that is served in a ramekin, a thin layer of cool jelly and a sliver of truffle over its top. This satiny terrine seems to have a spot of cognac in it, which at once intensifies and mellows the strong flavor of duck liver. Something billed as Croustade de Crevettes consists of a handful of shrimp in a flaky well-browned pastry, served with a polished white sauce made slightly pink with wine—these shrimp have a clarity of flavor that comes of their being fresh and not overcooked. If you are fortunate enough to come on one of the nights when the chef chooses to make snails, you will be able to sample a startling preparation. The snails are not served in their shells, but instead in what may as well be called a snail plate, a circular piece of pottery with six snail-size concavities, into each of which a snail is fitted with hot butter flavored with Pernod. Across the top, grated cheese has been spread and browned during the final baking. You probably would not have dreamed up the unlikely combination of snails, Pernod and cheese, but it works very well, particularly with the plump tender snails you get here.

The soups are good, if not consistent. The cold cucumber soup, which has been a summertime cliché in New York restaurants for more than a decade, is here made in a version that is distinguished from the others by a powerful overriding flavor of vividly fresh dill. But on one occasion the cucumber and yogurt flavors were lost, though another time, when the cucumber was in sizable crisp chunks, all the tastes were clear. A far greater tragedy is the fact that the Crème de Fenouille is not invariably what it can be. At its best, this thick soup of fennel and potato in a chicken-stock base has a quality of primal nourishment, as of the flavors of the earth. Sounds pretty good? Well, on another occasion it had been puréed too far, its slightly grainy quality gone, a thin smoothness (as of too long in the blender) in its place. That slight change kills the whole thing.

You order the Carré d'Agneau à la Menthe Fraîche, and you specify that you would like it rare. The owner/chef makes one of his frequent trips to the dining room to inform you that the lamb has been roasted to medium and that there is no more lamb in the house with which to start over. At any rate, it is good lamb, presumably even better when it is cooked to order, and it is served with a dollop of a deep-green sauce that is essence of fresh mint, lightly moistened and seasoned—just a bit of it livens up the overcooked lamb and would even improve rarer meat.

With so brief a menu, the management displays an admirable audacity by listing liver among the handful of main courses, particularly as this preparation is not liver in disguise, but rather, liver that retains its smooth texture and flavor, even though it is moistened with the winy deep-brown sauce studded with bits of black truffle—a spectacular dish.

There must be better ways to exploit the chef's talents than with Filet de Boeuf Sauce Fine Champagne. This is perfectly good beef and all that, but like most filets, it is relatively bland. This quality can be offset somewhat by grilling at high heat to form a crust, or by wrapping the rim of the filet in bacon before grilling, to impart the flavor of fat to a meat that has little of its own. Unfortunately, the filet here is grilled gently, and though it is sauced very nicely, in the same sauce that went on the liver (sans truffles), that does not rescue the steak.

Bass is served a number of ways, including a rendition with a cream sauce based on fish stock to which sautéed vegetables have been added for flavor and to which fresh lime juice is added just before serving. The fish is fresh, sweet and cooked to the right point, and the sauce transforms it into a startlingly piquant dish.

Salad. Three leaves of endive are set on a plate like three canoes, with a dollop in each hull of thick dressing made with a grainy mustard. Leaves of lettuce and sprigs of watercress surround the endive. The menu does not so state, but you are offered cheese with your salad, different ones on different nights, and they are excellent.

The Vacherin Box Tree is one of the greatest desserts in town. This vacherin consists of a crown of hazelnut-flavored meringue filled with alternating layers of whipped cream and raspberries. On occasion, before slicing it up, your waiter will parade the whole thing through the dining room. It is worthy of at least one bow of the head. Plump liquored strawberries are also available, with a thick silken cream very akin to a French *crème fraîche*. The dish is called Fraises Romanoff, but if that is a dish you have come to know in New York restaurants, be assured this is to the usual thing what Escoffier is to the Good Humor man.

The place has its inanities. Females receive menus without prices (if there is a male in the party). There is background music (especially preposterous in a small crowded restaurant that is noisy enough with customer conversation and the sounds from the kitchen).

Your check arrives on a plate with a rose.

★ BRADLEY'S

70 University Place (near 11th Street)
LUNCH, MONDAY TO FRIDAY; DINNER, DAILY.
No reservations (CA 8–6440).
Credit cards: AE.
Medium-priced.

Bradley's is presided over by a fellow named Bradley. Bradley is a cartoon dinosaur, tall, ample, sage and weathered. His clothes hang on him like an old, softened shell. When he smiles, an arc of a hundred gleaming teeth bisects his leathery visage. To cope with the occasional difficulty, he puts on the look of the sleepy killer who will, if necessary, tiresome as it all is, dispatch with dispatch. He has it all down pat.

There is insistent jazz from musicians in a corner between the barroom and the back room. Up front there is the long bar under dim, low-hanging lights—you can study the back of your hand. (Here Bradley man-talks with the customers who have made it and has a hamburger when he is hungry.) In back are most of the dining tables. Throughout stride the busy waitresses (various degrees of stunning). Dark walls, wood-grained, glazed, hung with sriking art, spotlighted.

A singular fixture behind the bar: above the bottles an artfully placed tilted mirror, the length of the bar—you can scan the place and the people without turning your back on your drink. You consider the Village spectrum as it is currently composed, from the aging individualists (wry, cynical, taciturn), who drank in Village bars in the forties, to the communal young (optimistic, flagrantly sentimental, joyous). The generation gap is not a no man's land between embattled camps. The Village preserves its reputation as a haven for all kinds of nuts and sanes.

Bradley's is a good place to visit if you like hamburgers and steaks. The hamburgers are plump and juicy, and the flavor of the good beef is unsullied by bread crumbs or seasonings. The steaks are tender and accurately cooked. There is a big steak and a small steak, the latter much like the former, but smaller. The cottage fries are well-browned discs. And those are the high points, except for the bread. The bread should be your appetizer—it is delicious bread, from one of those Italian bread houses in the Village, and surpasses the underseasoned snails, frozen shrimp with bland cocktail sauce (horseradish should be brought), and the avocado stuffed with the kind of crabmeat salad that is acceptable as a sandwich filling at a drugstore—in a small town in Nebraska. If you really can't go for straight bread as your first course, the clams are your best bet. It is suggested that the Italian-bread supplier be approached and asked for the name of a good Italian cheese-cake supplier. There is ice cream. If you are into Gleam II, you will like the Mint Parfait.

The music starts at around nine-thirty.

★ BRASSERIE

100 East 53rd Street
NEVER CLOSES.
No reservations (751–4840).
Credit cards: AE, CB, DC, MC, V.
Medium-priced.

When the Brasserie was introduced to New York, in 1959, it finally became possible in this city for a suffering insomniac to surrender cheerfully to his affliction, get into something comfortable, and taxi to a steak and a bottle of wine at three o'clock in the morning. (The Brasserie, as almost everyone knows, never closed and never closes.) Not only was there food to eat and drink to drink on East 53rd Street while most of the city slept, but a lot to see as well. Instead of counting sheep, the hard-of-sleeping could count night people—they flowed through the revolving doors and down the brass-balustraded stairs in variety, in the good spirits of that day, in throngs. The middle of the night had been waiting for this place since Repeal.

The early-morning crowd came from Broadway, Carnegie and the Garden, from charity balls at the Waldorf and the night shift at the post office, from Third Avenue saloons and spent poker games. Never had democracy worked so well. Chinchillas waited in line behind Persian lamb, chesterfields behind mackinaws. Though there were no tables out on the street, this was New York's closest to a European café, not only in the colorful diversity of its clientele but also in the plain decency of the food. The onion soup was a small meal in a big bowl, the choucroute a civilized tour through meaty gluttony. You could read a paper and fiddle with a couple of drinks through changes of the season without being hustled, for the largely French floor staff had not yet absorbed the local obsession with turnover. The Brasserie was the antecedent of the easygoing eating and drinking that have become New York's predominant restaurant style.

To begin at three o'clock in the morning, your yellow cab drops you off at the familiar canopy on the north side of the Seagram Building, where you are greeted by a gent who sells early-morning flowers to those who are giddy and susceptible when the stars are out. You pass him by, knowing there are nosegays in Perrier bottles on the tables inside, and enter the front room, which is big and brown, low-ceilinged and softly lit. It is brightened by the dozens of red-and-white-checked cloths that drape the rows upon rows of tables. Off to your left, as you descend the stairs, is the massive rectangular dining counter, the island within it surmounted by festive displays—autumn leaves in October, bunting for the Fourth of July—that are changed a little less frequently than their themes or states of disintegration call for. You sit comfortably, in captain's chairs or deep banquettes. And the service is good. The place is patrolled by an international brigade of waiters and waitresses in red, white and blue, almost all of whom gild their English with the accents of a more musical first language. They know the menu, and they understand their jobs: to find out what you want and bring it.

Begin with some raw clams. They sell a lot of them here, so they are usually fresh, sweet enough to have with nothing added but lemon and a few grindings of black pepper. The kitchen will, if you are fool enough to permit it, convert them into clams casino by the admixture of a tasteless breading and the application of heat, which is a minor desecration that might be justifiably committed against the shrimp instead, for the cocktail de crevettes is picturesque and nothing more, the pink-tipped shrimp having been boiled to anonymity. The steak you have been building up to is of good, if not prime, beef; it is usually tender, accurately prepared, handsomely crusted, and served with an ample mound of French fries—long, slender strands of prettily goldened potatoes, slightly crisp on the outside, moist and tender within; good with salt. Sadly, that description does not always hold, for a serving now and then appears to have been deep-fried at least once too often. Raw meat was served almost nowhere in this city before the Brasserie, but this place promptly popularized steak tartare. It is still made with freshly ground meat here, which is essential; and if you explain to your waiter that you want it prepared with as much oil as it will hold without leaking, and with plenty of mustard and pepper, abundant minced onions and chopped anchovies, and capers galore, it is possible to get a terrific tartare in this place. Eat slowly, for there is much to see here during the suicide shift: repentant inebriates with coffee in one hand, head in the other; the remnants of theater parties having toasted bagels and smoked salmon (eschew) before the bleak drive to Queens; the exhausted, fresh from aerobic conditioning at the local discos, in boots and tuxes, T-shirts and silver pants, prolonging the mood with Mumm's and chocolate cake.

Onion soup is the big item at lunchtime. It is not what it once was, but the melted cheese that seals the soup and bread within the pot is genuine Gruyère, browned in the oven until it is almost bubbling, and its solidity and flavor save the dish. The choucroute is even further from its original self, the slabs of pork bled dry of their meaty substance, the sausages little more than excessively fatted ground meat, the sauerkraut in which all this is buried little more than warm vinegared cabbage. Big-business lunches do not take place here. It is the middle-income sensible who keep this place busy at the middle of the day, and they have learned that the daily fish special is always of fresh fish— on occasion whole flounder that are buttered and broiled until they are dark russet brown. The meat that you find beneath is white and flaky, almost fluffy—perfect fish. Once a mad scene at lunchtime, the place is busy nowadays but never to overflowing, and you can usually get a table as soon as you arrive. Mostly the lunchers are grabbing an hour or two of friendship at the centers of their mechanical business days.

Dinner is not recommended. Not that you cannot assemble a decent meal from what is offered; rather, the place is frequented at this time by grim, determined economizers. They have learned that two can get stuffed, drunk and away for as little as $25, for *French food,* and *without stiffing the waiter.* They are all around you, thinking about how inexpensively they are eating. This gives them a deep—*deep*—sense of accomplishment. You can see by their little eyes that they are continuously computing the economy of it all.

If you do not mind being surrounded by the obsessively pecunious, the big dinners, none higher than $8.95, commence with crudités that are accompanied by a thin tuna tapenade; proceed through such as a coarse and gamy pâté that is served with a rather thin Cumberland sauce, or an unexceptional fruit cup or consommé; continue to veal Cordon Bleu, a hefty slice of tender and pale meat wrapped around strong cheese and tame ham, all breaded and deep-fried until the dish takes on an almost violent heartiness; or to Surprise de Volaille Vigneronne, a solid and creamy stew of well-browned chicken that is served with an amazingly nutty and artfully seasoned purée of chestnuts.

For dessert there are good cheeses one night, tired ones the next—your waiter will clue you if you ask. The chocolate mousse is nowhere, but the chocolate cake—called Côte de Chevreuil—is dark, moist and deeply flavored of strong chocolate, and wrapped in a thick, polished icing that is black and sugary. The Black Forest Cake is light and rich, but only half black, dark layers alternating with strata of fluffy whipped cream, the top of the cake studded with candied cherries and strewn with chocolate shavings and powdered sugar.

★ BRAZILIAN PAVILION

141 East 52nd Street
LUNCH AND DINNER. CLOSED SUNDAY.
Reservations accepted for dinner only, PL 8–8129.
Credit cards: MC, V.
Medium-priced.

A pretty restaurant, smallish, made to seem larger by mirrored walls. There are colorful murals of Rio, simple caned chairs at the tables, much green and yellow, the colors of the Brazilian flag. The menu is extensive and authentic, the prices reasonable for a good restaurant in midtown Manhattan; and the place has become very popular. At lunchtime it gets a substantial share of the traffic from the nearby office buildings, and in the evening New York's casual and experimental young keep coming from all over town and help to keep the place busy. The Pavilion is a little noisy, a soothing hum, and part of the sound is the gentle, singsong sibilance of the Portuguese language, for the place is also frequented by members of New York's growing Brazilian population.

The assorted appetizer platters include a number of simple things (canned sardines, hearts of palm and olives), but also a terrific Portuguese sausage that is oily, spicy and fibrous, and best of all, shrimps that have been cooked in their shells, in oil—they are warm, crisp, strongly flavored (leaving the shell on does that) and satisfying.

None of the main courses here is what you would call a delicacy. Brazilian food is vigorous and full of contrasts, and this place, like the other Brazilian restaurants in New York, puts plenty of food on your plate. When you have eaten, you know that you have eaten.

Churrasco Gaucho is a delicious steak, marinated and accurately broiled. The meat, which is tender, has been marinated thoroughly (with onions, peppers and tomatoes), so that the flavor of the marinade has permeated the meat; and it is served in a thin sauce of the marinade itself, with rice and a mound of manioc meal, the zesty flour ground from the yuca root, which is a common starch in Latin America.

On Fridays there is Cod Fish "a Gomes de Sa," a heavy and hearty dish of cod fish, baked with potato salad and slices of hard-cooked egg—oily, salty, loud. It is sprinkled with parsley, which is something like garnishing a side of beef with a cherry tomato.

Virado a Paulista is a dish of pork chops that have been peppered and blackened, served with substantial discs of grilled sausage and black beans that are winey and thick, all surmounted by a fried egg, and served with kale and the manioc flour. This is about as vigorous a plate of food as you can imagine.

Marmelada com Queijo, as you probably guessed, is quince paste and cheese—a cool, hard block of sweet preserves served with a Brazilian cheese that is not likely to develop a substantial following outside Brazil. The caramel custard here is cool and jellylike, covered with shredded coconut. Powerful coffee that is very good.

• BRETT'S

304 East 78th Street
LUNCH AND DINNER. CLOSED SUNDAY.
Reservations, 628–3725.
Credit cards: AE, CB, DC, MC, V.
Medium-priced.

Everything about Brett's was designed to be cute. The very size of the place is playpen-cute and the napkin-size tables, of which there are more than a dozen, with ample room for perhaps eight, are cute too. It really isn't so bad to rub shoulder padding with the fellow at the next table, if only he wouldn't marvel throughout his dinner at his fish's extraordinary lack of bones. "Hey," he says to his enthralled undoubted wife, "there's no bones in here." And later: "You know, there's still no bones in here." It's his favorite subject. Even during the Gâteau Fromage.

The wallpaper is *Gray's Anatomy* seen through rose-colored glasses, your tiny tables are clothed in Brooks Brothers–shirt pink, and in a little room at the rear there is a cater-cornered bar under mirrors—it is meant to appear jewel-like, but instead it is smoke-filled. Downstairs are the facilities, identified by male and female frogs on the respective doors.

A bare-shouldered soubrette asks if you would like a cocktail, and recent movements notwithstanding, you cannot help but note that she is the best-looking item in the place.

The menu changes constantly, but on one occasion, moving your elegantly manicured fingernail down the effete menu, you pause and nod at Mousse au Parmesan—ooh, how marvelous, a *mousse,* mind you, made of Parmesan *cheese,* mind you. An atrocity, mind you. An entirely unnecessary reduction of strong cheese to mild putty, sprinkled with parsley. The house has a diabolical way of serving its better dishes in littler portions. The Bay Scallops au Gratin, for example, are idiotically served in a stainless steel "shell," in which they would promptly become cold if the serving were not so small that you eat it before there is time. The scallops are obscured in the spicy Mornay sauce, which is made with a pungent cheese. The Baked Salmon en Croûte, of salmon that is less than perfectly fresh, is a well-made dish of fish in a nice flaky crust. Something called Stuffed Mushrooms should be called Unstuffed Mushrooms— these, too, are served in stainless steel and should be eaten in a trice, before they refrigerate, but once again that will not be difficult, for you have been served about two forkings and a scrape—nice sautéed mushrooms, in a creamy sauce made with good stock, but too little here to let your friends have a taste.

Something styled Roast Pork Bell Fermière consists of pork chops roasted to utter, white devastation. The chops are rimmed with some more of that pastry the salmon was wrapped in—happily, the pastry clings to the fat of the meat—this sparse rimming being the only civilized sustenance in the dish. True, your Tournedos Henry IV (don't you love their *names*?) does not arrive rare, as you ordered it, but by now your hopes are not high. The beef is tasty and tender; it is ornamented with a hefty dab of pâté de fois and served in a dark, winy sauce that is at once sweet and nutlike. The scalloped potatoes that accompany are brown from long, long cooking, and still slightly crisp. The Blanquette de Veau is a dreary version of this common dish, made with cartilaginous lumps of veal. Your Suprêmes de Volaille Artichaut consists of an OK chicken breast in an OK white sauce (chicken-stock base) and a fresh artichoke heart.

The Kirsch Torte is a heavy, nutted, whip-creamed cake soaked in an excess of liqueur, an after-dinner drink that requires a fork. The ingredients are good, but they are excessive. Not too many places around town where you can get Chilled Sherried Syllabub, right? Turns out to be your midget ramekin of whipped cream that has been lightly livened with a bit of wine, lemon rind and chocolate—not bad. On occasion there is a definitely desirable carrot cake; it has a lovely, sweetened quality of the fresh vegetable, and is layered and topped with whipped cream.

★★BROADWAY JOE STEAK HOUSE

315 West 46th Street
DINNER. CLOSED SUNDAY.
Reservations, CI 6–6513.
Credit cards: AE, MC.
Expensive.

One is greeted at table by a bored, formally attired gentleman who puts down a basket of bread, twenty to forty pats of butter, and immediately poises his pen at his pad.

"May we have a menu?" (Innocently.)

"Ova here we got no menu." (Bored.)

"What do you have?" (Expectantly.)

"We got pâté, shrimp cocktail, herring, tomato juice, lamb chops, steak, chopped steak, French fries, baked, cottage fries, hashed browns. Salad comes." (Bored.)

Not bad. He omitted only the onion soup and the chicken.

"Is there a wine card?" (Excitedly.)

"We got Valpolicella, Soave, Beaujolais, St. Julien." (Very bored.)

Steak is all. The first courses range from bad (pâté and onion soup) to fair (a shrimp cocktail consisting of half a dozen shrimp, sometimes overcooked, and a good cocktail sauce that contains plenty of strong horseradish) to very decent (pickled herring, with onions that are not wilted and retain their bite, in fresh sour cream and chives, served on fresh iceberg lettuce).

But that's not what we came here for, right? Right. We came here for steak. Thick, bloody, tender sirloin, blackened, with potatoes: baked potatoes are included, and they have crisp skins, and firm but thoroughly cooked interiors, into which you may insert a fistful of that butter the man brought, or some sour cream (still in its half-pint container, with chives stirred in); or cottage fries—two-inch, golden-brown, crunchy discs; or French fries—a bit limp, it must be admitted; or best of all, hashed browns that are of the brown-through-and-through school, with tiny flecks of almost blackened potato throughout, like a built-in zest. The steaks are cooked accurately, and the servings of potatoes are more than ample. There are also lamb chops, about three ribs thick; giant chopped steaks of good meat; and broiled chicken, which is often over-cooked.

You get a huge salad, but you don't have to eat it. If you wish to eat it, be sure to specify the noninclusion of the house dressing (which is made with what tastes like a garlic substitute) and the substitution of oil and vinegar. Or you may have that most barbarous of salad creations—alternating half-inch slabs of tomato and raw onion—which is not recommended for before the theater unless you have a box of your own.

Nothing special for dessert—tortoni, spumoni, canned stewed fruit or, oddity, cookies.

"Are there any cookies left?"

"Sure. Why not?" (Still bored.)

There are lots of waiters at Broadway Joe, and though the service is cursory, it is never rude, and always available and prompt.

Broadway Joe is one of the two or three places on this restaurant block that do any business after show time, for the simple reason that many people eat here because they like it here, theaters nearby or not. At seven-thirty or so the ladies in creations and the men with pinky rings and pointed shoes are replaced by a more traditionally dressed set, to whom any dinner worthy of the trouble is by its nature too substantial to be a mere prelude to the theater. Such dinners, if they are preparatory at all, prepare one for pursuits more languorous than forced attention in an auditorium full of burpers.

Broadway Joe is a simple and comfortable restaurant—a barroom in front, with a huge mural of Broadway and Hollywood caricatures; a center room that is pointlessly but harmlessly papered in scenes of Colonial America; and a rear room of plain walls and beamed ceiling

• BRUSSELS

115 East 54th Street
LUNCH, MONDAY TO FRIDAY; DINNER, MONDAY TO SATURDAY. CLOSED SUNDAY.
Reservations, PL 8–0457.
Credit cards: AE, CB, DC, MC, V.
Very expensive.

New management. Victor is in ever-courtly attendance, offering sound wine advice to whoever asks for it, with the courtliest manner on Manhattan Island. Behind the bar in the cozy cocktail lounge, the statue of the young boy continues to perpetually relieve itself into a champagne cooler. The large dining room, with its delicately patterned maroon-and-gold wallpaper, walnut beams, heavy chandeliers and soft light, is as muted and old-world as ever. And, as ever, reading the elaborate menu is more rewarding than eating the foods it lists. What arrives on your plate is clean, studiously prepared, but it is not only utterly without inspiration but actually devoid of the quality of French food. It has no character. An occasional dish is good, nothing is ever actually bad, but if you come here five times you will invariably find yourself searching the menu for something you have not had before, in the hope of finding a dish you would gladly order twice.

In the old days, for a first course you would order the Anguilles au Vert à la Flamande—cold eel in a jellied green sauce, with a bit of garlic. It is sturdy stuff with a texture that appealed to few. Nowadays it is rarely available—perhaps because the desirable small eels are not to be had, as you are told, but more likely because the dish is rarely ordered. You can have Pâté de Fois Gras de Strasbourg en Gelée; it comes from there and it is *en gelée,* and that's about all you can say for it. You can have Jambon de Parme; it is that kind of ham, and there are better kinds of that kind. You can have Toast à la Moelle aux Champignons; the dish is toast with marrow *and* mushrooms, and this mushroom is very nicely sautéed but that one was soaking wet when they sautéed it, so it is stewed instead. The lobster bisque is nice and spicy, and your waiter will pour either brandy or sherry into it, but neither liquor nor wine can rescue this soup from its inferior lobster.

You order Pompano Grenobloise, and the fish seems fresh enough, but at this restaurant, as in most places in New York, Grenobloise means Grenobloise minus mushrooms. Even so made, the dish can be good if the floured fish is rapidly sautéed in very hot butter, but here the process is carried out much too slowly, and instead of a crisp crust you get a soft, breaded exterior. The roasted pigeon is OK, with its canned peas; Tournedos Niçoise turns out to be a filet mignon of unexceptional quality, with a delicious sauce Béarnaise, and a garnish of one stewed tomato to justify the regional name, and another wet mushroom, this one as a cap, to make the dish look like something special. One of the best dishes in the house is the Noisette de Chevreuil Grand Veneur. This restaurant imports some excellent venison—it is well aged, tender and sweet, and served with a good dark sauce that is sweetened and thickened with cream. The à la carte vegetables are not much, but as you might hope in a restaurant of Belgian pretensions, the braised endives (called chicorées) are very good—the vegetable is cooked in consommé and lemon until it is limp, dark and strong.

The Crêpe Soufflé (vanilla flavor) with crème Anglaise (vanilla flavor) is better than ice cream. The thick strawberry mousse lacks the flavor of fresh strawberries.

If only Victor could cook!

★★CAFÉ DES ARTISTES

1 West 67th Street
LUNCH, SUNDAY TO FRIDAY; DINNER, DAILY.
Reservations, TR 7–3500.
Credit cards: AE, DC, MC, V.
Medium-priced.

Ah, the past, recaptured and preserved as in an old movie, the place so redolent of the thirties that you automatically look down to see if the snappy clientele is wearing spats or silver slippers.

This is no relation to the egregious restaurant of the same name that occupied these premises in recent years. Very little in the way of renovation has been imposed on the Café except for some felt on once dingy walls, and artfully lowered lighting. But that is all it took to accentuate the jewel-like quality of these small rooms, the semidarkness brightened here and there by cavorting peachy nudes, the subjects of the famous Howard Chandler Christy murals. In the pretty barroom the mirrors are still present, and there are black-and-white prints hung on the new tan felt. Throughout there are tables, quite cheek-to-cheek along the banquettes, and in the barroom there are a few booths wherein one may appreciate a bit of privacy. Avoid tables near the front door —on icy days there are chilling blasts.

The printed menu is a matrix of printed categories (chilled soup, veal, etc.) and some always-available dishes (gravlax salmon, gazpacho, etc.) onto which are dittoed, in purple ink, a couple of dozen additional items available the day of your visit. Among these are Oysters or, at a 25-cent premium, Oysters Saucisse. As these mollusks are not invariably the morning's catch (though they are certainly not over the hill), set aside the notion of having them with just a squeeze of lemon and a couple of turns of the pepper mill. Surely any slight incorrectness of taste will be obscured by the cocktail sauce, but it is firmly recommended that you try the Saucisse version, in which the circle of raw oysters surrounds a little ramekin of tomato-flavored beef broth and chopped sausages, into which you dip the oysters before eating them. For some strange reason this hefty sauce does well with the oysters, and if there is a hint of off taste, the sauce eliminates it while permitting the sweet taste of fresh oysters to show through—a good dish. The aforementioned gravlax is billed as Gravlax Salmon, Dill Marinated. This is the famous Scandinavian dish of raw salmon that has been marinated in salt and pepper, sugar and dill, served, traditionally, with a sweetened dill-and-mustard sauce. The Café's version is quite terrific, several slices of the deep-red tender and sweet fish sprinkled with coarsely ground pepper and served with a strong and sparkling version of the mustard sauce.

Each day a pasta dish is listed. One of these is Spinach Noodles with Mussels in Cream, and it is a semisuccessful essay. In re the noodles, instead of long, even strands we have shreds, as if these are the result of a first try on an at-home noodle-making machine; they are not overcooked, and they retain a subtle spinach flavor, but it's frustrating to eat the slippery slivers with a fork. As to the mussels in their cream sauce, the thickened cream is perfectly nice, but the quite fresh mussels are not quite perfectly rinsed—a single grain of sand in every single mussel. Your waiter brings what looks like a pencil sharpener, in which there are chunks of Parmesan cheese—a few turns of the handle liven the dish.

Unusual preparations of snails are becoming fashionable around town, and the Café is right there with Garlic Snails Sautéed with Prosciutto & Onions. These are snails without shells, tossed in an oily pan with the ham, onions and tomato and served on a layer of what seems to be sautéed garlic. The snails are at once metallic, oily and briny —sea-gamy—and the slivers of ham are an excellent foil to the rich snails.

Young Duckling with Pear in Williamin Brandy—the duck itself will give you a good notion of how to roast a bird. This one is crisp and moist, and the listing "Young" duckling is apparently true, for it is juicy and tender. The pear-and-pear-brandy treatment, however, yields a sauce so delicately flavored as to be overpowered by the rich bird.

That New York is not a pork city is the only conclusion that can be drawn from pork's almost universal absence from New York menus. And in fact it is not regularly listed here, which is a pity, for the Tenderloin of Pork, purpled in under "spit-roast," and served in a brown, gravylike sauce, arrives, surprisingly, as several slices of meat and one chop, and it has the sweet, fatty succulence that makes pork the richest of meats. The pork is surrounded by garnishes—nicely browned and creamy scalloped potatoes and a buttery purée of broccoli.

Escallopine of Veal, Gypsy Style, does not flaunt its Romany origins. The dish is made with perfect pale, buttery meat, but the sautéing is carried out at too low a temperature, and the cutlets are not properly browned. They are surmounted by strands of tongue, the whole thing served in a creamy sauce—an excellent dish that would be even better if the meat were more carefully cooked.

Olive-Cured Mozzarella is the regularly available house cheese. It is queer stuff, fibrous and permeated with olive-sourness—pickled cheese. But sometimes other cheeses are available, and some of them can be just as odd, including something called Crème de Gruyère, which tastes like candied cheese, while some others can be quite normal, such as a good, strong French Roquefort.

Pass up the temptingly named Strawberry Collage, a three-container ensemble of (1) merely decent berries, some of them unripe, (2) sticks of sponge cake, most of them a little dried out, and (3) whipped cream which is of real cream, but "whipped" by a machine, so that it lacks the buttery quality of the real thing—it is only light. Opt, rather, for the pumpkin pie, when it is available—it is brightly spiced with cinnamon and cloves; or for the chocolate tart, an almost black cake under an equally dark icing, crushed nuts in every bite.

★★ CAFÉ EUROPA/LA BRIOCHE

347 East 54th Street
LUNCH, MONDAY TO FRIDAY; DINNER, MONDAY TO SATURDAY. CLOSED SUNDAY.
Reservations, 755–0160.
Credit cards: AE, CB, DC, MC, V.
Medium-priced.

This is one of the simplest and most straightforward neighborhood restaurants in New York. It is also reasonably priced. The present site is its third since the restaurant first opened as Peter's Café Europa more than a decade ago. The present expanded name reflects an expansion of the menu by an additional menu of large, stew-filled brioches which are good value for some imaginative food.

There is a quasi garden wherein it never rains—a small room in the back which, with its skylight, glass wall, floor of simulated red tiles, and plants, feels very much like a garden. The main dining area, with space for about twenty tables, has the dim, soothing atmosphere of a cool, deeply shaded house in some hot part of the world. The walls are of bare plaster, overlaid here and there with stripped cabinetry, tapestries and cracked oil paintings. The illumination is from a couple of pewter chandeliers with dim lanterns, and from candles on each table. Oriental rugs fail to absorb the shock of the heavy-footed; the wooden floor is creaky, and when a customer or waiter goes by, you may feel it through your chair.

Mussels Marinière are the always-available appetizer, and they are well made—in a buttery broth of wine, seasonings, abundant fresh parsley and, adding an unusual tang, minced scallions. The alternate first course varies from week to week, and it is rarely a humdrum item: on occasion there is something the house refers to as Shrimp Castillo—a little hot sandwich of minced shrimp, flavored with spices and lemon, between two slices of well-browned French toast; at times a very decent ham-and-asparagus quiche. The invariable soup is gazpacho. This dish has too often been called a liquid salad, but the version made here really merits the description. It consists of very finely minced vegetables—tomatoes, celery, cucumber, onions, etc.—in their own juices, with very little oil, no thickening of bread and hardly any garlic, all very fresh, refreshing, nourishing and thinning, but it should be listed as V-8 Maison. Among the alternate soups one is likely to prefer are a mulligatawny that is sometimes available cold, sometimes hot, sometimes both ways; but hot is best because the soup is a thick, curried, puréed vegetable made with a chicken base, and curry when it is cold is a little queer. There is also, on occasion, a cucumber soup (sometimes hot, sometimes cold) which is very thick and has a strong flavoring of dill.

Broiled lamb chops, it would seem, should not be tampered with. Get some good chops and broil them, but not too long. The result, as everyone knows, is a simple, perfect dish, and anyone who can't consume sixteen baby ribs at a sitting is a sissy. Well, you don't get sixteen ribs here, and they are tampered with, but in such a way that the simple dish is actually improved. The chops are marinated in soy sauce, sake and ginger before they are broiled. The marination lasts only long enough to flavor the outside of the meat, and the subsequent broiling creates a brilliantly flavored crust—the lamb on the three-rib chops is excellent, but even better are the highly flavored bits and pieces one finds when the nearly denuded bones are finally picked up and nibbled at. Amazingly, the chops are served with *fresh peas.*

The Duck à l'Orange here, as in almost every restaurant, has a sauce that is too candied; its sweetness is not as exaggerated as in some places, but it is a bit excessive. The bird is perfectly roasted, however; the sauce is served in a separate dish, and using just a little helps. There is also Chicken Kiev (yes, the butter spurts out when you cut into it), and Beef Wellington (no, it is not overcooked).

Then there is this matter of the brioches. Each one is the size of a cantaloupe. The conical top is pulled out of the brioche, the center is hollowed and filled with the stew of your choice, and the plug replaced. Among the available fillings is an excellent Chicken Basquaise—chicken cooked in wine, with strong ham and green peppers. There is also a good Veal Marengo, made with fresh sautéed mushrooms, onions, celery and tomatoes; a spicy Curried Beef (with nuts, fruits and chutney); Crab Gumbo; and something named Shrimp & Mushroom Polonaise. In all of these the flavors of the ingredients are preserved, and the combinations are well balanced. You will get more brioche than gravy with which to moisten it—spread the remainder with butter and eat it that way.

The salad is nothing special. Among the desserts, there are several good reasons to pass up the chocolate mousse. It must be on the menu because it sells well, and it is made with good, dark chocolate, but it is airless, like a pudding rather than a mousse.

Have, instead, the macédoine of fresh fruit—the apples are crisp, as if they were just cut; the strawberries are ripe and juicy; the blueberries are large and firm; the orange sections are seeded and sweet; there is no sugar added, and the fruit arrives in the juice that comes of cutting it up—very pure, though a little bloodless. Better still are the crêpes, in a sauce of wine, lemon and sugar. Best of all are the bananas au rhum—bananas baked soft in a custard—very sweet, with just a suggestion of the edgy flavor of cooked milk, and a strong flavor of dark rum.

If every part of New York had a handful of sensibly priced neighborhood restaurants like this one, the supermarkets would be reduced to their natural commerce—dog food and soap.

★★CAFÉ LOUP

18 East 13th Street
LUNCH, MONDAY TO FRIDAY; DINNER, DAILY.
Reservations, 255–4746.
Credit cards: AE, DC.
Medium-priced.

A ten-stool bar at the front and a dozen or so tables in the back are all of Café Loup, but if every neighborhood in New York had a dozen like it, the supermarkets would fold and the mom-and-pop stores would go back to the middle-of-the-night sandwich trade. The food here is simple and good, if never wondrous; the prices are reasonable, if not exactly low; the surroundings are comfortable; the service is efficient, friendly and unpretentious (though occasionally a waiter will sniff a cork); and the people at the next table do not grunt. This is a civilized place, and one senses no generation gap between the young people who wait on tables and tend bar and the contented middle-aged crowd that has made this its neighborhood joint. The walls are beige and hung with prints. Pots and pans and little vases of dried flowers are on display on little shelves. The bar and tables are of unstained wood, and at every place setting there is a deep-blue napkin in the bowl of a large wineglass. Blackboard menus circulate to where they are needed—when it is time for you to look at one, one is placed on a blond bentwood chair near your table.

You are offered different soups on different days—sometimes pea soup, ham and noodles in it, thick, only mildly seasoned, Germanic, a good first course if you missed lunch. Otherwise try the mushrooms à la Grecque, very crunchy, in an herbed and onioned marinade that is perhaps a bit too sweet, but good. Splendid snails are served without shells, with mushrooms, in a thick and garlicky sauce, a hefty chunk of toast buried therein, which makes for a lovely hardness against the rich food.

The place is a bird house: good duck Montmorency, the skin crisp, the dark meat rich, the cherry sauce not excessively sweet; and good poulet moutarde, a simple dish of nicely browned chicken with a mild mustard sauce; and, best of the lot, Cornish hen aux fines herbes, the skin of the little bird almost black without being burned, intensely flavored with the taste of herbs.

The sautéed calf's liver is okay, strewn with sautéed onions, the meat pink and moist, though it could do with a crisper surface. And the almost excessive richness that is natural to sweetbreads is leavened by the sharp dark sauce and strands of ham that are served in this version. The steaks, at around $10, are the most expensive items in the place. The grilled steak is fine, but the steak with garlic is marvelous—fragrant and bloody.

Fresh vegetables, simply prepared, are served with all the main courses.

The desserts have cute names, like "Peter's Pan Chocolate Cake," which, name aside, is memorable for the raisins and nuts the rich cake is studded with. The cheese cake is the heavy, cream-cheese variety—it is brightly lemoned, sweet and extremely thick. There is carrot cake, and it is spicy, moist, pleasantly pebbly. And there is strawberry shortcake, made with plump ripe berries and good whipped cream—it would be better still on a biscuit instead of this pallid sponge cake. Very good coffee.

A near-singularity for these days: juice for sours and such is squeezed from fresh fruit, at the bar, when the drinks are ordered.

★★CAFFÈ DA ALFREDO

17 Perry Street (near Seventh Avenue)
LUNCH, WEDNESDAY TO SUNDAY; DINNER, TUESDAY TO SUNDAY. CLOSED MONDAY.
Reservations, 989–7028.
No credit cards.
No liquor.
Medium-priced.

A dozen black-topped tables in a storefront that barely holds them all. A bit of room has been set aside for a little jungle of greenery. An Italian copper fountain, which gurgles when functioning, is presided over by an Italian copper boy. A couple of the tables are nestled under broad blue-and-red Cinzano umbrellas, for a café note. The floor is of simulated, ornately patterned Florentine tiles. The place is a jumble, the simple wooden chairs competing in the aisles for space urgently needed by the hustling waiters. At lunchtime things are slow, the front windows let in light and a feeling of openness, and the place is easygoing. But at night things can be hectic. People waiting for tables have no place to wait. Still they wait, adding to the human clutter. But reservations are well handled, and if you arrive at the appointed hour, you will usually be seated promptly. Once you are, however, the rhythm of your meal may not be a toe-tapping one, the intervals between courses sometimes being unpredictably lengthy. So remember to bring your own wine, see to it that you get glasses and a corkscrew at once, and tipple while you wait. The crowd is young and makes a colorful show.

The seafood salad is not on the menu, but it is often on hand, a cool and crunchy scramble of mussels and shrimp, squid and scallops, a smattering of mushrooms, and a sour, biting dressing that is heavily garlicked and parsleyed. If you add lemon, things get even livelier. Also unlisted are the stuffed mushrooms—six inverted caps, served in a little casserole dish, filled with bits of shrimp and a covering of melted cheese, sizzling oil all about. Occasionally stuffed zucchini is available, and this is the best first course in the house. Half-cylinders of the vegetable are stuffed with spiced meat that is flavored with onions and herbs, and the dish is baked under a topping of strong cheese that melts and mingles with the meat. It is served with a thick red sauce that is heavily flavored with garlic.

Good pasta, including a Spaghetti Carbonara that is solid without being heavy, little squares of meaty bacon livening the rich mixture of noodles, eggs and cheese. The Trenette Verdi al Pesto is a dish of broad green noodles in a fresh basil sauce that is pleasantly coarse of its ground cheeses and pine nuts—the flavors of the fresh herb and garlic are wonderfully high. The pasta is carefully cooked, and in all the dishes it arrives tender but very firm.

When the first of Alfredo's restaurants opened—the Trattoria da Alfredo, on Hudson Street—one of the most popular dishes was of poached vegetables served with a cool green sauce. This establishment is no longer owned by Alfredo himself, but by his daughter, and she dishonors the past with her version—Cassoeula Milanese with Salsaverde. The vegetables are vastly overcooked, the splendid sauce no help to to the soggy stuff—the waiters know it is dreadful and try to prod you away from the fiasco.

The fish, veal and chicken dishes vary from day to day, what is available indicated by title cards stapled to the menu: Pollastrino Ripieno, for example, a little bird that is stuffed with ground veal, cheese and mushrooms, all served in a lightly tomatoed sauce flavored with pepper and herbs; Scaloppine Vivandiera, something less than perfect veal in an excellent, slightly sour, cheese-thickened sauce that is studded with peas, onions, ham and mushrooms—lovely food, the imperfect meat notwithstanding; an ever-changing series of sauced fish dishes, in which the fish is invariably fresh.

Limited desserts, including good cheeses, fresh fruit and ripe strawberries in a zabaglione sauce that is, happily, not served ice-cold.

The pasta dishes are inexpensive; the meat, chicken and fish are not.

★★★ LA CARAVELLE

33 West 55th Street
LUNCH AND DINNER. CLOSED SUNDAY.
Reservations, JU 6–4252.
No credit cards.
Very expensive.

Perfections and a well-bred lid on passion have been the marks of the Caravelle kitchen. But the latter is hard to take without the former. It was never the business of this place to dramatize the flavors of the produce of the earth and the waters, but rather to demonstrate how elegantly they could be tamed or transformed or concealed. That is a kind of magic that is, if it is executed artfully, its own excuse. But magic, to justify itself, must work perfectly. The failure is total, not partial, if while sawing the lady in half you draw even a little blood. The crimson droplets have been spotted at La Caravelle. It is no longer a great restaurant. Plenty of wonderful food, and you may have a delightful time, but the magic is gone.

Which is a pity. M. Meyzen, the portly and—to some—frightening proprietor who operates this institution, will be sorry to learn it. For Meyzen, who is actually a courtly pussycat, is no happier than when his customers are happy. And thereby, maybe, depends the key. They are happy no matter what.

La Caravelle is banker-and-broker heaven, the most sanitary clientele in town, and a very well-educated lot. They know the names of things, and they know which names are better than which names. But they do not know the substances the names represent. In this way of life, substances do not matter, only that they have the right names. La Caravelle, of course, has one of the right names. It is therefore, by definition, marvelous. With customers like these, it may be humanly difficult to maintain standards. From a financial point of view no standards are necessary. The customers come to the name "La Caravelle," never mind what it is.

Take, for a for-instance, this well-tailored jurist on your left. He would like a bottle of Château d'Yquem with his dinner (no objection from his frau), and you wonder if he would have tasted it clearly enough to have regretted his choice had not his captain steered him to something sane. International clusters of businessmen glare at each other in four languages, stuck with one another's company until the big deal is made. Matrons and their patrons, every hair nailed into place, sip their 1945 châteaux casually, not because it is a lifetime habit, but because they do not realize they are drinking something special. (The bottles are selected, of course, by their three-figure price tags.) On Friday and Saturday nights there is a bit of gaiety in the air, a smile at this table, an actual tune of laughter at that one. But the rest of the week ladies in print dresses stick out like gypsies at a bishop's funeral, gentlemen in plaid suits are taken for bookies.

You enter to a red-velvet anteroom, where a display of hors d'oeuvres and desserts is reflected in a great polished mirror. Your coat is taken by a demure clerk whose smile remains engraved in place for as long as you wish to gaze at it. You are led first through a mural-lined corridor, tables along each side, with seating on banquettes of that same red velvet. Ordinarily, in restaurants of this rank, front tables like these are the choice spots, from which the lucky holders thereof may see, and be seen by, all who come and go, with particular attention to the celebrated. But this pass is too nakedly exposed and close for that, it is front-row orchestra—a bit vulgar, don't you know—not the grand tier, and it is given over to families with minors, females without males, strays. The rest of us march grandly through, looking neither to the left nor right, colonial governors between ranks of native mendicants.

The main dining room is your basic posh. More of those velvet banquettes rim the room and are formed into semicircular settees around large tables in the center. Mirrored walls and columns reflect glowing sconces. Murals of the parks and streets of Paris save the scene; they are pale, they glow with the soft light of that city, and they are made bright with spots of strong color—the Tricolor waves in all of them. Glowing linen, shining solid flatware and gleaming china, stemware with sailing ships engraved on the bowls—"Les Caravelles" made water crossings before they were fitted out with jet engines.

Your captain will be with you in a moment, for he is at work serving a silver bowl of Le Caviar de Béluga to your neighbors. *Zing.* He has scooped up and swallowed a spoon of the stuff so quickly that only the bright eye of a clear-headed observer catches it. Confronted by you moments later with the fact that he has been caught out, he shrugs and allows that he really does not much like the stuff. What may be made of all this? Much, actually. The dining-room staff does its job well, but not seriously, reflecting a commitment to efficiency but not to excellence. They are cheerful and friendly as well. But no one here is shocked if a thing goes wrong.

Les Moules Caravelle have gone a little wrong. They are perfectly fresh, you understand, almost every one of them free of grit, and they are dressed in a pinked mayonnaise that is smooth and rich, but totally forgettable. Much better La Cervelle Vinaigrette, cool chunks of calf's brains that have been cooked with bit of vinegar, the tartness of which eliminates the otherwise cloying richness of this organ meat—the dressing is light, made spiky with bits of minced red pepper and parsley. Your captain suggests that a dollop of Le Céleri Rémoulade would garnish the cervelle nicely. The root is crisp and nutty in the lightly lemoned dressing, but there is missing the clear flavor of fresh celery that characterizes this dish at its best. Le Pâté Toulousain is splendid, fatty and loud, garnished with cool jelly and powerfully sour little pickles.

La Caravelle has always listed as its first-course specialty Le Pain de Brochet, a mousse of pike prepared as if for quenelles, but cooked in a loaf and served by the slice. They are still at it, the mousse is light and the flavor of the fish is vivid, but a trace of fishiness has been detected on occasion, and it is not undone by the lightly tomatoed white-wine sauce that is poured over it, or by the crunchy little button mushrooms or plump white grapes therein—a superb dish with a slight but devastating flaw.

Le Homard Washington, Friday's lobster (the listing of main courses changes a little from day to day), is a crustacean elegance of tender and fresh lobster meat that has been poached to the perfect point; it is then served in a white sauce that has been fortified with bourbon whiskey and port wine. If you are a lobster freak, this dish is not for you, for the lobster, as such, is not glorified in this treatment—the heady sauce is the dominant element of this dish, the strength of the liquor tamed to the point at which its hard edge conflicts superbly with the seafood. It is a magical dish, at the expense of the magic of lobster.

Half the house, it seems, orders duck, and the birds flow from the kitchen in their copper pans by the dozen, to be ritualistically carved by assiduous waiters who go through the motions hardly looking. The house is famous for its sauce Smitane, of sour cream and green pepper, but on certain nights it offers instead Le Caneton rôti au Poivre, a winy sauce that bristles with nodules of the pungent spice, making an excellent slight harshness against the rich bird. But the kitchen makes those birds by the score, and they do not get the attention each one deserves, and once in a while the bird is underdone—red and a bit tough near the bone. The duck is garnished with a mound of wild rice that is unsullied by ordinary rice—it is the plain thing itself, and its strong, grainy flavor is a perfect foil for these rich sauces. Pigeons, too, including a Véronique —you are served the entire bird, crisp skin and supple dark meat, with a sauce that has the depth of a good stock. There are warm white grapes in the sauce, and their juiciness is a pleasure against the rich bird.

L'Escalopine de Veau au Citron is like a song that is sung unaccompanied in a hall with clear acoustics. If anything goes wrong, you cannot miss it. This is a simple dish of veal sautéed in butter, a bit of sauce made in the pan by the addition of lemon and seasoning. Perfect veal, admirably browned, but you cannot taste the lemon for the salt —magic in reverse, sleight-of-hand ruination. You console yourself with the little balls of roasted potato—golden skins of browned butter around soft, steamy potato cores— and with the chopped spinach, which is strong, spicy, smooth. Excellent steaks of all shapes and cuts.

Fine apple tarts and banana tarts, fresh berries filmed over with a light crème Anglaise, a Bavarian cream that is purple with the juice of dark berries, lofty soufflés. But Les Crêpes "Ma Pomme" (for two) are the specialty of the house. If you order them, Meyzen himself may trot over to finish the dish at your tableside. But first you learn, as the menu does not state, that this dish takes time. Your captain suggests you sample the half-dozen cheeses with half a bottle of wine while your dessert is working (the menu does not even mention their availability), and you find that they vary from good to super, and later you learn that there is no extra charge. Meanwhile, back in the kitchen, chunks of apple are being sautéed in brown sugar, for your crêpes, until they are candied and crusted; they are brought to the dining room when you have dispatched your cheese, and Meyzen wraps them in large, thin pancakes, and then cooks the bundles very slowly and long in cognac and calvados, until they are soaked and browned in the brandies. He explains that he invented the dish himself, which explains his concern for their preparation. While he works he continues his friendly lecture, pointing out that anyone can flame a crêpe dish to the ceiling, but that it is the slow preparation that achieves the desired concentration of flavor. It turns out a very good dessert, spirited and perfumed, and you tame it with big dollops from the pitcher of whipped cream. You are brought a plate of glazed fruit to nibble on, the grapes and berries and orange sections encased in sugar that is as clear as glass.

★★ CARROUSEL

1307 Third Avenue (near 75th Street)
DINNER, MONDAY TO SATURDAY. CLOSED SUNDAY.
Reservations, 744–4978.
Credit cards: AE, DC, MC, V.
Medium-priced.

For some reason, despite the phenomenal success French restaurants have enjoyed in New York, in particular the constantly thriving bistro-like places in the West Forties and West Fifties, the East Side has largely done without. Along come these pioneers, to break new ground. But these are timorous adventurers, undertaking to settle hardly more than a twenty-five-foot storefront, and sure enough, the place is no sooner in business than it is jammed.

Carrousel is the quintessential theater-district French restaurant, transported piece by piece to this foreign ground. The walls are of a deep salmon pink that should age very well, and if you thought that the cluttered look of many French restaurants is a condition arrived at through years of aimless acquisition and installation, this place is a jumble from the start. There is a framed poster on every patch of wall; where the space to be filled is three-dimensionable, there is a green plant. A tiny vestibule is separated from the dining room by a partition of engraved glass, and through this minuscule space the diners come and the diners go, which is bad enough, but hooks on the wall must accommodate coats, and when there is chill or rain in the air, you walk through a jungle of cheviot, gabardine and poplin to reach your harried host.

If you have experience piling families of six into a subcompact, you have some idea of how the tables were inserted into this space. Well, you have all seen crowded restaurants before, but they are usually eschewed by the kinds of customers you find here. It appears that inflation and recession have caught up with even our moguls, and here they are, their male frames in tailor-made suits, female ones in one-of-a-kinds, supping at lower prices than once was their wont, now that the economies are just around the corner. Yes, this is a reasonably priced little place, but you can be certain the prices will get stiffer if this level of business continues; and, yes, it is a hectic one, but somehow it is all OK, once you are comfortably ensconced in your chair; the action and chatter all around you are like the rain and lightning outside your family-filled, sealed Volkswagen.

The menu is brief, and it follows, though not slavishly, the pattern of most French menus in town. Among the deviations is the Feuilleté au Roquefort—a hot first course of Roquefort cheese and custard baked in a pie. The strength of the cheese is heightened by heat, and it is offset by the creamy custard and by the browned and flaky pastry.

48

Of the handful of appetizers on this menu, this is the best. But if strong cheese is not your meat, the Escargots are a bit above average in that the snails themselves are plump and tender, and the sauce, milder than many in its spare use of garlic, is well-balanced and herby—the snail butter is an excellent moistener for a few tufts of the good bread served here. Of course there is pâté, but this one is more like cold meat loaf, *too* cold, slablike, though its flavor is not bad.

Fish baked in a crust is becoming a familiar item in French restaurants around town. Here it is called Filet de "Bass" en croûte (someone is yet to do that study on the use of quotation marks in menus), and it is, in this version, a simple and very good dish —a section of impeccably fresh bass wrapped in a pastry envelope. The tender fish and a hot buttery sauce are sealed in the pastry, which is delicately browned. The magic of any sealed-in cooking is that moisture and flavor are kept where they belong, in the food, instead of in the air.

The ambiguously named Escalope de Veau is a cutlet of properly pale veal, browned in butter and served with browned fresh mushrooms in a delicately seasoned, creamy, wine sauce—your basic scallop of veal.

Not all is well. The Steak au Poivre Vert is of beef that is mild, as if it is too young; the green pepper is used sparingly, which is to say *too* sparingly, and the thin sauce makes little impression even against this pale steak.

Yes, there is mousse, and moreover, it need not be chocolate, if you prefer orange or coffee; all of them are good, none is spectacular. The best desserts are the fruit tarts —blueberry, strawberry or apple, when those fresh fruits are available, and the flaky pastry and light custard are piled high with the plump berries, piled low with thin slivers of apple.

What is most surprising about this new place is the excellence of the waiters and the orderliness of the dining room in the face of this pace of business.

★★★ CASA BRASIL

406 East 85th Street
DINNER. CLOSED SUNDAY.
Reservations essential, 288-5284.
No credit cards.
No liquor.
Expensive.

Originally a six-table, twenty-seat restaurant a couple of blocks from the present site, Casa Brasil was successful enough to move to these larger quarters—a brownstone with two dining rooms on the ground floor, and seats for about fifty. The tables are set with immaculately fresh, flower-printed cloths, good china and flatware, and excellent wine glasses—large and thin—for the wine you bring. There are always fresh flowers, in good condition, on every table.

There is no printed menu. The first appetizer is set, and the second is a choice of two; there are three or four main courses to choose from (except on Wednesdays); and four or five desserts. On Wednesdays the main course is feijoada, the national dish of Brazil. (More accurately, it is the Brazilian way of eating meats. It can include pork, beef and beef tongue; fresh, smoked or dried, or all three; and sausages.)

The first course has often been hearts of palm in a pungent cheese sauce flavored with ham, pepper and hard-boiled eggs, and garnished with a couple of black olives. The dish is extremely vigorous and, at the same time, very light. It stimulates your appetite, without beginning to satisfy it.

The second appetizer is a choice of crabmeat in seasoned mayonnaise and sour cream (it comes on a few lettuce leaves which are in better shape than the lettuce in most restaurant salads) or melon and prosciutto—a rather bland prosciutto, but the Persian melon, served cut from its shell, is perfectly ripe, and extremely sweet and juicy. This course is accompanied by a basket of bread equal to the best in New York (the recent introduction of Interbaco notwithstanding). The basket contains croissants of such an airy and buttery quality that almost none of the little rolls return to the kitchen. They always arrive warm—never hot, never cool. Wisely, they are not served from the start of the meal. They are as easy to eat as it is to breathe, and they could displace several courses.

At this point—the wrong point—a good salad is served. The break following two appetizers is a good spot for a freshener—a light salad or a sherbet—but if only one such course is to be served, it should follow the main course and precede the dessert, where it is needed in a long dinner. That aside, the salad is fine—not a speck of brown on the fresh Boston lettuce in a lemon-and-oil dressing flavored with puréed garlic, onion and parsley. The dressing is made up daily, probably just before mealtime, because the flavor of raw onion is especially fugitive once an onion has been sliced, chopped or puréed, and the onion flavor in this dressing is absolutely pristine.

Among the main courses, Casa Brasil offers a Beef Wellington which, it appears, is on the menu because there is a demand for it, or because it is expected in this kind of restaurant. Beef Wellington is really a silly dish—filet mignon wrapped in pâté and pastry, and served in a brown sauce flavored with a deglazing of the beef. Filet mignon is the most delicately flavored of all beef, and pâté overpowers it, so its flavor must somehow be built up, or get lost. Moreover, pastry and meat do not cook the same way, so separate preparations of each are required before they are combined. Trouble is no argument, if a dish is worth it, but these ingredients do not long for each other, do not get along when wed, and all the ooh-ing and ah-ing is at the *sight* of the complex thing. These problems are recognized at Casa Brasil, and there is just a hint of pâté, but there is a clear lack of enthusiasm in the preparation; even the sauce, which *can* save it, is cursory, and the whole thing is tasteless. But the customers love it.

The roast duck is another matter, served *without a sauce!* If you know how to roast a duck, you can get away with that. Here it is crisp, moist, done to the bone, but not stringy.

The scallops of veal in a winy cream sauce are very good. The chanterelles are not fresh, but very well handled. Most important, the veal is *white,* and delicate, able to pick up the flavors it is cooked with, which is the whole idea of veal.

Bowls of four or five vegetables are served. Better to serve two or three, if the peas and artichoke hearts are to come from packages. A puréed squash, with lots of butter and nutmeg, is excellent; there is some very good rice, flavored, oddly, with sage; and an excellent warm compote of stewed apricot, pear and pineapple.

The Wednesday-night feijoada is a completely different world of food. Ordinarily it is a coarse dish, but the version served here is a slight deflection toward something more delicate, without any loss of character. The ingredients (each in its own bowl or plate) include rice cooked in stock and flavored with hot pepper; and the black beans, cooked with Portuguese sausages, and flavored with garlic and pepper. These two, combined, are the starch of the dinner. Two kinds of meats are served at Casa Brasil, both beef: one fried very rare with onions, in a pan gravy thick with blood; the other a fricassee —sautéed beef braised in wine. There are garnishes of fresh orange, very ripe bananas fried in butter and brown sugar (for these the only word is succulent), and a farina of the yuca plant, used as a zest, like salt and pepper. The food is heavy, but difficult to stop eating. It is one of the most distinctive meals in New York.

Of the good desserts, one is singular and stunning—tapioca poached in wine, covered with a crème Anglaise. The tapioca takes on the appearance of purple berries, and the flavor of concentrated wine, the alcohol removed. The other desserts include strawberries in a raspberry glaze; raspberries (better ones do not grow) with whipped cream; and an excellent nut cake, extremely moist, made with walnuts, almonds, pecans and dates, also covered with fresh whipped cream. The coffee, as you would expect, is perfect.

There are a few shortcomings in the management of this place, including the proprietress/chef's short fuse. As a rule she is grand and gracious, which suits her position and talent. But her occasional pique at a customer, though understandable, is audible and visible enough to discomfit others. She terminates the early sitting by abruptly turning up the lights (the rooms are small enough for an announcement to be audible). The waiters—food carriers really—don't know the answers to simple questions about the food, though the menu hardly varies. But in some ways, they're well trained: if you bring two kinds of wine, they change your glasses when you switch. Signed testimonials on the walls—from André Kostelanetz, Joan Crawford, etc.—are superfluous and not decorative. This sort of thing puts a restaurant in doubt, as if it needs something beyond its own performance to persuade the public of its quality.

★★CEDARS OF LEBANON

39 East 30th Street
LUNCH AND DINNER.
Reservations, MU 6–9634.
Credit cards: AE, CB, DC, MC, V.
Medium-priced.

Good and cheap, even by pre-inflation criteria. Once a seedy place with plastic tablecloths and splintery walls, Cedars of Lebanon has been COMPLETELY REDECORATED and now looks like all the successful Armenian restaurants in New York, even though it is Lebanese. But, miraculously, the shift to posh has not been attended by a parallel movement to steep. Here—amid the pictorial velvet rugs hanging on rosewood walls, ornate chandeliers, sculptured red napkins standing on white linen, and swarthy waiters in red jackets and bow ties—you can still get a complete dinner for $7 if you select from the lower-priced main courses and restrict yourself to the on-the-dinner appetizers. Employers seeking to attract staff to this unfashionable neighborhood can point out the fringe benefits of working far from the temptations of Saks and Bloomie's and near the $4 lunches at Cedars of Lebanon.

Precisely what distinguishes the dishes of Lebanon from those of Syria, Egypt, Turkey, etc., is, one feels certain, well-known to the Lebanese, Syrians, Egyptians, Turks and etceterese. But in New York the restaurants of these countries offer menus that are indistinguishable from one another. No matter, we do not come to study, but to eat, and one begins here with a little plate of oily hot peppers (pale gold) and a basket (plastic gold) of triangles of flat bread, cut from the circle. The moist heat of the peppers is alleviated by the dense, bland bread. The bread is double-layered, like an envelope, and after you have dispensed with the peppers, studied the menu and ordered the first courses, you may fill a few of the envelopes with homus, the Middle Eastern paste of chickpeas and sesame oil. The version served here is among the best in town—freshly made each day, thick yet moist, so redolent of the flavor of sesame that the stuff tastes almost like halvah, soft, slightly grainy, rich and heavy. The mashed eggplant with sesame oil (which all the world knows as "ba ba ghannouj") is not particularly notable for the vividness of its eggplant flavor, but the baked vegetable is freshly mixed with an abundance of oil, spices and garlic, making it nice and gooey, a hint of texture lent by the eggplant seeds. Here are not New York's best stuffed grape leaves, though it is not easy to put your little finger on the problem—they are a bit too loglike, rather overly sour, the leaves somewhat tough; none of these grossly offensive, but the total off the mark in several directions at once. Listed under the salads, but served as an appetizer, is a sparkling item called tabboule, which consists of very coarsely chopped parsley, minced scallion greens and little chunks of tomato, all dressed in oil and lots of lemon juice. Mint leaves belong but are not in evidence; the scallion greens are visible but rare; and in the company of the fragrant parsley, the bits of tomato are a textural note rather than a flavor; but the resilient parsley, fragrant and slightly chewy, is especially stimulating when stirred up by the tart lemon and the other, more fugitive ingredients. This is a good place to come to with a few people—an assortment of these appetizers, each on its own little plate, arranged in the center of a table, is a lovely and tempting sight.

Kibbee is many things, in its most primitive form raw ground lamb and cracked wheat. When it is taken beyond that stage, it is called Kibbee This or Kibbee That. Among the Cedars' kibbees is one called Kibbee Shish Barak, in which the kibbee is stuffed into sausage-shaped patties of yet another lamb mixture—lamb and pine nuts —sautéed, and served in a lemony broth that has been enriched with yogurt. The meat is spiced, the grainy outer layer hardened to a crunchy crust, the inner filling soft and moist—you alternate bites of the little dumplings with spoons of the sour and creamy broth. Then there is couscous (Class, what is the distance between Lebanon and North Africa?). Couscous is also many things, ranging from a fiery vegetable, pasta and semolina stew augmented by several meats, to sweetened steamed grain, eaten as a dessert. The Cedars' couscous is approximately what most people think of when they hear the term—a broth containing grain and vegetables (here the grain is fine and slightly nubbly, the chickpeas crunchy, the onions tender and sweet), surmounted by browned chicken that is thoroughly cooked but still tender and moist. The thing comes off as an Eastern competitor in the chicken-in-the-pot stakes and wins handily. Naturally there is shish kebab, but this one is not made of great lamb, which is a matter of immateriality when the lamb is (a) only one step below the best and (b) either stewed or ground. But in shish kebab you are eating chunks of lamb that have been marinated and broiled, which is a revealing preparation. It is on the menu because the public expects it to be on the menu in Eastern restaurants, but at Cedars of Lebanon you are better off with the more complicated and more highly flavored lamb dishes.

Your waiter escorts you to the display of desserts at the front of the restaurant and explains the desserts to you. Then the proprietor rises from his table near the display of desserts and explains the waiter's English to you. The best thing in the place is something they have decided to call Ladyfingers—a log of sweetened ground walnuts that is baked in a wrapping of buttered onion-skin-thin filo pastry, cooled, and moistened with honey just before it is served. The worst is something called Bird Nest, which is apparently made of pistachio nuts and mothballs. In between are good versions of two varieties of baklava—the standard thing and a variant in which cheese is substituted for the walnuts. The Lebanese coffee is thick, strong and delicious.

★★CELLAR IN THE SKY

1 World Trade Center
DINNER, ONE SEATING.
Reservations required, 938–1111.
Credit cards: AE, CB, DC, MC, V.
Very expensive.

A subsidiary of Windows on the World, and situated within the walls of that hive, Cellar in the Sky is milord's retreat from the mob that teems through the public rooms of the parent company and presses its collective nose against the panes that give on views of Metro New York. While the shovers and gapers are being dazzled by food and wine as varied and sundry as the characters in the *Collected Works of William Shakespeare,* the few, mellow and wise, tolerant of the masses but having seen all they will ever see, take instead to this cloister, in search of excellence in simplicity. But the elegant dinners-cum-wine-tastings that are the intended stock-in-trade of Cellar in the Sky are only a little more ordered than a restless dream. There is some excellence in almost all the dishes and wines, to be sure, but little art in their assemblage. For all its refinement, a principal appeal of the place will be to the gluttonous and intemperate —for the flat fee of $45 per person, two are served food that would hold a string quartet and enough wine to fill the cello.

After your quarter-mile ascent on a high-speed elevator that shimmies like Sister Kate, you kiss the carpeted ground just outside its sliding doors and follow the wide-eyed crowd through crystalline corridors that lead to Windows. But the favored—those heading for Cellar—make a subtle left at the next-to-last minute, through gold-handled doors, into this quasi-cave, wherein the wine-cellar theme is sounded lightly—this is a stone floor, but the stones are blocks of white marble; the pillars that lead up to arches are of white stucco and support only themselves; hundreds of bottles of wine line the room, ensconced in glinting racks of tubular steel; and the bare wooden tables at which one might do a bit of businesslike tasting in a cool underground are here transformed to handsome polished oak, about a dozen tables in all, surrounded by oak-frame chairs to which broad seats and backs of heavy tan leather are belted. This is a comfortable spot, and when you are finally seated to settings of handsome flatware and simple stemmed crystal in a handful of sizes you judge that whatever the quality of the fixed dinner, the time spent over it will pass pleasantly, for by now you have not only sized the place up, you have been greeted by Pepe!

Pepe is your charming captain; he is recently arrived from Spain, he pronounces "olives" with three syllables, and he pronounces lots of other things funny too. This is perfect, for the silliest part of Pepe's job is to make a little speech about each wine he serves, and as the prescribed content of these recitations is geographic and vinicultural, they add nothing to one's enjoyment of dinner. Pepe's accent converts, however, empty words to music. He also knows good wine from lesser wine, and though he solemnly champions each new bottle when he brings it, he fails to conceal his approbation when you taste wine 4 and decide to stay with wine 3.

Dinners here consist of seven courses accompanied by several wines, and though the wines suit the dishes they accompany fairly well, the wines themselves have no relationship to each other. Switching from one to the next is like jumping TV channels.

Chorizos and olives seem to be the mainstay first course, with sherry. The thirty slices of the Spanish sausage they serve up to two people are hard to resist if you have been restraining yourselves all day in anticipation of this complex dinner. The heavily fatted meat is slightly chewy itself, in a tender casing, the flavor of the meat vaguely gamy, and it is saturated with mild red pepper that is flavor instead of fire. But, if you can believe it, the sausage is overshadowed by the remarkable olives, of which there are three kinds: little green ones that are juicy and salty; big green ones that are drenched in oil—they are sour and firm, almost crackling, and their high flavor approaches rankness, but is never unpleasant; and ripe brown ones that are sharp and strong enough to clear a head that has had too much sherry.

Soup follows—more specifically consommé, one time flavored with spinach that has been filtered away, another time with fennel. These are terrific broths, steamy and deep, spooned with a silver ladle from a silver tureen into a handsome ramekin. The spinach consommé is accompanied by pirogin, light pastries filled with herbed meat; the fennel consommé by crisp flat biscuits that are sprinkled with roasted fennel seeds.

So far everything has been perfect. But the fish courses have been less than that. Half of an impeccable baked potato, firm but cooked through, in a crisp skin, bathed in sweet butter, surmounted by shad roe that is fresh and tender, but without any crisping, so that it is almost bland; another time Scallops à l'Armoricaine turn out to be tasty but tough, in a pink sauce of no distinction. But they have come up with some marvelous wines for their seafood—a Freemark Abbey Pinot Chardonnay of 1974, heady cold wine that is at once metallic and spicy; and with the scallops a Wehlener Sonnenuhr of 1973, a Moselle of such refinement, complexity and vibrance that it is insane to serve it this early in a dinner and then expect anyone to switch to lesser reds.

They seem to be making a point here, that foods native to very different parts of the planet can be combined into harmonious dinners in New York. Accordingly, a saddle of lamb and a roast rack of veal are served with, respectively, sautéed Chinese mushrooms and sautéed snow peas. The Oriental vegetables are marvelous with the Western roasts, and they were both served crisp and oily—the mushrooms fresh and smoky, the peas very sweet. The lamb is perfect tender meat, pink and tasty; but the veal, though perfectly made, suffers from being roast veal. The rack is cut into chops and the edges of each chop, where the meat was exposed to the direct heat of the oven, are browned and delicious, but the pink meat at the center needs help—roasting large pieces of veal is a minor barbarism.

Salads of impeccable ingredients, variously fresh mushrooms, watercress, arugula, in fine light dressings; good cheese, one time an assortment of goat served with a rather coarse Spanish wine—Marques de Caceres 1970—that seemed just right with that pungent food; another time cheeses from around the world, including a splendid rich blue-veined cheese from Indiana that Pepe identifies as "Maytag."

It is flattering to be served an orange soufflé just out of the oven and just your size —each diner gets his own little product. The flavor is not great, but the soufflé is light and perfectly risen, and preferable to the Lemon Bavarian Cream with Berries served another time . . . too much gelatin in the cream, making it—well, gelatinous. Good berries. Cookies and candies with your coffee.

With its flaws, the place is extraordinarily pleasant, a lovely setting for a dinner spun out over three or four hours. There is a flamenco guitarist who strums gently, Pepe's waiters are as gentlemanly as he is, and if a black thought chances into your head, they are right there with the wine.

★★★ CHALET SUISSE

6 East 48th Street
LUNCH AND DINNER. CLOSED SATURDAY AND SUNDAY.
Reservations, 355–0855.
Credit cards: AE, CB, DC, MC.
Expensive.

If you believe what you see, and if, therefore, you are frequently disappointed, you must come to the Chalet Suisse, if only to reinforce your confidence in first impressions. The place is immediately prepossessing: comfortable, elegant rusticity—rough plaster ivory walls, dark beams on the ceiling, soft lighting; the large tables are surrounded by wooden slat-backed chairs with cushions on the seats. They are occupied by comfort-loving regulars, who look like they have been coming here for many years without losing any of their taste for the place—at lunchtime they fill the restaurant, at dinner the place is quieter but far from dead. Whenever you come, if you linger, even to the point where you are the last customer, dawdling over a superfluous brandy and a second cigar, you are attended to as if time had no end.

The owners, man and woman, are ever-present, unobtrusively overseeing, not above filling your wineglass or coffee cup if your waitress is engaged elsewhere. And the waitresses, these incredible waitresses in their nifty, crisp, pretty Swiss costumes—they know the menu utterly, and they explain it thoroughly, concisely; they are watchful and available. And thoughtful. "Is it all right with you if I take some of this veal back to the kitchen to keep it warm until you are ready for more?" "Yes, of course. Very good idea. And by the way, while you're at it, if you don't mind, will you marry me?"

If you flinch at the idea of eating brains, how do you feel about *cold* brains? Just as ivory-white and slippery as the hot kind, but also kind of clammy—they are marinated in a lovely dressing, with minced, pickled vegetables (crisp), parsley (fresh) and capers (sour); you get a lot, and it is delicious. Pretty much the same color and texture, but hot—actually steamy—is the Onion and Cheese Pie, a kind of quiche actually, but predominantly cheese and very pully. The cheese, of course, is from Switzerland, and it has a strong, nutlike flavor that is quite powerful when it is hot and browned. Even stronger-tasting is the Bundnerfleisch—a smoked beef, served in thin slices, fibrous and peppery.

Nine times out of ten, when you read a menu introduction like "SPECIALTIES of our Executive Chef Mr. Erwin Herger," you know you're being sold what you don't want to buy. That kind of pronunciamento almost never precedes a dish of the quality of Médaillons de Veau aux Morilles, and when you're told, additionally, that these are "The finest Veal Steaks in a rich Cream Sauce with imported Mushrooms," you have every right to expect that you are in a boob trap. Unfortunately for rules of thumb, but happily otherwise, the dish is as good as its description. The veal is very pale, and lightly sautéed, so that it is moist and rosy, and the sauce is thick, buttery, well herbed and strongly seasoned.

There are humbler items on the menu, like Liver and Kidney à la Suisse, a fricassee of browned slices of liver and kidney made in a strong stock; you soak up the thick brown sauce with hunks of the good bread you get here. Naturally, there are fondues. And if you don't mind working for as well as paying for your sustenance, the cheese fondue is worth struggling with, particularly if you let it bubble for a while over its flame —it improves with extra cooking. The dish is made with good cheese, a little kirsch and a touch of garlic, and the knowing drink the vaguely sparkling white wine called Fendant with this dish—a good one is available here.

Excellent vegetables: the spinach is strong, lightly seasoned with nutmeg; the string beans are fresh and moist, and they are served in a little bundle, wrapped in a strip of bacon; the rösti potatoes are moist and salty under their perfectly browned crust.

The desserts are as successful as the dishes on the rest of the menu, but the listing is not especially interesting. The chocolate fondue, of course, is made with superb chocolate as well as hazelnuts—you dip the almost black stuff out of its pot with bits of pastry or pineapple or sections of mandarin orange. The Aargauer Rueblitorte is a sweet, crunchy cake of carrots and almonds topped with a dollop of whipped cream that is so startlingly light, so happily unsweetened, so elemental, that it is like a sniff of country air to a lifelong city dweller.

Plenty of good Swiss wine on the list.

★ CHARLEY O'S BAR & GRILL & BAR

33 West 48th Street
LUNCH AND DINNER.
Reservations, 582-7141.
Credit cards: AE, CB, DC, MC, V.
Medium-priced.

"I only drink to make other people interesting."
—George Jean Nathan
"A gourmet who thinks of calories is like a tart who looks at her watch."
—James Beard
"New York is a catastrophe, but it is a magnificent catastrophe."
—Le Corbusier

These photograph captions (there are dozens more) and the establishment's motto, "Solid drink and good food. That's my theory," set the tone—pre-lib masculine with stand-up lunch: hefty sandwiches; shrimps, clams and oysters sold by the piece, to people who know just what they want. "I'll have four shrimp, two clams, an oyster, a CB on rye, a Harp's on draft, and a small Guinness for color" is the ultimate lunch order, to be eaten, of course, by a 6-foot 2-inch, 185-pound advertising killer, who ruins the effect by tossing a Master Charge card on the bar instead of a ten-dollar bill, and signing his name with exaggerated loops.

But don't laugh. That lunch was delicious. The oyster and the clams were opened a few minutes before they were eaten, the huge shrimp were cold and not overcooked, and the spicy corned beef arrived on two slabs of crusty rye bread. When you're in the mood for body contact, have lunch at Charley O's. Clear a place for your food by sweeping your arm over a square yard of counter, remove your raincoat and eat.

Or come at dinnertime (not cocktail time, when the lunch mob has either returned or not yet left), when the place is metamorphosed into an elegant eating house, with crisp linen, polite, competent waiters and good food.

There is a wonderful assortment of appetizers, including a huge serving of pâté which is strong and coarse, pigs' knuckles in a gamy jelly, soused shrimp (marinated in lemon, oil and raw onions), and the same good clams and oysters.

It's not unusual for one of the seven daily specials to be out by seven-thirty, but it's assuredly irritating. The best of these are a roast duck with a sauce of chestnuts and peaches, and a sirloin of beef braised in cider. The regular menu offers the inevitable corned beef and cabbage, good steaks, an excellent lamb stew, and fried prawns in beer batter. Whatever you have, have the Irish fried potatoes—diced, par-boiled potatoes, fried to a luscious dark brown in grease, with salt and pepper. It's difficult to believe that anything this good is obtainable in Ireland, where the reputed high level of serious drinking is due to the fact that the best-tasting stuff in the country comes out of a bottle.

The strawberries and cream are usually good here. The whiskey cream pie is literally intoxicating, but the hot apple pie is not. It is an individual little pie, in a crust simulated of Melba toast, and it tastes awful. Calling it apple pie is a misrepresentation—if not technically, then morally.

★ CHARLIE BROWN'S ALE & CHOPHOUSE

200 Park Avenue (Pan Am Building)
LUNCH AND DINNER. CLOSED SATURDAY AND SUNDAY.
Reservations, MO 1–2520.
Credit cards: AE, CB, DC, MC, V.
Medium-priced.

Charlie Brown's is a handsome place—brick walls, stocky brick pillars, beamed ceiling, red tiled floor in a brickwork pattern, a bustling open kitchen, spacious booths along the walls, good-sized tables with captain's chairs, and handsome pewter table settings.

The food is, for the most part, Improved English and variations thereof, including, among the first courses, a refreshing dish of mussels in a cold, sharp curry cream, sprinkled with chives; the herring, which has always been superb; a salty Scotch egg (a hard-cooked egg wrapped in spiced meat). The egg comes with a tangy sweet-and-tart relish of red pepper and pickles, which is desperately needed—the leaden dish itself is something only a Briton could love.

Among the main courses there is a pretty good beefsteak, kidney and mushroom pie. Technically this is a difficult dish to make. The stewed filling must cook under the crust, and the steam from the boiling concoction should not prevent the pastry from becoming crisp and brown; at the same time, the vapors from the stew add flavor to the pastry. Here the whole issue is sidestepped. The meat is prepared in one place, the pastry is baked in another part of the oven, and they meet on your plate. This simplifies things in the kitchen and assures a good flaky pastry, but it tastes rather French.

There is excellent roast beef here, served with the aforementioned horseradish sauce. But the so-called Yorkshire pudding that comes with it is flat, heavy, and to judge from its flavor, not made in suet or beef drippings—not Yorkshire pudding at all, just a popover. The filet mignon in a crust is a small triumph. Grilled with dough over it and stuck under the broiler to brown the crust, it is served with a good sauce Bordelaise, including a slice of the marrowbone fat with which it is made. The sauce permeates the crust (this dish is also more French than English), and no one is complaining.

Pretty good fish and chips—the fish crisp and flaky, but the potatoes, like all the French fries here, rather limp; here authenticity would serve well.

Deep-dish Sour Cherry Pie is really sour, and the crust is a real lard crust—a sprinkling of coarse sugar provides just the right accent. Strawberries are served with that mellifluous, vaguely chalky, tender stuff called Devonshire cream.

The bar is usually packed, jam-packed, or, especially on Friday evenings, packed to paralysis. This presents a problem, because one must pass through the bar to reach the dining room. No suggestions.

★★LE CHÂTEAU RICHELIEU

48 East 52nd Street
LUNCH, MONDAY TO FRIDAY; DINNER, MONDAY TO SATURDAY. CLOSED SUNDAY.
Reservations, PL 1–6565.
Credit cards: AE, CB, DC, MC, V.
Very expensive.

There has been a Château Richelieu in New York for many, many years, and one at this spot for more than fifteen. The ownership has not changed. Mr. Robotti was always the proprietor, but he made his big money in other enterprises. When he amassed enough, he took a good piece of it and created the restaurant of his fantasies. Those who enter here are thereby privy to Mr. Robotti's private visions. What he visioned was a distinctly posh place, with mirrored walls and crimson walls of silken damask reaching to a lofty ceiling, deep banquettes of glistening French blue and plush red carpeting. The walls of the grandiose room are adorned with gilt sculptures (back-lighted), grand displays of cut flowers stand here and there. The restaurant is in Technicolor.

The customers are in gray: substantial, corporate types in gray suits, their spouses in gray hair. If they consort with other than their spouses, they are not here. Here is for grim marking of birthdays, ritual pretheater dinners. They are called "Mr. This" or "Mr. That" or "sir" by the fawning captains. If you look like you "don't belong" in the place—that is, if you seem to be stretching your budget for a special night out —the captains turn on the boredom and the short answers. Like most such types, however, they readily revert to servility if they are merely looked at with a bit of contempt. A glance of amused scorn is *very* effective. It is not necessary actually to *say* anything.

Journalists want to dislike this restaurant. Its trappings are too obvious, the food too pretentiously *haute cuisine* in such a worn-out way, with an almost endless list of incomprehensible modifiers scattered over the menu: this is à la Parisienne, that Royale, something else Diplomate, Maréchale, Jurassienne, Grand Veneur, Marguery, Henry IV, Lucullus, Rothschild. If you know someone who doesn't like all those fancy sauces, this is what he doesn't like and probably doesn't understand. But for what it is—fancy food—it is pretty good. And you can get good versions of dishes that are so familiar that almost everyone has forgotten what they can and should taste like.

For example, Oysters Rockefeller about as well made as you can find them in New York. The oysters are filled with a spinach stuffing that has been seasoned and flavored with Pernod, and they are baked until the buttery filling is bubbling and browned, but not too long, so the oysters themselves are juicy and tender. The whole thing is permeated with the licorice fragrance of Pernod. This is a very substantial appetizer, and there is no rule against having two orders (one dozen) as a main course. Smoked trout is on many menus, and it is almost always the commercially available stuff—good as long as it kept refrigerated and moist. The sauce, however, is the restaurant's contribution, and in this place it is fabulous—sharp horseradish and airy whipped cream. One wishes the fish itself were not a bit dry, and that the lemon, artfully serrated, did not look as if the artist came in only once a week. There are snails, plump and tender, in a sauce that is deep-green with parsley and more heavily flavored with shallots than with garlic.

Among the fancy main dishes is one styled Ris de Veau Braises Financière, which is to say sweetbreads braised in stock and served in a wine sauce to which the braising liquid has been added. One looks in vain for the truffles the dish is ideally made with, but the sweetbreads themselves are so hearty and rich, the sauce so sharp and deep— the perfect contrast to the sensuous meat—that it's hard to quarrel with it. Les Médaillons de Veau Vallée d'Auge is a typical Normandy preparation of veal. Thin slices of the pale and tender meat are browned, as are some fresh mushrooms, and the two are served in a sauce that is mostly Calvados and cream. This is a simple dish, made with good ingredients. The Noisettes d'Agneau Mascotte consists of slices of roast lamb (very rare) in a sauce made of the roasting-pan juices, to which browned artichoke hearts and delicious little roasted potatoes have been added. The à la carte vegetables are very expensive, but they are carefully prepared. The grilled mushrooms, for example, are fresh, well-browned, crunchy and fragrant.

There is an unspoken agreement among the more thrifty (to put it nicely) New York restaurant customers and the more entrepreneurial (to put it bluntly) New York restaurant captains and waiters. When salad time comes, toward the end of dinner (not long before tipping time), the parsimonious diner considers his finances and orders something like one salad for two, or three salads for five, or whatever. The functionary considers *his* finances and portions out plates of salad that are more copious than anyone wants, charging according to the number of salads ordered. He is, as you see, in the salad business, but with no costs. The watercress and endives are fresh and crisp, and the oily dressing, with freshly ground pepper and just a little mustard, is first-rate.

A good dessert cart, including, at times, a hot Christmas pudding—a dark, spicy and sweet amalgam of nuts, fruits, rinds and brandy, served with a heavily liquored and rather liquid hard sauce. The chocolate mousse is rich and thick, and is served in a cakelike crust, with excellent whipped cream. The tarts are something rare—the usual fruit and pastry, but with a layer of marzipan. Now, marzipan is out of the world of pastry into the world of candy, and unless you have a special liking for the stuff, you may find these tarts a bit much.

This place is known for its lengthy wine list. The prices at the low end are insane: $12 for a bottle of ordinary Beaujolais. But the prices are not proportionately higher for wines that are many times better. To save a few dollars you may drink what the wine list refers to as "Native wines." There is a cover, but those entrepreneurs sometimes forget to include it in the final calculation. Business is business.

★★CHEZ NAPOLEON

365 West 50th Street
LUNCH, MONDAY TO FRIDAY; DINNER, MONDAY TO SATURDAY. CLOSED SUNDAY.
Reservations, CO 5–6980.
Credit cards: AE, MC, V.
Medium-priced.

Of the twenty or so moderately priced French restaurants in the West Forties and Fifties near Eighth and Ninth avenues, not all are worth entering for any reason other than getting in out of the weather. But Chez Napoleon is one. Not only are there a couple of surprises on the menu, but the familiar dishes are carefully made of good ingredients. Moreover, the service has not deteriorated over the years, despite steady, good business—the waitresses are intelligent and good-humored, and except during the very busy weekend dinners and at the peak of the lunch hour, prompt.

Dinner begins with a plate of good-quality black and green olives to hold you while the menu is read. An experimentally inclined guest consumed them by the plateful to determine how frequently the house would refill the plate. The management's generosity outlasted the diner's taste for olives, but this may have had something to do with the customer's excellent native French, a useful passport to good treatment in all of these West Side bistros.

At any rate, don't eat too many olives, because the listed first courses (and subsequent courses) are far more interesting. The mackerel in white wine, which in many restaurants should be labeled "pickled fish," is here a tart, strong appetite builder, the fish marinade made of lemon juice as well as white wine, flavored with vegetables and slivers of pickle. The pâté maison is simple, coarse, strongly flavored with garlic and served with real French cornichons instead of the usual domestic gherkins. The snails are small and tender, but the preparation is rather bland. The Mussels Biarritz, on the other hand, are something else; served in addition to the run-of-restaurant Moules Ravigote, they are breaded, seasoned with garlic and parsley, moistened with butter and oil, and baked—much the way snails are usually prepared—and it is a pleasant change to have mussels this way.

Another surprise is the rabbit cooked in white wine. Rabbit is rarely found on New York menus, and here the meat is well browned before the stewing, the bones go into the pot, which helps to make for a thick, rich sauce, and sautéed onions and mushrooms add a perfect accent. The Coq au Vin is easy on the red wine, heavy on a strong chicken stock—a difficult preparation to bring off. The Duck à l'Orange is far better than one expects in this caliber of restaurant—the duck is moist, the skin crisp, and the sauce carefully built.

Chez Napoleon is best known for its bouillabaisse, available, unfortunately, only on Friday, a very crowded evening at this restaurant. (You may avoid the crowd by coming late, but by that time the bouillabaisse is frequently all gone.) This is an eccentric bouillabaisse, very heavily flavored with fennel, but it is made with a variety of good ingredients—red snapper, sea bass, eel, lobster, clams, mussels. The fish is cooked to flakiness, not mush; the shellfish to firmness, not leather; all in a fragrant, thick soup.

To most palates the salad dressing will seem far too oily—understandably, as it is almost pure oil. Ask to have it made with a bit more vinegar than usual, or if you prefer a Roquefort dressing, here it is made with real French Roquefort.

Of the desserts, the cheeses are refrigerated, and the Crêpes Suzette—well, this is not a Crêpes Suzette restaurant. They are flamed in a few droplets of Grand Marnier, which yields almost no sauce. They are much too dry. If you must have a flame, the Cherries Jubilee are good. The *café filtre* is superb.

★★★ CHEZ PASCAL

151 East 82nd Street
DINNER.
Reservations necessary, 249-1334.
Credit cards: AE.
Very expensive.

In carving out this place, the old plaster has been removed to reveal walls of rosy brick (warmer and softer than any paint, and, oh, so durable); the ancient stamped-tin ceiling has been silvered to a dark luster, as of burnished zinc; the floors are stripped to bare wood. Within these pristine planes, illuminated by the gentle glow of opaline chandeliers, the luxurious appointments seem to be in a warehouse, *en passant* between the maker and a posh apartment. Plump banquettes of gray suede opposite French period chairs in white and wicker, here a wall of wine bottles, there a display of appetizers and desserts, on the walls unobjectionable art, everywhere lovely flowers. And before each seat, white octagonal plates which will be decorated (once you are seated) with a slice of saucisson en croûte while you consider the wine list and the menu. That unexpected morsel is, happily, superb and of a quality that foretells excellences to come—the sausage at once sharp and fatty, the pastry that rims it moist and flaky, and the mustard that accompanies it the perfect sharp foil for the glistening and rich meat.

That wine list, by the way, consists of a paddle to which are affixed an assortment of wine labels, under glass. Included are a couple of house wines—white and red—at very reasonable prices for such eminently drinkable, if small, potions.

The waiters wear long aprons, the captains spiffy civvies, the clientele a spectrum of finery extending from Bond Street to Job's Lane; and this place has their numbers, perfectly. Some of these folk are more than the least bit stuffy (the last thing in the world they want believed), and Chez Pascal, with its armory air, helps them to feel that they are ever-so-slightly slumming, that the rose petal in the finger bowl is satiric rather than *riche,* the steep prices larky rather than *bourgeois.* Here on East 82nd Street, where $80 tabs for an intimate little supper for two are signed blind, those revelers, in their nostalgic fantasies, are courting in the neighborhood joint.

That is a tough revery to nurture if you order Pascal's Trois Terrines. Those terrines arrive as three slabs, each the size of a package of filter kings. A wooden spoon is dipped in a gallon jug, and you are garnished with those little French pickles called cornichons. These are good terrines, one porky, one livery, one studded with ham, and though you can easily praise their quality and distinguish them by their differences, they are simply in too narrow a range, and this appetizer ends up being too much of a good thing. You will enjoy it more if you share it than if you tackle it alone. Another ambitious first course is something called La Salade Royale, also a prodigious item to undertake: a mound the size of a grapefruit, made up of crisp, barely cooked strands of stringbean; spears of fresh and perfectly poached asparagus, a bit too fibrous, having not been peeled before the boiling; hearts of fresh artichoke, cooked not a minute too long; chunks of crabmeat and shrimp; and a few spears of endive, all dressed in a vinaigrette that is strengthened with minced onions and mustard. This is a perfectly nice salad of better-than-average vegetables and seafood, but the mélange has little character—you feel as if you have eaten good things, but not a good dish. Eschew all but the artichoke, by ordering Artichaut Vinaigrette, and this time you even get the leaves—one wishes the article were not so recently taken from the refrigerator.

If you come to Chez Pascal just once, you would do well to order Le Bass en Croûte Monloup. You are presented with a huge oval platter, its perimeter graced with string beans, braised endive, grilled tomatoes; its center occupied by a browned cross-hatched pastry in the shape of a fish, the pastry thus cueing you to its contents: a small bass that has been spread with a duxelles of mushrooms, which in itself sounds like a wonderful idea. The dish is completed when your waiter turns back a section of the crust and pours in a creamy sauce of fish stock, white wine, shallots and abundant butter. Chez Pascal offers a grilled lobster, a preparation not usually found in these parts, where one is either an adherent of boiling, steaming or broiling, or one is a fool. But careful grilling yields a lobster equal to any—to grill a lobster, it is immersed in boiling water for a couple of minutes, to make the meat firm, and then it is finished by turning it in a hot well-buttered pan until the meat is thoroughly cooked but not dried. They seem to do it perfectly Chez Pascal, bits of charring here and there, the lobster fresh and moist, the silken sauce that comes with it sweet and buttery.

There is a pigeon offered whose meat is so rich you could mistake it for liver; it is surrounded by the usual little peas and the unusual slivers of black truffle. The bird, browned and moist, is as good a pigeon as you will find in New York. And sometimes there is Gigot d'Agneau, the lamb slices showing bright pink centers and crusty browned edges. The gamy meat is surrounded by browned scalloped potatoes and a slightly sour grilled tomato that is plump, moist and generously herbed.

There is a simplicity of desserts, including a very refreshing lemon mousse; an orange tart of deeply darkened pastry, a smooth thin layer of custard, and discs of darkened fresh orange, sweet, tart and juicy; a cake, the principal ingredients of which are a purée of chestnuts and a mousse of chocolate, and the main qualities of which are a smooth airiness, somehow combined with solidity and richness; raspberries, soft and firm, in a Crème Chantilly, which, you should understand, is a lightly sweetened and vanilla-flavored whipped cream.

Study your bill to the accompaniment of some lovely petits fours.

★★ CHEZ RAYMOND

240 West 56th Street
LUNCH, MONDAY TO FRIDAY; DINNER, MONDAY TO SATURDAY. CLOSED SUNDAY.
Reservations, 245–3656.
Credit cards: AE, DC, MC, V.
Expensive.

Chez Raymond is a spotty restaurant, but for its best items it's worth knowing about. The place looks like dozens of French restaurants in New York—a small bar at the front, with a few tables around it along the wall; in the back room there are wood paneling, framed murals, a gold-colored banquette, fresh flowers on the white linen. It is ever so slightly gaudy, in an innocuous way, tasteless but inoffensive.

In this simple setting, devoid, as it is, of distractions, the food is the thing, and you can have it with some quite nice wine.

Don't begin with the Moules Ravigote—the mussels, if they are not canned, might as well be. But there are any number of good things you *can* begin with. The stuffed oysters, for one, are sweet, briny and tender. They are not really stuffed, but sprinkled with chopped shallots and parsley, and covered with a small slice of bacon. The oysters are put in the broiler very close to the fire so that the bacon becomes slightly charred before the oyster has a chance to toughen. A dish like this requires careful timing, and when it is properly made, the warm but still raw-tasting oyster is perfectly accented by the sharp, slightly smoky bacon.

Or you can begin with saucisson chaud—the warm, spicy sausage always served with potatoes in oil. You get two thick slices of the sturdy sausage here, and the potatoes are firm but thoroughly cooked. The problem with this dish is that after an hour you will not yet be hungry. There are also such standard first courses as marinated mushrooms—they are fresh and strongly perfumed with spices and herbs; and céleri rémoulade—the root is crisp and radishy, and the rémoulade sauce is slightly tart and lemony. All in all, this is a better version of this dish than you get in most French restaurants of this class.

If you want soup, the onion soup is sweet, hot, admittedly made with a rather weak stock, but topped with excellent Swiss cheese, nicely browned. The special soups of the day include a watercress soup, which is principally potatoes, butter and fresh watercress, and a fairly similar hot leek-and-potato soup, in which the chicken and the strong flavor of leeks blend very nicely with the sharp taste of cooked cream and the succulent one of chicken fat—a really first-rate dish.

The outstanding dish of the house is Le Pintadeau en Croûte aux Chanterelles Monbazillac, which, in case you are wondering, is guinea hen and the delicious wild mushrooms called chanterelles, baked in stock, wine and herbs under a glazed crust.

The pot arrives at your place with the crown of pastry intact, and when you break it, an extraordinarily sweet and earthy fragrance fills the air. Guinea hen is a rather delicately flavored bird, like pheasant, but it is the preparation rather than the bird that makes this spectacular dish. If you come to this restaurant once, this is the dish to have.

There is a very good poached striped bass, moist and flaky, served with a thick and lemony hollandaise, and the broiled beef and lamb dishes are good. One dish that is good but could often be better is the Filet de Boeuf, Sauce Périgourdine. The whole filet is roasted at the start of dinner, and when you order the dish, a couple of slices are cut for you and served in the thick, sweet sauce that was deglazed from the roasting pan. This is all to the good, but because the meat was prepared early in the evening, it may be too well done by, say, nine o'clock, and the house is not above dabbing the slices of meat with that bloody-looking liquid sometimes called "paint" that some restaurants keep around to convert well-done meat to "rare."

The salad course is taken seriously here. You get good ingredients, like watercress, endive, Boston lettuce, and an oily vinaigrette made sharp and vibrant with plenty of strong mustard. There is usually Brie in good condition.

For some reason many of the regular customers here order soufflés for dessert. There is no special oven for them in the kitchen, and during the busiest part of the dinner hour they are baked at the temperatures demanded by the other dishes with which they must share the oven space. Even late at night, when they can be treated a little better, the results are heavy and improperly flavored. You are better off with the pastries—the napoleon is made with a sweet, rich custard and a very flaky pastry. The fruit tarts are good too.

Occasionally the rather officious proprietor dresses down a waiter in the dining room, which he should do in the kitchen. And occasionally it seems as if the floor is under-staffed, so this may not be the place for a quick dinner before the theater or before a concert at nearby Carnegie Hall. But those are minor shortcomings, and you can have an excellent dinner here if you order carefully.

★★★ CHRIST CELLA

160 East 46th Street
LUNCH, MONDAY TO FRIDAY; DINNER, MONDAY TO SATURDAY. CLOSED SUNDAY.
Reservations, OX 7–2479.
Credit cards: AE, CB, DC, MC, V.
Very expensive.

You are greeted by a host who, when you reject the first couple of tables he shows you to, does not, directly or by suggestion or by gesture, imply that Christ Cella can do without fussy customers. This is remarkable because Christ Cella *can* do without fussy customers. It has plenty of all kinds, and they pay more than liberally for the pleasure of eating in this establishment. But your host listens to your objections care-fully, no sooner does he grasp them than you are escorted to the bar, and as soon as a table is available that meets your specifications (not in the traffic, not near the door), he comes to get you. The amazing policy of this restaurant is: you pay your money and you take *your* choice.

That bar where you waited for your table is very much of the place. The downstairs of this two-story restaurant is made up of many small rooms, and one of them is the handsome wood-paneled barroom, the bar the length of one wall, the three tables opposite spaced well apart. There are no stools at the bar (this is not primarily a drinking place), and the polished walls and the mounted antelope head notwithstanding, the room is not clubbily masculine, just comfortable. Then there are all the other rooms, with their pale-green walls hung with prints and photographs. At the back is the immaculate kitchen, open to view, with accommodations for a handful of regular customers who find that eating in the kitchen at an unlinened table, under the clamor of the pots and pans and kitchen patter, is a fillip that spices the simple pleasures this restaurant provides. Upstairs the rooms are large, bare and forbidding—a good place for big parties, where your companions are also your scenery.

Christ Cella has an Old New York feel to it, like a restaurant born in the Depression; it is Spartan in its appointments and lavish of quality, as if it knew and remembered the value of a customer and never learned the show-biz side of the food biz.

The customers have more than a touch of class—conservative but not stuffy, people who do not brandish their individuality, who are not dazed by their own success. The clothes worn here are neither uniforms nor political statements. (Of course, that is at dinner. At lunchtime the restaurant is just another place in the midtown business district, and the place is loaded with guys who seem more important outside their offices than at their programmed tasks performed at standard desks.)

There is no printed menu. The waiter tells you what there is, all of which is simple food. The crabmeat cocktail is copious, tender, fresh, with a brightly flavored cocktail sauce—not inherently a great dish, but as good as it can be for what it is. Shrimp and lobster cocktails of comparable quality, but no clams or oysters.

Perfectly broiled fish is available, on occasion roast beef, good liver. But the standard dishes here, making up probably 90 percent of the main-course orders, are steaks and lobsters, and they are more consistently excellent than in any other steak/lobster house in this Steak Row neighborhood, or, for that matter, in New York. The steaks are fibrous, tender, seared (but not burnt), so the juice of the meat is sealed into the center of the steak. The filet mignon is at least three inches thick, adorned with a few fresh mushrooms; the sirloin is not that deep, but it is substantial enough to be cooked for more than a moment and still come out rare. By and large, the degree of doneness of your steak is as you request it in this restaurant, and deviations are slight. The steaks are sprinkled abundantly with fresh parsley.

The lobsters are big but not huge, they are broiled, and they are fresh, unbelievably moist, faintly imbued with the taste of the charred shell. Unrequested, your waiter separates most of the lobster from its shell, so that even a child can eat it with a knife and fork; the meat from the claws is brought to you extricated from its housing and served up in a little bowl. Still, grown diners are up to their elbows in drawn butter by the time they have worked their way through one of these things, their wineglasses coated with the stuff, as if it wouldn't be a lobster without the mess. The hashed brown potatoes are lightly blackened and crunchy outside, soft within. The baked potatoes are done perfectly. The salads are of fresh, unblemished greens in a tart, limpid dressing —the arugula, for example, has a full, strong fragrance, as if it were just picked.

Excessive desserts, but good of their kind. The cheese cake at this restaurant is not what it was a few years back, but it is one of the best of its type in town—extremely rich and creamy, very heavily lemoned. The napoleon is made up, elementally, of thick layers of custard between very flaky layers of pastry. If all of that sounds like too much, which it should be if you have eaten well to this point, there is a more than decent raspberry sherbet served in more than indecent quantity.

★★ LE CIRQUE

58 East 65th Street
LUNCH AND DINNER. CLOSED SUNDAY.
Reservations, 794–9292.
Credit cards: AE, DC.
Very expensive.

It is an almost unfailing rule that any restaurant that serves both French and Italian food is no good at either—the breadth of the menu is a search for a broader clientele, and a signal that someone in charge cares not what he serves, as long as it sells. This place serves several Italian dishes in addition to its preponderance of French food, and you can tell that this is not an economically motivated pandering to the supposed tastes of the wished-for customers. The handful of Italian dishes are not the standard New York items, they are on the menu because someone who decides what is being served here likes to serve them, which is a heartening sign that the place is governed by an ego, not a calculator.

This establishment is built into the Mayfair Hotel, where no restaurant was before, and they have chosen to go the route of Champs-Elysées posh, which is, in this version, harmless enough—but it has dragged in the most uniformly stuffy crowd outside Quo Vadis. The softly lit room is papered in an ivory-and-tan trellis pattern, with pastel murals, in a certain low order of French humor, of monkeys doing human things—Le Cirque is The Circus; in one mural we have monkeys chatting, in another dining, then dancing, then flirting . . . they stop short. The furniture is Louis the Something (with oval-backed chairs in pink upholstery); there are mirrored columns, flowers on the tables, candlelight; and a gentle murmur from the well-breds that besport themselves along the taupe banquette of glistening suede that meanders through the room. It is all very other-worldly, with nary a black or a beard or a denimed derrière in the place —they could have called it Le Musée—but perfectly comfortable in its anachronistic way.

To begin with one of the Italian items, you may drop $5 for a delicacy which is styled Carpaccio Toscane—three small thin slices of superb raw beef, served with a cold green sauce. The meat is freshly sliced from the filet, and the sauce is a thick composite of minced capers, parsley, a bit of garlic, a touch of anchovy, and oil—a good idea is to wrap one third of your sauce in each slice of meat and eat with your fingers. To begin with one of the French items, you may sacrifice $3.75 for Crêpes Le Cirque—these are a usual thing, two pancakes rolled up and stuffed with curried seafood, mostly crab-meat, served with a mustard sauce (a pool of it on one side of your dish) and a spicy tomato sauce (another pool, at the other side)—nice, but nothing special.

When the soup of the day is hot leek-and-potato, do not pass it up. It is simply a buttery broth (chicken-stock base), infused with the flavor of leeks, with a layer of crunchy bits of potato at the bottom of the bowl—elemental and very satisfying.

An ambitious duck, and, by and large, a successful one. Called, without commas, Le Canard Rôti au Citron Pommes et Raisins, it is a very good rich bird, against which the sharp flavors of citrus rind, the sweet and spicy taste of cinnamoned apples, and the plump ripeness of dark little raisins are all perfect complements. La Selle de Pré Salé Desossée Grillée is your lamb as beef, a thick steak of it, served with a mustard-and-tomato sauce (like an excellent barbecue sauce). The sauce is not needed—the lamb steak is good just the way it is. Pretty good vegetables, including zucchini that is sugared and browned until leathery.

A limited number of desserts of interest—an unlisted Tarte à la Tatin is just a humdrum apple tart covered with a whipped cream that is all air; the chocolate cake is rich, moist, solid without being heavy.

★★CLOS NORMAND

42 East 52nd Street
LUNCH AND DINNER. CLOSED SUNDAY.
Reservations, PL 3–3348.
Credit cards: AE, CB, DC, MC, V.
Medium-priced.

This is a lovely restaurant; the food is usually good, often excellent; the service, once you get past the officious host, is intelligent and industrious; and the prices, though moderately expensive at lunch (à la carte), are very reasonable at dinner (prix fixe), as a result of which the place does almost as much business in the evening as it does at noon, which is rare for all but the most *haute cuisine* of New York's midtown restaurants.

There are dozens of French restaurants in New York in the East and West Forties and Fifties, and the daytime office population in these neighborhoods is so dense that it's almost impossible for a restaurant to fail unless it is shut down by the health department. So it's admirable when any of them goes to the trouble, first, of preparing the conventional dishes with care and originality, and second, of augmenting the standard French menu with unusual dishes.

There is pâté all over town, but the terrine served at lunch here is of game, and it is pink, moist, rich, and accented with crisp nuts and firm black truffles. In the evening you may wish to pass up the terrine, however, because a crock of fluffy liver mousse, strong and perfectly salted, is placed on the table to divert you while you read the menu, and perhaps decide to start with Moules Normande, one of the best mussel appetizers in New York. This is a giant pot of at least two dozen fresh mussels that have been steamed in their own juice, milk, wine, herbs and shallots; the tangy white soup that remains when you have eaten the mussels is worth the $1.75 premium alone. Even jellied consommé is good here—cool cubes of strong beef broth. And the pink Bayonne ham, served with ripe melon, is tender, just a little smoky, and sliced elegantly thin.

This restaurant makes some of the better quenelles in New York, and though they are served with what the menu calls lobster sauce, it's not the usual sauce Nantua. On the other hand, the word "lobster" doesn't seem quite right either. The white dumplings come in assorted shapes, which gives them a pleasant homemade look. They are tender, not rubbery, intensely flavored without being fishy, and they are covered with a strong brown sauce containing mussels, fresh mushrooms and breath of lobster. Well, lobsters are sky-high. At lunch there is a seafood quiche which is loaded with huge chunks of pink-skinned crabmeat.

Clos Normand is one of the few places that consents to prepare a rack of lamb for one person. It is served in the juice of the lamb, not converted into a sauce, and the meat is smeared with a potent amalgam of garlic, shallots and herbs. The duck with figs is a juicy bird, but the figs are only a garnish and do not enter into the preparation, and are canned, anyway, so you are disappointed if you expect something that lives up to Le Caneton aux Figues.

Most fixed-price dinner houses do not include a salad in the price of your dinner. Here you not only get a salad, but a great one—tender Boston lettuce, crisp watercress and loads of thinly sliced raw mushrooms in a truly French dressing of mostly oil and mustard, with just a little vinegar.

The Mont Blanc here is disappointing—a commercial meringue, an excessively sweet canned chestnut purée and whipped cream. It's just too much. In its original form this dish is made with *crème fraîche,* not whipped cream, and *crème fraîche* has an edge to it that can relieve the overwhelming sweetness of the purée. Better are Les Délices du Chef, which are little babas covered with a runny custard and toasted almonds, all in a puddle of powerfully sweet caramel sauce. The Crêpe Surprise is a browned crêpe around a ball of pecan ice cream, all in the same honeylike caramel sauce—sort of a French sundae. There is a sensible policy here of stocking only one or two cheeses, but of keeping them at room temperature, and available in good condition. You get a large pot of very good coffee.

Tan plaster walls, beams, rough-hewn wooden pillars, rustic-looking wall sconces, banquettes of coarse red wool, and large, delicately shaded murals of foggy Normandy —cities, towns and a beautiful long beach in hazy sunlight. This is one of the prettiest restaurants in town, though it is rather crowded and noisy, which tends to offset the effect.

The proprietor here is a stiff type who peers at you dubiously over his steel-rimmed glasses. He considers it a sin to seat anyone at once, empty tables or no, reservation or no. His stiff frame collapses and is reassembled into a limp posture of abject respect when big spenders show up. But he is a minor obstacle, and he wilts under a firm complaint.

★ COACH HOUSE

110 Waverly Place (near Sixth Avenue)
DINNER, TUESDAY TO SUNDAY. CLOSED MONDAY.
Reservations required, SP 7–0303.
Credit cards: AE, CB, DC, MC.
Very expensive.

Visualize, if you will, a color photograph of the perfect slice of roast beef, served, in the American way, an inch thick and attached to its rib. You might even think of this vision as a panoramic backlighted transparency, like those mounted by Eastman

Kodak in Grand Central Station, in which every tint is true, lifelike and yet—glorified. Of such impact is your first sight of the Coach House's Prime Rib of Beef, a gigantic chop of pink meat, its edges browned and crusted, the center moist and glinting, inviting the stroke of the knife that will pass through its tenderness like a glider through still air. And yet to eat one of these works of art, a certified hypertensive must defy medical opinion and inundate the thing with a blizzard of common table sodium chloride, for on its own the roast has all the flavor of raw Wonder Bread.

And therein is the story of this fabled place. Not, you understand, that all the food is pretty and tasteless, for much of it is neither; rather that this establishment is an illusion, so nourished by its well-fed reputation that the hordes of tourists and tri-generational old-line New York families that make up the bulk of its clientele pass through in states of unconscious, unquestioning rapture. One is reminded of the opium den that operated for years without so much as a single brief closure. Everyone assumed high-level police connections. Nothing of the sort. It was just that the pipes were prepared without a speck of laudanum, the deceived customers achieving their highs on atmosphere and imagination.

This den has been going so smoothly so long that it needs no help from the boss. Nevertheless, he is always here. Anywhere else his demeanor would be an insuperable liability, but in this place he could spit in their eye without losing a customer. He is tall, skeletal and graying, formal in his dark suit; yet he stands about sucking his teeth and gently scratching himself. He regards his patrons with the bored contempt of a porn-shop proprietor making change for the men who feed quarters to dirty-movie machines. He points you to your table with the tossed gesture of the butler directing the delivery boy to the service entrance.

With him setting the tone it is remarkable that the help displays any courtesy at all. Still they do, stiltedly mouthing little speeches in answer to your questions, the younger members of the staff aping the vacuous suavity of those who have been here for decades. But you can ask for the wine list the moment you sit down, order a bottle when the captain tries, prematurely, to get your food order, remind him about it again when you do finally let him know what you want to eat, mention it to the waiter when your first course is delivered and still not see it until—salvation!—it arrives with that dreary roast beef.

The Coach House has the look that every Colonial motel dining room aspires to, but they do it better here, excellently as a matter of fact, a special Bloomie's room it could almost be. This is one of the few restaurants in New York in which the framed art is a notch above inoffensive—the still lifes live, the old sporting scenes can make you long, for a moment, for the simple life of another day. There is a beamed ceiling, exposed brick, leather banquettes of pure, vivid red. The peach-colored tablecloths are a bit icky, but the crimson napkins at each place are a hearty note. Flowers are all about, also great displays of food and wine, the whole scene illuminated by large, graceful, airy brass chandeliers. The place is busy and it hums, and almost everyone is having a good time —old-liners are so relaxed when they are not slumming.

There is an à la carte menu and a prix-fixe menu. If you go with the former, do not go with the Hors d'Oeuvres Variés, an ill-assorted miscellany of items carefully selected to clash: the swell herring, firm and tart in its smooth cream sauce, is ridiculous next to the undistinguished pâté that is studded with pistachio nuts; nor does a hard-cooked egg (its yolk tinged with green), surmounted by cocktail sauce and crossed anchovies, make any sense next to these musty Mushrooms à la Grecque; the platter is completed with a dab of Eggplant Provençale, cool and heavily garlicked, the skin of the well-cooked vegetable pleasantly leathery, the pine nuts crunchy, the whole thing in a thick, strong tomato sauce. They get $5 for that cacophony. Choose instead the Escargots de Bourgogne Sautéed with Croutons in Garlic Butter (for two), each serving consisting of eight snails on toasted crusts of French bread, the sauce that is poured over very much like a buttery green soup, the snails themselves plump and tender, everything redolent of pungent fresh garlic.

Nothing is more typical of this establishment than the contrast between the reputation and the reality of its Black Bean Soup Madeira. Mention the restaurant and someone will immediately mention the soup. And yet this is nothing more than a perfectly decent bowl, thick and dark, bits of egg and lemon therein—it is hearty and satisfying, but it lacks any distinctive character.

It would be unfortunate if side stepping the roast beef causes you to trip over the Mignonettes of Veal à la Campagne with Glazed Chestnuts, for the meat is likely to be dry, the sauce candied, the mushrooms and small onions in the sauce nice notes on their own, but having little to do with the dish as a whole. You are wise to turn instead to the Rack of Spring Lamb Roasted to a Crisp. They use strong, almost muttony lamb here, full of slightly gamy flavor; the little roast is accurately prepared, and the many ribs of red meat should hold you for quite a while. One of the best dishes in the place is Fresh Lump Crab Meat Baltimore, Sautéed with Julienne Ham. What makes the dish is the sweet, gentle flavor, slightly oceanic, of crabmeat that is truly fresh—it is served in a simple sauce that is mostly butter and parsley, with bits of strong ham for sharp contrast. But then there is the American Chicken Pie, not a pie at all, but a pallid stew, a disc of barely cooked dough added as a "crust" to justify the title—institutional food. The green vegetables are usually limp, sometimes cold.

Almost every method of preparing salads badly has been mastered by the Coach House. Occasionally the greens are wet or brown or both. The "Italian" dressing, described as "with herbs" lacks herbs and has in its place slightly rancid oil. The blue-cheese dressing is blenderized, so that instead of the bits of sharp cheese here and there that can make a salad exciting, we have goo. Something described as "French" dressing is merely sour.

It is apparent that the cheeses are in and out of the refrigerator from day to day, so if you are lucky you get a decent slice of Brie; less lucky, and you are served chalky Gruyère.

The virtuosity of the Fresh Apple Tart cannot be overlooked. The slivers of apple are almost black, and they have an odd prunelike flavor; the crust is thick, brown and crumbly; almonds are sprinkled on top. But if you close your eyes to the vision and just taste the dessert, it is little more than a good apple pie. God knows what would happen if you asked for a scoop of ice cream to go with it. The dacquoise is an excellent stack of layers, hazelnut meringue and mocha cream. Wonderful Hot Fudge Ice Cream Cake—fresh sponge cake with rich ice cream, topped with real thick, unsweetened hot fudge. Good tarts, made with fresh berries, and better than average pecan pie. Good coffee.

The wine list is extensive, expensive and uncluttered by vintage-year designations.

★★ LA COCOTTE

147 East 60th Street
LUNCH AND DINNER. CLOSED SUNDAY.
Reservations, 832–8972.
Credit cards: AE, CB, DC, MC, V.
Expensive.

La Cocotte is now a large restaurant—a small front room, a somewhat larger back room, and a spacious room downstairs built into what was once the garden. It still has some of the feeling of a garden because two of the walls are almost entirely of glass, through which a little foliage can be seen, and at lunch, a little daylight. The other walls are papered—huge green ferns.

La Cocotte is a very classy restaurant—everything is clean, neat and relaxed. And nothing can be more comfortable than the East Siders who take it over for dinner. The people who come here for lunch are comfortable too; they have found a restaurant where the daytime prices are competitive with some of the most mediocre French restaurants in New York, but where the food is far better—on occasion, superb.

"Coquille" is a word that is so familiar on New York appetizer listings that one almost automatically reads right by it in the search for something more interesting. But *coquille* means "shell," the contents can be anything, and here the dish is called Coquille Thermidor, not St. Jacques. The contents are sautéed mushrooms, tender little shrimp and red-skinned lobster meat, as well as scallops, all in a sweet, thick Thermidor sauce, the whole sprinkled with cheese and lightly browned just before serving. The search for a mussel variant has led to Moules Mignonette, which is soft, well-cleaned, steamed mussels, out of their shells, marinated in vinegar and pepper, and served with lemon, which gives the dish even more sparkle. The plate of Hors d'Oeuvres Variées is indeed *variées,* but you will have to hunt through it to find something worth a tumble. The oysters here are good, though the management operates under the delusion that tiny ones are better than big ones. And there are the usual smoked salmon, shrimp cocktail and a good pâté de campagne, with the pistachio nuts without which the East Side would not put up.

The steak tartare is very good. The meat is ground just before the preparation, and it is moist and red, which is the basic requirement of a dish made with raw meat. However, if the captain spends too long making it, the Tournedos Périgourdine, destined for the same table, may get overcooked while the tartare's middle-of-the-dining-room preparation is interrupted by the demands of diners who should but can't be assisted by any of the numerous waiters who are standing about in clusters discussing politics. Aside from the timing problem, the preparation of these tournedos is quite expert—the sautéed truffles and sautéed filet mignon are covered with a superb madeira-flavored brown sauce. But the addition of a cap of pâté de foie gras is ridiculous— it's wrong for the dish (the flavor of the pâté is overwhelmed by the beef, sauce and truffles), and it's clearly aimed at the kinds of customers who are the more delighted the greater the number of fancy ingredients they find on their plates.

One of the best dishes here is the rack of lamb (served for two). The delicate, very young baby lamb is studded with garlic, roasted and carved across the ribs, to produce eight long slices of pink meat. These are moistened with a light sauce made in the roasting pan, sprinkled with parsley, surrounded with the now denuded ribs and served with watercress and some very good Pommes Anna (a cake of sliced, seasoned potatoes baked in clarified butter to the point of brown crust, and soft, white interior).

There is a delicate dish of sautéed veal scallops moistened in a cider-based sauce; and a good grilled bass covered with sauce Choron (tomato-flavored Béarnaise). The salads are of excellent crisp greens in a very tart and mustardy vinaigrette.

There are nice fruit tarts, a good coffee mousse, flaky and creamy Napoleons, perfectly decent Cherries Jubilee, and a light and refreshing crème caramel, etc. The wine list is rather brief for a restaurant of this caliber.

★★ LA COLOMBE D'OR

134 East 26th Street
LUNCH, MONDAY TO FRIDAY; DINNER, MONDAY TO SATURDAY. CLOSED SUNDAY.
Reservations, MU 9–0666.
Credit cards: AE, DC, MC, V.
Expensive.

Bored we are, and novelty is a virtue. La Colombe d'Or is unlike any other French restaurant in New York, and we fall into it in relief, like dogged Christmas shoppers taking the consolation of an after-Altman's cocktail.

There is more to French food than Manhattan Island's familiar extremes—*haute cuisine et la cuisine bourgeoise*—and local eating places often put themselves forward as "Normand," or "Brittany," or "Périgord," et al. But their justifications are little more than the odd dish or two among the dozens of familiars. You could, for example, collect all the menus of the French restaurants in New York's theater district, shuffle them and redistribute them at random—those kitchens, despite their suddenly "new" bills of fare, could continue operations without skipping a beat. But drop this establishment's menu on an uptown chef, and you send him to his books.

La Colombe d'Or has named itself, though it does not model itself, after a legendary eating place in the town of St. Paul, in Provence—a land of sunshine and olive oil, herbs and garlic, bouillabaisse by the sea, spicy stews of meats, fowls, sausages, vegetables in the fertile countryside that lies inland from the Mediterranean. Like the restaurants in that part of the world, this one on East 26th Street offers no duck à l'orange, no tripe à la mode de Caen, no Dover sole—neither real nor imagined. The listings are so relentlessly southern, so free of deference to local custom, that reading through them engenders—are you ready?—curiosity! But there's too many a slip, alas. The singularity of the undertaking is matched by the variability of its success—the food here is never less than OK, mind you, but from such heady promise the more than occasional disappointments are commensurately disappointing.

La Colombe d'Or is a charming little place. When it was new, its ivories and beiges and freshened sand-colored brick gleamed a bit brightly. But The Golden Dove has been around awhile now; it has been—if not lived in—eaten in, it is humanly scuffed here and there, its edges beveled by brushes with human sleeves, an orderly clutter around its dozen or so tables. There are clumps of flowers here and there, the vividly-colored forms of Léger prints on the walls, benchlike banquettes with cushions in a French country print of small florets on a dark-green field—which goods is repeated in the curtains on the front windows, repeated again in the pinafores on the nubile waitresses. At lunchtime the place is frequented by the gentle editors of the genteel publishing houses that have eschewed uptown in favor of this old neighborhood. And resident Gramercy Parkers have discovered the place, some of them now eating in a restaurant within walking distance of their own town houses for the first time since they got the sulks when Madison Avenue was made a one-way street.

Everyone goes for the cold spinach appetizer, given as Epinards à l'Huile d'Olives, the fresh leafy vegetable in smooth olive oil, accented with browned sesame seeds and the little black olives of southern France—sometimes the dish is crackling and vibrant, but now and again it is limp. The Mousse aux 4 Poissons, a pale-green fish pâté that is studded with bits of whole fish in among the otherwise thoroughly ground meat, is powerfully flavored with fresh dill, which accounts for its color; and it is garnished with a tomato-flavored mayonnaise and crushed black and green olives. Unfortunately, the mousse itself is strong but short of character; it has flavor but not the distinctive liveliness of fresh seafood. The Brochette de Crevettes is a simple dish of shrimp that are herbed and broiled—the shrimp are plump and crunchy, and the herbing is delicate but sufficient to liven the shrimp. A good, spicy ratatouille is available, too, and it, like all the appetizers, is wonderful with the strong, sour bread you get here—served with sweet butter and with an alternative spread, a tapenade of anchovies, tuna, oil and olives, ground fine to a vibrant paste.

Along the Mediterranean they eat a lot of fish, one of them an especially ugly variety called *lotte*. The *lotte* never actually swims across the Atlantic, and the dish that Colombe d'Or gives us in French as Lotte à la Façon du Pétit Nice, is very freely translated by them as "monk fish, scalloped & sautéed à la provençale." The monk fish, better known as angle fish or anglerfish, is a fairly close approximation of its subtropical swimmer cousin, both in the horribleness of its appearance and the light sweetness of its flavor. In this preparation it arrives in a thick and slightly oily sauce that is studded with capers and black olives; the sauce is peppery, the flavor of its tomatoes heightened with fresh herbs, the whole dish strewn plentifully with fresh parsley. Bass is on the menu in a simple preparation—braised with tomatoes and herbs, the braising liquid then made into a sauce that is spiked with anchovies and olives—and the bass is good that way, for the fish here is always fresh. But on occasion you can have your bass in a buttery sauce that is aswim with mushrooms, onions, parsley. The seasoning is artful, bringing out all the flavors in the sauce and fish without overpowering them—it is a subtler, more balanced preparation. These are both good bass dishes, but once in a while the fish is under- or over-cooked.

When the highest-priced main course on a menu is a kidney dish, you figure they do something special with that unpopular organ, and in fact Rognons aux Morilles is one of the best items in the place. The kidneys have been carefully cleansed of their acids, and they are sweet and crunchy; the forest flavor of the wild morel mushrooms is heightened by the brandy that fortifies the creamy and slightly fatty sauce. The steaming dish is wonderful in the clarity of its textures—crisp kidneys, tender mushrooms, the two bound together by a sauce that is at once thick and polished.

Not every dish is an obscure one. Cassoulet is sold all over town, but this is an especially good one: a couple of sausages and hefty chunks of lamb and duck buried in a little pot of white beans, the top of which has been breaded and crusted. And the coq au vin, though a familiar title, is of better-than-average quality, the chicken thoroughly stewed, after browning, in wine and vegetables, the cooking liquid then made into an earthy sauce to which mushrooms and little onions are added late, so that they stand out in a lively way from the solid, sauced meat. The vegetable garnishes can be swell—thin, crisp French fries; or dreary—limp zucchini; or very interesting—dandelion in broth, with bits of pork fat adding body to the leafy greens.

A good selection of cheeses at room temperature may be had with a variety of salads, all of which are fresh and crisp. Many of the sweet desserts are supplied by outsiders, and they are fine, but the Paris Brest is made here, and it is a rather remarkable cassis-flavored airy cream between layers of light pastry. The pear, poached in wine, is firm but cooked thoroughly, and its winy syrup is sweet and refreshing. Good coffee.

If you drink wine by the glass, your needs are taken care of during the periodic trips taken through the dining room by a member of the staff, carrying a bottle—he or she refills your glass at the nod of your head. The wines by the bottle are mostly overpriced, but half a dozen inexpensive and quite drinkable ones are available.

★★ COPENHAGEN

68 West 58th Street
LUNCH AND DINNER. CLOSED SUNDAY.
Reservations, MU 8–3690.
Credit cards: AE, CB, DC, MC.
Medium-priced.

This is a wonderful restaurant in many ways, but one wishes that the host and hostess would turn it over to managers who are not enslaved by the petty pecking order of an established restaurant with an established clientele.

An apparently unrecognized couple arrive for dinner, and though the room is only half filled, they are seated at a small table behind a post, while a larger table beside it (as well as many others elsewhere in the room) is unused for the balance of the evening. When two beautiful young ladies arrive for lunch in casual dress, the plump, dimpled, blond boss lady sizes them up as in over their heads (and anyway, we all know that women alone don't spend) and leads them to a rarely used table in a remote corner; eventually she has it set up for eating, while better-situated tables, all ready with their rolled napkins, flowers and crystal, wait for customers who never come. But the host and hostess are minor obstacles; the waiters one deals with after they are out of the way are far more courteous, and the food makes it easy to overlook the deficient hospitality.

Danish food is famous for "det kolde bord" (a more or less elaborate buffet), and smørrebrød (open-faced sandwiches, available, in good restaurants in Denmark, in imponderable variety). At this restaurant the buffet is served at lunch and dinner, the sandwiches only at lunch.

The buffet table at Copenhagen is circular, so one can begin at any point, but the standard place to start is at the herrings and other cured fish. One marches from his table to the buffet, takes a plate from the stack and begins. There is sweet herring in a tart curry sauce, and a pickled herring with dill and cucumber, both of which are stimulating; a very strong smoked herring which is positively invigorating; and a mustard herring, with dill, which, by comparison, is merely refreshing. These, with a few slices of smoked salmon and a helping of cold beet salad are a good selection for the first trip. When all is consumed, with, it is suggested, beer and Akvavit (the Danish caraway-flavored stimulant, which is brought to the table in a bottle sheathed in a sleeve of ice), one waits a moment for the plate to be removed and repairs to the buffet for a fresh plate and some milder seafood. There is a whole cold salmon under a blanket of mayonnaise, sprinkled with little shrimp. Take some of that. Then there are some very nice halves of cold boiled lobster. Take one or two of those. Enough for this trip, except perhaps for a little potato salad. Return to your table, arrange for some more beer, and perhaps a second Akvavit. By this time the waiter will recognize you as the salt of the earth, and he may suggest a double Akvavit, for efficiency and economy. Not a bad idea.

Mousse of liver, cold roast beef, cold roast duck and chicken, melon (it could be riper) and an excellent smoked ham are good reasons for a third trip (very good with beer and Akvavit). Avoid the half-dozen hot foods, because they range from bad to worse. At this point one may decide to repeat one or two previously eaten items, or ease into dessert with some strawberry preserve and cottage cheese on plate number four. Desserts proper are served at your table, and they include a delectable apple concoction with whipped cream and sweetened pastry crumbs, a light lemon chiffon and a chocolate mousse, all served by the waiters in gigantic platefuls.

At lunchtime the menu that one is handed does not mention the availability of smørrebrød, but many of the customers are seen eating open-faced sandwiches. The waiter must be asked for the smørrebrød list—a slip of paper on which you check off your selections. The selection is meager, by Danish standards, and outrageously expensive by any standards, but the sandwiches are excellent. They are decoratively composed by the artist in the kitchen, who always begins by covering the bread with a half-inch layer of butter.

Many of the sandwiches are of items available at the buffet, but there are several additional interesting possibilities: the good smoked salmon with scrambled egg; a little tartar steak with egg yolk, capers, horseradish, onions and beets, which is sensational; seasoned roast veal, reclining under aspic and onion rings; and cold roast duck with beets, prunes, orange, apple and red cabbage. It's quite amazing to see how successfully so many items are combined on a normal-sized slice of bread. Simpler sandwiches of Blue cheese, egg-and-tomato, and so on, are also available.

Copenhagen has an extensive list of hot foods on its menu, but they are generally of less interest than the cold buffet and smørrebrød. There is a boiled codfish, with mustard sauce and horseradish, which is apparently heaven to a Dane but slightly stupefying to anyone else; and Danish fricadeller, the national dish of Denmark—meatballs served with red cabbage and potatoes—which is also mainly for the home-sick.

Three kinds of Carlsberg beer available: light, dark and elephant. Décor is *nouveau* Danish Bronx, with gold banquettes. No pipe smoking.

★★ LA CÔTE BASQUE

5 East 55th Street
LUNCH AND DINNER. CLOSED SUNDAY.
Reservations, MU 8–6525.
No credit cards.
Very expensive.

This is one of the prettiest restaurants in New York. The murals set in the ivory walls are not the bland background illustrations that panel many of New York's midtown French restaurants—their colors are brilliant, painterly; and their presence is assertive and actually delightful. (It's as if you entered a restaurant where you have learned to suffer the Muzak to savor the mousse, and found the Muzak replaced by Mozart, and the speakers by Stern, Rose and Istomin, in the flesh). The curved back wall is a gorgeous, panoramic view of a Mediterranean harbor vibrating in subtropical light, dotted with hundreds of little boats and surrounded by a density of tile-roofed houses. There is a sense of casual, elegant gaiety about La Côte Basque. The table linen is of soft red-and-green striped cotton, there are flowers on all the tables, and if you're not swooning just to be here, the side chairs may help—they sway to the tune of about five degrees from the perpendicular. It's true, this grand relic is opening up at the seams. La Côte Basque, Henri Soulé's fun house, built to look like the transformation of a manor house into a party retreat, is stiffening and cracking. It's not only the chairs, of course. Everything about it is less. The food is less. The utter relaxation of its former self is now rendered in dismal imitation, by captains who exchange a few casual remarks about this and that as the menu is explained, add a few more as the food is served and —disaster!—keep talking as that moment arrives when you're ready to convert food, wine and conversation into dinner, the moment when a professional captain would instinctively absent himself. La Côte Basque is now a museum. Perhaps the thing to do is drop in, look at the pictures and leave. Not that you can't get a good meal here, but you may get the wrong idea; this is not the Côte Basque. The place is legally entitled to the name, and its lineage is impeccable, but the restaurant is trying to survive by perpetual imitation of itself. The real thing has to be re-created, every day, by the creator, and Soulé is dead.

Some restaurants in New York are known as places where married men take women to whom they are not married. To La Côte Basque they take their wives. The close-tonsured, iron-gray heads barely turn to the stone faces on their left or right. At the little place around the corner from the office, these guys would be leaning, squirming and patting with every virile anecdote. There the food doesn't matter. Here, where it *is* the thing, it will not invariably offset the company, though when it is at its best it equals the food of the old Côte Basque.

Among the dishes which are of that quality, you may number an unlisted item that is occasionally available—a mousse of sole, served with two sauces. The mousse itself is fluffy and firm, yet it has a deep, clear flavor of fresh fish. It is served with an herby white sauce, made with a well-flavored *court-bouillon,* and a delicate brown sauce in which there is a distinct flavor of wine. If you begin your dinner with smoked salmon, you'll find that La Côte Basque obtains the best (you couldn't beat it at Zabar's), and on occasion forgets to serve oil with it. You want the Terrine Maison? Good idea. It is made with chunks of ham and tongue in among the pork, and it is fragrant with garlic. The plate of hors d'oeuvres includes some excellent crisp shrimp in, it must be admitted, very good Russian dressing; crunchy mushrooms that have been marinated to a turn in oil and herbs; a refreshing salad of tuna and celery, amalgamated in a clear-tasting vinaigrette; dressed tomatoes; and hard-cooked eggs in thick house-made mayonnaise, which raises the pedestrian to a position of semi-nobility. The billi-bi is odd—this cold soup in the version served here lacks the almost overwhelming concentration of mussel flavor that characterizes most good renditions of it. This one is spicy and briny, with the mussels detectable as an aftertaste, but it is delicious nevertheless.

If you're going to spend what it takes to have dinner at La Côte Basque, spend a lot more and have the best. The Noisettes d'Agneau Edouard VII are offered at a large premium above the regular fixed dinner price. It's not that the lamb is so splendid— it is good, but of the American kind, which means mild and not gamy; and it's not that the accompanying vegetables are short of disgraceful, because the little balls of roasted potato seem re-roasted and the artichoke heart is overcooked—it's that the sauce is thick without seeming thickened, it is meaty and buttery without being cloying and it is utterly infused with the nutlike flavor of truffles—the sauce is dense with little black chunks of the stuff.

Fine. But what does one make of this Côte de Veau aux Cèpes? The mushrooms are nice, but the sauce is raw—raw wine and raw stock, hardly melded, and insufficiently enriched, so that it seems like a kitchen cocktail, and the veal chop itself is coarse. The Caneton aux Pêches is not bad, but in a restaurant of this caliber, the sauce and the fruit should be a creation, not a combination—not peaches in sauce of duck.

Perfectly rendered soufflés; a mille-feuille of thin, crinkly layers of pastry and a filling of thick cream; fruit tarts that are of good fresh fruit.

★ LE COUP DE FUSIL

160 East 64th Street
LUNCH AND DINNER. CLOSED SUNDAY.
Reservations, 751–9110.
Credit cards: AE, DC, MC, V.
Very expensive.

Literally the phrase chosen for the name of this restaurant means "rifle shot"; idiomatically its meaning is more appropriate, for "coup de fusil" is a restaurant overcharge and this is a pricy little spot. Of course it is more than that; it is coy and pretentious, cute in a turn-of-the-century New Orleans–bordello style, amateur in its dining room staff, and, astonishingly, talented in its kitchen crew. That talent, however, is not invariably turned to deserving tasks, for many of the concoctions served here are gussied up, fancified mistreatments of—there is no denying it—excellent basic ingredients. But this is unpredictable New York, and some of the city's brightest-looking people are here squeezing themselves into minuscule allotments of space to be seen in one of the day's most popular meccas of the chic and would-be's.

This store has been a couple of other aspiring eateries in the last few years, but the only feature retained from the previous enterprises is the stamped-tin ceiling, painted a dull, zinclike silver. Ghastly though it is, your eyes turn to it for relief in these unrelievedly hideous rooms.

Most of the light is provided by sconces that are clusters of tentacles, incandescent bulbs at their ends, each bulb at the center of glowing white milk-glass petals. To make the sconces doubly awful, they are mounted on mirrored walls. What the lights illumine and the mirrors reflect are red-flocked walls that you could probably overlook if the painful intensity of their color were not perfectly emphasized by the contrasting pink linen on the tables. Here and there murky oils, in the corners plants that were apparently chosen for their slender, hairlike leaves. Perhaps someone thinks this is the time for another Art Nouveau revival. With this in the forefront, no one is going to take up the rear.

Fashionable New York eats late. Turnover is the name of the commercial restaurant game. You call for an eight-thirty reservation. "We are very heavily booked," you are informed. "Could you make it eight sharp?" Another time you try for eight and are coaxed to seven-thirty. Of course the bookings are imaginary, you linger long, and there is still a handful of unoccupied tables when you leave very near closing time. The tables, by actual measure, are twenty-four inches by two feet. A tour through the cramped rooms in search of something a bit more comfortable, for two, reveals a couple of circular tables at the rear, situated in the corners of the crimson banquettes—it is recommended that those who wish to experience this environment reserve one of those particular spots.

You have not been fortunate enough to obtain one of those favored situations and you idiotically choose a table nearby, as if by proximity you will enjoy perhaps a smidgen of ease. The corners are not merely cramped. The waiter, with all good intention, jostles your shoulder perhaps a dozen times during a three-hour dinner. When he is chatting with your neighbors, parts of him are violating the air space over your bread plate. Then he turns to you, a youngster in love with every word he has been trained to utter. "We have both red and white wine." Later, when you order approximately half the dishes offered by the extremely brief menu, he commends you on the wisdom of your choices.

Considerations of space notwithstanding, first courses are served on plates that are, again by actual measure, close to eleven inches in diameter. And depending on the distribution of wine and water, bread and butter on the meager acreage, they are served —believe it or not, Ripley—so that a few inches of plate violate the air space over your lap.

The first courses do not make the high points of meals here. The best of them is the Soupe du Marché, a purée of a dozen vegetables on a chicken-stock base. It is dominated by peas and the clear flavor of celery, but a sturdier stock would have made for an even stouter soup. Then there is the Salade de Marron au Cresson. Chestnuts in the salad, you say to yourself, gimmicks, gimmicks, gimmicks. Well, you are right, but this gimmick cannot harm a decent salad. The chestnuts are not fresh and they haven't much flavor, but they add a nice note of crunchiness to huge, marvelously fresh and crisp sprigs of watercress, good lettuce and a few slices of orange, all in a light vinaigrette. Oranges in salads take a bit of getting accustomed to. If it is hard for you, don't force yourself—the end is but a minor pleasure.

Two fish appetizers are offered, neither good. The Pâté de Poisson chaud aux Pistaches, you figure, has pistachio nuts in it. Well, the slice on the table next to yours does, but yours does not. Too bad, for the ground fish in this pâté, speckled as it is with bits of red and green vegetable, is virtually flavorless, the green core of spinach harshly spiced and metallic. The Mousseline de Snapper aux Pointes d'Asperge seems like the same ground fish, this time with an intentional absence of pistachio nuts—*most* of the ingredients here are good, not all, and these asparagus points are canned and horrid.

If you tell them to hold the honey from the sauce, you can get a lovely steak here, tender, accurately grilled, but why a simple wine pan sauce should be sweetened with honey is hard to guess—the smallest touch of it might add an interesting note, but this sauce is dominated by syrupy sweetness. Much better is Le Petit Poulet au Pot, a simple poached chicken in broth, surrounded by crisp carrots and celery and onions—the vegetables were added late to the stew and they retain their garden flavor. The waiter's description of this dish is interesting. "The chicken is cooked," he says, "in its own juice."

The Bass à la Julienne de Légumes may astonish you for the utter sweetness of the fresh fish, poached not a moment too long; the white sauce is smooth but beside the point, adding no point of its own. The strands of vegetables that garnish the fish are fine. The big deal is the Navarin de Homard à la Truffe Noire—lots of tender and sweetly oceanic lobster meat, with carrots and turnips, in a thick sauce of white wine and cream that has been flavored with lobster shell. It is strong of its flavors, albeit excessively salted, but the strands of truffle are obscured in this potent dish.

The Brie is cool, but it would be good otherwise. If you think you will want cheese, ask them to remove a slice from the refrigerator for you early on. If they can still find it two hours later, be surprised. The Vacherin Coup de Fusil consists of a meringue shell around a chestnut sherbet—very pretty and little more. The winning dessert is the Tarte Fine aux Pommes—slivers of sweetened apple baked on a crêpe. It is like the essence of a fruit tart, the crust purified down to a simple browned crêpe, the fruit to a glazed parchment.

As the evening wears on, you overhear one waiter inform his customer that if he doesn't order "now," he is not certain when he will be able to get back to him. Nor will the hatcheck attendant let you get away easily. "That will be fifty cents a coat," says she when you give her a mere seventy-five for two.

★★ CUISINE OF SZECHUAN

33 Irving Place (near 16th Street)
LUNCH AND DINNER.
Reservations, 982-5678.
No credit cards.
No liquor.
Inexpensive.

If the nation's shortage of resources engenders utilitarian chic, Cuisine of Szechuan will, to its astonishment and without so much as the flick of a warped chopstick, find itself aglitter with galaxies of awards of three- and four-star ratings for undécor. From the white plastic frame just inside the door, wherein the pay telephone once rested but which now serves as a resting place for your elbow when there is a wait for tables, to the twisted metal hangers waiting for your coat on the flaking, formerly chromed pipe rack, this little place is a hair-down, jeans-up, boots-on repair from the pretensions of Gramercy Park—plain white walls and strands of plain white air-conditioning duct across the dreary acoustical ceiling, an enameled red rear wall echoes the plastic red of the booths along the sides. (In recent years the paper place mats on Formica tabletops have been replaced by white linen—a dangerous trend.) Functional, and the shirt-sleeved waiters merely function—they record, deliver and bill. Consultants they are not. But as in many neighborhood Chinese restaurants around town where each copy of the printed menu serves its purpose through a full cycle of the four seasons, you get your advice from clients who have come before—they leave check marks next to recommended dishes (valuable restaurant lore: this is usually sound guidance), the urban equivalent of the Welcome Wagon.

One of your predecessors has checked Aromatic Sliced Beef, so you send for a platter of this cold dish while you and your companions determine the highest check-mark scores among four menus. You have plenty of time for the arithmetic, since the platter of cold beef is rather immense, which is nice because the dark slices of tender, fibrous meat are saturated with the flavor of peanut oil (though the meat is not oily) and accented with the sharpness of the chopped scallion greens that have been sprinkled over.

Three check marks out of a possible four to Smoked Duck with Camphor and Tea —the duck, in the Chinese manner, cross-sectionally slabbed through skin, fat, meat and bone, the outer layer crisped and dark-brown, plenty of fat just under it, the meat saturated with the smoky flavor of tea, some of the bones crumbly enough to eat, all served with a thick plum sauce and shafts of glistening scallion.

In a tie with the duck for the three-check-mark lead is the mis-Anglicized "Dried Sautéed String Beans." Fear not—the string beans are not dried but dry-sautéed, which means they are stirred about in a barely oiled and very hot pan. This process yields beans that are cooked, but as firm and bright-green as raw ones, at once crisp and chewy. They are served tossed with heavily seasoned ground pork, the earthy and oily meat a perfect garnish for the vibrant freshness of the beans.

Many, many two-check-mark entries, including Bean Curd, Szechuan Style—a fiery, weighty porridge, inexplicably not flagged with the red asterisk that denotes "Hot Spiced Flavor" (doubtless a typographer's oversight). It is like the rice, potatoes or noodles that are the starchy bulk of meals designed in other sections of the world. To a Szechuanite, of course, such stuff would be undetectable (if not unpalatable) in the context of this blazing cuisine. The ubiquitous scallions are present.

For $1.25 you get a giant bowl of two-check-mark Cold Noodle with Sesame Sauce. By the time the dish reaches your table, the sesame oil, peanut oil and soy sauce will have drained to the bottom—stir the noodles well in the liquid, even go so far as to obtain a spoon with which to ladle the salty mixture over the firm strands. The dish has an intensity of peanut flavor almost like that of peanut butter, and of course, this richness is offset with a sprinkling of, you guessed it, minced scallions.

Now you have grown confident. You are no longer dependent on and therefore shun the advice of the early pioneers who left their marks and went on. You hack out a path of your own—Hot Spiced Sautéed Kidney. Really have to credit those first settlers, don't you? Next time, it's back to the check-mark system, right? Nothing actually wrong with the food, what with its crisp water chestnuts, tender mushrooms and impeccably rinsed kidneys all in a spicy brown sauce, but nothing special.

Hurry to Cuisine of Szechuan before they lay in a supply of clean menus. Bring enough beer (it is not sold on the premises), which, with this food, is about a quart per person.

★★★★ LE CYGNE

53 East 54th Street
LUNCH, MONDAY TO FRIDAY; DINNER, MONDAY TO SATURDAY. CLOSED SUNDAY.
Reservations, PL 9–5941.
Credit cards: AE, DC.
Very expensive.

When Le Cygne was young, aspiring and not quite succeeding, it offset its short-comings (1) by underselling its *haute cuisine* competitors and (2) by making much of its elaborate service and suave *politesse*. There are now clear signs not only that Le Cygne has arrived but that Le Cygne knows it and is relaxed in the knowledge. The lid has been taken off the prices, and they have been permitted to reach their unnatural level; and the mindless reverence that once infused the demeanor of the host, captains and waiters has been replaced by a bemused savoir-faire that bespeaks a cool confidence not only in themselves but in what they are selling. The captain smiles lightly as he listens to and answers your questions about this dish or that—"Why do you ask all these questions," he seems to be saying, "when whatever you order will be superb?" Not only superb (by and large), but virtuosic—the kitchen, apparently bored by merely turning out, six days a week, terrific versions of the dishes listed on a fairly elaborate menu, keeps itself in shape with fanciful, ever-changing augments thereof. This is one of those restaurants where one may eschew the menu and just ask for the day's specials (to avoid eating the same old thing, day after day)—the main courses tend to be roasts (excellent, but not fascinating), but the appetizers are complex, often startling surprises, and you should not pass them up lightly.

Among these miracles, on occasion, is a quiche in which you will discern minced sweetbreads and strong green olives, and the singular effect of this particular combination of ingredients is to render the spicy quiche at once stronger and richer—the custard is light, firm and perfectly browned, and the crust is dark and crunchy. This is to run-of-restaurants quiche what love is to larceny. Another off-the-menu, elegant variant on a mundane theme is the saucisson chaud—an amalgam of well-spiced coarse meat, with plenty of fat left in, wrapped in a flaky pastry that is warm and moist with grease. It is served here with a deep sauce instead of the usual jar of mustard on the side, and that little touch lifts the dish well above the level of ordinary charcuterie. It is to run-of-restaurants saucisson chaud what Watergate is to larceny. Yet a third unlisted appetizer, sometimes available, is an almost unspeakably delicate feuilletée filled with striped bass and herbs (a feuilletée is a stuffed puff pastry, and the pastry here is almost fugitive in its lightness—just as you have begun to experience its flavor, it is gone). The fish and herbs, however, are clear and vivid, and the white sauce (made with a fish stock) that is poured over the tender dish is like liquid marble—weighty, polished.

Of course, there are first courses that *are* listed on the menu, and available whenever the place is open. The greatest of these are not the Moules à la Moutarde. Understand, they are flawless, and if you love mussels you will love this dish because the mussels have a clear fresh taste, and the sauce is vibrant with the flavor of good strong mustard, but the dish will bring to mind other good food you have had before, it will not astonish you—can't have that! Not to say that the listed items never make it—the Little Necks des Gourmets (ghastly name), for example, are perfectly tender and sweet, which means that their baking, under a topping of mushroom purée and a little bit of garlic, is very carefully controlled. The six mollusks arrive in a pool of buttery clam broth with parsley—you spoon the briny liquid over the browned mushroom topping before swallowing the freshly moistened morsels. There will be a good bit of the broth left over when you have finished your clams—if you are concerned about your girth, you drink it from a spoon, otherwise you eat it soaked into chunks of the excellent bread.

L'Emincé de Filet de Boeuf Bercy (a lunchtime dish) should not be read as minced beef. The slices of beef are small, but their sautéeing is so carefully attended to that each slice is like a perfect miniature steak, pink within, browned outside. The meat itself is extremely tender but with no loss of texture, and the sauce it is served in is made with an exceptionally sturdy beef stock and red wine that would be quite good enough to drink even with this exceptional dish. If there is a dish in this restaurant that is quintessentially French, it is L'Escalopine de Veau au Champagne—three slices of delicate white veal, sautéed in butter until a few points and edges of the meat are chocolate-brown, most of the surface just sprinkled with flecks of brown, the meat taking on the nutlike flavor of heated butter; the meat is served with a delicate white sauce, the abundance of which is more than enough for the little cutlets, a circumstance that is provided for by a mound of superb rice—huge firm kernels (apparently cooked in stock, so they are very tasty) which you slide through the sauce before consuming it. Butter, perfect meat, a simple sauce and a simple starch—perfect French food.

Le Caneton Smitane is still on the menu, and though it is still not up to the version served at La Caravelle, it is much improved from what it was a couple of years back. The bird itself is at once sharp and rich, with a perfectly browned skin and ample moisture in the meat, but the sour-cream sauce, though much better than the old version (which tasted far too strongly of raw sour cream), is now obscured by the excellent bird instead of providing a contrast to it. The dish is merely delicious.

The Quenelles de Brochet which are served at lunchtime are very refined pike dumplings in a crayfish sauce that is at once oceanic and honeylike. One of the three dumplings is surmounted by a sautéed mushroom, a sort of lark. The mingling of sweetness and of the two distinct seafood flavors is an amazing harmony, the mushroom a grace note.

Wonderful mocha mousse, made with excellent chocolate and what tastes like a fresh brew of strong coffee. A pear tart in which the fruit is in an eggy custard, on a breadlike pastry—delicious, but not sweet, it takes a position toward the end of a meal that is more like cheese.

But, of course, almost everyone skips that kind of stuff and orders soufflés. It is something to observe them emerging from the kitchen—they are browned, but not deeply, which will lead you to expect that they are a bit unfinished and will promptly collapse. They do not. They are simply made with such exquisite care that they are moist but not wet, firm but not breadlike, light but substantial. Try the one that is served with a sauce of Calvados and minced apples—the vibrant liquid and crunchy apples are a perfect sauce to the tender and sweet soufflé.

The service that was once hovering is now attentive, but there are still a few idiocies. At the busy lunchtime there is a sheet of paper in a glass on every table which is designed to give you the impression that each table has been assigned to a specific reservation, in case you want to refuse the first table you are led to. Of course, if you look at the sheets of paper, you will note that they are blank—you are led to a table selected by Mr. Whim. But in the slower evenings the whole business of seating is handled with much grace, and couples are offered side-by-side tables for two if neither member wants to face the wall. Best of all, the clientele is not what the steep prices would lead you to expect. During the day there are, of course, midtown executives reinforcing their own sense of importance. But much of the crowd, at lunchtime as well as in the evening, are relaxed pleasure lovers rather than big spenders (though of necessity in this place they must be the latter as well); it is not all sharkskin suits and sculptured hair—this is a classless restaurant in every sense except the economic.

★ CZECHOSLOVAK PRAHA

1358 First Avenue (at 73rd Street)
LUNCH AND DINNER.
Reservations, YU 8–3505.
Credit cards: AE.
Medium-priced.

There are three well-known Czechoslovakian restaurants in the Seventies near First and Second avenues. Ruc is rustic; Vašata is like a comfortable European upper-middle-class café; Czechoslovak Praha is the most Americanized of the three—soft lights, carpeting, golden draperies, a separate barroom with (color) TV, plastic flowers (tulips and daisies). The main dining room is dominated by a huge black-and-white engraving of the city of Prague. If you don't want to look at that, there are two tables at the front windows, and you can look at First Avenue. Sometimes there is music, and if you make arrangements you can have "Happy Birthday" played (not sung) by a duet of one stout man on accordion and one thin one who plays a huge metal clarinet that sounds like a tenor saxophone. Notwithstanding the slightly vulgar touches, this is a comfortable and well-run place. The bad taste is the kind of bad taste that is in good taste, the kitchen turns out food in the kind of good taste that tastes good, and the service is winning. The customers, as in all the Middle European restaurants in this neighborhood, relax into the ways of the old country—the talk is polite, and when the food comes, there is much less of the talk.

The delicious headcheese, mostly tongue, in a firm and cool jelly that is heavily peppered and herbed, is served with minced onions and garnishes of olives, small tomatoes and radishes. It's unthinkable (well, a mistake) not to accompany this stuff with the superb beer from Czechoslovakia (Pilsner Urquell) which is on tap out by the TV. The beer is just as good with what is called Prague ham, but the ham, though it may be from Prague, is not the smoky, fat-rimmed thing you get at Vašata—it is just OK. An experienced restaurant goer will read Eggs à la Praha and smugly say to himself, "A lot of fuss about a couple of hard-cooked eggs." Wrong. It's true about the eggs, but the salad of chopped ham and pickles in mayonnaise, with a couple of slices of lemon squeezed over it, is sparkling and appetizing; there is no question but that it is made daily because there isn't a trace of that held-in-the-fridge flavor which ruins many mayonnaise salads. There is a similar salad, called Gypsy Salad, which is just as good—coarsely chopped beef, chicken, green peppers and onions in mayonnaise.

At the coarsest, but by no means lowest, level of main courses, there is a suggestive Czechoslovak Sausage Platter. You are served up three firm cylinders: number one is Jirtnice—pale, hot, moist and vibrant; then comes Klobasa—red and very potent; the third is Debrecinka—spicy, fatty and explosive. Of course you'll want beer. For something more relaxing there is Boiled Beef with Dill Sauce, one of the best boiled beef dishes around, in that the meat is not poached to extinction—it is served, oddly, off the bone, in thin slices. It is tender, but still textured and tasty, and it comes with a creamy sauce that is infused with a powerful flavor of fresh dill and parsley. Up the scale of culinary refinement by a degree, to what the menu calls Rabbits in Cream Sauce —peppered joints of rabbit in a slightly tart sauerbraten-type sauce, with caraway. You eat the extra sauce on slabs of bread dumpling. And finally, to the pinnacle—roast goose, with a crinkly skin, firm dark meat and a pitcher of strong consommé to liven it up as you slowly work your way through the huge portion.

The vaunted fruit dumpling dessert is a comedown—a canned peach in a dumpling under a mixture of sugar and cottage cheese or sugar and poppy seeds. It is heavy stuff, but it would be good anyway if the fruit inside had any character; the menu reads Fruit Dumpling *in Season*—we learn from this that canned peaches have a season. The strudels are pretty good—poppy-seed strudel, or nut strudel, or apple strudel; the pastry is flaky, the fillings are moist and fresh, and they are sprinkled with powdered sugar.

★★DARDANELLES

86 University Place (near 12th Street)
LUNCH, MONDAY TO SATURDAY; DINNER, DAILY.
Reservations, CH 2–8990.
Credit cards: AE, CB, DC, MC, V.
Inexpensive.

There are only a handful of Armenian restaurants in New York, and they are all pretty good. They look very much the same—like a Hollywood notion of a middle-class Arabian living room. Serious art (framed prints of mosques), red broadloom, wood paneling, brass sconces with dim amber lights and textured wallpaper are typical. The Dardanelles goes all the way. The restaurant is just as conventional in its menu— authentic Armenian food, all right, and mostly well prepared, but selected, and in some instances modified, for the local palate.

The best of the familiar appetizers here are the fassoulia poulaki (crunchy white beans, lots of dill, stewed carrots and celery, all in plenty of thin oil), cheese boerek (a warm appetizer of a strong egg-and-cheese mixture, with parsley, in a flaky pastry) and enguinar (the heart and core of artichokes, in the shape of large mushrooms, cooked in oil with onions and carrots; the artichokes are firm and soft, and they take on the flavors of the vegetables they were cooked with). But the chickpea spread (homus) is terribly bland, the stuffed mussels are greasy and absurdly overflavored with cinnamon, and the cold stuffed grape leaves are wilted, with a mushy and sugary filling of rice and pine nuts. The hot yogurt soup is good, but no mint at all would be better than the dried mint used here (and everywhere else).

There is at least one outstanding dish which you will not find in many other Armenian restaurants. It is called harpout keufta, and is a mixture of spicy ground lamb and pine nuts shaped into balls and rolled in cracked wheat before cooking, and served in a thick and strong meat broth. There is an excellent baked lamb shank, tender and not stringy, and a very good chopped-lamb dish called Scarra Keufta—two broiled banana-sized patties served with cracked wheat and rice. If you ask for Lulé Kebab, you get the same dish, but powerfully and deliciously flavored with red pepper. Of course there is shish kebab, made with tomatoes, onions and green peppers; better lamb is served elsewhere, but this is good.

The usual desserts are above average here. The baklava is served slightly warm— the walnuts and almonds are crunchy, the pastry crisp, and the honey clear and pure. There is a very rich ekmek kadayiff, an overwhelmingly sweet pastry made by baking toasted bread in honey; it is served with kaymak, the concentrated cream of the Middle East. This cream has no sugar in it, and is composed of butterfat and milk solids—its dry flavor and texture are the perfect complement to honeyed desserts. The Armenian coffee is one delicious gulp from a tiny cup.

The waiters here, at first impression, look like TV Arabs—smooth and sinister. They are, in fact, mostly young students, eager, polite, helpful. On Friday and Saturday evenings there is an oud player or two. They also wail softly. Very nice.

When busy, this is a festive restaurant, and it gets its share of the Village's diverse populace (impoverished poets explaining economics to their middle-class girl friends, who are paying; members of the N.Y.U. faculty debating the meaning of tenure in a discontinued department).

★★ DaSILVANO

260 Sixth Avenue (near Bleecker Street)
LUNCH AND DINNER.
Reservations, 982–0090.
No credit cards.
Medium-priced.

About a dozen crisply linened tables in a neat little room, ivory walls plus one of bare brick, greenery at the front window, a tiny espresso station in a rear corner, with a gleaming coffee machine on the counter, a bowl of fruit beside it, bottles of liquor on the shelves behind. From certain tables in the dining room the gleaming white-tiled kitchen is visible. All is orderly.

The seafood salad is a perfectly respectable mixture of squid and mussels, flavored with fresh parsley and moistened with an unimpeachable, if uninspired, vinaigrette. You are better off with the dishes that are peculiar to the place, which includes panzanella, or bread salad. Relax, it is not a salad of bread. It is, rather, a salad of cucumbers, green peppers, raw onions, lightly cooked string beans that are cool and crisp, chunks of tomato and herbs, dressed with morsels of bread and bread crumbs that have been soaked in a strongly vinegared dressing. The bread serves to hold large quantities of the dressing, so that each forkful of salad is heavily dressed; the bread also adds a pleasantly grainy texture to the crisp salad.

An item that seems to be borrowed from French and Jewish cuisines is called Crostini. It consists of slices of Italian bread spread with a thick, heavy paste of abundantly oiled and strongly seasoned ground liver. It is the use of olive oil instead of butter that gives this simple dish its unmistakable Italian quality.

Among the few pasta dishes is one called Puttanesco, which is spaghetti, perfectly cooked, served in a pungent dressing of black olives, strands of sautéed anchovies, and small chunks of tomato. This is an exceptional spaghetti dish, the sauce positively profound of these strong dark flavors. DaSilvano also serves a Tortellini alla Panna that is at distinct variance from the usual thing. The tortellini themselves are standard, little circlets of pasta wrapped around a filling of chicken and cheese and served in a sauce of cream and cheese; but this sauce is heavily seasoned with nutmeg, which gives the dish that spice's distinctly fragrant quality.

Pollo Umbriago is something akin to chicken in the pot, except that the broth has been enriched to a sauce made slightly bitter by an admixture of beer. Understand, this is not a fricassee, for the chicken is not browned before it is poached in the beer; you must be a fan of plain boiled chicken if you are to accept this Italian variant.

Listed on the blackboard is a veal dish of the day, sometimes a veal stew, which is a nice enough dish, the veal well-browned before it is slowly stewed for at least a couple of hours—the meat retains its shape, and it is tender and has taken on some of the flavors of white wine, carrots and butter.

There is also a fish of the day, sometimes codfish, fresh and moist, served in a simple and herby tomato sauce—a dish of perfect simplicity.

The vegetable garnishes are a step above the usual—nicely browned chunks of roasted potatoes, for example, or sautéed zucchini, sometimes sprinkled with rosemary. And there are cool salads if you wish, including white beans and raw onions, heavily parsleyed and served in a good vinaigrette. The dish suffers a bit from the onions being chopped long before the salad is served, which robs them of much of their strength.

The desserts are fruit, cheese, fruit and cheese, and a wondrous green-grape pie that comes with thick whipped cream.

• DAVID K'S CHUNG KUO YUAN

1115 Third Avenue (near 65th Street)
LUNCH AND DINNER.
Reservations, 371–9090.
Credit cards: AE.
Very expensive.

The back page of the menu is headed "WHY 'CHUNG KUO YUAN'?" There follow 600 words of piffle but no answer to the question. Chung Kuo Yuan is because to find out how much the suckers will pay through their big noses. [Editor's note: *Big nose,* a Chinese colloquialism for a non-Chinese.] Though the message on the menu fails to answer the big question, it does provide you with more than you want to know about a lot of things you couldn't care less about. Also a true confession: "In planning this restaurant, I have done everything I possibly can to avoid the usual trap that every Chinese restaurant before this has fallen into. There is no reason, for example, that a Chinese restaurant should look like Hollywood's gaudy version of a Buddhist temple. There is no reason also that the tablecloth has to be greasy, the china dirty, and the flatware cheap. There certainly is no reason at all that service need be haphazard and the waiters insolent." This is a message from David Keh, proprietor of this pretentious establishment, who, elsewhere in his sermon, informs us that he used to run many of those very Chinese restaurants. Mr. Keh has apparently deluded himself into thinking that he has reached a pinnacle, that he may now safely kick at those beneath him without fear of surprise attacks from above. Poor David, mired in this most mundane sanctimony, he doesn't know he is standing on his head and looking down.

What Mr. Keh has created is a Chinese restaurant that, except for the food, is not Chinese. It isn't anything else, either, unless it is Marriott Antiseptic or Suburban Hospital. The place is clean, there are lots of flowers, and it is instantly convertible to, say, a Scandinavian restaurant by replacement of the current help with cool-eyed blonds. Give us, please, Hollywood's gaudy version of a Buddhist temple, even if the greasy tablecloth has to come with it.

You descend the grand stairway to the beige-carpeted, flower-bedecked dining room, hanging plants, a frightening tree that reaches its grotesque arms to the ceiling, an attached "garden" dining room, enclosed and windowed, under a sloping ceiling of green glass. This is just an inexpensively spruced-up nonrejuvenation of the premises of the former restaurant tenant—Bruce Rogers—and the place is utterly without character. Something like dozens of men wander around in black suits and matching hair. Such uniformity is ominous, the only feeling the place may give you. The boss is in a black suit, too, but he permits himself to stand out from the others by smoking a pipe.

The help is in the image of Mr. Keh. They talk like the back of the menu reads. You must learn the phrase "THANK YOU VERY MUCH," and you must practice uttering it, sternly, in the middle of one of your captain's syllables, else you will be lengthily told, while you would rather be eating, drinking or talking to your companions, that this is very fresh, this very traditional, this never before served in New York, this in some other way tiresome.

With the warped chopsticks this restaurant specializes in (never before served in New York) you manage some of the assorted cold appetizers, including hacked chicken in a fiery sauce that cannot conceal the flavor of this too-often-thawed frozen chicken, and marinated beef that is a tired imitation of this usually vibrant dish. The assorted hot appetizers are four minuscule dumplings, oiled and slippery, filled with minced chicken, lobster, shrimp, combinations thereof—you dip them in a spicy sour sauce, and you find no substantial fault.

All is not lost, except your bankroll. For a cool $14 you may have seasoned barbecued squab, or if you find that a tongue-twister, Ts'ui P'i Ju Ko. This is a nice enough little bird, laid out head and all in a symmetrical pattern on a clean plate, the skin brown and crisp, the meat only a little dry. You are supplied with slices of lemon, and the lemon juice is a good livener for this dish, but the seasoned salt that comes as well is harsh and should be passed up or used sparingly. The sliced duck with asparagus, water

chestnuts, and much ginger is your standard Chinese conglomer
by an abundance of minced scallions. The sliced filet of beef wit!
fiery, and one serving is almost inedible with fewer than three bott'
prawns with hot spicy sauce achieve their effect by their very
condition—huge, crisp shrimp, tasting almost fresh, but in a sau
insipidly sweet, and nothing more. Scallops with Garlic Sauce is
browned seafood full of sea flavor, the taste of fresh garlic m
obscuring the other. Any of these dishes is made more enjoyable by an accomp
of cold green noodles with sesame sauce—firm noodles, with a fresh grassy flavor,
lightly charred by pan-frying and dressed with fiery oil.

"May we have fortune cookies?" "We don't serve, not Chinese." "You serve French
wine." Off he goes, mumbling.

★★ DELSOMMA

266 West 47th Street
LUNCH AND DINNER. CLOSED SUNDAY.
Reservations, PL 7–9079.
Credit cards: AE, CB, DC, MC, V.
Medium-priced.

The brilliant neon sign is an incongruous beacon on this dingy block. This is an
incongruous restaurant in this rundown neighborhood, something like Reverend Moon
posters on abandoned buildings, or a forties Warner Bros. Technicolor musical in a
Bowery movie house. But once you are inside, behind the hanging strands of huge beads
that fill the front windows, you are not inside the Bowery movie house, but in the
musical. Delsomma is a slickly appointed joint—solid shining bar in the dimly lit
drinking section (lounge) off to one side (TV at the ready for major sports events), in
which well-heeled and well-fed gents in snug suits drink and discuss deals while their
ladies silently sport their duds and diamonds, and from whence their occasional boister-
ousness and the perpetual background music emanates. The dining room gleams—slick
white plaster walls, walls of wine bottles, walnut-paneled walls; a gleaming patent-
leather butterscotch-yellow banquette rims the room; the linened tables are large and
well-spaced, fringes of dark-green cloth showing beneath the white; and under all, plush
red carpeting. There are nautical notes: a sailfish leaping up one wall, nautical plaques,
and at the center of the room (where the gleaming red espresso station forms an oasis
of warmth in the frigid air conditioning), a model sailing ship in full red sail.

The nautical theme augurs a seafood emphasis—not in the written menu, which is
burdened with the usual encyclopedic listings of pastas and veal dishes, but in the
urgings of your host, a gravel-voiced toughie with an overlay of politesse, who suggests,
"Read da menu fa fi' minutes. Den we talk." Meanwhile you sip some of the red wine
you ordered ("We'll have a bottle of Chianti." "You want dat at room temperature?"),
and enjoy the commodiousness of your well-placed huge table—with all his gruffness
Mr. Gravel does not lead strangers to obscure corner tables when better ones are
available, which is a good sign.

The secret of Delsomma (big secret) is that after you read da menu fa fi' minutes, scard whatever decisions you may have arrived at in favor of Mr. G's recommendations. He advises, for example, that you pass over the listing of appetizers (good advice, for it eats as dully as it reads) and begin with Shrimps Fiorentina, an easy thing to do, as the dish consists of an even number of shrimps, six, which is divisible by either two or three. This quite superb delicacy consists of huge shrimps that have been battered and then sautéed in butter, wine, lemon and parsley. They are served in the delicious and well-seasoned sauce this preparation yields, the shrimps crunchy, their batter crusts soaked in the liquid, with plenty of additional sauce left over for improvement of the excellent bread.

Delsomma makes a good Lobster Fra Diavolo, but what is perhaps more important, you can get in on someone else's lobster, if one is in preparation, to have an unlisted spaghetti and lobster sauce. G will keep you informed. The pasta here is cooked when ordered, so it is never gummy, and the lobster sauce is a sparkling harmony of the flavors of clear, fresh lobster, hot-peppered tomatoes and good, strong garlic.

Old Grav will try to steer you toward more seafood, including some good striped bass or squid, but if you insist that you would like to return to land, he knows his way around the veal and chicken dishes, too. He suggests that you might be amused, whatever your deepest feelings, by Scallopine of Veal Pagliacci, an asymmetric sandwich of sautéed eggplant and sautéed veal between melted cheese and escarole—two stacks to an order, excellent for noncombative sharing. The veal is tender and white, the eggplant browned and soaked in the sautéeing oil, the cheese pleasantly gooey and loud, the escarole sharp and lightly metallic. A dish difficult to fault.

The secret chicken is Chicken Arreganate, unlisted—chunks of moist chicken, on the bone, browned in oil, served in a dark and salty sauce that has been flavored with oregano. All the sauces are good here, and this is another one that will make you glad there is bread.

No cheese cake! Well, occasionally there is cheese cake. The rum cake is the usual excessive confection; the pastries are mediocre; the zabaglione is fine.

★★DÉZALEY

54 East 58th Street
LUNCH, MONDAY TO FRIDAY; DINNER, MONDAY TO SATURDAY. CLOSED SUNDAY.
Reservations, 755–8546.
Credit cards: AE, CB, DC, MC, V.
Medium-priced.

It is unfortunate that a kitchen as competent as this one sends its end products to a dining room fit for faster foods. Nothing hideous about it, you understand, it is just that the row of tables down one side is hardly any further from the row on the opposite side than the distance between rows of double seats on a Greyhound bus. The furniture itself, much walnut in no-frills modern, has a comfortable look about it under ivory walls decorated only with simple sconces. Planters of greenery here and there soften the impression somewhat, and large dark mirrors go a short way toward making the place feel spacious. Naturally, in these close quarters the tables are wee; and with little to soften the sound, you fail to overhear the people at the next table, because they are drowned out by the people at all the other tables.

So, what makes this place so hot? For one thing, the management reveals a mature sense of responsibility by insisting that all the food preparation be undertaken in the kitchen, so that when it reaches your table all you have to do is eat it—put differently, there are no fondues on this Swiss menu. Hooray. And for another of several things, it offers a sparkling white Dézaley (Dézaley is a wine and wine region of Switzerland) in little seven-ounce carafes, so you can drink as little or as much of this refreshing wine as you want, at a reasonable price.

Get a little of that Dézaley and begin your dinner with Escargots Café de Paris, which arrives on a wooden board out of which declivities have been carved. In one of these there is snugly fitted a thick skillet with six declivities of its own, in which your snails are waiting; in another there is a sliced roll, to be used for the soaking up of the snail sauce. The snails are plump and tasty, and there is a bit of garlic in this preparation as well as butter, but it is the strong flavor of brandy that distinguishes this from most snail dishes—very good. Or you may start with Tortellini Maison (in Swiss cooking, all's fair from France to Italy to Germany), and in this very good version the little crescent-shaped pasta pouches are filled with ham and served in a creamy tomato sauce that is thickened with cheese and studded with crisp mushrooms—the sharp flavors of the ham and cheese perfectly balance the richness of the sauce and the weight of the pasta.

For some reason the Swiss have a way with soups. Consider, for example, this establishment's Essence queue de boeuf, or oxtail soup, which is a clear broth, dark and strong, with the pungent flavor of bones and a fragrance of herbs. The liquid arrives in a steaming copper pot and is ladled into a broad soup plate. In a completely different example of this Swiss talent, there is Soupe aux tomates froide, a cool purée of tomato, flavored with celery, nicely spiced, and decorated with slivers of unpuréed tomato.

Combinations of fruit and meat are common in Swiss cuisine, and Dézaley offers calf's liver with bananas and bacon. The liver is perhaps a bit thicker than it should be, but it is well grilled in a skillet sufficiently hot to brown it without overcooking the inside; it is surmounted by two full lengths of sautéed banana and a single length of crisp bacon; it is flanked by three little boiled potatoes that have been cooked to the perfect point of firm tenderness, then buttered; and it is moistened by a sturdy mustard-flavored pan sauce which, miraculously, manages to make harmony of the diverse ingredients. This is a very solid and very delicious dish.

Going from fantasy to mere oddity, we are offered boned trout poached in red wine with shallots. The wine does less than you might expect in the way of altering the flavor of the fish, but the dark sauce made from the poaching liquid is polished and stout, and the layer of sautéed minced shallots you find under your trout is sweet and fragrant.

A limited selection of desserts, with the Swiss specialties far superior to the French pastries. Which is to say that the Meringue glacée au chocolate, for instance—a crisp meringue, topped with rich vanilla ice cream and thick whipped cream, and served with a small pot of warm Swiss chocolate, to which chopped nuts have been added—is much better than the apricot tart, a wedge-shaped section of a large, circular pastry that consists of some perfectly nice apricot preserves under a sweet syrup and on a doughy crust.

In addition to the carafe wines there is a good selection of bottled Swiss wines.

• DUCK JOINT

1382 First Avenue (near 73rd Street)
DINNER. CLOSED MONDAY.
Reservations, 861–1102.
Credit cards: AE, MC.
Medium-priced.

This was a good idea for a restaurant when it opened, and it is still a good idea, but unless you know what to order, the idea will be superior to your dinner.

The menu is built around ducks and geese, and nothing is thrown away but the feathers. "How about a treat for your pet!" says the table card. "We have fresh goose and duck gizzards cooked in natural gravy, quick frozen and conveniently packed in 1 lb. containers 45¢." The other side reads: "Did you ever try to cook with goose fat?? or dip a piece of crisp bread in it? it is incredibly goooood! Handy containers of pure rendered goose fat 85¢ lb."

The appetizer of potted goose livers is an example of Middle European cooking for which one must have a taste. The potted livers are stuck with whole cloves and served cold, buried in pure goose fat. The idea is to eat the livers with bread spread with the fat. Unfortunately, this restaurant seems to buy only day-old bread, which they make into garlic bread. Bizarre, particularly with this wonderful dish on the menu; garlic bread is simply wrong with clove-flavored livers and goose fat. Of the other appetizers there is a delicate and creamy Duck Liver Mousse en Gelée, an excellent Russian Egg on Ham Salad, a Smokehouse Selection (a good sausage and a bad one), and Various Pâtés (two again, both mediocre).

The regular menu lists only three main courses—roast goose, roast duck, and braised duck with grapes—but a supplemental menu ("For our friends who do not like Duck or Goose") lists "Wiener Schnitzel as Only the Viennese Can Do It," which is fair warning, since the management here is Czech; Bauernschmaus—a Middle European choucroute—made with excellent sauerkraut, but with only moderately good pork and with sausages which, even without chemical analysis, are food for Ralph Nader's anti-hot-dog campaign; and roast baby lamb, served with huge slices of dumpling and a good sauce of wine, rosemary and garlic.

To get back to the main menu, braising is an excellent method of preparing duck or goose—the bird remains moist, gives up most of its fat and picks up the flavors of the braising liquid. But if you braise a duck and then serve it with seedy, sour grapes, you get sour customers. Who wants sour customers? The roast duck and roast goose are much better, though not invariably perfect. They are served with little pitchers of natural gravy and a brandied cherry sauce, and a delicious stewed cabbage flavored with caraway is served with all main courses.

For dessert there is a very well made apple strudel which, unbelievably, is served at refrigerator temperature instead of at room temperature (which is better) or a little warmer (which is best). The Sacher Torte is rich and covered with Schlag. The fresh strawberries, on occasion, have been fresh for an unnaturally long time. A couple of good cheeses can usually be found on the board, but they must be eaten with crackers, as fresh bread is not available. The fruits that accompany the cheese may well be in bad condition, except perhaps for the orange, but an orange is, of course, an absolutely wrong fruit with cheese and wine. Well, dessert is not the Duck Joint's strength.

This is a handsome restaurant, with the atmosphere of a European inn. The tables are large and well spaced, and the service is friendly, if amateurish. One senses that the management could do much better but doesn't have to.

★★EAST-WEST COOKERY

105 East 9th Street
DINNER.
Reservations, 260–1994.
No credit cards.
No liquor.
Inexpensive.

Natural food, health food, organic food. Who is not put off by the antiseptic phrases? Yet this stuff need not taste like undoctored shredded wheat. Set aside for the moment the fact that the terms are vague at best, meaningless most likely, that they suggest plain food, unsauced food, intact food, unbleached and nonchemicalized food, berries and nuts, salads of weeds and stews of tubers—in short, medical repasts; and call to mind for the same moment your knowledge that things take on identities only when they are given names: had the pizza parlors leaped onto the health-food bandwagon at the beginning (whole-grain crust, vine-ripened tomato sauce, certified-milk cheese), we would associate lithe bodies and clear eyes with the red-and-white pies. But no particular kind of food has monopolized the fad, and though there is a pretty consistent tendency in the movement to eschew red blood, there are natural-food restaurants in New York where you can get steaks and chops with your seaweed. Perhaps because Japanese food, as perceived by Americans, has a Spartan quality, it is a natural for the sound-body freaks, and this restaurant serves up its health à la Japanese, with a preponderance of tempura on the menu. Tempura, of course, is deep-fried food, usually shrimp, fish, vegetables. Wasn't fried food once the antithesis of health food?

East-West Cookery is a low-luxury but comfortable little place, perfectly suited to its youthful clientele. They come in their sandals, jeans, long flower-print skirts, sleeveless tops, splendiferous hair; they park themselves on the ledge under the hanging plants at the front window to wait patiently for one of the little tables, even more patiently for one of the burlap-upholstered booths along the side. The walls are of raw redwood clapboard, the slat ceiling is vaguely Japanese, there are white paper place mats on the red-clothed tables.

This is a bring-your-own-wine-or- beer establishment, but the innocents drink mostly tea (no charge for tea) or tap water (no charge for tap water) or spring water from the water cooler, just like the one in your office (10 cents for spring water) or mineral water.

The food is rather elegantly made; it has, it cannot be denied, freshness, purity, life; you eat it with chopsticks (the little Japanese ones that come joined and wrapped) unless you want to advertise yourself as an alien.

There is a charge for bread, 40 cents, a dime more if you have it with miso spread (soybean paste). Pay the charges. The bread is extraordinarily assertive in its vibrant scent and flavor of wheat, and the miso, warm and oily, is the perfect succulent foil to the dry bread.

Begin with shrimp tempura. The shrimps (several) seem to be fresh, as are the broccoli, carrots and green peppers, and they are all very artfully battered and rapidly deep-fried in very hot and, it must be, frequently changed oil. The ingredients of the dish are just barely cooked, and the batter is crisp and airy, all in all the equal or superior of the same dish in Japanese restaurants that are actually run by Japanese. Move on to a soup of the day, which, when it is split-pea and zucchini soup, is a substantial bowl of thick pea soup, rather heavy, relieved by chunks of moist zucchini —a nice idea.

In line with the "East-West" theme, there is a dish called Scallops Champignon, the Orientalism of which is in the dish itself, the Westernism in the title. This is a gigantic stew of scallops (the big ones from the ocean, not the little ones from the bay), mushrooms and other vegetables, in a briny broth. The food lacks character, but the excellence of the ingredients and the straightforward preparation yield a pretty satisfying plate. Better is the broiled fish—immaculately fresh bluefish, for example, broiled in butter and flavored with rosemary; flaky and moist, the rich fish retains its robust character, and the browned skin, crisp and buttery, is like a built-in sharp seasoning. As a garnish to whatever you eat, there is (are you ready?) seaweed du jour.

Domestic desserts, displayed on a counter just below the window at the back of the room, through which you may observe the activity in the bustling kitchen. The banana cake consists of a dark, moist, banana-flavored cake, a banana-flavored icing and chunks of banana-flavored bananas. Excellent. Good pies, and pretty good apple strudel, with crisp apples and lots of cinnamon, wrapped in a flaky pastry.

• ELAINE'S

1703 Second Avenue (near 88th Street)
LUNCH AND DINNER.
Reservations, TE 1–9558.
Credit cards: AE.
Medium-priced.

Elaine's (the restaurant) is famous for Elaine's (the proprietress's) icy or, at best, cool reception of any customer she does not know. On her own territory Elaine is the boss, and she wants everyone to realize it. For this endearing trait (and, it appears, for this alone) the literati have made Elaine's their restaurant and Elaine their Buddha. But is there another Elaine? Under that tough veneer, is there another veneer? Does this coarse exterior conceal a heart? And if so, what is it made of?

Being the darling of any fashionable set sure can get you into trouble. The set may not realize that the darling is not so darling off her turf; on neutral ground Elaine has trouble—after all, it's tough to throw someone out when he's not in your restaurant. Elaine gets invited to parties, and when the company is sophisticated, suave and unruffled—when, in short, they are not begging for a table at Elaine's—Elaine sits in a corner, going forth frequently, but only to replenish her plate, New York's most popular wallflower preserving her figure.

"To understand all makes us very indulgent," quoth Madame de Staël, so we overlook the symptoms of Elaine's pathology in search of pleasure in her restaurant. We must also, it is true, disregard the reflected malady sometimes seen in the waiters, but their crust is seamed, and if their witless brevity is countered with glazed indifference, they relent and struggle to gain favor. The food is decent, sometimes good, the customers picturesque, each sex in its way, and to the extent possible within the restrictions of literary etiquette, the mood is relaxed, even a little gay. (The etiquette, by the way, is a simple one. You speak only to those at your own table. To stride across the room, hand outstretched, to "Hi-Charlie" Charlie is an act of such abject gaucherie that ripples of empathic, nauseated embarrassment cause customers to close their eyes and cringe at the opposite end of the room. But there is heat beneath the cool, and if you walk in confident and unknown, and act, generally, as if Elaine's is your oyster, you will be warmed by curious glances.)

Elaine's consists of two long, narrow adjacent stores. The place is dim, the walls are dark and vaguely muraled, the tables are well spaced (no two are adjacent). The waiters strike odd poses—this one wanders down the aisle as he removes the cork from a bottle of wine; that one delivers a pot of espresso while clutching a rolled-up tablecloth under his arm. When there is nothing to do, they protrude their stomachs for the purpose of making a place to rest their crossed arms. There is a bar near the front, at the end of which Elaine takes her post until she sits herself down to eat late in the evening. When most of the customers have gone home, the cloths are removed from the black-topped tables and a core of regulars hangs on for a few more hours, for a bit of serious drinking.

There is a menu. It does not, for example, list the squid salad, the best appetizer in the place. It's hard to figure out why it is called squid salad instead of seafood salad, when it also includes shrimp and mussels, but it is made of fresh-tasting ingredients, including string beans, onions, capers and parsley as well as the seafood, all in a fresh vinaigrette. The steamed mussels (not on the menu, not invariably available) are carefully prepared, fresh and tender. The steaming liquid is a bit of lemon and the liquid from the mussels, and the result is a very pure dish. On occasion there are pretty fair stuffed mushrooms (stuffed with bread crumbs, chopped mushroom stems and parsley, blanketed with a thin slice of cheese and stuck under the broiler), and sometimes there is a simple shrimp salad (shrimp, chopped celery, mayonnaise) in half an avocado— the shrimp are firm and the avocado is soft and ripe.

We slip a bit when we come to pasta and meat. The Fettuccine Alfredo arrives suspiciously soon after it is ordered, and sure enough, it is gummy, as if it has been waiting for you. Something called Chicken Toscana, described by the waiter as "chicken with brown sauce," whatever that means, turns out to be sautéed chicken, sautéed not enough, in a sauce which, it's true, is brown, but tasteless. The Veal Parmigiana is better—the veal is pale and tender, there is flavor in the tomato sauce, and the cheese is a decent mozzarella. You're much better off with a broiled steak (tender, seared, accurately cooked), or with the Mixed Seafood (steamed clams and mussels, shrimp, and unfortunately, a tasteless lobster tail, all in a thick, garlicky marinara sauce of the most fundamental, aggressive and delicious character).

Avoid the chocolate mousse—it is a misnamed chocolate pudding. The pecan tart is a small pecan pie of no particular distinction. When there is cold zabaglione and strawberries, have that—the zabaglione is thick and heavily flavored with Marsala, and the strawberries are ripe.

Take your time about ordering. Wait until two or three waiters have approached and told you what is available—their versions will vary, one from the other, but a pretty fair outline can be put together if you get more than one set of clues.

○ EMPIRE DINER

210 Tenth Avenue (at 22nd Street)
NEVER CLOSES.
No reservations (243–2736).
No credit cards.
Medium-priced.

This place was put together with no purpose other than to get itself talked about and written about, to get people to wonder what it is like, to get them to come and find out. Naturally, people who fall for this line of promotion might even, on visiting the place, conclude that it is a good restaurant. Actually it is an absurdity. All silver and black, the hideous stainless steel still behind the counter of this not-long-ago diner, coffee urns and all, chrome chairs upholstered in black plastic, black plate glass on the counter top and tabletops, flashes of mirror here and there, an upright piano (black) stuck into a little space at one end. White tapers on the tables do manage to look something like stars in here at night, which is pretty. And they must be commended for their artistic flexibility; the black and white and silver rigidity of the design was relaxed so that the orange and blue and tan tiles would not have to be replaced. The old appointments—the counter stools and pie stands and coffee urns—add a little warmth to the otherwise austere front room, but the overflow chamber to the north is unrelievedly bleak—the same black glass on the tables, dull-silver silhouettes of the Empire State Building on the mirrored walls. The only relief back here is the garish light and noise that emanate from the closet-size kitchen.

The place is staffed by a mostly young crew. Some of them so content that they have landed a job where everything's at, as they might put it, they treat innocent customers with amused contempt, presumably because *they* have not. Others of them are sweet, innocent, actually recommending some of this food as if, as one of them put it, "It's great!"

The Escarole Soup that introduces one of the fixed-price dinners is a vegetable soup on a chicken-broth (not stock) base that might as well be called Celery Soup. Let's call it Vegetable Soup. Whatever it is, it is not bad. At this point you are brought a salad, and had they omitted the out-of-place raw zucchini, this assemblage of watercress and romaine lettuce in a decent vinaigrette would have been commendable.

Now the cowbell rings insistently from the kitchen, signaling the readiness of your Chicken Breast with Bacon and Cheese. Why anyone would bother to concoct this when something equally dreadful can be obtained ready-made from a factory is puzzling. There is no flavor of chicken, none of cheese, one of burnt bacon, a texture of clay. Limp zucchini accompanies. If you pass up the complete dinner, you can have the sliced-steak sandwich that started the big argument. *She* said the sauce on it was canned beef-and-mushroom gravy. *He* said it was blenderized dogfood. Now they're not talking.

That chicken shows up again, this time cold, in the chef's salad, in strands. There are strands of ham as well, and they taste like the strands of chicken.

It is a miracle, but you can get a beef stew here that tastes like honest food: huge chunks of well-browned beef that have been simmered long, served mingled with potatoes and onions and carrots that are only a little limp—altogether not bad with the warm bread.

Bad desserts, including angel-food chalk under a machined substance that could be called Mocha Whip. A similar creation is called vanilla cake with chocolate frosting and it, too, is merely sweet. Then there is the hazel-walnut cake with brandied whipped cream, but you can figure it out. There are ice creams.

★ EL FARO

823 Greenwich Street (at Horatio Street)
LUNCH AND DINNER.
No reservations (WA 9–8210).
No credit cards.
Medium-priced.

El Faro means "the lighthouse," which is probably the least appropriate name this place could have. El Faro is situated in a section of the West Village that is virtually dead after sundown, and the place does not call attention to itself. To find it you must know where it is, with confidence; for years more people have been finding it than the place knows what to do with. This is one of the oldest and most popular restaurants in Greenwich Village, and it is an astonishment to approach it down dim, deserted streets to discover, when you go in, that the place is clamorous. You enter into a small, low-ceilinged barroom, complete with beer-sign clocks, juke box, coatrack, cigarette machine, air-conditioning machine, and customers at various points of alcoholic contentment, depending on how long they have been waiting for their turn for the next available table.

The dining room is small, efficiently filled with Formica-topped tables, and somberly, anciently muraled with grimed-over flamenco dancers. Between the tightly packed tables skip the red-vested waiters—more of them than you will find in other restaurants this size, but they are busy all the time.

It is the way of these busy places—to keep you quiet they bring your salad right away; but in a way that is *not* the way of these places, it is made of fresh lettuce and crisp red cabbage, in a thick, red, peppery Spanish dressing. ("Our Salad Dressing is available to Our Customers," it says on the menu.)

The food here is usually good; the first courses always best. The Broiled Chorizos are discs of spicy Spanish sausage, crisped and browned on the outside, served in warm, peppery oil—they make you thirsty. Ham and olives is referred to as Ham and Olives Spanish Style. Well, they look like ham and olives, and they taste, respectively, smoky and salty—they make you thirsty. Salpicon is crabmeat salad, a piquant and peppery mélange of crabmeat, minced eggs, green peppers, raw onions and parsley in a lemony dressing. It will *not* make you particularly thirsty, though the Galician Soup may— this is the familiar Caldo Gallego, the thick bean soup made with meats or sausages and turnip greens. The version served here is thick and loud.

Your waiter refers to the Cornish hen as *perdiz.* It is the only word you know in Spanish, but you leap at the opportunity to insist that he not misrepresent a domestic hen as a partridge. He's impressed with your knowledge of the Romance languages and waffles uncomfortably for a bit. The minor misrepresentation notwithstanding, this is a splendid dish—you get a big enameled iron pot in which there are several moist, plump parts of a moist, plump bird, in two inches of an oily gravy that is powerfully and fragrantly flavored with clove, onions and bay. If you're going to come here once, the hen is the dish to have. There is, of course, pork with almonds. It is pretty good, the thick slices tender and moist and all that, but the almond sauce lacks an edge, so the dish is satisfying without being exciting. There are shrimp dishes and there are lobster dishes. If you want seafood, eschew the latter in favor of the former. Lobsters do not suffer well the perils of freezing and casual cooking. To overcook a frozen lobster is to add toughness to fibrousness. The green sauce you can have it in is thick and winy, but it does not rescue the lobster. The Shrimp al Ajillo, however, is something else— the shrimps themselves are just OK, but the sauce has character: it is fiery and spicy, redolent of garlic, and uncompromisingly oily.

Spanish desserts are, admit it, dull. Perhaps not to Spaniards. Anyway, the ones you get here are about as good as they ever get: firm, red, crunchy guava shells with a chunk of cream cheese and crisp saltine crackers, for example, can be simple and delicious if all the elements are fresh; the flan is cool, firm and nicely flavored with the lightly burnt sugar; and there is natilla, the *other* custard, gooey and vanilla-flavored and very sugary.

★ FLEUR DE LIS

141 West 69th Street
LUNCH AND DINNER.
Reservations, 874–9060.
Credit cards: AE, CB, DC, MC, V.
Medium-priced.

Frequented in large measure by old-time West Siders—semiradical intellectual entrepreneurs, music teachers, Viennese reminiscers and small-time diamond traders —supplemented by an admixture of new West Siders—Juilliard students, young unmarrieds and boutique operators—this straightforward restaurant sometimes fails to please lovers of *haute cuisine* because of the vigorous quality of its definitely unsubtle food and service.

The menu here is startlingly elaborate, but then, this place does a very steady level of very good business. Of more than twenty-five appetizers, several are of genuine interest. The gallantine of pork is, in fact, a hearty headcheese, heavily weighted toward tongue. It is bound in a strong jelly, and tastes great with bread, strong mustard and white wine. The Bismarck herring is as good as Zabar's best, which is saying a great deal. It is served with pickled raw onions, and it is firm, shiny, spicy and brilliantly sour

—not exactly French, but a superb appetizer. One first-course oddity is the Salad Niçoise, which in this country is usually thought of as a complete lunch. This is a small Niçoise, with the usual tuna, tomato, hard-boiled eggs and anchovies. But a sprinkling of slivers of superb green olives, raw onions and green peppers, and a dressing of a good, mustardy vinaigrette, help to convert it into a stimulating first course.

The pâté is a simple, garlicky country version, and the garlic sausage is a savory chain of discs of powerful charcuterie laid over a mountain of delicious potato salad—very oily, well-peppered, loaded with parsley and lightly flavored with onion.

This is not exactly a restaurant for fancy food. Not that there is anything wrong with the Seafood Cardinale or even with the Lobster Thermidore; rather, better versions are available elsewhere and Fleur de Lis is more adept at, for example, grilled fresh salmon, with butter and parsley, which is bright pink, flaky and strong, or grilled halibut, a fish which is almost invariably ruined by cooks determined to eliminate its oiliness and thereby end up with something that seems to have been woven. Be assured, the halibut here is oily.

Game in season is often available, and the venison stew (Civet of Venison au Beaujolais) is gamy, tender and authoritative—the sauce is a deep mahogany; the meat, which is thoroughly browned, keeps its shape through long cooking; and as is usual here, one's portion is enough for one's family. The stew is inundated with sautéed onions and mushrooms.

Fleur de Lis, if it is famous at all, is famous for its cassoulet. Unfortunately, in one respect it is not what it once was—that is to say, it is no longer enough for three stevedores after a twelve-hour shift in December. It can only be concluded that the former portions were left unfinished so frequently that the management felt justified in reducing their scope. This is to be deplored, because cassoulet is a dish which must be copious to be itself. A small serving of cassoulet is like a little bit of love. The dish, as served, is still redolent of pork, mutton, sausage, beans, herbs, garlic and white wine, and, therefore, it is still delicious, and there is no restriction against ordering a second portion.

Salmis is a rare but marvelous cooking method in which a bird is roasted for about two thirds of its cooking time, and braised in a sauce, with vegetables, for the remaining third. This yields a more tender, juicier bird than roasting permits, and a heartier texture and taste of skin than is possible in a fricassee, even when the bird is thoroughly browned beforehand. The Salmis of Pheasant is one of the best dishes at Fleur de Lis —it tastes like a roasted bird, and also like a stewed bird, and the thick sauce in which the pheasant is finished is strongly flavored of Chablis, onions, mushrooms and pork. There are few dishes like this available in New York, and if one is to make a single visit to this restaurant, this is the dish to try.

The green salads are large, the cheeses, unfortunately, are refrigerated, and the desserts are something of a comedown. The pastries are only OK; better strawberries are available in other parts of town than one usually gets here; the rum cake is yellow and tastes sort of yellow.

★★LA FORÊT

208 East 60th Street
LUNCH AND DINNER. CLOSED SUNDAY.
Reservations, 759–7766.
Credit cards: AE.
Medium-priced.

A little brick-walled barroom, then a tunnel-like path past the hatcheck to a couple of cozy, low-ceilinged rooms, fireplace (cum fire) in the first one. Sepia murals of pine forests reaching to the low ceiling alternate with broad panels of the pale stucco walls. If you sit along the walls, your seat is of loose velvet cushions—antiqued brown; opposite these and at the tables in the middle of the rooms you sit in captain's chairs that are comfy with chintzy seat cushions. Dark carpeting and light from deeply shaded sconces contribute to the warmth of the place, as does the demeanor of the staff—they are extremely polite and solicitous without being at all obtrusive. There is so much courtesy here you wonder if you are being put on. How can they like you so much if they hardly know you?

You select from a menu that is nominally prix-fixe, varying with the price of the main course. In fact, naturally, most of the hors d'oeuvres command a premium, which renders the entire system slightly absurd. If it offends, then you can stubbornly insist on paying no premiums and still commence well—with the Poireaux Vinaigrette, for example, three shafts of dull-gold poached leeks moistened with a very smooth and mustardy dressing; or with the Pâté du Chef, a coarse and salty loaf of spiced and herbed meat freshened with cool jelly and garnished with a couple of crisp cornichons; or even with the vichyssoise, which is at once creamy and sharp, with the flavors of both leeks and potato vividly clear. For those who disdain cost, there are Escargots de Bourgogne, requiring of you an extra $3, which is almost worth it, for the plump snails are flavored, at once elegantly and powerfully, with a well-balanced combination of butter, shallots, garlic and fresh parsley.

Let us dispense at once with the unpleasantness—the Loup de Mer Froid, or cold striped bass. To begin with, *loup de mer* is not French for any fish that swims around here, but they apparently did not want to call it *bar,* because that is the name for their *hot* bass. Therein, probably, hides the secret: today's cold bass was originally obtained to fill the orders for hot bass of a few days ago, for this fish is clearly over the hill. Moreover, the simple-minded sauce in which it is served seems to consist of one part tomatoes, one part onions, and one part sugar. Dreadful candy.

So let us turn forthwith to contentments, one of which is the Carré d'Agneau Persillé. Happily, this rack of lamb is served to as few as one, and new as the restaurant is, this dish has already developed a cult—individuals who, suddenly taken with a lust for lamb, hasten here for these little chops. This is truly baby lamb; it is served pink— approaching red—and each chop is crusted with a thick garlic breading that was deeply browned when the rack was roasted. The garnish of crisp oiled string beans serves the excellent purpose of slowing the devouring of the tender meat. Very good tournedos —two thick slices of filet mignon, tender and accurately cooked, served with a mound of roasted potatoes. The Poussin Bûcheronne is that rare thing, a good baby chicken roasted to the perfect point, at which it is crisp, cooked through, and still moist. It is served with some more of those roasted potatoes mingled with mushrooms that have been sautéed until they are limp and pungent. Considering the better items in the house, the duck suffers, though by comparison to competitors' ducks, this one is praiseworthy. The roasted bird (served only for two) is flamed in brandy in view of the audience, and it is served with an orange sauce that is perhaps a bit too sweet. It's a nice bird and all that, served with a great mound of earthy, crunchy wild rice, but the distinct sense that you are eating *duck* is missing, for the sauce, and the mandarin oranges that are part of it, fail to emphasize the flavor of the meat; instead they conceal it.

Good Brie; respectable mousse; a more than respectable chocolate mousse cake, light and rich alternating layers under a cool, smooth icing; flaky napoleons; and an assortment of the usual ice cream things.

The wine list is brief, supplies no information about vintages, but is not overpriced by today's measures. They sell a lot of the Mâcon Blanc called "La Forêt"—a simple, crisp white Burgundy that is especially good with this restaurant's chicken dishes. A cheerful, bustling place, with eminently decent food.

★★ FORLINI'S

93 Baxter Street (near Canal Street)
LUNCH AND DINNER.
Reservations, 349–6779.
Credit cards: AE, CB, DC, MC, V.
Medium-priced.

Forlini's has been here for almost twenty years. It was a seedy place at first, but almost immediately successful, and each year a portion of the profits is invested in improvements—one year the fake wood paneling, another year the nondescript murals, another time the color TV—so that the locals who drink beer and eat meatball sandwiches at the long, massive front-room bar will keep coming back. Forlini's is one of the best restaurants in Little Italy. The solid food is served by brusque but competent waiters to solidly built customers, their trailer-truck physiques maintained by habitual ingestion of the rather heavy stuff that is the stock in trade of this restaurant.

The first courses are not particularly interesting. There are the usual baked stuffed clams and mussels, and stuffed mushrooms (listed as a vegetable). The clams may on occasion be a little tough from being cooked too long, but the mushrooms are excellently sautéed, and their breading is herby and well seasoned. The broth here is strong and salty, almost briny, and it is a nice setting for the little tortellini you can have in it—these are stuffed ring-shaped pouches filled with ricotta cheese, farina and fresh parsley.

Good pasta, including an item listed as Linguini Clam Shrimp Crabmeat Fra Diavolo. And sure enough, the casual syntax notwithstanding, that is what it is—the linguine is *al dente,* each of the three kinds of seafood is present, each retains its own flavor, and the sauce Fra Diavolo is strong and heavily flavored with garlic. The lasagna is firm, stuffed with gooey, melted ricotta cheese and covered with a red, peppery meat sauce that is studded with discs of hot Italian sausage. For an extra half a dollar you can have it with extra sausage, by which is meant not a few more discs, but two substantial lengths of the strong stuff, which converts this dish into a complete dinner.

You will not find a better saltimbocca than the one you get here—tender white veal, strong red ham, melted cheese that seems to be Emmenthal, all served on a pile of fresh spinach that has been sautéed in oil with plenty of garlic. Every element is delicious, and it adds up to an extremely hearty dish. There is an item here called Diced Shell Steak—it consists of more steak than one normally eats, in chunks the size of children's blocks, sautéed with celery, mushrooms, green peppers and onions. The beef is tender, the vegetables are rendered very tasty by their sautéeing, and the strange dish can feed you and a friend and a small dog.

When it is in season, this restaurant serves Broccoli di Rapa, that tender wild broccoli which is pleasantly bitter—a little like a cross between broccoli and escarole. Forlini's variant in the deep-fried-zucchini competition is to start with thick cross-sectional slices of the vegetable instead of with strands; this makes it possible to brown the outside batter very thoroughly and still retain a moist, barely warmed interior. The little side order of salad is made up of chicory, onions, fresh Italian parsley and bits of tomato and green pepper, all in an oily dressing with a bit of garlic—very good.

Good cheese cake (very creamy and smooth, with graham-cracker crumbs on top), and zabaglione (very thick, intensely sweet and loaded with wine), and the usual ice cream desserts.

★★FOUR SEASONS

99 East 52nd Street
LUNCH AND DINNER. CLOSED SUNDAY.
Reservations, 754-9494.
Credit cards: AE, CB, DC, MC, V.
Very expensive.

Once the marginally profitable flagship of the Restaurant Associates chain, the Four Seasons is now the commercially successful enterprise of a couple of gentlemen who once ran the place for the big corporate mother. A few years ago the boys took it over from the parent, and what has since been gained financially has been lost artistically. The Four Seasons has mislaid some of what once made it singular. It is still unique, nothing like it in New York or anywhere else, but what the place really needed was the support of a charitable foundation. The Four Seasons is an opera, after all, with vast and elaborate settings and costumes and a cast of dozens, maybe hundreds; but like many a great production this one is kept alive by the cutting of corners in its revivals. Probably we should be grateful, for if the Four Seasons were not given its intermittent and ongoing doses of plasma—guest chefs imported from France, wine tastings, snappy little businessmen's lunches in the Grill Room, pre- and after-theater low-price dinners from a menu that is a dull abbreviation of the real thing—we might be out the whole works. But they cannot go much further. You can have a tarnished masterpiece, but not half a masterpiece. You cannot have the Two Seasons. We may already be down to Three.

The discreet East 52nd Street entrance. Within—marble and modern art, flowers and Barcelona chairs. The lighting is soft, a grand stairway leads up and away, but something is most assuredly wrong. It is the atmosphere! a *very* clean smell—they use strong soap in these lavatories, and one wonders if they change the fragrance, like the menu, every season.

This restaurant consists of two vast rooms connected by a marble-and-glass walkway that looks onto the lobby of the Seagram Building and, through the glass of the building's front entrance, Park Avenue. The rooms themselves are three stories high, dominated by lofty walls of polished, mahogany-colored wood, and windows, reaching from the floor to the ceiling, that are hung with arcs of copper-colored chains, thousands upon thousands of dark metallic strands that ripple and cascade constantly in the convection currents that form just inside the plate glass windows. It is a flaw, of course. The place was designed to be great and still, dramatically somber, stark, awe-inspiring. But from the first, when the chains were not replaced with something that would preserve the quiet of the original design, the integrity of the architect's intention has been compromised—in small ways, it is true, surely not to the point of destroying it, but compromised nevertheless.

The low point of the Four Seasons is the bar. The thing itself is fine, a square of polished wood surrounded by banquettes and cocktail tables, but the crowd is often beery and morose, they seem to be sitting under the dramatic Lippold sculpture of thousands of brass rods held in place by threadlike wires, in perfect readiness for the moment when it falls. Nearby, in giant pots, there are trees that reach to the ceiling, casually placed shrubbery here and there. That sculpture has a smaller mate, at the opposite side of the Grill Room, and under that the editors and agents and writers conduct the lunches of which the publishing business consists. Serious eating is undertaken in the so-called Pool Room and you are led to your table there, through that walkway, under the immense Picasso tapestry, past the thousands of bottles of wine (behind glass) by a youthful page in a nifty pink jacket.

This room looks its best when the adjacent, ten-steps-up mezzanine is closed and invisible, which is to say all the time except at weekend dinners. At that best it is blocklike, a giant deep-brown cube, at the center of its base a square white bubbling pool, a rubber tree at each corner, each tree illuminated from below, casting shadows on the distant ceiling. But rubber trees are a dreary choice for this dramatic setting. They are clumpy, they have no reach, no matter how tall they may be. And those chains do ripple, and plants hang from the ceiling in front of each lengthy window, one more bit of destruction of the grand spareness that was intended. But once you are seated it is easy to overlook the flaws, for the tables are large, they are set with lovely beige linen, huge silver serving plates at each place, and you are seated on commodious leather banquettes which it would be a pleasure never to have to leave. You are presented with warm bread; a bowl of cracked ice that is adorned with scallions and radishes and cherry tomatoes and some of the sharpest ripe olives ever to reach these shores; and a huge menu, one side of which sports this establishment's extraordinary wine list—around 250 bottles from eight countries, including one of the best assortments of American wines available in New York.

The Quenelle of Pike, Nantua, is very much the usual thing, the quenelle acceptably light, the flavor of pike perhaps a bit vague—though the dish is clearly made of fresh fish—the sauce surely a little thin; the dumpling is ornamented with a sliver of truffle, but that does not make for a fair tradeoff. They must have sold a million orders of

Crisped Shrimp Filled with Mustard Fruits since this place first opened, and now they are coasting, for the dish is not what it once was. The huge shrimp, battered and deep-fried, are still glorious to look upon when they arrive, but the crust is a bit coarse, the shrimp a little loud, the mustard sauce not recognizably of fruit as well—once a wonderful appetizer, this is now a dish of show. An appetizer oddity on the new menu is Ragout of Baby Lamb with Saffron, a little pot with two or three ounces of substance in it at a cool $6.50. This is a very elegant stew, tender meat in a thick sauce, with a heady flavor of saffron, but it is somehow not an appetizer—presumably enough of it as a main course would set you back $30, and they figure the traffic will not bear it. The Pâté of Salmon and Crab Meat is both more satisfying and more expensive—a muffin of pastry filled with the two ground meats, the flavor of each vivid, and a rich white sauce that is slightly sour of the sorrel that flavors it.

Come on now, credit where it's due—how many restaurants in New York have either the style or the grand insouciance to serve lamb chops with nothing sharper than a butter knife? Perhaps they are making a statement, that lamb chops are picked up and eaten like corn on the cob. However you manage the task, these are perfect chops, requiring something less sharp than a steak knife but more sharp than the side of your fork. The Escalope of Plume de Veau with Crabmeat and Asparagus is simply an absurd, does-not-work dish; and one wonders how the place can have veal in the house at all and be, as the captain insists, "out of" Veal Paillard. The Stuffed Baby Pheasant is a moist, rich, sweet bird, perfectly crisped, with a light stuffing and a smooth tomato sauce that is sweet and delicately lemoned. The superb Sautéed Calf's Liver gains nothing from the sliced avocado that is part of the dish, but do not carp, this is perfect, delicate liver, not a hint of gaminess, and it is sautéed in a very hot pan, so that the exterior is deeply browned, the inner meat pink and moist.The Classic Truite au Bleu, as they call it, seems not to have been poached in water that had vinegar added, and that must account for the blandness of the fish. (It is listed as "classic," but your captain pooh-poohs your request for hollandaise.) The Grilled Gravlax with Dill-Mustard Sauce is almost as good as the standard thing—ungrilled gravlax with dill-mustard sauce. And the so-called Four Seasons Lobster Soufflé is surely confusingly named, if not deceptively so. This is not a lobster soufflé at all, but a cheese soufflé served with a sauced lobster. Your waiter slices the top off the little soufflé, pours the lobster mixture over the bottom, and puts the top back on. Nice food, the soufflé fairly well made, the lobster meat only slightly tough in its winy pink sauce, but something of a comedown. Some of the garnishes and à la carte vegetables: deep-fried grapes do not work (they come with the quails); perfect boiled potatoes, probably cooked in sea-salted water, the essence of pure potato flavor; a shallot soufflé is nowhere near as good as a pristine shallot; if you have eaten roesti potatoes in good Swiss restaurants, you will be disappointed in these; excellent, crisp broccoli; the asparagus is peeled, firm and strong, and you wish you hadn't ordered it with Hazelnut Butter, Parmesan and Prosciutto, which is, apparently, still being perfected.

The lesser of these captains will lie as readily as he will blink, and he informs you, unblinkingly, that there are no desserts on the menu that are not on the cart and that therefore you need not look at the menu again. He does not want the trouble that crêpes entail, or to spend the time waiting for soufflés, or to take the walk to wherever the cheeses are kept. The famous chocolate cake is good, the bits of whole chocolate always a nice surprise. The lime mousse is frothy and slightly acidic, the walnut tart is unfortunately on a humdrum pastry, and the Coffee Cup Soufflé still tastes as it always has—like instant-coffee ice cream. As ever, good sherbets, with the vivid flavors of fresh fruit.

This is an expensive place, but you can offset that a little by sticking to those wines, and there are several, that are relative bargains.

• 468 WEST BROADWAY

468 West Broadway (near West Houston Street)
LUNCH AND DINNER.
Reservations, 260–6779.
Credit cards: AE, V.
Medium-priced.

SoHo's are America's most self-consciously casual eateries, and your waiter, a little embarrassed because he is wearing both shoes and socks, must tell you of "Les Spécialités du Jour" in an exaggerated French accent, while rubbing his hands together and swiveling his hips, lest you mistake him for an uptowny. You put him at ease by stripping to the waist, unplaiting your beard and pounding on the table, while firmly chanting your mantra, which is "Fresh Fish Daily." This makes the waiter laugh, for, as it turns out, 468 West Broadway, SoHo's principal fish house, has fresh fish only on delivery day—every other full moon.

Stark, cavernous space, made cozy, is the style of the restaurants of SoHo (please, exception us not your exceptions), and this half-acre has been artfully subdivided, so that wherever you are seated you can see the far-flung borders and yet have the sense of being in a discrete locale within them. They stripped the premises to the shell and skeleton. The floors are of bare wood, the walls of rosy brick. Pipes, ducts and conduits carry their assorted juices up the walls and across the tin ceilings. At the front, big plate-glass windows have been installed, yielding a gray view of the craggy streets of this grim-looking part of town. To your right as you enter, rows of large wooden tables, surrounded by captain's chairs. This is where you eat, amid abundant space, diverted by little more than a fresh flower or two on the tables, hanging and standing greenery, and a huge misplaced mural of sky and clouds at the back. No carpeting on the floors, no linen on the tables, little more than the tools of the eating habit. Accordingly the customers: nary a soigné SoHo gallery owner; perhaps an artist or two, but none with paint in his hair or tragedy on his face; just the kind of simple folk you expect to be contentedly eating this ordinary food.

Ancient, twelve-by-twelve massive wooden beams support the floors above, and a few of them stand between the dining area and the playground. In the latter a long sinuous bar that curves around behind itself. Near it, for nonbarfly drinkers, the world's longest cocktail table, fifteen feet of waxed wood, on legs, beside a lengthy banquette, where youths meet and drink and play a little. When things get crowded, the table doubles as bench; you can face in either direction, strangers become acquainted by back signals.

You order smoked trout and get smoked whitefish; they thought you wouldn't know the difference. The difference in wholesale price is considerable. Keeping up the deception, instead of raw onions and bagels, you get sauce Raifort, fresh cream and strong horseradish; it is all delicious, but it is not smoked trout. Clams and oysters are sold by the piece, and they sell enough of them so that they are usually fresh, if rarely pristine. As the place specializes in seafood, they do not know how to ruin the Melon with Prosciutto—fresh melon, lots of well-fatted, smoky and spicy ham.

Great platters of mussels flow out of the kitchen in abundance. Half the tables in the place have sent for an order or two of these so-called Steamed Mussels Dijonnaises, one of the most egregious dishes of food ever exchanged for good money from people who are impressed by heaped plates of food. Never mind the preparation, for the mussels were not cleaned to begin with, and they are carbuncled and gritty; nor were the quick and the dead separated, and many of the ghosts of these mollusks started new lives mussel-generations ago.

You simply cannot rely on the fish being fresh, so one time you get a fine striped bass, another a wilted bluefish. There is a steak on the menu and it is not bad—steak, after all, can improve with age. The preparations of both the fish and meat are fine—it is the condition of the ingredients that causes the problems.

Lovely slices of fresh fruit, spread on ice, are served with horrid little wrapped triangles of Camembert. The mousse is heavy, the chocolate cake ordinary, the cheese cake without finesse. You can eat safely here from the hors d'oeuvres menu—oysters, clams, smoked trout/whitefish, melon, prosciutto and salads of fresh, crisp greens. You may even find a waiter who will clue you to what arrived today—one such prince touted some superb bay scallops, but if he didn't tout enough of them on Monday, there is always Tuesday, Wednesday . . .

★ FRANKIE AND JOHNNIE'S

269 West 45th Street
DINNER. CLOSED SUNDAY.
Reservations, Cl 5-9717.
Credit cards: AE, DC, MC.
Expensive.

This is an upstairs restaurant, once a speak-easy, and it is still like a lair. The windows are shuttered; the limited space is allocated stingily—a tiny bar (framed *Playbill* covers, photographs of ball players, actresses and archbishops) directly across a narrow aisle from a minuscule kitchen (multilingually boisterous, though the noise cannot compete with the customers), and more tables than there is room for (including one so close to the gas-heated coffee station that it is accepted only by novices, and usually abandoned for something better after a couple of minutes of perspiration).

The tuxedoed, middle-aged waiters are selected for reasons of nostalgia: there are Edward G. Robinson, Clifton Fadiman, George Jessel, Boris Karloff and Dick Tracy —at least good stand-ins for them. Many of the customers they serve are appropriately theatrical. They are noisy and sexy: enter a couple of disparate age—his cauliflower face goes unnoticed as the entire room easily estimates the dimensions under her casual scarf top; other customers give their names to the host and tell him they are expecting calls from their producers; lots of kisses are blown. And the younger people here eat like actors too—ravenously, as if each meal is a miracle, perhaps never to be repeated.

It's not a miracle, but it's not bad. Most New York steak restaurants augment their steakhouse menus with a handful of Italian dishes, but here the exotic items are mostly Jewish, so you can start your dinner with a homey dish of chopped chicken liver—the stuff is spread on the bottom of a plate, like jam on a cracker. It is rather bland, but that's OK because it is covered with oil, and garnished with minced raw onions and a chopped hard-boiled egg, and you eat it with the thick slices of fresh rye bread that are part of the complement of motley items in the bread basket (Melba toast, salt sticks, seeded rolls and the rye). There is also matzo-ball soup, but most of the first courses are what you expect: clams and oysters, in good condition; a shrimp cocktail which, as in many New York restaurants, has been attenuated to five (5) shrimp, and they are overcooked and mealy, anyway; melon (a gigantic slice—a smaller, riper one would suit); and a decent pickled herring.

But broilings and potatoes are the main events here, and they can be pretty good. The steaks are not the thickest in New York, but they are not the most expensive either —a little cheaper than at Broadway Joe's, a couple of blocks away, cheaper still than at the places across town on Steak Row. There is a steak ritual: the waiter shows you your steak, you nod or murmur; from his inside coat pocket he withdraws a small scabbard, from that a small knife; he grabs a fork from somewhere and carves the meat off the bone. In like manner he separates the eye from the rib of the thick, delicious, juicy lamb chop (best item here), and the breast from the wing of the chicken (blackened skin, moist meat, made to order). Even the liver is pretty nice here—it is, as stated, calf's liver; it is fresh and bloody, and it is garnished with bacon (not dried out) or sautéed onions. Chicken in the pot, with matzo balls; chicken à la king.

Everything is à la carte. Lyonnaise potatoes (home fries with onions), home fries (lyonnaise without onions), cottage fries (re-fries, really, and hardened, like wooden nickels), French fries, potato pancakes. Skip them all and have the broiled mushrooms —almost everyone does. They are certainly the best vegetable—how can you go wrong if you butter fresh mushroom caps and broil them? The French fried onions are lightly battered, thin and crinkly—pretty good stuff. Everyone also seems to have the Frankie and Johnnie Special Salad—it is huge, made up of crisp lettuce, strong raw onions, tomatoes that are pretty good for these days, green peppers and anchovies, all in a forthright red-vinegar dressing.

The blueberry pie with whipped cream is not what those simple words suggest, but rather a thick slab of fresh cake under half a pint of stewed berries that are covered with half a pint of whipped cream, which, in turn, is embellished with a great dollop of blueberry sauce—a child's blueberry fantasy, for adults. The strawberries are OK, and the cheese cake is steakhouse cheese cake. Better to share one of the blueberry extravanganzas with a friend.

Frankie and Johnnie's is an erratically busy place, and sometimes your table will not be available at the appointed hour. The beverage of choice with dinner seems to be the martini; tourists who do find the place (it is in the theater district, and it is in the guidebooks) prefer coffee; the wine is overpriced; there is beer.

After you've been here a few times you hardly notice the constantly ringing bell that summons the waiters to the serving counter. It contributes to a cheerful din that assures conversational privacy. This is far from a great restaurant, but it has a distinct New York Broadway flavor that can't be found anywhere else in so well-preserved a state. The clear-skinned ingénues, heavily made up former ingénues and their bluff escorts, but for their clothing, seem like museum pieces.

○ FRAUNCES TAVERN

54 Pearl Street (at Broad Street)
LUNCH AND DINNER. CLOSED SATURDAY AND SUNDAY.
Credit cards: AE, CB, DC, MC, V.
Medium-priced.

Here Washington said goodbye to his officers (and if he had any sense, to the tavern as well). The successive proprietors of this place have been exploiting that bit of history for decades. The notion of exploiting the taste of good food has apparently never occurred to them. And anyway, flavors and smells would be out of place here. After all, the building has "Landmark Status." And so do half the customers. They are upright. They sit at the tables in very upright postures. They have developed the miraculous ability to stare straight ahead while conveying so-called food from plate to head. They think American Gothic is the national emblem and they are mastering the expression. They bring their children along. Some of the children are so young they smile occasionally. Those are half the customers.

The other half cannot feel anything either. They are drunk. There is a whole separate room set aside for them to get drunk in. Or if they prefer, they can get drunk at one of the tables in the dining roon. Many prefer to get drunk in the drinking room first and then stumble into the dining room to "eat."

No one knows what would happen if any of these people were given tasty food. The drunk people would probably survive, but what would happen to the upright people?

Every New England motel wants to look like this place. You know—stained-wood walls, fireplaces flickering across rag rugs, leather wing chairs, mahogany and cut-glass sideboards, pewter on the tables, George Washington in bronze on a window sill. Were Colonial waiters this bored, do you think? Did their eyelids descend thirty degrees while they stood at tableside and waited for their customers to make up their minds?

Did Washington know that you cannot rescue waterlogged lobster with a salty ketchup called cocktail sauce? And that frozen crabmeat tastes especially bad just before it has thawed? The shrimps are a cross between the flaws of the two. If you are stuck here, order raw oysters or clams—they are not invariably fresh, but this is a busy place, and they often are. Do not under any circumstances go anywhere near the "French onion soup, baked with cheese and crouton, encrock." They said it. Encrock.

You are informed, in print, that "The Specialty of the House" is BAKED CHICKEN A LA WASHINGTON." Chicken à la king into which huge quantities of rice have been stirred. Hoping to find something harmless tucked away in some remote corner of the menu, you hunt and hunt. Here! Sautéed calf's liver. You try it. You live and you learn. They do not know how to sauté. They manage to cook the inside of the liver precisely as much as the outside. Is it possible that this most venerable of eating places is sautéing with a microwave oven?

These people are still fighting the Revolutionary War, heaving insults across the Atlantic. What they call English Mixed Grill consists in part of a marvelous imitation of Jones Breakfast Sausage, a grilled tomato that is as tough as a golf ball under melted cheese and bread crumbs which, if given a little time, may become sandpaper. There is a charcoal grill in the kitchen, and the items prepared thereon are not bad; naturally, if you order something rare, such as some lovely, plump lamb chops, you may receive them raw. But think of how much better off you are than the folks who ordered the Broiled Fresh Red Snapper and received clapboard. You get decent home fries here, oily and brown and strong, but the vegetables are just terrible after their hours on the steam table.

They may well get some of the desserts from outside sources—the pecan pie is loaded with crisp nuts, and the crust is well-browned, but tell them to leave off the whipped cream, which is of their own making. "Our Spectacular Chocolate Mousse" tastes like syrup, and "An Exceptionally Light French Cheese Cake" is medium weight and excessively sweet.

All the Colonial hocus pocus notwithstanding, the rooms are comfortable. The place is often mobbed at lunchtime, but you can usually just drop in at dinner and put together a decent meal of oysters or clams, broiled meat, potatoes, and ice cream. The wine list bears little relationship to the wine stocks, but if you keep sending your waiter back when he brings you B because he is out of A, you may end up with a decent bottle —a number of good California varietals are available.

★★GAGE & TOLLNER

372 Fulton Street, Brooklyn (near Borough Hall)
LUNCH, MONDAY TO FRIDAY; DINNER, MONDAY TO SATURDAY. CLOSED SUNDAY.
Reservations, TR 5-5181.
Credit cards: AE, DC, MC, V.
Medium-priced.

During the famous power blackout, Gage & Tollner was one of the few places in New York with illumination. The gaslights, still in place in their nineteenth-century chandeliers and regularly turned on on Mondays, Tuesdays and Saturdays during winter months, were on that famous occasion pressed into emergency service. Unaided by electric bulbs, they cast a rather dim glow, but adequate. The customers felt lucky, privileged, even wise to be in that place on that night.

On Friday nights the remnants of Brooklyn's upper classes emerge from their door-man-protected enclaves in Brooklyn Heights with their families for Gage & Tollner dinners, as do those Brooklyn boys who made it big in Manhattan but still cross the river to sleep, and as do the powers in Brooklyn politics, looking very bored out of the arena, e.g., Mr. Cuite, seated glumly across the table from their wives. These types make it to Manhattan on Saturdays, or to their country retreats, and they are replaced by the up-and-comings from the so-called brownstone revival communities in Boerum Hill, Cobble Hill and Clinton Hill—stockbrokers, assistant curators and twenty-minute-movie makers. Brooklyn isn't what it was, but all of the patrons are trying to clarify a memory or to experience a first taste of it in this well-preserved relic—huge arched mirrors from front to back, well-worn mahogany tables, cane-seated chairs, carpeted floors (rubber runners in the main aisles, rain or shine), which dim even further the restrained sounds of these eaters.

The eight-page menu, famed for its length, is slightly promotional, but only on the cover, and so awkward and amateurish that it is a point of charm. On the cover we find an illustration of a black waiter, tray in hand, leaning forward, and the only thing missing is the caption "At your humble suhvice." A homily signed by the proprietor is innocently redundant: ". . . We intend to preserve the nostalgic atmosphere that serves to bring back fond recollections . . ." etc. And, further down: "Our waiters wear service emblems: Gold Eagle—25 years; Gold Star—5 years; Gold Bar—1 year." And, they might add, no Afros.

On the inner pages, however, things are quite honest, and among the appetizers and soups are a few items unique in New York. Soft Clam Belly Broil Appetizer consists of the contents (sans necks) of a dozen soft-shell clams, lightly breaded in corn meal, briefly broiled over anthracite coal, and served on toast, with half a lemon. Tender, elemental, superb. Shell roast clams and oysters (littlenecks or cherrystone clams; bluepoint or larger oysters) are baked in their shells (until they open) and served in the halves with melted butter. They are delicate, oceanic, sweet, soothing, pure—a wonderful preparation for clams or oysters. It's difficult to choose among the shellfish appetizers here—oysters and soft- and hard-shell clams are also available broiled with celery or in milk, or both, broiled plain, stewed in cream, fried, and on and on. They can also be had fricasseed (sautéed in butter, stewed in milk), but this double preparation usually toughens the meat and is the least successful of the many clam and oyster dishes.

The bisques—basically white sauces of shellfish stock combined with minced cooked oysters or clams or lobster, further enriched with cream and eggs—are extremely thick and strongly flavored. Have only a cup. If you eat a bowl, your meal will be over.

You might consider making a meal of items on the appetizer, soup and shellfish lists only, because the fish is OK, but nothing you can't get elsewhere. A dozen varieties of fish are listed, and four or five are usually available, served broiled only; there is bluefish, snapper, lemon sole, sea bass. The lobsters are good, but often not available if market conditions are bad and prices up. Scallops (the real thing—little bay scallops) are served in all the ways that the oysters and clams are, and not as Coquille St. Jacques.

Gage & Tollner is not exclusively a seafood restaurant, but that is the bulk of its menu and reputation. There are good steaks; there are mutton chops that are, like those at Keen's, mild for mutton, though here they are at least broiled to order and therefore tender and juicy. The fried chicken is crisped without breading and served with good corn fritters which are made brilliantly successful by the addition of the dark, clear maple syrup that arrives in a little pitcher with them.

Shredded cabbage here is shredded cabbage, not cole slaw. It is covered with a sparkling red-pepper dressing. The hashed brown and lyonnaise potatoes are very good, and the French fries are not. There is something called Spaghetti au Gratin.

For dessert: moist applesauce spice cake; blueberry pie with huge berries, a lattice crust and a five-inch arc; and sweet-potato pie that is superior to pumpkin pie in exactly the way sweet potatoes are superior to pumpkins.

The waiters are kind and they know their stuff, but some of them keep it a secret:
"What are Shell Roast Clams?"
"I'll get you some nice casinos." (He's writing already.)
"What are Baltimore Broiled Scallops?"
"You'll like them."
"What's the difference in the four kinds of Welsh rabbit?"
"Which one do you want to know about?"
But they are not all like that.

Miscellaneous items: scrambled eggs, milk toast, chicken sandwich, hot chocolate. No marshmallows.

Half portions of most items are available at a small premium.

• GALLAGHER'S

228 West 52nd Street
LUNCH AND DINNER.
Reservations, CI 5-5336.
Credit cards: AE, CB, DC, MC, V.
Expensive.

The mahogany walls of this famous masculine Mecca, where fame is all and how you got it little, are crowded with sporting engravings and paintings, caricatures of jockeys in brightly colored silks, pen-and-ink sketches of lovable Broadway characters, and hundreds of photographs of pugilists and ballplayers, pols of the past (derbied, smiling thinly), race horses (head and shoulders, in brown or chestnut, against very blue skies), their owners (proudly holding the reins in the winner's circle), actors (in full dress) and actresses (in a little less). No epicures, however, are so honored, no gastronomes, no gourmets or famous gluttons, no chefs, no brewers or distillers even—the closest we come is a picture of the H. M. Stevens family.

Men come here, where the famous have been, to indulge their manly fantasies—pairs of men, groups of men, men alone—to read the paper and have clams, steak and beer. Ladies do not come here; ladies are brought here. And they wear skirts, mind you, *skirts.* Pants are rare. Men wear pants. The drinks are big and strong, and the food is big and (sometimes) tough.

Insular, speak-easy ethics govern. Not to suggest in any way that this is a violent establishment, but when one clown gets off his bar stool to knock another off his, the disputants are merely separated and the more flagrant offender asked to leave. "No police" is an ancient rule in these places, not always unspoken. (The mysterious explanation: "We don't want any trouble.") The house comes first, and men in dark-blue uniforms make certain regular customers uncomfortable.

You can predict 90 percent of the menu, but you can't predict the conversation.

"Microcosms are boring as hell," he explains to her, as he poisons his perfectly good oyster with a jigger of cocktail sauce. She lowers her eyes in respect, simultaneously forking a lump of tasteless chopped liver.

"I *never* make love to a woman I don't like," he remonstrates a bit later on, finding it difficult to handle her sudden insight while attempting to carve the resilient London broil (here peddled as Sliced Beefsteak on Toast and served with a sauce of watered Bahamian mustard). He by-passes that obstacle by changing the subject, and she learns that "Opera is Italian, orchestra is German" while learning, too, that the fried shrimp in beer batter are delicious—done in hot fat, crisp, moist, huge, tender. He's really fielding them now, and he does not notice that the French fried onion rings are coarse, greasy and wilted, because he is explaining, "Sure you're married. But you're married in Brooklyn. This is Manhattan."

They have a good laugh over that one, and she, happily surrendering to his good-humored but irresistible flow of virile logic, polishes off 75 percent of their delicious lyonnaise potatoes, and then makes the serious mistake of ordering Apple Pie Mel Ott. She errs again by not returning the tasteless mess to the outfield. He orders Kid Chocolate Pie on the assumption, presumably, that—like the Kid—it will be feather-weight, when, in fact, it is overweight, dried out and past its prime. He doesn't care, because they are relaxing into a comfortable interlude of reviews of common acquaint-ances. "Martin? He reads a lot, goes to the track, and has a medium-sized circle of intellectual friends. Still, he's not a bad guy." She rinses out with coffee that arrives in a hospital carafe (Gallagher's Special Coffee), and he, now confident, and with the gracious generosity that comes of impending success, buys a couple of drinks for the yokels at the next table, who giggle and sip as he makes Mr. feel comfortable by settling with him into a discussion of grain futures ("I know for an absolute fact you're crazy not to buy corn tomorrow") while she enlightens Mother, complete with addresses written on matchbooks, about upstairs places where the "finest furs" are "less than wholesale."

That main course of fried shrimp makes an excellent appetizer for two. Good clams, oysters, herring, steaks, chops and roast beef; the grilled bass is reliable, but the accompanying stewed tomatoes come from an institutional container. The salad is nourishing. Michelob beer on tap. Bad desserts, though the strawberries are sometimes in good condition; they can be seen in the same glass-walled refrigerator near the front door in which the beef is aged and displayed.

Gallagher's is a comfortable restaurant: a handsome, commodious bar; large-enough tables, spaced well apart; captain's chairs and red-leather banquettes; and soft lighting from hanging fixtures of crossed logs and copper cones. At one time the logs were real, but the bark began to shed into the food.

The service is available, mechanical and bored. The waiters are at their best when no questions are asked.

★ EL GAUCHO

93 MacDougal Street (near Bleecker Street)
DINNER.
Reservations, 260–5350.
Credit cards: AE, CB, DC, V.
Medium-priced.

Juke box, cigarette machine, open kitchen in the rear. All this is perceived through a haze of smoke, not because the place is particularly crowded with smokers, but because almost everyone orders the mixed grill (read on), and the mixed grill is planted on your table on a little hibachi, glowing, smoking coals within. True, there is white linen on the tables (red napkins forming diamonds thereon), but there the elegance ends. El Gaucho is a primitive place.

What little there is of a South American population in Greenwich Village keeps El Gaucho busy, with a little help from some of the old-family locals who have discovered that, though Argentine food bears little resemblance to the food of southern Italy, it is just as sturdy. The customers come late, casually dressed, including whole families, complete with kiddies—it seems that our Spanish-speaking neighbors have never learned that children should be in bed by eight if they want to grow up to be big and strong.

Your waiter did not attend a Swiss hospitality school, so it is a good idea to find some excuse for an altercation with him before your dinner is well under way. This will not accomplish anything in the way of the progress of your meal, but it will establish that you are someone to be reckoned with, respected, and on subsequent visits you will be shown an esteem usually reserved for the town mayor, which does not necessarily include pronto service.

In deference to the neighborhood, the platter of assorted appetizers is called Antipasto El Gaucho, and it includes discs of various potent sausages, slices of tender, oily ham, and substantial slabs of marinated eggplant. It also includes one slice of Matambre (also available in a four-slice platter of its own). This is the famous Argentine dish of marinated beef, stuffed with garlic, herbs, vegetables, hard-cooked eggs and spices, poached in stock and (usually) served cold. It is stimulating, but also satisfying, and the satisfaction will soon overtake the stimulation—consume one order and you may want nothing more. Something exaggerated as Perdiz en Escabeche on the Spanish side of the menu is more modestly and more accurately referred to as Cornish Hen Special Sauce on the English side. This is a dish of cold Cornish hen, a bird that is usually too dry to bother with. But this preparation is just the thing—the hen is cooked in stock, with vegetables, herbs, garlic and lots of black pepper, and permitted to cool. The liquid is thickened in the process, the bird moistened and flavored—the bits of garlic, green pepper and onions are delicious against the oily sauce and the fibrous meat.

That mixed grill is an impressive affair. The little smoking grill is piled high with assorted meats and sausages. You spear what you like before your companions know what hit them, and leave the liver and sweetbreads to them, or the kidney, or the blood sausage, or the meat sausage, or the "butcher's tenderloin" steak. That blood sausage is bloody, black, bready and rich, in a crackling casing (don't fight, you can order extra blood sausages). The kidney is cartilaginous, gamy, a little tough, and much aided by the charcoal flavor imparted by the smoking coals. There are chunks of red pepper in among the pieces of meat, and they are very good with the sweetbreads and liver. And there is a little pot of an extremely fiery onion-and-hot-pepper relish on every table, and that is a particularly well chosen additive for the fibrous, charred steak.

Naturally, in an Argentine restaurant you can order a straight sirloin steak, described as "The Most Famous Steak in Town." Notice how cleverly the name of the town is not given. The steak is huge, of good meat, though not prime, aged and tender. It comes with terrible French fries. Strenuously avoid the Milanesas, the Completa, and the Napolitana. These are breaded beef cutlets, variously treated, and there is very little you can do in the service of breaded beef.

No desserts worth bothering about, and after two courses of solid food at this place, dessert would be unthinkable anyway.

★★ GAYLORD

50 East 58th Street
LUNCH, MONDAY TO FRIDAY; DINNER, DAILY.
Reservations, PL 9–1710.
Credit cards: AE, CB, DC, MC, V.
Medium-priced.

New York seems to expect a kind of economic authenticity in its restaurants of foreign cuisine. If a country is not among the so-called advanced nations, its New York restaurants must be cheap and seedy. Consider, for example, the Spanish Pavilion and Toledo, posh Spanish restaurants, now both defunct, while a couple of dozen comparatively grubby Spanish restaurants have survived, in some instances thrived, for years. Notice that grandeur in Chinese restaurants was accepted only when it became generally recognized that China was not a nation of starving peasants and scrawny coolies. Oblivious to this law, an international chain of high-class Indian restaurants has taken on the New York market.

Gaylord is a luxuriously and colorfully appointed place. The main dining room is rimmed with plump comfortable sofas; the chairs that face them from the other side of the ample tables are high-backed and covered with pale-blue, soft wool. At your place there is a giant plate of gleaming brass. There are chandeliers of the same polished metal. Hanging along the cloth-covered walls are tall macramé lamps of pale string interwoven with patterns of brilliant color. In between there are panels of hanging beads with, behind them, back-lighted, translucent pictures of Indians doing Indian things.

Indians, apparently, are accustomed to extremely polite but very leisurely service, which is the only kind anyone gets here. You will be treated very well, but not necessarily right away. When he comes, however, the captain will explain the menu to you patiently and informatively, and if you have already made your selections and he considers them badly matched, he will tell you so, and why. Then he goes away, and you nurse your wine, and you nurse it and nurse it. The quality of the food you finally get indicates that it is made to your order, which explains the delay; and if you are sitting near the front of the dining room, you can watch it being made—there is a windowed wall, behind which a couple of men in white kitchen linen, their skins gleaming, their performances enveloped in clouds of steam and smoke, prepare some of your dinner. The glass is soundproof, and their labors are like mime.

If you are a sampler, you may begin here with the Special Indian Hors d'Oeuvres, which will provide you with a taste of samosa—a deep-fried pastry filled with fresh peas and potatoes; of pakora (which is a generic term for vegetables that are coated with a paste of chickpeas, and deep-fried) made with ripe plantains (big bananas to you), very sweet and moist; of shami kebab, spicy patties of ground lamb; and of papadum, a crisp, spiced wafer of fried unrisen bread. None of the food here is particularly spicy, but it has an unmistakable quality of authenticity—it has character, singularity. These first courses, though you may find them in more potent versions in other Indian restaurants, do not seem to be compromised for the American palate. They seem, rather, to be refined urban versions of strong Indian food.

There is an extensive assortment of main courses at Gaylord, including very good versions of some of the most familiar Indian dishes. The Tandoori Chicken is bright red, moist, firm, with the nice flavor of the edges being slightly burnt. The Boti Kebab (skewered lamb) is of cubes of meat that have been marinated in curd, onions and spices, and broiled with raw onions—very good. A quite different lamb dish is the one called Lamb Pasanda—the meat is marinated in yogurt and stewed in cream with sweet spices, mainly cinnamon—very, but not excessively, rich.

There is an item on the menu called Tandoori Prawns. This is a bastardized dish, because seafood is not part of the original tandoori cooking, but that should not bother you, particularly as this illegitimacy seems to have been the result of love. The prawns have been marinated in herbs, they are oily and slightly spicy, though their brilliant redness makes you expect something hotter than what you get, and they are coolly garnished with minced onions, cucumbers and tomatoes.

The dish called Chicken Bhuna Masala seems Western, which should not prevent you from trying it. The chicken is stewed in an herbed sauce of vegetables, dominated by tomato—the flavors are strong without being spicy, as of fresh vegetables and herbs highly concentrated.

With all of these things, one may choose from an assortment of side dishes: Special Indian Pickles are inflamed zucchini—it is not necessary to actually eat them, just wave them around to clear the air. The paratha here is not the rich deep-fried bread you get in most of New York's Indian restaurants—this version is comparatively dry and may seem tasteless if you have come to like the oilier kind.

The desserts are like candies. For $1.50, the menu informs you, you make "Selection from Trolly (Any two pieces)." The man wheels over the trolly and you point to Rasgalla and promptly regret having been seduced by the pretty little balls that taste precisely like chalk in rose water, which is close to what they are. You try the pistachio candy, an excellent heavy pistachio-dominated nut cake—much better.

If you have eaten highly flavored food, a thoughtful man may come around and offer you dried anise and cardamom seeds. Hold out your hand, and he will spoon some into the palm. You place them on the impeccable cloth before you and meditatively chew them as you talk, fancying yourself all the while a philosophical Indian with all the time in the world. The seeds *are* refreshing.

★★ GIAMBELLI

238 Madison Avenue (near 37th Street)
LUNCH, MONDAY TO FRIDAY; DINNER, MONDAY TO SATURDAY. CLOSED SUNDAY.
Reservations, 685–8727.
Credit cards: AE, CB, DC, MC, V.
Expensive.

This is a rather garishly appointed restaurant. You enter by way of the well-trafficked bar; beyond it, down half a dozen steps, are two rooms into which are crammed an inordinate number of tables at night, and that many plus a few extras at lunchtime. (The lunch menu, by the way, is like the dinner menu, but with no appetizers of interest.) The illumination emanates from crystal discs flush against the ceiling, and there are prints and paintings along the walls which, unfortunately, have lights of their own. By day this is a businessmen's restaurant in which businessmen take businessmen to lunch. At night it is a businessmen's restaurant in which businessmen take business-women to dinner.

There are few dishes in any cuisine that consist of a fish sauce on meat. The cold Italian dish of Vitello Tonnato is probably the best-known, and the version served here is very hard to beat. It is made with tender, pale veal; and the tuna-fish sauce, flavored with anchovies and lemon, and rendered creamy by thoroughly blending it with olive oil and stock, is at once sparkling and rich.

Rice is a nice occasional alternative to pasta. But the risotto with mushrooms served here is a big comedown; compared with the version served at Mama Laura, it is an insult. And when you realize that they give it to you for $6.50, it's a triumph of materialism over mind that they ever sell any. On occasion the rice is not merely *al dente* but pebbly, and when that doesn't happen you find that the dish consists merely of coarse-grained rice that has been boiled in an undistinguished chicken broth, and then combined with sautéed mushrooms.

The pasta dishes are generally better, including a good version of Spaghetti alla Matriciana, which is made here with the thinnest of spaghetti and a heavily parsleyed tomato sauce in which the onions are only lightly sautéed and still firm, and in which there is an abundance of tiny slices of good ham. Plenty of red pepper makes the sauce very lively. You can also get those little containers called tortellini, here filled with ground chicken and served either with meat sauce or with a creamy sauce which you complete with a heavy dose of grated cheese and fresh pepper.

Excellent brains are served here—they are carefully prepared by marinating and poaching so that they are rich and vaguely sour, and then dipped in flour and eggs and rapidly sautéed in hot butter. You can also get Veal Piccata, and so on, but as in lots of Italian restaurants, the veal scaloppine dishes are disappointing because the various sauces all start with the same beginnings, to which a little lemon is added for piccata, or a little Marsala for something else, or a few vegetables for yet another dish. Try, instead, the Veal Paillard, in which the veal is flavored with garlic and grilled very rapidly, so there is a pattern of lines on the outside of the veal that is almost black, while the inside is creamy white and tender—the garlic is delicate, but not lost. There is a chicken dish here called Pollo dei Castelli Romani which is made with fresh artichokes and mushrooms. There is a minor miracle in that the chicken actually takes on the flavor of the artichokes, but there is a major idiocy in that the slices of artichoke reach you with the choke and the inedible, hard portion of the leaves still attached.

The cheese cake is the real thing, made with ricotta instead of cream cheese, but it lacks moisture. The otherwise competent captains are not particularly careful about their zabaglione—they make it right there before your eyes, and they spoon it into your dish, and it is cold. Perhaps the best dessert here is the Banana Vesuvio, an adult sundae, made with ripe bananas that are sort of sautéed in simple syrup (to which Grand Marnier and brandy are added) and flamed. All that is then combined with vanilla ice cream. As a rule such concoctions do not add up, but this one does, and it can make you forget the sins of the recent past. At best, one of the better Italian restaurants in New York, but there is carelessness in the preparation of the food at almost any meal.

★★ GIAMBELLI 50TH

46 East 50th Street
LUNCH AND DINNER. CLOSED SUNDAY.
Reservations, MU 8–2760.
Credit cards: AE, CB, DC, MC, V.
Expensive.

The bartender chews while he pours, laughs merrily, says "Wrong again" every time he gets the drinks mixed up, shakes his head and smiles with tolerant indulgence at his little faults, and tries again. Well, this is only the bar, you say, but on visits to this restaurant you almost invariably spend some time here because your table is not ready for your reservations. *Unless,* big unless, you are willing to sit *upstairs* (Coventry), where no one will see you, and you will see no one. *But,* big but, where the place is not populated to within a millimeter of the swinging door leading to the kitchen, and where there is service, not only when you trip up a waiter, but sometimes if you simply catch his eye. The service downstairs, which is simply terrible, suffers not from lack of help, but from lack of room for help. A few more people downstairs, and the traffic, which now has two speeds—slow and stop—would have one speed. Rule No. 1: Eat upstairs. Rule No. 2: Bring plenty of money.

Rule No. 3: Don't eat the Antipasti Variati. These so-called "Italian Hors d'Oeuvres" come from American, Portuguese, Spanish and Mexican cans, with a few items in domestic casing: a slice of ham, another of salami. Instead, have the Spiedino Valdostana—a series of squares of ham, Fontina cheese, dough, ham, cheese, dough, etc., impaled on a skewer, fried and served under a strong sauce of tomatoes, peppers, capers and anchovies—an eminently Italian dish, strong, heavy and satisfying. Or have the Mussels Riviera—mussels steamed in their own liquid, oil, parsley, garlic, onions and tomatoes, and served on toasted Italian bread—tender mussels, and a delicious broth.

Or if you wish to start with a pasta, have the Trenette al Pesto. For "Trenette" read "Linguine," as it is simply the Genoese term for that particular shape of macaroni. And for "Pesto" read one of the best basil sauces in New York, made with garlic sautéed in oil, chopped fresh basil, a little cream, consommé, pine nuts and grated cheese, all warmed together with the pasta, lots of parsley added near the end. The captains here, particularly upstairs, where they have the time, put on elaborate shows of twirling it in the sautéing pan, as if they were coiffing the head of a great lady. It does not hurt the food, and they seem to enjoy doing it. The high flavor of the pesto seems literally to vibrate.

The Tortellini al Sugo di Carne, on the other hand—pasta tubes filled with ground dark meat of chicken (the white meat is reserved for a couple of $7 Chicken Suprême numbers)—tastes not of chicken under its overpowering and not particularly brilliant sauce of cheese, cream, tomato and garlic.

But the pasta should be shared, or eaten in small portions, to allow for such main courses as Red Snapper with Clams. The snapper is done in the same sauce as the appetizer of mussels, but with little necks, which add a sharpness that changes the sauce slightly but significantly, making it brinier, though the clams are added only at the end of the cooking of the fish, so that they are still tender when you get them.

The Osso Buco is tender, falling off the knuckle, served with a fettuccine, all under a simple tomato sauce—not bad. And the Pollo Napoletano—chunks of chicken and chicken livers, sautéed with shallots, is a plain, rather heavy dish which should perhaps not be preceded by pasta; it's good, but it's an awful lot of solid meat. A long, slow sautéeing in olive oil makes the Eggplant Parmigiana almost intolerably rich, under its layer of melted cheese. It is listed as a vegetable, but if it is ordered for one person, little else may be needed.

Ricotta is the cheese used in the cheese cake here—not Philadelphia cream—so the cake is dry but tasty, and moistened with rum and candied fruits. Strawberries Portofino is a simple sweet of strawberries. They are warmed in butter and flavored with Grand Marnier, which yields a honeylike sauce. This is served over ice cream and whipped cream.

Posh surroundings; a different perfume at every table, so you may have to keep your nose to your plate to enjoy your food. There are more than 150 items on the menu, of which most are nothing, but the English translations make clear what is what—Coppa di Frutta Fresca, you understand, is fruit cup, and Sofliola alla Mandorla is Sole Amandine. Order items whose English definitions seem to speak in Italian—like Veal Scaloppine with Prosciutto, Sage, Artichokes and Peas, or Disjointed Chicken with Peppers and Mushrooms, and *not* Sogliola Inglese Gratellata al Burro, which is not Heart of Grateful Donkey, but English Sole Maître d'Hôtel.

The French wines are priced for comic relief. A spotty restaurant, but sometimes the food is inspired.

• GINGER MAN

51 West 64th Street
LUNCH AND DINNER.
Reservations, SC 4–7272.
Credit cards: AE, CB, DC, MC, V.
Expensive.

Over the years the Ginger Man has managed to receive considerable notice in the local press. The place has always been treated *seriously,* as if it were a restaurant to be reckoned with, as if someone, having eaten there, would thereafter be ever so interested in any bit of news or comment about the place. Most recently the Ginger Man made the headlines because its latest chef is a *woman!* This should hardly be startling, particularly at the Ginger Man, where the very first chef was a woman—the late Dione Lucas. Having eaten some of the current food, one may safely conclude that the latest lady in the kitchen was hired for her publicity potential, not for any ability with a stove.

This is one of New York's first tries at a British-style pub. There are hideous oil paintings all around, by way of carefully chosen idiosyncrasy, and sure enough, the hidden spotlights are played on that very art. Dark wood, exposed brick, semidimness. The sidewalk café, of half a dozen tables, is enclosed, and it is used the year around.

You nab a wandering host and you explain to him that after obtaining some wine there has been no sign of a waiter for twenty minutes and that you wish to order immediately and receive food promptly thereafter, or you will leave and pay for nothing. "In that case," he says, "I'll take the order myself." *In that case.*

Eventually your waiter arrives, and after he addresses the usual question, you wonder why, if he asks "Who gets the coe-keel?" for coquille, he does not ask "Who gets the pate?" for pâté. Something to think about while you consider your food: a cool and spicy pâté, served with the lovely little sour pickles called cornichons; a decent coquille, actually made with bay scallops as well as tiny shrimps and mushrooms, all in a competent white sauce under a layer of bread crumbs—you squeeze on lemon to bring the dish to life. There are artichokes, and occasionally they are not overcooked—their dressing is made with an abundance of mustard. And there is onion soup, but because the onions are not cooked until brown, the result is simply beef stock with onions, and not a strong stock at that—the tasty melted cheese on top almost rescues the dish.

The Canard à l'Orange is almost blackened in the attempt at a crisp skin, and there are myriad mandarin orange sections in the thick but undistinguished sauce. At $10.95 your filet mignon should be of first-class beef—it is not; and the so-called sauce Béarnaise, which pours from the pitcher like lava, is predominantly salty, short on the flavor of tarragon.

Among the supper dishes, the steak sandwich, once a bargain, now mocks your money at $5.95, though the meat is tasty, particularly with a dab of mustard. This is where the Spinach Salad with Mushrooms & Bacon got its big start, and you still get a good one here—very fresh, well-cleaned spinach leaves, a couple of handfuls of slices of raw mushrooms, and a few strips of bacon—that undistinguished dressing that you had on your artichoke is, unfortunately, repeated here.

The fruit salad no longer has the shredded citrus rind that used to distinguish it from dozens of others. But the Austrian Nut Roll is as creamy, sugary and delicate as ever.

★★ GIRAFE

208 East 58th Street
LUNCH, MONDAY TO FRIDAY; DINNER, MONDAY TO SATURDAY. CLOSED SUNDAY.
Reservations, PL 2-3054.
Credit cards: AE, CB, DC, MC, V.
Expensive.

Formerly a hangout for guys in pinky rings and dolls in noisy dresses, this place was taken over by people formerly connected with San Marco, an elegant Italian restaurant a few blocks to the south and west. The emphasis has shifted from business conferences and seductions to good food and memories.

This is a two-story restaurant, with an irrelevant wild-animal theme, which has not been altered by the new proprietors. Grainy enlargements of beasts in the wild are on view as murals, if you can see in this dim light. There is tropical greenery here and there, and a spiral stairway that leads to a smaller dining room on the floor above, where the painted brick wall is hung with a zebra skin, and where a few paintings and a bit of statuary complete the gestures to the downstairs motif. Upstairs is considered Siberia by regulars, but it is calm and comfortable; downstairs is heavy intimacy—among you, your company and the people at the adjacent tables.

Not only are the Vongole Fresche fresh, and therefore fine for eating straight, but you can have them transformed into Vongole Cassino, in which the clams are lightly breaded, spiced and oiled, and served hot in a pool of briny butter mildly flavored with tomato. They unabashedly call their shrimp appetizer Gamberi Girafe, which is hard to order with a straight face, but good to eat—huge shrimp, breaded and browned, served with a creamy tomato sauce that is just the moisture the crusty dish calls for. But the winner is Spiedino di Mozzarella, that wonderful battered and deep-fried multiple sandwich of bread and cheese, served in a thick anchovy sauce—the airy crust is marvelous with the oily, salty sauce.

You pay $7 or more for a plate of pasta in this place, and though you may feel that such a tariff is inherently absurd, nevertheless they do wonderful things here with the noodle. The Cannelloni Fiorentina is huge envelopes of pasta stuffed with a mixture of spinach and spiced meat—cheese has been melted over those and a thick meat sauce poured over the works. Sturdy stuff. Your waiter detects that you are a creature of discernment and good taste, and he suggests that you sample a dish that is not on the menu—Tortellini alla Giuseppi, which, it develops, are the usual little crescent-shaped dumplings of meat and cheese wrapped in pasta. They are a bit mushy, which is a pity, for the creamy sauce that is laced with peas and prosciutto is rich without being thick, and the whole dish is given a note of sharpness by being sprinkled with cheese and quickly browned. If you prefer that some of the action take place before your very eyes, the Spaghetti Carbonara, except for the actual boiling of the spaghetti, is prepared in the dining room. The onions are sautéed in butter, the mound of noodles added and stirred, the crisped bacon is sprinkled in, the egg cracked over the mound of noodles, the pepper mill turned to the waiter's taste. You add the cheese yourself.

Wondering what kidneys are doing on a New York Italian menu, you find out by ordering Rognone al Barbera, which you promptly regret. The kidneys are not perfectly clean, which makes them loud in an unpleasant, acidic way, and the garnish of canned artichoke hearts does not help. Shaken, you retreat to the safety of your waiter's advice, and he comes up with another secret of the house—the unlisted Vitello Martini, a gentle dish of pale, tender scallops of veal that are sandwiched with mild cheese, breaded and sautéed, and served with a light sauce of wine and butter—you may think of it as Italian mother's-milk food. The Chicken Scarpariello is fine, the chunks of chicken moist and well-browned, bits of garlic clinging to the skin, but you probably expect sage or rosemary in this dish, and at Girafe it is missing, which is too bad. The seafood dishes are made with fresh fish, and the Spigola alla Livornese is flaky, moist bass in a thick and tasty version of the familiar tomato sauce studded with olives and capers.

Something they call a napoleon is a simple and rich compound of flaky pastry, fresh and unsweetened whipped cream, and chocolate shavings—what could be bad? The zabaglione is hot and winy, and you can have it over ripe strawberries. The cheese cake is moist, pebbly of its ricotta cheese, and extremely sweet.

★★GLOUCESTER HOUSE

37 East 50th Street
LUNCH AND DINNER.
Reservations, PL 5–7394.
Credit cards: AE, CB, DC, MC, V.
Very expensive.

Gloucester House does what it can to perpetuate Puritan propriety, economic stratification, racial separation and bluenose privacy. To keep the riffraff out, gentlemen are required to arrive with coats and ties and about a pound of bank notes—the à la carte prices are insane.

The room itself is rather severe, though not unattractive or uncomfortable. There are sanded tabletops on the main level and finished ones on the level above, all unclothed; there are comfortable captain's chairs just like the ones on the customers' boats; an interior window display of ship models; and a plaque of sailor's knots. To this Northern severity is added a plantation note: the serving staff is almost exclusively of color, and their supervisors uniformly pink.

You're greeted at the door (and inspected) by a type who carefully checks your name against a list and turns you over to one of the handwringing floorwalkers. (They say "Ahem" a great deal, and look back every few steps as they lead you to your table.)

And yet, unfortunately, this is probably the best seafood restaurant in New York—in part because Gloucester House serves some superb food, and in part because the other fish restaurants in New York are terrible, or OK, or even, on occasion, good—but only on occasion.

Many New York restaurants list a number of oyster varieties in addition to local ones (usually bluepoints), but Gloucester House sometimes goes so far as to actually sell them. These oysters are not superior to New York oysters, just different. Cape Cods, for example, are clearer-tasting, less metallic, less oily, rather stimulating. Chincoteagues (from Virginia) are also available on occasion. The menu says: "Please state your choice: large or small oysters." Ask for large ones—unlike large clams, large oysters are as good as little ones, and they are bigger. Eat them with lemon juice and a few grains from a pepper mill; if you're going to bury them in cocktail sauce, they might as well be pickled onions.

The crabmeat at Gloucester House is *fresh*. You can have it straight, in a cocktail, or wrapped in bacon and broiled—a nice dish, though only four morsels, each the size of a child's thumb. The littlenecks (8) are, happily, minuscule; the steamers are sandy, though the hot clam broth is hearty and lightly celeried; the roasted shrimp in garlic butter are tender and just lightly garlicked; the "Freshly opened Clam Juice" is from freshly opened clams, not bottles; and if nothing else will serve, half a cold lobster is an elegant first course. There are good chowders and shellfish stews, and while all this is getting under way, superb, fluffy hot biscuits, just out of the oven, are brought to your table when you ask for them, and sometimes even when you do not.

There are about thirty varieties of fish listed on the menu, and on a given day about a dozen prices are written in, indicating that those kinds are available, or at least that they were at the beginning of the day. They are fresh, and broiled carefully, so that each variety maintains its character—dark, succulent bluefish, flaky snapper; strong, oily halibut; nutlike flounder, and so on. The shad roe, as in most places, is a little over-cooked unless you specify that you want it rare. The overcooking is a gesture to those who want the luxury of eating shad roe but don't actually like the stuff—it is moist and jellylike when it is cooked properly, but it tastes much better that way. After all, fish eggs—what did you expect? The roe is served, bizarrely, with a poor hollandaise sauce, presumably to offset the overcooking. A better solution is melted butter and lemon.

The broiled and steamed lobsters are done perfectly, and each arrives with a num-bered tag on a plastic pole, like the ducks at Tour d'Argent. God knows why. The lobster bibs are of nice soft linen.

Terrific vegetables: thin, thin, delicious, crisp, deep-fried onion rings; delicate, fluffy discs of fried zucchini; good charcoal-broiled eggplant. The French fried potatoes are called "Raw French Fried Potatoes," which means they are not parboiled early in the day for future frying, which is the right approach, but the eventual frying is not hot enough to make a really crispy potato. Fresh corn on the cob is available.

At least one of the desserts is a peerless masterpiece, called Gloucester House Special. It is an airy froth of fresh orange juice and whipped cream, garnished with a tangy marmalade made on the premises. Blueberry Slump is stewed blueberries with whipped cream—in winter, when scrawny Mexican blueberries are used, it is just so-so; much better in summer, when large local berries are available. The delicate strawberry mousse is uncompromising in its purity—nothing is done to emphasize the strawberry flavor, which is naturally thinned out a little in the preparation. The strawberry shortcake is authentic—fresh berries on a light biscuit, covered with unsweetened whipped cream. The apple pie is fairly good.

Next to a number of items on the Gloucester House menu are the words "When Available," which is fairly uninformative, as none of the items can be had when they are not available. But the clear implication is that everything else is almost always available (setting aside the unpriced fish varieties). Which brings up a problem here. Take, for example, the soused shrimp, mussels in curry sauce, billi-bi, turtle soup, various desserts, twenty of thirty wines, and four of six listed beers, most of which were not available at three of three lunches and dinners. When engaged in conversation on the subject, the plump, close-cropped, narrow-lapelled proctor smiled tolerantly and explained that late in the day certain items run out. At lunch the same authority attributed shortages to the weather. He mumbled and became a little hesitant when challenged about the wines, but recovered his poise at once when asked about the chronic unavailability of guilfords (listed in three places on the menu). He stood up even straighter than before and won that one with "We had those last Tuesday!," emphasized with an orator's index finger pointed heavenward.

The proprietor is a white-haired patrician giant who concerns himself primarily with the placement of nautical paintings on the walls. On occasion he takes a seat in the dining room and gazes, over the heads of the diners, out to sea.

★★LA GOULUE

28 East 70th Street
LUNCH AND DINNER. CLOSED SUNDAY.
Reservations, 988–8169.
Credit cards: AE, DC, MC.
Very expensive.

La Goulue is an effort to replicate, with nothing less than movie-set realism, a bit of old Paris. Visually the performance is impeccable; and, much delayed blessing, the food these days is so consistently above reproach (albeit uninspired) that anyone wishing to soak-in these lovely quarters may do so without fear of distaste.

Under a deep-brown tin ceiling, somber notes make a pretty tune. The walls are paneled in dark wood and mirrors, the silver backs peeling and flaking here and there, as if this really were a French restaurant that has survived since the turn of the century. The room is rimmed with high-backed banquettes the color of caramel, above which a thin brass railing gleams from bracket to bracket, pointlessly and beautifully. Light is cast from Art Nouveau brass sconces on the many-too-many little tables that are covered with snowy linen and set with simple china. One rose per table, in tall, slender glass vases. The first room includes a little zinc-topped bar, a few cocktail tables, and a handful of eating tables for two along the wall, for those who are without reservations, or just want dessert, or want to avoid the slight bustle of the dining rooms proper. The dark colors of the place, with just the brightness of the linen and the flowers, mirrors seen from an angle, the waiters in black and white, the almost invariable elegance of the crowd—gents in dark suits, ladies in simple little numbers—make for a scene of almost breath-taking respectability, not to say taste. We have here an admixture of high fashion and the senior partners of some very old law firms. It is true that excessive jewelry has been seen at the early end of the dinner hour and a bit of tipsy youth as midnight approaches. But the place takes no notice, remains its proper self withal.

La Goulue is getting old now, and it has settled down. The once hectic service is calm and available even at the busiest times, the waiters are confident and knowing, even pleasant, and everything is so utterly under control that when the host's pals arrive, he joins them for a drink in the front room, they in their evening-out clothes hardly distinguishable from him in his tux. What could be more civilized?

Well, the food could be more civilized. Though one could argue that the Assiette de Crudités is *too* civilized—four raw vegetables moistened with very nice vinaigrette, a slice of melon placed away from the dressing. As mama said, this you can have at home, though mama's ingredients were not invariably so crisp and fresh. Considerably less perfection with a bit more excitement are available in the Terrine de Canard, which is loudly livery, short on the flavor of duck meat, moist and spicy, served, happily, with pungent little cornichons. A good version of your standard snails. A bland one of onion soup.

The bass that is listed on the menu seems to be a symbol for a fish of the day; it is often not to be had, another fish available in its place. Sometimes it is poached salmon —an utterly fresh slice of the pink fish, unfortunately cooked a bit too long, so that the meat has lost its slight natural oiliness. It comes with a smooth hollandaise that has strong touches of spice and acid. Nice food. The Canard à l'Orange is the basic familiar item, very darkly roasted, garnished with slices of fruit, moistened with a tasty if far from deep sauce. The lamb here is served oddly. Called Medaillons de Selle d'Agneau, the dish consists of three substantial eyes of meat carved from their ribs, after the short rack was roasted in a dressing of bread crumbs that were oiled and flavored with garlic and herbs—good strong meat, but the dressing is somehow not integrated into the dish, perhaps because its flavors have not permeated. The Côte de Veau aux Morilles consists of a couple of eyes of veal chop, perfectly sautéed, so that the tender meat is lightly browned; but the creamy sauce of wild mushrooms lacks sparkle. Ask the waiter to substitute French fries and grilled tomatoes for whatever would otherwise come with your main course—they are the best vegetables in the house.

Good ripe Brie, at room temperature, served with excellent French bread. The Bombe Praline is a delicious sweet of little more than layers of almond paste and coffee ice cream. Good fruit tarts, in the simplest French manner, barely cooked fruit and flaky pastry.

With all its chic, the place is sedate.

★ GRANADOS

125 MacDougal Street (at Third Street)
LUNCH, SUNDAY; DINNER, TUESDAY TO SUNDAY. CLOSED MONDAY.
Reservations, OR 3–5576.
Credit cards: AE, DC, MC.
Medium-priced.

The growth in number of New York's Spanish restaurants is a reflection of increase within the families that own them. As a family of Spanish restaurant proprietors grows, it requires new restaurants to support itself. Thus the recent appearance of Spanish eating places in lower Manhattan, Queens, Nassau County. Old family hands ship out to oversee the new stores, leaving the established establishments to coast in well-worn grooves under the watch of scions new to their seniority. At ancient Granados the last couple of years, this was disastrous. In service of a youthful ego, treats flowed freely to favored habitués, solvency suffered, suppliers came begging, while old customers shook their heads at pointless revisions in one of the town's most venerable menus and at the deterioration of the kitchen. Then the doors were closed.

Then the doors were opened. The ancestors had come to the rescue. During the hiatus the old place was cleaned and tidied, but with little sacrifice of its jaunty primitiveness—the Goya etchings still hang next to the electrical conduit, the former now within restored gilt frames and freshened glass, the latter under new whitewash. The food, however, is not quite what it once was, though nary a morsel offends.

Even the exterior has been painted, and until the sun has set, a drink at one of the outdoor tables on this most sleazy corner of Greenwich Village is possible, if one is not depressed by the vista of parking garages, strolling trippers and the grim brick flank of the NYU law school. Access to the dining room is through the bar, a dim room with garish electric lights that somehow fail to illuminate, overstuffed black barstools, and machines that vend cigarettes or music. You eat in the back room, where those Goyas that occupy an entire wall are supplemented by mandatory art—a bullfighter fighting, a flamenco dancer dancing—a slowly spinning ceiling fan, and plastic ferns, all leftovers from the original regime. The tabletops are of pretty blue-and-green Spanish tiles (except for the larger linen-topped ones in the corners), the courteous waiters wear red jackets and make themselves easily available. You can have the place virtually to yourself if you eat at the standard American hour—as ever, Granados rarely begins to fill with its Village regulars until about ten o'clock, and it is often busy well past its official closing hour.

Familiarity and abundance are the game at Granados, and you may begin your dinner with a platter of Broiled Spanish Sausages that will provide morsels for a couple of couples. These are discs of simple sausage, little more than pork, fat and hot red pepper, broiled until they are crusty and almost completely drained of their grease, and brought to the table still sizzling. The Stuffed Mushrooms are comparatively tame, the caps filled with a mild white sauce, a bit of crab meat, and lots of fresh parsley, all adding up to a texture that is at once gooey and crisp. The standard Spanish Ham and Olives holds no surprises—the pink, slightly smoky cured meat hides the big platter it is served on, and it comes with vividly salty olives—very stimulating if you have not made contact with your appetite or thirst by the time you sit down to eat.

To Village octopus-eaters, Spanish octopus usually means El Rincon de Espana, an eating place a couple of blocks east of here that sports an outstanding and flavorful dish of that exotic meat. Granados' seafood dishes are prepared in the more elemental manner of the other side of the Iberian peninsula, and its Pulpo Salpicon is good, but in a plain way—lots of firm but tender chunks of the pale and slightly rubbery seafood, in a spicy, limpid sauce that is principally oil and pepper. Food for a simple hunger.

The Mariscada Ajillo is a substantial comedown. *Ajillo* means garlic, and though you can see dozens of bits of the minced bulb dancing about in the bubbling sauce, you must close your eyes and think hard to find its flavor behind the raw spice that inflames the liquid. The shrimp, sea scallops, mussels and little clams are not all those animals might be—a loud mussel here, a slightly pulpy shrimp there—but all is not for nothing, for the oily saffroned rice served with all main courses is splendid when moistened by the sauce of this dish. Good, if unspectacular, green-sauce dishes—crab meat, shrimp, lobster—the seafood itself suffers the occasional imperfections noted in the Mariscada, but the sauce is smooth, heavily laden with fresh parsely, rich and fragrant.

The pork with almond sauce is not what it once was. The thin slices of marinated meat are sweet and tender, but they lack the blackened crusty edges that made the dish; and the almond sauce, though generously studded with slivered nuts, has been thickened with starch or some such, and it is cloying. For each loser, however, there is a winner, in this instance the Veal Estremena, a powerful stew of browned veal, with green and red peppers, onions, peas and—the life of the party—chunks of strong Spanish sausage.

It must be noted that the revived Granados has turned its back on some of the best of its past—the game birds are gone from the menu. Tradition is served by the last course, as Granados passes the blindfold Spanish dessert test—the flan, natilla and guava with cream cheese are indistinguishable, by even the most refined of palates, from those served in 99 percent of New York's other Spanish restaurants.

★★ GRAND CAFÉ

28 East 63rd Street
LUNCH, MONDAY TO FRIDAY; DINNER, MONDAY TO SATURDAY. CLOSED SUNDAY.
Reservations, EL 5–2121.
Credit cards: AE, CB, DC, MC, V.
Expensive.

You probably didn't notice the demise of Passy, former occupant of these premises and, at the time of its belated passing, one of the most venerable (if no longer venerated) of New York's eating places. Passy (to give it a bit more space—after all, it was past forty before put to rest) was the grave of that ancient set that oscillated restlessly between Sutton Place and Newport in the days when those places were those places. The relationship between life expectancy and gender being what it is, Passy became a little-old-ladies' restaurant, complete with little old ladies. But they eat so little. And drink so little. Passy had to go.

The cup passeth—to New Jersey dentists (the early sittings only) and those to whom the source of money is virtually forgotten, how to dispose of it gracefully ingrained (they come later at night, to avoid the drillers). For the Grand Café is instantaneously in. And the past is part of the picture, the studiously faded elegance of the old place now so gaily burnished and prettied that we can indulge our lust for nostalgia without suffering any dust in our nose. Passy was originally put together when Art Deco was living its first life—that is to say, with restraint. As the proselyte out-adores the prophet, so this Deco revival outshines Passy.

You enter to a lofty anteroom watched over by murals of colorful goddesses of the Egyptian-sorceress persuasion: molded hair, tiaras, their bodies draped in brilliantly colored vestments, on their slender faces expressions of heavenly imperiousness. Under their gaze you may tipple, your torso ensconced in dove-gray velvet chairs, and heels of your shoes on buttonlike ottomans, your drink prettily set on glistening tables of jet-black glass.

Down the marble stairs to the spacious dining rooms, the dark-coral-pink walls spotted with circular mirrors the size of small ponds; massive pillars with ribbons of blue mirror running their full height; more of those Egyptian goddesses, these etched into the great sheets of glass that serve as partitions between the rooms; chandeliers of sinuously curved brass and white glass, strands of crystal beads hanging therefrom. And throughout, upon the plush and glowing carpet of rose and pale blue, are large, well-spaced tables covered with pearly gray linen. The Grand Café is a pretty place.

Even the food is pretty. Consider for example the Crabmeat and Spinach Pâté, looking so much like the national flag of a tasteful nation: a long narrow stripe of dark green between two broad bands of roseate white, this banner framed picturesquely by the contrasting colors of ripe tomato and herbed mayonnaise. That mayo is perhaps too salty, but the clear fresh taste of the ground crabmeat (studded with substantial chunks which avoided the grinder) carries the dish. The most ambitious and probably the best first course in the house is that Russian creation long ago affectionately adopted by the French, called Coulibiac. This exotic item consists of a flaky crust of brioche pastry filled with salmon that has been wrapped in rice, bits of egg and parsley. The secret of making this dish well is in the preparation of the individual ingredients—cooking the rice in fish broth, sautéeing the salmon with wine or shellfish or whatever will bring out the flavor, and the baking of the entire dish until the pastry is dark-gold and crackling. You get it that way here. Other perfectly good first courses include cold bass—flaky and fresh, not the least bit overcooked, but unfortunately served with that vastly oversalted green mayonnaise; slices of tender smoked turkey draped over chunks of unexceptional melon; and, in season, long thin shoots of asparagus in a splendid mustardy vinaigrette.

Both the lunch and dinner menus feature an inoffensive gimmick, explained this way: "Please note that each of the Grand Café's entrées are prepared in two styles—American and French." Perhaps this is just a polite but unenthusiastic gesture to us, for the only truly unacceptable food this establishment has served was a sautéed fish of the day, sole, in which the fish was so long past its freshness that one self-consciously expected aversive sniffs from nearby tables. But at the same time the house provides a splendid rolled filet of bass bathed in a pink crayfish sauce that is laced with chunks of shrimp—but this of course is a French preparation. You gamble again on the American column, and you do considerably better with "Crisp roasted duckling served with sweet plum sauce." The description is accurate; the duck sports a crisped skin (albeit somewhat toughened in the process), the meat is moist, if perhaps a bit too much of the fat has been drained off in the roasting, and the mound of dark, warm sweetened plums which surmounts the bird is velvet and wine—and if you artfully combine some of the fruit with every morsel of the bird, quibbles will be obviated. A bird in the French column is given to us as Poulet Sauté Richelieu, and described for us as "chicken sautéed with artichoke bottoms, carrots and celery," which, you will discover on sampling, establishes that hospital food need not be awful. For this is a simple dish—plain sautéed chicken, strands of vegetable across the top, nary a sauce in sight—but the ingredients are all so clearly of themselves, the chicken so tender, the fresh vegetables so assertive of their earthy flavors that the dish becomes an essay in support of the school of cooking which favors ingredients over improvements.

This establishment prepares what may be the best veal chop in town. Despite its admirable thickness, the center of this broiled chop is thoroughly cooked, without any toughening of the exterior. The white meat is moist and fibrous, the specks of brown are evidence of the butter that gives the meat a vaguely nutlike edge. That is the American version. For the French you simply add a crêpe and a creamy sauce that has been suffused with the vibrant flavor of green peppercorns—a strong flavor, to be sure, but one which does not conceal the sweetness of the chop. At lunchtime the house offers an interesting-sounding liver dish, Foie de Veau à l'Orange. Sounds fascinating, and it is therefore disappointing: perfectly decent liver, though sliced too thick, nicely grilled with a bit of flour on the meat to enhance the browning—but you wondered how they were going to make liver work with orange, and the answer is that they weren't. A dark sweet sauce with a vague memory of orange and a couple of minuscule sections of the fruit resting on the meat do not quite justify "à l'Orange." Lovely garnishes of fresh vegetables—mostly purées—accompany the main courses.

One fabulous dessert. A house-styled dacquoise which turns out to be an airy assemblage of crunchy meringue, abundant and ephemeral whipped cream, crumbs of pistachio nut, and glistening strawberries. There is really little point in deviating from that, for you may select from not much more than a couple of decent cheeses, fresh fruits, sherbets and ice cream. Don't pass up the dacquoise.

★★★★ LA GRENOUILLE

3 East 52nd Street
LUNCH AND DINNER. CLOSED SUNDAY.
Reservations, PL 2–1495.
Credit cards: AE.
Very expensive.

When Charles Masson died there was speculation as to the future of the famous restaurant he had built up. Surely his was the principal responsibility for the creation of this marvelous establishment. But in the care of his survivor, Gisèle Masson, it is today better than ever. Her method is simple: she is everywhere, watching, and setting an example of concern for detail that her employees follow. She is elegant and always unobtrusive, though the sometimes boorish crowd that mobs this place on weekend nights occasionally wears down her graciousness—leaving only a sturdy calm. On those occasions her maître, a mechanical little functionary who looks you directly over the right shoulder when you address him, has been known to hold tables near the front of the room while customers with reservations that were not honored on time are made to wait for something to open up in the back. This is an unpleasant fact of life for which Madame may well be ashamed. She gives no such sign. But Monday through Thursday the place is populated by ladies and gents who have just dropped in for a casual hundred-dollar dinner, little attention is paid to segregating money-come-latelies from the friends of the house, and the place is just one big happy family.

La Grenouille does something you want it to do—it dazzles, literally. You enter to a small room with a tiny, well-polished bar, a stunner on a perch behind the cash register, yet another behind the little counter in the hatcheck room. Just to the right of the entrance door is the great array of hors d'oeuvres and desserts, and to your left the dining room, with dozens of glowing sconces reflected in tall, broad mirrors, making the place shimmer. There are little lamps, like those on the walls, on all the tables along the rim of the room. And on every table, and in every corner, brilliantly colored flowers, thousands of them in all, so many that they are like part of the crowd. The expanses of the walls are painted a pale pea-green, and they are hung with scenic oils chosen for their predominance of darker greens—all that seems to recede, and everything about the place directs your attention to what glitters around you at table level.

Perhaps everyone who works here, with the exception of that maître, is a saint, or perhaps it is the effect of Madame's almost constant circulation in the aisles, but once you are seated, whether at the front, or back near the kitchen, you are treated like the prince you are—or should be. A waiter's jaw has been seen to drop like a weight when an empty water glass was pointed out to him. And the captains do not go off in search of a busboy to get you some bread when they are free to give it to you themselves. Madame's inquiries as to whether everything is all right are so warm, you fear that some of this Saturday-night crowd's metal-and-plastic hair and clothing will melt in her glow.

So you eat. From the assortment of hors d'oeuvres you select what you wish: an extraordinary céleri remoulade, in which the crisp strands of perfumed root are served in a sparkling, lemony dressing—it is almost a crime to eat this dish here, for once you do, it will taste right almost nowhere else; plump shrimp that seem to burst when you bite into them, in what must be called Russian dressing, though this is a mayonnaise that was made pink and seasoned the day you eat it; cool bass in more of that creamy mayonnaise, this batch flavored with fresh herbs and a rather heavy dose of salt; slivers of cucumber in a dressing that is little more than vibrant white vinegar; pungent pâté de campagne; slivered avocado, firm and nutty, in a polished, mustard-thickened vinaigrette.

You order a Truite Fumée and your captain displays the smoked fish to you on a silver platter. You nod. Off he goes to filet it, returning it to you with a pitcher of Sauce Raifort. The fish itself is perhaps no better than good smoked trout anywhere, but this horseradish-spiked whipped cream is at once airy and creamy and sharp.

Les Little Necks Corsini are served here by the hundreds every night, tiny clams in their shells, awash in melted butter that has been strengthened with good, sharp salt and made sweet and a little crunchy with coarsely chopped parsley—the clams are delicately garlicked, and though they are hot, they are impeccably tender. They have the sweetness of the clams of the day.

The Billi Bi aux Paillettes commands a premium of $2.75, which seems larky where the dinner prix fixe is $28.75, but whim will have its way. This is amazing soup, especially in that the strong flavor of the mussels in this thick and creamy broth is sharpened with brandy—lots of it, as much as such a soup could take without being made into a silly vehicle for a stiff drink—but it does not go over the edge. You have downed your cup and consumed the mussels you found at the bottom. Presently your captain blessedly shows up with a silver pot that holds yet another cup, and with his ladle he restores your delirious contentment.

How they get Sole Anglaise from Angleterre to East 52nd Street in this buttery condition should not concern you, since you are paying for whatever method they use. They do it, and they serve it as La Sole Anglaise des Gourmets, filets of the supple, gentle fish concealing a duxelles, under a white sauce that may give gilding the lily a good name. That duxelles, a hash of minced sautéed mushrooms, is of such concentrated mushroom flavor as to seem like the good earth itself. They may well have a special source for every special ingredient, for Les Grenouilles Provençale are made from the tiniest legs of the littlest frogs. They are lightly breaded and sautéed in a trice in garlic and butter; they are juicy and sharp and a little crisp, and they are graced with tomatoes that were cooked down with herbs until the resulting paste is like a dozen vine-ripened beauties concentrated into the volume of one.

La Poularde Poêlée à l'Estragon is a simple dish, a chicken roasted in a covered pot, its meat moist, its skin salty and a little crisp, served with a dark tarragon sauce that bristles with branches of the fresh herb; it is so thick with leaves of the herb that when you spoon the sauce over the bird, a green sediment is left on the meat—the scent of tarragon that rises from this dish is dizzying, the wild flavor of the dish almost shocking in its intensity. La Grenouille has always done wonders with chicken.

Surprisingly they list it as a specialty, for Le Steak au Poivre à la Fine does not seem like their kind of thing, steak studded with coarsely ground peppercorns being, simply, coarse. But if elegance can be made of this rather obvious invention, this is how it is done, with a brandied sauce of such rarefied headiness that the brusqueness of the spiced meat is overcome by the liquor. It is garnished, perfectly, with a small head of celery that has been braised apparently forever, until it is gentle, but somehow with no loss of strength.

La Grenouille makes dessert soufflés its own way, which is to say without egg yolks. The results are odd creations in which the browned tops have the flavor of meringues, the flavored centers the airiness and spirit of light mousses. The marvelous soufflé of raspberries is shot through with bits of berries, and it is moistened with a hot raspberry sauce—a wondrous, light dessert. Good fruit tarts; a chocolate cake in which the layers of dark moist cake alternate with layers of good mocha cream; the chocolate mousse is very rich without being at all insipid, though it is served with a crème Anglaise that is on occasion watery and dull. You are brought a fanciful plate of petits fours, in which the assorted cookies are laid out in the shape of a lobster. There aren't ten restaurants in New York where the best dessert is as lively as this little throwaway.

This place has far from the most extensive wine list in town.

★ GROTTA AZZURRA

387 Broome Street (near Mulberry Street)
LUNCH AND DINNER. CLOSED MONDAY.
No reservations (CA 6–9283).
No credit cards.
Beer and wine.
Medium-priced.

To love the Grotta Azzurra, as many do, you must suspend half a dozen common predispositions about comfort and courtesy. Except at off-hours, you must wait in line to get a table at this restaurant. If you're near the front of the line, you're one of perhaps eight people in a five-by-five vestibule just inside the front door—photographs of celebrities, plastic flowers, unspeakable writhing when, simultaneously, customers attempt to leave and those up next are summoned to the just-vacated table. Farther back in the queue, you wait on a marble stairway which descends to the aforementioned waiting room at an angle that is not quite sheer. You join with your neighbors in applauding the departing customers as they leave, bleary and contented, cigarettes hanging from their lips, each of them one obstacle less between food and you. At the very rear you're on the Broome Street sidewalk, under a plastic canopy—you regret not having brought a book; you discuss alternate restaurants within walking distance, and customers behind you tell you of the joys of Luna's, Forlini's, Angelo's; you try not to think about food. Once inside and seated, you ask a nearby waiter for a bottle of wine. He's not your waiter, so he just forgets about it. Five minutes later you ask another waiter, pointing out that you tried once before. He explains, with only a trace of contempt, that if you ask a waiter who is not your waiter, you can't expect to get what you ask for or anything else for that matter. You proceed to ask *him* ("your" waiter) for the bottle of wine, but it's sort of late, he yawns broadly while you ask, shudders, shakes off the sleeps and looks at you quizzically, so you ask again for, say, a bottle of Bardolino. On a good night he asks if you want it at room temperature or if you want it cold; on a bad night you just get it cold. On a good night you get Bardolino; on a bad night you get something else, already opened. On a good night the something else is Valpolicella, which is at least from the same country; on a bad night you get a bottle of something the label describes as "Claret wine" (from France), and, in fact, it is red, and it may have reached this country by way of France, but no more can be said for it.

The Grotta Azzurra is just a little hole in the ground that turned out to be a gold mine. It is small, low-ceilinged, garishly lighted, mirrored and muraled. There is sawdust on the tile floor. At the rear a handful of impassive, well-disciplined kitchen men are visible through a semicircular hole in the wall that is framed with copper pans. At the nearby register, Mama, under fifteen inches of copper hair, takes the cash. The boss, a couple of hundred very healthy pounds, barbershop-tanned, wanders around. He has grown into his diamond-studded ring so snugly that the stones barely peak out —only the most bloodthirsty mugger will ever get it off him. His tailored suits fit him more lightly, and his silver ties match his hairline mustache.

Although forty million New Yorkers can be wrong, in this case they are not entirely. With all its grotesqueries, this manages to be a good restaurant, partly as a result of the undampable good spirits of the customers (for them d'Grotta, as they call it, is a wondrous treat), and partly because of the sturdy, highly flavored food. Here heavy-duty eating and drinking are the thing—the terribly audible conversations are mostly between courses or between the waiters and the customers. One waiter to a large party: "Oo wants cannoli?" (six hands); "Oo wants chisscake?" (eight hands); "Oo wants spumoni?" (a chorus of boos); "Oo wants coffee?" (fourteen hands). The figures check.

The Steamed Clams Italian Style (they don't come any other style) are served in a sauce you will hear much of here—thick tomato sauce studded with chunks of garlic. The clams themselves, however, are of three generations, and in a seafood restaurant the grandfathers would be reserved for clam chowder—here it is not on the menu. The stuffed pepper is a huge red vegetable sautéed in oil, stuffed with a loud combination of capers, eggplant, chopped meat and chunks of garlic, and served under the Universal Sauce. If you tire of the sauce, you might try the stuffed artichoke—the vegetable itself is overcooked, so that the ends of the leaves are rather mushy, but the bread stuffing is nice and oily and spicy, and the heart tastes pretty good when you dip chunks of it in the pool of oil and garlic the thing is served in.

Of course there is pasta, with the usual sauces. But for an unusual sauce there is mussel sauce—good oil, fresh mussels, a few sautéed fresh mushrooms, the unavoidable garlic, and a handful of fresh parsley, served over carefully cooked linguine. Or you can have your pasta Sicilian style, which means with eggplant, and here the eggplant is battered and deep-fried before it is combined with the tomato sauce, blanketed with cheese and baked; not bad, and the dish contains a lot of garlic.

You ask that your "Calves Liver, Sauté Garlic & Oil" be served rare. "Of course," Mr. Waiter says, not exactly in polite acquiescence, rather in tones of disbelief that such a thing need even be mentioned. When it arrives you find you have no fork. And the waiter is gone! Presently he reappears, his arms burdened with gleaming metal casserole dishes, huge china platters, bowls of pasta. All for some other table. But he approaches to within three inches of *your nose.* Why? Then you perceive that from among the solidly balanced pyramid of plates protrude the tines of a fork. He knew! You extract it, he proceeds to the big table, and you proceed to eat what is a good change from the usual Liver Veneziana—garlic instead of onions, and the liver is tender and tasty.

For something really solid, and for at least three people, there is Chicken, Steak and

Sausage Contadino—a monster platter of sautéed chicken, strong sausages, chunks of beef (not your prime sirloin), red peppers, fresh mushrooms, and you guessed it, large pieces of garlic; to make the whole dinner "family style," you order Mixed Fried Vegetables—battered and deep-fried: zucchini (good, but not up to the best deep-fried zucchini in town—too much taste of batter, too little crispness of zucchini); mushrooms; fresh cauliflower (it, too, could be crisper); rice balls mixed with cheese; pieces of mozzarella cheese that are gooey and pully inside their crisp wrapper; and potato croquettes.

The famous cheese cake is nothing much. The cannoli are filled with a thick custard that is flavored with anise. The coffee is good and comes in a glass, spoon standing within.

Get out your low-cut, bare-midriff whatever, your dark glasses; make sure your hair is blue; a couple of over-the-shoulder pelts would be nice. His glasses should have half-inch-thick frames; his fingernails should be shiny. And wait in line. Before six-thirty and after ten you can usually get a table promptly. Frank Costello no longer comes here. When he did, he did not wait in line.

• HARVEY'S CHELSEA RESTAURANT

108 West 18th Street
LUNCH AND DINNER.
Reservations, CH 3–5644.
No credit cards.
Medium-priced.

Someone has found an ancient saloon that, beneath its ninety years of grime, was solid mahogany and sparkling glass. He scraped it all down, polished it up, added a few brass touches of his own, and brought forth this child of the turn of the century. The long bar is on your right as you enter, behind it a great triptych of huge mirrors, elaborately carved-and-lathed wood ornamentation, cabinets fronted by cut-glass doors, an aged clock with a gleaming pendulum. Restaurant or no, this is surely Chelsea's most commodious drinking place, and the broad and handsome wooden counter is being regularly buffed by a rainbow of tweeded elbows. This may be the seed of the rebirth (or is it the first birth?) of Chelsea, in recent years New York's dullest enclave.

Opposite the bar there are a handful of tables, unclothed, supplied with paper napkins, and to these one repairs if a number of drinks yield an unplanned hunger, the kind that may be assuaged by hamburgers, Reuben sandwiches and such. But when calling ahead, specify a table in the back room (not the downstairs spare room), for here, under a deep-green ceiling and chandeliers of frosted-glass lanterns, surrounded by hanging plants in clay pots that are suspended on brass chains, one has something of the sense of being back in the long ago. You hang your coat on one of the brass coat hooks mounted on the polished wooden walls, sit yourself at one of the white-linened tables, munch, in an instant compulsion, on the hot, raisin-studded soda bread that was delivered by a waiter who is wearing a long-sleeved white shirt, black bow tie, and a white apron that reaches almost to the floor, and order from a menu that is a conglomerate of traditional German, British and American food, with a little indeterminate Continental thrown in.

The last category is the one to avoid, as in Quiche Lorraine, made on a well-browned crust, but this peppery stuff is far from the light custard you have a right to expect from anything going by the name. Never mind the Herring in Sour Cream, too, for if this does not come from a jar, it might as well; it lacks the spanking vibrance of freshly pickled herring, and the onions in the sour cream are limp. Opt instead for the Split Pea & Ham Soup, thick and spicy, studded with bits of salty meat and crisp croutons. And avoid with determination the soup listed as Onion au Gratin, au horrors, the American cheese with which this bland broth is topped is still square and orange and tasteless when it reaches you.

If at this point you cancel the balance of your order and leave, you would be making a decision that in most such instances would be sound. But, astonishment, many of the main courses here are good to eat, such as the Roast Duck in Plum Sauce. That sauce is hardly more than a bit of lightly fruited moisture, but the bird is crisply roasted, its meat lightly fatted and tender, and it is served with good rice and, on occasion, crisp, vividly green broccoli. Then there is the German Mixed Stew. Now this is a *stew*, not a fricassee, which means that the meat is not browned before it is cooked in its liquid. This is an assortment of meats, lamb, pork and beef, boiled with potatoes and strewn with peas and carrots, a weighty dish almost totally without sharp flavors, but satisfying if you don't insist on sparkle in everything you eat. The Alsatian Sausage & Hot Potato Salad is another winner, a hefty and well-fatted sausage in a crackling casing, heavily peppered, served with a hot potato salad that is strongly flavored with mustard and herbs and vinegar. The Broiled Scallops are simply terrible.

The Pecan Pie seems, on one occasion, to be walnut pie, served with decent whipped cream—the pie is heavily flavored with cinnamon, the nuts are many and crunchy. The Apple Strudel is not bad, and the Black Forest Cake, yet another vehicle for much whipped cream, is a kind of baker's sundae, a black cake garnished with the cream, ground nuts and cherries.

Your check arrives with a stein of after-dinner mints—*such* a nifty touch. And when you pay it your money is rung up in a huge, gilded cash register. The hamburgers, sausages and sandwiches are good and inexpensive, but the steaks are priced in the uptown manner and they are not worth the cost.

★ HERMITAGE

251 East 53rd Street
LUNCH AND DINNER. CLOSED SUNDAY.
Reservations, 421–5360.
Credit cards: AE, DC.
Very expensive.

Most of New York's more pretentious French restaurants are blondes and strawberry blondes, their pastel and pale citron colors illuminated with golden light, the velvets and flowers and bright murals like ribbons and pretty dresses on golden girls. But this place has darker good looks, umber-colored beams crisscrossed on rough plaster that is the color of old ivory, dark-brown leather banquettes, black-enameled chairs, dusky carpeting. The walls of beveled mirrors, like myriad window panes in their cream-colored frames, are jewelry against these dark, dressy colors. The white linen is set with white china that is rimmed with black and a bit of gold; there are dark flowers in gray pewter pitchers; little pewter lamps with jet-black shades make islands of light on each table.

You enter to an anteroom that has a glittering little bar and a few cocktail tables with tops of crystalline glass. You are greeted by a gentleman who can only be described as tall and handsome. He is also at once brisk and unctuous, a combination he manages by vigorously rubbing his hands together while he nods, grins and heaves his chest. He bends over to the kisses of disagreeable old women. If there is a man behind these manners, he is a continent from his work, which is carried out for him by a switched-on glad-hander who resides in his body. You are led to your table promptly enough, but there is always the danger that, sometime during your repast, Good Looking will approach to ask if everything is quite all right.

It is a relief from The Land of Smiles to be in the hands of either of the two captains who work this place. Not only do they conduct their discourse with you in the manner of one civilized mortal to another, but they know the menu, they answer questions patiently and fully, and they grin only appropriately.

The menu is a rare one for these parts, dominated by fish and shellfish in an extensive range of French preparations and sauces that is slightly fascinating. You figure that whoever made up this selection has a passion, and that is usually a good sign. But one must conclude that this enthusiasm is not a passion at all, but a matter of marketing. Apparently this place, like its clientele, is following not zeal, but fashion—the trend to seafood among diners in New York's French restaurants—for the food, though mostly fine, lacks the touch of a zealot chef.

Your captain suggests Malpeque oysters, not listed on the menu, all the way from Canada, special. You are enthusiastic. On the trip south, alas, they have lost the plump, firm, juicy brilliance that characterizes this breed of mollusk at its best. When oysters and clams are really fresh, they are not only tender, but resilient; the bluepoints and littlenecks you get here are usually that way, the Malpeques not. Smoked trout is available all over town, but this place, happily, serves smoked eel as well. You are brought four substantial shafts of the pale meat, delicate and sea-gamy: unfortunately, it is garnished with a shortcut sauce Raifort—horseradish in sour cream—which is nice; instead of the real thing—horseradish in whipped cream—which can be marvelous. So is the very good cold bass, which is utterly fresh, the meat falling into moist flakes at the prod of your fork, but the herb sauce that comes with it, which could have a clear, green flavor, is almost killed by an excess of salt.

Surely the most picturesque item in the house is the Terrine de Poisson, a rosy-pale slice of fish pâté at the center of your plate, a pool of thick sauce, burnt orange in color, around it. The ground fish is a little bland, though it is sweet and delicately peppered, but the sauce makes the dish: it is like a subtle gazpacho, a thick, herbed tomato purée that is polished with oil and lightly garlicked. There is a red-meat pâté as well, a good coarse version, spicy and well fatted, bits of truffle throughout.

A couple of hot first courses are first-rate. The Mousse de Brochet is an airy, fluffy fish dumpling, the size of a cupcake, with the vivid flavor of lightly peppered pike. It is covered with a pink crayfish sauce on one side—it has a clear but restrained flavor of lobster shell—and a polished white-wine sauce on the other.

Hermitage is famous for its fish soup, a heavy brown liquid, oily and oceanic, studded with bits of seafood and strands of firm noodle. Slices of dark toasted bread come in each serving, their crustiness marvelous against the powerful flavor of the soup. If that is not enough, you may spoon in a thick, strong garlic sauce as well.

Sole, salmon, red snapper, striped bass and turbot are all on the menu, but you take your chances here when you drop $12 to $16 for fish and sauce. They brought this turbot from a long way away, and they serve it with a hollandaise that is rich and tart —but the fish has been poached until flat. And this bass, which is from nearby waters, was clearly a day or two on the ice. But then on another day you get perfect snapper, delicately fibrous, nutty, artfully broiled, with a Béarnaise sauce that is about as good as you can make it, lacking fresh tarragon. Best of the lot is the salmon in sorrel sauce —the fish is broiled to the point at which its flavor is sharpened by light browning, without being dried; it is served with a pale and gentle sauce that is accented with a bit of sorrel. La Timbale de Homard Robert is an odd admixture of lobster, lamb kidneys and scallops, in a sauce that is like lobster bisque, served up in a casserole with a circlet of browned mashed potatoes around its rim. Anything is possible, but here this does not blend; moreover, the scallops are overcooked and tough, and the kidneys lack the sweetness perfect rinsing would give them. Les Crevettes Espagnole Provençale is a nice enough dish of fresh, crunchy shrimp in a frank tomato sauce that has been fortified with hot pepper.

For seafood unenthusiasts an excellent steak is available in a lightly vinegared sauce, which just sets off the juicy meat; and a perfectly roasted chicken in tarragon sauce that would be superb if the man in the kitchen had a tasty bird to begin with.

The salad of watercress, endive and bibb lettuce is crisp, refreshing and immense.

Your captain confesses that the cheese is kept in the icebox—this clientele knows not of cheese. The soufflés are good, if not spectacular, the chocolate version notable for a fine intensity of bitter-chocolate flavor. The Paris Brest, that sometimes marvelous dessert of hazelnut cream between layers of pastry, is here made with good, nut-flavored cream and tough dough. Decent mousse and tarts.

All Smiles bows you out with words of devotion.

★★HISAE'S FISH PLACE

570 Hudson Street (at 11th Street)
DINNER.
Reservations, CH 3–4212.
No credit cards.
Inexpensive.

Growing boys are the natural clientele of this feed box. The giant servings look like mirages of the starving. The youngsters' gratification is not only enough, but instant, for there are crudités waiting for them on the table when they sit down. Hisae's Fish Place is a misplaced enclave of the little-known Sino-Japanesque-Italianate Seafood Gobblers (a cult that adores New England desserts), and so there are bean sprouts in among the strands of carrot, discs of zucchini, florets of broccoli. To dip any of the last three into the jigger of mustardy sauce is easy. To dip a bean sprout is not. It bends, refuses to pierce the surface by force of its weight. All around the room the lads are experimenting to determine which end of the sprout punctures best. Then they munch the wonderful whole-wheat bread while evaluating their data.

Actually, it is the young of all ages and genders who come here. The youthful clean traipse all the way across the Village from NYU to eat very inexpensively, as do Christopher Street gays, cautious Dutch-treaters. No limousines waiting at the curb, cabs do not pull up, there is not a perm or a tiepin in the place.

The pine walls are hung with photos and prints, coats and hats. Brick, green plants and plain wooden tables emphasize the innocuous cliché, the bar contradicts it, the posters of fruits and breads fight back: a dozen or so varieties of peaches, fuzzy skins showing in the full views, pits in the cross sections; apples, pears; Near Eastern breads and Jewish breads at peace on one chart. They do not say the word, but "healthfood" is in the air, and the waiters and waitresses, youthful and cheerful, advertise it well. The middle-aged come here to be depressed.

The copiousness of the portions of Sautéed Beansprouts with Nuts and Raisins is limited only by the size and shape of the platters they are served on. This is a wonderful first course, the grassy sprouts crisp, oiled and garlicked, intermingled with walnut halves and juicy black raisins. Equally massive is the Broccoli in Garlic Oil, an inverted chandelier of the green vegetable, crunchy and hot, its buds in a pool of oil that is loud with the flavor of fresh garlic. Regulars know that either of those appetizers will suffice for two; newcomers are so advised by the help. The artichoke is too cold, it is occasionally overcooked, and it is too gentle a vegetable to be served with strong mustard sauce. An off-the-menu appetizer of conch salad consists of chunks of the gray shellfish meat and strands of translucent onion in oil and garlic; squeeze on the lemon—it is essential to complete the dressing—but nothing will help the slight toughness of the conch itself.

The best main courses are the whole fishes, however prepared. The Brook Trout with Black Mushrooms & Sesame Seeds is about as good as a trout can be when it has not been assassinated a moment before its preparation. It is tender, flaky and sweet, and comes in a soy-sauce broth aswim with browned sesame seeds, mushrooms and scallions. The Sea Bass with Black Beans & Ginger is about as long as the tables are wide, and as fresh as sea air. It comes in the same soy-sauce broth as the trout, the black beans and ginger tasty, but with little effect on the liquid. Much of the food available any given day is not listed on the menu—on occasion red snapper. They select only the snapper that could feed a small family, sauté it until the snowy meat is bursting through the copper scales of its skin, and serve it under dunes of sautéed, browned garlic bits and chopped parsley—a simple and wondrous dish.

They steam lobsters well, if not invariably to the perfect point, but, aside from that, shellfish is not their strength. The Shrimp with Oriental Vegetables—an array of Chinese greens, all of them crunchy, mingled with metallic-tasting shrimp—is an exercise in marathon chewing, for there are a million miles of fiber in all this celery and Chinese cabbage, broccoli, snow peas and bean sprouts. The Broiled Sea Scallops are plump, nicely browned, tender and, somehow, devoid of richness—they are adorned only with a sprinkling of parsley.

Splendid desserts, displayed on a couple of counters near the back. The yogurt prune cake is little more than a good moist cake in a thin icing, its yogurt content taken on faith; but the layer of nuts and pitted prunes just below the top surface makes the dish rich and vaguely exotic. Good carrot cake, spicy and nutted and moist. There is a rich chocolate mocha cake and a Key lime pie on a crunchy graham-cracker crust that has a vivid flavor of fresh lime. A substantial dollop of thick whipped cream is available with all of these, and also with the strawberries, of which a few, on occasion, are not first-class. Fruit pies, tarts, cobblers. Good coffee.

The most you can pay for a bottle of wine is $6. The background music is mostly Mozart. The cigarette machine is in the men's room.

★★HO'S PAVILION

324 East 44th Street
LUNCH AND DINNER.
Reservations, 986–3775.
Credit cards: AE, DC, MC, V.
Medium-priced.

A lengthy menu of almost unparalleled breadth and a range of quality almost as wide. They only rarely come up with a truly bad dish of food, and so, what with the moderate prices, you can satisfy an awful lot of culinary curiosity by eating here once a week for a year, hardly repeat yourself, encounter a good bit of surprising food, and almost never have a disappointing meal. Ho's serves dishes of all the currently fashionable provinces, and though you might reasonably expect them to do one region better than another, no such pattern has been detected.

The Pavilion has gone to no lengths to revolutionize the look of Chinese restaurants, though your reception, by a fetching Occidental in a Chinese dress just this side of topless, is steakhouse cheery—like many such functionaries, she walks you to your table with a drum majorette's strut but merely slinks back to her post. Copper-colored metallic walls, others of patterned gold, paper lanterns, Chinese paintings, a burly Buddha, the Chinese-restaurant-works—but in this dim light it all seems cheerful. And despite its recent vintage, the place has its regulars; they like the place, and they roll up their sleeves to eat.

If you opt to participate in the Ho's Pavilion Gourmet Dinner ($9.75 p.p.), you start off with Assorted Hot Appetizers. Now, you are dealing here with charming young waiters whose English is best described as ardent, and when you cup your hand behind your ear and say "Eh?," the man's misassembled words are repeated as was, no rebuilding having intervened. Thus one element of the Hot Appetizers, conveyed, one swears, as "crabmeat roll," must be described as a disc of pork sausage, like a Chinese saucisson chaud, circled by a ribbon of pastry—it is spicy and warm, and it glistens with oil. The dish that most Chinese menus give as Cellophane Wrapped Chicken is made here in aluminum foil—you break open the wrapper and you find that your little cutlet of chicken is steamy, moist and smoky—very good, and too little of it. The spring roll, unfortunately, is in a dough that puts one in mind of a street vendor's rewarmed blintz, and the house is fresh out of sour cream. The Hot and Sour Soup is not particularly hot and not especially tart, and the noodles and bean curd and water chestnuts therein are wilted. But if you lost interest in wonton soup a generation or so back, set aside your ancient prejudice, for this is an exceptional version, studded with strands of strong ham, peas and shrimp, and the wonton itself, a crisp little noodle bow tie stuffed with delicate meat is, perfect.

Among the more impressive productions of the establishment is the one called simply Crisp Fish. This is a great, craggy striped bass that has been battered and deep-fried until its exterior is as rugged-looking as gnarled bark—but within is this abundance of flaky fish, and the dish is served with a thick spicy sauce snappy with fresh ginger and scallions. The Hot Spiced Lobster is fresh and copious, served virtually buried in a thick and crunchy sauce, the fiery spice of which is augmented with scallions and garlic. This place prepares a splendid version of Hunan Beef, and what differentiates it from most Chinese beef dishes around town is the restrained but very hot sautéeing applied to the meat, so that it is deeply browned, pink and moist within—true of every little morsel of beef that appears on your dish. It is garnished with fresh watercress, and both the meat and the green are moistened with hot, peppered oil. Amazingly, the very same establishment produces this so-called Pressed Duck, in which boned duck is compacted into rectangular solids about half the size of children's building blocks. These tasteless objects are stacked like cobblestones at the curb and brought to you with a sauce that may well be a compound of flour and canned gravy. The Tangy and Spicy String Beans are sautéed with ground pork in a peppery oil; they are crisp and slightly and pleasantly leathery, and the bits of blackening here and there add a smoky flavor.

Better-than-average Banana Fritters: they use ripe bananas, which they cook until hot, coat with honey and sesame seeds, and cool until crusty—the soft, sweet bananas within remain warm.

★★HUNAM

845 Second Avenue (near 45th Street)
LUNCH AND DINNER.
Reservations, MU 7–7471.
Credit cards: AE, CB, DC.
Medium-priced.

When this place first appeared, the *Times* announced that heaven had opened a branch on Second Avenue. Anyone can make a mistake. But then, about a year later, the *Times* checked and *confirmed* that heaven was doing business on Second Avenue. People who know heaven when they eat at it pooh-poohed and entertained uncharitable Emersonian thoughts about the dimensions of minds that are foolishly consistent. This restaurant serves some paradisaic food, but also some that is quite mundane. This restaurant is to be thanked for introducing the food of Hunan to the citizens of New York. But much about the place is hell on earth.

Hunam is a noisy madhouse of a restaurant. If you manage to overhear any conversation at the table that is one inch from your own, like as not what you hear will be "What did you say?"

So is it worth it? Well, yes. But try this restaurant in the off-hours, unless you dig aural and optical cacophony. And try to start your dinner with Turnip Cake—balls of moist ground turnip, crisp outside, only vaguely turnipy, sweet, light, appetizing. Do *not* start your dinner with Crisp Chicken with Peanuts—slabs of dry, puttylike chicken, crisped, and coated with stale-tasting peanuts. Proceed, most assuredly, to Hunam Preserved Duck, a singular dish (your captain may try to talk you out of it, explaining that most customers don't like it, but persist). The dish does have one off-putting characteristic—abundant duck fat, but when duck is steamed this way, with the fat in place, the meat remains astonishingly moist. It is steamed over ground pork, and the entire product tastes vaguely smoky and has a subtle citrus-fruit flavor—wondrous.

The dish here that has received a great deal of publicity is Hunam Beef. This is eminently edible food—the beef in a hot, clear, oily sauce made with red peppers and an intensity of garlic, the watercress a crisp, leafy garnish that sets it off perfectly. Beef is also served here in the form of Orange Flavor Beef, and unlike most of the orange-flavored dishes served in the Szechuan and Hunan restaurants around town, the flavoring in this dish is of the juicy inside of the orange, not the rind. The dish is hot and spicy, the beef is tender, there are bamboo shoots here and there, and to eat it is to decide that almost anything can be successfully cooked with almost anything. Who would have featured beef cooked with orange juice?

The Sliced Leg of Lamb, Hunam Style, is a very highly flavored as well as seasoned dish, so much so that the flavor of the meat is virtually obscured. It must be lamb, but it is hard to tell. In any event, the dish is made with an abundance of huge shiny mushrooms, crisp scallions, and onions, all in a thick fiery sauce that is densely flavored with garlic—good stuff.

Another good dish is something called Shrimp Puff in Ginger Sauce, and what is meant by "puff" nobody knows. The dish consists of a huge mound of good firm shrimp in a dark viscous sauce that is thoroughly gingered. Avoid, however, Fillet of Sea Bass with Shrimp Roe Sauce. Sounds interesting? Comes out flavorless fish with snow peas.

The Honey Crisp Bananas are dreadful, and you will not be surprised to learn that the *Stuffed* Honey Crisp Bananas are also dreadful.

★★ HUNGARIA

153 East 53rd Street
LUNCH AND DINNER.
Reservations, 755–6088.
Credit Cards: AE, DC, MC, V.
Expensive.

At Hungaria five Hungarian gentlemen play musical instruments while you dine. They are a "gypsy orchestra," we are told, from Budapest. During their gypsy wanderings they have picked up, among other things, "Lady of Spain," "Granada," the "Saber Dance," "Whispering" and, available by request, "Happy Birthday." These men have the bored mechanical demeanor of hack musicians everywhere. When the violinist retires to the back of the room to suck on cigarettes, the lead is taken by a clarinetist given to acrobatic, squeaky tootlings. The schmaltzy Gypsy fiddling is thin on sentiment; the fast and furious dance music lacks the essential touch of frenzy. No one seems to mind. The clientele are largely members of New York's *Mitteleuropean* expatriate community, and they are delighted to have a new gathering place. Sometimes four of the five musicians wander among the tables to play for tips (the fifth goes for a smoke because he cannot carry his instrument—the cembalom—with him), and the customers attend eagerly, following them with happy homesick eyes. This restaurant is fun. The scene is at once a little sad and a little hilarious.

There is a massive triangular bar just off the front of the restaurant, a few tables opposite one side, semiprivate draped booths—with sofas—adjacent to another; side three gives directly on the dining room proper, which is fitted out with crockery on the papered walls, homey little framed photographs, lampposts, folk art, Magyar murals, leather-upholstered benches with big brass Old World upholstery tacks. The most ridiculous *objet* in the place is the so-called "sausage tree," a pathetic leafless sapling, or rendition thereof, sausages hanging from its branches—it is the centerpiece of the restaurant. There are two small rooms off the main room, made to look like middle-class dining rooms in comfortable middle-class houses, complete with clumpy dining tables and straight-backed wooden chairs; and there is a quasi-pantry at the rear, with cabinets and drawers and a blue tile counter. But with all the paraphernalia, when the place is less than crowded, it has the quality of a bare room with lots of things in it. You get the impression that with one truck to empty the place and another to bring stuff in, this could be an Italian restaurant in twenty-four hours.

But some of the food is delicious, a lot of it is new to these parts, and the service —though often inadequate to the press of business, and plagued by plates and tray stands that insist on flinging themselves to the hardwood floor—has been earnest and charming in the face of much impatience. Try this place, but not when you are in a hurry.

The sausages from the tree make up saját felvágottaink, Asztalos hentes módján (hereafter no more Magyar), a decent but uninspired selection of strong sausages. Pass up the mousse of chicken liver, which is wet and sour, and eschew the calf's brains and scrambled eggs—often a marvelous dish in New York's Hungarian restaurants—served here in a limp version that suggests it is made in batches and held until ordered. Choose instead the wine-marinated cold carp, tart breaded fish, suffused with the flavor of its marinade, deserving of a stronger garnish than these tired onions.

The best first course in the house is the fried pancake Fehervar, a crusted, deep-fried crêpe roulade, stuffed with ground meat and sautéed green peppers, served with a hot vegetable stew of peppers, tomatoes, onions and salt pork. A close contender is the gulyas soup, the hot potato-thickened broth studded with chunks of meat, slivers of red pepper, and little chunks of dumpling.

What is marvelous about the homemade skillet-fried sausages is that the three varieties are so vividly different from one another: one is iron-gray, stretched with rice, spicy, mellifluous; the second is fatty and red, heavily flavored with strong paprika; the third is black and bloody. They are served with sweet cabbage and a pork chop, the relatively dry meat of the chop a nice contrast to the juicy sausages. The venison with plum sauce is a medallion of tender browned meat with a lovely garnish of stewed plums and oranges—the dish is served with something called a "pheasant dumpling," which does a terrific imitation of a baseball of bread stuffing. Good roasted veal shank, blackened, crusted and tender, though this kind of a dish is better when it is cooked until it is almost falling apart—it is served with a tasty sauce/stew of vegetables, liver and bacon. The most notable fact about the dish of grilled meats on a skewer is that it is served on a board that occupies a third of your rather wee table—the beef, pork and veal, though artfully browned, are undistinguished meat, but the peppers and onions that alternate with them on the skewer are nice and crisp. The paprika chicken is fine, and the sometimes available roast chicken Transylvania is crisp and spicy, though it is burdened with a lifeless stuffing.

Such items as the stuffed filet of beef and the stuffed dilled cabbage with pork chops and sausage are dishes of such unrelieved weightiness as to be unappealing to anyone who was not brought up on that kind of thing.

The heavy meals here can be leavened with a very crispy, tart, subtly sweetened cucumber salad or a nice dish of sauerkraut stuffed into red peppers.

Other than the purée of chestnuts with whipped cream—a frankly rich dessert that makes no pretense of being anything more—and a nice apple strudel made with firm, tart apples, the desserts are comedowns. The poppy-seed strudel is heavy and greasy, the stuffed pancakes leaden. The coffee, it seems, is never good. The best closer in the place is the Hungarian Tokay, a strong wine that is tangy and sweet without being sugary.

★★ INDIA PAVILION

325 East 54th Street
LUNCH, MONDAY TO FRIDAY; DINNER, DAILY
Reservations, 838–9702.
Credit cards: AE.
No liquor.
Inexpensive.

This little cave is a bit ramshackle, but that is obscured by the gay cheer of the young people who often crowd it from end to end of its long narrow dining room. The ceiling is low, almost everyone sits at one of the long row of small tables; for larger parties there are a couple of booths and two large tables at the rear, on a platform. The cursory decorations include carved wooden screens, a hammered brass medallion, an Indian stringed instument mounted on the wall. During the days of intense cold a space heater glowed from a cranny at the rear. The menus have been heavily emended by hand, but they still sport some of the lowest prices for good food anywhere in midtown Manhattan. You bring your own alcohol, too, so eating here is like putting aside a little something for your dotage. Many domestic jugs and imported magnums are in evidence —this food creates thirst.

The greeting and much of the serving are performed by a stocky, swarthy Indian whose smile makes of his face a dark sun and whose accent makes of the English language a melody played on a golden horn. Sometimes he is assissted by a lady, a compatriot of ample substance, in a snug coverall. They are a casual two, to be sure, friendly and smiling, but they take their work, as they say, to heart, which gives them and the place dignity.

Begin your dinner here with the India Fried Shrimp, small crunchy shrimp in a thick, dark sauce that is at once hot and sweet. Do not make the error of drinking beer with this kind of food, for these sauces are laced with vegetables and sweet spices, and wines of all kinds are fine with them, beer all wrong. Another good way to start is with the Assorted Hors d'Oeuvres, a collection of fruit and vegetable turnovers and fritters, battered, deep-fried—gentle food, each of the items distinctive of its principal component: chickpeas and green peas, bananas and potatoes, eggplant and whatever. They are served with a heavy sauce that is like a thick plum preserve. The

Mulligatawny is like a heavy split-pea soup laced with a leafy vegetable, and you wish it were much hotter, for it is a little leaden at this tepid temperature.

Your Chicken Tandoori is the familiar dramatic thing, red and black, spicy and moist, the lightly burnt edges of the rather huge half-bird like a built in zest. The dish is not made from a great chicken—it is probably frozen—but the preparation yields a sturdy plate of food. A Mrs. Kalayaniwalla, the menu informs you, is a winner of many prizes for cooking in India, and you are informed further that she has released her secret recipe for Moghali Badami Duck to our own India Pavilion. This is a spiced roasted duck, moist and crisp, almost crackling, and it is served with a vividly contrasting sauce that is as grainy as cereal, slightly sweetened, and made high by a heavy dose of coriander leaves—this is a long way from the underspiced spicy food you get in most Indian restaurants.

Those curries and vindaloos are served here, too, and according to yet another pronouncement on the menu, "Our curries are medium spiced. Hot sauce served on request." Don't make the request, for one man's medium is another's massacre, and a searingly hot sauce that is but a dash of salt to an Indian is probably the obliteration of all flavor to your unaccustomed palate. If you like the aroma of lamb, cooking, you will probably like the Lamb Curry here, for the aroma of lamb on the fire is principally that of lamb fat, and this spicy stew is like a distillate of that flavor, gamy and rich, perfumed with coriander. The Beef Vindaloo is yet another powerful stew, filled with huge chunks of fibrous beef, the thick and spicy sauce suggesting oils and vegetables. These things come with fluffy, buttery rice, mysteriously tasty, though the saffron with which it is allegedly made is difficult to detect. Of the breads, the paratha lacks the richness of the best versions, but the puri, that airy pillow of glistening, glazed dough is superbly delicate next to this substantial food. The pickles, chutneys and yogurt are fine, the usual thing. The dahl, the tradional purée of lentils, is tastier than most because it is mingled with those fragrant coriander leaves. Sometimes you think they do things just for laughs, and as you sample an unheralded garnish of spicy raw onions, you realize you are being watched by your host. "Onions too hot for you, sir?" He seems to sing the question, smiling a little like a prankster. You need something to quiet those onions: "May I have a little more rice?" "By all means! Lot more!"

Splendid Bakhlawa, a flaky top, center of crunchy honeyed nuts, a bottom crust of browned and honey-soaked pastry. The two other Eastern desserts will strike you perhaps as interesting. There is ice cream and, surprisingly, awful tea.

The slightly mournful strains of Indian music make a background of soft sound. When things are slow a sinister chap in sweater, scarf and apron seems to make several extra trips from the kitchen through the dining room to the facilities. Sometimes the lights go off when a novice customer brushes the light switch while hanging his coat in the self-service coat room.

★★ITALIAN PAVILION

24 West 55th Street
LUNCH AND DINNER. CLOSED SATURDAY AND SUNDAY.
Reservations, JU 6–5950.
Credit cards: AE, CB, DC.
Expensive.

This is a gracious and comfortable restaurant with food that is always reliable, occasionally excellent. It has long been a lunchtime hangout for the publishing world. Nobody knows why. More mysterious is why they choose to eat in the commonplace, albeit comfortable, front room, when the year-round garden room, with its tall windows, is bright and airy and pleasant, despite the inelegant vista of a New York backyard planted in vines. Perhaps the dim interior is a fitter setting for the cunning proposals that lure literary talents into the traps of the book industry.

Between lunchtime proposals you might try the Fonduta—a thickened mixture of cheese and eggs, cooked together and then fried, to form a nice brown crust; or perhaps the thinly sliced, pale, slightly smoky ham, with a couple of slices of ripe melon. Since most of the appetizers here are items you can get anywhere—clams, oysters, shrimp, smoked salmon or trout—the pastas are a more interesting beginning. The linguine with white clam sauce, for one, is made with an abundance of fresh clams, added to the sauce just as it is being completed, so that they are tender and briny. If you like this dish made with lots of garlic, you had better so specify because the inclination of the house is toward a rather pure but slightly bland version. A specialty of the house is Fettuccine Pavilion—the noodles are carefully prepared, so that they are neither gummy nor hard, and the sauce is a thick and oily tomato sauce, heavily flavored with garlic and mixed with chunks of smoky ham. The Cannelloni Bolognese are stuffed with herbed veal and covered with a mature meat sauce that you can awaken and improve by adding a couple of ample spoons of the good grated Parmesan cheese that is served here.

In season the Italian Pavilion offers shad roe, and as in most restaurants, it is cooked too long, so that the rich and oily quality is lost. You're better off with some of the dishes for which the place is known. What is Suprema di Pollo alla Doria? It is tender, white chicken, sautéed until it is nicely browned, served in a thick, thick sauce of cream and cucumbers; it is very intelligently served with perfectly made white rice on which you spoon your extra sauce when you have finished your chicken. What is the Osso Buco like here? It is tender—falling off the bone, as they say—browned outside but still moist, and served with Risotto Milanese—rice heavily flavored with fragrant saffron. Good vegetables: the asparagus is carefully peeled, so that it is tender, not stringy, and it is served under a filmy layer of melted cheese and a lightly fried egg; if you order your spinach with garlic, it is made to your order, and the distinctive mineral taste of the fresh spinach is well seasoned with fresh garlic.

The desserts are few and traditional. A moist, rummy Zuppa Inglese, carefully prepared zabaglione, and the usual ice cream and custard things. Better to order some more red wine and dunk your Amoretti. It takes about 150 Amoretti to soak up one bottle of wine, so you may wish to drink as well as dip.

There is an abundance of help at this restaurant, strained only when every table is taken, and the service is professional—available, polite, friendly. The captains wander around in search of wishes to fill.

★★ LE JACQUES COEUR

448 East 79th Street
DINNER, TUESDAY TO SUNDAY. CLOSED MONDAY.
Reservations, 249–4920.
Credit cards: AE, MC, V.
Medium-priced.

A neat little bar at the front, a couple of rows of tables in the back, perhaps a dozen, along two parallel banquettes. Simple modern armchairs of bentwood and woven-cane seats. The carpeting is warm red. One wall is dark-mirrored, the one opposite is ivory, hung with prints and plates. At the back a glass-doored refrigerator with desserts and cold wine. All is prim and trim, bordering on the antiseptic, but managing to avoid it. There are flowers on the tables, but *the* flower is your hostess, a pleasant and efficient young woman recently from France. She seems to have made many friends since she opened this place, and the restaurant is occasionally busy. She never wastes a moment while never hastening when she talks to you—she is all patience and courtesy, and the place runs along purringly because it is small enough for her to be on top of everything. It is a rare moment when you cannot catch her eye. Already this is a neighborhood, drop-in restaurant to which solitary men repair with their newspapers, to which young couples come when their hard day at the office discourages them from thinking about the kitchen stove at home. If the city were ordered by the patron saint of restaurants and their customers, there would be a place like this every half mile or so, up and down all the avenues, along all the streets.

That lady of the place, with whom you have instantly fallen in love, performs the miracle of deftly opening your bottle of wine while discussing the menu. She answers one question while pouring the wine for its tasting, two more while filling the glasses after you have expressed your approval, yet another while she puts it on ice within your reach. By the standards of New York restaurants this is virtuosity comparable to playing a Beethoven violin sonata in the manner of Isaac Stern while accompanying yourself on the piano. Elsewhere around town everyone is still struggling with the right-handed circular motion on the tummy in counterpoint with a left-handed patting motion on the head.

Begin gently with Crème de Cresson, a simple creamed soup on a base of potatoes and chicken stock that has been brought to life by crisp watercress added shortly before it is served. Or start somewhat more firmly, with an appetizer of Quenelle de Brochet, which is listed among the main courses, but which, happily, your sainted lady makes available in a smaller portion. Yes, the dumpling is a bit heavier than you would like it to be, but the lobster sauce is fine, tasting more of lobster meat than shell in this version, and it is served with wondrous rice, warm and tender, each grain a vivid little pleasure. The Jambon Fumé et Melon features a rather coarsely cured ham, smoky and salty and fibrous, pleasantly resilient without being tough. Sadly, the melon is not perfectly ripe.

The menu is not an attempt to alter New Yorkers' tastes in French food and there is much that is familiar on it, including Steak au Poivre Vert, composed of good beef and served in a creamy pepper sauce—the meat is accurately prepared and the sauce is heavily flavored of pepper without being particularly strong. The Carré d'Agneau is a rack of lamb, roasted after being infused with fresh garlic, carved into four chops per person at a serving stand beside your table and served prettily arranged on your plate —this is good, young lamb, and the garlic, though vivid, does not overpower its flavor. Splendid Ris de Veau Braisé Forestière, the sweetbreads cooked until the rich meat falls easily into firm, moist flakes, served in a light tomato sauce that is mingled with fresh sautéed mushrooms—one of the better sweetbread dishes in town. The green vegetable garnishes are not invariably any better than colorful, but the potatoes, cooked in oil, are stout stuff.

Your main course entitles you to a simple green salad in a light dressing. The only cheese on hand is Roquefort, sharp and buttery.

The best of the desserts is the almost-black chocolate mousse, nodules of solid, bittersweet chocolate here and there in the sweet stuff—it is served with true whipped cream. The apple tart is a comedown, mushy apples on a wet crust; but a cake of the house, a dark pastry with an almond-paste filling that is without the cloying sweetness of marzipan, is well-baked, flaky and sufficiently heavy to appease any lingering hunger.

The wine list is brief but well-chosen.

★ JOE ALLEN

326 West 46th Street
LUNCH AND DINNER.
Reservations, 581–6464.
Credit cards: MC, V.
Medium-priced.

If you don't work in the theater, you may feel out of place here. Of the fifteen or so restaurants in this block, Joe Allen is one of the two or three that do any business to speak of after the local curtains go up. It appears that everyone who has nothing to do on stage is here, wishing they had.

Joe Allen is an example of the classic two-room-restaurant-and-bar. The bar itself is in the entrance room (with a handful of tables) and most of the eating is done in the back room, at the rear of which is the kitchen, for all to see, looking like a clean, cute little installation at a small prison: dreary, pale-green tiles, gray duct work, and for color, a red fire extinguisher. The barroom and the dining room are separated by a brick wall with arched, unpaned windows, and most of the rest of the interior is brick too, hung with sporting and nautical photographs, theatrical posters, plus, in the dining room, large slates on which are chalked the available dishes—shrimp cocktail (not bad), chopped liver (bland), Caesar salad (made with powdered garlic—yuk!), strong, heavy chili, good steaks and chops, broiled fish, shish kebab (in an excess of Middle Eastern-ism, it is sprinkled with crushed wheat), shrimp in ale batter (five large, moist shrimp, served with sliced tomatoes), chicken pot pie, ham and other burgers, and standard desserts, including a very tasty and crunchy pecan pie. The food is solid stuff, reliable, uninspired and rarely disappointing. It is best accompanied by beer (Bass Ale on tap), and one's enjoyment of it varies directly with the intensity of one's hunger, perhaps even more directly with the degree of diversity and activity at nearby tables.

The people here seem to be permanently in costume. At one table a plump strabismic has equal billing with a spit-curled soubrette and a bun-headed mother-in-law. At another, Tarzan holds hands with Isadora Duncan. Some are boisterous eater-drinker-talkers, others intimate nibbler-sippers, but at either end of the gustatorial and conversational spectrum, the subject matter is the same:

"Darling, you il*lu*minated the part. She [sneer] milked it."

"He took one look at her you-know-whats, and the other tryouts were just a formality."

The waiters make their contributions too:

"I'm sorry this is late. I forgot all about it." Not surprising; half the help here hug and kiss half the arriving customers—the misemployed consoling the unemployed.

★★ JOE & ROSE

745 Third Avenue (near 46th Street)
LUNCH, MONDAY TO FRIDAY; DINNER, MONDAY TO SATURDAY. CLOSED SUNDAY.
Reservations, 355–8874.
Credit cards: AE, DC.
Expensive.

This is Old New York. The customers, some of them, are out of thirties movies, the ones about newspapermen and underworld figures and men about town in the days when such types didn't know any better and wore their hair short and slicked down, had their suits made with narrow lapels, wore stick pins in their ties, bought corsages for their ladies, who, in turn, spoke only when spoken to, and then adoringly, unless they were Rosalind Russell.

A series of homey little rooms, one of them with a bar, the others with tables and chairs and booths. The walls are a dusky tan, and they are hung with an assortment of prints, etchings, oils, watercolors, a few of them plumb. Above all that, of course, is the stamped-tin ceiling.

The place has a hustle-bustle air about it, within which the calm, competent waiters seem doubly self-composed, their tasks well in hand. You ask one of them for a bottle of good Chianti, and he offers an Antinori—he *does* know what he is about.

Joe & Rose is one of a type—the Italian steakhouse. It is generally not thought of as one of the Steak Row restaurants, though it is no farther from the Row than, say, the Palm. But there is something so relaxed about the place, and there is so little of the studied masculinity affected by the other Steak Row restaurants and their customers that this seems a place apart.

"First we'll split a manicotti." "Good," answers the waiter, and you get the impression that you are in fact being favored with an expert opinion and that favorable opinions are not the only ones he delivers. The manicotti is immense, a simple thing of pasta stuffed with creamy ricotta cheese and covered with a rich and oily meat sauce —this is hearty food, perfectly and freshly prepared. You can get excellent clams and oysters and shrimp here, but to give the Italian side of the place its due, a little pasta is recommended.

The steaks are of perfect beef, accurately broiled—lightly blackened outside; fibrous, tender and bloody within. During soft-shell season you get a different notion of soft-shell crabs when you eat them here. They are sautéed in olive oil rather than in butter, which gives them a distinctly Italian quality without sacrificing any of the delicacy of the crabs themselves, which are tender, fresh and sweet.

A good side-order house: lyonnaise potatoes that are almost spectacularly variegated, within the limits of lyonnaise potatoes—there are butter-soaked and soft slices of potato, slices that are leathery and brown, slices that are crisp, and in among these are the onions, limp and juicy, some almost burnt, some barely at the translucent stage; French fried onions that are crunchy and salty, made in a clean batter, so that the coating seems to crackle on the crisp onions. The orders are mammoth.

The desserts are pretty bad, but you won't want them if you didn't fight with yourself over whether to finish your potatoes.

★★ JOE'S

79 MacDougal Street (near Bleecker Street)
LUNCH AND DINNER. CLOSED TUESDAY.
Reservations, 764–1838.
No credit cards.
Medium-priced.

Joe's has always been one of the best of the old-style Italian restaurants in Greenwich Village: a little out of the way; a little more expensive and more elegantly appointed than most of its competitors; not frequented by the Bohemian side of Village society, rather by the stolid types whose supposed affiliations were whispered about; and serving food that went well beyond the narrow range of red sauces over noodles and veal that made up the bulk of what was served in the places with the checkered tablecloths and candles in Chianti bottles.

In the old days the riffraff stayed away; perhaps they still do; but now it is difficult to tell—it is fashionable to dress like riffraff no matter what your status, and these T-shirted and dungareed neighbors may pay their checks and pull away in a chauffeured limousine that is just like the one waiting for those obviously moneyed advertising types making all the noise. There are still a few seeming-underground potentates around—they are very stiff, apparently offended by the relaxation of standards.

You ask for the fried zucchini as soon as you sit down. This establishes you as one who knows his way around the customs and secrets of this place and, in addition, provides you with some excellent fried zucchini! It is traditionally munched, in this restaurant, during perusal of the menu, on which, by the way, you will not find said fried zucchini. (Think of the insular types—there must be such—who have been eating here for decades and have never had the famous zucchini.) The stuff comes wrapped in a napkin—the thin strands of the vegetable have been lightly breaded and deep-fried in extremely hot oil, so that the breading is extremely crisp, the strong-tasting squash barely cooked. You eat it with your fingers.

Meanwhile you have ordered your dinner, beginning, probably, with the quite remarkable stuffed mushrooms. These stuffed mushrooms are unlike any other stuffed mushrooms in town—no oiled, herbed breading; no minced mushroom stems; just cheese—ricotta and something much louder on top, the mushrooms themselves sautéed until dark, the cheese lightly browned. One order consists of four such mushrooms, which seems paltry, but they are worth more than the price. There are excellent baked clams, juicy, tender, the breading delicately browned. And you can have one of the clams and one of the mushrooms as part of the pretty good hot antipasto, which also includes some thoroughly sautéed eggplant and a huge shrimp. What distinguishes this hot antipasto from all others is its red sauce—it is studded with huge capers and loud olives.

Nowadays when you order the Home Made Egg Noodles, Carbonara Sauce, you are getting green noodles. True, green noodles are made with eggs, but one does not think of something called an egg noodle as being green. Hues aside, the food is delicious. The noodles clearly *are* made on the premises; they retain the flavor of spinach, and they are served in a thick, creamy egg-and-cheese sauce that has been mixed with slivers of smoky ham. The same noodles can be had in a very meaty meat sauce—spicy and oily —to which fresh mushrooms have been added. For something more primitively red, there is a sharp and acidic tomato sauce on the manicotti—the pasta is thin, tender and firm, and the filling is a simple one of steaming ricotta cheese.

Chicken Livers Cacciatore: soft, succulent livers; crisp mushrooms; a bright tomato sauce; a garnish of one potato croquette, fluffy, spicy and perfectly browned. Chicken Scarpariello: chunks of chicken on short lengths of bone, sautéed until browned, with chunks of garlic, big slices of mushroom and herbs. Veal Francese: good veal, if not the best, in a smooth and lemony sauce with slices of ham in the sauce, a nice variant; all in all, one of the best versions of this dish around. The stuffed veal cutlet, a sometime daily special, is good, but basically no more than a run-of-New York veal Parmigiana.

Good vegetables, including sautéed escarole that is dry, fibrous, salty, and mingled with the chunks of sautéed garlic that contribute to its potent flavor. Good salads, including, when available, very fresh and crisp arugula, in a clear, strong and salty vinegar dressing.

Joe's serves one of the best cheese cakes in New York. It is wildly excessive, very wet, intensely sweet, heavy and thickly studded with candied fruit. And an excellent zabaglione, hot and thick, and strongly flavored with good Marsala wine.

Joe's is a brightly lit, clean, comfortable place. The immaculate kitchen is visible through a portal at the rear of the front room. The waiters are at once casual and quick.

○ JOE'S PIER 52

144 West 52nd Street
LUNCH AND DINNER.
Reservations, 245–6652.
Credit cards: AE, CB, DC, MC, V.
Expensive.

Middle Americans with weighted middles and mountains of plasticized and/or metallicized hair compete boisterously ("Charlie, on you dat bib looks like a necktie") with a steel band of busboys who clear away dishes with a cacophonous vigor that must break 30 percent of them. Flat-faced waiters, arms folded, sucking their teeth, watch bored while others, frantic and inept ("Who gets scrod? Who gets crabs?"), serve a group of ten in such fashion that when the last dish is put down, the first is quite cold. Waiters and busboys fight it out on the dining-room floor. ("Hey! Water over here! More budda fer dese nice people!")

Thousands of clams and oysters must be served each day in this busy restaurant, and they are always fresh. But the distinction between littlenecks and cherrystones is honored only if inventory is in balance. An order of littlenecks may arrive with two cherrystones. ("May I exchange these two cherrystones for three littlenecks?" "Sorry, no substitutions." "What about two for two?" "Look, dat's what dey gamey. Dat's it.")

A promotional piece on the table:

The Original Joe's Stone Crabs . . . Presented the way they have been winning acclaim from the critics of the world for the past fifty years in Miami Beach. CONTINUOUS PERFORMANCES DAILY.

Not true: they are often not available, even in season; and though they are served hot or cold in Florida, Pier 52 serves them only cold. Their temperature is not specified on the menu, but mention of drawn butter suggests hot shellfish. (If you dip a lump of cold crabmeat into melted butter and then stare at the moist object for a moment or two, you can see the butter revert to its congealed state right before your eyes.) Waiters and captains (well, cocktail pushers) are incredulous at the suggestion that a Floridian would eat a stone crab hot.

A specialty here is red snapper stuffed with spinach. And when they say red, they mean red. Painted with paprika when it was first cooked, and repainted and stuck under the broiler before serving, this delicious Florida fish arrives mushy, and as tasteless as this restaurant's white bread. The spinach tastes like new-mown artificial lawn. The whole mess may be one of the ten worst dishes served in any restaurant in New York. It is accompanied by a potato which has been baked in an aluminum-foil shield for ten days or two weeks. The jacket is limp, and the potato is floury. Tons of salt, pepper and butter are needed to make it edible.

The apple pie consists of undercooked sour apples, a few raisins and a cup of powdered cinnamon between two strata of unleavened brick. The pecan pie is topped with a bent cylinder of toothpaste from an elephantine tube. You're OK if you just pick out the nuts.

If you must eat here, choose the food that requires no preparation (clams, oysters), or food that doesn't suffer much from early preparation (chowders and seafood stews), or food that is made to order (lobster, steak).

The check arrives with the coffee.

★★KITCHO

22 West 46th Street
LUNCH, MONDAY TO FRIDAY; DINNER, SUNDAY TO FRIDAY. CLOSED SATURDAY.
Reservations, 575–8880.
Credit cards: AE, DC.
Medium-priced.

The fancier of New York's Japanese restaurants are supported, principally, by the thousands of youngish Japanese male executives who work for Japanese companies in New York. These restaurants are their social centers, they come here in groups, dressed, almost uniformly, in dark worsted suits, white shirts and ties. They talk business, golf and baseball. They stack their attaché cases on empty chairs. Americans come to these places too, and they sit around and talk about Japanese food.

Past the elevator leading to the upper floors of the modern office building that houses this sleek establishment, to the little bar lined with Japanese men sipping beers and Bloody Marys and, often as not, watching baseball on the color TV. Farther back, rows of nifty black-topped tables under spherical paper lanterns that hang from the ceiling; farther back still, a square dining room similarly furnished, but with a hint of a Japanese interior in the otherwise smooth, Western-modern rooms—rice-paper panels and a wall of wooden slats. Everything in the place is tasteful, if a little sterile, right down to the handsome stoneware ashtrays and tiny vases for the flowers on each table.

The waitresses here are motherly, which is good and bad. Unless you are Japanese, they try to steer you away from what Occidentals before you have not enjoyed, and efforts to learn the ins and outs of the Japanese-language menu that is printed on the back of the regular menu lead almost invariably to the allegation that all those things are really the same as the English-language items. Nevertheless, there is plenty of good food here, none that is bad.

As in most Japanese restaurants that do not specialize in raw-fish dishes, the sushi and sashimi lack the sparkle of what you get at the places with the busy sushi bars— the fish is perfectly fresh, you understand, and the mustard and the vinegared rice that fortify the sushi are lively, but the fish lacks a certain sprightliness.

So begin your dinner with Sunomono, a Japanese salad of crabmeat and cucumber —the seafood and the crisp, thin slivers of cucumber are flavored with a gentle vinegar and a little ginger, which combine to make the dish sing. Red caviar and horseradish, called Suzuko, may strike you as unlikely, and the caviar is in no way extraordinary, but the horseradish is—instead of the hotness you expect, you get the powerful and earthy flavor of a root just pulled out of the ground; it makes a dramatic contrast to the fish eggs. In Japan, warm clams are served with paper-thin rounds of lime; what seems to be a variant of that dish, designed for American taste, is served here as Yaki Hama. The clams are broiled until they are warm but not colored; they are surmounted with thin circles of lemon or lime, and they are served with a cousin, several times removed, of cocktail sauce—a garlicked tomato purée that seems more Italian than either Japanese or American. Odd but good.

The shrimp tempura cannot be recommended—the shrimp are not fresh, and these days you almost have to expect that, but they have the loud taste of iodine; and the tempura batter here is a little thick or the frying oil is insufficiently hot, for the crust is heavy and barely crisp. The Yaki-Tori is described on the menu as "Broiled Chicken and Scallion, Skewered," but the chunks of chicken are alternated on the little wooden skewers with slices of ordinary onion instead, which tames this dish. The meat and onions are dipped in sweetened sake and soy sauce before they are broiled, which sweetens and spices the chicken, and it is no contrast at all against the onions, which become sweet anyway when cooked. Shio-Yaki is broiled, salted fish—you can have it made of mackerel (a little loud) or salmon (rich); the fish is fresh, it is perfectly broiled, moist and flaky, and if you moisten the horseradish garnish with a bit of soy sauce, it makes a perfect condiment.

To-Banyaki is the solid climax to most of the dinners here, especially substantial if you have the version made with pork. This is a steaming stew that arrives in a deep ceramic pot with a close-fitting lid. The slabs of tender meat are rimmed with fat, there are chunks of soft bean curd and slices of crisp squash alongside, all in a meaty broth that is heavily flavored with sesame. For all its solidity, there is no heaviness to this stout food.

Beer is the best drink here. Unfortunately, the house does not sell Kirin, and the Sapporo that they push is a little dull in comparison.

★ LADY ASTOR'S

430 Lafayette Street (near Astor Place)
LUNCH AND DINNER.
Reservations, 228–7888.
No credit cards.
Expensive.

Like parti-colored clowns in a cathedral are these SoHo Bohemians and off-Broadway theatrical types in the men's-club solemnity of these plush, spacious halls. Lady Astor's sports pretty girls and pretty boys, dreamy onlookers and slumming voyeurs. When things are busy the bowling alley–length bar, which runs along one side of the main dining room, looks like the rear view of a multiple-edition mummers' last supper.

Lady Astor's is situated in a grim old commercial neighborhood. At night one is confronted on these streets by the huge bleak façades, behind which by day light industry industriously throbs. But in recent years Off- and Off-Off-Broadway have established beachheads, the so-called East Village is only a couple of blocks off, SoHo and the real Village are not much farther; these are the cultures that are the culture on which a handful of new restaurants down here feed.

The small, dimly lit yellow canopy barely calls attention to the place. Up a few steps and through unpretentious apartment house–vestibule doors into the grandeur that was your grandfather's rarely used musty library and study. The dark maroon walls are illuminated by crystal chandeliers and graced by great and ornately framed mirrors. Dark-green linen on the tables, dark-green leather and brass nailheads on the comfortable armchairs, deep carpeting across the vast floor. Through it traipse the waiters, waitresses and busboys, trancelike, as though just released from solitary to be pressed into this service, barely awake to the world around them; behind it sounds the background music—late Beethoven quartets followed by the Benny Goodman Quintet followed by Billie Holiday.

The food is ambitious and not invariably successful. Lady Astor's has discovered the "tenderloin of chicken," and they sauté these small sections of the chicken in butter and flame them in brandy. To sauté the breast of chicken is an exacting proposition —you must cut off the cooking at the moment the meat has become cooked, just before it begins to dry out. With only that objective in mind, the house is to be praised. Moreover, the dish is good to eat, the lightly brandied lengths of chicken served on a mound of buttery rice that is, rather startlingly, sweetened with an admixture of white raisins, warm and juicy. Sweetbreads are prepared in a pretentious way—they are braised, the braising liquid is thickened with foie gras and flavored with bits of truffle, and the meat is served in a pool of the sauce, amid chunks of pastry crust (pâté brisée), with which you soak up the remainder of the thick polished sauce.

Everyone is offering steak au poivre these days. This one is studded with abundant black pepper before it is broiled and served in a creamy and brandied pan sauce. The peppering must be done well in advance, for you discover that the treatment has implanted a potent pepper flavor to the unsuspecting beef. The sauce is creamy and strong, but the meat itself is not first rate—a little tough and not particularly tasty.

Naturally there is chocolate mousse, and here it is served in a large stemmed wineglass. It is loaded with concentrated chocolate flavor, it is so thick it is almost sticky, and if you are really flying, you can have yours with a huge dollop of whipped cream. There is an equally solid cheese cake, American style in that it is made with cream cheese and strongly flavored with lemon, Italian in that it is soaking wet—good stuff.

★★★ LE LAVANDOU

134 East 61st Street
LUNCH AND DINNER. CLOSED SUNDAY.
Reservations, TE 8-7987.
Credit cards: AE.
Very expensive.

You enter to a vestibule heavily hung with citations, diplomata, certificates of achievement, ratifications of victory, confirmations of award. You are duly impressed, you proceed to the dining room, and you decide that the chef's honors are not for originality if his restaurant's appearance is clue to his creativity. This is Paris posh, as middle as class can be, with a crimson velvet banquette circling the room under ivory walls, dark mirrors, scenic and sunny oils, bronzed sconces. There is potted greenery in each corner, flowers on every neatly-set table. Down to the red carpeting, you have seen it all before. The French restaurant in New York is such a successful institution, that newcomers are happy to get lost in the crowd.

Your *déjà vu,* however, will wane when you eat, for Le Lavandou, particularly when you select from its list of specialties, produces some very classy fare. Accordingly, you opt for La Cassolette d'Escargots des Pinêdes, and receive, blessedly, a small baking dish with six snail-size declivities, in each of which, besides a plump and tender snail, you will find a few crunchy pine nuts and a clear and buttery sauce, mildly herbed, and amply flavored with Pernod. You are happy with one specialty, so next time you try another, specifically La Quenelle de Brochet au Pernod (did the man get his recipes from the back of a Pernod bottle?). The little dumplings of pike are firm, tender, and peppery, with a bright and clear flavor of fresh fish—that is to say, what any good quenelle de brochet would be; but the house ennobles the already aristocratic dish by serving with it a smooth white sauce that is heady with Pernod and populated by half a dozen fresh mussels—lovely.

Veering from the red-letter items, you encounter Asperges de France Hollandaise, and the way they got those French asparagus spears to the USA is by can. Well, withal, they speak only faintly of the tin, and as white asparagus are so rare here that few have a notion of how they taste when fresh, they seem quite delicious in their preserved form, cool and sharp; but this establishment's hollandaise lacks sufficient lemon to undo its exceptional richness. Once more eschewing the featured dishes, you ask for the Terrine de Canard Truffée, and you are brought a wheeled serving stand, from which you are served any number of things in addition to the listed terrine, which is spicy and rich: a head cheese that is an array of textures, from nodules of white fat, to a cool jelly, to chunks of fibrous tongue; take it or leave it, but a "pâté en croûte" that is not in a crust, one that is predominantly ham and pork, accented with whole filberts; and a mousse of chicken liver that is light, loud, and rich.

Returning to the list of specialties of the house, you find the least likely kind of thing you will want after four pâtés and terrines—Le Cassoulet du Chef Toulousain. Well, have it anyway. This is a heady and heavy composition of meats, birds, and sausages in a thickness of beans. The pork and pigeon are moist, the sausage is fragrant of fennel, and the final heating of the dish with a sprinkling of bread crumbs provides a crusty contrast to the moist ingredients.

To something more refined, Les Délices de Veau aux Chanterelles. It arrives prettily enough, the glistening meat and mushrooms colorfully surrounded by crisp string beans, grilled tomatoes, and browned zucchini. The excellent veal pale—almost creamy —and the chanterelles moistened by a polished dark sauce. But in a dish like this, the sauce is all, and this one is low on character—perfectly good food and all that, but unexciting.

Le Tournedos aux Cêpes Sauce Truffe, however, is something else. The perfectly grilled beef is dressed with a sauce that is creamy, sweet and mingled with the extremely delicate mushrooms—the cêpes are best eaten alone, for their fugitive flavor is masked by strong meat. The sauced tournedos is garnished with a disc of goose liver pâté which is sprinkled with bits of truffle, and this, in its way, adds fat to the dish, the filet mignon being the leanest of beef.

Birds, too, as in La Dodine Pintadotte Périgourdine, in which goose liver and truffles play parts again. A breast of chicken has been removed from its bone, wrapped around the delicate mousse of liver, browned until the pale meat is thoroughly cooked and the liver warmed, and served in a beefy, truffle-studded sauce. It is garnished with fluted mushroom caps, zucchini in a thick tomato sauce, crisp carrots, and green beans.

There is a white cake with pink sherbet, flavored with anisette; good tarts served with dollops of whipped cream; a chocolate mousse wrapped in plain cake and whipped cream, sprinkled with shavings of chocolate for identification. Buttery petits fours arrive with your coffee.

If you wonder about the name "Lavandou," your waiter explains that it is a town in Provence where the chef took his holidays when he was a "leetle keed."

○ LÜCHOW'S

110 East 14th Street
LUNCH AND DINNER.
Reservations, GR 7–4860.
Credit cards: AE, CB, DC, MC, V.
Medium-priced.

High up on one of the muraled two-story walls, prehistoric man, lean and muscular, is competing with wild beasts for his daily meat, and across the room, blond, red-cheeked Valkyries aboard their steeds are escorting the souls of the heroic dead to Valhalla. Down below, the rotund customers drink a lot of beer, don the management-supplied red Tyrolean hats (green feather) and wax moody with the music—sometimes a squad of flushed tootlers and blarers, in short pants that reveal knobby knees, instills martial feelings; at other times a chamber trio spins out violinistic medleys of Franz Lehár operetta tunes while, at the tables, stubby fingers clutch at plump knees in a romantic, aromatic haze of weinkraut and cigar smoke. Stuffed moose look down, impassive.

It has been said that all of the food at Lüchow's is terrible. Of course, nobody knows. There are close to 200 items on the menu, and many of them engender so little curiosity that only some kind of crazy, obsessive investigator/cataloguer would ever look into them all. Are you, for instance, interested in getting the scoop on the Vegetable Plate of Green Beans, Baby Carrots, Asparagus Tips, Creamed Spinach, New Peas and Boiled Potato? Or are your awe and wonder aroused, rather, by Berliner Eisbein (Boiled Corned Pig's Knuckle) with Sauerkraut and Mashed Potatoes? Perhaps you would be more interested in getting the low-down on Home Made Bratwurst, Sauerkraut, Mashed Potatoes. Well, don't bother. It has been established that a blindfolded man, sober, admittedly without the aid of mind-expanding drugs, could not differentiate between the sausage and the mashed.

But some of the food here is good. The Schwarzwälder Pfifferlinge are little pointed-cap mushrooms, imported in perfect condition from Germany, sautéed in butter and served in a lovely warm dill sauce. You can have a good bit of it as a main course, or considerably less as an appetizer. It is one of the few dishes here that would do credit to a first-rate restaurant. There are excellent herrings, including a really sour but not acidic Bismarck, and soft, sweet maatjes. The so-called chopped chicken liver is just a tasteless mousse, and the headcheese a dismal amalgam of variety meats. There is a hot, peppery, thick lentil soup, which is satisfying despite the peregrinations of homeless frankfurter discs therein.

The main courses are the real comedown. The boiled baked beef is a satisfactory pot roast, and the knackwurst is spicy and properly fatty, but such items as Kassler Rippchen and the braised veal knuckle really test your control of the gag reflex. One bite, and you know what it feels like to be in the last stages of an eating contest.

The desserts are mostly stewed fruits in cloth pancakes or leaden pastry, plus such heavyweights as cheese cake and marzipan torte.

But, with all that, this place is really something to see. Had Wagner written a comic opera, this would be the set. The waiters bungle on a grand scale, and the customers eat on a cosmic one. The servings here will hold you through the Ring cycle. During the Sommerfest a well-advertised dessert for two consists of "one and one half feet of Apfel Kuchen."

There is an amazing selection of wines, with about thirty-five German ones and as many from France listed on the menu, and many others available. But the wines are overpriced, and anyway, the proper drink with the food here is Alka-Seltzer.

★★ LUNDY'S

Ocean and Emmons Avenues, Sheepshead Bay, Brooklyn
  Emmons Avenue exit on the Belt Parkway
LUNCH AND DINNER. CLOSED MONDAY.
No reservations (646–9879).
No credit cards.
Inexpensive.

Lundy's is probably the largest restaurant in New York. A block long by a block wide, and two stories high (the upper floor hasn't been used in a number of years), Brooklyn Moorish by design (sand-colored columns and lofty arches) but Fulton Fish in spirit, this unbelievable relic (in good repair) looks like a movie set converted into an officers' mess. The crowd scene stretches to a dim horizon, but the backdrop is real, not painted scenery.

The menu is basic seafood—always fresh—augmented by the usual steaks and chops, plus broiled chicken. (To hold you while the casual service catches up with your needs, an oversupply of hot biscuits, pilot crackers and Oysterettes is planted before you, with enough butter to fossilize an elephant's aorta.) Only simple preparations are available, and the prices are positively nostalgic. Where else in New York can you sit down at a large table with comfortable chairs, and be brought a dozen littlenecks, six oysters, good chowders, strong clam broth, a giant plate of steamers, at prices from 50 cents to $2?

Lobsters are alive until cooked (never over), and the fish, broiled or fried, are firm and flaky—bluefish (the whole animal), sea bass and smelts are available. Not on the menu, and, therefore, long favored by cognoscenti, is a lobster stuffed with crabmeat, but now, with crabmeat very dear, it is overly breaded, and to be avoided. The steaks and chops are rather heavily charcoaled, but the meat is good and cooked as ordered. If you are really hungry, there are complete dinners at discounts—Shore Dinner, Cold Lobster Dinner, Fish Dinner, Chicken Dinner, Chops and Steak Dinner (their nomenclature).

154

The sleepers here are the à la carte vegetables. Skip the green ones, and try hashed brown potatoes—perfectly seasoned, artfully browned, firm and copious; or lyonnaise —the same partly cooked potatoes fried in good grease, made even more irresistible by an intermixture of lightly fried onions. Not better, but more surprising, are the French fried onions—lightly breaded, crisp on the outside, the onions still crunchy within; and julienne potatoes—the matchstick French fries which, in most places, are either hard from overcooking, or limp from under-, but here are usually crisp, soft inside. Another item not listed is potatoes au gratin—not as good as those mentioned, but if you order them, you look like an old-timer. The desserts are OK, the blueberry pie actually quite good, but the best food appears higher up on the menu.

In summer the beach bugs by the thousands, enervated but happy, trudge from the hot sand to their apartments, hotels, rooming houses and summer sublets to shower away the salt and then sprint to Lundy's, where they wait interminably, but happily, for a table—perhaps, God willing, in a nook beside a window. (Even an amphitheater can have a nook.)

This stable's colors are orange and green, and chair slats, washroom tiles and the waiters' uniforms carry out the scheme. There is a long clam and oyster bar, where people too restless to wait can get quick service. A surviving Lundy lives upstairs, and each morning, it is said, he loads a score of dogs into his miniature bus and drives them out to Long Island for a romp.

For most New Yorkers, there is not a more foreign, or more genuine, cultural encounter, *au restaurant,* than an evening at this bustling mausoleum. The archaism of an all-black serving staff is irksome, but the clientele is like a memory of Brooklyn's forgotten working classes. Italians find no pasta here, blacks no soul food, Jews no chicken soup, but they all come, and at Lundy's even a lobster is kosher.

★★★★ LUTÈCE

249 East 50th Street
LUNCH, TUESDAY TO FRIDAY; DINNER, MONDAY TO SATURDAY. CLOSED SUNDAY.
Reservations essential, PL 2-2225.
Credit cards: AE.
Very expensive.

During the first decade or so of its existence, the kitchen at Lutèce turned out the best restaurant food obtainable in New York. At the same time, certain members of the dining room staff, with the encouragement of one of this establishment's proprietors, did what they could to keep people from enjoying it. M. Surmain's contempt for all but a rich and/or famous few was given by analysts of the parvenu mind as the key to the intense demand that obtained for the privilege of eating in this place; other analysts of minds, while not necessarily quarreling with that theory, held that the underlying purpose of Surmain's pompous hauteur was to obscure his bourgeois beginnings. Surmain's motives, always a boring subject, are now an irrelevant issue, for, happily, he divorced himself from his baby a few years ago, leaving Lutèce entirely in the more capable hands of his former partner, André Soltner, who has always been its chef. Perhaps snobbery was the lure that drew them in when this place was getting started. Still, arrogance departed right behind Surmain, and the customers have not. Today Lutèce is the most charming and relaxed of New York's famous restaurants. Anyone who is uncomfortable here is uncomfortable.

You are greeted by Madame. Her attitude toward her customers is—get this—that of one human being to another. A little better, even, for she is all concern for your wishes. Unknown customers, for example, are asked whether they would like to sit upstairs or down, and then they are led to the best open table on the floor they choose. If they prefer another table, and that one is free, it is theirs.

But all that is a bit previous, for first you will want a drink in the little front room, four tiny tables and a miniature zinc bar, behind which there is a barman who seems to enjoy his work. He polishes glasses until they are crystalline and stirs cocktails until they are icy, ever serious when at work, smiling a French elf's smile when exchanging small talk with the customers. Though there is hardly room for them, you sit in ample wicker chairs while you sip your drinks and stare about you. The walls are innocently adorned with a mural of Paris, a street sign from the same city (Place de Furstenberg, 6° Arr.), *Holiday* magazine awards and a letter of tribute from the *Mobil Guide.* Those publications, displayed in this place, are getting the better of the bargain. Off this room coats are checked, in a wee closet, and bills are processed, at a minute cashier's counter; and the crowds—of customers around the *vestiaire* and of waiters around the little desk —make for an occasional congestion that would infuriate anywhere else: at Lutèce everyone is so relentlessly civilized that the principal delays result from everyone's eagerness to defer to everyone else.

You may eat upstairs, where a couple of small, comfortable and comparatively formal rooms accommodate a handful of tables each. But if you want the feeling of being where this restaurant is, eat on the ground floor, in the famous "garden."

You are led through a narrow corridor (past a reclining nude smoked salmon) to, first, the antegarden, a small, cozy room with a table in each corner, grotesque paper of cavorting fern fronds on the walls and a view through glass paneling and a glass door of the garden proper, a fantasy candyland of outdoors elegance, pink stucco walls behind snowy latticework, columns of whitewashed brick supporting palms in great brass pots. You walk on flagstones and look up to a vaulted glass ceiling lined with pale-green blinds—by day the sun shines through. The tables are in two rows, surrounded by deep wicker chairs and set with white linen and china, glinting silver, gleaming crystal.

M. Soltner is a restless cook, so it is wise to discuss with your captain the chef's whims of the day, which are in addition to the menu listings and frequently of special interest. Failure to do so may lead, for example, to your humbly ordering Foie Gras en Brioche, only to then have your captain point out that it is foolish to have your foie gras in bread, when only this morning the chef packed the stuff into quails. The little birds (they are about the size of a fist) have been boned (but for their legs), roasted, stuffed with the foie gras, coated with aspic and cooled. Your quail is bisected on a carving board near your table and served to you, a couple of eccentric doughnuts of pink bird meat, a leg protruding from each, a bull's-eye of the buttery concentrate of liver at each center. This is, of course, a visual conceit, the flesh of the quail playing the part of the brioche bread, the dark jelly that of the crust, the fois gras doing a terrific imitation of itself. A few white grapes garnish the little masterpiece.

Remarkable hot first courses, including this establishment's famous snails, styled as Timbales d'Escargots à la Chablisienne. They are not served in snail shells, but in eyecup-size ceramic pots, the tender morsels submerged in a liquid butter that is winy and powerfully scented with fresh herbs. Equally deserving of all the syllables are Pélerines à la Méridionale, bay scallops that are the size of sea scallops, sautéed until they are lightly browned, but not a second too long, so that all their sweet richness is retained, no toughness added. Though you get about a dozen of them, they are so fluffy and airy that they are not excessive; they are served in a sauce of such profundity and fulfillment that it controls your entire attention—a dark and oily concentrate of tomatoes, garlic and mushrooms that is poured over the shellfish and over a crust of toasted bread as well—which supplies a crusty texture that rounds out the otherwise supple dish. The Truite Fraîche à l'Oseille is a gentle dish—a skinned trout, separated from its outer bones but still attached to the central ones along the spine, in a pool of buttery sauce made colorful and tasty with chopped sorrel and parsley and strands of carrot. The trout is firm and sweet and moist. The scent of a wild perfume seems to rise from its plate.

It is called Cassolette de Crabe "Vieille France," but this main dish is made with the best American crabmeat fished from the water. This is a stewlike dish, arriving in a little pot under a pastry top. When that crust is inverted onto your plate and the contents of the pot spooned over it, a vivid aroma of crayfish shell and wild mushrooms permeates the air. The crabmeat is almost unbelievably delicate and sweet, the light-brown sauce at once clear and deep, the copper-colored flaky pastry something you toy with to prolong the remarkable experience. The Poussin Basquaise is a whole young chicken, browned and moist, in an earthy sauce that is studded with wild mushrooms; artichoke hearts—fresh, firm, delicately acidic; and nuggets of tomato—cooked down until they have reached an extreme intensity of concentrated tomato flavor.

When local venison is available, this establishment prepares it as if it were beef—the meat grilled, moistened with a polished wine sauce that has a few mushrooms in it and served with salty noodles that make an excellent foil for the sweet, tender meat. Technically this is game meat, but there is nothing gamy about it or its preparation: classical cooking applied to a slightly unfamiliar meat, and the results are perfect. All is not heaven, though little approaches the mundane. What does is Délice de Veau aux Girolles, which turns out to be that most indelicate of dishes, veal Cordon Bleu, in a house variant that includes the crinkly mushrooms called chanterelles. The crust around the veal, ham and cheese is deeply browned, and the meat and cheese within form a hefty sandwich, lightened and sharpened a bit by lemon. But even the vaguely wild flavor of the mushrooms fails to ennoble this earthbound item. Good vegetables, including spinach that seems to have its natural flavor greatly magnified; morels that are at once cartilaginous and tender, in a creamy brandied sauce.

If you are one of those in whom abundant eating begets further gluttony, you may want cheese before your dessert. The bread here is crusty and strong, and the selection of cheeses, though conventional—Brie, Roquefort, Pont l'Evêque, etc.,—is remarkable for its consistently high quality. If, however, your hunger has been oversated, you may proceed at once to mere sweets. Did you know that there is such a thing as *marc* of Gewürtztraminer? There wasn't until only a few years back. Now that it is here, of course, it may be toyed with, and at this establishment it has been discovered that this cousin of brandy makes a head-clearing sherbet; has in it more than a hint of the Alsatian grapes of which the eau-de-vie was made. Half the customers have the "Soufflé Glacé" aux Framboises, and toward the end of the dinner hour white ceramic pots of the deep-pink sweet are dispensed with rapid regularity. This extraordinary dessert consists of cool layers of raspberry-flavored frozen cream and crumbly cake, over which fresh raspberries are poured, in a raspberry sauce that is so strongly flavored of the fruit that it is almost a liquor. This place manages to serve you berries out of season that seem just off the bush. While everyone is competing to caramelize the apples in their Tartes Tatin to the color of deeply stained mahogany, Lutèce, these days, is giving the apples a light treatment, so that they retain a good bit of the flavor of the fruit. Naturally, they start with tasty apples, and the result is sweet, slightly acidic fruit on crumbly, deeply browned pastry.

The captains are all courtesy, their jobs so well in hand they seem free to discuss the menu with you endlessly. The waiters are simple seriousness, the occasional awkward-nesses of these young Frenchmen actually charming.

There is a wine book with runs of great wines, prices into the hundreds of dollars. Most people order from the secondary list of around two dozen wines at prices of $11 to $14. No other restaurant of this class makes so extensive an offering of good wines at these prices. Lunch reservations can usually be had on a couple of days' notice, as can weekday dinner reservations. Weekend evenings, however, are usually booked a week or two in advance.

★ MA BELLS

218 West 45th Street
LUNCH AND DINNER.
Reservations, VO 9–0110.
Credit cards: AE, CB, DC, MC, V.
Medium-priced.

Ma Bells is a spacious, airy, relaxed saloon. It is Original Joe's and Charley O's; O'Neals' Baloon without the vulgarity; a sprawling frontier tavern with a plate-glass revolving door.

Ma Bell, as you know, is Wall Street's name for AT&T, and if you get a table along the wall, you get a table with a telephone on it—please, only local calls. The old-fashioned, stand-up instrument is made by Norelco.

The green-and-white tiled floor does not have sawdust on it, thank you, but it looks like the kind that usually does. The tables are of handsome dark wood. There is a bar, eighty feet long, we are told, and if there is a burst of thirst during a coincidence of intermissions here in the theater district, no bar nearby can accommodate as many shoes on the brass rail as this one. If you want something longer and more confidential than a quick one to help you through Act II, there are enclosed booths along one side —no drawn curtain, the portal is open, but they are excellent for long, serious drinking, interrupted now and again by a sandwich or two to renew the capacity. Find a friend with a despair commensurate with one of your own, settle in and spend the day. The service is good enough to keep the frights away, and for further distraction you can watch the slowly spinning ceiling lamps. Real saloons—that is to say, saloons that seem to be where they are out of some inevitability of place and community—are usually festooned with devices of the day and of earlier days. To fill this perceived gap we are given large and very large photos, mainly of motion-picture celebrities in scenes from old movies, telephone in hand, with fanciful captions that are meant to be amusing.

There is a lunch menu, a dinner menu and a supper menu, and they are pretty much the same, each a rearrangement of the other. What's good is the Crock of Onion Soup with Calvados. The dish is filled almost entirely with cheese and onions, what there is of the broth is thick and sweet, the cheese is gummy and strong, and you can taste a bit of brandy and a slight accent of burnt onions. What's not so good are the shrimp —either in the cocktail (with a better-than-everyday cocktail sauce) or in the Shrimp Salad Louis (with a very good Green Garden Sauce: mayonnaise and vinegar, and enough puréed parsley to make the thing green). But the shrimp, good grief, are past their prime.

What else is good is the steak, and you know what a fairly good steak is like. But what else is not so good is the French fries—gross oblongs of Idaho potato that are soggy and limp. The hash is satisfying—abundant, spicy and heavy, and served with poached eggs that run all over the hash when you break into them. Tell them to hold the sauce (an unpleasant Worcestershire-and-tomato mess) and bring the ketchup (ketchup has its place). The sandwiches are thick.

Cheese cake made of cream cheese is inherently bad food. But if you disagree, you may disagree more when you taste the version served here—there is a layer of caramel between the filling and the crust, which jazzes up this otherwise excessive dessert. If you and your friend both want to try it, order only one, which is quite enough of this extremely sweet substance. The chocolate cake is called Chocolate-Chocolate Cake, and as you might have guessed, it is very chocolaty.

During the day there are peanuts on the bar; at cocktail time, crocks of cheese and plates of crackers. There is no free lunch.

★★★ MADAME ROMAINE DE LYON

32 East 61st Street
LUNCH.
Reservations accepted for five or more, 758-2422.
No credit cards.
Beer and wine.
Medium-priced.

Hatpin handicapping is a race track system for the selection of horses. One purchases a program of the day's races, and without opening the booklet, pierces it at an arbitrary point on the front cover, through to the back cover, with a hatpin. The hatpin is removed, returned to its hat, and the program opened. The selections for the day's races are the horses whose allotted spaces on each page are perforated.

This system is indispensable at Madame Romaine de Lyon. It's impossible to decide that one omelette is preferable to 519 others, and as the 520 omelettes offered here are listed on 16 pages, a hatpin reduces the problem by 97 percent, from 520 to 16. The patron is still faced with a dilemma, but one of human proportions.

A selection of 520 omelettes is such a wonderful gimmick that a restaurant could succeed even if the omelettes were bad. Madame Romaine produces omelettes that are the equal of the best on earth. Not only are the eggs fresh, the butter sweet, the pan hot, the preparation rapid, and the delivery instantaneous (omelettes go bad in just a few minutes), but the ingredients—the beef, brains, mushrooms, chicken livers, etc.—are pre-cooked superbly: the beef is sautéed, the brains marinated, the bacon fried (but not to a crisp) by an expert who could have stopped right there and still delivered an excellent dish.

There is a palpable pleasure in simply reviewing the names and ingredients of some of these fabulous concoctions: Rochambeau (spinach, sausages, mushrooms, cheese); Jourdan (caviar, ham, bacon, onions, mushrooms, cheese); Maxim's (beef, foie gras, mushrooms, spinach, tomatoes, walnuts, Courvoisier sauce); Suprême (chestnuts, chocolate sauce).

No main courses except omelettes are served, but brioches, croissants and rolls are available, as well as a salad of good greens and a light, refreshing dressing. Desserts are a huge assortment of pastries, a chocolate mousse of the heavy, black, you-can't-be-hungry-after-this variety, and a macédoine of fruits which the menu happily defines as "all kinds of fruits mixed."

Assuming that the hours are lengthened, and that one eats three meals a day here, seven days a week, it would require twenty-four weeks, five days and a breakfast to consume one of each omelette.

★★★ LE MADRIGAL

216 East 53rd Street
LUNCH, MONDAY TO FRIDAY; DINNER, MONDAY TO SATURDAY. CLOSED SUNDAY.
Reservations, 355–0322.
Credit cards: AE.
Very expensive.

The difference between the new Madrigal of a few years back and the older Madrigal of today is little more than time and its ripening and mellowing effects. Take, for example, your host, the diminutive gray-haired chap with the smile. That thin arching of the lips once scarcely concealed his distaste for some of the sources of his livelihood. Little as he liked it, and from the first, for every bearer of old money that walked in his front door, two with new came to see. On the theory that the old has been multiplying for generations (and apparently unaware that fecundity is a property of youth), Le Madrigal raised its already exorbitant prices in search of a level at which mere high-earners would wince, while coupon-clippers would go on never even reading the right-hand columns of their menus. The fixed-price dinner has been replaced by an à la carte listing in which the lowest-price main course is $9.25, which means that if you consume nothing else, your food bill will be $10.75 because there is a leetle item in leetle print at the top of the page—Cover Charge $1.50. And if a couple of people eat and drink in this place with regard only to what they want, not to its cost, they will part with $65 or more before they leave. So what do you think happened? Right. Today, for every bearer of old money that walks in the front door, two with new come to see.

So, saith the wise man, if you can't divorce 'em, love 'em, and your host, along in years and loath to enter senescence without wisdom, has taken the advice. He now smiles with equal warmth on bankers and loan sharks, ambassadors and middlemen. His staff follows his cues; this has become one of the city's most cordially run dining rooms, and in the waiters' and captains' pockets and in the house bank account, all kinds of money happily comingle.

Always one of the prettiest restaurants in town, and one of the most comfortable if you avoid the cramped little "garden" room appended to the rear, you must now enjoy it without the pleasure of stiffing the captain. The place is all sunny golden light, and nowadays the men in uniform seem to give off some of it.

On your left as you enter is a pretty array of platters, the makings of a refreshing plate of Hors d'Oeuvres Variés, including slices of perfectly ripe but not the least bit soft avocado; tomatoes of rare redness and flavor for these days, and (touch of old elegance), the tomatoes are skinned; mushrooms, the stems trimmed down to a stump, so that they are crunchy little nuggets—they have been marinated in oil, vinegar and herbs; two kinds of saucisson sec—one peppery, the other smoky, both sausages firm, dark-red and abundantly fatted; chickpeas that are crisp—there is someone in the kitchen here who does not let a thing cook too long—and dressed with an oil that is fragrantly flavored with bay. You can have excellent ham, tender and smoky. The fresh clams and oysters are served on deep plates that have been filled with crushed ice— the littlenecks are *tiny*. The smoked trout is the usual thing, firm and flaky, and what differentiates one place from another as far as this dish goes is the horseradish sauce —this one is thick and heavy, made with cream that has been whipped until very stiff, and strong fresh horseradish.

If two of you want fish, you qualify for "Striped Bass Flambée Madrigal (For Two) $21.00 (45 Minutes Waiting Time)." This is a variant of the famous dish of Provence in which *loup* (a fish of the Mediterranean) is cooked over burning fennel branches. The real thing cannot be made in New York because *loups* do not frequent the Atlantic, but this will do. The fish is poached with the fennel branches, delivered to within viewing distance of your table, the twigs of fennel still protruding from the core of the fish, and flamed in Pernod, yielding, at the bottom of the pan, a buttery broth with a fennel flavor. Your captain separates the meat of the huge fish from the sticks and bones, piles it onto a couple of plates and spoons the sauce over it. The sauce is rather obvious, but it is good anyway, and the fish used here is impeccably fresh and thoroughly cooked without being in the least softened—a gay dish.

More in the tradition is the Caneton à l'Orange, and the one you get here is the honest article, not candied duck—the sauce is deep, slightly acidic, polished, velvety; the bird is moist and oily, without a trace of excess fat, wrapped in skin that has been browned to a glistening reddish umber.

If the two who had fish want to go all the way together, there are well-made soufflés, their tops like huge golden mushroom caps above the white porcelain soufflé dishes, available in all the standard sweet flavors, at a not falsely modest $7.50. The dessert cart carries an unabashedly sweet, thick, almost sticky chocolate mousse; a bowl of whipped cream that can be spooned on the mousse or on the strawberries (a couple of unripe ones here and there) in kirsch; a rich bread-and-butter pudding; crisp pears cooked in white wine and sugar.

Vestiges of the days when they were trying so hard to keep the riffraff out—at the bottom of the menu: "Appetisers [sic] Served and Not Followed by a Main Course will be charged as a Main Course"; and "One Portion Served for One Person Only." Nothing worked. The rowdies are still here, guffawing and giggling as they stumble out.

• MAMMA LEONE'S

239 West 48th Street
LUNCH, MONDAY TO FRIDAY; DINNER, DAILY.
Reservations, JU 6–5151.
Credit cards: AE, CB, DC, MC, V.
Medium-priced.

Mamma Leone's has been called the most underrated restaurant in New York, which tells us more about the ratings than about the restaurant. There are worse restaurants in New York, but those are the ones which cannot be described in words, the ones that can only be rendered by example or anecdote. The English language can cope, however, with Mamma's place—it is stunningly garish and ugly, the food is decent, the service automatic, the customers contented and unliberated cows with bulls and broods in tow. The place may well make more money than any other restaurant in town—the tourists come here in droves.

First of all, the restaurant is mammoth, and to fill a place like this, you need a lot of stuff, right? So you get some red plastic lobsters and stick them on the mirrors, frame the mirrors in gold tinsel and hang green fish net over the whole thing. (Sometimes you substitute a green paper anchor for the lobster.) You slice life preservers in half (the way you bisect a bagel for a sandwich) and stick them on the ceiling. Then you acquire a batch of heraldic pennants and give over the ceiling of at least one room to these. Also, you should get lots of paintings for the walls—for instance, a nice oil of a couple of voracious, poorly shaven monks salivating comically over their dinner (a good place for such an *objet* would be near the coat room, between signs that read "No Furs Checked"). Larger, more heroic canvases are also needed, for the grander rooms—such as swooning seminudes, giraffe-size; and heavenly encounters of godlike folk looking heroic.

But these are merely decorations. The place has to be filled—the space, not the walls —so we need Sculpture. Somebody in the sculpture game had Mamma's number, and as soon as he learned it, he started chiseling and selling, selling and chiseling, and she took it all. And what did this sweet little old lady like? You guessed it—good-looking girls, their clothes falling off, in pain. The stuff is all over the place. (There is so much of it that you may fail to notice the matched portraits of Eisenhower and Leone.) The statues are on pedestals, standing on the floor, in niches—all of them well-built females with troubles. The crass waiters (a pox on them) insert stray menus in these statues —under their arms, and you can imagine where else.

But the place needs still more. It needs action. So we get strolling (well, shuffling) musicians—sawyers and squeezers, the kind that wander from room to room appraising with bored, half-closed eyes each and every table, looking for the clue to the $5 tip. They throw a tune or two in that direction, snatch a couple of puffs and continue their search—cynical musical prostitutes whose mothers made them take lessons.

But this is a restaurant. So when you sit down you are brought celery, olives, tomatoes, and a block of soap the size of half a loaf of Wonder bread, and you cut off a hunk and go to the washroom to wash before dinner, and a few old hands restrain you good-naturedly and say no, no, that's cheese, for to eat, not soap. And you say no, no, it's soap, I can tell from the taste. And they say oh no you can't, because it doesn't have any taste! And everyone has a good laugh.

The menu at Mamma Leone's is a statistically perfect compendium of the most familiar dishes in New York's Italian restaurants. There is shrimp cocktail; anchovies and peppers (green ones, sautéed, not canned pimentos); an antipasto which includes those items as well as decent cabbage, beet and onion salad, insufficiently sautéed eggplant (tastes raw), melon, paper-thin prosciutto, a tube of bologna wrapped around a bread stick, a slice of good Genoa salami, and so on.

There is a soup called "Fresh" Chicken Soup, which either means fresh from the chicken or fresh from the pot. At any rate, it is listed as "pasta." The manicotti are literally fluffy, with a good strong meat sauce. The white clam sauce is too obviously thickened to retain the briny quality this sauce should have—it tastes like salty goo.

The main courses are the big comedowns. To satisfy out-of-town people, the over-cooked Italian sausage has as much taste as a drugstore hamburger—neither hot nor sweet. God forbid your roast chicken should be moist, so it is dry and stringy. And so on: bland Veal Piccata (theoretically a contradiction in terms), dismal Saltimbocca.

Pasty cheese cake with a layer of Ann Page pineapple preserves; rum cake decorated with pastel icing; a Zuppa Inglese that is much like the rum cake, but with good whipped cream instead of the toothpaste.

Mamma Leone's is such a solid tourist attraction that there are more horse-drawn cabs waiting for customers in front of Mamma's than there are on Central Park South. Lots of knee-length skirts and kiddies in crew cuts and suits with short pants. The waiters take the orders because the captains are busy snapping family group photos with the customers' own Instamatics. (As the man said at the Last Supper, everyone who wants to be in the picture better come around to this side of the table.)

★★MARCHI'S

251 East 31st Street (near Second Avenue)
DINNER. CLOSED SUNDAY.
Reservations, Monday to Thursday, 679–2494.
Credit cards: AE.
Medium-priced.

The food at Marchi's demonstrates the degree of perfection which should be achieved by a restaurant that serves a limited or fixed menu. With the possible exception of the lasagna, none of the food here suggests a particularly inspired hand in the kitchen. What it does reveal is simple preparation, with exquisite attention to time, temperature and proportions; and fresh ingredients of first quality. Anyone can do it, it would seem, but Marchi's, despite its success, has no imitators.

Marchi's has been serving its five-stage dinner in these spacious dining rooms for over forty years. The place is comfortable, the dining rooms well lighted, clean and carpeted, and the service very simple and correct; the stiff manner of the staff suggests a stern disciplinarian in the wings.

Dinner begins with a huge antipasto of celery, radishes, tomatoes, fennel (the winter celery with an anise-like flavor), melon (always ripe), parchment-thin slices of superb Genoa salami, and a mixed Lorenzo Salad of green olives, capers, chopped celery, red cabbage, parsley and a hint of tuna fish. In many neighborhoods in New York, one could go from store to store for a day and not be able to assemble the quantity of vegetables, in perfect condition, that is placed on a table for two at Marchi's. There is not a brown spot on the celery or fennel, the radishes are firm, the melon, though ripe, is not beginning to rot here and there. Even the tomatoes, virtually unobtainable in good and tasty condition in many years, are sound, if not what we remember from the days when tomatoes were tomatoes. It's best not to eat all that is served at this course, as there is much more to come, the aforementioned lasagna being next. This pasta dish, as prepared at Marchi's, is very sexy. The flat noodles are soft and firm—no hard edges, no binding together of gluey strata. The lightly tomatoed meat sauce is the single culinary accomplishment of this restaurant that seems more than simply perfect—in fact inspired.

The lasagna is succeeded by fish which has been lightly floured and fried to the point of crisp skin, and flaky, perfectly cooked flesh. The type of fish varies from time to time; occasionally one is served whole little smelts, sometimes small steaks from a larger fish. The fish is accompanied by barely cooked, crunchy, cold beets, and cooked green beans at room temperature, in a simple dressing.

Roast chicken, with skin crisped to the flakiness of parchment pastry, and roast beef, with a spoon of pan gravy, are the meat of the main course. These are served with an oversufficiency of sautéed mushrooms, and a salad of very crisp greens in a clear, sharp dressing.

Dessert consists of deep-fried lemon fritters, a disc of rather mild provolone cheese (port would go nicely here), a bowl of fresh fruit (nary a worm), and a huge stack of cristoli, those twists of dough which are here deep-fried to a brittle crust and sprinkled with powdered sugar. The espresso is perfect.

• MARKET DINING ROOMS & BAR

1 World Trade Center, on the Concourse
LUNCH, MONDAY TO FRIDAY; DINNER, MONDAY TO SATURDAY. CLOSED SUNDAY.
Reservations, 938–1155.
Credit cards: AE, CB, DC, MC, V.
Expensive.

Inhilco (horrid corporate name), a division of a division of Trans World Airlines, has a restaurant monopoly at the World Trade Center. Just as no one competes with it, so it does not compete with itself. For the Center's vast street-level shopping concourse, Inhilco has developed a restaurant—the Market Dining Rooms & Bar—that aims at customers quite apart from those courted by the pretentious establishments on the 107th floor (Windows on the World and Cellar in the Sky). MDR&B peddles itself as a temple to flavor and abundance, old comforts and fresh ingredients. And it advertises the creed with every trapping short of fish tanks and sawdust. Yet much of what arrives on your table is contrived or lifeless. The contented crowd has been had by the persuasive setting.

You approach the place through a field of café tables, pass through a matched pair of big untidy bars, and make your final leg through more tables—full-size, bare-topped and gingham-topped. This room, the prelude to the real thing, is for light eating and heavy drinking, office flirtations and fresh clams, peppery bean salads and too loud laughter. Giant burgers are sold by the gross, and these are a foretaste of the disparity between idea and reality that characterizes the food in the main restaurant—the burgers are gloriously browned but usually bloodless. You may order from the full menu out here, but that would be idiotic, for the only undiluted virtues of this whole complicated enterprise are the look and feel of the main dining room, and the service therein.

So you proceed under a sign that says DINING ROOM, then through a portal. You are greeted by a gentleman in a doctor's coat who is standing among crates of vegetables and a tray of eggs. Why you do not ask. He leads you to a table in a big glowing room that is dominated by polished oak and white linen, brass railings and frosted lamps, rugged oaken banker's chairs and soft banquettes upholstered in a nubbly black cloth that is crisscrossed with white chalk stripes. The stepped ceiling is painted a warm terra-cotta, the walls are of heavy wood stripping, stained brown. The spaciousness of the room is tempered by partitions—oak, surmounted by etched-glass panels—that make cozy islands of groups of tables. A little service bar, under a handful of eyeshade-green lamps, is a jewel-like touch. Here and there, antique oak tables are surrounded by assorted old oak chairs, a striking note of variety in the handsome room. Rising above it all are tall marble posts—at their tops brass statuettes of livestock standing within circles of lights. A comfortable place.

You find that your ample napkin has a buttonhole sewn in one corner, which makes it fastenable to your shirt. Cute. Your menu is replete with propaganda. Boring. The pumpernickel bread is chocolate-brown, fresh and light—terrific with the good sweet butter.

The best food in the place is that to which the least is done. The raw littleneck clams and Cotuit oysters are as fresh as you can find them. But when they bake the oysters with saffron and tomato, or devil them with mustard and bread crumbs, they look very pretty and taste like Coney Island. Avoid the hot clams too, except for the shell-roasted —these are buttery and lightly garlicked, the sweet flavor of the clams vivid in the strongly flavored juice. Good pickled herring, firm and tart, in crisp onions and cream; the kitchen adds a variant of its own—chopped green peppers, a misjudgment posing as originality. The Meatmarket pâté comes in a serving the size of a paperback book; it looks like a headcheese in a fatted pastry crust, gelatinous and cartilaginous and weighty—a texture dish, if you like that kind of thing. There is another house-styled pâté, this one a core of spinach in a doughnut of gnocchi—the spinach has lost most of its flavor but retains just enough to obscure the potato pasta. A ridiculous dish. Start instead with the fettuccine, a rare preparation, the tender eggy noodles mingled with crisp, barely cooked green vegetables—often, fresh peas, snow-pea pods, discs of zuc-chini, shafts of fibrous celery, and florets of crunchy broccoli, all bathed in cream and butter, fragrant with nutmeg, and livened with grindings of Parmesan cheese and fresh black pepper. This is one of the few plates of first-class food you can get in this place.

"Fish & Shellfish Are Delivered Fresh Each Day," quoth the menu. Carefully worded. That they are served the day they are delivered it not stated. Take for example the striped bass, baked on leeks and tomatoes: but for the sand in the leeks and the slightly noisome fish, it would be fine. And though the bay scallops may be fresh, they are defeated by their separated sauce of sorrel and cream, substances that do nothing for scallops except complicate them. What, you wonder, do they do with oysters that are no longer fresh? Why, they bury them in a dish of pan-fried shrimp and oysters, served with smoked sausage in tomato sauce, a compendium that wouldn't work even if the oysters were ten minutes from their beds.

One section of the menu lists dishes under the names of their suppliers. You are informed, for example, that your duck is supplied by H & H Purveyors, your chicken by DeBragga and Spitler. A shipper's name on a Burgundy may help you judge an unopened bottle, but you can't judge a duck by H & H if Inhilco intervenes. Duck is a fatty bird, and all over the world it is served in acidic sauces—cuts the grease, don't you know. Here it is served with a heavy gravy, than which nothing could be more redundant.

Some places sell the steak, some the sizzle. Here you barely get either. The skillet-grilled sirloin is just OK beef in (if you want it) a heavy brown sauce. The chopped steak is awful—dry and tasteless—and the storm of dried rosemary that is rained on it does not help. The charcoal-broiled leg of lamb—slices of rare meat with well-crusted edges—is not bad, but you are much better off with the double-rib chops, which are plump and juicy.

The platter of half a dozen vegetables is big and colorful. On occasion the components are limp and tired. Splendid kohlrabi gratinée (Hollaender, Gould & Murray Company, N.V.), the crisp discs pleasantly bitter, coated with strong browned cheese. Splendid hashed brown potatoes, crusty outside, moist within.

Not many desserts. The Bassett's (of Philadelphia) vanilla ice cream is marvelously rich, the maple syrup on it lost in the overpowering cream. The moist and strong chocolate cake is soaked in Grand Marnier, and the frozen chocolate soufflé is just a superb imitation of chocolate ice cream, its burnt-almond sauce adding a nice edge. Every pot of coffee is delicious.

A very brief list of inexpensive and drinkable wines. A slogan at the top of the list: "We'll Sell You Half-a-Bottle at Half-the-Price *Everytime!*" Looked at another way, a full bottle costs fully twice as much as a half bottle. At these prices—$5.50 and up for full bottles—the gimmick is only mildly offensive.

Your waiter offers to wrap up some of the excellent bread for you to take home. Sweet. On your way out, the doctor gives you a couple of those eggs. Next morning you discover they have double yolks. Cute again.

★ LE MARMITON

216 East 49th Street
LUNCH, MONDAY TO FRIDAY; DINNER, MONDAY TO SATURDAY. CLOSED SUNDAY.
Reservations, 688–1232.
Credit cards: AE, CB, DC, MC, V.
Medium-priced.

Time was when through the front door informality was not allowed to pass— gentlemen were required to be dressed in jacket and tie; and that tended to set a certain tone. And time was when through the kitchen door, food that failed to meet standards was similarly rebuffed, and that accounted for a reputation. Unfortunately, the relaxation of standards has been all but pervasive. You may come as you are, and the food on a given visit may not equal that of a previous visit. Some things, however, never change—you are expected to pay full price at all times.

This is still a commodious place, though the years have frayed its edges a bit. The small-patterned wallpaper, beamed ceilings, decorative copper utensils and cushy carpeting are slightly dimmed by the patina of time, but somewhere along the way a colorful mural has been added to the east wall of the dining room—of a narrow street in a French town in springtime, with leafy trees, orange awnings, blue sky—and if it fails to rejuvenate the staid surroundings, it does nothing to diminish their conventionality.

They still make a fine Pâté du Chef. Carve out a substantial slab from the red pot in which it was baked, in which it reposes under a blanket of jelly, and they still leave the pot right on your large table, for those of you who side with the more-is-better school. The Assiette de Hors d'Oeuvre is various but dull, including a nice little shrimp in cocktail sauce, slices of strong salami, the usual hard-boiled egg in Russian dressing, marinated mushrooms and a couple of items that should have been left in their cans. The Moules Ravigote are distinctly disappointing—the mussels themselves are a little tough and something less than perfectly fresh, and the so-called ravigote is nothing more than sandwich-shop Russian dressing. The snails are plump and tender, but oddly grassy and only mildly seasoned. This is a prix-fixe menu of the old style, so you are entitled to soup in addition to appetizer. The sorrel soup and watercress soup, when they are the soups of the day, are thick and hearty and sport the strong clear flavor of their greens, but the onion soup is dreary, despite its pungent cheese, and the Cold Jelly Consommé is virtually tasteless—squeeze on the lemon, and all you taste is the lemon.

The Roast Squab Chicken is a whole little bird, crisply roasted—its flavor is slight, but its sauce is studded with white onions and bits of ham, and that livens the dish. The Grenadin of Veal Normande is one of the best dishes in the place: pale veal in a creamy and buttery sauce that has been laced with calvados, to which has been added abundant sautéed mushrooms—tender meat, crunchy mushrooms and a velvety sauce, perfect textures. You expect a great deal of the lobster, billed as Maine Lobster Marmiton. It is perfectly nice, but its adornment of one scallop and several shrimp are a classic cliché—gilding the lily. The dish is served with melted butter that has been thickened with the lobster's tomalley. Not on the menu, but sometimes suggested by your host —"If you like it"—is Tête de Veau. One's first tête de veau (calf's head) is a rite of passage, like one's first moonshine, except that the calf takes more getting used to. This dish is an assortment of fibrous meats, cartilaginous jellies, resilient sinews—gamy and mild, tender and tough, depending on the particular morsel. It is served with a strong vinaigrette and plump boiled potatoes. This is challenging food, but one can become addicted to it. Sturdy dishes like this, as well as stews and fricassees, are what this restaurant does best.

The chocolate mousse is gentle, the coffee mousse gentler still—both are freshly made and airy. On occasion there is a vanilla mousse, suffused with the flavor of almonds. The fruit tarts are OK; the Macedoine de Fruits au Kirsch only vaguely liquored.

★ MAXWELL'S PLUM

1181 First Avenue (at 64th Street)
LUNCH AND DINNER.
Reservations, 628–2100.
Credit cards: AE, CB, DC, MC, V.
Expensive.

Maxwell's Plum suffers for its singles' bar reputation. That is not to say that its business suffers—as the prices go up, the intensity of the demand for tables seems to go up—but no one quite takes the Plum seriously as an eating place. It's true that in this three-ring circus, the center ring, between the elevated, ornate back room and the informal, street-level café, is a densely populated horseshoe bar at which the day's ration of, say, 1,000 customers buys precisely 1,000 drinks for the privilege of commencing conversations with strangers on territory where that is socially condoned. But the food in the outer rings is pretty good, in some instances original; the wine list is extensive and sanely priced; the service is available and pleasant; and the surroundings are a sight to see.

You arrive for your back-room reservation as part of an endlessly entering throng (something like the four-abreast Chinese who are somewhere perpetually throwing themselves off a cliff), most of which is heading headlong for the sexual gold mine at stage center ("If we can't make out here, we might as well give up"). You give your name to the gent behind the book, and he informs you that coats are checked downstairs, and that when you return, Van will show you to your table. "Van?" Your gaze is directed to a waiting figure who closes his eyes gently, smiles thinly, bows slightly and all in all makes it quite clear that he will wait patiently for your return from the hatcheck factory on the lower level. Or you show up for your café reservation, and your table is not ready, so you are instructed to keep your eye on the flashing lights over the entranceway, and when your number comes up, you're a winner.

Maxwell's Plum makes the Sign of the Dove look like a monastery. The ceiling is of molded plaster in many places, painted to look like hammered copper; that is, except for the ceiling in the back room, which is an acre of glowing stained glass illuminating a room papered in pointillist pink nudes against a pointillist blue-green ground. There are flickering gas lamps, ornate mirrors, statuary, velvet banquettes, flowers on all the tables. Here, when someone orders one of what the wine list refers to as "Rare and Extraordinary Wines," a busboy holds a candle while, by the light of it, a captain decants and examines the precious fluid. The café tables are covered with cloths of chrome-yellow gingham, there are hundreds of ceramic animals hanging from the canopy over the sidewalk section, hanging plants at the windows, banks of flowering shrubbery, and pillars of painted brick.

The Hors d'Oeuvres Variés include a few interesting items, such as a rather mild guacamole made with good, ripe avocado; marinated fish that is flaky and lemony; well-garlicked cold ratatouille; Russian eggs, with a powerful dressing; and so on. For a more luxuriant assortment you may begin with a platter of Scottish salmon, smoked trout and smoked sturgeon. Admittedly, the quality of these foods is no tribute to the kitchen, but they are obtained from good sources and brought to the table in good condition—at room temperature, but with no sign of drying out—and they are served with a sparkling whipped-cream-and-horseradish sauce.

You can get what they call Roast Wild Boar here, but though it may be roasted, it seems to have been battered and then sautéed. The meat is sweet, and it is served with slivered apples (they are slightly acid, which is good with this rich meat). Or you can have a cassoulet, here made with gamy meats and sausages, cooked until they have lightly burnt edges, all buried in crunchy white beans. Such a complex dish as Salmon en Croûte with Sorrel doesn't come off as well, although it *looks* lovely. The waiter expertly peals back the crust to cover the fish with a puréed mushroom sauce, but the sorrel stuffing has lost its sourness, the fish is overcooked, and the very good mushroom sauce can't really save tasteless fish, tasteless stuffing and tasteless pastry. If you want fish, order something simple, like grilled red snapper—the fish is perfectly cooked and lightly browned, and it is served with a delicate mustard sauce.

The pies and cakes are all good: a Black Forest cake that is part chocolate cake and part light chocolate mousse; good pecan pie that is loaded with nuts and cinnamon; banana fritters that are made with very ripe bananas, so that the crisp, deep-fried crust contrasts nicely with the sweet mushy center—this is served with a sauce of honey and cinnamon.

Sandwiches are available in the café.

★★ LA MÉTAIRIE

189 West 10th Street
LUNCH AND DINNER. CLOSED MONDAY.
Reservations, 989–0343.
No credit cards.
Wine.
Expensive.

You are greeted by your host, a tall, bronzed, handsomely weathered, robust-looking gent who is often wearing an *après*-ski sweater; his accent is the guttural growl of a French peasant, but his demeanor is suave. Your waitress is one of a small, earnest corps of youthful, well-nourished, long-haired angels, fetchingly costumed in dark, delicately patterned French country cottons; the star of the group turns your head one extra painless twist with musical speech that is measured out in a gentle cadence of the British Isles. If you dine late, you meet yet another of the notable staff, for the chef goes public at the end of the dinner hour and visits briefly at the tables in the dining room to determine how the evening's efforts went over. This cook is not your ordinary *chef de cuisine,* however, for the kitchen whites hang from the shoulders of a diminutive young woman whose sidewalks–of–New York accent has not been seasoned by her immersion in French food. She wears no *toque blanche* (perhaps because it would double her height), and the chipper enthusiasm with which she discusses her food is unsullied by hucksterism—she does not conceal her chagrin when any of the evening's results is less than what she had hoped. None of her disappointments is devastating, however; in fact, the food here is always decent, often delicious, sometimes superb, making La Métairie the best French restaurant in Greenwich Village and a very good one by any measure.

If you knew the former restaurant on these premises, La Petite Ferme (*en anglais,* "the little farm"), now situated uptown, you know the general physical outlines of La Métairie (*en anglais,* "the little farm"), its somewhat imitative successor: a handful of tables and hardly more than twenty chairs very tightly strung along the circumference of a minuscule, white, rough-plastered room, duplicative, we take it on faith, of the interior of a rustic cottage off a dirt road hard by a rocky, hand-tended field of struggling salsify.

The tablecloths are dark-green; your napkin is a heavy dish towel of green-and-white plaid; a basket of flowers and dried grasses hangs from the wall; and a candle burns on every table. As in the old Ferme, there are a couple of cooing doves, but this pair is housed in a comparatively posh bamboo cage, as against the crude wooden bars provided by the predecessor. Ears of maize and chains of garlic adorn the walls, and charcuterie, cheeses and desserts are on display on a little table and shelf. When the little place is filled, as it often is with well-dressed types, it has the air of too large a festivity, prosperous cousins invited, at a poor relation's too small house.

You are shown a little slate. The dishes of the day are chalked on one side, wines on the other. You are brought good French bread, slightly warmed, and a little pot of sweet butter adorned with a sprig of parsley. They go well with the "chochonnaille," a selection of the charcuterie that includes a coarse, heavily herbed pâté and rillettes, pounded meat that is spiced and fatted almost to the point of excess. It is served with crisp, tart, vibrant little pickles that sparkle in contrast to the enriched meats.

On occasion there is a mousse of sole, an exceptionally fluffy and sweet refinement of fresh fish, with a couple of crisp shrimp for contrast, in a polished sauce that is made slightly pink with a touch of tomato. And sometimes there is a salade du pêcheur— plump scallops, fresh-tasting shrimp, mussels, and a sprinkling of capers in a mayonnaise whose extreme richness suggests it was made on the premises.

The blackboard listing "Salade Jeannette" represents different things on different nights: one time, firm strands of beet and celery with whole marinated mushrooms on a few leaves of tender lettuce, the entire little production moistened with a lively vinaigrette; another time, a simple lentil salad, the firm and tender beans oily, peppered and solidly satisfying.

The talents of that woman in the kitchen are particularly suited to seafood, as she demonstrates in merlan aux câpres, a splendidly browned slice of whiting, moist and flaky within its crust, adorned with capers (she loves capers) and surrounded by crisp vegetables and fluffy rice. Capers again in the sole Métairie, an odd dish in which the delicate fish is covered with a well-seasoned fish purée studded with capers and shrimp. The bar aux raisins is a simple dish of bass in a white sauce with a good bit of wine in it and plump white grapes; the hot and juicy fruit is a nice foil to the tender fish.

The steaks and liver are always well made: excellent meat accurately grilled, crusty outside, tender and bloody inside, moistened with a bit of sauce made in the pan— elegant dishes. But the escalopes de veau provençale, though of pale and tender veal, suffers from a tomato sauce that, with its peppers and olives and garlic, is too much a vegetable stew, not the sprightly sauce it is meant to be. Poulet au vinaigre is a more than decent country dish—lightly browned chicken, stewed and served in a slightly sour sauce.

Good cheese, fresh and at room temperature, is always on hand. If you want a pear with yours, someone peels one for you. Of the desserts, the big production is the tarte Tatin—dark, almost caramelized apples on a well-browned crust, served flaming in Calvados.

★ MINETTA TAVERN

113 MacDougal Street (at Minetta Lane)
LUNCH AND DINNER.
Reservations, 473-8907.
Credit cards: AE, DC, MC, V.
Medium-priced.

The type has almost passed—the Village saloon, to which, in the days when the Village was the Village, aspiring admen and editors repaired (having made the quick change from young exec to Bohemian by loosening their four-in-hands on the south-bound Fifth Avenue bus) to booze up in the front room and then sober up on strong food at a table in the back. Invariably these establishments were decorated with carica-tures of those regular customers who were also pals of the boss, and dozens of the old drawings, framed and behind glass, cover a couple of the walls of the front room; there is a painting of Joe Gould, the quintessential Greenwich Village nonconformist; and throughout the place, framed photographs of the former long-time proprietor, slim, trim, dapper Eddie "Minetta" Sieveri, as he is referred to in all the captions, with the likes of Tami Mauriello or Linda Darnell or Willie Pep, even the famous self-conscious in their poses.

The front room has a long, shiny bar, red lights, cut glass, a handful of bare, polished tables with bowls of pretzels. The dining room is vaguely Moorish, with a couple of plaster arches descending to pillars of simulated brick, and along one wall, red drapes hanging from the ceiling to the floor, tied back to facilitate the waiters' access to the kitchen and yours to the facilities. There are wooden booths, and the tables are covered with white linen. But if you lift your eyes to the upper reaches of the other—undraped —walls, there you will see the happily preserved and annotated old murals of the Village as it was in the days before there was a Minetta Tavern. There is Mori's, one of the fanciest and most expensive supper clubs in all of Manhattan, doing business on Bleecker Street near West Broadway (God knows what is doing business there now), and in front of the place, a uniformed chauffeur at the wheel of a luxurious sedan, reading, waiting for the revelers. There is Washington Square North, with nothing behind the row of houses but open sky, and with horse-drawn carriages passing through the uncluttered street. There is the Washington Square arch high over a park that looks nothing at all like a jungle. There is the Sixth Avenue El. The whole panorama is rendered with such innocence! Certainly the El could never have been anything but a noisy nuisance. And Mori's was something of a clip joint. But whoever painted it all, when it was not yet very old, apparently knew that to future eyes it would be seen, most easily, as a fairyland.

When you turn your thoughts to the purpose of your visit and your eyes to the bill of fare, you will find that Minetta Tavern offers a conventional, albeit lengthy, Italian menu. What you will not learn from reading the lists is that this is a sauce restaurant

—*good* sauces—wherein the ingredient to be sauced is not invariably the equal of its liquid garnish, unless that ingredient is pasta. Accordingly, you may wish to come here for a simple dinner of a cool appetizer, a big plate of spaghetti, dessert and coffee— and if you do, you will not be disappointed. But the meat and fish dishes are not disasters, and a number of them are more than decent.

To begin there is a not bad stuffed artichoke—the stuffing is an oily, herbed breading, the vegetable itself is perhaps overcooked; but it is cooked in consommé, with considerable oil, and this flavorful liquid is what you dip the leaves and heart in. The cold appetizer called Mixed Sea Salad is composed of small chunks of crisp shrimp, circlets of tender squid (cones, if you get the end of the little torso), the odd sardine, anchovies and stretchers of tomato, and diced celery, all in a bright garlic dressing, with lots of parsley and oregano.

The pasta courses are the best. Rigatoni Sorrentina is a thick, tubular noodle in a meat sauce that has been mixed with ricotta cheese. This particular combination has a mysterious succulence that seems to derive from the sauce being at once creamy and meaty. Spaghettini Caruso is a dish made of thin pasta with perfectly sautéed chicken livers, onions and thinly sliced fresh mushrooms. Another good pasta dressing in this restaurant is the sauce Matriciana, here made with tomatoes and onions, plenty of red and black pepper, considerable salt (which it takes on without tasting excessively salty), and lots of sage and bay.

Among the veal dishes there is a very decent Veal Pizzaiola—the red sauce is fiery and heavily flavored with oregano—but the veal itself is not first-rate. The Calf's Liver Veneziana is also pretty good—chunks of liver, sautéed so that they are pink in the middle, and lots of onions—but the liver itself is not perfectly delicate. The scungilli served here comes in a terrific red sauce—peppery and oily and abundantly flavored with garlic—but the scungilli (conch) itself is mature and rather tough. None of these main courses is less than good to eat, but each of them suffers a little from carelessly selected basic ingredients.

The zabaglione seems to be a mistake. You order it once, and it is snow-white for lack of Marsala, and you order it again and it is exactly the same—it is sweet, hot, frothy and liquored with something or other, but it does not taste like zabaglione. The cheese cake is better; made with ricotta and plenty of lemon, it is moist, and somehow at once filling and refreshing. Good espresso.

• MR. & MRS. FOSTER'S PLACE

242 East 81st Street
DINNER. CLOSED SUNDAY AND MONDAY.
Reservations essential, LE 5–1234.
No credit cards.
Wine and beer.
Expensive.

After overcharging twenty-five patrons twice a night, six nights a week, for a number of years, Mrs. Foster, the sole proprietor, apparently still can't afford larger quarters for her establishment, or the elimination of a couple of tables so that the remaining diners could eat comfortably. At one dinner a gentleman facing west was locking elbows with a man facing east at another table, while a couple of feet away, on a skimpy banquette, the third guest at a table too small for two had the options of (1) not facing his food, (2) eating sideways or (3) standing up.

"This is a jacket-and-tie place," Mrs. Foster informs you over the telephone, after accepting your reservation and food order (the latter required in advance), but she neglects to mention that the place is for Hobbits.

The odium of comparison will be noted more by Mrs. Foster than by Madame Helma (of Casa Brasil). The comparison is unavoidable because, superficially, the two restaurants resemble each other. Perhaps this place should shut down for a few months while Mrs. Foster, who obviously knows how to cook, serves an apprenticeship in other aspects of restaurant management at her neighbor's place only a few blocks away.

Dinner at Mr. and Mrs. Foster's Place begins with a minuscule ramequin of chicken livers sautéed in butter and madeira, and served with buttered toast. The livers are superb, and the toast would seem excellent at the counter of a hotel coffee shop. The next course is a small, excellent blini stuffed (well, almost filled) with red caviar and sour cream, and served with lemon and watercress. These are so delicious that it's a crime to serve only one, but a thread of sadism seems to run through this place.

Then comes your tiny corn bread, made in a corn-shaped mold, and very crispy. It is meant to accompany the soup, but that arrives later still. Negotiations for more bread may be undertaken and concluded satisfactorily, but the second piece never actually arrives. The soups include an excellent cold apple, made with white wine and served with sour cream; a tepid mushroom consommé; and a good lentil soup flavored with parsnip and nutmeg, and served with lemon and sour cream.

At this wrong juncture the vegetable salad arrives, composed of cold, parboiled broccoli, string beans and carrots; tomato, blanched to remove the skin; and lettuce; all moistened with a good French dressing.

After your waiter returns your fork to the table from your salad plate, you're ready for the main course. Mrs. Foster serves Beef Wellington made without pâté, and if she eliminated the pastry as well, we would really be getting places. Beef Wellington (whatever one may think of the pretentious dish) without pâté is the equivalent of ham and eggs without eggs. Whatever you call it, the dish is excellent here—served with a well-flavored madeira sauce. It is available only when ordered for two.

Something called Burgundy Beef is sautéed beef and sautéed vegetables (celery, carrots, white beans and onions) in a sauce made with a strong stock, a little wine and a heavy enrichment of butter.

The shellfish dishes are all good, including a very large lobster (at an immense price) stuffed with crabmeat and shrimp; and crayfish flavored with parsley and dill.

The desserts are disappointing: a dismal mousse made, it seems, with milk chocolate; a vanilla pudding named "Snow" but reminiscent of junket; a dull cherry torte; and a chocolate cheese cake which seems to have been coagulated rather than baked.

When asked what this or that dish is flavored with, Mrs. Foster caresses the back of her hair, giggles girlishly and announces that she never gives her secrets away. Her best-kept secret is how she gets the customers to come back.

Your check arrives when the waiter decides it's time. This is the same genius who, besides his corn-bread and salad-fork ploys, can't remember which of two soups is for which of two people, never fills an empty water glass unless he is asked, and grandly decides for you that the wine is OK, simply plunking the bottle down on the table. (If you want your white wine kept cool in a bucket, you must so plead.)

Most of the food is good. Almost everything else is not. Pay, and pick your way out carefully.

★★ IL MONELLO

1460 Second Avenue (near 76th Street)
LUNCH, MONDAY TO FRIDAY; DINNER, MONDAY TO SATURDAY. CLOSED SUNDAY.
Reservations, 535–9310.
Credit cards: AE, CB, DC, MC, V.
Expensive.

One thin, thin page, not without its blemishes and errata, added to the very thin book entitled "Estimable Italian Restaurants of New York's Upper East Side." (Do not turn down the fragile leaves.) So we give thanks. Also a bit of advice. Your host is a gracious gentleman, he aims to please. In fact, his good will extends even to the help, from whom he does not demand the good manners he expects of himself. He sets an example which may or may not be followed, almost certainly not by the captains. You innocently ask one of these bored officials the difference in preparation between the mussels (Muscoli Portofino) and the clams (Vongole Positano). "It's da same thing," he says to the section of wall just over your head. On another occasion you order the Misto di Pesce fra Diavolo, but as the occasion is a Friday, when the daily special is Zuppa di Pesce Livornese, you are brought the daily special, which is ready, instead of the food of your choice, which is not. You remonstrate, and you are assured, in no-compromise terms, that the food before you is precisely what you ordered. Risotto con Funghi, a rice dish, is listed under "Farinacci," to which list is appended the legend "half order of pasta served as an appetizer." You request a half order of risotto. No dice, full orders only. (He is peeved—the rice takes forty-five minutes, which info does not persuade you to change your mind.)

Il Monello is a pretty big place, plaques and crossed swords on the walls, garish chandeliers hanging from the acoustical ceiling, white linen on the tables. There is, of course, a bar, over which well-fed guys exchange wisdom with the bartender while the ladies are off powdering their noses—no quotes, this is a family publication. Though the captains are in formals, the waiters wear only long-sleeved pink shirts (open at the collar), as if they were a crew of dashing unemployed actors—on the portly and/or bald the outfit looks delusional, like aviator glasses on a spinster. But in this crowd there can be no anomalies—Seventh Avenue mingles with Wall Street; whispered, spiritual seductions with young marrieds comparing prosperities—"What was your average wedding present?" one husband wants to know of another.

Begin with Insalata di Funghi Freschi. You cannot tell from the name, even if you read Italian, that this mushroom salad is 50 percent celery, but you will know at first taste that slivered fresh mushrooms and crisp celery, in a slightly garlicked dressing of oil and little else, is a stunningly appetizing first course, particularly when the ingredients are impeccably fresh—who would have figured, mushrooms and celery? Or else divide a main course of Muscoli Portofino, in which fresh mussels are steamed in white wine and garlic. The mussels seem newly plucked from the sea, they are not oversteamed, so they are tender, and the broth in your plate, a layer of minced garlic at the bottom, is briny and strong.

Proceed to Tortellini alla Panna, those little crescents of pasta stuffed with ground chicken, each of them firm, in a sauce of thick cream and strong cheese. This is mother's-milk kind of food, warm and comforting, but it can be converted to something more stimulating by grinding on the fresh pepper. That rice you were warned would take forty-five minutes comes in half an hour and is worth the pause. The magic of these Italian rice dishes is in the sautéeing of the ingredients, including the rice, before the grain is cooked in a strong broth. To make the sauce, butter and/or cheese are added at the end. This version is close to perfect, each grain of rice separate, the thick sauce pungent and vaguely smoky, the bits of mushroom here and there almost lost among these powerful tastes, so that it is best to eat them separately.

Well, you can put up a giant fuss, or you can eat the Zuppa di Pesce Livornese (which you received in place of the Misto di Pesce fra Diavolo that you ordered). Minister to your feelings with a glass of Barbera (before your captain vanishes your bottle) and proceed with your alternate dinner. This is a Friday special, apparently made in batches, and the clams and mussels toughen a bit as they wait for your arrival. The dish also includes chunks of fish, big scallops and squid, all in a spicy and oily sauce —strong, satisfying food, in abundant amount, but without finesse. Just to prove they can do unqualifiedly ill, Il Monello is kind enough to destroy a dish that you can get good versions of in dozens of other places. The chicken dish called Pollo Scarpariello consists of chunks of chicken which have become oil-logged in their sautéeing; it is served in a milky red sauce, and it is garnished with canned artichokes, the makings of a total mistake. However, another dish you can get almost anywhere—Saltimbocca Fiorentina—is made here in an exceptionally vivid version: there is across the top the usual layer of ham, but here the meat seems to have been grilled or broiled briefly, which accentuates the sharp flavor of the red meat; the veal just below is white and buttery; the spinach the meats rest on is pure and strong; and over it all there is a smooth sauce, buttered and slightly lemony, which livens the dish. An order of deep-fried zucchini is one time soggy and limp, another time crisp and lightly browned.

Your helpful captain makes special arrangements for the delivery of menus by the busboy so that you may select desserts. Then he returns to hear your selections. Then he informs you that your selections are not available. Had he brain one, he would have told you that in the first place. You figure this is basically a good Italian restaurant, and you calculate that, therefore, the house must have real Italian Parmesan cheese in the kitchen. You are right, and it is hard, sharp, head-clearing. You may have it with melon that is not invariably ripe. You may skip the whole thing and have a cheese cake that is of the cream-cheese variety—rich, gooey, and sweet. Or you may get even with Il Capitano by ordering a zabaglione. He makes a good one, eggy, with lots of hot wine.

○ MONK'S INN

35 West 64th Street
LUNCH AND DINNER.
Reservations, 874–2710.
Credit cards: AE, CB, DC, MC, V.
Medium-priced.

In restaurant journalism, eating places are often rated separately for different aspects of their operation. Thus, one place may be scored very high for food but very low for cleanliness, or good for "atmosphere" but bad for service—which raises certain questions. Should someone in search of dinner repair to, say, O. Henry's, with its mindless menu, vulgar service and dirty floors, to sample a portion of its ambience?

Among the restaurants in New York that trade (successfully) on one restaurant feature, giving indifferent attention to the others, is Monk's Inn, where interior design is all, and food, service and cleanliness (and you) are nothing. A local mag refers to its "monastic mood." It's the customers who must be in a monastic mood to tolerate the place, and apparently they are. Their saintly indifference to mistreatment and their Zen relish of discomfort are manifested daily. Hundreds of them, paralyzed to abject faith by the overwhelming air of the place, line up—wide-eyed masochists, grinning, eager to be playthings in the management's and waiters' sport.

The waiters are dressed in knee-length monk's habits—baggy pants and scruffy shoes protruding from the bottoms, shaggy heads from the tops. The restaurant itself is a huge brick-walled, street-level dungeon, dimly lit by tabletop candles, each set in a wine bottle. The candles are fast-burning, and new ones are installed at every table at almost every meal, a service attended to far more rigorously than the delivery of food and drink, or the removal of the detritus of previous courses. The drippings of the candles have accumulated pyramidally around their bases, and the encroachment of candle wax seriously compromises the serviceability of the already wee tabletops. In time, when the tables are completely useless, they will be removed, and the worshipers will eat from their laps with one hand, holding the candle-bottle in the other hand, and twice as many of the faithful will be accommodated (if that is the correct word).

The waiters are brinksman penance inflicters, always testing to see how far the devout will let them go before they cry "Enough!" (The management will let them go as far as their ingenuity carries them.)

When you sit down at your checkered, encrusted tablecloth, you will be presented with a couple of slabs of complimentary cheese. Leyden and smoky Wisconsin Cheddar are an odd appetizer, but this is the best part of the meal, so eat it when you can, which may be five minutes later when your sticky silverware arrives, or five after that, when the bread materializes (with a couple of apples), or if you are stubborn, later still, when the waiter, in his flight, drops off the butter.

The first courses are soups: Soupe Montagnarde, described as "Lumber Jack Style Soup," and undoubtedly, some lumberjacks eat vegetable soup, au college dormitory; Potage Esau—*Then Jacob gave Esau bread and pottage of lentiles; and he did eat and drink* (Gen. xxv. 34)—get it?; Gratinée des Halles "Onion Soup Halles Style," though one would have to look all over Paris, let alone in the district of Les Halles, to find an onion soup that can't stand up to a glass of tea. More interesting than comparing the soups with their descriptions is finding a place for them on the table, by now already overburdened; but the waiter moves your cheese plate to the left of your fork, places the breadbasket half over the edge of the table, snuggles the salt into the ashtray and forces the soups into position.

Now comes the main course, and you thought the waiter was going to remove the soup dishes, didn't you? They are piled one on top of the other, the ashtray (still with the salt in it) is lowered into the space you left in the breadbasket when you ate one of the apples (you couldn't eat the other, because it was resting in its own fermenting liquor), the wine and water glasses are forced against the base of Mount Candle, the cheese board (you remember the Leyden and Cheddar?) is placed atop the soup dishes, and you are served, say, La Raclette Valaisanne, "A Swiss Aged Bagne Cheese scraped from the Wheel at the Stove served with Potato and Assorted Relishes" (capitals theirs), which is tasteless cheese, melted directly on a very thin metal plate (which promptly gets cold, the cheese with it), decorated with Heinz pickles, gimlet onions, frozen kernel corn (golden yellow) and a cold, soggy boiled potato. Or else you may sample the Bratwurst aux Pommes Lyonnaises, which tastes like a hot dog—not at Nedick's, not at Nathan's, not at a Sabrett hot-dog stand, no, more like the rubber hose Harry Stevens serves to his captive clientele at the Big A. A call for mustard means the saltcellar must be removed from the ashtray (which, you will recall, is in the breadbasket) and placed between the stems of the adjacent water glasses so that this essential spice, brought in a saucer, can be placed on the ashtray.

Dessert? Well, that means you are through with your main courses, which simplifies everything. The large plates are placed one atop the other, the breadbasket atop these, and luxurious space is available for Crêpe aux Groseilles Flambées (an excess of lingonberries wrapped in suede, burned in kirsch), and *café,* which is mud in a cup in a pudding dish (the saucer is busy with the mustard).

This restaurant wasn't bad when it first opened—at least the food was edible. But now the chef, not content to be outdone by the dining-room staff, matches the penance they exact with forced fasting. The famous table of cheeses flaunts a Bel Paese with the telltale map of North and South America, and a Brie which not only runs but shouts. The wine list is a joke.

★★★ MON PARIS

111 East 29th Street
LUNCH, MONDAY TO FRIDAY; DINNER, MONDAY TO SATURDAY. CLOSED SUNDAY.
Reservations, 683–4255.
Credit cards: AE.
Expensive.

Crimson fleurs-de-lis of velvety flocking adorn the walls; carpeting cushions the floor; there are street lanterns, framed travel posters, jolly art; chandeliers that are bouquets of little red lampshades shine down on tables snowy with stiff white linen. The waiters serving you are in scarlet doublets; their boss, ever-present and watchful, mindful that they do it well, is portly and contented in his snug, too long jacket. He is a kind of burghermaster among the self-made middlemen spending their money here. The rather obvious posh of the institution he presides over fulfills the early dreams of the jobbers, head bookkeepers, salesmen and bejeweled housewives who compose the couples, and clusters of couples, that fill this place.

No one here was born with a three-bedroom apartment and a terrace in his mouth; there is nary a prep-school diploma or B-School master's in the house. They are all perfectly well off, you understand, but their pleasures are not quite taken for granted, and while they betray considerable satisfaction in the comfort and solid food they find here, and visit with each other heartily about such subjects as making connections between Acapulco and San Juan during what is known as the height of the season, their preoccupation with the wherewithal to prosper again another day is rarely more than just under the skin of their conversations. A cocktail or two, a little time with the menu, two minutes with the waiters—hardly have the crevettes Provençale arrived when talk among the men switches to market conditions, among the ladies to supermarket conditions and the chances of getting Himself to spring again for a fortnight on the sunny sands.

You, however, will give all your attention to those shrimp Provençale; plump, crunchy and sweet, they are moistened with a garlicked sauce that is red, tart and heavy, glistening with oil, thick with little chunks of tomato, prettied with a liberal sprinkling of fresh, fragrant parsley. The escargots de Bourgogne are equally blunt, served in New York's most forthright snail butter, so nubbly with bits of minced garlic that it has the texture of cereal, and so pungent of garlic flavor that the abundance of parsley can be detected only by its vivid green color.

Cooler beginnings include smoked trout with a sauce Raifort that is made with plenty of horseradish and little finesse, and the Terrine de Canard, heavy with duck meat and liver, salty and thickly fatted, very good with the crusty bread served here and some cold white wine.

It is a sign of the familiarity of the customers with the peculiarities of the house that about half the tables order a dish that is never listed on the menu—a profound lobster bisque that seems to crackle with the essence of lobster shell. It is deep and winy soup.

The secret of the bisque, of course, is the availability of lobster shells, and they are in abundant supply here because of the popularity of Le Homard sauté à l'Armoricaine. This is not a dish for lobster purists, being several removes from the elemental thing you dip in butter. The crustacean arrives in hefty chunks—meat and shell—that are piled to the rim of a deep bowl. The bowl is filled with a spicy, dark-brown broth that is heavily tomatoed, lively of wine. Blatant food. The frogs' legs are subtle by comparison, though the nicely crusted, tender thighs are liberally sprinkled with sautéed minced garlic and moistened with a strong tomato sauce.

Jump not quickly to conclusions, for many dishes here lack even a hint of tomato, among them brains in black butter, a good version, tender, smooth and a little tart, crusted and browned, moistened with a carefully burned butter that is studded with sour capers. The Poulet au Vin Rouge is the standard thing, the chicken well browned before it is simmered in wine and stock. The bird is a good one, with the clear— nowadays rare—flavor of fresh chicken; and its cooking liquid has an earthy taste that is imparted by the fresh mushrooms that are part of the stew. A more interesting dish, and not just for its rarity hereabouts, is Le Pigeon Grillé Maître d'Hôtel. The entire little bird, spread open, is herbed and buttered, and broiled until its skin is almost blackened, its dark meat, hot and moist, at a peak of high, sweet flavor. Splendid lamb chops are available here, as well as good steaks—they are of tasty and tender meat, accurately prepared and handsomely crusted. The accompanying vegetables for all of these are a bit sad, but many of the main courses come with puffed potatoes, tiny golden balloons that you can have with any main course if you so command. A crisp salad of fresh greens in a lively vinaigrette comes with your dinner.

Sometimes the cheeses are fine, sometimes not. You may send for them, look at them and judge for yourself. The remainder of the printed dessert list is boring—mousse, peach Melba, coupe aux marrons, commercial pastries, etc. Regular customers, as soon as they arrive, order the unlisted soufflés, and late in the evening these flow from the kitchen by the dozen, their browned tops high above their white ceramic pots. They are not the greatest soufflés in town, but they are fine—though the Grand Marnier is a little heavier than the ideal, and one wishes the accompanying crème Anglaise were not cool; the chocolate soufflé would be more exciting if its flavor were more intense.

• MORTIMER'S

1057 Lexington Avenue (at 75th Street)
LUNCH AND DINNER.
No reservations (861–2481).
Credit cards: AE, DC, MC, V.
Medium-priced.

Famous people, people who look famous, gents and ladies in colorful duds and tanned skins, scented folk, laughing folk, earnest folk, tipsy folk. Much waving to friends across the room and blowing of kisses. Plenty of colorful cocktails shaken for the cheerfully waiting loungers at the bar—no reservations, boys and girls, and the boys and girls love the suspense of not knowing when they'll ever eat. "Who cares?" is the motto of this carefree crowd.

Mortimer's has been straightforwardly laid out, a large, square, high-ceilinged room with brick walls, giant mirrors framed in dark wood, a lengthy bar along one side (behind which as many as three bartenders are kept busy). Old-fashioned opaline lights provide the illumination for your crisply linened tables and simple cane-seated chairs, for your potted greenery here and there in the slightly hazy atmosphere, for the organdy drapes that grace the front windows (which would make of this place a lace-curtain P. J. Clarke's were P.J.'s drunks ever to join Mort's crowd). But this is distinctly not an inebriate's hangout, no matter how much drunkenness you may spot.

No, this restaurant has been set aside for a specific type: he may be drunk or sober (he will not deny being either), he may be old or young (he will not advertise the former); she may be single or married (she'd hate to allow she's never been the latter). He is a sportsman, she the devil-may-care companion. She is casually chic, comfortable on a little something Daddy gives her. They are the Year-Round Hamptonists, whose plans for the summer germinate in October, are discussed, considered and revised all winter. So if you don't know where your friends are, this may be the place.

Mortimer's may be a perfect place of its kind if only it did not take itself seriously. Word has been let out that its "chef" was "formerly of" someplace or other. The menu is sprinkled with French accent marks (about half as many as its text calls for). The listed food includes such exoticisms as Crab en Gelée, Kipper Pâté and Carrots Glacé. And you can get a bottle of Dom Pérignon for thirty-six clams. But only a modicum of skepticism is needed to put the place and your expectations in reasonable perspective —Mortimer's is a combination feedbox/watering hole, a perfectly respectable form of retail establishment, this one already much honored in the observance.

You arrive early, and your host, a hip and modish Briton, proffers a table near the front window. You accept. He then plants his tail on the adjacent sill, to discuss your preferences with you. Later, when the place is packed, no such leisurely visits are possible—he flies by, his shirt collar rising above his jacket, his temperature rising above normal, his color above pink.

The highest-price-tag first course is the Crab en Gelée. It shows up in a small oval ramekin, the crabmeat and a decorative cross section of hard-cooked egg visible through the cloudy and firm aspic. This is certainly OK crabmeat, albeit frozen rather than fresh, but the jelly is harsh, too briny, and the dab of creamy mayonnaise that arrives on a lettuce leaf alongside the little porcelain pot must be used copiously if the gamy quality of the jelly is to be tamed. Stay away from the Kipper Pâté—it looks, smells and (one guesses) tastes like cat food. Opt, rather, for the Cold Cucumber Soup —served here in a low-dill, high-parsley version which is creamy and refreshing.

One assumes that when a restaurant appends its name to one of the dishes it serves, it does so with a touch of pride, that the dish is one of the kitchen's more meritorious achievements. Thus one orders Chicken Hash Mortimer with the conviction that, good or bad as it may be, everything else will be worse. But just as one must not take this restaurant terribly seriously, one must not be unduly taken with one's powers of reason. Chicken Hash Mortimer is neither "hash" nor much more than OK. It is, rather, creamed chicken, altogether satisfying, utterly unspectacular, and the abundance of huge chunks of white meat moistened by a pale sauce which is lightly sharpened with lemon, the whole creation surmounted by a crisp crêpe. A secondary recommendation is implied in the title of Broiled Chicken, Chef's Style, and sure enough, this is an ambitious venture, a carefully broiled half-bird, but this time the chicken's absence of flavor reveals its provenance (a freezer); and the buttery sauce, peppery and lightly herbed, and the nicely browned skin cannot rescue it from mere acceptability. Your Shell Steak is as rare as you wish and perhaps tougher than its price tag calls for. The Calves (sic) Liver Sauté is the sleeper, the thin slices grilled very rapidly, so that they are crisp and dark outside, pink and moist within. Fettucini Alfredo is here rendered in a version in which the thick sauce of eggs, cream and cheese is augmented by fresh peas and mushrooms. The noodles are firm, the white sauce slightly sharp of the sturdy cheese that went into it, and the vegetables are little nuggets of nature's own flavors amid the more contrived ones of the noodles and sauce.

A brief choice of OK desserts: a perfectly good apple tart which would be splendid if it weren't kept in the refrigerator right until the time you order it; a sweet entitled Trifle Mortimer, consisting of chunks of cake and cakecrust, raisins, a hefty dollop of good whipped cream, and a heavily brandied sweet sauce. Pass up the cheese—it is old, and it is presented to you with such unlikely accompaniments as icy tangerines and tasteless "Delicious" apples.

The host cannot pronounce the names of the wines he recommends; the waiters, in white shirts, black ties and long white aprons, perspire easily; the busboys work very hard and never neglect to return your fish fork to its original position on the linen, where it will be handy for your cheese cake. At 10 P.M. the lights are lowered. You get coffee beans in your Sambucca.

★★NAKAGAWA

7 West 44th Street
LUNCH AND DINNER. CLOSED SUNDAY.
Reservations, 869–8077.
Credit cards: AE, DC, MC.
Medium-priced.

Spic-and-span Japan, sleekly furnished in unstained wood, soft carpeting, and just as a reminder, a little rice paper here and there for filtration of the illumination. The cheerful young kimonoed waitresses wear gingham aprons with pockets in them for their order books. Your host is in black jacket and bow tie, but there are paper napkins at your place.

You enter to a little bar. At noon it is softly lit by the daylight that filters through the bamboo shades over the front windows, and the bar is populated by a scattering of midtown lunchers waiting for their companions. At night the little barroom is almost dark, and every stool is topped by a Japanese male in his thirties. They smoke and drink strong drinks. Just beyond the liquor bar is a long, narrow room, sushi bar along one side, tables along the other. At the rear, a sunken dining room, with more tables. At night, throughout, more Japanese males in their thirties, every one of them dressed like a B-School graduate in the Eisenhower era. Is Japan controlling its population by exiling its educated males during their procreative years? They do not seem to mind. They gather here happily and ignore the waitresses. Let us hope, as we begin, that this disposition is not a by-product of the cuisine.

The cuisine, its elegant presentation, some of the prettiest-arriving food in town, the good looks, from dish to dish, reflecting the food itself—assortments of sushi, cool and glistening, spread casually on wooden boards; strongly flavored foods in angular arrays; crusty foods formed into lightly browned cylinders. The plates, boards, bowls—curved rectangles, crescents, platforms, shallow cones; in earth colors, cool glazes, gleaming enamels.

The food is almost as good as it looks. Sushi that includes little blankets of deep-red tuna over vinegared rice, moistened with a soy sauce that is almost chocolatelike, at once warm and sharp; sheets of seaweed wrapped around crisp raw zucchini and rice; silky raw squid; fried egg loaf with a belt of seaweed holding it to a patty of rice; a layer of red fish roe over one of rice, in a cylinder of the seaweed.

A few of the dinnertime appetizers, which are orderable by number, no transliterations of the Japanese characters given. Try No. 12, a little dish of sliced squid, seasoned with salmon roe and cod roe, the squid silky and oily, the gamy roe dressing laden with salt. No. 13 consists of radish that has been grated down to a paste, buried in a mound of minuscule fish, each of them no larger than half an inch of string—the contrasting textures are the appeal of the elusively flavored dish. No. 3 is described on the menu as "Chopped squid seasoned with sea chestnut," and it is recommended for those in search of a flavor so intensely concentrated and animal-like that it is almost rank. A couple of bottles of beer will help you through a couple of ounces of this stuff, but in the process you may break a barrier.

At lunchtime some of the main courses are apparently made available especially for the pink-skinned types who frequent the place during daylight hours—Fried Salmon, for example, a battered and deep-fried crescent of red fish served with a slice of raw orange and a misplaced sauce that is a terrific imitation of Worcestershire. But people in all kinds of skin like the Kakiage—a splendid loaf of chopped shrimp and onions in a tempura batter, crisp and light and voluminous, like a craggy seafood soufflé. There is also, of course, straight tempura, not in the airiest batter you can find in New York, but the ingredients—fish and vegetables—are good, even including a sheet of deep-fried seaweed.

A terrific eel dish, one of the best plates of food in the place, called Unagi-Kabayaki. Three three-inch lengths of eel are split, spread into three-inch squares, and broiled until lightly blackened. The meat is rich, oily, not salty, but sharp, and it looks a little frightening lined up in its chevron formation on a rectangle of porcelain.

No desserts of interest. The best beverages are beer or sake.

★★ NANNI'S

146 East 46th Street
LUNCH, MONDAY TO FRIDAY; DINNER, MONDAY TO SATURDAY. CLOSED SUNDAY.
Reservations, 697–4161.
Credit cards: AE, CB, DC, MC, V.
Medium-priced.

There is a captain here who somewhere picked up the notion that nothing will impress an American more than a restaurant wherein the chef is also the owner. The dining room here is small, and throughout dinner you will hear the captain working the fact into his presentations that the owner of Nanni's is also its chef. These lectures seem always to begin with a reminder that in a good restaurant the menu is merely the starting point, and they then proceed with the assurance that Nanni, the chef, the owner, will make for you anything you want, which comes down to anything on the menu plus three or four specials of the day.

"You won't find it on the menu, but if you like, Nanni, the chef, the owner, will make for you a cold seafood salad as an appetizer, which you can have with some cold white wine we have which is very special." The gentleman does a Balinese hand dance as he talks, with a counterpoint of Western mime, explaining how this is delicately seasoned (he pinches off a small piece of air), that carefully prepared (he eyes an imaginary pan on your table, waiting for the moment when . . .) with some perfect ingredient (he kisses a wild vegetable with his eyes closed). At first it is sort of amusing.

Nanni's is a simple enough place. You walk along a narrow corridor past the bar, into a room decorated with Italian travel posters. There are three rows of tables—about fifteen in total—and on each table there is a small lamp with a red shade. There is little room for the waiters to get from here to there, and the place is noisy when it is half full.

Among the items which Nanni, the chef (the owner) will make for you sometimes, other than the starting points on the menu, is the brilliant seafood salad, composed of small, crunchy shrimp, very tender little mussels, bits of bass, chopped cucumbers, celery, onions and parsley, all marinated in oil and wine.

Nanni will be delighted also to make for you a pasta course of Capellini d'Angelo (angel's hair) in sauce Nanni—"Tin, tin, tin little spaghetties, with Nanni's own sauce" (a whisper that is barely a hiss, emphasizing how svelte is the noodle). Chef Nanni's sauce is a delicate mixture of creamed tomatoes, peas, sautéed mushrooms, wine and a little strong cheese. It is not just a tomato sauce, with other stuff thrown in, but a balanced mixture, with the tomato in the background. Of course angel's hair is not kosher, and if that concerns you, you may have Tortellini alla Nanni—the same sauce, on little tubes of pasta that are stuffed with spiced ground veal—very heavy going, but redeemed by the great sauce.

The owner's main courses are easily oversold by the captain. One is talked into "breast of chicken taken off the bone, and pounded very, very thin. Then sautéed. And also is sautéed some mushrooms and prosciutto ham. All together with some cheese on top, and baked." (Fifteen inches in front of your nose he is holding his vision of the breast in his hand.) The breast is actually still on the bone. It may have been petted, but not pounded, and that of course ruins the dish—it is heavy rather than tender. The veal, roasted with mushrooms and truffles, is of second-rate meat—a kind of near-beef. They hate to admit it, but their thing is veal scaloppine, and they do it all the usual ways—piccata, Parmigiana, Milanese, zingara. The bass baked with mussels is splendid. The side orders of vegetables are often superior to what they garnish—sometimes crisp broccoli, at other times barely cooked zucchini under a thin sheet of browned cheese.

Crushed garlic is the most noticeable ingredient in the salad dressing here—good greens, including arugula when it is available, strong wine vinegar, oil and lots of that raw garlic. If that's what you want before dessert, you got it. It is good for what it is, and it is best between the pasta and the main course.

Zuppa Inglese here is an excessively sweet, very rummy cake, with a barely cooked meringue. If you want even more rum, there is a straight rum cake—Sacra Pantina—so loaded with alcohol that it can literally intoxicate; it doesn't taste bad either—lots of almond paste. But for something that does not rely on excess for its effect, there is fruit (peaches and strawberries) marinated in sweetened Marsala—fresh fruit, lots of fortified wine and a long marination—the best dessert in the place. Complimentary macaroons.

★★NICOLA PAONE

207 East 34th Street
LUNCH, MONDAY TO FRIDAY; DINNER, MONDAY TO SATURDAY. CLOSED SUNDAY.
Reservations, 889–3239.
Credit cards: AE, DC.
Expensive.

William F. Buckley Jr. has written that Nicola Paone is the best restaurant in New York. This is erroneous. However, though liberals may comfort themselves that this nonsense confirms the poverty of Mr. Buckley's judgment, and though conservatives may answer that his powers of intellect and discernment are husbanded for battles in the intellectuo-politico-socio-econo arena and are portioned stingily to gastronomo-oeno, the fact is that Nicola Paone is a splendid restaurant of its kind—a leisurely, comfortable den—serving Italian food to successful men (sometimes accompanied by successful women) who keep their jackets on but never lose their cool, and who make this place their fraternity house, albeit one in which nonmembers are quite welcome.

For the selection of food one is presented with a simulated slate on which are painted, in simulated chalk, such informative entries as Boom Boom, Nightgown, Non M'Importa (at $9 it must be at least fairly important), Serenata in Minore, Chicken Baci Baci (it must be chicken) and Primavera (it must be spring). If you're left for ten minutes with this incomprehensible document, don't fret; use the time to take in the surroundings: mock sandstone building blocks and pillars, stained-glass windows, a linoleum floor in a pattern of red clay tiles, and as in all Roman abodes, phonograph-album covers on the walls, in abundance, picturing the man of the house and his guitar.

When the captain finally returns to your table, you can find out what the slate is all about. The pre-pasta courses here are not especially mystifying and are the least interesting items available. There are baked clams in a fairly good version of this common dish, with a strong flavoring of Italian parsley in the breading; stuffed mushrooms, in which the mushroom caps are filled with a well-seasoned stuffing of minced mushroom stems (waste not); and if you try the hot antipasto, your sampling of these items will be augmented with sautéed eggplant filled with cheese and tomatoes, stuffed peppers and a lone baked shrimp. There is a Zuppa Pavese, which, it develops, is chicken soup wherein an egg has been poached (it's still there), on a slice of toast (which any poached egg deserves). A harmless broth.

The pasta dishes here are a much better starting point than the official first courses, and one of them in particular is really outstanding. It is called Serenata in Minore and turns out to be wide noodles tossed with ricotta cheese, sprinkled with more cheese on top, the whole then briefly browned under the broiler. The pasta, which is cooked to order, is tender and firm; the excellent cheese makes a delicate but extremely rich sauce, and the stronger flavor of the browned cheese on top is a perfect accent—a marvelous dish.

A man who ordered Nightgown, because he likes them, discovered that it consists of a pair of cylinders of veal, cheese and prosciutto which have been baked, then wrapped in eggplant, breaded, baked again, painted with a sauce of cheese and tomato, and browned briefly in the broiler. This is quite a production, the serving is immense, and this kind of solid, highly flavored and satisfying food calls for an adequacy, perhaps an abundance, of wine.

Chicken Coraggioso is an excellent sautéed chicken. One of the things that is really outstanding about the preparation of this dish is the superior browning of the chicken. In most restaurants so-called sautéed meats are hardly browned, if at all; they are mostly stewed in oil or butter, and liquid. This brave chicken is made dark-brown and crisp on every visible square inch of its skin before being simmered in white wine, mushrooms and Genoa salami—which makes for a very hearty feast, particularly as the portion could feed a small family.

The desserts are pretty—presented by a flying squad of waiters, a different edifice of whipped cream, mocha, mousse, fruit, etc., in each hand. But these lovely-looking items are mediocre in the quality of the cake, in the purity of the cream, and in the flavor of the custards—only the fruits are of first quality. To eat wisely here is to have pasta, a main course, salad and then the strong espresso coffee in squat, heavy glasses—their rims coated with lemon-moistened sugar.

The service is very leisurely (you may call it slow if you are in a hurry), but this is in part because the food is made when ordered, and it has that bright, strong quality of flavors just brought to their peak. The staff works together well, and they seem loyal to their boss:

"Who is Nicola Paone?"

The captain's face lights up. "He owns this place! He's a celebrity! He's an entertainer! He sings! He plays the guitar! He makes records! He writes songs! He cooks! *He makes the pastry!*"

"Does he make love?"

"Eh. I donno about that."

There is one large table in the small rear dining room, where the walls are lined with wine bottles. Contemplative, aimless background music of Nicola plucking. (Says the captain, "Everything is homemade here, even the music.")

★ NIPPON

145 East 52nd Street
LUNCH, MONDAY TO FRIDAY; DINNER, MONDAY TO SATURDAY. CLOSED SUNDAY.
Reservations, PL 8–0226.
Credit cards: AE, CB, DC, MC.
Expensive.

An order of sashimi, at $4, consists of a small slice of raw squid, one of snapper, and two of striped bass. "This is four dollars?" you ask the waitress. "Yes, because the chef cuts it. You can get it for two dollars at another restaurant, but this is the best *expensive* restaurant." This is uttered with such bright-eyed, innocent enthusiasm that it's several moments before you fully realize that any pursuit of the subtle conundrum germinated by this exchange could lead to more inquiry and explication than you're willing to undertake across a cultural barrier. This may well be the Cadillac of Japanese restaurants in New York—solid and expensive—but it is not the best place for the raw fish dishes. The prices are bizarre, and the fish is not invariably served at that point of sweet freshness past which delicate Occidental olfaction takes offense.

But the cooked food here is so uniformly well made that there are any number of good reasons to visit this popular place. The small order of tempura which the menu suggests you have with your drinks consists of shrimp, fish, green peppers and onions, lightly battered and rapidly fried in hot oil, and each item is in crisp condition. The consommé is available with a selection of added garnitures. The broth itself is hot, clear, faintly flavored, and you can have it with crisp broccoli, firm and slightly rubbery abalone, carrots, and so on.

You may be shocked to see that the Japanese casseroles are cooked right at your table in Corning Ware, on a hot plate, but this does not Westernize the food. One of these dishes, called Hama Nabe, is a stout stew of fresh clams, chunks of bean curd the size of children's blocks, mushrooms, onions and scallions. When you have finished with the solid contents of the pot, you may feel a wee bit unsatisfied, but when you have asked for bowls and drunk the heavy broth, all will be well.

Most of the American customers look at the menu with dismay and end up ordering one of the house dinners, in which the main courses are sukiyaki, teriyaki, yakitori or one of the other Japanese dishes they have eaten before. Turn the page and you will find the à la carte menu, where there are listed such comparative New York rarities as Uni-Yaki (broiled seasoned squid, served with strong pickled ginger), and Shichimi-Yaki (marinated chicken that has been seasoned with red pepper, sprinkled with sesame seeds, and broiled until very crisp and almost black). There are a number of good side dishes too: if you have gotten past the mental block (now, don't deny it) between you and raw fish, perhaps you're ready for raw chicken. Torisashi is just that—the un-cooked, pink chicken meat is sweet and moist, served with cold spinach and shredded roots. If you really are in the mood for culture shock, order a box of Yakinori, which is thin, dried seaweed, several blackish-green sheets of it, each the size of a calling card; its strange, metallic taste is rather marvelous. All this, with the excellent beer from Japan called Kirin, can make a splendid meal.

Nippon is a sprawling restaurant with bare tables close together, rice-paper lamps, a sushi bar, and to your left as you enter, a small bar and lounge, entered over a little bridge, under hanging branches—this was built to the scale of the builders, so keep your head down. At the rear there are tatami rooms where you may eat while sitting on the floor. (Except on weekends, about half the customers here are Japanese, and they, who know a good thing, seem to prefer chairs.) It's more fun than a circus to watch the pink-skinned experimenters on the floor discover that they seem to have an extra thigh.

★★NIRVANA

30 Central Park South (near Sixth Avenue)
LUNCH AND DINNER.
Reservations, 752–0270.
No credit cards.
Medium-priced.

You are greeted by a dark-haired, sari-clad young woman with a rose behind her ear, a spot on her brow, a diamond on her nostril and a very throaty delivery. This vision is not the result of light-headedness after your fourteen-floor voyage to this aerie overlooking Central Park and points north, for of all the Indian restaurants in New York, Nirvana lays on the subcontinental schmaltz with the heaviest hand, and your hostess, born to it though she may be, plays the part of her exoticism with operatic breadth. Even her gleaming eyes and sparkling teeth seem to be acts of volitional electricity here in these dim rooms.

Professional basketball players and other lengthies must, from the moment they disembark from the elevator, take care not to brush their heads against the garish, bejeweled cloths that billow down as low ceilings in all the rooms of this place. The reds and blacks, gold and turquoise are repeated in wall hangings that surround the gilt-framed Indian art. If you want a choice table, you may have to wait in the anteroom, among wicker chairs, a couple of private tables hidden behind carved screens, and a short bar, behind which a comely Occidental lass is getting the old colonial treatment in repayment for British transgressions. She must sprint through her shift like an Olympic potato racer, taking orders at the tables, mixing drinks at her station, delivering them back to the tables all while making the most of casual conversation from entranced observers at the bar. She stirs a mean martini, however—Bombay gin, of course.

What you were waiting for at the bar was a table with a view in the oblong main dining room, one lengthy wall of which consists of picture windows that look out on Manhattan's great rectangle of trees, traffic and assault. From up here all you can see are the first two, and the auto lights look very pretty carving their way through the jungle. You are attended to by gentle young men in gauze shirts that hang loosely over their trousers. They are solicitous, which does not entirely offset their rudimentary English. Have your waiter bring you another martini or beer, for the wine list here is ludicrous, as to price, and of abysmal quality, especially the inexpensive bottles.

A shrewd menu, with all the conventional dishes that will satisfy the once-a-year sampler of Indian food, and a goodly number of rarities for sophisticates. If you choose the complete-dinner plan, you will begin with Assorted Appetizers, which consists of nothing new, but much that is well-made, including the sweet and spicy onion fritters called Piazi; a stuffed puri, called Dal Puri, in which the light bread is filled with a solid and steamy mash of chickpeas; and Singara, a thin whole-wheat bread filled with curried vegetables that are mild enough to be fairly called bland. But if you eschew the prix fixe for more adventurous essays, you may precede or surround your main courses with such obscurities as Anda Bhaji, a lightly oiled mix of eggs and vegetables, stir-cooked until it is almost pebbly, flavored with green peppers, onions and herbs—the solid substance of the ingredients notwithstanding, the dish is light; or with Bagon Bharta, baked eggplant that has been mashed with onions, peppers and fragrant coriander leaves—this, on the other hand, is not light at all, but solid and oily and extremely satisfying in that way; or with Mach Bhaja, fried fish with a deep-brown exterior that is like a filament of sweet spices—this is fresh-water fish, and the pale meat seems especially delicate next to its tasty crust.

Nirvana doesn't manage to obtain better shrimp than most of its restaurant competitors these days, so you would do well to pass up the shrimp curry. And though you may be inclined to leap at a goat-meat curry, for no other reason than its rarity in New York restaurants, this sturdy stew betrays none of the particular character of kid. Do not therefore abandon the whole idea of trying the rarities, for the curry of lamb brains is one of the best dishes available in any Indian restaurant in New York, a rich and solid stew that is powerfully herbed and fragrant of sweet spices. And if you sensibly wish to by-pass lamb because it is so much the usual thing, pause at least briefly at the special lamb curry made with spinach—the green vegetable gives the dish a wild and intensely grassy flavor. Good chutneys are available, strong or sweet, and the rice that accompanies your meal is light, buttery and flavored invariably with saffron and with different spices as well, which vary from day to day—cloves give this rice a particularly heady quality. The breads here are good—the poori is the size of a soccer ball, but much lighter, and the parata is browned and buttery, with the strong clear taste of whole wheat.

Much of the brief dessert menu is often unavailable. The rice pudding is pleasantly musty, studded with nuts and raisins. The ice cream the menu refers to as "celestial" is mundane. On occasion the tea is sour, as if it has steeped long past its bedtime.

As the evening wears on, the recorded background music gives way to a sitar player and a gentleman who taps lightly on little drums. They do their thing from comfortable positions on the floor.

○ O. HENRY'S STEAK HOUSE

345 Sixth Avenue (at West 4th Street)
LUNCH AND DINNER.
Reservations, CH 2–2000.
Credit cards: AE, CB, DC, MC, V.
Medium-priced.

When Di Lucia & Di Lucia, despite concerted community opposition and support, elected to preserve and transform an erstwhile meat store into a so-called restaurant, it was in the then new spirit (now so forgotten and revered) of Destructive Rehabilitation (which anticipated, before its time, the movement toward Preventive Restoration which has now engendered the Retrospective Futurism of tomorrow) that they—with a financial hindsight and a commercial foresight rarely encountered in brothers who are at once restaurateurs and patrons of an architectural style that can, thank God, be called singular—elected to provide the northwest corner of West 4th Street and Sixth Avenue, Greenwich Village, our City and the World not only with an eating place wherein (and whereout during the summer months) one could in fact eat but also with a visual encounter, the reverberations of which are yet to be fully ventilated, beyond the oft-recorded impressions of quasi-historic unsanitation, intramural optical sexual review and (particularly in re the garb and manner of the professional staff) medical manhandling, both inpatient and outpatient.

Still to be explored (surely Cockshell and Stutts, despite the diligence of their research—an actual meal actually consumed in the actual room—cannot be accepted—he wore sunglasses, she is blind) are the repose and strength of the Northwest Walk-In Refrigerator Room, with its floor-to-ceiling, wall-to-wall original icebox tubing, shrewdly preserved in a cigarette-ash white to suggest, without slavishly capitulating to, the frost of yore (some say the coolant rests yet within), against a grotesque but stimulating field of lamp black. The strident and touching rendering of the overhead carcass chains, in a straightforward ventricular red, eliminates the need for further inquiry. With a rare openness (so useful), the initial essay in this area, the *South*west Walk-In Refrigerator Room (which fronts, or backs, on West 4th Street) is left as was. It tackled the problem with the more timid leverage of ornament, giving us the *loops* in red, the meathooks in putty (!); only the bold sooty walls were perfectly to the point and ultimately carried over to the climactic Northwest treatise.

The main Saloon, with its gargantuan serving counter (ingeniously spotted alongside fifteen stools), and the elegant simplicity of its table distribution (one behind another, another behind that, and so on), is ringed by the Sidewalk Café, which faithfully follows the store frontage, traversing as it does a reversed L, the trunk of which adheres rigorously to the north-south axis of the Avenue of the Americas, the leg to West 4th Street's not yet deviated east-west course. The border of flat-topped tables, under a fringe of flag-striped canopy artfully positioned to keep out the sun while letting in the rain, attracts a bizarre and colorful clientele of popeyed bipeds occupied with the study and mental notation of the physical characteristics of all erect females the circumstances of whose lives bring them past this now historic corner.

The total complex is unified by a dry slush of well-trod sawdust, constantly redistributed by the sliding shoes of straw-hatted waiters, their long white coats, from waist to ankle, gilded with a butcher's patina of coal-black and blood-red.

No shrimp cocktail; the tomato juice is chilled; the grapefruit juice is unsweetened; the Sauté Mushrooms seem stewed; tough, inaccurately prepared steaks cooked over "real live charcoal"; baked potatoes steamed to powder in aluminum foil; French fries with the texture of noodles; noodles with the texture of gum; golden-brown, crispy, crunchy, tasteless "Confederate" fried chicken; good hamburgers (ground meat cannot be tough); cheeseburgers that taste like hamburgers (the yellow stuff is visible but not tasteable); sugary-sweet apple pie on a ginger-snap crust (sans snap); the cheese cake is insipid and gluelike.

In recent years the Di Lucia brothers have had the opportunity to reevaluate, and to rededicate themselves to the refinement of their opus. With reluctance, but with fierce purpose, the butcherblock cocktail tables were removed when it was determined, once and for all time, that American adults will not manipulate their knees under a tabletop that is eighteen inches thick. But more important, the release of the long-coveted storefront property directly to the north of the Saloon has made possible a fresh approach to the original challenge. White, all white, has been their clear response, except for the sawdust, the waiters' coats and a green trellis that echoes the diamond pattern of the stamped-tin ceiling and walls. This is the first Di L. & Di L. environment in which it has been possible actually to see after sundown, and the visibility of the food has precipitated certain difficulties which, eventually, will have to be dealt with as firmly as the inflexible cocktail tables. Many of the pilgrims who climax their voyages here are from the Land Between the Hudson and the Pacific, and of her illuminated goulash, one said, "Christ, it's stew."

★★ OH-HO-SO

395 West Broadway (near Spring Street)
LUNCH AND DINNER.
Reservations, 966–6110.
Credit cards: AE.
Medium-priced.

But that the kitchen produces some terrific Cantonese food, Oh-Ho-So is most of the things New Yorkers have come to think of as what a Chinese restaurant is not. Where, please, just to begin at the beginning, is your big, bold and brassy Chinese menu, complete, as we have come to expect, with endless lists of available dishes, rendered in both ornamental Chinese characters and garbled English. And what of these surroundings? How are the skeptics to be persuaded that Oh-Ho-So is in fact a Chinese restaurant, when not a gilded ornament catches the eye, not a gewgawed chandelier, nary a square inch of pink Formica, nor a swatch of gold-flecked hanging cloth (parted to reveal a mural of bamboo forest or a wallpaper of cavorting dragons)?

You are about to leave, of course, having obviously come to the wrong place, when an alert Oriental in platform wedgies and illustrated stockings sprints up to you, smiling prettily, and with delicate fingers caressing your flaccid bicep, coaxes you back into what looks like Penn Station—the *old* Penn Station, the one with the lofty ceiling you could see on a clear day; for this Sino-SoHo renovation is in the South of Houston mold, sure enough, but on a Kennedy Airport scale.

Oh-Ho-So is a lofty carving out of old commercial-loft space. You enter a dim, roomy saloon, a long bar cutting through it diagonally, behind which a lengthy mirror, from shoulder-height to ceiling, tilted into the room at the top, reflects the scene: a polished hardwood floor, small tables randomly distributed thereon, brick walls that reach up to a complex of rafters. The house and the customers provide the sound—the management installed the juke box, the customers insert the quarters—and you get gentle strumming of soft rock against the hard-edged quarters. The cleanest Bohemians of our day lounge on bar stools and loll contentedly at table, beside their imported beers. There is not an unwashed hair in the crowd. You spot Hell's Angel tops over Ali Baba pantaloons, velvet suits and velvet shoes, sunglasses with a blue lens and a red one, glimpses of denim foundation garment, denim umbrellas, denim denims. All squeaky clean.

You proceed through that cool, carefully staged theater of casual chic to the capacious dining room, dozens of vintage wooden tables, row after row of refurbished oak surrounded by a hundred sizes and shapes of straight-backed chairs; at the back of the room, a second level, a mezzanine, with more rows; all in this giant box of earth-colored walls under a dark, electric-blue ceiling of conduits and pipes, from which, on long cords, hang the simple shaded lamps that cast islands of light on many of the tables.

The Orientals who greet may be the only ones you will meet, for this is one out of perhaps one Chinese restaurant in town where you are waited on by locals, in this instance youngsters of just-out-of-college age. But not just any such—these, as befits SoHoers, are the avant-garde, and this is the first place in town in which *unprinted* T-shirts have been sported. Also in style is a bit of surreptitious munching while they bus tables, and intersexual flirting (*this* is the avant-garde?) among the working boys and girls before the fashionably late 9:30-on diners and revelers arrive, flashing the snazzy duds that are the signs of freedom from constraint among the topsy-turvy dissenters of our day. But do not, because of these signs, hold in suspicion the merchandise dispensed at Oh-Ho-So. For one thing, you will from time to time encounter Chinese family parties within these walls, so the place passes New York's traditional test of Chinese authenticity; and for another, the ardent young waiters and waitresses inform you, when you try to pin them down for more information about the food than is provided by the menu, that the sources of additional info are the chaps in the kitchen, and they, you learn, merely gesture and giggle when addressed in English, so recent is their arrival from old Hong Kong. Chicky, the immigration cops!

For no reason at all, the printed menu appears on circular pieces of paper affixed to paper plates. For good reason, to the left of each listed dish there is a number, for it is by numbers that the dining room staff communicates the patrons' orders to the kitchen. You may begin by ordering *1. Oh-Ho-So Spare Ribs (the asterisk next to this and other dishes denotes "First time served in New York"), and you conclude that this is precedent by presence of a very subtle ingredient, for these seem to be your standard ribs, moist, slightly crisped, in a barely present sweet and syrupy sauce. Much more interesting is *3. Oh-Ho-So Barbecue Pork, which consists of sturdy chunks of meat and sections of green pepper impaled on a skewer, and served in a pool of a meaty broth that is principally soy sauce, beside a garnish (a peculiarity of the place) of lettuce and tomato. This is not a subtle dish; it is strong and satisfying, the meat well-salted and spiced, the peppers oiled and, here and there, blackened.

You move forward to what the menu mysteriously calls "Entries," and after viewing the parade to the post, you decide to risk $5.50 on number 12, Coconut Chicken, and your choice, though out of the money (finishing fourth behind Braised Flounder, Crazy Drunk Chicken, and Rice Noodles), performs creditably enough and could be a winner in cheaper company. Coconut Chicken is coconut candy made out of chicken, the large cross-sectional slabs of bird little more than carriers for the sweet coconut sauce. Everything seems to be just as it is meant to be—the meat of the chicken moist and tender, the sauce smooth and polished—but this is a dish you would have to grow up with to want twice. On the other hand, *13. Crazy Drunk Chicken appeals even if first encountered late in life. It is a many-flavored, many-textured scramble, like innumerable Cantonese dishes, and like the best of them it has individuality despite the range of its ingredients. The singularity of this dish stems from its abundance of peanuts. Unlike many Chinese peanut dishes, as they are served in New York, the nuts in this have neither the taste nor texture of the thirst-making things you find in converted ashtrays on New York bars. These peanuts are cooked *into* the stew until they have the soft flaky texture of moist chickpeas, and it is the breakdown of the peanuts that thickens the Chinese-wine–flavored sauce in which there are, in addition to the chunks of chicken and peanuts, Chinese cabbage and parsley, that mysterious mushroom called cloud ears, and occasional stimulating strands of fresh ginger.

Because *27. Baked Stuffed Crab Shells is listed under "Sea Food," you leap, without looking, to the conclusion that the crab shells are stuffed with seafood. *Au contraire.* The dish is simply a meaty method of not wasting the shells of hard-shelled crabs after the crab meat has been used in something else. The five shells per order are stuffed with a spicy forcemeat of pork and herbs, they are moistened with an almost black sauce that has a concentrated and briny flavor of strong fish, and they are sprinkled with an abundance of sharp chopped scallions and fragrant Chinese parsley. This is a far-out dish by domestic standards, principally because the flavors of fish and meat are so closely juxtaposed.

You will be relieved to learn that under the heading "Sea Food" there are actually a number of seafood dishes, though in the nomenclature of some of these there are other puzzlements. For example, *29. Braised Flounder is not braised, though it is a splendidly prepared flounder. The fault here probably is with the expert brought in to provide the English equivalents—he may know English, he may know cooking, but not both. In any event, what you get shortly after ordering this dish is a browned, crisped and fish-shaped item spread on a platter. The biggest mistake you can make is to permit your young server to bone it for you, unless you are happy to let 25 percent of it go to the cat in the kitchen. Filleters they are not yet. Within the apparently deep-fried shell there is a tender and perfectly fresh flounder, garnishing it strands of strong ginger and sprigs of Chinese parsley.

The fish tanks in the dining room are not merely decorative, the carp swimming within are doomed according to your order. There is an unnumbered item on the menu, indicated by the suggestion "Try our live fish . . ." Be not afraid, it is dead when you get it, and you can have it killed either by deep-frying or by steaming. Either way, this is a very bony fish, served with nothing but clumps of the very strong fresh ginger it was prepared with. This is simple, elegant food, the steamed version rather spare, the fried one providing a bit of crust next to the tender meat of the fish.

Under the brief listing of "Rice & Noodles" there is mentioned a cold dish of Rice Noodles w. Bean Sprout in Wine. This is a copious serving of cool, inch-wide, cloudy-white strands of rice noodle, slippery in their slightly sweetened oil, accented with sesame seeds and crisp bean sprouts.

The menu announces, "We have desserts." They haven't, unless you accept canned lichees and such as such.

○ OLD HOMESTEAD

56 Ninth Avenue (near 15th Street)
LUNCH AND DINNER.
Reservations, CH 2–9040.
Credit cards: AE, CB, DC, MC, V.
Expensive.

The tables are too small, the background music is too loud, the air conditioning is arctic, and the doggy-bags leak. The Old Homestead bills itself as "New York's Oldest Steak House," and it bedecks itself with hideous turn-of-the-century accoutrements, which bedazzle some of New York's visitors: "This is a *historic* place," says he, his gaze dwelling reverently, now on the brass chandeliers (Lampland), now on the art (Artland); her gaze follows his; the stuffed moose (not from Mooseland, but moldering; possibly c. 1868, when the place opened) gaze straight ahead.

Not to slight the local customers—they constitute the bulk of the clientele, and they are mostly what Manhattanites imagine their Queens neighbors to be. She, ventricose and pendulously bosomed, obscures her chair as she sits down beside the table and waits for his move; he, columnar and hard, takes his position opposite, and with the seat of his chair in his hands, by little hops, inches himself and the table toward her, forcing it between her upper and nether protuberances; she crosses right thigh over left, lifting her abdomen and establishing the family grip through meal's end. They smoke throughout, he a cool young Kent with his shrimp, a full-bodied Bering with his "Heavy Cut Boneless Sirloin Steak. For the trencherman who isn't satisfied with the average portion. About a pound and a half of our prime boneless sirloin. More than a match for the heartiest eater. Our steaks are aged for four weeks in our scientifically controlled aging boxes"; she sticking by her Pall Malls (you can light either end) from lobster cocktail through "Extra Heavy Cut Prime Ribs of Beef Au Jus." If you thought the next generation long ago turned from the crass ways of its antecedents, come to the Homestead, where up-and-coming goons court their fishwives-to-be. Martinis and beer do nothing to unbend the silent, ritual courtship dinners of these doomed robots. Only the groups of young men (full-time jobs and no obligations) seem to do any laughing.

They know their customers, the management here, and they give them even less than they deserve. You're greeted by one of a pair of confused schedulers. She assures you that there will be a wait of ten minutes, appends your name to a list and departs. Her male counterpart materializes within the minute and leads you to a table at once. (Perhaps they are competitors and she is just now learning the ropes; perhaps they are paid piecework, per seated body, and there is a whole section of the many-roomed place that she does not know about.) The food is dreadful—from the waterlogged shrimp or lobster cocktail, or the limp herring, to the mealy, tasteless roast beef and the resilient steak, accompanied by leathery cottage fries or powdery home fries, through the claylike cheese cake. Miraculously, there is a decent apple pie, made with green apples, cinnamon and a good lard crust. The waiters are almost workmanlike—sooner or later you get what you ask for.

★ L'OLIVIER

248 East 49th Street
LUNCH, MONDAY TO FRIDAY; DINNER, MONDAY TO SATURDAY. CLOSED SUNDAY.
Reservations, EL 5–1810.
Credit cards: AE, DC, MC.
Expensive.

A pleasant enclosed garden and an occasional wonderful dish recommend the place. And you cannot easily fault the service. But for some reason, these aspiring proprietors have gone the pretension-and-high-price route, and here at Forty-ninth and Second, hard by restaurants with even loftier ambitions that are much more nearly achieved, L'Olivier is the sure-fire also-ran, a plater in the Belmont, entered to satisfy the owner's desire to see his colors go by in the big race. Certainly they could have given us instead an easy winner in a secondary event, the bistro this neighborhood could use.

The previous occupant of these premises was Chez Renée, a nifty and comfortable spot which was on the culinary decline in recent years. The new place is a light renovation of the old, hardly more than a single coat of French Provincial over the shipshape but anonymous interior; not enough to qualify as kitsch, but all it takes to make the place recognizable anywhere as a New York French restaurant of the seventies. The long narrow room has been given the standard walls of rough plaster, beamed ceiling and carpeted floor; there is a little display of cheeses and fruits and berries just to your right as you enter, the tidy little up-front bar that is all but inevitable to your left; along the smooth brown banquettes, rows of immaculately white-linened tables adorned with fresh flowers in little pitchers; paned mirrors are in this year, and they are in here, as are the innocuous prints that have been in for decades. But when the weather is fine and you have arranged ahead, you may pass through this pretty cliché to the enclosed garden at the rear.

Gardens are few in New York restaurants, so the style has not been set; L'Olivier had little to go on, no one to turn to but themselves. They have come up with less than art, but this tiny plot of broadloomed land is an uncommonly agreeable site for summer dinner, particularly if the chaps and ladies at the other tables modulate the audibility of their good spirits—excellent acoustics back here. The massive trunk of an ailanthus pierces through the prettily striped translucent gable roof that is the wall-to-wall skylight. There are screened, louvered windows in the white masonry wall along one side, white trelliswork over the wall on the other. At the rear there is an actual strip of land in which actual greenery grows. The dozen or so prettily set tables are surrounded by chairs of natural wood that have seats of strung twine. The casual look extends even to the waiters, young Frenchmen mostly, in black vests over long-sleeved white shirts that are open at the neck to reveal casually tied handkerchiefs—veree sportee. Happily, their informal uniforms do not set the style for their demeanor, which is polite without being stiff, not a trace of snootiness even when one optimistic lady asks, "What do you have that's *like* a '71 Montrachet or a d'Yquem?" An essay question.

Your nattily suited and tonsured Gallic host recommends the specials of the day promptly after you are seated. You mistakenly sample the suggested Terrine of Bass, a totally uninteresting fish pâté that you might just as well smother in the quasi–sauce Gribiche that accompanies it—mayo studded with chopped pickled things. Of course if you make a practice of ignoring suggestions, you will miss the Seafood Salad that is sometimes available, which would be too bad. The salad is composed of crisp, fresh-tasting shrimp and tender squid; it is garnished with a dollop of an unlikely but delicious orange-flavored mayonnaise, and it is topped with halves of a hard-cooked quail egg, which, if they are a touch sour, are surely as decorative as the socks on a lamb chop, and edible to boot. Memories of a wonderful Feuilleté de Roquefort, served not far away at Le Chanteclair, lead you to hope for its equal when you order it here. No dice. This is some sort of joke food: a couple of circular layers of pastry (airy and admirably browned, it is true) between which has been spread an obscurity of (apparently) emasculated cheese—perfection without personality. You are safe with the Jambon de Parme, an abundance of thinly sliced strong, smoky ham, salty and a little fibrous, sprinkled with crunchy cornichons.

Your host outlines for you the three different ways you may sample the house's excellent fresh salmon: poached, with hollandaise; poached, with sorrel sauce; grilled, with Béarnaise—and the kitchen proceeds to prepare it yet a fourth—poached, with Béarnaise. Perfect fish, however, firm and moist and flaky, served with a sauce that is a bit watery, easy on the tarragon, which is the herb this sauce is all about, and too heavy on the salt, a frequent error of this kitchen. There is too much salt again in the braised endive that accompanies the Caneton au Poivre Vert. But the bird itself is judiciously roasted, with browned and crisp skin around moist meat, and it is served in a very buttery sauce that has a vivid pepper flavor and more than a hint of vinegar —probably the liquid in which the pepper was packed. A marvelous little tart of riced potatoes, deeply browned, is served with many of the main courses, and it is a perfect foil to the juicy bird. Impeccable lamb chops, four single-ribs, cooked accurately, a lump of herbed butter on each. Inedible Civet de Lapin—the waiter observes that this is of course not wild rabbit, but fails to point out that nevertheless it got its roadwork —the stew is in a wonderful, almost purple sauce, thickened with blood, but the meat itself is the sinew of a marathon runner.

The cheeses are fresh, they are at room temperature, and the French bread is crusty and tasty, much like the genuine Parisian article. If you are interested in baked desserts, a couple of waiters arrive at the side of table displaying tarts and cakes and smiling faces. The tarts are on crusty pastry, and there is a thin layer of good custard under the plump berries. The Tarte Tatin sports chunks of brown, spicy apple, but it is served with a lifeless crème Anglaise. For $3.50 you may have yourself a little soufflé, though when you suggest the idea your waiter is discomposed and holds a hastily called whispered conference with the maître before everything is arranged. The chocolate soufflé is moist and light, but it surely could use another two or three minutes in the oven to set it and dry it a bit so that it will be a soufflé, not a pudding. Its chocolate flavor lacks punch.

At the old Chez Renée the garden was unusable in the hottest weather because the daytime sun baked the place and it took at least an overnight to cool it off. L'Olivier has no provision for offsetting the condition. And when Chez Renée closed its garden for the wintertime, it opened its upstairs dining room, wherein there was a cheerful fireplace. This room has been prettied up and is in use.

• O'NEALS' BALOON

48 West 63rd Street
LUNCH AND DINNER.
Reservations accepted for large parties, 399–2353.
No credit cards.
Medium-priced.

O'Neals' Baloon is an American brasserie. People come for just a drink, or for coffee and cake, or for three-course meals. The place is angular, sprawling, garish, noisy, active, and despite many kinds of illumination (clusters of brilliant, unfrosted bulbs at the ends of bent wands; red-and-white movie EXIT signs; pale chartreuse globes, Tiffany lamps; antique ceiling fixtures) it is dark and a little sinister because the walls and ceiling are an unrelieved black but for the glum paintings, posters, mirrors, ducts and pipes. The L-shaped sidewalk café is of a piece (dozens of little tables in rows, under a long green awning) but inside we have a jumble of rooms (up a few steps for this one, around this corner for that one), all of them filled with bare-topped, wooden tables (a bottle of Heinz on each), red chairs, coatracks, the sounds of the juke box, at the south end the competing sounds of the exposed kitchen, at the north end the lesser, guzzling noises of an active bar.

Everyone here is theatrical or musical, or at least a little bit exhibitionistic: Juilliard students; West Side semiprofessionals whose occasional theatrical earnings barely cover their Equity dues; members of the chorus and corps de ballet at the Met and the City Opera; and a few more-successful types, though most of these prefer the Ginger Man or Le Poulailler after an evening at Lincoln Center. The waiters, of course, are either *manqués* (gray-haired and wry) or aspirers (King Valiant hair and pimpled), all in red newsboy aprons.

No one has ever been heard to say "Let's go to the Baloon—I love their——." But if you know what to avoid, you can put together a decent little meal here if you select from:

O'Neals' Chili Con Carne: crunchy beans, chopped meat, a modicum of hot pepper, and if you wish, a garnish of chopped raw onions.

Avocado Vinaigrette—a ripe avocado, sliced, dressed with a good, thick, mustardy vinaigrette, and garnished with a few slices of pimento for color, and chopped raw onions for the hell of it.

Hamburgers, Cheeseburgers, Bacon-Burgers, Chili-Burgers, Cheese-Bacon-Burgers: good stuff.

Southern Fried Chicken, Shoestring Potatoes in Basket—the chicken is moist inside, crispy outside, and there is plenty of it. But the fries suffer from being shoved under the chicken, and they arrive wilted.

Fish & Chips in Basket—read the previous item and substitute fish (flounder) for chicken.

Spinach, Mushroom & Bacon Salad—the West Side staple, made with fresh spinach, crisp raw mushrooms, crumbled bacon and mustardy dressing.

Good cheese cake, a pecan pie that has a buttery filling, and hot chocolate in the cold season.

★ 162 SPRING STREET RESTAURANT

401 West Broadway (at Spring Street)
LUNCH AND DINNER.
Reservations, 431-7637.
Credit cards: AE, MC, V.
Medium-priced.

You get into a cab and you remain in the lean-forward position after instructing the driver to take you to the corner of Spring Street and West Broadway, because you assume that he has heard of Broadway, but not West Broadway, and that he has never heard of Spring Street. But if your driver is young and bearded, he may turn and ask, eagerly, "Are you going to the *Spring Street Bar?*" (the place is known as the Spring Street Bar), and you will have begun to discover that this out-of-the-way SoHo tavern is to the SoHo community what your local OTB office is to your local horse degenerates —not only a hangout, but where the action is.

To call it the Max's Kansas City of a decade later is glib and false. Studiously groovy ambience and all, this place is a real restaurant, serious about the wine and food it serves, if not invariably successful with it; and the best meal you got at Max's cannot compare with an average one here.

You enter into an oddly laid out barroom, through which the gleaming bar cuts a diagonal line. Lots of people hang around, glass in hand, talking or looking for someone to talk to. The rest of the establishment is dark-brown: two dining rooms, one with brick walls, one with dark-brown painted walls; strings of the world's dimmest spotlights offer a pale glow from the distant ceiling; the tables are dark-brown; the china is dark-brown. The dining rooms fill late, and they become noisy and cheerful. The prices are high, and the customers can afford them; no starving artists; everyone is clean; SoHo's struggle was brief (it is now a middle-class neighborhood), and the struggle is now out of style.

The former strugglers often begin with the Quiche Lorraine—a pretty terrific, very cheesy pie on a dark crust with chunks of dark ham throughout. On other occasions they enjoy their new-found prosperity with ratatouille (hot or cold)—an oily, wet, heavily garlicked soup of sautéed vegetables, including oily slices of green pepper, strands of sweet onion, and chunks of tomato. Continuing to enjoy themselves, on their next visit they learn about saucisson with potato salad—the loud sausage wrapped in a pastry and sliced thin; the cool, crisp potatoes mixed with strong, freshly chopped raw onions and fresh parsley. Then they discover that this prosperity thing isn't all roses, because the snails here are, atypically, inadequately seasoned, though they are nice and buttery.

The regular *nouveaux* have learned about the pork chops and skip them; the trichinosis scare is at work, so the chops are pre-cooked and then re-cooked, and they arrive dried-out and fibrous. Sensibly, they order the roast leg of lamb—many, many slices of pink lamb arrayed on a large platter, the meat well flavored with garlic and moistened with good gravy. Eminently American roast chicken, with a moist, peppery stuffing that will remind you of Thanksgiving. Something called John's Lemon Steak is a dissonance of beef, lemon juice, dried thyme and dried oregano.

The waiters and waitresses here are nothing if not opinionated, and less if not outspoken. "How's the fruit salad?" "It *can* be boring." "The pecan pie?" "Doesn't make it." You are given a strong recommendation for "David Eyres Pancake, for two —30 minutes to order $4.00."—a deep, pot-shaped popover filled with stewed apples (flavored with lemon and cinnamon), and about a pint of perfect, airy whipped cream. Can't miss. If you don't want to wait, the fruit tarts are warm, made with fresh fruit and served in warm fruit syrup. Good chocolate cake with dark-brown icing.

If you get a table near a West Broadway window, you have a beautiful view of the Goldman Pressing Machine Corp. at No. 402 and the Hoffman Boiler Co. at No. 400. When the Hoffmans and Goldmans have gone home, there is not a domestic car at the curbs. Getting here by cab is easy, but finding one in this neighborhood late at night is a little tougher.

★★ ORSINI'S

41 West 56th Street
LUNCH AND DINNER. CLOSED SUNDAY.
Reservations, PL 7–1698.
Credit cards: AE, CB, DC, MC.
Expensive.

This is the famous, intensely romantic hideaway where grown men eat in the dark beside cool, slender nymphs. Why, then, does the house provide us with Muzak, specifically "Una Furtiva Lagrima" on a muted (but well amplified) trumpet, followed, even more grotesquely, by "Casta Diva," rendered the same way? Your host, perceiving that you have noted the music, explains that not all the customers like it, and that some even ask to have it turned down!

There is a lot of nonsense about Orsini's—that the favored get tables in the front, the unknown clean in the rear, lepers one flight up; that the food you get is not the same as the food *they* get; that if you are not a tiger, this place will humiliate you and then impoverish you with its haughty treatment and high prices. This stuff is believed by people who want to believe it, to flatter themselves, or to take comfort in their imagined persecution. In fact Orsini's is a fairly straightforward place. The service is polite, the food is reliable, if never inspired, and the prices, particularly for wine, are below San Marco's, Romeo Salta's and Giambelli's. The mythology is ridiculous on its face. If this place were the private preserve of the international set, they might, it is true, not object to the sour note of the Muzak. But would they tolerate being taken for less than top dollar?

Downstairs it is dark. There are red velvet walls and red velvet love seats. There are paintings with simulated century-old grime. Dim crystal chandeliers barely cut the gloom. Wrought-iron partitions form intimate corners.

Upstairs it is sunny. The walls are of rosy brick and creamy plaster. The tall windows at the front are hung with printed curtains, tied back to reveal rows of flower pots at the windowpanes. The chairs are straightbacked and rustic, with red-and-white fitted cushions.

Scampi—good, crisp shrimp, in a fresh-tasting buttery sauce, with garlic and lots of green parsley. Mozzarella in Carrozza—slabs of mild mozzarella cheese, lightly breaded and deep-fried until crisp outside and gooey inside, delicious with squeezed lemon. Vongole Sorrentina—rather ordinary breaded clams, utterly mis-described on the menu as "clams in tomato broth." Crostini alla Romana—the familiar deep-fried cheese-and-anchovy sandwich, but the batter is a little too sweet, like a fritter.

The gnocchi in pesto sauce are rather heavy, but the sauce is oily, loaded with garlic, powerfully perfumed of sweet basil and edged with an accent of Parmesan cheese. The pasta usually comes out of the kitchen in good condition, but the sauces that are made by the captains are as different as the captains themselves—this one of the mellifluous manner gives you an Alfredo of eggs, butter and little else; that one sharply flashes his teeth under his black mustache as he grinds and grinds the black pepper and sprinkles and sprinkles the grated Parmesan cheese. The menu describes the Risotto Milanese as "rice, veal marrow, saffron and wine." Pretty fanciful. It can be made that way, but it isn't. This is good rice, cooked in consommé and flavored with saffron, but it is not the kind of rice you want as a separate course, because it is just a step removed from plain rice.

Very good Osso Buco, tender, flaking off the shank, in a lemony tomato sauce enriched by the cooking of the veal bone. The Veal Chop all'Orsini is stuffed with cheese and good prosciutto, and it is served in a nice, slightly sharp sauce of tomato, white wine, lemon and cream—the veal itself white and tender. Something called Mignonette Peperonata is an elemental dish of grilled filet mignon, sautéed green peppers and a simple tomato sauce—not a silly concoction, despite the disparity of the elements, but a well-balanced dish.

The salads are good. You ask for spinach, and you get spinach with a bonus of slivered raw mushrooms. The Caesar salad is of good fresh lettuce, but the croutons are apparently allowed to age in the dressing, and they are mushy, not crisp.

The cheese is cool (not cold), and this does not really hurt a cheese like Gorgonzola. Orsini's is, how you call, not a dessert house. The Zuppa Inglese is an acceptable almond-flavored cake, with layers of chocolate, custard and preserves, all soaked in rum —not bad.

Orsini's has one distinct advantage over many of the most popular midtown Italian restaurants. It is not a mad scene. You do not wait for your table at a packed bar. Even where the tables are fairly close together (upstairs), there is a feeling of space.

★ OSCAR'S SALT OF THE SEA

1155 Third Avenue (near 68th Street)
LUNCH AND DINNER.
No reservations (TR 9–1199).
No credit cards.
Medium-priced.

Oscar's is a three-room restaurant with such a heavy volume of business that fully a third of the store space is given over to the amenities and mechanics of handling the flow of customers. The center one of the three large rooms in series (the shape-up area) includes the entrance to the restaurant; a booth at which a comely thing takes names for future seating in order of arrival (the wait can be an hour); the mechanized coat-check apparatus; rows of seats, movie style, in which the patient sit and stare so blankly and intently that one turns and looks automatically for the television set that isn't there; and a giant square bar which holds forty comfortably, seventy-five usually, behind which shirt-sleeved mixer-pourers stir and make change like plugged-in automatons. Through it all a wanderer with a clipboard (he has Miss Comely's list of names now) traipses and calls "Mr. Brllumpy. Mr. Brllumpy? Mr. Brllumpy!" as tables become available.

Today's Oscar's is a modernization and expansion of a smaller place that did business at this site when the El shaded Third Avenue. Today the place looks almost Scandinavian—walls of polished wood or white brick, rows of white globes in the dining-room ceilings, ranks of polished wooden tables. The food, however, is old-fashioned, and there are few surprises on the menu except the prices, which are among the lowest of any decent fish restaurant in New York.

There are the usual raw clams and bluepoints, and as you would expect in a place this busy, they are always fresh. The fish chowder has lots of fish, dill and pepper in it, but it is a dull soup, rather leaden; the New England chowder, though light on clams, has a nice smoky pork taste, and cubes of potatoes that are added shortly before serving, so that they are just done. The mussels with garlic broth are a much more interesting matter. The mountain of mussels (imperfectly scrubbed, it's true, many still wearing beards) has been steamed with great quantities of onions, carrots and celery, and immense branches of fresh dill (a favored Oscar's herb). It is served with the cooking liquid thickened with butter and strongly flavored with garlic—a splendid solution to the problem of what to do with the billions of mussels that line local shores. There are baked oysters (whole); baked clams (minced) in which bread crumbs and paprika play major roles; and steamers, shellfish cocktails, and so forth. But the mussels take the prize.

At Oscar's you can have your fish broiled, deep-fried or steamed plain, or steamed with the same mixture of vegetables and dill used in the mussel dish. The broiling cannot be faulted. Many of the unaccompanied middle-aged men who take a lot of their meals here get their daily ration of cosseting at the same time. The motherly waitresses lean over them solicitously and record in detail the instructions for the exact broiling procedure: leave the fish whole and make the skin crisp; split it and remove the skin;

bone it and split it; remove the tail but leave the head (imagine). Deep-frying should be reserved for fish and chips, and steaming removes the oil from a fish—it's a bad preparation for, say, bluefish (with or without the vegetables), but it works out pretty well for salmon. There are sixteen varieties of fish on the menu, and blackboards in the shape-up room list the ones that are out (not many) and the extra varieties available on a given day.

The Clam Fry is delicious if you like fried clams, the Shrimp Fry not quite so successful—but these are gestures to the Howard Johnson crowd, served with a shiny bottle of Heinz ketchup. There is something called Shrimp with Clam Sauce, which only sounds Cantonese—the shrimp arrive in a flour-thickened, oregano-flavored clam soup. It's a bad thing to do to shrimp, and the clams come off no better.

The desserts are a good reason to make the most of the earlier sections of the menu.

This is a no-nonsense restaurant, and if you linger at your table during the busy hours, the busboy will quietly pick up everything but your cigarette lighter, to let you know your time has come. Go.

★★OYSTER BAR & RESTAURANT

Grand Central Station, lower level
LUNCH AND DINNER. CLOSED SATURDAY AND SUNDAY.
Reservations, 532–3888.
Credit cards: AE, CB, DC, MC, V.
Medium-priced.

The refreshed Oyster Bar is an affectionate restoration of a bit of Old New York, a rediscovered underground cave much like an abandoned subway station, long and cavernous, its vaulted ceilings of tan tiles newly polished and glinting as if half a century of accumulated grime had preserved their sheen for us; the installation of simple and cheerful appointments has converted these potentially somber halls (for the last few decades they *have* been dreary) into a subterranean surprise, picnic grounds in a grotto.

The familiar winding counter at one end of the longish premises has been resurfaced in white. The long bar that adjoins is topped with the old red marble, gleaming stainless-steel appliances behind, including the familiar hemispherical pots the shellfish stews are made in. At the eastern end the terrazzo and red-tile floor has been sprinkled with tables that are gaily linened with blue-and-white gingham. At the center, just inside the glass-and-ironwork entrance doors are the lobster tanks. And at either end, high up on the varnished wooden walls, there are railroad clocks, complete with the correct time—long ago, before it was an OTB office, Grand Central was a railroad station, and in those days the Oyster Bar never closed. Offer up a fervent word of fervent thanks: this may be the only seafood restaurant in New York that has eschewed the usual hanging junk—no stuffed fish, no buoys or watercolor seascapes, nary a seine. This is a straight restaurant, peddling little more than honest food in comfortable surroundings. And the casually uniformed young people in navy blue (light-blue vests on the waiters, light-blue aprons on the waitresses) handle the service cheerfully and efficiently.

For all these virtues New York has turned out, madly at lunchtime, and with just enough enthusiasm to keep the place busy but not booming at night. Solitary late-working commuters have a fish *cum* newspaper before training home for two hours of TV and then bed. Brave city people come by subway, eat, go home by subway, setting foot on city streets only at the beginning and end of their evenings out. Others arrive by cab at the Vanderbilt Avenue entrance—no chichi, at least not of the day, but there have been some dignified-looking arrivals who appear to have ventured from their apartments for the first time since the war (WW II) on the rumor that a piece of the lost city has been located.

You will like the menu, that is, the physical thing itself: a sheet of paper the size of a small pillowcase on which are listed about 125 items of food, 100 or so with prices alongside; no price means not available, and new menus are printed daily, with revisions.

Six kinds of oysters is a big deal these days, when most restaurants merely list "oysters," and you take what they have. But there was a time when a mere six varieties would have been the stock in trade of a street vendor, when respectable seafood restaurants had listings that read like the complete roster of an Eastern milk train. Take, for example, this collection, reported by Joseph Mitchell, in 1945, as an old man's memories of the good old days: Shrewsburys, Maurice River Coves, Narragansetts, Wickfords, Cotuits, Buzzards Bays, Cape Cods, Chincoteagues, Lynnhavens, Poko-mokes, Mobjacks, Horn Harbors, York Rivers, Hampton Bars, Rappahannocks, Goose Creeks—the list goes on and on. With overdredged and polluted waters, that romance is over, and we are well off with this restaurant's six, plus the usual clams, herring, chowders, over thirty varieties of fish (with more than half of them available on any given day), live lobsters, five preparations of shrimp, several cold fish dishes, a dozen different stews and pan roasts, and a handful of international seafood preparations.

OK, very nice. But it must be told that all is not exactly delicious—nothing actually bad (or less than fresh), you understand, but you can be disappointed by a gross cooking one time, a careless one another.

Those raw clams and oysters are fresh, but the most interesting items in the mollusk category are the cooked oysters. The trick in cooking oysters is to preserve all the qualities of the raw oyster—that tender and oily sweetness, the briny, almost gamy edge —heighten them by the addition of heat, that is, give them the quality of actually being *cooked,* and surround them with flavors and textures that enhance but do not obscure the oysters themselves. And the trickiest part of the trick is to not toughen the oysters in the process. Very tricky, this Oyster Bar. You can get some extraordinary oysters broiled in anchovy butter. The deep bluepoint shells are filled to the brim with hot melted butter that is brown and sharp with its admixture of ground anchovies, and at the center of each shell sits a plump oyster, tender and rich, with, actually, a broiled (emphasized) taste to it, and nothing of its freshness lost. And you can get an impeccably prepared oyster stew—a simple dish of oysters that are gently poached in their own liquid, milk and cream, butter and seasonings. This is a rich bowl of food, well-populated with oysters, distinctly American cooking in its warmth and simplicity.

Rhode Island is represented by Point Judith Herring, and the Oyster Bar by the dill sauce served with it. The silvery cutlet of fish is at once sweet and tart, firm and tender without any of the mushiness you find in commercial herring; and the dill sauce is a simple thing of sour cream and fresh dill. Happily, the sauce is not made in big batches in advance of mealtimes, but apparently to order, for the dill has all its delicate springiness and pungent flavor.

There is another herringlike entry on the menu, inappropriately listed under "Today's Catch." This is Lake Winnipeg goldeye, a flaky reddish-gold fish that is salted and smoked before shipping and steamed to your order. The meat is almost buttery and because it is salted it seems like a rich herring—a terrific plate of fish.

If you have wondered why all the sturgeon you run across is smoked, the reason is not merely that smoked sturgeon tastes good, but that fresh sturgeon does not. Fresh sturgeon is on the menu here, broiled, and it is a dry and stringy thing. You are safe with familiar fish—bluefish, striped bass, shad—they are fresh and usually accurately broiled, in butter. On occasion fried whitebait is available, but the little sliverlike bodies are rather heavily battered and deep-fried overly long—their flavor is too near that of the heavy and far-from-crisp French fries that accompany the dish.

Desserts include a couple of decent pies, ice cream and sundaes, a "strawberry shortcake" that is not strawberry shortcake, but nice sponge cake with strawberries and whipped cream.

★★ PALACE

420 East 59th Street
DINNER. CLOSED SUNDAY.
Reservations required, 355–5150.
Credit cards: AE, CB, DC, MC, V.
Very expensive.

You walk in the grim shadows of the hulking approaches to the Queensborough Bridge to reach the unobtrusive entrance to this highly touted, out-of-the-way place. You recall other slightly legendary, obscurely situated, dim-fronted restaurants to which the knowing repair in numbers. In New York there are El Faro, Ballato; after sundown Mon Paris seems to be sitting in the middle of nowhere. The magic of such establishments is that they are oases—good food, warmth, even gaiety, in the middle of gray city wilds. But the Palace is where it belongs, suits where it is.

This must be the point at which money finally mortifies. It is tough for two people to have dinner here and get out alive for less than $300—the prix-fixe dinner is $75; the lowest-priced wines on the list are $40 the bottle (there are dozens at over $200), and with three to four hours for dinner, normal couples will need at least two. Add a house-charged 23 percent gratuity *"en sus,"* as they delicately put it, plus tax, and you may, with the aid of your little pocket calculator, compute the burden in advance. The apparent effect of this is deadening. No one in the place is having a good time. Or a bad time, for that matter. Or any other kind of time. What they are doing is Eating at the Palace, an activity that seems to exist outside the pleasure continuum. Here they are, commemorating an anniversary or a divorce, entertaining a billion-dollar customer from Kuwait. Some people eat here regularly—"Only place you can get a decent dinner," says one businessman repeatedly to his bored, unimpressed guest. No one here is just having dinner. In the consciousness of those present the usual mixed awareness, of consumption and companionship, is heavily weighted to the former. As a substantial proportion of each is essential to pleasure in the other, the people at the Palace are miserable. They are having kisses without hugs. From the twenty tables in the place the only guffaws or laughs a stray investigator hears come from his own.

They aimed for grandeur and achieved baroque fanciness, Telemann instead of Mozart. The walls are covered with dull-gold brocade, the floor with floral carpeting that can only be called broadloom. Where harmless scenic oils do not hang between the voluptuous brass sconces, elaborately framed massive mirrors do. The doorways are hung with discreetly patterned silks, tied back, as are the windows; the armchairs and settees are upholstered with similar stuff. Bless them, the tables are immense, laden with arrays of stemmed cut glass, roses in crystal vases on little silver trays, tall white candles in heavy silver candlesticks. The pale ivory china is rimmed with gold. The help are in black and white, they are nice, even pleasant, and hard as they may be working, they seem to be having a better time than the clientele. And they don't just tell you where the facilities are, either, boy, they lead you there and bow you in. Makes you want to go often.

The menu is in a foreign language. This does not affect the food, which tastes fine no matter what you speak, but the French they use is coy French. It puzzles even those who have a fair working knowledge of the language, and one wonders whether this contrived opacity is not just your old-fashioned exoticism for the sake of the higher prices such mystifications bring. There are no hors d'oeuvres on this menu, no appetizers or first courses, oh, no. We get instead Emaux et Camées (enamels and cameos, you idiots). But the chaps in the kitchen have sharper wits than the joker who produced the script, and the Terrine de Foie Gras Frais aux Truffes is wondrous under any heading: comes a two-inch hemisphere of heavily buttered goose liver, encased in a glistening crust of black truffle, set in a ring of minced jelly. It is so rich that the light buttered toast points are almost essential to its consumption, a glass of wine of considerable assistance. Almost as small, and arriving at the center of just as huge a plate, is the Roulade de Saumon d'Ecosse Fourrée au Caviar, a crunchy pastry boat of lovely Scottish smoked salmon rolled around some superb gray caviar, dabs of whipped cream at each end of the boat.

The place seems bent on conveying the notion that nothing served here is served anywhere else in the world. Your captain, on the other hand, has been around, and when you ask what, please, is Potage au Coulis de Homard, he must confess that it is lobster bisque—they have nothing to be ashamed of, for outside of Mon Paris you won't find a better one in New York. It is deep, spicy and strong, and the couple of spoons of lobster meat added at the last moment provide little more than a textural contrast to the creamy steaming soup. They also refuse to say billi bi, preferring Soupe de Moules au Safran. This, at least, is a distinct variant of the famous mussel soup, the flavor of the mollusks less than forthright, the creamy soup very thick, its richness offset by strands of crisp vegetable but reinforced, in turn, by chunks of the velvety scallops with which the soup is laced—fabulous.

The third course is the fish course, which they convey as Relèves—the changing of the guard. Your chosen fishes are presented for your approval on a tray adorned with a glistening castle. No harm there. The fish preparations are very good, including a Darne d'Espadon Grillée, Sauce Collioure, which is a swordfish steak fired on an open grill (the blackened hatchwork on the white flesh plain to see). The charring imparts a wonderful edgy flavor to the perfectly fresh fish, and one wishes the firm and slightly fibrous meat had not been dried in the process. The swordfish is served with a white sauce that has been slightly sharpened with anchovy and a bit of garlic. One of the world's ugliest fishes is also one of the lightest and mildest. It is called *lotte* and has no consistently used English name, though your captain consistently calls it bellyfish. The *lotte* is delicate and delicately browned, served in a light sorrel sauce that is at once sour and sweet, with a garnish of stewed white raisins. This is one of the few dishes in the house that has an airy quality, and one could put away a barrel of it quite casually.

A cooling lemon ice arrives between the fish and the meat.

If you want the rack of veal, you must settle for Carré de Veau Etuvé dans son Jus Forestière, and like most of the meat courses, it is served for no fewer than two people. This item is one of the comedowns of the place. It is lovely to see the giant cylinder of veal carved away from the series of eight ribs and, sure enough, the meat has been carefully roasted, so that there is a bit of pink at its center. But this is simply not a good preparation of veal, the elegance of the light, winy sauce notwithstanding. It is almost impossible to get away without browning veal or exposing it in some way to direct fire or heat and, unfortunately, what is served here is veal that has been roasted within the protection of ribs and fat, and it lacks life. Make sure you get those ribs— they are browned and crisped, and the minuscule morsels found thereon are the best of the meat of this dish. Better still are the vegetable garnishes: sautéed mushrooms, buttery and garlicked; a spectacularly crusted potato cake, salty and oily. Whether or not you ate the ribs with your fingers, you get a finger bowl—a crystal dish of steamy water afloat with rose petals.

A rather impeccable little salad arrives, of arugula, endive and mango, in a very mild dressing. Then a tray of cheeses—Brie among them, of course—with a bowl of rather hangdog fruit. Then the desserts. A frozen soufflé is wheeled through the aisles, and everyone gets a substantial slab of the cool white sweet—it is studded with nutted meringue and berries and softened with good, unsweetened whipped cream. More desserts come, including an apple tart moistened with apricot preserves; a chocolate cake under a black icing, with layers of mousse and sprinklings of nuts; candies (bad); petits fours (not bad). Pretty good coffee to go with the brandy or liqueur you select from the cart that travels by.

But, but. The Palace is the home of linear man. It is sexless and stuffy. Its prices are the highest of any restaurant in town and it qualifies, thereby, as the best to people who have no other way of judging. Here they are, the first citizens of Consumerville, and Mr. & Mrs. Frank Valenza (les "Proprietaires," the menu informs you) got 'em. A joyless achievement.

• PALM

837 Second Avenue (near 45th Street)
LUNCH, MONDAY TO FRIDAY; DINNER, MONDAY TO SATURDAY. CLOSED SUNDAY.
Reservations for lunch only, 687–2953.
Credit cards: AE, CB, DC, MC, V.
Very expensive.

This venerable institution is certainly one of the most unusual-*looking* restaurants in New York. The narrow downstairs rooms and the more commodious upstairs dining area are painted a pale-coffee stain, and the walls and some of the ceilings are adorned, if that is the correct word, with painted caricatures, some forty years old. There is sawdust on the brown floor, the lights are bright, and from the choice window seats, there is a spectacular view of Second Avenue.

The Palm is one of those places in which there is no printed or written menu—the waiter recites the available dishes. There are about half a dozen things wrong with this idiotic system. To begin with, one makes his choice under the more or less impatient or bored gaze of the waiter, as he stands now on one foot, now on the other. Here at the Palm, where the listing is brief, some of the waiters recite less than all of it, anyway, and only initiates (who remember meals past) are in fact choosing from the complete selection. Naturally, when there is no menu, there is no posted list of prices; your waiter at the Palm may inform you of the prices, and then again he may not; and of course there is no document against which to check the accuracy of the bill.

Fully 99 percent of the customers here have lobster, sirloin steak or filet mignon, preceded by shrimp cocktail or clams, accompanied by some fried potatoes, and followed by cheese cake and coffee. Deviates cause some of the waiters to lift their eyes heavenward.

A sample encounter:

Waiter: "What can I do for you?"

Customer: "What do you have?"

W: "Anything your little heart desires, my little lady." He pats her arm.

C: (Innocently) "Do you have steak?"

W: "You want filet or sirloin? How do you want it?"

C: "Just a minute. Do you have anything else?"

W: "We got lobster."

C: "That's all? Steak and lobster?"

W: "Anything your little heart desires, my little lady." He pats her arm again.

(Pause, while the waiter greets two customers, kissing the woman, shaking hands with the gent, happily getting *that* straight.)

C: "Could you tell us everything you have?"

W: "Sure. We got steak, lobster, chop steak, lamb chops, pork chops, roast beef."

C: "No fish?"

W: "We got sole."

It takes an additional five minutes to determine that there are two kinds of potatoes: cottage fries (good when they are pale; tasteless and pointless when they are dark) and home fries (a huge platter of deliciously fried and browned spuds, made without tossing, so that there are gradations of brownness and crispness through the dish); three kinds of salad dressings: Russian, Roquefort (made with the real thing) and oil-and-vinegar; that there is wine, but that there is no wine card to choose from, and so on.

The steaks and chops are good, though not invariably cooked as ordered. The lobsters are an achievement—they appear to weigh about four pounds and completely disprove the notion that large lobsters are tough or tasteless. They are broiled to perfection, tender and juicy, and the meat picks up an interesting flavor from the charred shell. Desserts are good, though undistinguished: cheese cake, ice cream and melon.

Strictly speaking, this is not a restaurant. It's a club for people who like it—people who like to wait for tables in the middle of a cramped dining room, since the house refuses to take dinner reservations (officially) because that would sacrifice a little business for customer convenience, and customers can wait; people who like to talk at the tops of their voices, or at least don't mind when people at nearby tables do; people who like to swagger and be recognized at a place where people swagger; people who don't like to be greeted by a host but prefer to be fought over by finger-snapping waiters when the place is not full; people who don't mind an occasional rotten tomato in their salad. These people come here by the thousands, and presumably there is something positive that they like about the place other than the food, which is not peerless. It's so casual, you can almost remove your shoes. Maybe that's it.

• EL PARADOR CAFÉ

325 East 34th Street
DINNER. CLOSED SUNDAY.
No reservations (679–6812).
No credit cards.
Medium-priced.

Its proponents claim that what distinguishes El Parador from the myriad of mediocre Mexican restaurants that are beginning to line Manhattan's avenues in the middle-income neighborhoods is not the food based on the tortilla—no, the tacos, tamales and tostadas at El Parador, they admit, are just junk food, sound excuses for an evening of beer drinking. It is, they claim, the more pretentious specialties that make this quite pretentious establishment. It is true, they are better than the junk food.

El Parador is a busy restaurant, but it is not the mob scene it once was. Nevertheless, when you arrive and there are tables empty and ready (and they cannot be ready for anyone in particular, because the house does not accept reservations), you are told that there will be a wait at the bar, you are assured that it will not exceed thirty minutes, and the scene has been set—here on 'way-East 34th Street, what can you head for and be sure to be seated in much less than thirty minutes? So you hit the bar, order the two drinks the whole charade is designed to sell, and as soon as that transaction is completed you are seated at one of the several available tables. And your host is so gracious! Shame, *shame*, Señor Jacott. Just to sell a couple of your excellent Margueritas? You are led to your table by a waiter carrying your barely sipped drinks, lambs from the slaughter.

Seviche is a marvelous dish of raw fish that has been "cooked" by marination in lemon or lime juice and any of several other ingredients, depending on which Latin country is the source of the recipe. If we may take it that the seviche at El Parador is typical of the Mexican method of preparing this dish, then we may conclude that Peruvians, Bolivians, Cubans, etc., enjoy it more. They start out with a nice fish here —red snapper—and they marinate it in lemon juice, but somehow some of the fish becomes chewy in the process. Then they garnish it with a couple of slices of avocado whose quite brown, loud overripeness could not have been concealed in a guacamole, and serve it on a pile of shredded iceberg lettuce that becomes limp in the drained-off marinade from the fish. The production is strewn with fresh peas. Unusual. The latest sampling of guacamole at El Parador is superior to the bland stuff this restaurant used to serve—it is garlicky and sharp, almost winy, and it would be first rate if it were not served at refrigerator temperature.

You were warned when seated that your Chicken a El Parado would take thirty minutes. You should have been warned twice. Eventually it arrives, a giant serving of crusty, garlicked fried chicken, garnished with a huge poached onion and a scattering of fresh peas. This is good fried chicken, albeit a bit heavy, but its reputation is not on its merit, but on its comparison with most Mexican food in New York. It may be the best dish in the place, but that is not a particularly exalted position. There is a pretty fair dish of shrimps in green sauce served here—good shrimps in a sauce that has a loud, clear flavor of fresh parsley. Unfortunately, the sauce is watery and if you spoon it over the excellent rice that is served with the main courses, you ruin the rice.

Slightly better than average Mexican-restaurant desserts, including nice guava shells, grainy and tart, with a creamy cheese and crisp saltine crackers—homey but good.

El Parador is a dim, sexy place, but avoid the downstairs room—Grand Rapids brick and ornate mirrors, and every time the kitchen door opens, the glaring white light jars.

★★★ PARIOLI, ROMANISSIMO

1466 First Avenue (near 76th Street)
DINNER, TUESDAY TO SATURDAY. CLOSED SUNDAY AND MONDAY.
Reservations required, 288-2391.
Credit cards: AE, CB, DC.
Very expensive.

This is a dark little den through which waiters wander by the seeming dozen. They are dark-haired, immaculately tonsured and handsome, and they are suited up in formal blacks, their shirt fronts and ties stiff and snowy. There is something religious about their uniform look and courtliness, but when they unbend and hover over your uttered wishes and over the tasks of carrying them out, it is the soma that is being nourished, not the soul. And very well, too—Parioli manages to serve some of the best Italian food in New York.

In the hierarchy of the priesthood of pleasure everything is upside down: the captain of the waiters is distinguished from his fellows by the rakish cut of his suit and by the broad wings and gay color of his bow tie; and your host, who carries out many captainly functions—discussing the menu with you and announcing and pushing special unlisted selections of the day—is resplendent in mufti and luxuriant hair. The moral is, When you make it to the top you can relax. And folk who have made it sufficiently high up the economic ladder to be seen in this steep place are very much at home here. Parioli, Romanissimo, is kept busy by a small but devout following of prosperous Upper East Side New Yorkers: the professionals come early in the evening, and the place is medically and legally sober for a few hours; then come the creatives, sporting their stylish hair and duds, chairs are pushed a few inches farther from the tables, and the sounds of gay but restrained cheer that filled the room at eight are replaced by a slightly cacophonous din—this room can be noisy.

You enter through a handsome wrought-iron street door to a tiny vestibule, wherein strays are rejected by the snooty sign: "By Reservation Only." Having arranged ahead, you proceed, into a longish room which, by a separated, two-steps-up level on the right, a turn to the left at the back, and wrought-iron partitions here and there, is divided into intimate sections. That raised level is given a light garden treatment—a few potted plants, the suggestion of an awning, metal chairs painted white—while the rest of the place, unblushingly unrealistic about the absence of a separating wall, suggests the interior of the parent house—gold wallpaper, racks of wine, framed mirrors, in one corner a spectacular arrangement of cut flowers, the single bright note in this dim fairyland. Parioli is something of a jumble, but the soft light calms it.

This is one of those establishments that are famous for their secrets, where frequenters push aside the proferred menu and ask about the day's unlisted items. This is most useful in selecting first courses, for though the various stuffed clams, scampi and prosciutto are unimpeachable, an occasional specialty like the Vitello Tonnato borders on the amazing—cutlets of cool veal, pale and tender, under a tuna mayonnaise that is at once creamy and light, sharpened with lemon.

While the rage among New York's food freaks is making one's own pasta on one's own little pasta machine or, at the very least, buying fresh pasta at one of the several outlets around town where it is manufactured each day for prompt sale, this place, bound to a more old-fashioned snobbism, imports its macaroni, dried, from Italy. It is difficult to believe that anyone's spaghetti in clam sauce could surpass this one, no matter what the provenance of the noodle. The spaghetti is extremely thin—vermicelli, actually—boiled to that perfect point at which it has lost all hardness without showing even a trace of mushiness; and it is served in a briny broth redolent of garlic and studded with an abundance of minced fresh clams that are as firm and tender as littlenecks two minutes out of the sea. The dish comes adorned with a couple of whole clams still in their shells and a small cloudburst of fresh parsley. By comparison the Tortellini Bolognese should not be asked to suffer, for these are nice enough little crescents of pasta wrapped around ground meat; and the sauce, a nubbly thickness of ground beef, mingled with oil, spices and chunks of tomato, is totally satisfying, if far from elegant.

The most expensive seafood dish on the menu, Pescatora alla Veneziana, can be the most disappointing item in the house. This is stew, principally of shellfish and squid, in a brothlike sauce made fiery with fresh red pepper. But the circlets of squid are tough, the mussels limp, the flavors of the shrimp and clams obscure in this setting; what is worst is the slice of fish at the center of the abundant mound—it is cooked beyond any flavor or texture other than that of wet cotton wool.

The same kitchen produces Piccata di Vitello al Limone, probably the best version of veal in a lemon sauce available in New York. The meat is buttery, the sauce creamy and sparkling with the vibrance of fresh lemon. The Suprema di Pollo al Cognac is a sautéed chicken breast inundated in sautéed fresh mushrooms and a cream sauce that is thick and lightly brandied—rich, smooth, polished food. Rare for New York's Italian restaurants, even the steaks are good, not to mention joyously labeled. Try, for example, the Lombatina di Manzo alla Toscanini, a section of filet mignon about the size of your fist, tender, accurately cooked, and served in a sauce of wine and green peppers that livens the meat. It is true of almost all the sauces here that they have character and individuality and that they brighten the meats they adorn—these are sauces with a function beyond fanciness. Good vegetables and salads, including Spinaci all'Aglio e Olio, a remarkable spinach dish in which the leaves of the vegetable retain their texture even though they are utterly imbued with the smoothness of oil and the strong scent and flavor of abundant garlic. Perfect greens—sharp, sweet, crisp endive and fragrant arugula—in a dressing that will wake you up.

The zabaglione is ceremoniously prepared in a copper pot at a serving stand near your table and it is not bad—frothy and winy. And there are perfectly fine cheeses with fruit. But the facts are that you must have the chocolate cake or the cheese cake. The chocolate is airy and moist, and it has a flavor that will remind you of the aroma of real cocoa when a fresh package is just opened—the thick whipped cream on top verges on light butter. The cheese cake is something else—a velvety and sweetened richness of ricotta cheese, sparkling with chunks of fruit, the blackened exterior of the cake making for a delicately bitter accent. A minor wonder.

★★PARIS BISTRO

48 Barrow Street (near Bedford Street)
DINNER.
Reservations, 989–5460.
Credit cards: AE, CB, DC, MC, V.
Medium-priced.

A hectic Greenwich Village restaurant, casual, relatively inexpensive. Two rooms, connected by a passage through the kitchen—in front a nondescript den, a bar at one end—brick walls, ornate mirrors, low ceiling, late-night joviality, comfort; in back there is outdoor dining (indoor in wintertime, when the overhead roll-away green-and-white awnings are un-rolled-away, and the heaters are turned on, and the fire in the fireplace is lit), under hanging white globes, hanging plants, very gay. The food is good and medium-priced, the wine is cheap, the service is positively in-passing.

The snails are plump and tender and served in a buttery sauce that is thick with parsley and garlic. These are not the greatest snails—they were not cooked in a profound stock—but they are totally satisfying. The Crevettes à la Marinade are perfect shrimps, big and firm, the surface a shiny flamingo pink, served with lemon. These shrimps seem to have got most of the cooking in the marinating, rather than in boiling water, and they retain a bright, clear taste. The Moules Ravigote are almost as good —the mussels are plump, tender and fresh, and the sauce ravigote is a nice variant— lots of mustard, fresh dill, and a sprinkling of capers. The pâté is the least of the appetizers, but still it is livery, loud and good.

The onion soup is good in all but its broth. The melted cheese on top is an excellent Swiss product, the crusts of bread that protrude from the cheese have been nicely toasted when the cheese was browned, but the stock is a bit thin, though more than palatable. Onion soup is a simple thing—the stronger and deeper the stock, the better the soup, and it should not take much to improve this version.

Your waiter drops by to chat, caressing his beard as he does so. He allows as how he likes the food here too, as he picks up the plates from your first courses and heads away with them. He returns with an afterthought—"Should I order your main courses now?" "Good idea." And off he goes to the kitchen to order your main courses, having taken an order for a second bottle of wine, as you figure to need a little something to hold you in the interim. Perhaps he knew what he was doing.

The steak au poivre here is really sturdy stuff. To some tastes this thick coating of peppercorns (barely ground) may be excessive, and the strongly brandied sauce may be, too, but the meat is good, the brandy is cognac, and it is thoroughly cooked down to make a rich, thick sauce; and the broiling is accurate. There is also a more than decent Carbonnade à la Flamande served here, the oddly sour beef stew made with beer —this version is thick and tender, and the serving is ample. Pretty nice vegetables, including excellent boiled new potatoes, cooked in their skins, bursting from them, coated with butter; tender rice, parsleyed and buttered; carrots that are barely cooked so that they are crisp—unfortunately this treatment is disastrous when it is applied to hefty, old carrots.

An utterly nowhere, commercial-seeming mocha cake, tasting refrigerated and feeling hard. You are better off with the pear poached in red wine—the wine is thickened in the process, and the good, fresh pear is firm and infused with the wine and sugar.

Careful attention to the limited number of items on the menu, sensible prices and the contented clientele that contributes to the light-hearted air of the place are the principal assets.

★★PATRISSY'S

98 Kenmare Street (near Mulberry Street)
LUNCH AND DINNER.
Reservations, CA 6–8509.
Credit cards: AE, CB, DC, MC, V.
Medium-priced.

Patrissy's is not far from the old Police Headquarters building, and it was always a policemen's hangout. You still see a lot of men in hats. They wear them at the bar and when wandering about, though the chapeau *is* removed at table. A jacket not removed despite profuse perspiration over a Lobster Fra Diavolo suggests that your suspicions about the bulge under the left shoulder are sound. You are well-protected here.

The dining room has the look of the thirties, though the black and crimson overlays of paint and wallpaper, undertaken in more recent decades, add a men's-club note which is supported by the heavily framed paintings, mounted sailfish, scimitar over the doors to the kitchen, solid captain's chairs surrounding the linened tables. Among the waiters a pattern has been observed—the locals are gruff and brief; those from the old country will talk as long as you want. They all know the menu and their jobs. It's just that domestic courtesies, unlike the imported, are extended grudgingly. These domestics have not been domesticated; perhaps they are policemen *manqués.*

Patrissy's is principally a Neapolitan restaurant, which means that the Zuppa di Mussels (their Italian) is made by steaming in the presence of tomato in addition to the usual wine, garlic and herbs. Fresh mussels and a strong and briny sauce—good stuff. But for a restaurant of the southern persuasion, this Frutti di Mare is surprisingly mild—chunks of octopus, squid, shrimp and conch, plus black olives, in a lightly garlicked and oily dressing with lots of parsley—also good stuff.

Marinara sauce is a basic industry in restaurants of this sort, and Patrissy's version is nuggety. The soft part of the sauce is a thickness of vegetables, the more solid ingredients chunks of tomato, and less frequently encountered and pleasantly startling, chunks of garlic; the heady flavor of basil pervades. Whatever shape of pasta you have it on, the noodles are cooked to order and arrive properly *al dente*. The wide noodles here are not the commercial, dried variety, and the sauce Carbonara you can have with them is thick with cheese, accented with bacon, and livened with parsley.

Those lobsters are carefully prepared, and, happily, the Lobster Fra Diavolo is very much Lobster Marinara, with the same potent sauce you can have with pasta. The Striped Bass Livornese is of good fish, and you will even enjoy the sauce, though this version, with its millions of capers against mere hordes of olives and oodles of tomato, is a bit unbalanced.

More cloves of garlic in the Chicken Scarpariello, not to mention sections of crisped and oily chicken and sautéed fresh mushrooms. Garlic yet again in the Special Contadina Dish, a hectic assortment of charcoaled slivers of beef, joints of chicken and lengths of strong sausage mingled with fried potatoes, mushrooms and peppers, the whole mélange flavored with oregano—sturdy stuff. To accompany the miscellany with a medley, have the Mixed Fried Vegetables—in addition to the expected cauliflower and zucchini, fairly crisp within their crusts, you will find a deep-fried clump of spinach and a hot, crusted-over hard-boiled egg.

Little of interest among the desserts.

★★PAUL'S

313 East 58th Street
DINNER. CLOSED SUNDAY.
Reservations, 752–9199.
Credit cards: AE, DC.
Very expensive.

Someday someone is going to put together a first-class French restaurant that reflects nothing but one man's ideas, never mind what the competition is doing, never mind what the press is likely to think, never mind, for that matter, what restaurant-goers seem to be going for. This is what I like, this fellow will say, and this is what I am going to do. If he is an artist, his work will be appreciated.

Paul is not an artist. His restaurant is, as they say in marketing-research circles, targeted—at jaded New Yorkers in search of culinary thrills. For all its undeniable virtues, Paul's is not an effort to do, but to outdo, to be different from, posher than, more wow. We have here excess in place of excellence, deviance for originality. The look is restrained elegance, with just enough opulence to satisfy even the summertime-mink-stole/wintertime-glorious-tan set; but the food sneers at its mostly Gallic past, which is hypocrisy, for the best dishes are the ones that are closest to classic forms, while the creative combos—beef with honey, duck and lobster, et al.—are, how shall we say, "Very interesting, please pass the bread and butter." Moreover, everything here is so correct that it is wrong, at least for a restaurant. There is little gaiety in the air, no abandon at all. You keep wishing someone would get drunk, or at least giggle. Partly, of course, the religiosity is a function of the clientele, solemn hedonists in diligent pursuit of experiences; and as the canons of their order dictate that they be among the first by whom the new is tried, here they all are. But the house itself is far from blameless. From the towering, tuxedoed and ruffle-shirted eminence who greets you (with the high seriousness of David Susskind welcoming a panel of deep-thinking gossip columnists), through the quart of pure Mountain Valley Water that is placed on every table (and decanted, idiotically, over ice cubes of city tap water), to the bill that is gravely presented in a discreet, unmarked envelope (rag content, you may be sure, and at $28.50 the three-course dinner, they do have a lot to hide), Paul's does what it can to create an environment that would befit a trial for high crimes. But what do you care? Most of the food, its cuteness notwithstanding, is OK to splendid, you can tell them to hold the ice cubes (or else drink wine from the extensive list), and the excessive cost will be somewhat offset by the greater than normal pleasure you will take in your own cheer when it is set against this ceremonious backdrop.

Paul's occupies an ancient two-story frame house. Its landmark exterior has been preserved and prettily freshened with a coat of white paint and dark trim. Its interior, however, is a thing of the day, the full W. & J. Sloane treatment applied after a thorough gutting. I feel PINK this year, the designer said as he threw his arms apart and turned his beaming face upward to the god who had sent his inspiration, pink, pink, PINK.

You enter to a spacious alcove, lushly carpeted, softly lit, paintings on a brick wall reflected in the mirrored siding of the stairway that leads to the floor above; under the art 'a row of tables under ice-pink linen, set against a banquette of dusty-rose velvet; across one corner a grand mahogany desk, behind it an impeccable functionary in a perfectly smashing knee-length number. Only moments before, she strode out of a Bonwit's window, now she is engrossed in her reservations and cancellations. She pauses to turn on her orthodontist's smile and to inform you that his grace will attend you anon. Presently, down the stairs he floats, the minister of culture, his face a mask, behind it long thoughts of correct table manners and library decorum. He parades you back to the dining room, a pink-and-crystal fantasy, with mirrored walls and stained-oak paneling, carved mirrors and ornate sconces thereon, plants and bursts of flowers here and there, large pink tables, broad aisles. If, instead, you are taken upstairs, you will find the glittering little service bar in place of the desk below, built-in wine racks in place of the bricks and art. Upstairs the pink linen is retained, the blushing velvet upholstery appears on cushioned and caned chairs and settees, the walls are of oak. A huge Oriental rug in soft colors covers most of the broad-beamed floor. At the back, sliding plate-glass panels lead to a little terrace with grass carpeting and potted roses. But another view of the outdoors is available—through a giant skylight of bubble windows, under which hang potted plants, with clusters of fresh flowers that are stuck in daily. It is all perfect, and a little dead. Perhaps after use it will take on the patina of a place touched by humanity.

If you have been eating in New York's more expensive restaurants in recent years, you have met these captains. They know their business, they are relaxed about it, they explain the menu knowledgeably. They are, in fact, the most relaxed members of the hierarchy, the waiters being somewhat nervous and jerky, as if they are intimidated by the importance of this place—they sprint breathlessly.

With a billing like Pâtés et Terrines Assortis, and the description "assortment of pâtés—mousses and galantines," you expect something more impressive than one pâté de campagne plus one pale assemblage of goose meat and goose liver. The pâté de campagne is superb—strong, slightly fibrous meat, coarsely ground, heavily seasoned and liberally cognacked, studded with pistachios, wrapped in fat that has kept it moist, marvelous with the good bread served here and with cold white wine. Its companion is wooden, the core of white meat tasteless, the liver and truffles around it vaguely flavored—a nothing extravaganza made doubly silly by being served next to something that is powerfully tasty. These are served with a wonderful cucumber salad—heavily vinegared cucumbers in a good mayonnaise that gentles the strong, sour flavor. A hot absurdity from the same department is given as Petit Saucisson au Champagne, Chaud, fancifully described as "grilled sausage made of veal and champagne." If they used carbonated Almadén Chablis it would not have made much difference, for these are rubbery little logs of spiced ground meat, served in a dark, sweet sauce.

Nevertheless, you let your adventurousness have its day and you send for some Anguille au Vert, semi-informatively described as "cold eel in green herb sauce." Now, eel, no matter its frightening reputation, when skinned and simply cooked, is not a particularly powerfully flavored meat, and when it is merely strands in a fish pâté that is strongly seasoned, it is little more than one texture against another. This tastes more like gefüllte fish than anything else, which is OK if you like that sort of thing, but its marriage to this heavily oiled and mustardy herb sauce is like a wedding from opposite sides of the track. Then they try a match between lobster and duck. Geneticists they are not. The Salade de Canard et Homard aux Légumes is made up of cool chunks of the shellfish meat, slivers of the bird, and crisp poached vegetables in a light dressing —for the extra $3.75 you can find out for yourself how much less the whole is than the sum of its parts, though there is no quarrel with the excellent lobster meat and the very decent duck. Fresh oysters and clams available—not a bad idea.

Pity this is not an à la carte menu, for the main courses are from another world. There is no explanation of what "two butters" in Darne de Bass Grillé aux Deux Beurres refers to (perhaps Hotel Bar and Land o' Lakes), but this grilled bass is as fresh, moist and flaky as this fish can ever be. It is browned lightly, without the assistance of flour or paprika, and it is served in a light, buttery sauce that is slightly acidic, marvelous next to the juicy fish.

You can do even better with the Coquelet aux Morilles, a tiny chicken roasted until the skin is brown and crackling, without a speck of charring, the meat within sporting the clear, warming flavor of fowl that has never been frozen. The bird is served with a perfect cream sauce that is fortified with cognac and wild mushrooms—simple, impeccable food.

The Médaillons de Veau au Basilique is a good dish, though it takes a small misguided step away from traditional French fare. The thick slices of veal are of the palest, tenderest meat available, and they are very well sautéed, though the touch of pinkness at the center is unfortunate; the sauce of concentrated basil in oil, though marvelous in itself, is strange with this meat, at least on first trial, though this is miles from the cacophony of some of the first-course combinations. The Filet d'Agneau Poêlé aux Purées de Légumes is a plain dish of pan-grilled lamb with vegetable purées. The meat itself is ridiculously mild for lamb, but it is nicely browned, rare within; the three puréed vegetables are a cut or two above baby food.

They have no shame. Restaurants push their tarts and pastries for dessert because they are already prepared and can be served to you from the dessert cart in a twinkling. If they are not sold tonight they must be discarded. One continues to naïvely expect that at restaurants of a certain pretended caliber no one will ever push too hard in these regards. Nevertheless, when you pooh-pooh the dessert cart and request instead the Tarte Fine aux Pommes Acidulées, you are informed, as if it were tragic news, that this will require all of twenty minutes. You do not mind. But they do, so they come back with a revised estimate—thirty minutes. You do not mind. At forty minutes you request your check. At forty-five minutes his eminence arrives and, lying as automatically as you breathe, announces that the tart "did not come out right," and that therefore he would not permit it to be served. Would you care for something else? At forty-eight minutes you are leaving, and a young waiter, not in on the story, comes running with your Tarte Fine.

They don't fight as hard against making a soufflé, for these command a $7 premium for two—they are well-made and light, but the chocolate version is sexless. The pre-prepared tarts are good, made with plump sweet berries on well-browned crusts—thick, unsweetened whipped cream is available as a bonus. A so-called homemade napoleon consists of a couple of inches of good pastry cream between a couple of flaky sheets of pastry—not bad. The chocolate mousse cake is marvelous, a strongly flavored and airy mousse under a crumbling sheet of smooth chocolate. The baked cakes are fresh, sweet, some of them liquored, and dull.

Sometimes Paul, a portly fellow in a toque blanche, emerges from somewhere and approaches tables of diners with a smile that suggests he is delivering indulgences. If you do not stand up and drop a curtsy, he goes away.

★ PEARL'S

38 West 48th Street
LUNCH, MONDAY TO FRIDAY; DINNER, SUNDAY TO FRIDAY. CLOSED SATURDAY.
Reservations, 586–1060.
No credit cards.
Medium-priced.

This is the *new* Pearl's, but with the same jokes on the menu—under "American" we have Chicken Chow Mein, Chicken Chop Suey, Pepper Steak, etc., just like in the old days at the old place. This is a system whereby the house can sell the stuff and still be above that sort of thing.

The old Pearl's was nondescript, the new one is anything but. The long narrow room is sleek, silvery, mirrored and sterile, which is appropriate to the traditionally icy service and to Miss Pearl's glacial demeanor. Surrounded by throngs of customers, she has a way of absent-mindedly straightening a place setting which suggests a search for tasks that will distract her from contact with the clientele. The customers do not mind. Pearl's is in the great tradition of Toots Shor's, Elaine's, and of course, Pearl's itself, those restaurants famous for their contemptuous owners, to which the rich and famous repair to demonstrate, we must conclude, that they are not held in contempt by the contemptuous owners and, therefore, that they must be rich and famous. Aspirers follow.

Each of these places garners its celebrities from a different world. The Pearl's world is the moneyed side of the media—TV, slick publishing. (The aspirers are from Seventh Avenue.) How different these journalists and hangers-on are from the four-eyed, hirsute intellectuals at Elaine's. Here you see *blazers*! And *crew cuts*! And sculptured, metalli-cized hair, and perfect teeth in perfect smiles, and suntans. Many are actually ringers for manicured dogs. At hangouts the food is not the thing, generally, but in this regard Pearl's is better than the others. Lots of humdrum stuff served here, but also some dishes that are terrific, so you can come here to ogle and also eat well, if you know your way around the bill of fare.

Look around, and what do you see? Everybody starts off with Yook Soong (you'll recognize it right away). You get a dish of lettuce leaves (crisp iceberg), a dish of hoisin sauce (thick, sweet and spicy), a dish of the stuff itself (an oily mixture of pork and crisp water chestnuts), and on request, a set of instructions from the waiter ("quarter tea-spoon sauce, some pork, wrap in lettuce, eat with fingers"). The combination of cool greens, the succulent meat mixture, the sharp sweet sauce and a few bits of strong scallion make for an extraordinary first course. This place is also big on dumplings, and for something homier than the Yook Soong, the Har Gow is coarsely ground shrimp, slightly oiled, wrapped in a tender noodle bundle.

Among the best of the big-deal dishes is Pork with Black Bean and Garlic Sauce and Mustard Greens (to put it exactly as it is put on the menu). This is a hearty stewlike dish, made with large chunks of slightly fibrous and slightly chewy pork, heavily peppered, served in an oily sauce with two-inch lengths of scallions—winter food. Among the least of the big-deal dishes, albeit one of the most famous, is the Lemon Chicken. The appeal of this dish must be its peculiarity—it is composed of slivers of chicken (hardly identifiable as such from their taste), strands of lemon rind, and bits of shredded lettuce, all fused together in a cloyingly sweet flavor of lemon. The Poached Sea Bass with Pickled Cucumber and Scallions is also a sweet dish, but a much better one. It is made with fresh fish, and the vegetables are a nice contrast to the almost caramelized thick sauce.

On Sunday evenings there are three sittings—at five, seven-thirty, and at ten. The last of these is the fashionable one, with lots of big names and famous faces.

★★ LE PÉRIGORD

405 East 52nd Street
LUNCH, MONDAY TO FRIDAY; DINNER, MONDAY TO SATURDAY. CLOSED SUNDAY.
Reservations, PL 5–6244.
Credit cards: AE, DC.
Very expensive.

Like father like son like father. At least that is the intention. Le Périgord sired Le Périgord Park, beheld its work and decided to emulate it. Le Périgord gets an E for emulate, which, the *Random House College Dictionary* tells us, means "to *try* [italics added] to equal or excel." The word also connotes some degree of success, and, it must be credited, Le Périgord is a better restaurant today then it was before it was attracted to its offspring's ways. The *cuisine* is a bit more *haute,* the captains a bit hautier (nothing serious—you just have to bellyache a little bit about the first table you are led to if your face is unfamiliar to his tuxedoed majesty, said table being perhaps a pitiful little island that stands in the center of the flow of traffic between the front and back rooms), and the prices up more than 20 percent in the last couple of years.

To make all this appropriate, there has been a bit of sprucing up. The intentionally-comic-but-not-in-the-way-intended murals in the back room have been replaced by sylvan scenes, though the marbelized mirrors have been retained. You are better off in the front room, which is larger, where there is a bar, where the action is—it has a festive ambience, it is where the regulars are seated.

But assuming you do not mind throwing your displeasure around or, alternatively, suffering your own disposal into the back room, you can eat well at Le Périgord. At lunchtime there is a saucisson chaud that is commendable more for what accompanies it than for itself. The sausage is properly spicy and oily, really a rather substantial item for an afternoon appetizer (and one wonders why it is offered only then and not in the evening), but it comes with impeccably poached little new potatoes, abundantly buttered and sprinkled with parsley—gloriously elemental potato. What price an appetizer of potatoes, please? You can also get a pretty terrific Terrine de Canard—a coarse pâté rimmed with white fat, moist, spicy and rich; shrimps that actually taste fresh, which is unlikely, but one is willing to be fooled by artful freezing; an excellent cold poached bass, flaky and sweet, garnished with crisp little marinated mushrooms; a firm artichoke, served with a thick tart dressing. This restaurant still pushes its Mousse de Brochet Tout Paris as a *Spécialité,* and these quenelles are very good, with a clear bright flavor of fish, albeit the dumplings are a little bready. The sauce, however, is outstanding, thick and honeylike, the whole dish fortunately served with a little mound of white rice, the perfect vehicle for the extra sauce.

If you eat around, and you do so for variety of food rather than for changes of scenery, the thing to do is to try the rarities wherever you are. Here one of the rarities is Poulard Poelée Demi-Deuil, which, as anyone who reads French knows, is a semi-despondent chicken, its ambiguous mood honored by swatches of black truffle worn under its translucent skin. The poached bird is very good, very moist, and it is served in a doubly thickened, very buttery sauce made on a base of chicken stock. The bird and its sauce are accompanied by rice that has been pepped up with bits of yet more truffle, and by celery that has been poached with garlic.

You can save a $3 upcharge by not bothering with the bouillabaisse.

A veal roast of the day is rather coarse, a sole in mustard sauce rather rubbery, though the sauce itself is rare for a mustard sauce in that it has the clear tangy flavor of the spice without being overpowered by it.

This is a busy restaurant, apparently busy enough to turn over enough cheese so that what you get is new and newly brought to room temperature—thoroughly ripened Brie, earthy and sexy between chalk-white skins; Roquefort that is at once buttery and sharp.

Poaching fruit in wine is a simple thing rarely done well—the wine must not be watered, and the fruit must be firm to begin with, and still firm when the process is stopped. They do it well here, sometimes peaches, sometimes pears, and the fruit, in its sugary and syrupy wine, is positively springlike. An excellent blueberry tart—plump berries, untouched by sugar, their sweetness natural, sprinkled with bits of pistachio nut, on a dark and flaky pastry.

★★★ LE PÉRIGORD PARK

575 Park Avenue (at 63rd Street)
LUNCH, MONDAY TO FRIDAY; DINNER, DAILY.
Reservations, 752–0050.
Credit cards: AE, DC.
Very expensive.

This restaurant, the aristocratic offspring of the plebeian Le Périgord, is one of the most elegantly designed eating places in New York. The large main dining room is brightly lighted with an ivory glow that is at once so soft and intense that it seems like gentle sunlight. There are crystal chandeliers and gold-colored banquettes, and apparently to ensure that the classical surroundings not create an atmosphere of overbred restraint, there are irreverent wall paintings of strolling characters in puckish garments who regard (or disregard) the proceedings with a jester's humor and superiority.

A few steps up is the second dining room—vaulted tan stucco ceilings, booths of dark wood and leather, and dim light; and a few steps farther up, the same furnishings in an intimate, low-ceilinged third room.

Le Périgord Park has one of the most reliable kitchens of the French restaurants in New York, the service is competent and professional without being stiff, and the regular clientele, many from the surrounding neighborhood, seems comfortable and keeps the rooms busy.

The food is not invariably to one's taste, but it's a matter of disagreement, not failure —the results are the intended ones, if not accepted ones. Terrine de Canard Truffée et Pistachée is a case in point. This is a powerful, livery terrine, at once refined and strong, but somehow the pistachio nuts seem out of place, too discordant; however, the garnish of celery root, in a very mustardy rémoulade, is a lovely touch. This terrine, on the good bread served here, with cold white wine, is a pleasant way to pass the time while waiting for main courses, as are the Clams aux Fines Herbes et Vin Blanc. These sweet clams are carefully baked with parsley, white wine, and most important, the juice of the clams; one wishes that only the tiniest clams were used because the larger ones overpower the delicate broth, both with their strong flavor and heavy texture. The appetizer of cold striped bass, with cucumbers and sauce rémoulade, is superb—a rich fish in a rich sauce, with crisp, dressed cucumbers as the very refreshing, tart relief.

Business is good at Sunday dinner. This is partly because most of New York's other fancy French restaurants are closed on Sunday, and partly because the splendid special main course every Sunday is the roast lamb "comme en Provence." The meat is excellently roasted—crisp outside, pink within—lightly flavored with garlic, and moistened with a glaze of good stock and the strong pan juices that lamb provides. There is a very good roast pigeon every day, but it is uninspired—called Le Pigeon dans Son Jus, it could use a little of someone else's *jus.*

Something on the menu is called Truite Inspiration du Chef. This, to begin with, seems to be sea trout, or else not a live fresh-water trout, which is not a misrepresentation, simply a disappointment. The chef's inspiration is a chocolate-brown sauce with mushrooms; it is very good, but he does a little better when he goes by the book. Good salad—lettuce and endive in perfect condition, the dressing made with excellent mustard.

There is a lot of flaming of desserts here, Mousse à l'Armagnac, soufflés of any flavor. But the cart of pastries and other sweets is more interesting: very light Floating Island; fluffy chocolate mousse; beautifully bronzed apricot tarts. After a large meal the bright pink raspberry mousse is a perfect sweet conclusion without too much weight.

• PETER LUGER

178 Broadway (Brooklyn)
LUNCH AND DINNER.
Reservations, EV 7-7400.
No credit cards.
Expensive.

Some of the legends that have developed about the New York restaurant scene are all-pervasive and indestructible. Ask a hundred people to name the six or eight best steak restaurants in New York, and 90 percent of them will include Peter Luger on their list. Most of them have never been to the place, because it is under the Brooklyn end of the Williamsburg Bridge, if that means anything to you. But nevertheless, they are correct. It is one of the six or eight best steak restaurants in New York, but what of it?

A wine expert, on the remote subject of vermouth, writes that "Vermouth-making is a complicated but not a great art." It can be said that steak-making is a simple but not a great art. The steak may be great, but the art is not. So for a steak place to be a fine restaurant, we look elsewhere for its art, and there is little to be found at Peter Luger. The art, or rather the imagination, is supplied by the customers, who attribute great value to such appurtenances as the simple, bare wooden tables—the honest color of unstained oak; and to the simple, bare wooden floor—a somewhat grayer but equally honest color. How much value can be found in the simple, rather tasteless home fried potatoes; or in the unstained and also uncooked pie crust under the apple pie; or in the simple wine list which is also almost bare; or in the simple cheese cake, which is simply insipid and barely worthy of a stand-in-line cafeteria?

But now for the good (well, better) news. The shrimp cocktail comes with a good, tangy sauce, and the shrimp have a fresh taste and they are firm. The other appetizer consists of a plate of alternating slabs of tomatoes and raw onions. The tomatoes are good for these days, red and fairly juicy, instead of the usual items of pulp and dry seeds; and the onions are freshly sliced, moist and strong. There is a pitcher of red stuff on the table—the famous house dressing—and it is sweet and spicy.

Peter Luger serves the best steaks in Brooklyn—huge porterhouses, the equal of any steak in Manhattan. But they tend to cook them rarer than you want, unless you ask for them rare, and you can't very well send them back for more cooking because they arrive at your table already sliced, and to broil or grill a sliced steak is to drive all the moisture out of it. You have to demand a new steak, and you can imagine what kind of reaction that generates.

Sometimes there is roast beef, and sometimes there is not, and sometimes there are lamb chops, but not always. These items are competently prepared, but you can't be sure of the availability of anything but porterhouse steak.

The place is certainly unpretentious and comfortable—when you arrive you hang your coat on one of the coat hooks that are all along the walls. And when you sit down you are promptly brought a basket of rolls and good rye bread and a plate of cool butter by one of the corps of waiters, who are almost invariably courteous, friendly and alert. And if what you want is a dinner of shrimp cocktail, steak and ice cream, you will have difficulty faulting this restaurant.

★★★ LA PETITE FERME

973 Lexington Avenue (near 70th Street)
LUNCH AND DINNER. CLOSED SUNDAY.
Reservations, 249–3272.
Credit cards: AE, DC, MC, V.
Expensive.

M. Chevillot has moved his Pure Food and Butter Act from Greenwich Village to the neighborhood from which many of his customers used to come in taxis and chauffeur-driven cars. The move was not, however, in honor of the energy crisis. Chevillot did not love his art beyond the logic of economics, and he has chosen not to settle for the livelihood that the mere twenty chairs downtown provided.

The new Ferme is not nearly as Petite as the old—twice and a half as large, in fact. Nor unfortunately, is it as Ferme—much charm has been lost in the transportation. The tiny spot on West Tenth Street was as nearly a farmhouse as a room could be on Manhattan Island. The new just has the clues painted on.

But New York is better off with a solvent Chevillot and a less-bucolic restaurant than it would be with neither. And if this Lexington Avenue establishment were La Petite Ferme's first life, no one would compare and carp. It would be celebrated for what it is: the best exponent of simple French cooking in town. One comes to La Petite Ferme for food that is little more than its pristine self, in superb form. There are sauces and garnishes, of course, but they never conceal essential character. Rather they set it off, like a pretty ribbon or two in the hair of an otherwise unencumbered nude.

All is studied simplicity. A deep, narrow store, floors of bare wood, walls of smooth white plaster—with floral patterns stenciled on here and there, pale, as if they faded long ago. An ancient rake stands in one corner, its foot-long tines black, twisted and pointed skyward. The little wooden cage of cooing doves has been brought uptown, and it hangs, birds within, high on a back wall. No plush banquettes here, but along one side simple benches with thin cushions. The pine tables are otherwise surrounded by tiny chairs of bare wood and twine rushing, Spartan pads tied to the seats. The chairs, like everything about this place, are a couple of sizes too small for the well-fed clientele, and it is difficult for a substantial occupant to rise from one casually without knocking it over backwards—you will see it happen at just about every meal. But the glamorous faces that appear here attract prosperous crowds. So not only the chairs are small, but the tables as well. What was designed as a deuce must accommodate four; a comfortable spot for a pair of couples must seat six. And they do talk, and the noise does reverberate.

This is a swell spot to take someone who doesn't speak your language. The noise does not drown out smiles.

Your napkin is a large blue-and-white plaid dishcloth. There are wild flowers in little vases on the tables. The menu is chalked on a small framed slate, food on one side, wine on the other. You are attended to by a corps of youngsters in elegant country garb, a few of them with mesmerizing French accents. And the food they deliver is very much what it was in the old place, and no more, the larger quarters having engendered no additional length in the little menu that changes a little from day to day. The youngsters' youthfulness, by the way, is essential, for the kitchen is a flight up.

One is horrified that the world-famous mussel appetizer, which used to be delivered in gigantic wooden bowls, arrives in a container barely large enough to hold the dozens of shells—this is realism, for these tables could not accommodate those old bowls plus one of your elbows as well. These tender mussels, over which a superbly tart vinaigrette —a bit of mustard in it—has been poured, with red onions, just chopped, sparkle.

Somewhere they must have a little person who does nothing but peel asparagus, even the thinnest stalks, down to the pale white core. Then someone poaches them, not an instant too long, and they are brought to you hot, drenched in sweet butter, their earthy flavor that of the youngest shoots the moment they are pulled from the ground.

"Truite Poché Sauce Chevillot," the blackboard reads, nowhere suggesting that they start with live trout. But they bring the fish to you in broken shapes, as if you were having truite au bleu; there is the unmistakable flavor of vinegar in the cooking liquid, also as in that dish; and the taste of the fish is indistinguishable from the live thing just done in. It is juicy and sweet, the sauce Chevillot little more than the man's ever-ready sweet butter, a bit of sautéed shallot therein. Similarly the lobster. No lobster tank is mentioned, but the poached crustacean has all the bright, sweet oceanic flavor of the most recently assassinated item—more of that shallot butter obviates dipping. The Poisson aux Truffes is a good little bird, all of her, a couple of truffle slivers on the artfully browned skin, in an herbed sauce made of a sturdy stock. The Entrecôte Maître d'Hôtel is an unimpeachable steak surmounted by a lump of herbed butter which you spread across the tender, crusty and lightly salted meat with your knife. Shredded zucchini and slivers of carrot, both buttery, accompany the main courses—they are crisp and tasty.

Half a dozen cheeses, all in blossoming condition, are brought on a big, thick wooden board: a powerful, almost gamy goat cheese, at once creamy and chalky; strong, hard regional cheeses; elegant, soft-ripening ones, like Brie; creamy and sharp Roquefort— a selection that would befit a restaurant five times this size.

Good ripe and sweet raspberries on a crumbly pastry, though the tart is cold, unaccountably. But when the berries are served in the bowl of a big wineglass, with a dollop of whipped cream that has been sharpened and sweetened with Grand Marnier, no faults are apparent. The thick chocolate mousse is, happily, almost devoid of sugar, and it is studded with bits of bitter chocolate.

There is a little terrace out back, with tables and chairs, where you may have an apéritif when the weather is fine. Quails wander about, minding their business.

★★LA PETITE MARMITE

5 Mitchell Place (near First Avenue and East 49th Street)
LUNCH, MONDAY TO FRIDAY; DINNER, MONDAY TO SATURDAY. CLOSED SUNDAY.
Reservations, 826–1084.
Credit cards: AE, CB, DC, MC.
Expensive.

Even among the best French restaurants in New York you will not find the consistency and reliability of La Petite Marmite. The menu is conventional (almost boring in the appetizers, your eyes may glaze over as you read the listing of desserts), with a few flashes of originality among the main courses, but it is virtually impossible to obtain a plate of food here that can be called "off." In addition, the service in this comfortable place is available, attentive, intelligent, unobtrusive. To come here is to take no chances. But it is more than that—the food is not only right, but good, sometimes better than good.

La Petite Marmite has enjoyed success since it moved into these quarters under new management a few years back, and what was once a makeshift-looking place had its skin smoothed with an overdue refurbishing. The uninspired appointments—dim floral wallpaper, wood paneling, idiotic little oil paintings, red velvet banquettes—have nothing to recommend them individually, but their sum effect is greatly more pleasant than the parts, particularly if you remove your glasses.

Those familiar appetizers are commonplace only as to the available assortment—the items themselves are of superior quality. There is, for example, the smoked trout available in many French restaurants around town, and from the admittedly excellent flavor of the product, it can be judged that it all comes from one smokery. But the trout you get here has not been waiting for you and drying out in the process—you get three shafts of the oily meat (three fourths of a trout, that is), and it is flaky and moist, utterly freed of bones, and served with a sauce that is a perfect balance of horseradish and cream, though some versions, in which the cream is whipped stiff before it is combined with the horseradish, have an airier texture. The Maquereau au Vin Blanc, an equally familiar item, is equally good, in the coarse way of this dish—the marinated fish is pungently sour, oddly flavored with *cloves,* garnished with the limp, sweetened onions of the marinade and decorated with slivers of fresh tomato. Order ham and melon, and you get thinly sliced huge sheets of dark, marbled, smoky meat over juicy, sugary melon; order saucisson sec and you get a platter of three-inch discs of a salami that is at once succulent and spicy.

Of course La Petite Marmite serves a petite marmite—a powerful broth with chunks of meat and crisp vegetable reposing at the bottom of the little crockery pot.

A nice little big deal is made of showing you the main courses in the pans before the food is served onto plates. Here comes your duck, for example, nestled into an oval pan, the skin dark-brown, as you can see, and the meat moist and slightly fatty, as you will soon discover. You will also discover that the orange sauce is not orange at all, but a deep mahogany, and that its meaty flavor, with vague overtones of herbs and liquor, is only subtly touched with fruit. Le Tournedos au Poivre Vert is a very substantial slice of filet mignon, aged and tender and tasty, grilled accurately, and served coated with a polished dark-pink sauce flavored with uncured pepper. At lunchtime you can get a simple roasted chicken here, browned and buttery, and served, as are most of the main courses, with little balls of roasted potatoes that have had thin brown skins formed as they cooked in drippings—lightly salted, crisp and quite delicious. Also at lunchtime, during the warm weather, there is on occasion a special of cold roast sirloin—rare, tender, served with superb hot mustard and with cold string beans that are crisp, barely poached, lightly tossed in a mustard dressing—excellent summer food. This establishment seems to know what it does especially well, and, happily, the Bass Amandine and the calf's liver with raisins are still on the menu.

The waiter confides that the cheese is in and out of the icebox from one meal and from one day to the next. You are grateful for the information, particularly as it deflects you toward the chocolate mousse—thick, yet airy, sweet, with a dense flavor of dark chocolate. On lucky days there is a roulade, a dark moist cake rolled around crushed raspberries and a lemon-flavored cream; and on most days there are tarts—lightly browned fruit on good pastry. For purists there is purity—huge ripe strawberries, solid and sweet, or a little mound of raspberries, juicy and fragrant of their own perfume, both with good unsweetened whipped cream.

A relaxed place with a starchy clientele. The management, however, does not favor the stiff collar and silk tie over shapeless denim. Contrary to the rule in many restaurants, unknowns are led to the best tables in the house if they are available—bad corners are given to the last customers rather than to the least-known.

★ LE PETIT PRÉ

170 Waverly Place (at Grove Street)
DINNER.
Reservations, 675-3915.
No credit cards.
No liquor.
Medium-priced.

This tidy little restaurant, installed in a venerable Village storefront just off Sheridan Square, differs from most of its similarly casual neighborhood competitors—for Le Petit Pré is operated by young bred-in-France Frenchmen, and the food they purvey bears the unmistakable and authoritative stamp of tradition.

Two small rooms, their walls covered with a neatly patterned brown-and-white fabric; a dozen tables in all, spread with white linen and set with huge stemmed water glasses, from each of which a large brown napkin sprouts, like an unfolded fan; daisies on the tables in slender vases; bowls of flowers and baskets of fresh vegetables on the window sills.

One of those baskets of vegetables will be brought from its window sill to your table when you order Le Panier de Crudités (served only to two or more). It is accompanied by a pitcher of thick, mustardy vinaigrette—an ear-splitting half-hour may be spent munching this crisp produce in its piquant dressing: florets of cauliflower, pale silken-skinned mushrooms, strong radishes and stronger scallions, immaculate lengths of carrot and celery, red peppers and red cabbage, lettuce and tomatoes, and more. More conventionally you may begin with La Tarte aux Légumes, a little quiche, hot and steamy on its well-browned crust, sautéed onions and green peppers throughout the light custard; or with the Artichaut Vinaigrette, firm and cool, served with that same vinaigrette; or with the crisp and crisp-tasting Salade du Petit Pré—romaine lettuce, walnut halves, and little cubes of Swiss cheese.

You are asked if you would like your duckling "crisp? or very crisp?" And you get this Canard à l'Orange just the way you ask for it, a splendid bird, moist and gorgeously browned, bathed in a sauce that is at once tangy and deep, and garnished, prettily, with a whole orange, sans rind. Equal luck with Les Rognons Grillés aux Herbes, a skewer of grilled lamb kidneys and tomatoes, moistened with a beefy sauce that is fragrant of fresh herbs. The secret of this dish is in the kidneys, for they have been immaculately freed of their acids, and they are at once crunchy and sweet. Less good fortune with Le Veau à la Crème, for the slivers of veal have been cooked to obliteration of all flavor, either in the sautéeing, the cognac flaming, or—more likely—both. The thick and creamy sauce, however, heavily flavored of brandy, almost saves the dish. The sauce Béarnaise that accompanies the filet mignon is heavy, vaguely tart, redolent of the smoky flavor of tarragon, spiced to the perfect point; the steak itself, however, though of decent beef, may be inaccurately grilled. Do not be taken in by the rather tempting description of La Casserole Villageoise—"Casserole of ham and endive gratinée." Though covered over with excellent cheese, crusted and browned, the ham is ordinary, like ham from a can, and endives become more bitter than ever when cooked. The à la carte vegetables include grilled tomatoes in thick red slabs, heavily oiled and powerfully garlicked; and crisp cauliflower gratinée, just a bit of cheese on the crisp vegetable plus an artful insinuation of anise.

Chocolate mousse in a wine glass, lightly flavored of orange rind and topped with good whipped cream and walnuts. When berries are in season the house gets good ones, and you can have them in wine or with that good whipped cream. You bring your own wine.

★★★ PHOENIX GARDEN

46 Bowery (in the arcade, near Elizabeth Street)
LUNCH AND DINNER.
Reservations, 962–8934.
No credit cards.
No liquor.
Inexpensive.

From the Bowery to Elizabeth Street a new street has been carved out, more storefronts for the commercially insatiable, retail-obsessed merchants of Chinatown. The arcade is a few years old now, and fully occupied. It's one of the places the locals go for pizza. There is a candy store that sells beer, for the patrons of the restaurants that don't. But the principal attractions along this chain of baubles are the Chinese restaurants, and no one can tell, just by appearances, which of these gilded boxes is worth looking into. This is the place.

The place looks like the inside of a refrigerator with the light on, all white polished surfaces, with here and there some hardware, ducks and chickens hanging at the front near the stainless-steel counter, a bustling little kitchen at the rear just beyond the stainless-steel coffee urns. The stainless-steel silverware is available on request; otherwise you get chopsticks.

Cantonese cooking has, of recent years, been looked down the turned-up nose upon. The foods of the provinces to the north and west have been the local favorites and fads. Your Chinese-restaurant goer doesn't merely utter the word "Cantonese," he expletes it, a one-word dismissal of a restaurant. There is an explanation, of course: hundreds of dreadful Cantonese restaurants in New York. But no, the Cantonese are not to China what the Dutch and Germans are to Europe, that is, plain ignorant about food; it is we, rather, who are ignorant (those of us who are not Cantonese), though admittedly at the hands of unscrupulous restaurateurs who have for years purveyed slop as Cantonese food, to the miseducation of the locals. At its best, Cantonese food is simple and subtle and light (rice provides the weight), emphasizing the basic ingredients and textures more than the flavorings and seasonings, a relationship that is reversed as you move away from Canton. Please, exception us not with exceptions to the rule.

Begin with "Pepper & Salty Shrimp (in shell)," which is not what it says, being peppery, not pepper, and thereby a good introduction to the English served here. These remarkable shrimps are either fresh or so carefully frozen that virtually no damage has been done to the sweet flavor and crisp texture. They arrive pink, bursting from their crackling shells, lightly spotted with bits of black pepper and moistened with an oil which is flecked with slivers of scallion and fresh ginger—everything conspires to emphasize the pristine flavor of the shrimps themselves.

Fried Fresh Milk with Crab Meat will strike you as yet another typo, and there are perhaps better translations of whatever the Chinese name for this dish might be, but as the dish is singular, it might as well go by this unique title. What arrives looks like a giant mound of moist white soufflé; dig around under it and you find crabmeat and crisp rice noodles. The meat is moist and firm; the noodles, included for texture, are crisp and slightly chewy; and the "soufflé" is glistening white, light and airy, and only faintly flavored with the slightly burnt taste of cooked milk. You may not like it, but that is merely culture shock.

Steam Flounder is not a new kind of flounder, but a steamed flounder. Now, you may say to yourself, "Steamed flounder, big deal." Well, first of all, this flounder is *fresh,* almost sugary in its sweetness, so fluffy it is difficult to hold it in chopsticks. It should be eaten alone because it arrives at a point of steamy perfection from which it deteriorates, since it continues to cook in its own heat. Quickly now, while the glistening silver fish is still somewhat hidden in the hot rising water vapor, push away the bony edges of the fish, pluck the moist, snowy meat from the spine and large central bones, and swallow it down. When it is all gone (in about two minutes), you can concentrate on the mushrooms and scallions you left behind in the broth the flounder was steamed in.

Fried Stuffed Bean Curd is, you guessed it, bean-curd sheet stuffed with bean curd, crinkly layers of the sheet around bricks of the soft and mealy bean paste, in a brown sauce that is oily and just vaguely fishy. This is a mother's-milk kind of dish, warm and satisfying, like buttered noodles, or bread and jam, or grits, and neither a fine nose nor tuned palate is needed to appreciate the simple oral pleasure of gumming it down.

Another good transition dish (we are heading toward birds and beasts) is Mixed Vegetables with Noodles, which is a party on a plate, here a carrot, orange and crisp and cut in the shape of a butterfly, and there one in the shape of a fish; ears of baby corn and brilliantly green snow peas; straw mushrooms and cloud ears, the mysteriously smoky fungi of your mysterious East; soft and buttery gingko nuts. The vegetables are not married, just joined in a gentle syrup, with rice noodles for a contrasting texture of dry crispness.

Head and all, here comes your Phoenix Special Roast Squab, much pushed by the waiters, advice that is much appreciated by first-time starters. The former bird arrives disjointed, skin browned but still soft, meat fibrous but still tender and moist, some of the little bones sufficiently crisped to be chewed down and appreciated for their salty oiliness. The bird is good as is, better when dipped in the seasoned salt that accompanies it, and utterly transformed when moistened with the lemon that is supplied. Enthusiasts eat the head.

Those birds hanging in the front window are not just for atmosphere. You can eat them. Recommended is the Roast Duck, listed under "Barbecue" on the menu. Your relentlessly sensible waiter (the one who insisted you eat your flounder in a trice) suggests most seriously that you have the duck as is, at room temperature, not reheated and dried out. Sure enough, it is profoundly succulent, not to be tampered with, served, in a way that seems French, over white beans that are in a bit of peppery gravy. To make one bite a little different from another, you dip it in the little dish of sweet ginger sauce.

You get your beer across the arcade.

★★ PIETRO'S

201 East 45th Street
LUNCH, MONDAY TO FRIDAY; DINNER, MONDAY TO SATURDAY. CLOSED SUNDAY.
Reservations, MU 2–9760.
No credit cards.
Very expensive.

Pietro's is busy and little-known. It thrives on the commerce of a small, addicted following. The peer of the best steak restaurants here on Steak Row or anywhere else in town, it is rarely mentioned when the talk turns, as it tediously often does among New York's restaurant freaks, to favorite steakhouses (when everyone gets down on the floor and wrestles over the Palm vs. Christ Cella vs. Peter Luger, et al., in an effort to establish who is tougher about what is tenderer).

Pietro's is a memory of New York. If you were out of town, unborn, or interred in the Bronx in the thirties and forties of this century, Pietro's is a glimpse from which you may extrapolate a city and an era, a time when a public eating place was a room with rows of tables. Atmosphere had not been devised. Menus were mostly in English. It was the waiter's function to find out what you wanted to eat and bring it to you. Your host was a supervisor, a hail-fellow only in passing, if at all. Conspicuous consumption had been invented, to be sure, but had recently suffered a grave setback— eating was too serious a business to be carried out ostentatiously. Something has changed all that, but hardly at all at Pietro's, a restaurant best defined by what it is an escape from: Section C of the *Times,* Lincoln Center for the Performing Arts, and universal psychotherapy. Pietro's gives us the simple life. Take one, please.

Up a flight of stairs to a tiny vestibule, where you present yourself to the man. He has a bundle of three-by-five slips in his jacket pocket (a unique reservation system). You announce yourself (very loudly and clearly in this din) and he leafs through the slips as if looking for the joker in a pack of cards. Tipplers at the bar, a dozen or so customers waiting for their assignments, hustling waiters sprinting through—this is a well-worn little room. And it gives directly, through large doorless portals, on two additional centers of dense activity.

To one side there are seven men in white in a garishly lit stainless-steel closet that is the kitchen. They have been working so long under the direct gaze of customers that all self-consciousness has gone. Julia Child has taught us that "When you are alone in the kitchen, no one can see you" as she retrieves a slippery chicken from the floor. Perhaps these fellows think they are looking out through one-way glass, but it is not exactly an oddity to observe one of them pinch a clump of clams from the top of a diner's plate of spaghetti and plop them into his mouth as he stares directly at (through?) you. Kitchen nibbling occurs all over town, you can be sure, but rarely in view of the audience.

Opposite the kitchen is the dining room, a dozen-and-a-half tables in a room that could not hold many more. The paint on the walls is fresh, the floor is polished, the paintings are undistracting. The choice tables are beside the curtained windows. This is where the action is, and this is where everyone wants to eat, but if a bit of calm is what you need, there is another dining room, like this one but smaller, another flight up. The food is the same, the noise is less, and reservations that may not be honored on time down below can usually be taken care of at once upstairs.

It is possible that Pietro's has the best serving staff in town. The waiters are at ease, polite, available and prompt. They ask for specifications you had not thought to specify. They understand what you say the first time you say it. They do not intrude, they do not visibly suffer, they seem to like their work even when they are carrying heavily laden trays of food up the stairs. They even look good—in old-fashioned crisp blue-linen jackets that are somehow much more professional than the quasi-formals or carefully designed casuals that are the rule in most of this city's spots.

The customers avoid chic as they skirt vulgarity. Very little denim, few pinky rings, and no Wildroot Cream Oil Charlie. Cigars and plaid suits; coiffed hair and knee-length skirts; tans. But they eat like starved children of the Depression who have struck it rich —you get enough food here to handle today's hunger and yesterday's as well, and these folks dispatch it casually. They may have hocked their jewels to come here, however, for the prices are impressive.

Appetizers appear on the menu in three categories. Under Antipasti we have your basic dollar-a-shrimp shrimp cocktail—five immense, snowy, pink-flecked crustaceans, sweet and crisp, so carefully removed from their shells that each of them is intact down to the last millimeter of its tail; and Clams Sauté, a singularity of the house, a handful of littlenecks, out of their shells, breaded, gently sautéed so that they are not toughened, served in a pool of butter, sprinkled with chives—the breading soaks up a lot of that butter, making for a richness that obscures the clear flavor of the clams, but a generous squeezing on of lemon brings them to life. The heading Spaghetti covers a few pastas of other shapes, but mostly the noodles are the thin strings of the title. The clam sau the chef's taste for it notwithstanding, is less than wonderful, despite fresh clam much butter and parsley—the dish needs garlic or salt or pepper or thyme to to life. And then there are the so-called Salads, including one called Broccoli, which is the best and sanest kind of item with which to preface Pietro's main courses: huge branches of the crunchy green, blanketed with broad lengths of roasted red pepper— a little sweet, a little sour and vaguely burnt—the whole wet with oil and lemon. A great dish.

But of course steak is the thing. You may have a large steak (sirloin) or a larger one (sirloin) or a double one (sirloin, not listed on the menu). They are of superb beef, tender without being mushy, juicy within their seared crusts, and cooked with uncommon accuracy. The thing to have is a friend with whom to share the double steak, for these are carved by the waiters into ten red discs with dark brown borders, served five discs to a plate. That kind of beef with a monster platter of thin and tangy French Fried Onions and/or a crusty hillock of Hash Brown Potatoes has been known to make grownups slowly shake their heads, as at a first encounter with Chapman's Homer.

You order Calf's Liver and your waiter asks whether you want slices of liver or a "liver steak." As the latter had never occurred to you, you opt for that, and you receive, exactly as you requested, a calf's liver. Or certainly most of it. When a portion of liver this large is cooked rare, its center may be too, shall we say, natural? But this is wondrous liver, tender and delicate, cross-hatched with dark stripes from the grill. It is served with sautéed onions that are made vividly sharp by the bits of blackened onion in among the tender oily strands; and with lengths of very good bacon.

Pietro's is also an Italian restaurant, and in this regard it is not unbeatable. The Veal Cacciatore is a wonderful stew, but the scaloppine dishes, though perfectly decent, are not much more; among them a Veal Française which, though of tender, pale veal, has a crust that is so eggy and browned that the dish tastes vaguely like an omelet. An item called House Special Chicken consists of chicken that has been sautéed with prosciutto and mushrooms.—wonderful ham and terrific mushrooms, but the chicken itself is the too familiar, bland current product—the only meat in the place that is less than first quality. Those sautéed mushrooms are available as an à la carte vegetable—a mere $4 for a casserole dish of them, and they are profoundly garlicked, heavily salted and cooked until they are dark-brown and strong.

Blessedly the dessert menu is a cursory gesture in a direction no one takes here. The rum cake consists of well-rummed layers of white cake among layers of icing, pastry cream and chocolate custard—not worth bothering about. There are the usual Italian ice cream things.

Most everything that goes on here is on the up and up, but Pietro's is just being discovered for its potential as a secret rendezvous. That could change everything!

★★★ PINOCCHIO

170 East 81st Street
DINNER, WEDNESDAY TO SUNDAY. CLOSED MONDAY
Reservations, 650–1513.
Wine and beer.
No credit cards.
Medium-priced.

Father cooks, son and daughter work the dining room. There are but a dozen tables in this tiny place, and with a seemingly well-knit family attending to its limited requirements, it is not surprising that virtually nothing goes wrong.

The marble bust of a poet stands on the radiator; vaguely Italianate bas-reliefs hang on the bare-brick wall. The stamped-tin ceiling is of a lipstick red that would be garish if there were enough light in the place to get a good look at it. You are presented with a menu that is handwritten on a sheet of paper that is torn from a spiral-bound sketch pad. There is a pipe rack just inside the front door, whereon you hang your own coat. Most of the illumination is supplied by a chandelier of glass grape clusters, electric lights therein. Can such perfect innocence be for real? Is there a man with soul so free of pretension that his hero is Pinocchio? Who is so artless in his adoration that he names his livelihood after the nosy fellow, but sets up no greater altars to his paragon than a doll figure astride the partition between the dining room and the kitchen, another in each of the two front windows? Ask no further. There may be danger in finding out.

Despite the signs, this is not a bring-your-own-wine restaurant. You contemplate the reasonably priced wine list while eating butter on crusty warm bread. Be advised, in this place you do not get warm bread when you sit down, cold bread later. Whenever you get bread, it is warm bread. So butter up and prepare for a lengthy series of wonderful foods, almost all of them made from scratch in the little kitchen at the back of this homey place, of ingredients as fresh as you can get them.

Carpaccio, thin slices of raw beef spread all across a good-size plate, decorated with green stripes of a thick, crunchy and oily sauce of capers and onions and parsley. Cacciatorini, a half dozen hefty slices of sausage, fatty and garlicked, garnished with a sliver of marinated red pepper that is sour and sharp. Caponato, a collection of marinated vegetables, eggplant, zucchini, celery, garnished with pimento—one wishes the marinade had not been so sugary and that the eggplant had been given more time, for it is slightly leathery. Stuffed Mushrooms, filled with ham, spinach, mozzarella cheese that tastes, miraculously, like cheese, all these flavors conspiring, somehow, to make these fresh sautéed mushrooms doubly vivid. Stuffed Eggplant al'Olio, thin cutlets of white eggplant, marinated and sour, wrapped around an oiled breading that is salty and herbed—they are like tart crunchy sausages. Fettucini Alfredo, powerfully eggy noodles, aswim in a sauce of eggs and cream, you add your own cheese from the bowl of the redolent stuff that is placed before you, and you grind on the fragrant pepper from a hefty columnar mill—the proportions hardly matter, these are superb ingredients.

This is an elemental Saltim Bocca—thin slices of pale, sautéed veal folded over thin

rp, salty ham. A bit of garlic introduced somewhere along the way empha-
meats; you may squeeze on lemon, and that makes the dish sparkle. Boneless
Marsala—cutlets of boned chicken and sautéed fresh mushrooms powerfully
ed with chunks of garlic and moistened with a bit of wine sauce—is, like most
he dishes here, simple and elemental and strong, but with none of the flavors hidden
any of the others. Fegato Veneziana—rapidly sautéed morsels of tender liver,
browned yet moist, mingled with sautéed onions—is served in a substantial mound that
tiny people have been known to dispatch in a twinkling.

A limited number of desserts, among them a hot and frothy zabaglione that could
do with a bit more wine—if you wish, you can have it served on some pretty good
strawberries. The Warm Brandy Cake is a fresh, nut-flavored spongy baba soaked in
hot liquor. Good coffees, plain and fancy.

The tables at the front suffer a bit from the ventilation through the louvered front
door, even more from gusts when the door is opened. The customers are couples and
couples of couples, young and earnest mostly, and very content in this, their marvelous
neighborhood joint. As the place empties out, the tape deck is turned on, and you are
serenaded by Benjamino Gigli, Jussi Björling, Enrico Caruso, and such, which makes
the face of the male offspring sparkle. "My father has a nice voice, too," he says.

• PIRANDELLO

7 Washington Place (at Mercer Street)
LUNCH, MONDAY TO FRIDAY; DINNER, DAILY.
Reservations, 260–3066.
Credit cards: AE.
Medium-priced.

Loft-living spreads beyond SoHo apace, and with it a certain style—seen principally in art galleries, but also in restaurants and other places of public accommodation
—of commercial space turned to more humanistic uses. High ceilings that once shel-
tered tall machines now look down on lofty rooms, barely furnished and airy; and vast
windows that once provided bright illumination for the busy fingers of light industry
are now hung with gauzy fabrics that soften the glare of the sun and streetlights. The
look is already hackneyed, like gingham-cloths-and-candlelight in eateries. This fledg-
ling establishment, had the new style not been available to it, surely would have opted
for the red-and-white table linen and the tapers in bottles in baskets, for by its menu
it reveals itself to be a child of minds that are given to habitual, if not imitative, thought.
Pirandello is an old cliché housed in a new one, and its clientele, trendy but slow, is
of sufficient numbers to suggest that our style makers had better change direction at
once if they are not to be run down by their followers.

This corner store is two floors high, and almost everything in it is chalk-white. But
for the black-and-white checkerboard floor and the black ice cream chairs (with white
plastic seats) it would be difficult to walk around inside the place without walking into
a wall. To be in here is to be snow-blind and half deaf, for the noise is intense when
the place is busy. You are safe enough in the entrance room, which has a wall of glazed
brick, a little bar and a bit of activity, it being the gateway to the kitchen. So insist on

one of the tables back here if you want to retain your bearings, for a look into the main room reveals that the huge windows, hung with white matchstick blinds and gossamer curtains, create a dense haze of light, early in the dinner hour, in which the seated diners look like figures in a blizzard. Plants (in white pots) hang from the distant stamped-tin ceiling, and there are candles on the tables. The abstract acrylics on the walls were done for the place, in matching dabs of black or green on a white ground. But the waiters are of the old school; whether friendly or curt, they are casual and semi-informed— you ask about wine, and you are told, with considerable smugness, that the house has both red and white, that therefore there is no need for a list. You are reminded of certain places in olden days where the availability of both red and white automatically added the choice of rosé, which was composed of a judicious mixture of the first two. We have come a short way.

A glance at the menu reveals that Zucchine Fritte can be had. As you are in the Village, where nibbling fried zucchini and driving away the day with a bottle of wine, while considering the menu, is a way of life, you go along, reminding yourself, if you have prior knowledge, that this is the zenith of your dinner—for the thin strands of crisp and juicy zucchini are crackling and steamy in their lightly crisped batter, positively sparkling after you have squeezed on a bit of lemon, and nothing you sample hereafter will match these high points.

Points much lower include the Funghi Ripieni, which might be edible if the mushrooms were adequately reheated, though the barely rewarmed cheese topping is tasteless. The Cozze alla Crema is a decent enough dish of steamed mussels, the "Crema" of the title absent, the fairly fresh mussels steamed in nothing more than wine, garlic, parsley and considerable pepper—several rejectable mussels among the good ones. Not all is beyond this kitchen, however, for the Peperoni Arrosto, roasted red peppers served at room temperature with anchovies and lemon, are simple and delicious.

Of the pasta dishes the most expensive is the least desirable, Linguine "Tutto Mare" (inexplicable quotes theirs). In the struggle to provide *al dente* noodles, they sometimes send forth tough linguine here, and the leathery clams, rubbery squid and muscular shrimps that are elements in the coarse seafood sauce compete with the noodles heroically. On the other hand, it is virtually impossible to undercook green noodles as long as you immerse them in boiling water at all, so it is perhaps wise to specify the green if you order the Tagliatelle all'Alfredo—wide noodles in a sauce that is thick with eggs and cream. Cheese and fresh pepper are added at the table, which means they are not cooked in, making for a somewhat unfinished dish. The Tortellini alla Panna, stuffed with spiced ham, are a bit hard, though the simple parsleyed cream sauce gentles them.

Getting a decent plate of seafood or meat in this place seems to be a matter of you and the fates, for though the shrimp in that pasta dish were dreadful on one occasion, the Scampi alla Posillipo were fine on another, the giant crustaceans tender and tasty in their thick and heavily garlicked tomato sauce. The Scaloppine al Limone would be splendid if it weren't sautéed in slightly rancid oil, and the Polla alla "Vecchia Romagna," sautéed chicken in a light sauce that is studded with ham, mushrooms and peas, would be sublime if the ingredients were not uniformly pallid. If the boss takes a fancy to you, he may also take your order, instead of leaving you to struggle with one of the non-English-speaking waiters. And if he absolutely adores you, he may even let you know that there are dishes available that are not on the menu—not everyone is provided with this fact. He suggests some striped bass, and as it is a special of the day, you figure it may be fresh of the day, and you are right. It is also tepid of the day, for it was prepared early in the day.

The cheese cake is dry, the zabaglione low on Marsala, the fruit cup dreary—you can have it liquored if you wish, which helps.

• P. J. CLARKE'S

915 Third Avenue (at 55th Street)
LUNCH AND DINNER.
Reservations, PL 9–1650.
No credit cards.
Medium-priced.

P. J. Clarke's is a saloon with a back room. A gigantic skyscraper was designed around it. Famous people eat in its little dining rooms.

In the front room the mirror behind the ancient, sagging bar has lost almost all its silver, and your image in it looks like an old photograph of a corpse, under a flag of the Irish Free State. The floor is of barbershop tiles, and the grandfather's clock gives the correct time twice a day. The juke box fails to drown out the beery middle-management pencil pushers who loudly exchange virile improvements on their pasts, ignored by the good-sport secretaries who accept liquid favors from dandy ad execs.

The back dining room is much like the front room, complete with bar, here used only for waiter service, and there are lots of little red-checked tables, and it is dark and clubby. The menu is chalked on a slate at the rear, and the white-shirted, long-aproned waiters (two generations—old, portly, red-nosed; young, thin, pink-nosed) move around a lot, exchange *macho* humor, and manage, finally, to get food and drink to the tables. And what does that consist of? Simple stuff, mostly, with a few anomalies: the ham in the ham-and-melon appetizer is sliced thick, spread on a plate and strewn with chunks of fairly ripe melon; the watercress soup, on a coarse potato base, has an honest, leafy taste (served with individual, cellophane-wrapped package of saltines); the really sparkling mushroom-and-spinach salad, usually eaten as an appetizer, has an accent of minced scallions and a nice lemony dressing.

The main courses include a perfectly good steak at $6.75, and a perfectly odd one called Steak Diane, which turns out to be tender sliced beef in warm Worcestershire sauce. (Yes, Virginia, there is a Steak Diane but this isn't it, which is all right, but this isn't anything, which isn't.) The Steak Tartare is of good, freshly ground beef, with capers and onions, and so on, but no oil or mustard. (Yes, Virginia, there is a Steak Tartare, etc.) You can have something called "smothered" for 50 cents—it consists of fried mushrooms and onions, it is delicious, and you can put it on anything.

The chef's salad is made up of lots of large chunks of moist, white chicken, hard-boiled eggs, tomatoes, onions, radishes and lettuce, all in good condition, and in a powerful blue-cheese dressing—good with beer. The very nice hamburgers are delivered on toasted, buttered buns. The vegetables are overcooked, the potatoes are OK.

There is a bouncer here who would frighten a whale, and a strutting host named Franky who walks on his heels, sucks up to the famous, and makes a federal case out of the most elementary responsibilities of his job. He looks around a lot as he walks, now behind him over his left shoulder, now over his right, as if to catch out by surprise waiter and customer derelictions of decorum. He finds nothing, invariably, shoots his cuffs and struts some more. An odious presence.

★★★ LE PONT NEUF

212 East 53rd Street
LUNCH, MONDAY TO FRIDAY; DINNER, MONDAY TO SATURDAY. CLOSED SUNDAY.
Reservations, PL 1–0373.
Credit cards: AE, CB, DC, MC, V.
Expensive.

There is no explanation for this restaurant's continued lack of exalted reputation, except that the place does not look like what it is—one of the half dozen or so best French restaurants in New York. Where is the grandeur, the spaciousness, the golden light illuminating muraled expanses? Where are the captains, and where are the impeccably tonsured magnates and their chic companions? Where, for that matter, is there anything visible to set the place apart from dozens of West Side bistros and East Side rendezvous? Only on the menu and on the plates. The listing is diverse, unusual and ambitious; and the dishes are, almost without exception, of character, distinctive and, moreover, good to eat. Picking out Le Pont Neuf from among the crowd of its competitors requires that ability to spot the star in the chorus line or, lacking that, a moderately discriminating palate. This is a professional establishment, as it has always been. Over the years the quality of the food has remained high, and the service, which was never bad, has improved—you can expect alertness and thoughtfulness from the waiters, intelligence and a thorough knowledge of the menu from the host. All this in a restaurant which is comfortable, a little informal and, it must be admitted, rather commonplace in appearance. You will find the plaques and folksy murals, and so on, dreadfully familiar—almost everything else, therefore, surprising.

There is a little blackboard mounted just outside the front door, whereon, in admirable tradition, are listed special dishes of the day, usually of seasonally available foods. Among these, often, are the crab "fingers" for which the restaurant has something of a reputation (that is, among those to whom the place *has* a reputation). The crab claws are battered and deep-fried until they are crusted to a dark golden brown, and they are served with a sauce of mild mustard and heavily herbed stock. Sometimes Moules Vinaigrettes are chalked on the board, and these are recommended too—the mussels are the tiny sweet ones, perfectly fresh, and served cool in a tart vinaigrette laced with minced Bermuda onions and lots of fresh parsley. The restaurant still makes some of the best quenelles around—tender dumplings of fish served with a smooth sauce flavored with crayfish. What distinguishes these quenelles from the run of the mill is their lightness and the vivid, sweet flavor of fresh fish.

When good venison is available, the blackboard sometimes lists venison stew. You have to be insane to pass it up. If this is not the best venison dish in New York, there is a miracle worker somewhere. The meat is marinated twice—in oil and vegetables, and then in wine. After it is stewed, the thick winy sauce is smoothed with currant jelly. The meat is almost unbelievably tender, still pink, vaguely sour in a way that contrasts perfectly with the gravy; and the stew is served to you surrounded by a great wall of chestnut purée, happily not sweetened to a candy, but prepared for what it is—a delicate vegetable with a nutlike flavor.

Bouillabaisse, we all know, is not *really* bouillabaisse once you get very far from the Mediterranean. But we do not sit around moping about it, right? We are mature, right? We do the best we can with what we have, right? Well, the best that Le Pont Neuf can is very good—a giant pot of *strong* briny broth, with clams, shrimps, chunks of lobster in the shell, and slabs of local fish. The thing is made right—rapidly—so that no ingredient has been toughened and no flavor has been lost. What with all the dipping of bread deep into the broth, holding the lobster with the fingers to suck out the meat, and generally abandoning all politesse, one slumps back in one's chair and gives oneself over to dreams of a warm wet napkin. No sooner dreamt than had. Your hot napkin replaces your bouillabaisse pot as naturally as your salad follows that. Good salad, too. Firm endives and crisp watercress in a creamy mustard dressing.

If there is one discomfort in this restaurant, it comes of the difficulty you will encounter concentrating on your own food when such delights as the superb rack of lamb is being carved for the people a table or two away—this is still one of the best racks of lamb in town, served for two, with little roasted potatoes, artichoke bottoms, and mushrooms in an herby lamb gravy.

At $7 the Soufflé au Grand Marnier should be better. It *tastes* delicious, sweet and liquored, with a perfectly browned dry crust, sprinkled with sugar. And it is served with a flawless crème Anglaise flavored with additional Grand Marnier. But the interior of the soufflé itself is a bit heavy and pudding-like. If you want to spring for a fancy dessert in this place, you are better off with the Crêpes Normande—next to which Crêpes Suzette taste like lollipops. The dessert is composed of thin pancakes and a thick sauce of orange rind, whipped cream, honey, Cointreau and Calvados, and it is superb.

★★ LE POULAILLER

43 West 65th Street
LUNCH AND DINNER. CLOSED SUNDAY.
Reservations, 799-7600.
Credit cards: AE, DC, MC, V.
Expensive.

This offspring of La Caravelle never quite matched the food of its progenitor, but it occasionally flashed a dish that could make a man's day. Those moments of brilliance are less frequent these days than they were a few years back, but this is still an uncommonly consistent restaurant, serving food that is comparable to that of all but the very best of Manhattan's midtown French restaurants, at prices that are lower than most—the prix-fixe dinner is $15.75 and you can eat very well within that budget, for there are plenty of good dishes on the menu that command no premium.

Perhaps most notable of those are the bluepoints. Not that there is anything spectacular about the presentation of a plate of good mollusks, but it is standard practice in New York's prix-fixe restaurants to assess you an extra $2 to $3 if you want to begin your dinner with raw oysters (or clams). For some blessed reason, Le Poulailler has always remained aloof from this custom and continues to. You get half a dozen bluepoints, fresh as if they were asea an hour before, sweet and tender, mildly briny, reposing in a few drops of juice—when they are at their best they can well be eaten pristine, without sauce, lemon, or pepper. Naturally, there is no requirement that you eschew premium-priced items, and the Striped Bass Froid is a temptation to extravagance—the cool fish is flaky and fresh; it is served with mayonnaise that has been brought to life with a heavy dosage of fresh parsley and with a garnish of cucumber salad in a slightly tart vinaigrette.

Compulsive investigators, evaluators, inspectors rely on Oeuf en Gelée to "test" a kitchen. This is perhaps a little silly, for the test of a kitchen is how good the food tastes, not whether certain dishes perform tricks. But for those of you who want more evidence than that of your palate, be advised that at Le Poulailler the Oeuf comes through with flying colors, in this case a runny yellow, for the "test" is whether the cooked egg within its jelly casing is done to that perfect point at which the white is firm, the yolk a slightly viscous liquid. The plump muffin of jelly is made from a stout stock, it is shot through with bits of chicken and strong ham, and it all adds up to a good dish. The saucisson chaud is made up of three hefty slices of warm oily sausage that has been heavily garlicked in the making, spread over a mound of slivered oiled potatoes. Your waiter spoons some hot Dijon mustard onto the edge of your plate—its sharpness is just right with this heavy meat.

The Grenouilles Provençale are, as almost everywhere, frozen frogs' legs. Offsetting this is the fact that they are impeccably prepared, breaded and garlicked and browned, served in a substantial tomato sauce that is strongly flavored of that fresh vegetable without being sour or acidic. The Foie de Veau aux Raisins consists of thinly sliced calf's liver, done to just the color you request, in a deep mahogany pan sauce that is sweetened by the white raisins that have been warmed in it. This is served with a mound of white beans, thoroughly cooked, but still a little crunchy.

A few dishes are in boldface, suggesting that they are specialties of the house. Among these is Le Rôti de Veau Ménagère—large thin slices of pale, almost white veal, looking for all the world like the breast meat of a turkey, moistened with a lightly wined and thoroughly buttered white sauce made on a veal-stock base. A few mushrooms have been warmed in the sauce as well, and a powerfully fragrant braised celery is served alongside. It is a minor crime that the veal has not been perfectly trimmed away from its gristle and that the meat is a bit fibrous, but this is a subtle dish that will distract your attention nevertheless. Another boldface item is Le Contrefilet de Boeuf Poulailler —this is not a steak, but a roast, nor is contrefilet the same as sirloin, the mistranslation on the menu notwithstanding. What you are getting is a kind of roast beef that lacks the juiciness and flavor of a prime rib, but the winy sauce it is served with adds a great deal of moisture, seasoning and taste. It is served with a thick purée of broccoli.

The so-called napoleon is nothing but layers of dark and flaky pastry alternating with layers of whipped cream, sprinkled with almonds—can't complain. The coffee mousse is syrupy and tastes like coffee candy, but the chocolate mousse is the real thing, airy, thick, sweet. The Crêpe au Fromage is a horrid thing of sweetened cream cheese in a tired crêpe, so pass it up for the apricot or strawberry tart, both on buttery pastries that are deeply browned, the slightly sour apricots on a layer of custard, the ripe berries on whipped cream. They have nice dessert customs here—you may, if you wish, have a little of everything on the cart.

This is a vast place, its ivory and lemony walls gaily adorned with pale drawings here, more colorful ones there. The light is golden. On busy nights, when a lot is going on at Lincoln Center, the place can be crowded, but often, even during the hours before concert time, a whole side of the main room is left unused. Once the performances have begun, the place is close to vacant, and the waiters and captains do more horsing around than a stern master would accept. But this master, a man who should be greeting you at the door, or at least at the entrance to the dining room, seems to spend the slow hours in hiding—often someone has to find him, so that a party may be seated at that one table, out of the dozens available, that he finds suitable. But Le Poulailler is well-tuned to the pre-performance cycle, and when their business is to feed a couple of hundred people in time for the first twitch of the baton, they work with speed and precision.

A simple and not particularly interesting supper menu is available from 10:30 P.M. until after midnight.

○ PRONTO

30 East 60th Street
LUNCH AND DINNER. CLOSED SUNDAY.
Reservations, 421–8151.
Credit cards: AE, DC.
Expensive.

Strolling East 60th of an evening, you spot and peer through the window of the brightly lit, white-tiled front room of this recent creation. There seems to be a good bit of action in that particular chamber and when you call to reserve, you specify that you wish to be seated there. When you arrive you are informed that your reservations "could not" have been taken on those conditions because that room is specifically set aside for patrons who have not called ahead. A pithy omen. You have been called a liar, and all it takes to get even is to tell the truth.

The street entrance is into that white-white front room—of which more later—then into the discotheque-dark of the bar, a murky, black-and-chrome customer staging area with a wall-size Naugahyde-and-brass étagère—some of its shelves are widely spaced, and sometimes pairs of pretties perch themselves thereon and look expectant. At the juncture of the bar and the long main dining room the major domo presides over his book. He demonstrates equivalent shock if you are five minutes late or five early. If you are precisely on time, he is not shocked at all, though he may have no place for you. Ultimately you are gestured grandly to a table, you seat yourself and discover that the overhanging lamps are cleverly positioned to shine directly into your eyes, an especial violence in a room that is otherwise quite dark. You summon a functionary and inform him that you have failed to bring your shades. He attends morosely, sulkingly loosens the bulb in the lamp, so that it no longer shines, and departs. Others on duty demur, and one of these comes by, and with a show of brisk, irritated adamance, tightens the bulb, relighting it. He leaves. Your duty is clear. You remove the bulb completely and place it on the floor under your table, making a silent resolution that if anyone tries to retrieve it you will crush it with the heel of your boot.

Mr. Adamant turns out to be your captain and when he much later materializes again, to take your order, he no longer cares whether you are lighted, for he has his mind on other things; and as you ask him questions and announce your order, he spins on his heel, now to the left, now to the right, his attention caught by everything in the room except you. Of course you do not permit him to go until he has read back your order and you have made corrections.

While he is gone you consider your surroundings, white-enameled wainscoting on the ceiling above, mirrored walls, hanging lamps over most of the tables, some of them draped with scarves to kill the glare, others for some reason not. You nab a waiter and ask him the quality of the inexpensive carafe wine. He tells you it is from Italy. Does he recommend it? The white, he allows, is drinkable. You opt for a labeled bottle from a brief, boring list.

Ultimately your food arrives, including an Antipasto Parmigiano, which includes a clump of tuna-fish salad that would even fail to grace two slices of sandwich bread, a couple of slivers of Genoa salami through which you could read the fine print of a phone book, tasteless ham, other items too dreary to recount, and, you have to give them credit, one fourth of a perfect hard-cooked egg. Salad Pronto reads like something anyone should be able to do—"arugula, bacon, eggs and mushrooms"—and, sure enough, there is a repeat of the unimpeachable hard-cooked egg, the arugula is fresh and strong, the bacon tasty and not excessively crisped. But the mushrooms, looking for all the world like mushrooms, taste for all the universe as if they were washed with the dishes.

To characterize Spaghetti alla Vigorelli on the printed menu as "with ham, mushrooms and tomato sauce," without mentioning that the sauce also includes peas, is to utterly misconvey what this dish is like. The pasta is tolerable enough, and not over-cooked, the creamy tomato sauce is even a bit velvety, the stray strands of ham and mushroom obscured by it, but the sweet nuggets of green pea actually give the dish a lively garden quality. Much is made of Pasta Fresca all' Uovo (homemade egg noodles), and, sure enough, they are almost as good as the elsewhere-made spaghetti. And if you order them Ai Frutti di Mare (with mussels and shrimp), you may well receive them with mussels and squid instead, the principal elements of a harsh, almost brackish sauce.

Your waiter arrives with your main courses, one of bass, the other of scallops, decides who gets what, and serves. You make the exchange and eat. Pronto is a busy place, so it is possible to get fresh fish here, and the Striped Bass Livornese is a perfectly respectable dish—a sizable slab of flaky fish in an uninspired but not seriously flawed tomato sauce that is studded with olives and capers. But the scallops, Conchiglie Saint Jacques alla Siciliana, are utterly without texture or flavor, like little balls of clarified suet, drenched in what has to be garlic salt.

By this time you will not be surprised that the Scaloppine Pronto, described as "veal, prosciutto, mozzarella, eggplant," tastes principally of lemon, albeit inoffensively; and that the Pollo alla Cacciatora, "chicken with fresh tomatoes, mushrooms, pepper and wine sauce," might just as well be called Chicken Nothing, for those ingredients miraculously cancel each other out. The deep-fried zucchini, $2.50 for a small mound, are limp.

The strawberries are not all ripe, and the zabaglione sauce in which they are served is deficient in wine. There is an adult sundae—Coppa Amalfi, biscuits soaked in Scotch and surmounted by three flavors of ice cream and mechanized whipped cream—edible.

You see things here you see nowhere else: even timid customers sending food back; every table in the good-size dining room occupied and not an employee in sight; now a waiter walks the length of the entire place, down the center aisle, never for a second looking to his left or right, lest a customer catch his eye; in that bright front room, where a kitchen island is surrounded by tables and chairs and diners, an awkward galoot in a white stovepipe dispatches fistfuls of pasta into pots of boiling water as if he fears the stuff might jump back out and bite him—nearby a little lady is giving artificial respiration to a pillow of pasta dough. You catch your waiter's eye and make the writing-in-the-air gesture which, all over the world, means you want your check —here it is not understood. When finally you obtain your tab and then hold it out with a $50 bill, your waiter, in his flight, snatches the check, the money and your fingers.

★★ P.S. 77

355 Amsterdam Avenue (at 77th Street)
DINNER.
Reservations, 873–6930.
Credit cards: AE, MC, V.
Expensive.

You enter to a snug brick-and-wood barroom and you are greeted, silently, by a coatrack, whereon, during bad weather and/or good business, are hung approximately twice as many coats as the fixture can comfortably accommodate. The customers' bodies, on the other hand, are somewhat more commodiously parked—at one of the several rows of white-linened tables, these in a prettily decorated room. Overhead the beamed ceiling; on the cream-white walls, children's art (New Yorkers will recognize this as a visual pun—P.S. 77, if it weren't a restaurant, would be a grade school—Public School 77), behind glass and neatly framed, like huge postage stamps; hanging and standing here and there, greenery; at the back of the dining room, a gleaming espresso station, a display fridge of desserts, and through a portal, a glimpse of a gleaming white kitchen. Along two sides of the dining room there are huge plate-glass windows, through which you have a panoramic view of the Texaco station on Amsterdam Avenue or the school playground on 77th—of course, you will probably prefer the look of your company because the playground is deserted during the dinner hour, and you may not wish to be reminded of the cost of gas.

The establishment is frequented by youngish West Side couples, some married—here a bit of hand-holding, there some spatting. She: "Why do you need another bottle of wine?" He: "Why do I need you?" Let's hope they don't have children.

Invariably on the menu are Escargots aux Champignons, three snails on three mushroom caps. These are quite lovely snails, plump and tender, the mushroom caps in which they are ensconced rather nicely sautéed, so that they retain most of the crunch of raw mushrooms while picking up that dark and smoky flavor mushrooms get when they are browned in butter and oil. On occasion there is available a simple avocado vinaigrette, and it is all you can ask for—the avocado perfectly ripe (pale pea-green and nary a hard spot) without being overripe at all (not a speck of brown). Within the hemispheric declivity formed by removal of the stone, you will find a pond of dressing—much clear-tasting oil, a faint echo of vinegar, and a distinct noticeability of sharp mustard—all very good.

The man who makes the sauces likes to make sauce Choron, for it is served with one fish one day, another another. Now, Class, what is sauce Choron? Right you are, it is sauce Béarnaise to which a bit of tomato has been added, and on occasion it is served with Quenelles de Saumon—little pink dumplings which are formed of puréed salmon, seasoning, egg white and cream, and then delicately poached. These have the required airy lightness, but the flavor of the fish itself is not perfectly clear and fresh; rather, it is just a bit fishy, as if the dumplings were made of fish which was half a day too old, and that is just enough to cause the flavor of the dumplings to overpower the sauce. It is a good sauce, thick and pink, rather easy on the tarragon and heavy on the shallots and parsley, but you will be able to appreciate it fully if you have it with a more delicate fish.

Then there is a Suprême de Volaille Zingara. A "Suprême de Volaille," as you know, is the breast meat of chicken, removed from its bones and usually pounded down to a thin cutlet. In this dish the cutlet is sautéed very artfully—the chicken is thoroughly cooked, but it has lost none of its moistness (in sautéeing thin suprêmes of chicken, if you cook for a minute too many, the meat is dried out and ruined), and it is dressed with a dark and spicy sauce heavily populated with slivers of tasty ham.

P.S. 77 includes a small salad in the cost of your main course. It is eminently decent —fresh greens and the sharp dressing you appreciated so much with your avocado. It is listed on the menu and served *after* the main course (unless, of course, you ask to have it sooner)—Upper West Side self-conscious sophistication.

There is Brandy Alexander Pie, an old *New York Times* recipe which was so popular that it can be found not only in the recipe folders of thousands of housewifes (and househusbands) but also on the menus of around half a dozen New York restaurants. As a few of you may already have guessed, this is a pie with the flavor of a Brandy Alexander, which is to say, a chocolate milk shake with cognac in it—if you think you will like it, you probably will. The Linzertorte is a lovely little tart—crumbly almond-flavored crust under a thick damson plum jelly.

★★PUERTA REAL

243 East 58th Street
LUNCH AND DINNER.
Reservations, 758-4756.
Credit cards: AE, CB, DC, MC, V.
Medium-priced.

Eleven tables in a cozy room, most of them occupied by prosperous East Siders who have discovered the place. In this setting of low ceiling and close walls of rough, chalky plaster, the softest sounds are converted into a minor din. If the place were not so dimly lit, it would be cutesy, but by this starlight one only vaguely senses the dark beams, shelves of folk crockery, false windows over painted country scenes. The tiny bar at the front is often rather crammed with waiting customers. In the dining room the service is of a certain kind—the waiters move very quickly, but they shift into a very polite "Park" when they are at your table; you sense, however, that the engine is idling fast, and sure enough, when the at-table service is done, they are off on their sprints.

To begin, have the Salpicon de Mariscos—a vibrant seafood salad of chunks of lobster, shrimps and mussels, with capers and minced hard-cooked eggs, in a tart dressing that rouses the flavors; the lobster and shrimps are firm and tasty, the mussels tender and vividly fresh. The specialty of the casa is Caracoles en Cazuela Puerta Real —plump, tender, salty snails in mushroom caps, in a deep pool of spicy oil; the dish is not brilliant, but the ingredients are so impeccable, the snails so soft and meaty, the mushrooms so fresh, crisp and browned, the oil so smooth and fiery that the food achieves elegance from simple perfection. There is a black-bean soup, Crema de Alubias Pintas—a thick purée, winy, enriched with cream and sharpened with red pepper.

There is a touch of hokum in the serving of the main courses, a bit of the passing of the pans of food over a flame before it is spooned onto plates, but it is more a gesture to a tradition than a pretense that any actual cooking is taking place on the serving stand, and the food is finally handled with such respect, it is so deftly spooned or speared, so artfully arranged on the dishes that one is not offended. The menu is like that of many Spanish restaurants in New York, but a few dishes are listed separately under "Our Specialties." Pollo en Cazuela del Jefe, for example, is a chicken dish with mushrooms, *lots* of chicken and *lots* of good mushrooms, but for some wholly inexplicable reason, there is an admixture therein of the kinds of little onions that come in jars to displace some of your Gibson. The chicken is fine, hot and moist, and like many of the dishes here, salty, though not beyond reason—but oh, those onions! You are better off with another of the specialties, Zarzuela de Mariscos del Jefe Antonio—tiny, tender little clams in their shells; fresh mussels in theirs; a good portion of lobster in its; all moistened with a superior sauce of sherry that has been laced with the licorice flavor of fennel; the extra sauce is fine on the delicious rice.

A flan that is different! Even in shape. This custard is cut from a loaf, and it is firm and moistened with caramel, as most are, but it is also studded with nuts and additionally flavored with a citrus liqueur—very nice. A dessert that is different! A pine-nut cake, light, liquored, with lots of crunchy nuts in the moist loaf.

★★LES PYRÉNÉES

251 West 51st Street
LUNCH AND DINNER. CLOSED SUNDAY.
Reservations, CI 6–0044.
Credit cards: AE, DC, MC, V.
Medium-priced.

Of the couple of dozen French restaurants in and near the theater district, Les Pyrénées is one of the better ones. It is also one of the few that keep their doors open late enough to serve post- as well as pre-theater customers.

The look of the place is corny in the French country manner, with copper pots and pans, a fireplace, pretty little plates hung on wood-paneled walls. There are cutesy slogans painted on wooden plaques—"A lunch without wine is like a woman without temperament," we are informed.

The food here is straight country cooking, with a few pretentious dishes on the menu that you will have the good sense to pass by. Stick to such appetizers as the pâté—it is wet, garlicked and spicy, delicious with bread and butter, and you get a portion the size of Monsieur's hand. Or have the Onion and Custard Pie, actually an onion quiche, and you get a slice the size of Monsieur's other hand, and a lot thicker. It has the sweet taste of sautéed onions, a touch of nutmeg and more than a touch of black pepper; though it is coarse, it is not heavy. Sometimes there is cold poached bass, and when there is, you can order it as an appetizer or as a main course. Either way, the fish is fresh and flaky, and it is served with a mellifluous mayonnaise that is made on the premises.

Of course there is Gigot aux Flageolets—roast leg of lamb with white beans—and the lamb is rare, slightly gamy and tender, and served in a thick gravy with beans that are thoroughly cooked but still firm. The braised capon is good—it is made with tarragon, and when it is brought to your table, or when a portion of it passes by, you will note an almost overpowering aroma of the mysterious herb. The sauce the bird was braised in is white and thick, streaked with the tarragon, and the dish is very sensibly served with rice, which is well suited to the task of soaking up the sauce. As in virtually all French restaurants of this class in New York, tripe is available, but here—shades of pretension!—they don't admit it at dinner, and you must get your tripe some day when you are in the neighborhood for a matinée. The tripe is slightly gummy, as it should be, and it is served in a fatty broth that is strongly flavored of bay and thyme. The rather sour flavor of the wet food is offset nicely by the firm boiled potato that arrives immersed in it. Even the side orders of vegetables are good here, particularly the oily, hot ratatouille, which is sometimes the vegetable of the day.

Your salad is dressed just before it is served, the greens are fresh and the vinaigrette is well balanced.

Why, in the peach season, is the peach tart made with canned peaches, when, in the simultaneous strawberry season, the strawberry tart is made with fresh berries? Hard to say, but the former suffers and the latter benefits, though not enough—the pastry is a little pasty. By evening the St. Honoré is also flat. The best desserts here are the caramel custard and the ice cream items. As to the cheeses, if you look like you know what you are doing, the waiter discourages you from that experiment.

This place has one of the most extensive wine cellars of any West Side French restaurant, both Burgundies and Bordeaux.

• QUO VADIS

26 East 63rd Street
LUNCH AND DINNER. CLOSED SUNDAY.
Reservations, TE 8–0590.
Credit cards: AE, CB, DC, MC.
Very expensive.

Quo Vadis is a high-priced, overstuffed hype. Once in a while you hit a really terrific dish here, but most of the food is simply passable. The dining rooms are decorated to the eyeballs, but the taste that inspired them is so banal, pompous and eclectic that the tastes that emanate from the kitchen are immediately suspect, and an experienced diner without professional obligation could take one look and leave.

The crimson carpeting is as velvety as the matching banquettes. The walls are silken. Crystal droplets depend from the wall sconces. There are somber paintings, of which one can say that they are genuine paintings. Nude statuary.

The dish of raw vegetables contains dirty radishes and canned olives. You may doctor the cocktail sauce that accompanies your crabmeat, shrimp, clams or oysters with the Tabasco that is presented alongside the Oysterettes. But of course this is a fancy restaurant, and you wouldn't order those anyway. You would order, if you're on your toes, Champignons Forestière au Gratin, and you would get one of the best dishes in the house—mushroom caps stuffed with minced stems and baked in a buttery cheese sauce that is lightly browned. The process brings out an overwhelmingly strong mushroom flavor. But if you're less fortunate you'll select the Pâté du Chef—a perfectly decent pâté, no worse than you can get in many West Side bistros, but at $3.50 it's a laugh, if you can laugh. Crêpes Quo Vadis are curried scallops in a pancake. At one time this dish was made with shrimp, lobster and crabmeat, in hollandaise. They haven't changed the name, and the item is still listed under *"Nos Spécialités."* They have simply reduced the cost, raised the price and insulted the public.

The listing of *Spécialités* is pretty amusing—it includes such masterpieces of the chef's talent as Beluga Caviar, Foie Gras de Strasbourg and Nova Scotia Salmon. By coincidence these are also the most expensive appetizers on the menu.

Perhaps you would like Le Caneton Rôti Normande. Sounds like something special, no? No. Roast duck, not crisp, some stewed fruit on the side. If they sold you the fruit by the pound in a jar, you could make the dish yourself at home! The Suprême de Volaille Gismonda is breaded chicken strewn with mushrooms; and the roast lamb is roast lamb.

Off in a corner of the kitchen somewhere, while the rest of the fellows are laughing it up, there is a vegetable cook who takes his job seriously. Among the à la carte vegetables, the delicious Aubergine Provençale is sautéed to the brink of being burned, and sharply flavored with garlic. The celery is braised in a rich brown gravy, and the asparagus, carefully scraped down to the soft white core, is served with a thick hollandaise into which no more butter could conceivably be incorporated, though it lacks lemon. The vegetables that accompany the main courses are very good too—including fresh, crisp, sweet string beans and very heavily buttered and spiced spinach.

They wheel over the dessert cart. You ask for the menu. They point out the delicious items on the cart. You insist on the menu. They inform you that the best things in the house are before your eyes, on the cart, but they promise to bring the menu as a reward after you have ordered. You point out your preference for having the menu before your eyes at once. It's an hour before closing. Soufflés? The waiter falls all over himself at the hysterical impossibility. Crêpes Suzette? His partner must also be carried off. The second team comes on. Cerises Jubilée? They embrace to hold each other up. You can have strawberries, oranges in liqueur, cake, ice cream.

There is a cover charge, surreptitiously listed as one of the hors d'oeuvres. It has a bitter taste.

★ RAOUL'S

180 Prince Street (near Sullivan Street)
DINNER.
Reservations, 966–3518.
Credit cards: AE.
Medium-priced.

You are wandering up and down Prince Street, looking for a restaurant. No restaurant. You enter a neighborhood saloon, in search of a telephone, to call for instructions about how to get to the recommended Raoul's. There you are. *You are in Raoul's.* Can you believe it? The place with the red-and-blue neon Ballantine Beer signs in the two front windows is Raoul's. Even if you walked right up to the storefront and pressed your nose against the window right under the Ballantine three rings, so that your face, as seen from inside, is bathed in a gaudy glow, you might still not know that this is Raoul's. Yes, now you notice, the name is painted on the windows, but one's sight does not pick the dim letters out under the gleaming neon.

Raoul's subtitles itself "The Bistro de SoHo." One might quarrel with "The," but not with "Bistro," for this is the Platonic Bistro à l'Américaine, a "small, unpretentious tavern or café," as the dictionary has "bistro," in the local manner, complete with elbow-worn bar along one side of the front room, opposite it such unlikelies as a hoary Frigidaire (the one that did away with the blocks of ice) and a rack bearing a roll of butcher paper (from which waiters tear off lengths of tablecloth), not to mention an ancient upright with eighty-eight black or yellow keys. The serving and eating, however, are done in the back room, where you will find not only the stamped-tin ceiling which stamps the premises as genuine, but even stamped-tin walls! (Sorry, the floor is of asphalt tiles.) The upholstered settees that form the booths are of two-toned plastic, and they are a little lumpy, what with these springs struggling to break through and attack the seated. Pipes of long-forgotten purpose wander along the ceilings; here and there pathetic, *fin-de-siècle* electric fans jut out from the walls, at the ready, should the leaning air-conditioning machine finally fall over. Murky paintings, prints and travel posters are hung with such seemingly random placement that one automatically suspects wall deformities behind them. A few plants and the kinds of overblown table lamps your grandmother had in the old place in Brooklyn complete the wreckage. You can't see the radio (which seems to play always), but you assume it has one of those bands of orange light with a center shadow which narrows as you sharpen the tuning. A house dog (shepherd) and cat (black) wander about.

You are approached by a muscular youth in a printed T-shirt who addresses you in a husky whisper and stands on one foot, then the other. Hurry up and order some of the pâté so that he can fetch it for you, with some good bread and a scrape of sweet butter which seems to have been gouged out of a vat with a wooden spatula. You notice for the first time the helter-skelter of the assorted china patterns, and you also notice that the substantial slab of pâté is not only enough to eat, but also moist, heavily herbed, abundantly fatty without being excessively so; moreover, it is served with those crisp *cornichons* (tiny pickles) that have the anise-flavored sparkle which attests to their having arrived in these parts in French jars.

There is usually a navarin listed on the blackboard menu, and it is made here in a coarse and satisfying version, composed of chunks of strong, muttony lamb in a thick and heavily seasoned gravy, with carrots and celery added well along in the stewing, so that they retain their flavors and crispness, and slivers of mushroom, added right near the end, so that they are still a bit crisp and faintly woodsy. You can also get brains in black butter, the tender and extremely rich innards delicately browned, served moistened by the black sauce of butter and vinegar and ornamented by a copious sprinkling of sour capers—solid stuff. Something listed as Poulet à la Moutarde is, surprisingly, hardly à la Moutarde at all; but the well-browned and moist bird has the clear, sweet flavor of never-frozen chicken, in itself a reward for your money, and the dark sauce traces back to a sturdy stock, mustard or no. If it is your habit to pass up all "amondine" dishes, because they are almost invariably made with canned almond slivers which have lost most of their almond flavor and impart little to the dish, your judgment is to be praised. But, though the almonds in the Filet de Bass Amondine are just what you expect, the fish is so perfectly fresh that the foolish nut-crust can be ignored—a squeezing on of lemon adds zest to the perfectly broiled and flaky fish. Such garnishes as zucchini in a slightly thickened tomato sauce seem to be held in large quantities in a steam table—they add nothing to your meal.

There is a selection of cheeses, and your eye or nose should be able to help you to select those that are fresh from those which have been refrigerated a few times—when the cheese tray is brought to you, the cheeses are at room temperature. Pretty good cakes, including a Gâteau aux Pecans—a moist nut-flavored cake under a mocha icing and a sprinkling of pecans.

★★RENÉ PUJOL

321 West 51st Street
LUNCH AND DINNER. CLOSED SUNDAY.
Reservations, 246-3023.
Credit cards: AE, MC, V.
Medium-priced.

Here on far-west 51st Street some of the densest French country kitsch in town may be waded through at the popular René Pujol: beamed ceilings and brick walls, copper pans and peasant crockery, a stuffed deer's head over the fireplace and an ancient grandfather clock that faithfully chimes the hours. No cliché has been left out, and Muzak has been left in. Withal, this is a comfortable place. West Side Gauls jaw in French at the gaudy bar up front. Some of them even eat here. Music teachers and social workers know this place, as do theatrical types who have not yet got their names in print. Lincoln Center people come here—many who may be heard from the pit, but few who have been seen onstage. An aspiring and youthful place, by and large, with lots of health and beards on view, and, though it is in the theater district, René Pujol does not empty just before curtain time, for this place serves its community much more than the town and country strays who periodically come around for theatrical rites.

The menu is no more inventive than the décor, which is perhaps just as well, for should you begin with one of its few oddities—"Les Little Necks aux Amandes"—you may leave at once with the wrong idea. These clams seem to have been stuffed with mashed potatoes and almonds. Try not to think about it. Think instead of the quiche Lorraine. Extremely rare for a restaurant quiche, it actually has some of the fluffiness and steaminess of the just-baked item and a deeply browned crust as well, and lots of strong and salty ham in the inch-thick custard filling. The snails are OK, powerfully garlicked and all that, but they lack character—they are strong rather than tasty.

You are not to be faulted if you long ago gave up ordering mushrooms à la Grecque, for it is a sorry item in most places. Here, however, the little champignons are marinated from a fresh start, and the perfume of their marinade is dominated by the sweet, spicy flavor and scent of coriander seeds. La Terrine du Chef is prepossessing for its design alone, each cross-sectional slice a mosaic of duck and spicy forcemeat, buttery foie gras and bits of black truffle, all bound in white fat, rimmed in darkened fat, and served with vibrant little pickles. You will see a side of smoked salmon on display just inside the door when you enter—order some, and thin slices of it are spread abundantly across a large plate. It is served with onions and capers, lemon and clear oil. Good food.

No effort is made to create a delicate dish out of the veal kidneys. These chunks of organ meat are gamy and cartilaginous, fat at their cores, and they are served in a mahogany-colored sauce that has the strength of blood and wine. For something else along that line, but nowhere near as far, there is boeuf bourguignon, a good stew of meat that is browned well and simmered long in its wine until the fibrous beef is succulent and tender.

Le Poulet au Calvados is a dish of sautéed chicken, with apples, in a white sauce that is flavored with apple brandy. On occasion the flour in this sauce is raw and obvious, but the dish is made with good birds, the skin browned artfully, the meat cooked until it is done, but still moist and tender; and the frankly creamy sauce is very satisfying in its simple way, especially when it is mingled with the rice that accompanies this chicken.

Good steaks, including a crusty steak au poivre that is peppery without obscuring the blood of the meat. The splendid racks of lamb are of tender young meat, each chop yielding up a plump morsel of pink juicy lamb and shreds of salty brown meat along the ribs; a bit of well-seasoned liquid from the roasting pan and an array of good fresh vegetables garnish the chops.

The quality of the cheese is a matter of chance. Usually there is a good cheese or two among those offered.

The house gets good berries, even out of season, and serves them with sugary whipped cream—what could be bad? They are a better choice than the merely decent pastries, tarts and fruit.

★★EL RINCON DE ESPANA

226 Thompson Street (near Bleecker Street)
DINNER.
Reservations, 475–9891.
Credit cards: AE, CB, DC, MC, V.
Medium-priced.

Buried among the garishly fronted restaurants and joints that make up the mini-strip along Thompson Street near Bleecker is this almost unnoticeable place; its little red awning protrudes hardly at all over the sidewalk. If you casually stroll the strip with the intention of eating in a place that catches your eye and takes your fancy, it is unlikely that you will end up here. Too bad. This is the best restaurant of the lot. You can eat well at Rocco's or New Port Alba or Portofino or Livorno, but you can also get some terribly ordinary food at those places. This Spanish restaurant has it all over its Italian competitors—you almost never get a bad dish of food in this humble establishment. The Greenwich Village locals know it, and the place is pretty busy—on weekend nights, right until midnight, you may find every one of the closely packed little tables in use, with customers waiting at the bar.

The bar. After hanging your coat on the makeshift coatrack just inside the entrance, repair to the bar. Behind it there is, of course, a bartender. Also a picture of the bartender, as well as pictures of the chef and of friends and relatives, and cluttered shelves of bottles, glasses, bills, reminder pads, an old-fashioned bedside alarm clock, the telephone, the chromed cash register (keys hanging from its buttons), the *pischkeh.* When things are slow it is the bar the waiters hang around, each of them red-jacketed, black-haired, long-sideburned, mustached, handsome. From the bar you can see into the kitchen (when the door swings open), and you see that it is the size of a shower stall and contains three full-size men. At the bar you also make a wise decision about your dinner beverage (you watch the bartender compound a pitcher of sangría, with *a lot* of ice, half an orange, several heaping spoons of sugar, about half a cup of brandy, and the very small amount of cheap red wine, from a giant jug kept under the bar, necessary to fill the remaining interstices between the ice cubes, all for $6), namely, to drink straight wine, from a labeled bottle, instead of sangría.

The restaurant proper is dungeony, the red walls hung with the required bullfight pictures, the rough plaster ceiling adorned with nonsupporting beams, the air filled with talk, and, at dinner, with the plinking and strumming of a flamenco guitar, and, at all times, with the fragrance of garlic—the specific Spanish persuasion here is Galician, which means food that is very much like other Spanish food, plus garlic.

Garlic, for example, in Mejillones à la Carlos, translated as Mussels Specialty of the Chef. The mussels arrive in a smooth oily sauce flavored with hot red pepper, sautéed onions, fresh parsley and the garlic, many slivers of it; the mussels may be big, but they are fresh and clear-tasting and tender, and very few customers fail to capture the residual oil at the bottom of the dish with a spoon or with bread. For something considerably milder you may have Jabas à la Plancha—shrimps sautéed in butter and white wine. The excellence of this dish derives from the fact that the shrimps are prepared in their shells, which strengthens and sweetens the flavor of the crunchy white meat. It is no tribute to the kitchen, but the Spanish ham you get here (the menu calls it Spanish Mountain Ham) is exceptional. Your large plate is covered with about a dozen thick slices of the slightly fibrous but tender, pink marbled meat—it is salty and loud, and you can make excellent little sandwiches of it if you are not prejudiced against sandwiches as a first course. Pretend you are at a picnic.

You may expect meat and/or sausages in your Caldo Gallego. You won't find either of them here. But the firm white beans, chunks of potato, and sharp greens, all in a buttery liquid, make for a decent soup just the same. Of course there is gazpacho. There is no such thing as correct gazpacho. If you have eaten gazpacho in restaurants in Spain, you know that there is approximately one version per cook. The bulk of the liquid you get here is solid—crisp little dice of green pepper and onion awash in an oily cold broth aggressively flavored with strong red pepper and garlic. You will note, but probably not taste among these pungent elements, plenty of chopped fresh parsley, too.

Your hosts, the menu informs you, are Carlos and Julio, and the former apparently works in the kitchen, as his name is appended to the dishes that are specialties of the chef. Among them is Pulpo [octopus] à la Carlos. First of all you have to not mind either the idea or the reality of eating octopus, that is to say, short lengths of a firm, slightly rubbery pale-gray meat, to which are attached unsightly little suckers; surmount that hurdle and you can treat yourself to a quite delicious dish, consisting of a substantial mound of the aforementioned stuff in an oily sauce that is thick with sautéed onions, slivers of garlic, parsley that is wilted in the hot oil, and a seasoning of strong red pepper; it is the taste of almost burnt onions that distinguishes this sauce from the many similar ones on the menu. There is also a very good Cangrejo con Salsa Verde (crabmeat in green sauce, to you). There are huge chunks of the tender crabmeat in a creamy sauce that is slightly winy, laden with parsley and strongly flavored with garlic.

To avoid garlic, if that is your wish, have Filete de Cerdo Barbacoa con Salsa de Almendra, which is pork with almond sauce. The slices of pork are tender and blackened at the edges, and the sauce is thick, sweet, flavored with citrus fruit juice and laced with slivers of almond. You might understandably suspect that Breast of Chicken with Almonds is much like pork with almonds. However, in among the almonds in this dish are slivers of garlic, disguised as slivers of almond; the sauce is white and thick and laden with parsley; and you get two immense quarters of the very good chicken. A lot to eat. There is also a hearty veal dish, made with green peppers and Spanish sausages, all in a thick gravy. It is called Ternera a la Estremena, and it is winter food.

The usual desserts: firm flan, with a sauce of caramelized sugar; guava jelly with cream cheese and saltines; etc.

Late at night there is occasionally a bit of boisterous gaiety—streams of laughter from the bar, energetic clapping in rhythm to the guitar. No dancing.

★ RIO-LISBOA

24 West 46th Street
LUNCH AND DINNER.
Reservations, 730–8247.
Credit cards: AE, DC, V.
Medium-priced.

There is a simply done, Old World look to this spacious establishment. The impression is created by the application of tan paint and brown trim to the rough stucco walls, by the placement of black ironwork lanterns and travel posters thereon, by the straightforward arrangement of the neatly linened tables in long rows. It is gracious in the way that an old hotel can be, when every rough edge has been worn off the appointments and the staff; for even though these are the salad days of Rio-Lisboa, its waiters have been matured at other places in earlier times, and their manners, at once amiable and restrained, are of a piece with the mellow hues of these quarters.

But that Old World was not *all* cordiality, it was a man's world, and where said man may have been every inch a prince, that was only on condition that his princess be every millimeter a mouse; and when a woman dares to enter this place unaccompanied, the host/prince will likely lead her to a lonely table in a remote corner, no one should behold such a disgrace; and when said disgrace then compounds her effrontery by turning down her first table assignment and pointing pointedly at a preferred one, her prince is reduced to prayer—mumbled imprecations as he obeys, marching the lady to her chosen place.

But do not permit this primitive to keep you from his place, for his ailment is not infectious—neither the waiters nor the foods they deliver are tainted by his anachronistic airs; and his eating place can afford you a fortifying dinner in pleasant surroundings, at prices that are reasonable for this extortionate section of midtown.

You may, however, be unconcerned about costs, in which case begin your dinner with the number that goes by the name of Ameijoas á Bulhao Pato in the Old World, "Clams in White Sauce" in the New. The clams are steamed in their own juice and wine, for liquid, with chunks of sausage, myriad slivers of garlic, and much pepper for strong flavor. The tender clams are very nice next to the crisp shafts of garlic and the chewy morsels of sausage; and the hot broth, briny and loud, is bracing. But you may be a slow starter, in which case commence with Sopa a Alentejana, a soup with which the menu translator could not cope, managing no better than "Alentejo Style Soup," your traditional, albeit strong, chicken broth, in which an egg has been cooked and to which a fistful of fresh parsley has been added—the steaming plate is fragrant and alive.

Pushing on, there is the Brazilian national dish, feijoada, a thick, hefty, almost black stew of beans, sausages and meats, the latter including blackened ribs, meaty and fatty, the complete cast awash in a thick and spicy sauce. The total production is augmented by slices of raw orange, a pungent green chard, and a small mound of the pale zest that Brazilians extract from the cassava plant—your cordial waiter, as he bows over your plate to spoon on some rice and more of the stew, explains that this plant is also the source of tapioca. The menu also lists Galinha Frita á Lisboeta, a similarly intimidating platter of food served with rice and beans. Once more your waiter bows to serve you, this time sautéed chicken, thoroughly browned after being rubbed with garlic; well-oiled black olives, green peppers, and onions, all cooked with the chicken, each of them also imbued with the flavor of garlic; and French fried potatoes, not, it must be admitted, the thin, crispy and delicate little strands you might prefer, but substantial rectangular logs, deeply browned, steamy at the center. If you chance on Rio-Lisboa on a Thursday, you may undertake Cosido á Rio-Lisboa, described by the menu as "Boiled Meat with Cabbage," yet another solid substance, this too served in weighty abundance, of which the preponderant ingredients are slabs of fat-rimmed meat, much like pot roast, red-peppery ribs, sausages, large chunks of potatoes, and, one must be grateful, boiled cabbage, which in this setting is distinctly light, an element of air in the otherwise heavy going. And of course there are Brazilian codfish dishes, including Bacalhau á Braz, which the menu also gives as "Cod Fish Braz Style," and which the kitchen prepares as a rich and salty dish of codfish and olives, bound together in an eggy sauce, and sprinkled with parsley—about as heavy a repast as you can contrive in a preparation that is principally fish.

Of course there are desserts, and they are not particularly interesting, except for the Doce de Leite com Queijo, a thick, syrupy and sweet milk caramel, which is garnished, for contrast, with a little nugget of sharp cheese—very nice.

The menu notes no penalty for serving one main course to two people; a single dinner here is enough for a man and his horse.

★★ RIVE GAUCHE

237 East 58th Street
LUNCH, MONDAY TO FRIDAY; DINNER, DAILY.
Reservations, 752–2113.
Credit cards: AE, DC, MC.
Medium-priced.

Midtown East is so strewn with middling little French restaurants that it is difficult to imagine making one and making it much different from its dozens of competitors. An obvious approach is to vary the ancient formula with a touch of the style of the day, which today is Art Deco—1939 World's Fair to you.

Deco, you will recall, is neat, and though the title of this place suggests a leftward-leaning disdain for order, what we have here is, nevertheless, positively spiffy, if not quite ultraconservative. Rive Gauche is little, a couple of dozen tables is all. Its walls are covered in a cloth of dusty-rose that bears a simple white geometric pattern. Chocolate-brown banquettes rim the room and jut out into the dining area, dividing it into small islands. The touches of Deco include polished brass sconces of sleek, slender figures holding aloft crystal balls; a boldfaced inoperative clock with a broad border of gleaming metal; the simple and bold RG logo on the etched-glass partitions just inside the front door; and a few examples of art of the era—flappers and their tuxedoed escorts. The white-linened tables, flowers thereon, derive from the ancient formula rather than from the revived style. The place is far from strikingly beautiful, but the thirties theme is sounded so mutedly that it avoids being vulgar.

There used to be a restaurant called the Little Royal that was famous for the atrocious spelling on its menu. They had the sense not to tamper with their orthography, and for a time the establishment prospered. It is believed that people came just to see the terrible words. Similarly, from the day it opened, customers have criticised the mussels at Rive Gauche for their sand. Presumably on the theory that it is better to have New York speak ill of you for your faults than to have it not speak of you at all, the sand in the mussels is now, apparently, the brand of the place, and the otherwise excellent Moules Poulettes—a sizable ceramic pot of fresh tender mussels, out of their shells, in a hot and creamy broth of herbed wine—are invariably delicately gritty. No grit in the Crab Meat Rive Gauche, but nothing else either—this is the most expensive appetizer on the menu, and it was forked out of a can. The winners are where you little expect: Avocado Prosciutto is the streamlined handle for a perfectly chosen fruit—firm, ripe and nutty, cut in a score of thin slices and covered with a polished dressing that has just a bit of mustard in it. It is garnished with slices of maroon-colored ham that are fibrous, gamy and loudly smoked, altogether an exemplary meat. The Saucisson Chaud Lyonnais is the usual dish in a superior version: three slices of well-fatted ground meat, heavily peppered, rimmed with flaky pastry and accompanied by a mound of hot potato salad, oiled and salty—a terrific dish.

Very good Bass en Croûte du Chef, a nicely browned pillow of pastry which your waiter punctures with a fork (revealing the fluffy fresh fish within), to pour in spoon after spoon of thick Béarnaise. Odd Canard au Poivre Vert, for the sauce is not only of green pepper, but also of orange fruit—the combination works well and the well-roasted, rich and oily bird is exciting against the hotness of the pepper. Almost impeccable Entrecôte Marchand de Vin—the meat grilled accurately, the wine sauce perfectly seasoned and slightly sweetened by sautéed shallots, though the meat itself is perhaps a bit firm. Delicate Escalopes de Veau aux Girolles—tender and buttery discs of veal, nicely sautéed and browned, in a creamy sauce that is marvelously redolent of the scent of fresh mushrooms.

Good Brie, mousse and tarts. The Fraises Cardinal are strewn with almond slivers, for no reason, and moistened with lovely puréed raspberries.

★★ RUC

312 East 72nd Street
LUNCH, SATURDAY AND SUNDAY; DINNER, DAILY.
Reservations, 650–1611.
Credit cards: AE, CB, DC.
Medium-priced.

New York's Middle European restaurants are among the most reliable eating places in town. It's almost impossible to get a bad meal in the Hungarian restaurants that line Second Avenue between 72nd and 86th streets, and the three Czechoslovakian restaurants in the lower Seventies are even better. When you're looking for a change from the familiar round of steakhouses and French and Italian restaurants, think of these places—not only is the food good, and the service positively courtly, but there is a feeling of such contentedness among the well-fed, superbly bourgeois customers that it's easy to forget whatever problems you bring into these adult fairylands.

Ruc seems to be a perfect evocation of home for the members of New York's Czechoslovakian community who regularly eat here. If we can't have Czechoslovakia in Czechoslovakia, they say, well, we'll have Czechoslovakia in New York. And since we are very nice people, we'll even permit these Americans to eat with us.

And lucky you are, because you can have headcheese, for example, a Czechoslovakian specialty—thick, firm slices of chunks of tongue, in jelly, with fresh chopped onions. Or you can have something called Meat Salad Gypsy—a cold mixture of coarsely shredded beef, onions, celery, green peppers and mayonnaise; it's like an excellent chicken salad, but made with red meat. Or you can have ham salad, which is like the Gypsy item, but made with finely minced ham (hold the celery and green peppers), and for an extra 35 cents it comes as Eggs à la Prague; that is, with hard-boiled eggs, a dollop of mayo over the eggs, and a garnish of black caviar.

There are different soups on different days, including an excellent giblet soup, and on other occasions, beef broth with liver dumplings. The dumplings are strong, and just before the hot soup is brought to the table, a large spoonful of chopped parsley is added. When the waiter pours from the silver cup into your large soup dish, you are enveloped by a powerful green aroma.

You won't get goose much better than the goose that Ruc often has on the Sunday menu. The skin is as flaky as a thin pastry, and the juicy and tender meat comes with thick slices of dumpling that you soak in the goose-dripping sauce. On occasion there is Cevabcici—ground veal, pork and beef, with onions and garlic, seasoned, rolled to the shape of sausages, and sautéed until the outside is dark brown and firm. The calf's brains with eggs are a rich, peppery amalgam, obviously done in the marvelous grease you get from ducks and geese. There is a good meat loaf called Prague Roast, and sometimes a roast tenderloin of beef—both are served with an unusual vegetable-based cream sauce that is redolent of celery, carrots and herbs. All the food arrives at your table in good condition; the main courses come with a crisp cucumber salad and either dumplings that are solid and bland, which means they are perfect for soaking up gravy, or else some kind of potatoes. Some of the dishes get this place's amazing sauerkraut; it is apparently cooked for weeks, and is sweet, utterly without acid, at once crisp and tender, and lightly accented with caraway seeds.

Some of the desserts you will not find everywhere. Apricot dumplings, for example, which are apricots, in dumplings, sprinkled with cheese, or with cinnamon, or with bread crumbs, or (best of all) with poppy seeds and sugar. The palacinky here are very good—thin, lightly browned pancakes with apricot preserves. Or if you are really hungry, have an Omelette Confiture—the same preserves in a thin, folded sheet of browned eggs, the whole thing sprinkled heavily with powdered sugar.

The older waiters here are of the European Café School. With napkins over their arms they walk extremely rapidly (they do not run) with their trays from barroom to dining room to kitchen. They make their explanations of the menu breathlessly but patiently. The younger help are blond, pink-cheeked and much admired for their awkward charm.

Ruc is a low-ceilinged place, decorated in plastic Bavarian—suspiciously shiny wood-paneled walls, hanging plates, wagon-wheel chandeliers with lanterns, and so on. The cruder front room holds a bar and three good-sized tables. In the summer this restaurant provides one of the pleasantest places for outdoor dining in New York—a terraced garden under overhanging trees.

Ruc is a good restaurant in which to eat alone, as there is much to see: When was the last time you saw a table of six at which three stout burghers were partnered by three ladies in black velvet hats? Where else are old-fashioned sultry blondes still in fashion, with their cigarette holders and long maroon fingernails? Greta Garbo would be just one of the girls here.

★★★ RUSSIAN TEA ROOM

150 West 57th Street
LUNCH AND DINNER.
Reservations, CO 5–0947.
Credit cards: AE, CB, DC, MC, V.
Expensive.

The Russian Tea Room, Carnegie Hall's West 57th Street neighbor, is the province of a low-ranking god who has been given the place as his small planet. But this deity is an undisciplined collector, his eyes bigger than his restaurant, and the glittering heterogeneity of things to eat, people, and objects that he has crammed into his little world would far exceed its physical limits were it not for his capacity to transcend physical bounds. The Russian Tea Room is possible in the same way that it is possible for all the angels in the universe to dance on a pin—by divine intervention.

Under a red canopy and through revolving doors you go, into the choice front room —theatrical posters and New York's smallest two-bartender bar, the saucy clash of lipstick-red banquettes against flamingo-pink table linen, the waiting line of the patiently waiting, the giant charcoal-and-ivory mural of a park café in a very civilized city somewhere long ago. Through this room the endless democracy flows—*grandes dames* in floor-length dresses, tomorrow's ingenue with last year's manager, musicians and musicians' mothers, opera freaks and lieder singers, children with their dates, drama critics with boring producers, rabbis with their wives, priests with other priests, purveyors of all culture, hustlers of all commodities, scribblers of all propaganda.

The deep-green walls of the big back room are hung with a hundred paintings and as many shining samovars; chandeliers and sconces glitter with golden tinsel; dark-red lanterns glow on the tables. Dozens of men in red or green bring and take away as they have for fifty years, and as they and their followers obviously will for fifty or a hundred more.

Remarkable food, like kholodetz—pickled calves' feet—cool blocks of firm jelly, textured with meat, garnished with whipped cream that is vibrant with powerful horseradish. Eggplant orientale, a rich, oily, tomatoed paste with a bit of garlic in it —you spread it on pumpernickel bread. The herring are firm and pungent, the smoked salmon pale and tender. And the caviar—four grades of the black are available—is superb.

The "cold" borscht is cool, polished, purple and creamy, its sweet beef flavor livened with slivers of seeded cucumber and lots of dill. The hot borscht is tart and salted, the dollop of cool sour cream lovely against the warm red broth and shredded beets.

The homiest foods are cotolette Pojarsky and luli kebab, the former veal-and-chicken patties, the latter lamb patties, the warm, spicy ground meats moistened with a pleasantly fatty and peppered mushroom sauce. And the most elegant main course is the blini with red caviar and sour cream, buckwheat pancakes that are browned, earthy and seemingly weightless. You soak them in melted butter, wrap them around the sour cream and pale amber-colored globules of salmon roe, and eat. The broiled lamb dishes —shaslik and lamb chops—are of tender and tasty meat, artfully charred. And such vegetarian oddities as mushrooms or eggplant au gratin are like thick vegetable stews, weighty with hot sour cream, served on rice.

A winy stew of prunes, pears and apples, in thick syrup, goes by the deceptive name of fruit compote. And the pastries, creams and custards that make up the fancy little desserts are all smooth and moist, polished and fresh and airy, their sweetness never excessive, the nuts and crusts and cakes browned, crisp and tender. Yes, tea comes in a glass.

Vodka and champagne are the drinks to drink. Vodka is ordered from the vodka menu.

○ RUSTY'S

1271 Third Avenue (at 73rd Street)
LUNCH AND DINNER.
Reservations, 861-4518.
Credit cards: AE, CB, DC, MC, V.
Medium-priced.

In the old days if a prize fighter or a ball player ran a restaurant, you knew what you were going to get—steaks and chops and no complications. Today famous athletes are, perforce, media personalities. They cannot appear on television and just grunt. So Rusty Staub, the baseball player who gives his name to this establishment, has put himself forward not just as an athlete, but as a *bec fin*. Millions have seen him on television, looking perfectly handsome and preparing Oysters Rockefeller at the same time. Fortunately for Staub and everyone else, the flavor of his oysters cannot be transmitted via high-frequency waves, and the pleasant myth of his gustatory refinement is preserved.

His restaurant has the standard accoutrements of the myriad places that strive for turn-of-the-century saloon cheer, as seen by a nineteen-seventies Third Avenue decorator—plain wooden floors, a stamped-in ceiling, bare-brick walls and brass rails. This harmless formula has been elaborated with baseball wallpaper here—brown basepaths on a green ground—beer posters etched in glass behind the big bar, and a genuine oil painting of a slugger swinging a bat. They may have been aiming to siphon off some of the action from the Upper East Side's fashionable saloons, but baseball, face it, is a rube's game, and all they've been getting are tourists, plus adolescents of all ages.

Those Oysters Rockefeller (two for $2) look like Oysters Rockefeller, feel like Oysters Rockefeller, and taste like Pernod and grass. Avoid the Plump Mussels with Special Mustard Sauce, which should be billed as Mustard Plaster Mussels. The herring is fine, sour and firm, in fresh dill and sour cream. But the Crêpe stuffed with Chicken and Mushrooms in Champagne Sauce is Horn & Hardart chicken à la king at best.

A steak is prepared with admirable accuracy, but it is not tender. A main-course quiche is so pully it can almost be called tough, its admixture of spinach, bacon and mushrooms miraculously adding no flavor. Your awkward young waiter delivers the vaunted Seafood New Orleans and gingerly ladles a couple of chunks of seafood from the aluminum pot onto your plate with the hesitant caution of a man handling cobras with chopsticks. You learn his problem when you try to amplify your serving—the steel ladle is short and its end is hot as the steaming broth it is meant to serve. This is not a bad plate of food—clams, mussels, shrimp in a sweet tomato broth that is flavored with onions and peppers. It contains a lobster tail as well, which is dreadful. A few items are listed as Rusty's Award Winning Recipes. They won prizes in a cooking competition among American League right fielders. But here on Manhattan Island, ol' Rust, these Shrimp de Maison (their actual name) seem ever so much like frozen shrimp, bread crumbs, dried herbs and stale oil, the kind, perhaps, that you rub into your fielder's mitt to soften it up. Good hamburgers have been had here, but only bad salads.

The Warm Open Faced Apple-Raisin Cake is too sweet and excessively cinnamoned, but it can be very much improved if you insist on a heavy dollop of the good whipped cream. There is no point to chocolate cake other than that it be outrageous. The one you get here should be called Live Another Day Chocolate Cake. On the other hand, cheese cake can be good any number of ways, as long as it retains the flavor of cheese. This one does not.

The house red tastes like ink, the white like water.

★ SABOR

20 Cornelia Street (near Bleecker Street)
DINNER.
Reservations, 243–9579.
Credit cards: AE, MC.
No liquor.
Medium-priced.

Amateur restaurants are materializing in the Village at the rate of about one a month, and of the dozen or so that are now struggling through their growing and/or failing pains, Sabor is the one that is most like a restaurant in the old-Village way. There is no kookiness about Sabor, no mirrored tabletops or bedspreads on the walls, no menu painted on the ceiling, no trees in the men's room. This is a clean, well-lit place; it has been put together with a certain respect for, if not a slavish adherence to, tradition.

Sabor is a long, narrow store, the walls painted cream-white and brown, the stamped-tin ceiling tan. The tables are covered with brown linen and white napkins, and they are surrounded by simple wooden chairs. You walk on an ancient, broad-beamed floor that has been sanded down, stained brownish red and polished to a warm glow. This is a Cuban restaurant, and some of the accouterments are intended to suggest that warm island—three-bladed fans hanging from the ceiling, maracas and native baskets on the walls, tropical greenery in the corners. But there are false notes, such as this waitress, during a slow hour, seated at a table in the rear, studying *Teach Yourself Spanish.*

If you have eaten in any number of New York's dozen or so Cuban restaurants, you have encountered most of the dishes available in this one, including escabeche, the cold, slightly spicy dish of pickled fish and vegetables. This version is made with fresh fish, and the vegetables (onions, carrots, peppers and olives) retain their crispness and individuality—lively food. A similar but much spicier dish goes as Camarones Picantes —shrimp that have been marinated in oil and hot pepper. The shrimp are crunchy, and their aftertaste is fiery and memorable. The warm appetizers include empanadas, your serving consisting of three of the crescent-shaped meat-filled pies—the ground meat is sweet and studded with currants, and the flaky pastry is browned and crisp. Of all the first courses in the place, however, the best is Frituras de Malanga. Malanga is a succulent Caribbean root with a nutlike flavor. Here it is puréed, mixed with spices and herbs, and deep-fried to a crusty fritter—very satisfying.

A certain amount of cynicism seems to have crept into the management of this establishment. You order the listed Pargo en Salsa Verde (red snapper in green sauce), and you are brought something like it, specifically cod in green sauce. Cod is cheap, dull fish, for which green sauce is inappropriate. The fish arrives in a casserole on a layer of buttery potatoes, the green sauce tastes vividly of parsley and spices, but the cod is a flaky, tasteless irrelevance. Yet most of the food you get is as advertised and good, including Fricase de Pollo, a chicken stew with raisins and olives, roots and herbs —not a great bird, but a straightforward dish of abundance and strong flavors. Do not be frightened by the translation of Pollo con Pina a la Antigua (chicken with pineapple). This is not Dole chicken, but a mildly coconut-flavored stew in which there is an assortment of fruits and vegetables—raisins and pineapple, olives and tomatoes—the meat is spicy, the sauce savory. They love raisins here, and the Picadillo (which the menu describes as "Like chili but better!") consists principally of heavily seasoned ground beef, black raisins and olives—as in all of the dishes here containing olives, beware of the pits. One of the coarsest and yet probably the most interesting main course is the Carne Estofada Mechada, a kind of pot roast of meat that has been stuffed with olives and spiced vegetables. Your plate arrives with three slices of the fibrous meat, each slice sporting a colorful eye that is its share of the stuffing, all in a thick and oily gravy—winter food.

If you have eaten two courses, you will have eaten amply at this point, and so there should be no great disappointment in discovering that the selection of desserts is very slight, including a Key lime pie that is well served by its thick topping of good whipped cream, for the lime chiffon under it lacks the convincing flavor of fresh fruit. You are far better off with Coco Quemado, a kind of coconut pie unlike any other you are likely to have had, for this one, on its cakey crust and under its rich whipped cream, has the strong sharp flavor of the actual fresh nut.

No one in the place talks with anything but the English of the continental United States, but the food has the unmistakable accent of authenticity.

Bring your own beer or wine.

★★SAKURA CHAYA

198 Columbus Avenue (at 69th Street)
DINNER. CLOSED MONDAY.
Reservations, 874–8536.
No credit cards.
No liquor.
Inexpensive.

The average age of the diners is twenty-six; the average income is below average; the average tab for two is $20, including beer, tax and tip; the average allocated floor space per diner is about two feet square; and the average attendance equals the total number of chairs plus 10 percent, except at the off-hours. But though the appeal is the low prices, at a sacrifice of commodiousness, the food is excellent, and this is certainly the best of the three Japanese restaurants that are neighbors on Columbus Avenue near 69th Street.

Japanese trappings are sprinkled about—bamboo screens, masks (one angry, one in ecstasy), paper parasols, fierce-face kites, paper lanterns (sans lamps), illustrated scrolls and painted screens—but the basic furnishings are domestic, including bare Formica tabletops, plastic-upholstered side chairs, and carpeting. There is a six-stool lunch counter, which may be the best place to sit. A genial gentleman (who likes his work and his customers), artfully, effortlessly and without the flashy display of talent that is found at the sushi bars in midtown Japanese restaurants, assembles lovely raw fish dishes—and these, sushi and sashimi, are made of perfectly fresh fish—better cannot be found in New York. They are variously delicate, sharp, tender, chewy, elusive or aggressive, but they are all near-perfect. For one visit the thing to order is the sushi-sashimi combination, for two reasons. Reason 1: you get to sample all the raw fish items; reason 2: if you are at a table rather than at the counter, the kimono-garbed waitress, who is all shy smiles and little bows, will startle you by ordering ONE COMBI! from the man behind the counter before she politely takes the remainder of your order.

Sushi, as everyone by now must know, is morsel-size combinations of fish (often raw) or vegetables and vinegared rice, sometimes wrapped in seaweed; and sashimi is strips of raw fish. They are served with soy sauce and with a powerful green horseradish paste, and with such garnishes as pickled ginger (served here in parchment-thin slices), cucumber and white radish. At this restaurant the seafoods that go into these dishes are raw tuna (it is the color of red beef when it is uncooked, but it is surprisingly delicate this way), squid and octopus, as well as varieties of local fish. This food is sparkling and stimulating, but subtle. Other cold fish dishes are served here, including a splendid salad of octopus, sesame seed, bean sprouts and cucumbers in a thin, tart dressing of vinegar and sesame oil.

Less common, and just as good in its way, is the raw beef served at Sakura Chaya. It is listed as Nama-Niku and consists of shredded beef, scallion greens and sesame seeds, dressed with soy sauce and garlic. It looks just like raw tuna, but it is strong and satisfying, and unlike the raw fish, which can be eaten endlessly, this stuff goes a long way.

There is an excellent tempura—shrimp and vegetables deep-fried in a very light batter, so that the resulting crusts are very delicate and crisp.

Sukiyaki, teriyaki, kushi-katsu and all the other familiar items are available here in good versions. None of the food is prepared at your table (no room), but this does not affect its quality. Included is a fish sukiyaki—a pungent fish stew made with octopus, tuna, clams, mussels, abalone, shrimp, mushrooms, bean sprouts and many other ingredients (including, unfortunately, a frozen, tough and tasteless lobster tail), in a strong fish broth. The varied ingredients retain their character, and each is modified in an interesting way by the powerful stuff it is cooked in. This is a wonderful dish, but some people may find it a bit too loud. The chicken teriyaki is of nicely browned chicken in a sweet thin sauce, with bean sprouts and lightly cooked carrots.

The desserts include ice cream, sherbet, fruit and yokan—a sweetened bean cake that may seem a little soapy if you're not used to it.

Almost no one here uses anything but chopsticks, but you can get a fork if you ask.

★★ SALTA IN BOCCA

179 Madison Avenue (near 34th Street)
LUNCH AND DINNER. CLOSED SUNDAY.
Reservations, 684-1757.
Credit cards: AE, DC.
Expensive.

A collection of hideous paintings on the walls can make a restaurant seem honest, as if the stuff is hung there by a proprietor who thinks the customers expect such things, but whose mind is elsewhere—on the food, perhaps. The glum salmon-pink of these walls was obviously selected by a relative known for excellent taste; the red carpeting is the necessary gesture to luxe. (None of this is surprising, for Salta in Bocca is an enterprise of the owners of Il Monello, on Second Avenue in the East Seventies; and they, after all, when taking over the hideous Villa Doria, left every stick in place.) The effect of it all is to direct your attention to what is placed before you, which is mostly good, sometimes wonderful.

If it is your habit when trying new eating places to look around to see what the regular customers order, you will have no trouble reaching at least one conclusion here. It seems that half the tables sport steamy bowls of Vongole e Muscoli al Vino Bianco —fresh clams and mussels, in their shells, mounded up over a deep pool of vibrant buttery broth that is strongly scented of garlic and parsley. You transfer the empty shells to the plate provided and drink the hot soup with a spoon. Very good Spiedino Romano, a crusty deep-fried, multi-layered sandwich of bread, cheese and ham in a strong anchovy sauce that is livened with capers—juicy food, wonderful with cold white wine.

This establishment prepares some of the best Spaghetti Carbonara in New York— very thin noodles, firm and tender, sliding around among themselves in a rich sauce of butter, sautéed onions and strands of tangy ham, all thickened with egg yolk and colorful with fresh parsley. Do not add cheese; the dish is impeccable the way it is. The Cannelloni di Carne is struggling along several furlongs behind the front-running

Carbonara—the ground, herbed meat within the pasta envelopes is dry and grainy, and the creamy tomato sauce, good as it is, cannot rescue the dish.

Cernia Livornese is snapper in the familiar Leghorn tomato sauce that is fortified with chopped olives and capers—this fish is, on occasion, a little overdone, and the sauce is a rather gentle version of this usually vibrant substance; but the dish is satisfactory nevertheless. The Pollo al Vino Bianco e Funghi is a nice little chicken dish, skinned breasts in a simple sauce of wine, mushrooms and onions.

But it is the veal that you should have. You would expect that the dish for which the restaurant is named, Salta in Bocca, would be the best in the house, and there is no denying the buttery tenderness of the veal, the stout flavor of the ham, the smoothness of the pale sauce they are served in, nor the freshness of the spinach garnish. But that is nothing next to the Costoletta alla Fiorentina, a butterflied veal chop that is stuffed with a fabulously rich mixture of ricotta cheese, spinach and bits of this establishment's excellent ham; the whole production is floured, dipped in egg and sautéed —superb meat, elegantly crusted and splendidly filled.

Good salads in tart dressings, including an excellent combination of spinach and mushrooms.

The cheese cake is a comedown; the Zuppa Inglese, buried in fluffy egg whites, is the very familiar sweet. The waiters are conscientious in the preparation of zabaglione here, dosing it with plenty of Marsala and beating it over the flame until it is frothy and hot. Unfortunately, this requires the use of burners in the dining room, and the principal shortcoming of this establishment is inadequate ventilation, yielding a smoky atmosphere that is aggravated by the alcohol fires. Asthmatics be warned.

A good restaurant. If you stick to the best dishes and wear your gas mask, a superb one.

★★ SAN MARCO

36 West 52nd Street
LUNCH, MONDAY TO FRIDAY; DINNER, MONDAY TO SATURDAY. CLOSED SUNDAY.
Reservations, CI 6–5340.
Credit cards: AE, CB, DC.
Expensive.

This new 52nd Street San Marco is to the old place on 55th as a carefully selected second spouse to an impulsively taken first—perfectly suitable and all that, but lacking a certain capacity, recalled with some nostalgia, to infuriate. At the old you suffered a bit of crush at the bar for the thirty minutes between the hour of your reservation and the time you were actually inserted into your tiny allotted space; you endured your neighbors' loud camaraderie, the staff's conflicts; you longed for escape from intimate bedlam, dreamed of a comfortable and civilized setting for the vigorous food and sturdy Italian wines.

Well, you got what you thought you wanted. "Never pray for a new king," said the wise man, "he will be worse than the old one." How we miss that old despotism. The new San Marco is benevolent, like a well-run clinic.

The place is long, wide and airy, the large tables in well-spaced rows across the generous spread, the lofty ivory walls made less bare by numerous paintings that have no other purpose. As in the previous San Marco, the ledge above the banquette that rims the room is strung with bottles of wine; and tall étagères of dark polished wood, open front and back, one-wine-bottle-deep, display hundreds of bottles more, and serve as "room dividers," to break up the cavernous volume. But these displays, for all they ought to suggest of alcoholic abandon, are coolly architected and, therefore, sterile. Maybe the place would feel OK if it weren't an *Italian* restaurant, but the assertive food of Italy in these spare surroundings is like a hot pastrami on Arnold Brick Oven White.

Accordingly the customers, particularly at lunchtime—here or there the token beard, there or here a woman with men, and beyond those, little but pairs and quartets of suited executives, discussing, with studied squinted eyes, the games of corporate business as if they were the conflicts of states. At night, however, things loosen up, and the signs of life San Marco needs are provided by New Yorkers who can afford the restaurant and enjoy their prosperity—you see colorful duds on fetching folk, hear smart talk and tipsy laughter.

The menu is very much the old menu, at prices that are no less immodest, including, as a dinnertime appetizer, a little $4.75 number called Spedino Romana—a row of alternating layers of mozzarella cheese and bread, grilled until the bread is toasted and the cheese strong and pully, served in an oily and salty anchovy sauce. It is a terrific dish, at once coarse and well-balanced, the sharp flavors offsetting the solid weight of the food. One ordinarily avoids liver pâté in Italian restaurants, because it is usually imported. The lunchtime menu at San Marco, however, informs you that the pâté is "homemade," and you investigate by placing an order for same. Well, you should have figured that an Italian pâté will be oily where a French one will be buttery, and you might have anticipated that the difference, to a predisposed palate, will be off-putting. This may be an acceptable dish, it is herby and far from flat, but you will have to approach it with a wide-open mind.

Cappelletti in Brodo means chicken dumplings in chicken broth—little pasta pouches stuffed with ground chicken and herbs, in a broth which has the gamy quality of chicken fat and plenty of seasoning; the tender dumplings are just right in the sharp soup.

Good noodles, with a strong egg flavor, cooked to order so they are firm but tender, and in Fettuccine alla Veneziana they are moistened with a vibrant sweet-and-sour tomato sauce in which peas and bits of ham are apparent, the flavor of rosemary very subtle.

Veal dishes do not seem to be San Marco's strength. You can actually get a Veal Scaloppine al Limone in which it is difficult to detect either the flavor of lemon or that of sautéed veal. The obscurity of the lemon is miscalculation, that of the veal indolence —it is barely browned, only on one side (the side that is "up" on your plate), and permitted to stew for a while in bubbling butter. This is ruination of a good ingredient. The veal birds (Involtini di Vitello) are somewhat better—hefty loaves formed of veal around a strongly herbed and spiced stuffing of cheese and ham, served in a winy mushroom gravy. At lunchtime the serving is augmented with a dozen or so gnocchi —firm little potato loaves that make a better match for the gravy than the birds themselves.

Sausages and Peppers (billed as "farmers style") is the kind of dish one thinks of in those Italian restaurants with checkered tablecloths and waiters in shirt sleeves. The San Marco version is no less vigorous than what you get in neighborhood places, succulent and spicy, but there are touches of class—an admixture, in the sausages themselves, of an exceptionally fragrant black pepper which, despite its abundance, does not overpower the dish but adds an unexpected piquancy. The meat is garnished with sautéed red peppers and fresh mushrooms.

For perfect, elegant simplicity, have Branzino alla Pescatora—a great slice of immaculately fresh striped bass, moistened with a delicate tomato sauce that is lightly garlicked. Purists who insist that fish should be no more than buttered and lemoned are the losers.

San Marco has always made a lovely event of the simple act of serving up a dish of zabaglione. To begin with, your captain prepares the dish in the dining room, with much grand stirring over the flame; and the result is hot, sweet and winy. Moreover, it is served up in a handsome porcelain goblet, the thick golden foam mounded high above the rim, some of the excess coursing down the sides and stem. Don't worry, your fingers will not be made sticky. You eat it with a spoon. The cheese cake has a smooth, custardlike quality; it is heavy and moist, laden with chopped fruits—very nice.

• SAN MARINO

236 East 53rd Street
LUNCH, MONDAY TO FRIDAY; DINNER, DAILY.
Reservations, PL 9–4130.
Credit cards: AE, MC, V.
Very expensive.

This long-established establishment changed hands a while back. The only visible sign of the transfer of power is the seemingly proprietary new face by whom you are greeted—a lengthy collegiate type in blazer, flannels, garish tie and mountainous hair. He moves around his province with the grace of King Kong in the kitchen. He is doing his schooled best; his hospitality has the stubborn warmth of a robot's. What a way to make a living, by going through the motions of liking people. He seems to have the relationship to the restaurant business that a newly prosperous plastic-toy manufacturer and theatrical angel has to his arty off-Broadway production: utter outsider, connected by a cord through which flows only money.

Running a restaurant has little kinship with making great art, but there are similarities. Unless the enterprise is informed by someone's tastes or preferences or passions or vision, it will fall flat. It may make money, but it won't leave a mark. So when someone comes along and buys San Marino and decides to leave it precisely as was, it cannot work, for whoever made the old place what it was is gone, and these mindless imitators in search of a buck don't have a single idea of their own. San Marino was never a great restaurant, but it was comfortable and straightforward, and the food was decent or better—the management liked things a certain way, lots of other people liked them that way too, and the place became something of an institution. Today's San Marino wishes to be no more than a slavish imitation of the original, and therefore it is a dull parody.

Just in case you don't recall, San Marino is an orderly-looking spot. A substantial barroom, with a curved bar and a few tables, is separated from the beige dining room by white ironwork panels, floor to ceiling. At the bar, gents in boldly patterned jackets belt shots and talk business conspiratorially. The dining-room clientele, equally unengaging, appear to be waiting, bored, for the world to come to an end.

Then there is Albert. Albert is the captain. He looks like the master of ceremonies at a Union City burlesque house, circa 1945. He is tuxedoed and gross. His head hangs forward as if it were weighted down by the pouches under his eyes and his pendulous second chin. His smile is tarnished. Most of his gestures are mechanical, as when he nods or shakes his head, miming the movements of a puppet controlled by strings, but he is all grace when he ceremoniously raises his index finger to his mouth, licks it and turns the page of his order pad. Albert sets the tone, and the desultory waiters follow. They wear gold badges on the navy-blue shawl lapels of their ill-fitting beige jackets. One of them approaches a table. "Fresh pepper?" he asks, brandishing the eighteen-inch mill like a mace.

Fruitta di Mare Salad (their spelling): once a vibrant assemblage of seafood in a powerful vinaigrette, the current version is a bit tame, albeit OK—chunks of squid, octopus, and shrimp, moistened with oil and lemon, flavored with garlic, raw onions, capers and herbs, all very sprightly. If you are here on the right day, the raw clams and oysters can be fine, but at other times they are a bit past perfection. The baked versions feature heavily oiled, undistinguished breadings. You are much better off with the Home Roasted Sweet Peppers—bright-red, carefully peeled, tender, oil-soaked, accented with the taste of charring, the clear flavor of sweet red peppers vivid nevertheless, garnished with a few anchovies, which do no harm.

Do not be disturbed when your Red Tagliarini with Prosciutto arrives two minutes after your order is placed. Red pasta is made red by an admixture of tomato, and it requires only a couple of minutes of boiling before this pasta is ready. The problem is that though it cooks with proper rapidity and is brought to you firm, it lacks life in the San Marino version—no sparkle of the tomato, no firmness of egg—and it sorely needs its sauce to make it a dish. Blessedly, the sauce is a good thing, slivers of strong ham and melted butter, and this dish would be really splendid if the pasta were more than a carrier for it. There is a dish always associated with the house: Quadrettini with Spinach and Prosciutto, little squares of pasta in a thick green sauce of the leafy vegetable and bits of meat—unfortunately, it has the harsh flavor of the frozen vegetable overseasoned.

There is room in New York for three or four freelance proofreaders who will hire themselves out to read menus before they go to press. Until the profession establishes itself, however, we will be privileged to place orders for such as Calamari Stuff with Crab Meat. Some Stuff. Leathery squid torsos packed tight with what might as well be triple-boiled rice, in a harsh tomato sauce that is laced with canned peas. Better, because it is painless, is Broiled Shrimp à la San Marino, in which the principal flavor is of the charred shells of the shrimp—you had been led to expect lemon and garlic, but these shrimp are aswim in a tasteless, bready oil.

Pass up the Veal Chop à la San Marino, for it is spread with cheese that has both the flavor and texture of chewing gum after a long day, all within a breading that is thick and soggy. The Italian Sausage Pizzaiola with Pepper reveals no especial presence of pepper, neither black nor green nor red, but the sausages themselves, four hefty logs, porky, greasy and strong, are fortifying, their thin tomato sauce virtually an irrelevance in this stout company. Albert advises that you can have your escarole made with

"Gollic, raisins, and nut pines." He needs a proofreader too, and the escarole is dreadful.

Terrible chocolate cake, like thickened syrup. Unripe strawberries in excessively sugared cream. Ice cream and ice cream things.

★ SAN STEFANO

322 East 14th Street
LUNCH, MONDAY TO FRIDAY; DINNER, MONDAY TO SATURDAY. CLOSED SUNDAY.
Reservations, 473–5953.
Credit cards: AE, DC.
Expensive.

The man is either a genius or a dreamer, for this is an unlikely location for a restaurant of immodest prices. And though the food here is not bad (on occasion even a little better than that), most New Yorkers can find its equal or better around the corner. But San Stefano is a comfortable and attractively appointed little joint, and when the days are long and the weather fair, this place is a likely terminus of a twenty-minute walk. And someday, when the Second Avenue subway is finally dug, San Stefano may be on the main line.

A little building on East 14th has been niftied up, right in the middle of an assortment of urban scars, and there is a dignified engraved metal plaque on the façade, announcing the existence of this place within. The main floor has been stripped to the rosy bricks, the low ceiling has fresh white plaster in which spotlights have been recessed, the ancient parquet floors have been sanded, stained dark and sealed. Beyond that the mode is Deco. Near the front the ceiling is mirrored to reflect the polished little bar and the boldly patterned geometric mirrors behind it. Copper sheathing on sections of the walls here and there adds to the warm glow of the place, as do the tall tapers on what looks like a desk at the head of the dining room—there is something a little religious about this place, and this monumental piece of formal furniture seems very much your host's holy station. The lighting is soft, so the patterned orange cloths that show as broad fringes under the white table linen are touches of soft color. The maître is at once formal, stiff and talkative; he assumes you are as interested in the restaurant business as he is. One wishes he were busier, not merely in the interest of his prosperity.

His prosperity will take care of itself if he sells enough of these Stuffed Artichokes at $3.75 a copy. The artichoke is served in a heavy oily broth, and it is stuffed with a garlicked breading, but the vegetable is vastly overcooked, making the heart mushy, the climax a failure. The Freshly Roasted Peppers and Anchovies are more successful, the tender green peppers oily and mellifluous, sprinkled with capers and freshened with the lemon you squeeze on; they are a good contrast to the sharp, salty anchovies. The Hot Antipasto di Casa is unexciting—acceptable shrimp under dollops of OK marinara sauce, mussels and clams stuffed with an excessively oiled breading, rather rubbery mushrooms stuffed with the same.

The Cannelloni di Casa are green; they are filled with spinach, cheese and ground veal, are immersed in white sauce, and lack life. You are better off with the simpler

Tagliatelle Verdi San Stefano, broad green noodles in a basic tomato and mushroom sauce—simple and satisfying.

Calamari Adriatico, a splendid dish but for the rubbery squid—the sauce is hot, vividly peppered, fragrant with parsley, but, oh, that coarse squid. The Chicken Scarpariello lacks the rosemary the title suggests, but the chunks of chicken are very well sautéed, browned and moist, enriched by oil and garlic. The Veal Chop San Stefano makes an imposing appearance, the huge rib projecting over the edge of its plate; the meat is pale and tender, inundated by a mound of sautéed onions, red peppers, olives and mushrooms—a good, hefty dish, though the meat and the vegetables fail to come together, might as well be served in separate plates.

Arid cheese cake, with almonds and bits of candied fruit; lemon chiffon pie that is sweet, light, harmless. Excellent espresso.

San Stefano has all the makings of that out-of-the-way place people would like to keep to themselves for special occasions—except wonderful food.

○ SARDI'S

234 West 44th Street
LUNCH AND DINNER.
Reservations, 221–8440.
Credit cards: AE, CB, DC, MC, V.
Expensive.

You enter to the checkroom, the untidy little bar, and the stairway to the upper level. Upstairs the principal bar, the busy three-deep one, newspaper men and newspaper women, actors and actresses (though nary a star stands here), and all the desk people and go-fer people that fill out the middle levels of those industries. The drinking is gay, rarely boisterous. This attic level of Sardi's is a little dingier than the main floor, a function of the lower ceiling. The dirty-salmon walls are much like those downstairs, the massive air-conditioning ducts somewhat more oppressive by virtue of their being closer to your head. And of course there is the checkerboard of colored-in caricatures the height and length of every wall. There is no pleasure in being surrounded by hundreds of grotesque heads, some of them up close. Lucille Ball at five feet, gaudily grinning at you in primary colors, is actually frightening. Up here there are a couple of islands of gingham-topped tables set aside for drinkers who want to avoid the bar-side crush. You get a pot of cheddar surrounded by Ritz crackers. The drinks are ample, the waiters city-wise. The place is patrolled by a tuxedoed gent with slicked-down hair, a beery complexion, jowls, and a constant preoccupation with a wad of gum. Things are a touch more gracious downstairs—all the tables under crisp white linen, the ceiling far enough away so that you hardly notice the patches in the cracked plaster that they mean to paint over one of these years. The overall feeling is of Old New York functionalism, rows of tables, plain chairs, wooden floor, nothing more than is needed to make eating possible—except those ghastly drawings.

You expect at least a decent shrimp cocktail in a place like this, but the shrimp are overcooked, and you are grateful for the horseradish and Tabasco that accompany the dish. Even the Smoked Brook Trout with Sour Cream and Horseradish Sauce, which every restaurant in town gets from the same few sources, is here so poorly handled that it is dried out by the time it reaches you—the horseradish sauce is useful, if lumpy, and the garnish of diced jelly is an irrelevance. As neither of these dishes is prepared to order, it is an astonishment to have them served ten minutes apart. Surely one would never take dining advice from any habitué of this place, but lovers of Sardi's do love Sardi's cannelloni (available as an appetizer or main course). Maybe the dish is all right early in the week—try it for Monday lunch perhaps—but it can be tough and rank, as though reheated on a radiator.

It is possible to get perfectly decent broilings in this place, and the lamb chops, for one, are very thick, tender, lightly charred and accurately prepared.

The specialties of the house on the regular menu are printed in capital letters, so you experiment with SUPREME OF CHICKEN SARDI, which turns out to be an abundance of tasteless chicken in a cheese sauce that has flavor only because it is burnt. This wretched stuff is served over asparagus that has been kept in hot water since early spring. Another fast-moving item here is the Deviled Roast Beef Bones. Though the title suggests that the bones themselves are deviled, there is nothing on them but a little meat, a lot of fat and too much breading, which serves to prevent much of the grease from running off—accompanying mustard sauce tastes as if it is made with Gulden's, which is to mustard as shells are to eggs. At lunchtime there are Fried Oysters—a tough crust around a lump of cotton wool. Avoid with care the so-called Fresh Spinach Salad. The spinach tastes as if it has been in cold storage since the last war, the mushrooms are tasteless, the zucchini plastic, the bacon overburdened with responsibility among these sorry partners.

Very ordinary desserts, for the most part, including sodden cheese cakes and tired pastries. But in this department the specialties are in fact superior to the rest of the list. The Frozen Cake, Zabaglione Sauce, is a splendid layered affair of good ice cream, startlingly tasty and berrylike strawberry sherbet, rich cake and silken icing, all moistened with a zabaglione that is loaded with Marsala. And the Bocconi Dolce is a more than tolerable and very picturesque combination of strawberries, whipped cream, dark cake and icing—when the berries are good, the dish is good, but you can't count on ripe berries every time.

The Sardi's dinner cycle is built around theater times—the place is quiet between curtain-up and curtain-down, busy before and after. You see pretty starlets with their gargoyle handlers (agents need not be good-looking). Much table-visiting and kissing. Yes, theater people do pronounce "darling" as "daaahling," and they do it a lot. Of all this establishment's faults, its contempt for the public is the most contemptible. Half a dozen pairs of desperate little ladies are standing around hoping to squeeze in a Sardi's lunch before the Wednesday matinee. They wait and wait. Along comes a customer with a familiar face, but no reservation. "Yes, Mr. X," says the host, "your table is ready, right this way."

★★ SEEDA

204 West 50th Street
LUNCH AND DINNER. CLOSED SUNDAY.
Reservations, 586–4513.
Credit cards: AE, DC, MC.
Inexpensive.

Buried in one of the Broadway area's seediest blocks, this is an astonishingly clean-cut little establishment, gaudily Thai-motel in its trappings, but spruce for all that. Wander around this neighborhood for an hour or two and then step in here. It is like a needle shower after a day in the mines. In fact, you can get here from underground—Seeda is just at the head of the IRT stairs.

Under wooden beams and rafters and hanging electric bulbs enclosed in perforated and bejeweled metal cylinders, within brick walls and mirrored walls broken by masonry columns, stand rows of tables draped in handsomely printed cloths of earth colors in abstract designs. The cloths are protected from your indiscretions by neatly fitted plate glass. The orange-plastic-upholstered little chairs look like they come from the five-and-ten-cent store, but they support your weight. You are served by cheerful young Oriental men in long hair and long-sleeved red T-shirts with the letters SEEDA across the front; their assistants, the busboys, are dressed the same but have shorter hair.

Much of the food is searingly hot, and the winner on that score is the Squid Salad, with the tenderest, least rubbery, freshest-tasting squid around. It is marinated in lime juice and a great abundance of fiery hot pepper—raw onions and coriander leaves add texture and fragrance to the inflammable food. The menu states that "the most famous Thai dish" is "Minced king fish & shrimps beaten with hot sauce, fried, served with cucumber sauce." Perhaps, but it is not likely to develop a great reputation in New York if this is a first-rate version of it. The silver-dollar-size discs of fried ground seafood may have a subtle appeal, but they lack a clear ocean flavor, and the sweet cucumber sauce is startlingly like confiture and could seem out of place to all but the most open-minded Western eaters. The Shrimp Rolls are like Chinese spring rolls, wrapped in a very crisp pastry, the shrimp and greens inside fresh and lively. Good hot soups here—strong clear broths with meats, scallions, bean curd, seafood, depending on the one you choose, all the floating ingredients fresh and tasty.

The Fried Red Snapper tastes good and will provide your dinner with a bit of theatricality as well—it is carried browned and sizzling and crackling on a great dark plate to your table, where it eventually calms down. This is a pretty terrific fish, very fresh, its skin crusty, the meat firm and juicy, the whole production strewn with chunks of hot celery, strands of fresh ginger and water chestnut, and spicy ground pork, all of which have been sautéed in oil. Then there is, to borrow the house language again, the Sauté Beef with Coconut Milk & Hot Sauce, slivers of browned meat with peas and hot green peppers (careful with those), in a smooth sauce that is at once buttery and beefy. There are interesting crabmeat dishes on the menu, but they suffer from the lack of good crabmeat in these parts. What they call rice sticks you call rice noodles. In any event, #161 on the menu consists of many textures of rice noodles, for they are fried in a big batch, so that some are browned and crisp, some are soft and moist—they are mingled with shrimps and bits of pork, and the whole dish is served in a lovely sweet sauce with a base of tamarind juice. The fried-rice dishes are much like the Chinese items of the same name, and they are well made—dark, lightly oiled rice mingled with tender bits of fried egg, the meat of your choice, strong scallion greens—superb filler if you are in search of a low-cost dinner.

Presumably the Thai beer served here, Amarit by brand, is the thing to drink, but it is watery and thin by comparison to, say, Kirin, which is also available.

★★ SHALIMAR

39 East 29th Street
LUNCH AND DINNER.
Reservations accepted, 889–1977.
Credit cards: AE, CB, DC, MC, V.
Inexpensive.

Shalimar is an Indian restaurant situated within an Indian enclave in Manhattan's East Twenties and Thirties. The place is not only a restaurant but something of a community center where Indians congregate, read the pinned-up notices of Indian cultural events, and of course, eat Indian food.

They don't seem to mind the eclecticism of the elements that combine to make up the ambience: the illumination is from those perforated-tin-can lamps that you find in Mexican restaurants; here they hang from a stamped-tin ceiling like the ones you find in old New York saloons; the place is broadloomed; the rough plaster walls are decorated with embedded bits of tile and mirror, in abstract patterns; the background music is sometimes of India and sometimes of other Asian nations. No one cares.

Among the items listed under "Appetizers" are papadums, which are thin deep-fried wafers about the size of dinner plates, with random perforations. The sheets are reddish brown, dry, crisp and salty. They taste like sublime potato chips, though they are made of a bean flour, and they are delicious with the cool relish of spiced raw onions that is brought to every table. Then there is samosa, the triangular pastries that are filled with spiced lamb and deep-fried just before they are served. Despite some strong ingredients, such as garlic, ginger and red pepper, the effect is subtle because the pastry takes the edge off the strong meat filling.

You will want bread, and paratha is a splendid, intensely oily bread of wheat flour fried in clarified butter (ghee). You can have it straight, or you can have a variation called Aloo Paratha which you will probably not like, because you probably will not like a sandwich of oily bread and spicy mashed potatoes. Then again you might. Indians do.

If India has a national dish, it's Chicken Tandoori. This dish is made by marinating whole chickens in saffron, spices (including hot spices) and yogurt, and then roasting them with a coating of clarified butter. This spicy and moist bird is very good with the rather bland purée of lentils called dal that accompanies your dinner in most Indian restaurants.

There is an enormous variety of vegetable cookery in India. Bhindi is a spicy and oily amalgam of onions, tomatoes, okra, salt and spices, fried in ghee. These rich dishes are very good with the cool condiments called raytas. Raytas are combinations of yogurt with one or another fruit or vegetable. The potato rayta is like a very refreshing rather than heavy potato salad; and the cucumber rayta may remind you of cold cucumber soups, except that it has substantial chunks of cucumber in the cool yogurt.

Indian desserts are hard to like, but for the record, something called Rosa Gola is described, in the inflated language of this menu, as "Snow White Succulent Cheese Balls, Rose Water Flavored," which may be translated as chalk balls in rose water. Then there is Gulab Jaman, a pleasant pastry in a thin honey syrup. And there is Firni, a custardlike pudding of rice flour, perfumed with rose water—pretty good.

★★SHEZAN

8 West 58th Street
LUNCH, MONDAY TO FRIDAY; DINNER, MONDAY TO SATURDAY. CLOSED SUNDAY.
Reservations, 371–1414.
Credit cards: AE, DC, MC, V.
Medium-priced.

It is decades now since the Indian subcontinent's partition and release from British domination, but the devoirs of the deferent colonial are not easily unlearned. The line between servility and cordiality is at least as wide as the Khyber Pass, but your hosts and servers at Shezan straddle it comfortably, bathing you in unctions that border on the extreme. The Briton's bearer, don't you know, knew what he was doing, for his endless "Yes, sahib" and repeated, languorous salaams, drove his crisp British master nuts. Wallahs, wallahs, cut it out, you are free, the British imperial sun has set.

But, no doubt, there are those among you who are not addled by being coddled, others who experience a pleasant puffing-up when you are attended to like a feverish child by a possessive mother, yet others gifted with the knack of summoning with a snap of the fingers, dismissing with a toss of the hand. All you chaps, come to Shezan. Much of the Pakistani and north-Indian food served here is both surprising and delicious, and the setting is not bad too.

Down the stairs to the warmest cool restaurant in New York, glinting modernity that isn't frigid—dimness, gray-carpeted walls throughout these two windowless basement rooms but for the wall of glass blocks that separates them; sand-colored suede on the banquettes, cream-colored linen on the tables; everything illuminated by candlelight that is reflected as a warm glow by a metallic acoustical ceiling. It is lovely, and as an environment of no specific function it adds up—but at this particular restaurant it misses. To serve the vivid, assertive food of Pakistan in this neutral setting is like displaying a brilliantly colored parrot in a delicate gilded cage, when the jungle is its natural setting. The festive air this menu calls for obtains only when the place is humming with people—fortunately it often is.

You are greeted by several dozen dark-suited gentlemen of various ages and a couple of matronly ladies, all of them washing their hands dryly. Their friendliness and courtesy are real, but of such quantity and intensity as to be almost maddening. You are escorted to your table like the President to the dais, hovered over, stared at with something approaching love. It is all you can do to get let alone.

You select wine from the international list, and soon a man materializes, bearing your bottle. He stands slightly behind you like a solicitous footman, a napkin over his left arm, his left thigh at your right shoulder. He bends forward and holds the bottle, in a basket, the perfect twelve-inch reading-distance from your nose. You read and nod solemnly. He moves not so much as a cork's length farther from you as he embarks on the elaborately choreographed *Opening of the Bottle,* complete with a neck and shoulder rubdown—God forbid a mote of dust—a careful peeling away of the foil— to yield a perfect eight-inch strand—the meticulous, painstaking dabbing away of bits of moisture from the as yet unpulled cork, the slow removal from a pocket and unfolding of the corkscrew, its turn-by-gentle-turn into the cork, its gentle popless levering out of said cork, all the while the napkin over that left arm flapping gently against your ear. It is particularly excruciating if you are thirsty. It could make a person order beer. But don't, for Western still wine, reds and whites, are very nice with Pakistani food, and Shezan's wide-ranging list is well-chosen.

You may begin elementally, with Yakhni, a generic name for clear stocks or bouillons which here represents a potent chicken consommé. It is probably prepared from roasted birds, for the resulting broth is dark-brown, almost beefy. The menu announces that it is "subtly flavored with whole spices and herbs," but there is nothing subtle about this steaming, robust liquid. More familiar, if perhaps less authentically of the region, is Mulligatawny, a much thicker soup, flavored with the hot spices of southern India; there are bits of succulent chicken at the bottom of the bowl and hints of the flavor of coconut—you squeeze in a bit of lemon if you wish to cut the richness.

Unless you object in advance, your waiter will portion out the main courses and any accompanying rice or vegetable dishes among all the diners at your table, which can amount to a four- or five-item display for enterprising eaters. This is fine, for the food here goes well with the food here. Moving counterclockwise, now, beginning at six o'clock, and disposing of the most obvious and the least impressive of this establishment's main courses, you embark on Tandoori Chicken. The version served at Shezan suffers from the quality of the bird—it does not taste like chicken. Its marination is apparently brief, and so it is not particularly redolent of spices; abundant lemon is in the marinade, and a bit of that flavor remains; its time over the charcoal is excessive, leaving sides of the bird black as pitch. Fret not, there are better things up at noon, Gurda Kapoora, an extraordinary stewlike affair of kidneys and sweetbreads in a spicy and gamy sauce that is studded with crunchy bits of black pepper. The meats have been marinated in yogurt, ginger and garlic, and the little morsels are at once sweet and lively.

A couple of terrific lamb dishes, including a complex one called Bhuna Gosht, in which chunks of lamb have been cooked in butter with ginger, garlic and spices—the meat is firm, tender and slightly fibrous, and the deep-brown sauce is thick, sweet and spicy. The same meat is also served as Sag Gosht, a simpler and more dramatic dish. The lamb is coated with a combination of ground spinach (the clear and sharp metallic flavor of the fresh article) and coriander leaves—that almost violently fragrant green.

Coriander green turns up again in abundance, this time accompanied by coriander seeds, in Chingiri Jhol: shrimp in a sauce, but not cocktail sauce—sweet spices, such as whole seeds of cardamom, stud the gravy, and the shrimp themselves are crisp, juicy, tasting of the sea.

Good rice dishes, the brown grains mingled with spices, herbs, bits of meat, onions;

different dahls each day—these are lentils, some days flavored with hot peppers and the almost ever-present coriander leaves, other days tasting blandly and pleasantly of little more than the basic bean; breads which to Western palates will seem almost tasteless, though matzoh fanciers may be at home with them.

Shezan serves what may be the best desserts of any Asian restaurant in New York. Taking them in numerical order (those of you who are unsure of your Hindi and Bengali may order dishes by their numbers), there are: Halwa Mumtaz Mahal, a hot pudding of minced fruits and almonds, flavored with saffron—its warm sweetness seems nourishing and wholesome; Kheer Khas, a milk that is thickened by cooking rice in it, but not to the point of rice pudding—the heavy and slightly spiced brew is sprinkled with slivers of almond; and the one that is truly amazing, Kulfi, the ice cream of the region—it differs in two important ways from Western ice creams: first, its flavor is that of grain; second, it is thickened with khoia, an extremely heavy reduction of milk. The result is more like respectable food and less like candy than what you know. All these desserts are covered with beaten silver—yes, thin sheets of the actual metal which, it turns out, is edible, tasteless and prettily decorative.

Occasional bumbling service, now and then an unpleasant waft of burning oil, and, of course, far too many inquiries as to whether you enjoyed your meal.

A 15 percent service charge is added to your check.

★★SHUN LEE DYNASTY

900 Second Avenue (at 48th Street)
LUNCH AND DINNER
Reservations, PL 5-3900.
Credit cards: AE, CB, DC.
Medium-priced.

It is possible to have a great dinner in this restaurant, equally possible to have a dreary one. One thing you won't get is *bad* food, so it's a safe showplace for visiting entertainees.

The Dynasty is, visually, a singular spot. If you wait for your table in the barroom, you will feel surrounded by tufted black leather and threatened by a twenty-foot paper lion over the length of the bar—the room is called the Lion's Den, but it is just a clubroom for the rows of guys in polo shirts, sitting on chairs, opposite rows of wives under blond soufflés, sitting on the massive banquette. The bartender, in civvies, slouches, drinks, chews peanuts, and wipes his hands on the glassware towel. Well, bring your own glassware. The dining room proper, however, is not just some more horsed-up New York bar. This is modern design, in spades: tall plastic wall panels, ceiling to floor, emblazoned with gay animal illustrations; booths made private by Mylar drapes; a ceiling centerpiece of hanging chains and chimes and pennants and dolls and fans, all in muted and softly lit golds and tans; and throughout the room massive enameled pillars. Carpeting, of course, the tables set with mustard-colored linen, sculptured napkins and ornate plates at each setting. The effect is blessedly somewhat diminished by restrained illumination.

You will not get better hacked chicken in New York, and you can order the dish in almost half the Chinese restaurants in town. This is the famous dish of cold, coarsely shredded chicken served in a peanut sauce; here the chicken carries the flavor of chicken, which is the flavor of chicken fat, and the sauce is spicy and heavy, almost mealy, somehow cocoa-like; the dish is sprinkled with bits of scallion and the almost overpoweringly fragrant Chinese parsley one must learn to like to like—its headiness is perfect against this rich dish.

The menu informs you that the Spicy Cucumber is "First Time Served in New York." This is a nice little number, cool and oily lengths of cucumber that have been marinated in sesame oil and spices, studded with bits of pepper and comingled with strands of carrot—a high-class pickle.

A couple of good Hunan dishes. Hunan Calf's Liver—thin, tender slivers of liver sautéed in a thickened oily sauce that is high on ginger and garlic, the sweet and sour elements combined into a kind of elegant relish; it is served with fresh, brilliantly clear-tasting, strong, metallic spinach, an audaciously right contrast. Hunan Smoked Duck—slabs of duck, skin, fat, meat, bone, served with a dish of salt, which diminishes quite perfectly the slightly excess oiliness of the bird and emphasizes the flavor of tea that the bird picked up in the smoking.

But the rest of the main-course menu is the compendium of OK cooking for which Shun Lee Dynasty has inexplicably always won the highest praise. Shrimp, Szechuan Style—prawns, crispy, in a thick sweet-and-sour sauce that is almost pebbly with bits of onion and scallion—is good food. Mandarin Beef—a meaningless though harmless mélange of beef, abalone, ham, chicken and vegetables; as the beef is overcooked and bloodless, you tend to eat around it. Slippery Chicken—strands of chicken browned in a honeylike sauce, served with a garnish of perfect spinach—more OK food.

Some find the service here overbearing, but it is really just a little dumb. You inform your waiter that you want the dishes served in series, one at a time; he announces that he will ask the captain's permission. Later, because of a change in the guard, your still-present waiter cannot accept any instructions and your yet-to-arrive waiter is yet to arrive. The folks love it.

★ SHUN LEE PALACE

155 East 55th Street
LUNCH AND DINNER.
Reservations, 371–8844.
Credit cards: AE, CB, DC.
Medium-priced.

The place looks like the lobby of a Miami Beach hotel and, appropriately enough, it is loaded with tourists. They have perhaps never been frightened by golden wallpaper before and they shriek a lot—delightedly when their attention is diverted to the blue flame that burns on the top tier of their Assorted Appetizers. Dozens of young waiters wander around during the slow periods (when the place is only half filled) and you are likely to be asked about drinks and such half a dozen times. You are not, unfortunately, furnished with Do Not Disturb signs and no amount of heavily applied facial boredom deters these couriers from their persistent appeals. The place is huge, and despite its various levels and sections and the turns in the walls, it seems barnlike. In so immense a setting it is not surprising that none of the staff has much of an idea what the rest of it is doing. Or perhaps it is their unwillingness to care in the service of so inelegant a clientele, for this is the home of some of the most contented and boisterous diners in town, comfy on these Naugahyde gold shantung banquettes, under these gilded chandeliers.

But the place has a persistent reputation as one of the best Chinese restaurants in New York and it is true that if you visit it a dozen times with a dozen friends, you will be able to learn enough about the menu to put together nothing but fine meals. If the establishment, however, is to be judged by everything it is willing to purvey—more than seventy items on the menu—it is not one of the city's best.

The Hacked Chicken in Hot Sauce is composed of strands of white chicken under a thick sauce apparently composed of peanut and oil—a thick, lively sauce with a vague quality of smoke in it, but the not-so-secret secret of this well-known dish is the chicken itself, for without the distinct taste of meat there is no foil to the sauce, and this chicken is flat. If you do not know your way around this place and if you are unknown to the management, they size you up (sometimes wrongly) and decide how little trouble they can get away with. You order some Fried Dumplings. They arrive in eight seconds. Naturally, they are not fried dumplings. They are steamed dumplings; the crust on one side that is formed by last-minute frying, to form fried dumplings from steamed dumplings, has not been bothered about. Terrific dumplings, you understand, lovely spiced ground pork accented with bits of strong parsley, wrapped in a firm noodle casing, and served with a bowl of tart sauce. But they are not fried dumplings. Assumptions are made. When three people request two orders (eight dumplings), your helpful servant dispenses three to him, three to him, and two to she.

A dish styled Frogs' Legs Wang Style (Chef Wang is the culinary king of Shun Lee country) might as well be made of rice noodles or cardboard for all the flavor of frogs' legs that can be detected in the dish. The taste of frozen frogs' legs is at best obscure and, for all the little green peppers and sautéed onions in this dish, nothing can rescue it from its overpoweringly sweet sauce. Disaster. The Velvet Shrimp Puffs are another world, the shrimp pounded down to light cutlets and served in a pale, oily sauce, mingled with morsels of crisp vegetables—snow peas, water chestnuts, mushrooms. A lovely, delicate dish.

Veal is rare on the menus of New York's Chinese restaurants and this place lists but one dish, Sliced Fillet of Veal, Hunan Style, a heavily garlicked dish of slivers of veal —pale and tender meat—with snow peas and green peppers, hot and spicy, but not searingly so, the diverse elements very well balanced. Wang's Amazing Chicken is a bit less, again because the chicken itself tastes like nothing in particular. It is combined with well-cooked eggplant, crisp mushrooms and snow peas, all heavily accented with Chinese parsley; all fine, but the second-rate chicken makes for a second-rate dish. The Eggplant, Family Style, loses the quality of eggplant in its sweet sauce.

Naturally, there are desserts for these people who look like they are stopping off at this posh restaurant after a trip to the supermarket (or are they on their way to the hardware store?), but the desserts are nothing.

Complete dinners for two—three dishes plus beer or drinks—around $30. If you learn your way around the menu, you can eat like a prince here, particularly if you pay like a prince. The Peking Duck, which, the menu says, must be ordered in advance, is $19. Sometimes it is available on immediate command, and it is terrific.

○ SIGN OF THE DOVE

1110 Third Avenue (near 65th Street)
LUNCH AND DINNER. CLOSED MONDAY.
Reservations, UN 1–8080.
Credit cards: AE, CB, DC, MC, V.
Expensive.

Potted trees, statuary, flowers; in one room a velvet ceiling; huge mirrors that are so smooth and polished that they look like open doorways; interior walls of stained glass; rosy brick pillars, walls and archways; a glass dome over what was once an interior courtyard (starry sky above); pink linen on the well-spaced tables; double-breasted navy-blue blazers and fawn-colored trousers (black silk stripes down the sides) on the mostly tall, dark and handsome, often mustached waiters. And that is just about it—because you can design a place, order it, get it and sure enough have it, but that procedure will not provide good food and decent service day in and day out. So when the host attempts to match the ceremony to the surroundings, he pirouettes to deliver his "Come with me" and glides you right up to a table that is very nice but covered with cake plates and coffee cups and lipsticked Kleenex. He solves the problem by forgetting your existence behind him, and is heading back to his post when you collar him and remind him of what he lately was about. Then there are the waiters, who seem to work in noncommunicative teams; three or four will ask for your order when you have already ordered. And then there are the busboys; your dinner plate is picked up, and then another is picked up and its contents dumped into the first so that a neat stack can be formed, and this process is continued until he has a column of perhaps a dozen dinner plates, a mound of bones, and other remains on the top one. And all this in such a pretty restaurant.

And such a pretty menu, too—a huge folder, silkscreened, with doves and berries and flowers and butterflies and things all flying around together. And then there are the listings within, so imaginative and informative. Lump crabmeat, for example, is served "on Snow," and we are told that the Roquefort cheese is "Made from Ewe's milk cured in Limestone Caves, Roquefort, France." Tell us please, where are these stuffed mushrooms from? Never mind; they are from yesterday, stuffed in a large batch, refrigerated, and heated under a broiler when they are ordered and served in an irrelevant, thickened beef stock. And is not the seafood in "A Variety of Sea Food, Gratinée Neptune" lacking in variety, since it is uniformly previously frozen and currently warmed up in a greasy sauce of oil and cheese?

But take heart, because it is possible to get palatable food here if you restrict yourself to the least pretentious dishes. You might, for example, fear that "Fresh Calf's Liver à l'Allemande (Bacon and Apple)" sounds too ambitious for so incompetent a kitchen, but in fact the ring of warm apple can be discarded as soon as it arrives, and you will find yourself with a dish of good liver and bacon. The broiled steaks and chops are good, and they must sell a lot of duck here because the "Brandied Duckling, Sign of the Dove" is apparently roasted the day you get it, and the brandied sauce, with a hint of chopped nuts, is sort of nice. The vegetables are not kept in a steam table, but in a warm bath.

At this point it may be a good idea to have salad, because the salads are good and the desserts are merely concoctions. The watercress and endive, for example, are served in two separate mounds, the endive sliced into long slivers, both items dressed in a clear vinaigrette. But if you want something sweet, and you accept a suggestion of mousse cake, you get something for which you will instantly think up several names better than mousse cake. How about brandy-candy-maraschino-chocolate-orange delight? It weighs a pound and hasn't an ounce of mousse in it. Would you like something a little simpler? OK, have an orange tart—visualize a triangle of tolerable pastry on which rests a triangle of custard of identical shape, surmounted by a few slices of the kind of orange that is not juicy enough for orange juice, not tasty enough to eat straight—now you know what they are for.

★ SILVER PALACE

50 Bowery (near Canal Street)
LUNCH AND DINNER.
Reservations, 964–1204.
Credit cards: AE, CB, DC, V.
No liquor.
Inexpensive.

This is Chinatown's largest restaurant and one of the biggest in New York. Accordingly, for the first time, it is now possible for the annual, semiannual, quarterly and monthly celebratory dinners of Chinese political organizations, trade groups, sects, tongs, tribes and block associations to be attended by the entire memberships, their spouses, friends and relations on weekend vacations, visiting firemen from San Francisco and points east, and the press.

Up the broad carpeted stairway or, if you are infirm or enjoy rides, up the purring escalator of a lobby that would befit a Chinese movie palace of Hong Kong's Great White Way, if there were such a thoroughfare, or even if there weren't, decorated, as it is, with tiles and lights and glitter and gilt. You achieve the upper landing, whip out your field glasses and scan the scene, which is a healthy block long, brightly lit, packed with tables that are, in turn, packed with people. The extensive ceiling is supported by columns that are faced with antiqued mirror. There is a backlighted mural of Hong Kong's harbor, garish painted tapestries, a fish mural (aglow), an icebox (with 7-Up, Coke, Nedick's Orange Soda, and a few fingers of Cutty Sark in a bottle stowed away for after hours). The food flies through on little nurses' carts pushed by the waiters at a hustling clip, flash bulbs pop, beer cans pop (you bring your own beer), applause crackles. Applause crackles? Applause crackles. For when the back two thirds of this place is set aside for a mammoth "affair," the deadly serious eating that goes on during these rites is sometimes followed by amplified speeches, which, in turn, are followed by polite smackings of hands. To Occidental ears at the Bowery end of the Silver Palace, the speeches will sound like the loudspeaker announcements on New York subways. For a clearer rendition, repair to the facilities, into which the proceedings are piped. No escape Big Brother. The place opens in the morning. One assumes it is quiet then.

There is also an extensive menu. Violate the Chinese order of things by beginning with Chinese Parsley with Sliced Fish, which is a violation because it is a soup, which traditionally is eaten later in the meal. Whenever you eat it, it is a strong fish broth, perfumed with the scent of coriander leaves and studded with slivers of fresh ginger and hefty chunks of fried fish. If you prefer your fish unmoistened, there is available a Fried Sweet and Sour Sea Bass, the whole immense fish presented on a platter, hot and crusty, inundated in a sweet red sauce and slivered vegetables—this is more of a production than a delicacy, but there is no denying the freshness of the fish. The Sauté Flounder Balls are not spherical, neither are they good—on occasion the chunks of flounder have been a day over the hill. The carrots and water chestnuts that are part of the potpourri are OK, and the chunks of zucchini that were dry-sautéed in oil before they were mingled in are juicy and crunchy and almost save the dish.

Sticking with the house orthography we move on to Szechuan Style Sauté Shrimp, a huge mound of crisp crustaceans in a hot oily sauce, all under a liberal sprinkling of scallion greens—an impeccable dish, even if the shrimp lack the flavor of the unfrozen article.

The title Preserved Bean Curd with Watercress may mislead you, for this is mainly the cress, an immense mound of it, strong and grassy, bits of ginger here and there, in a broth that is thickened with bean curd—wherefore the name.

Good duck dishes, including Braised Duck with Mushrooms, hefty slices of a juicy crisped bird, surrounded by crisp broccoli and covered over with broad mushroom caps that are dark, firm and nutty, everything lightly moistened with a salty brown sauce.

Avoid such things as Crispy Fried Spare Ribs with Sweet & Sour Sauce, a grotesque array of tomatoes, pineapple, green peppers and too much more. Avoid just as assiduously the Chinese Style Broiled Beef, a leaden pot roast that satisfies certain hungers for slabs of beef.

★★ SLOPPY LOUIE'S

92 South Street (near John Street)
LUNCH AND DINNER. CLOSED SATURDAY AND SUNDAY.
No reservations (952–9657).
No credit cards.
No liquor.
Inexpensive.

In appearance Sloppy Louie's is about as primitive a restaurant as you will find. In the dining room there are two rows of long wooden tables, one row along each side, six chairs at each table. The kitchen is behind the dining room, partially hidden from view by a mirrored partition. At one back corner there are coffee urns, and at the other there is a steel cabinet that holds glasses and silverware. In front there is a cash register, and near the door, a cigarette machine with a few extra chairs inverted on it. Three frosted-glass lamps hang from the wavy, stamped-tin ceiling. This is a seafood restaurant, and along the walls hand-lettered signs announce the varieties of fresh fish that are in season and available. There is also a printed menu. When the place is crowded, a rough line forms at the front just inside the door. The long tables are shared by strangers. This causes no problems.

On each table there is a bottle of ketchup, a bottle of Worcestershire sauce, and a bottle of Red Devil. The place is patrolled by waiters in assorted uniforms—this short, thin man in a neat blue linen jacket, that giant in a limp short-sleeved white shirt and a white apron down to his ankles. They are diligent and intelligent, and compared to the clowns at Sweets, around the corner, they are courtly, gallant, empathic, clairvoyant. The customers are diverse—respectably suited men come here from the financial district, second-generation Chinese walk over from Chinatown, people from SoHo come here, as do people from the low- and middle-income high-rise housing projects that are within walking distance of South Street. This restaurant is in the neighborhood of the old Fulton Street fish market, and here you can still get fish and shellfish that are as sweet and fresh as any in the city.

The thing to know about Sloppy Louie's is that you should order the simple dishes. Avoid the chowders, which are rather thick. The bouillabaisse is an artless and not particularly satisfying soup; the squid (or whatever) sautéed in garlic sauce is toughened in the process, though the sauce itself is very tasty. This leaves you with a lengthy assortment of shellfish and fish, raw, broiled or deep-fried, and you get them in perfect condition nearly every time.

If you start off with a shellfish "cocktail," you'll find, not surprisingly, that the oysters or clams are sweet and juicy. But the shrimp and crabmeat taste just as fresh, and that is rare. You can also have your oysters fried, and the dish is something of a miracle—true, the batter is dull, but it is perfectly crisped, and the frying is done so rapidly that the oysters are warmed without being the least bit toughened. When shad roe is in season, this is a good place to get it. The roe is carefully handled, so that the membrane that surrounds it is not broken; this keeps the moisture of the roe inside, where it belongs, and you get moist roe in a crisp, browned skin. The broiled fish at this restaurant is as good as any in New York. You can prove this five times at once by ordering the Seafood Combination Broiled. You will get lemon sole, striped bass, snapper, halibut and salmon, or, sometimes, another fish that is in season substituted for one of the listed ones. If all fish tastes the same to you, try this dish—each fish is so carefully prepared that its character is preserved, vividly clear, and after a few bites you will be a minor expert on the flavors of certain Eastern fish.

Little dishes of salad are served when you sit down: sometimes good cole slaw; sometimes cold beets that are pretty good; sometimes lettuce, in vinegar and paprika, which is bad. This is not, as they say, a dessert house—the strawberry shortcake, for example, is made with frozen strawberries. There is ice cream.

Customers continue to arrive right up until closing time. At seven fifty-eight you may order and be served and not be rushed. At eight the front door is firmly locked, and no more orders are taken.

In the middle of the afternoon this is a sleepy restaurant. The waiters, cooks and dishwashers nurse mugs of coffee at the back tables. A few regular customers sit down with them and gossip. A handful of people with no afternoon obligations let their lunches spin out, talking or reading. At first glance Sloppy Louie's looks like an end-of-the-line place, but in recollection it is shining clean.

★★SOHO CHARCUTERIE & RESTAURANT

195 Spring Street (at Sullivan Street)
LUNCH, DAILY; DINNER, MONDAY TO SATURDAY.
Reservations, 226–3545.
Credit cards: DC, V.
Very expensive.

They are not kidding with that complex title, for this is two retail establishments in one: the so-called Charcuterie what you would call a pretentious and not particularly ambitious deli; and the Restaurant what you would call a restaurant, with no questions about the claims and aims, for they are high.

By-pass the corner store for the eating house by going in through the Sullivan Street entrance, a quick passage from the jagged asphalt grays of Little Italy to the softness of dim light, pale ivories and soft whites, here and there a potted plant, a bit of J. S. Bach piping cheerfully in the background. The city is somehow hushed away within these walls, and even if you are seated at the windows—a great wall of glass panes framed in ivory—from which you behold the street you have just left, that street doesn't look the same, for you are seeing it as if from a sanctuary. By day it is quite another matter. The windows work the other way—skylight and sunlight pour in; the greenery, which at night is obscurely in corners, springs to life, and you are at a garden party, all spaciousness and air.

From time to time, roughly with the changing of the seasons, this establishment completely revises its menu, so that what you read about here may not be available when you come.

The word "sardine" unavoidably brings to mind flat tins from Maine or Portugal, but sardines are sea-faring beasts which may be handled like other ocean creatures. This place obtains them fresh, lightly batters the little bodies, sautés them rapidly in oil, and serves the by now formless shapes in a row of four, on a white rectangular plate, the unoccupied spaces around the little fish adorned with chunks of lemon and warmed, oiled quarters of tomato. The sardines are fresh and clear-tasting, delicate and crisp (you eat them bones and all), and the batter is airy and almost weightless—it is food that is utterly without heaviness, one could eat several dozen of them. But don't, for there are other estimable items with which to begin, such as Poireaux Braisés, leeks that have been simmered in butter, their bulbs wrapped in strong and smoky ham, the greens splayed out along a lengthy plate, served in a sauce which is an intense concentration of fragrant herbs. You get lucky if you find Barquettes d'Huîtres on the menu when you come, for this dish will convert the most obstinate of raw-only oyster-lovers to the miracles which can be accomplished when these mollusks are cooked. Your barquette is a pastry boat; it is filled with sautéed mushrooms and gently warmed oysters, the entire production bathed in a sauce of seasoned butter and wine—it is perfect balance, and it is made with immaculately sweet and clear-tasting oysters. On occasion there is an exceptionally pricey first course listed as Ris de Veau Financière, which is another item served on pastry, this one a slightly heavy pâte á choux. But the sweetbreads themselves are at once rich and light, they are commingled with mushrooms and chunks of black olive, and they are served in a sauce that has the quality of prunes and wine, a fruity sweetness that has depth, as of the earth. But the place is perfectly capable of coming up with an undistinguished duck pâté, complete with those now very fashionable pistachio nuts. This pâté does have the virtue of unmistakable duck flavors, both the meat and the liver, but it lacks restraint—you want to bury small chunks of it in very large slices of bread.

Something of a comedown, these main courses. You are not surprisingly made curious and even hopeful by the entry Poulet à la Bière Noire au Genièvre, for it has among its ingredients shallots and mushrooms, gin and cream, dark beer. You figure that as you like each of them, there is a chance you will like them all together. Tough luck, for the beer imparts an acid quality to the sauce which is not overcome by the other ingredients, and though the chicken is not from the freezer, it is rather tasteless. Eschew the veal dishes—when they sauté the cutlets they manage the miracle of removing what flavor the meat has while adding nothing—they don't brown the meat, even slightly, they just simmer it in butter, which is ruination. But choose with alacrity the Porc Normande, sautéed chunks of rich meat in a thick sweet sauce of prunes, apples and apple brandy. These flavors are well in excess of the simple sum of their parts —the meat is elegantly garnished with scalloped potatoes that are browned at their edges and very creamy.

If you have the impression that this establishment is given to elegant excess, the Croustade de Fruits de Mer will do nothing to alter it. This production consists of four seafood items—morsels of salmon, shrimp and scallops, and filets of sole—which have been poached in wine, married in a thick fish sauce, enriched with butter, and served in a shell of puff pastry. It succeeds completely.

A good dacquoise, very much like a layer cake, smooth mocha-flavored pastry cream alternating with layers of meringue, slivered almonds all about. Something the house calls strawberry mousse is more like a strawberry sherbet, but there is such an intensity of the lightly lemoned sweet berries, brightly accented with at least a shot of Kirsch per serving, that it almost earns the word mousse. When there are berries this place goes a little wild over them—raspberries and crème fraîche, or at least as close an American version as you will find; blueberry pie of plump berries and just a bit of jelly next to the crumbly brown crust. Your iced tea has fresh mint in it.

• LE STEAK

1089 Second Avenue (near 58th Street)
DINNER.
Reservations, 421–9072.
Credit cards: AE, DC.
Medium-priced.

You've heard of a tourist trap? This restaurant is a New Yorker trap. Same thing, but the deception is more carefully contrived, and the place is packed with New York businessmen, their customers, comrades and companions du jour, enjoying their special knowledge of this special out-of-the-way place, which serves a single, not so special, prix-fixe steak dinner. This dinner is hardly a dinner at all—the salad converted into the first course, French fries with the steak but no other vegetable, dessert and coffee. There are enormous economies in so limited a selection, which can be reflected in (1) perfectly prepared food, or (2) low prices, or (3) increased profits. Here the economies are channeled mainly into (3), and the food is only moderately good, the price no bargain.

One's (everyone's) dinner begins with a large salad of romaine lettuce and chicory, dressed with a good vinaigrette, and continues with what the menu refers to as "Le Steak Maison—steak served with unique herb sauce from Provence & thin French-fried potatoes." One area in which American cooking outshines the French is in the preparation of steak. The American method leaves a band of scored fat on the steak, which adds to the flavor and prevents overcooking at the edges. At Le Steak the steak is trimmed before grilling, and as the meat is not well marbled to begin with, the steaks are mediocre (though cooked as ordered). The mysterious sauce from Provence is a Beurre Maître d'Hôtel (parsley butter, with lemon, salt and pepper, here augmented with basil) in which the steak is basted. Before serving, the waitress goes through gestures of finishing the preparation over an alcohol burner on a serving stand. Actually, there is nothing for her to do but remove the food from the platter, put it on the plate and serve it, as the preparation is complete when the steak leaves the kitchen. Then the accompanying French fries are given the same magical toss over the fire on the steak platter, hocus pocus, abracadabra, and *voilà!*, steak and potatoes.

The French fries are good, but as the kitchen staff has little else to conquer (or to offer), an effort should be made to do them as well as they are done in any second-rate establishment in France. The reputation Le Steak has for its *pommes frites* must be attributed to the abysmal quality of most New York French fries rather than to any particular excellence here.

One may have either cheese or dessert. The cheeses are Brie and Camembert, from those four-inch export circles found in supermarkets. But they are served at room temperature, and can be acceptable. The Gâteau Maison is a chocolate excess. La Surprise de Monique, described as "parfait with chestnuts, whipped cream & grilled walnuts," is made of canned, candied chestnuts, good ice cream and whipped cream, and walnuts that have never seen a grill. The balance of the inspired selection: Peach Melba, chocolate mousse, crème caramel, fresh fruit. Wines are overpriced from a very limited selection.

With all its faults, the restaurant somehow adds up. The food is fairly good, the service, though bored, is efficient, and the room is cozy. The regulars who pack the place are, of course, never disappointed, so one is surrounded by happy people. And though the value is illusory, one is not being beaten out of very much.

★★ SUN HOP KEE

13 Mott Street (near Park Street)
LUNCH AND DINNER.
No reservations (349–9831).
No credit cards.
No liquor.
Inexpensive.

Lest they function, the acoustical tiles that are the ceiling have been brilliantined with white enamel, which reflects not only sound but stark light from the strands of exposed fluorescent tubing that provide the principal illumination in this garish noisery. The walls are a shiny mustard-and-olive moiré nightmare, the dozen or so tables are topped with remarkable marble—the pattern repeats. On the little shelf over the radiator are baby highchairs and the dispensers of paper napkins that are on the tables during the off-hours. A Model T gray-green air-conditioning machine totters at the rear. Limp gray jackets hang from the shoulders of the cheerful, if linguistically undeveloped, waiters who sprint around the premises. The boss spends a lot of his time at the cashier's desk–cum–cigarette stand just inside the front door, where he exchanges cheerful Chinese greetings with the large family groups that come here for casual feasts; it is all very musical in a brass-and-Chinese-gong orchestration. Children are part of the scene, on occasion as many as a dozen on hand, their big brown eyes enchanting even the most tragic Nordic visitors. At meal's end the adults are sometimes too sated to interfere with the toddlers that are chasing around on the tabletops.

There is a menu, and there are dozens of strips of paper affixed to the walls, Chinese characters thereon announcing what more is available. But if the Latin alphabet is your limit, one of the best ways to assemble a dinner here is to commandeer a waiter, escort him on a tour of tables occupied by knowing Orientals, and point to the dishes that catch your eye. Sometimes you can even elicit from the waiter the names of the things you are about to eat!

"Bitter melon," he says, is what you are about to eat, a mound of pale-green crescents that have been stir-fried in oil. They are served in a dark oil-and-garlic sauce that is studded with black beans. The vegetable is, in fact, slightly bitter; it is also crisp and juicy, also it is very easy to pick up pieces of it with chopsticks. Chinese broccoli is like wild broccoli, with leafy tops instead of budded ones, and an earthy, slightly sour flavor. This too is pan-fried, which preserves the resilient fibrousness of the thick dark-green stems and the almost parchment quality of the broad leaves. The oil with which it is moistened is dark and salty.

Immense flounders are to be seen on almost every table occupied by Chinese, so you send for one of those. You can have yours steamed or fried, but the locals unanimously prefer the former, and you go along. The fish is served up in an oily golden broth. It is impeccably fresh, so that its meat is sweet and delicate, and it is covered over with strands of scallion greens and leaves of crisp, strong ginger. This is a simple dish of simple perfection, and a bemused eater could casually work his way through the entire item alone. Everyone orders the crabs, for exercise. These are hard-shelled, and they yield few calories of sustenance per erg required to consume them, but the crabmeat, when you finally get at it, is firm and oceanic, and the sauce—of salty oil, ground pork, chopped eggs and greens—has an intensity of flavor that almost makes up for the sparsity of the dish's nourishment. Cherrystone clams do not turn up on many Chinese menus, and they are not exactly the high spot of this one. The clams are steamed a little too long, so they are a bit tough, though their flavor, like that of all the seafood here, is fresh and near-perfect. The clams arrive on a giant platter, in their shells, and the production has been copiously doused with a sweet-and-bitter sauce of black beans, scallion greens and slivers of green pepper, all in a dark and peppery oil.

There is, of course, a selection of your standard Chinese mélanges, including Lychee Roast Pork Kow, chunks of good meat in among a tangle of bamboo shoots, water chestnuts, snow peas and mushrooms, plus the sweet lychees of the title—good solid food. And there are rice and noodle dishes to settle you at the end of your meal, including Duck Lo Min, a salty and oily mound of brown rice studded with chunks of rich duck meat and leaves of fresh watercress; and Noodle with Beef & Tomato, slightly gummy pale noodles topped with chunks of hot tomato and strands of meat, all in a heavily salted oil.

When people get up to leave, the large tables look like the beach at Coney Island at the end of a hot Sunday. The Chinese leave empty Budweiser cans, the Westerners empty bottles of the Chinese beer that is available in the supermarket a few doors to the south.

★★ SUSHIKO

251 West 55th Street
LUNCH, MONDAY TO FRIDAY; DINNER, DAILY.
Reservations, 974–9721.
Credit cards: AE, CB, DC.
Inexpensive.

The neighborhood seems to be picketed, but the pickets are not carrying signs. In this part of town, hard by Eighth Avenue, there is much traipsing, up and down the streets, by bizarrely attired female humanoids whose leisurely gait tells much about their occupation. But assuming that the lure of raw fish is more compelling than their blandishments, or that by reason of gender the latter were not directed your way, you make it to and enter this humble restaurant in the humbler half of the humbler half of Manhattan's midtown. There are gilded paper lanterns hanging in the front window, but there the *luxe* ends. Within, there are splintery bamboo walls, yellow oilcloth on the dozen or so tables, rickety rice-paper lanterns. There are also adornments—a Kirin Beer calendar (scenic), a telephone (pay). Behind it all, the plinking and wailing of recorded Japanese music, and when that lets up, the murmur of the Japanese language. The place has a substantial Japanese clientele, including not just the neat and clean executives that habituate the swanker restaurants on the less humble, East Side half of midtown, but women and children and menials, too, drawn by the low prices and creating, in their aggregate, a more homey ambiance than the aura of officers' mess you experience when surrounded by dozens of close-tonsured black-haired men in impeccable suits.

The sushi bar that is the off-to-one-side hub of the dining room is manned by hirsute Japanese youths whose lank hair, casual white garb and offhand manner are no clues to the neat things they do with the fresh seafoods that are the principal ingredients in the sashimi and sushi served here. This is one of the best restaurants for raw fish in New York, and the place to enjoy it is on one of the half dozen stools at the little bar, where you can point at any item on display, ask its identity, struggle with the heavily accented polite answer, try it despite your lack of new information, and have a wonderful time.

You sit down to paper napkins, little chopsticks in a paper sheath; you are brought a warm moist square of terry cloth on a little bamboo canoe, and if you are at a table instead of at the bar or if you want hot food served to you at the sushi bar, a seven-page menu in a hangdog folder, the first page of which is an ardent paean to the pleasures of eating in Sushiko, albeit with some good advice: "Sushi is for the true connoisseur. . . . Eaten with beer, Sake or whiskey, there is no equal in this world." Hyperbole aside, those are the right beverages for this food.

You put yourself in the hands of the youngster behind the bar; he places a clump of moist pink pickled ginger before you, on a little board, the ginger shaped to a pyramid by his nimble fingers. (If you do not enjoy seeing the food you are about to get fingered, eat at a table.) You are started off with slices of dark-red tuna, soft and velvety, around moist rice and a sharp mustard that seems to clear the head. Then some mackerel, distinctly fishy compared to the tuna, also on rice, and sprinkled with sesame seeds on the silvery skin, for a crunchy, grainy accent. Next, though only for willing experimenters, raw abalone, a tough and inky-tasting and cartilaginous meat, with a stormy-oceanic flavor that calls for a calm interlude of raw squid—a very rich, almost buttery raw seafood that is enhanced by a moistening of soy sauce.

The second movement also begins with the tuna theme, but in this variation the fish and rice are formed into cylinders within a wrapping of crinkly seaweed sheet, and one-inch discs are cut off and served in pairs. Then we return to the abalone motif, but this time the resilient sinew has been tamed by boiling and made succulent with a sauce that is thick and brown, like warm chocolate—your server explains informatively that it is "special sauce." And if you have been swallowing everything placed before you without making a face, you qualify for some Japanese eel—it is salted and smoked in Japan, and it is behind the counter window in a little wooden box, and you will like it if you like smoked, rubbery, jellied salt.

Of course, you needn't go the whole route.

Having warmed up on seafood, you proceed to meat, which will, if you wish, be served to you at the sushi bar. And while you are waiting for it, you may observe an egg loaf, deep-yellow, lightly browned, being sliced behind the bar for delivery to some of the Japanese customers. Get a slice—it is steamy and sweet and firm, a rolled Japanese omelet, made in clear oil.

Now your Katsu Don arrives—thin slices of breaded pork, made in an eggy batter, served with onions and mushrooms, atop a bowl of rice. Or else your Gyu Don—beef that is barely steamed, very tender, with delicate slivers of sweet onion, on rice. Of course there are good versions of teriyaki and yakitori, and so on, but as the principal attraction of the place is the products of the sushi bar, a properly gluttonous approach to that may dictate a restrained one toward meat. You have to watch out for the man behind the bar. As you are about to wipe your lips for the last time, he hits you with some charcoaled tuna stomach, hot and sweet (you really do well here sampling what the knowing Orientals have made for them), and it is very hard to resist the oily fish with the sharp accent of the charred parts.

At the real end, someone will bring you a nice hot glass tea.

• SWEETS

2 Fulton Street (near South Street)
LUNCH AND DINNER. CLOSED SATURDAY AND SUNDAY.
No reservations (825–9786).
No credit cards.
Medium-priced.

The food is not bad, the service is not good. The waiters are the worst brand of sufferers. They wake up exasperated and become more and more impatient as the day wears on. Customers find themselves giving orders to elbows or trousers because these food handlers find it a bit beneath them to face a customer directly or attentively, though they appear eager enough when you sit down—they ask for your order before the menu is so much as unfolded, and they exchange significant glances with their counterparts at adjacent stations when you presume to read the thing before selecting from it.

This is the famous Sweets, where reservations are unheard of, and where the line extends down the stairs and into the street at the busiest part of the lunch hour. When you mount the last of the steps, you find yourself in a room that makes the Palm Restaurant look like the palace at Versailles. The floor slopes down toward the center of the restaurant from each end of the building at an angle of at least five degrees. There are oil paintings on the dingy walls which are not only hideous but for sale. The back dining room has a special air of excitement about it because it leads directly to the kitchen. The waiters open the swinging doors with solid kicks to the steel plates nailed thereon for the purpose, and while the doors are ajar, one is entertained by momentary amplification of the otherwise merely intense kitchen noises—a dishwashing machine powered by a prehistoric locomotive, and a constant exchange of pleasantries between the dining-room and kitchen staffs at sufficient volume never to require repetition: "Where's my herring?" "Look in ya pocket."

But as noted, there is the food. The deep-fried oysters have been lightly breaded and fried rapidly. They taste good and are tender, but somehow the oyster has been lost. The clam stew consists of milk, butter, clams and clam broth, artlessly compounded and innocuous. It is called Little Neck Stew and is made with huge, tough cherrystones, almost chowders, sometimes. It's best to begin a meal with raw clams here. (In this venerated seafood joint, raw oysters are not even on the menu.)

The broiled fish is pan-broiled, which is OK, and it is lightly breaded first, which is also OK, though corn meal would make a better breading than ordinary flour. A dozen varieties are listed, and most of them are usually available, including grey sole, flounder, haddock, pompano, shad, and so on. The broiling is expert, and you will get a very fresh, perfectly broiled fish here nine times out of ten. Avoid with great enthusiasm the Newburgs, au gratins, sautées and Creoles. They are, here, methods of defiling good food. But do try the finnan haddie, in the preparation pretentiously called "à la

Sweets." The fish is extremely smoky, rather salty, baked in milk (manna to the English), and a singular dish. It is made perfectly here.

A good vegetable: deep-fried eggplant—the moisture sealed inside by breading and by the use of very hot fat. The potatoes, other than the French fries, are OK.

One is rushed through one's dinner here (the used dishes are dropped loudly onto metal trays), and it is soon time for dessert. Don't have it. The Nesselrode pie is sickening and overwhelming—tutti-frutti within, shreds of bad chocolate atop. Ice cream, stewed prunes and orange juice are also listed.

In the old joke, you can lead a horse to water but if you can get him to float on his back, then you really have something. The horses who come here do a water ballet and pay for the privilege, then go forth to talk the place up.

A bad restaurant for a relaxed dinner, but a tolerable one for a fast lunch—the pace and noise seem appropriate to the noontime clientele, busy Wall Streeters.

★★ SWISS PAVILION

4 West 49th Street
LUNCH AND DINNER. CLOSED SUNDAY.
Reservations, 247–6545.
Credit cards: AE, CB, DC, MC, V.
Expensive.

This has always been potentially one of the best restaurants in New York. But there has always been one thing or another.

The food at the Swiss Pavilion is not only good but authentic. Even that is not necessarily a virtue, but this authenticity is more than just a matter of the right ingredients in the correct proportions; one has the feeling here that the food is prepared by people who grew up with it, people who care about its tasting the way it tasted in the original, who provide not just the technical quality called authenticity, but also authority grounded in tradition.

But the Swiss Pavilion seems to compromise itself, once it gets past the actual preparation of the food, by catering to certain popular tastes. The disproportionate number of flambés on the menu is one thing, of fondues another.

A third is the horseshoe bar, a before-dinner drink at which may lead you to suspect you have chanced into one of the many restaurant/dives in the neighborhood that make most of their money on the torrents of booze that pass over the bar during the cocktail hour. The customers, instead of the proprietors, run the place. It has become theirs, and it is noisy and sloppy, with empty bottles, messy-looking pots of cheese dip, stirrers, napkins and other assorted junk strewn about. You could overlook it, but sometimes the boys get a notion to have dinner here (not often), and when they do, they do not lower their voices.

In the handsome dining room, its walls hung with pennants, you are seated at settings of solid and graceful brown ware on soft, putty-colored linen. The service is not as professional as it once was (the dining room is no longer staffed by Swiss-trained Swiss, but by friendly and willing but still-learning South Americans of various nationalities). In the old days, for example, it would have been unthinkable for a captain to wave you back to the hatcheck room (if you got past it undetected and, thereby, got past the hostess); he would simply have seated you himself, or asked you to please wait while *he* went for the hostess.

But once the food starts coming, you are OK. You may begin with something called Ramequins—little quiches made with superior cheese and bits of meat and perfectly browned crusts; they are hot and aromatic, and they are delicious with cool red wine. Or you may start with Surprise au Céleri—a surprising and perfectly successful combination of poached apple, a delicate liver pâté, and crisp celery root, acidic, tasting almost raw, in a thick mayonnaise. If that does not seem ridiculous, take note that the dish is served with Cumberland sauce—lingonberries and orange—and that the sauce is delicious on these diverse ingredients.

The soups here are all very good, from the cold apricot soup to the hearty Basler Mehlsuppe, a beef-stock broth cooked with excellent strong-tasting flour. There is also one soup made on a base of chicken stock—it is called Schoppa Da Giuotta, and it is eggy, laden with big kernels of barley and bits of ham, and redolent of chicken fat—it is almost as thick as mayonnaise.

Among the flambés is one gaily entitled "Hühnerbrüstchen mit Orangen, flambiert." The chicken arrives at the serving stand already cooked—it is a chicken breast, stuffed with veal, nuts and honey. Your server combines this with orange, and he cooks it some more; he adds grapes and cooks it further, he tosses in some raisins and cooks and stirs again. Then he flames the event in Curaçao (after a couple of tries). The stuffing within the chicken breast is a little like a sausage, and the fruit-and-brandy sauce is very nice on the spicy meat. The dish is served with very good spinach, loud and salty.

The Tournedo aux Morilles is not invariably fashioned from a perfect slice of beef, but the sweet, crinkly mushrooms (morels) are spectacular, and the dish is served in a very good cream sauce made slightly sharp with a touch of brandy. The best things on the plate, however, are the almost unbelievable noodles—they are firm yet soft, the flavor of eggs is vivid without being in the least "eggy," and the butter they are moistened with is all they need—probably the best noodles in New York.

One very simple and good dessert: Öpfelchuechli. These (that's a plural) are apple rings that are deep-fried in beer batter right before your eyes (or under your nose, if you wish) and sprinkled with cinnamon and sugar. The inside is sweet and soft, the outside sweet and crisp—good stuff. The rhubarb pie is something else. It is quite tart, only slightly sweetened, and the excellent crust and good firm quality of the fruit notwithstanding, the dish requires learning to like.

★★ SZECHUAN

2536 Broadway (at 95th Street)
LUNCH AND DINNER.
Reservations, 663–8150.
Credit cards: AE, V.
Inexpensive.

This place lacks geographic appeal (the Broadway desperadoes up here make you wish you had eyes in the back of your head), atmospheric appeal (a large, garish room, a ceiling of acoustical tiles, long rows of tables and chairs) or service appeal (waiters who lounge against the cash register, hands in their pockets, sniffling—they come alive at around nine-thirty, when it is their turn to sup. They congregate around a couple of the large tables at the rear of the restaurant to eat, drink beer and exchange boisterous stories).

But for far-out taste appeal, this may be the place. Some of the dishes here are singular (for New York), and most of them are very well made.

The cold pickled cabbage that in some Chinese restaurants is provided free of charge will set you back half a dollar in this one, but it's worth it. The crisp shredded cabbage is mixed with carrots, celery and fresh ginger, and the vegetables are marinated in vinegar and the hot red peppers that separate the manly food of Szechuan from the boyish delicacies eaten in the other provinces. The peppers are easy to distinguish from the other elements of the dish—they are deep-purple, and if you neglect to separate them out by color, they will separate your gums from your teeth.

Ask for the Bean Curd Mixed with Preserved Egg. Chances are you will be informed that it is "out." Insist. The waiter will inquire if you have ever eaten it. He will intimate that most customers do not like it. Tell him you like it. In fact, you may *not* like it, but the only way to find out is to eat it. This extraordinary cold dish is composed of squared chunks of bean curd, firm green eggs in jelly (chopped), scallion greens and soy sauce. It looks hideous. But the nutlike quality of the soft bean curd, the intensified flavor of the eggs, and the sharp accents of the scallions and soy sauce combine into a robust, if slightly terrifying, plate of food.

Among the hot dishes there is something called Shredded Beef Dry-Sautéed, Szechuan Style. In the preparation of this dish, the thin strands of beef are rendered black and ropy by being cooked at high heat with almost no liquid, and you'll be at a disadvantage if you're not equipped with your natural teeth. But of course this texture is intentional: each individual piece of beef is small in itself; your occasional encounter with a bamboo shoot or a strand of carrot will renew confidence in your masticatory prowess; the spicy, blackened oil that moistens and flavors the entire dish lubricates the grinding process somewhat; and the fiery flavor and mixed textures are ingeniously well balanced.

For very little money you can have Noodles with Braised Beef—a huge bowl of dark, spicy broth (the braising liquid), in which you'll find a mound of noodles, a few peas, and chunks of coarse beef that have been cooked to tenderness in the liquid. This is an inelegant but satisfying dish.

The Diced Chicken with Hot Pepper Sauce is just that, with the chicken very thoroughly browned, and one-inch lengths of scallion to add a crunchy texture to the soft chicken. If you want strong flavor instead of fire, the Sliced Prawns with Garlic Sauce are made with plenty of fresh garlic, slices of crisp water chestnut, and that tender, leafy, mushroomlike fungus with a smoky flavor called "cloud ear."

Here you'll find Columbia University professors; Greenwich Village expatriate writers; young, second-generation locals emulating the cultural adventurousness of their collegiate peers; their collegiate peers emulating the primal pleasure-seeking of the young second-generation locals.

The management of the dining rooms is cursory, and the service ranges from casual friendly to casual lousy, but the food redeems the place.

○ TAVERN ON THE GREEN

Central Park, at 67th Street and Central Park West
LUNCH AND DINNER.
Reservations, 873–3200.
Credit cards: AE, CB, DC, MC, V.
Very expensive.

When Frederick Law Olmsted built Central Park more than a century ago, he copied nature with man-made lakes, forests and meadows. The essential structures and roadways were invisible from most points in the park, as was most of the city outside. The place was truly bucolic then, right down to its birds and beasts. No Manhattanite was more than an hour from serenity. Eventually, of course, the park's horizon was disfigured by the huge buildings that became this city's specialty. And what are usually referred to as special interests managed to convert tracts of the park to nonpastoral uses.

But even if these 840 acres were thrown into permanent shade by a World Trade Center on Central Park South, and if the 79th Street Lake were drained, filled in and paved for stock-car racing, the insult to Olmsted's vision that is the new edition of Tavern on the Green would hardly be matched. This is the effulgence of vulgar ego, initials carved on a landscape. Tavern on the Green, however, is no greater threat to New York than the potentates who permitted it on city land. Hope rests with the citizens, and there are good signs—yes, the Tavern is packing them in, but the place is clogged not with New Yorkers, but with suburbanites, Texans and drunks (happily siphoned off from some of our town's more gracious eating places). The miraculous fact that some of the food served here is good makes no difference to them. Balloon strings in hand, they gobble down the tasty with the egregious in states of glazed, indiscriminate glee.

Fortunately, Warner Leroy has not yet devised a way to polka-dot the sky, and it is possible to avoid much of this establishment's posh honky-tonk by eating on the patio, which they call the Garden. Here there are several dozen white-enameled tables, many of them under fringed umbrellas. You are attended to by youngsters in garish yellow shirts, black bow ties and red aprons. They bring drinks (you pay when you receive, else you might escape over the low retaining wall into the freedom of the park), a bowl of iced raw vegetables ($5), and a selection of foods from the Garden Menu, a brief version of the Elm Tree Room Menu, which is an expurgated rendition of the Crystal Room Menu. It is all hustle out here. A waiter takes your order, collects and goes off with, he hopes, a tip. Next round you are served by someone else, very likely. This minimizes customer-server bonds; and such niceties as clearing away the detritus of previous customers or your own accidents is attended to casually at best. At night, of course, it is dark out here, the illumination that is thrown on the bottom branches of the trees makes for little light on the ground, and hapless customers, some of them heavily sedated, have been seen stumbling and tripping over low-lying furniture and the borders of the swatches of earth that surround the trees. The Garden is L-shaped, and the best thing about it is that it is wrapped around the glass-walled Crystal Room, for the Crystal Room is a three-ring circus in one ring, which from outside looks like a silent movie of a three-ring circus in one ring, which is fun to watch.

The Crystal Room is a circular, glass-walled room containing ten crystal chandeliers that depend from a hard ceiling of pastel plaster, the petrified top of a birthday cake. Never mind that when you arrived at the Tavern you had to stand in line to tell a couple of arrogances that you were present, in hopes of being seated at the table you reserved for this very hour; never mind that this simply meant that you had to stand on yet another line; and never mind that these delays, which took you well past the hour of your reservation, led finally to a brief, escorted stroll to a table not yet made up. The simple facts are that people in glass houses shouldn't sing "Happy Birthday"; in this place you are sure to be serenaded with three or four shrieked, tuneless renditions of it per dinner; and within these hard walls every voice in the place is boosted to the tune of around eighty watts per channel. Glass, crystal, plaster, brick and hardwood floors —would anyone create a crowded restaurant room of these materials other than sadistically?

In much less demand is the Elm Tree Room (not far away, just down the corridor past the plaster reindeer). Here we have mostly wood, with brass and copper ornaments on the walls, partitions topped by long rows of golden globes the size of bowling balls, etched mirrors with park scenes of the nineteenth century. The room is roughly in two parts, the westernmost section, which includes the long curving bar, looks out on the parking lot, but when things are slow this is left unoccupied in favor of the several dozen tables near the kitchen. Now why do you suppose that is? Well, this room is a lot quieter than the Crystal Room, but when, as frequently happens, a busboy drops a tray of dishes when he collides with the dining-room side of the kitchen door, the unexpected report, like the sound of a hundred cannon in the newly improved acoustics of Avery Fisher Hall, is reflected at these very tables by a cannily positioned brick wall angled just for the purpose. Anyone who survives one of these events may sleep easy, for his cardiac arrest is not imminent.

To eat. Have a second choice ready, for half the things you order will be unavailable, often the very items the waiter recommends; and don't arrive too hungry, for there is no telling when you will be fed. Candidate for Worst Dish: Hot Pâté Périgourdine, rubbery sausages in a rubbery pastry—inedible. Contender: Quennelle of Pike with Sauce Nantua, a gelatinized and tasteless dumpling in a loud sauce that is only dimly of crayfish. Be smart: order the oysters, which are fresh; and command a pepper mill and use the lemon, for the horseradish was grated hours before and is moribund—who wants ketchup? (you get some in a thimble), and this third little cup that accompanies contains what must be a cleansing agent. Or a little less smart: Escargots Bourguignonne, about a dozen snails in a miniature frying pan that is laden with herbs in melted butter.

The menu informs you that "Tavern on the Green is proud to welcome as Chef de Cuisine the extraordinary Daniel Dunas, Recently Chef de Cuisine for 12 years at The Connaught Hotel, London." Like an idiot you therefore order Chicken Dunas, which is described as "Sautéed with Artichokes and Fresh Asparagus Velouté." You receive a half-cooked breast of chicken (it blushes within) drowning in a sauce that is little more than flour and water, some tolerable asparagus, and an artichoke heart that has been very gently simmered, for many hours, in a solution of brine and Tide. The Sweetbreads will put you in mind of the breaded veal cutlet you grew accustomed to when you were condemned to five school lunches a week.

And yet the fish is fresh, prepared to order and not overcooked, though the sauce that accompanies the Red Snapper Dijonnaise is little more than harsh mustard. And the Calf's Liver, Broiled Over Charcoal with Sage Butter is tender and accurately cooked, though the flavor of the charcoal is excessive, that of the sage imaginary.

Slivered almonds are added to the green salads, and that is not a bad note, though the dressing is too sour. A few cheeses are listed, but, as your waiter informs you at nine o'clock one evening, "Someone forgot to take it out of the icebox." Soufflés? "Sorry, we're not making them this evening." The sweet desserts are your basic plethoras. The Hazelnut Cheesecake with Strawberries must be eaten at once before it solidifies to concrete; the Chocolate Cake is insipid; something given as Praline & Strawberry Ice Cream Cake is a wedge-shaped sundae made with Hershey syrup; and the Banana Fritters come with a cinnamon sauce that tastes like a warm cinnamon lollipop soup, albeit the hot ripe bananas are pleasant in their crisp deep-fried batter.

Fashion note: diamond-studded cigarette holders are definitely in this season, as are little rhinestone butterflies directly on the lenses of the sunglasses that are on top of your hair. Dress flexibly, for the air conditioning is different things in different parts of the rooms.

The waiters are mostly young, earnest, well-meaning and really up against it in this madhouse. The wine list is extensive, and a couple of dozen of the wines have asterisks next to their names. The note informs you that these are "REASONABLY PRICED WINES." We may conclude that the others are unreasonably priced.

Your first fifteen minutes of parking are free.

★★TAVOLA CALDA DA ALFREDO

285 Bleecker Street (near Jones Street)
LUNCH AND DINNER. CLOSED WEDNESDAY.
No reservations (924–4789).
No credit cards.
Wine.
Medium-priced.

"Tavola Calda" is Italian for cafeteria, and the place does have a functional look. There are rows of little square tables in the front, a display and serving counter at the back. The walls are hung with blown-up photos of garishly costumed revelers cavorting in the presence of, and sometimes *with,* various forms of Italian food. What with green plants busily filling the front window, casually dressed waiters stretching themselves thin as they squeeze between tables, much calling and waving across the room between friends and enemies, and the traffic in and out of the kitchen colliding with the restless and hungry in the small waiting area at the rear, Tavola Calda da Alfredo is a jolly circus all around. In that waiting area, by the way, one waits not only for tables, but also for food to go—Tavola Calda was billed as mainly a take-out place when it opened, but it has not caught on as such—now it is 90 percent restaurant with a wine list, at, believe it or not, liquor-store prices. Drop by for some splendid food at reasonable prices, Italian wine at deflationary ones.

The menu reads "Stuffed Eggplant(3)," but if you are sharing with a friend, your thoughtful waiter will bring you "Stuffed Eggplant (4, small)." Sections of eggplant shell, like four-inch canoes, the exteriors blackened by a thorough baking in oil, are filled with a deeply browned and oily mixture of cheese, bread and ham, lightly spiced and sweetened. "Tomatoes Capricciose (2)" is a refreshing and simple dish consisting of two *halves* of tomato, filled with cool rice, lightly oiled, studded with bits of pro-sciutto ham and fresh parsley. Though listed further down on the menu, the Insalata Marinara, also served cool, is an eminently satisfactory first course—chunks of squid, whole scallops, slices of fresh mushrooms, and circlets of raw but tamed onion, translu-cent and slippery, all in a marinade of lemon and oil that is flavored with parsley and bay; it is a sparkling dish, astringent and brightly flavored, appetizing.

The "salads" are not what one usually thinks of as salads, and accordingly, they will often be eaten at odd junctures in one's meal. They are referred to, simply enough, as string-bean salad, cauliflower salad, broccoli salad, and asparagus salad, and depending on the whim of the proprietor, the season of the year, and the condition of the available produce, some or all of them are available daily. Of them the broccoli and cauliflower salads consist of the lightly poached vegetable, crisp and cool, in herby dressings of oil and garlic—simple and elegant food, of fresh ingredients respectfully prepared.

Alfredo's pastas are among the best in New York, at least in this one of his establish-ments. In addition to the half-dozen pasta dishes on the menu, there are usually a couple of specials of the day. To begin with a couple that are on the menu, there is, first, something called Cold Pasta e Fagioli alla Trasteverina, a version of the famous chickpea-and-pasta soup, here served cold. The beefy broth is a bit thin if you get here when the soup is still new and tepid; thick and grainy if it is a bit older and chilled. Either way it is powerfully salted, herbed (principally with Italian parsley) and teeming with crunchy chickpeas, lengths of husky tubular noodles, and shreds of meat. And then there is the Cannelloni della Trattoria, the double sheets of macaroni filled with a mixture of meat and herbs that is spiced with a heavy dose of cinnamon. The little bundles are baked in a thick meat-and-tomato sauce. Every texture is right, the pasta neither chewy nor soft, the sauce viscous without being dry, the filling tender and moist without being wet. The effect of the dish is at once nutlike and vibrant, its diverse flavors unpredictably yet perfectly blended. Among the occasional pasta specials of the day is a version of ravioli in which the pasta is filled with parsley and ricotta cheese, and served in a sauce of strong cheeses and walnuts—a singular and startling compound.

As usual, Alfredo's veal dishes are the least successful items he sells, including a Veal Française that is nicely flavored with lemon, but soggily crusted and drastically over-salted. His Chicken Scarpariello, on the other hand, consisting of chunks of chicken sautéed in oil and rosemary and served in a pan sauce made with white wine, is tender, the meat nicely browned and crisped. And sometimes there is a really extraordinary chicken dish in which the roasted and stuffed bird is served under a thick fruit sauce of black and white raisins, peaches and lemon rind. The chicken and veal dishes change from day to day—none is listed on the printed menu.

Not every restaurant offers a cheese cake of the day. You never know what you will find in or on your cheese cake at the Tavola Calda. First of all, this cake is more American than Italian—it is made with cream cheese rather than ricotta cheese, and it is baked on a graham-cracker crust. If the cheese cake is spread with blueberries or some other fruit, avoid it, for the heavy and dry cake is not made any lighter or moister by a topping. But if you have lucked out, and the cheese cake is filled with candied fruits and raisins, have it, for the moist fruits that have sunk down to the crust are the perfect juicy foil to the solid cake. You can also have strawberries and cream.

★ TAVOOS

30 West 52nd Street
LUNCH, MONDAY TO FRIDAY; DINNER, MONDAY TO SATURDAY. CLOSED SUNDAY.
Reservations, 541–7777.
Credit cards: AE, CB, DC, MC, V.
Medium-priced.

The prefabricated Arabian Nights posh, not grand to begin with, is further undone by canned music and the slightly dizzying sight of a turbulent floor, which turns out to be undulating broadloom (red, gold and black); when it gives a little under your foot here, it pops up a little there. The walls are deep-red, the banquettes and armchairs are upholstered in plumply tufted wool, all is illuminated by dim lights that are deeply recessed in the ceiling. The lengthy taper on your table is lighted when you sit, making for a silly little ritual, as if this must be done so that your captain can see you.

The place is vast, a two-story jeweled barroom at the front, a glass-enclosed kitchen at the rear, which seems to be on the next block. When business is slow these extensive spaces are dreary, but the crowds that occasionally come offset the bleak expanse. And the food is interesting, much of it good.

Tavoos is an Iranian restaurant, and the food, though it has similarities to Indian and Near Eastern cuisines, is in many ways singular. It is, unfortunately, much like other New York restaurant food in that many dishes seem to be prepared in advance and reheated when ordered.

Among the unusual items: an appetizer that goes by the name of Coucou Sabzi, a deep-green cake of spinach that has been powerfully flavored with dill and parsley, made crunchy with walnuts, slightly sweetened with currants—it is garnished with lemon and raw onions, and you must not chastize yourself unduly if you do not at once grasp the harmonies among these ingredients; another appetizer—this one called Kashk e Bademjan, a stew of sautéed eggplant and onions on which a hot yogurt sauce is poured, which is very loud indeed, goaty in fact, and perhaps a few preparatory drinks will help you to become intimate with it. Both these items are good with one of the special breads made here, Nan Tavoos, a hot pillow of unleavened dough that is stuffed with spiced minced chicken and vegetables—it is steamy and light.

Move along to Kabab Mahi, marinated fish that is both hot-spicy and sweet-spicy, red outside, lightly blackened here and there from its baking in a clay oven. Presumably in deference to a misapprehended local taste, it comes with lettuce and tomatoes. Megu Darbari is a preparation of shrimp with the same sweet and hot spices as in Kabab Mahi, but served in a moist dill-flavored sauce—the shrimp are firm, but neither fresh nor particularly tasty.

A handful of dishes is grouped under the heading "Our Chef KARIM Recommends." (His attitude toward the remainder of the menu is not given.) Among these is Khoreshe Fesenjan, which consists of a single breast of chicken, off the bone, in a thick sweet-and-sour sauce that is fruity, studded with walnuts and mildly spiced—very good with the rice that accompanies the main courses here. KARIM also pushes Chelo Kabab Sultani, which, you are further told, is the "national favorite of Iran." This is a dish of marinated slices of lamb that have been broiled until, unfortunately, the meat is firm, if not tough. It is flavorful, though, in the mixed-spice manner of most of the food here, and when you mingle the meat with the raw onions and raw egg that are its traditional accompaniments, you may flatter yourself that you are doing things right, even if you are not having a wonderful time. KARIM does not recommend, but you try anyway, Karisky Makhsoos—you are better off sticking with KARIM. Rare marinated lamb, substantial chunks of it, with overcooked wilted chicken livers, an incomprehensible platter of food, ornamented with lettuce and tomatoes. Whatever you have, order a side dish of Torshy Irani, a cold relish of pickled vegetables—celery, carrots, turnips and others—in a sour and spiced pickling juice. Stimulating stuff.

Only a few desserts, just one of them particularly native—Persian Pudding, a coconut-flavored custard with whipped cream. The more foreign-sounding Plumbier is a tutti frutti ice cream sherbet pineapple nut thing like those you gave up for martinis when you left school.

For some reason the place has attracted an inelegant clientele of brooding couples who wear tight tops over their ample figures and eat ploddingly. Tavoos, one guesses, had been aiming for something more chic, but the look of the place is so devoid of finesse or style that they never had a chance, particularly here in Rockefeller Center.

★★ EL TENAMPA

304 West 46th Street
LUNCH AND DINNER. CLOSED SUNDAY.
Reservations, 586–8039.
Credit card: DC.
No liquor.
Inexpensive.

The competition is dreary, so the distinction is perhaps worthy of no more than a bronze medal, but this is probably the best Mexican restaurant in New York. Difference, of course, is not superiority, and El Tenampa's menu being, as it is, experimental (by New York–Mexican-restaurant standards) does not alone win the award—just a good bit of gratitude for introducing some new dishes to the jaded town. What earns it is the brightness, freshness, just-prepared vibrance of the food, so that even the commonplace dishes seem like items you are encountering for the first time.

Kitsch and cleanliness. On the white plaster walls, a pay phone, colorful Mexican artifacts, blankets, costumes and travel posters. Unfolded napkins form white diamonds on the red table linen, you are seated on simple wooden chairs. At the rear of the little room an even littler kitchen, into which are crowded several members of the young proprietor's sizable family. In addition to his fatherly and husbandly duties, your host also serves as your waiter, delivering menus and a little basket of crisp corn chips when you arrive. He strives for a reserved dignity that borders on the sullen, but send for some guacamole to hold you while you decide what else to eat, then tell him how marvelous it is, and he is all boyish, enthusiastic cordiality. He explains that whenever possible he obtains California avocados—*so* superior to Florida's—and that each serving is prepared to order; and it must be, because it is brightly acidic and yet rich, hot, but not so that it obscures the flavor of the avocado. He also recommends the Quesadillas, a coarse dish of heavily oiled tortillas wrapped around melted cheese and served under strong tomato sauce and sour cream. Pass up such non-Mexican items as gazpacho—it arrives cold, sure enough, but only because there are four ice cubes in it—in favor of Sopa de Frijoles, a Mexican bean soup that is not particularly thick but very satisfying, a dark broth studded with black beans, onions and melted cheese.

The tortilla family is well served here, the meats and chicken in the fillings are fresh and moist, the shredded lettuce crisp, the spices pungent, the dabs of sour cream, a peculiarity of this place, a lovely cool note against the otherwise coarse food. But with luck you can get that kind of thing in acceptable versions in other local spots. But not Pipian Estilo Veracruz, a dish made either of chicken or pork, in which the tender meat is served in a peanut-butter sauce that is red with peppery spices. Nor are Chuletas de Puerco con Salsa Verde available everywhere—in fact, they are available at El Tenampa only with difficulty, for your considerate host fears you will not be able to eat these pork chops in their fiery sauce of green tomatoes, and he talks it down. This may be the hottest food in town, and you will have to scrape away all but a hint of the killing green sauce to enjoy the good meat, but as you work your way gingerly through the dish, consuming heavier and heavier doses of the spice as you go, you begin to appreciate that it is the firm texture of the meat against the powerful green tomato, more than the flavors, that makes this food. The Bistec Ranchero is a somewhat milder dish, cutlets of beef sautéed in chile sauce, served with chunks of pungent okra—earthy, satisfying food. The good rice and thick fried beans that come with the meat courses help to soften the impact of the spices. Beer is indispensable against your inevitable thirst. You may skip the desserts; the coffees are strong and fresh.

Tape-deck background music.

• TINO'S

235 East 58th Street
LUNCH, MONDAY TO FRIDAY; DINNER, DAILY.
Reservations, 751–0311.
Credit cards: AE, DC, MC, V.
Expensive.

The wholesome airiness of La Fleur (which these premises late housed) has been converted to a clubbier setting by a simple lowering of lights. The skylights, the rough-hewn beamed ceiling, the exposed brick are all in place—but when most of the illumination is from little candles on the tables, the country aspect is lost to the darkness. The mirrors that once appeared designed just to expand the room now make it seem jeweled and chic. There is a bar at the front—not much used—and a few tables around it; most of the action is in the rear, where the tables are a few steps up, which makès for a feeling of comfortable isolation.

The principal attraction of Tino's is the extensive list of pasta dishes, under which listing, by the way, there are a couple of risotto dishes—in certain parts of Italy rice dishes sometimes substitute for pasta. You may wish to look forward to this portion of the menu when you begin, for the first courses sometimes disappoint. The Mozzarella in Carrozza, for example; the deep-fried combination of cheese and bread is perfectly crisply rendered and absolutely dreadful, because it is made of American white sandwich bread and cheese that must come from the same source. The baked clams are fiercely flavored, although the clams themselves are not injured in the process. If you order the assorted hot antipasto, you will get mussels prepared the same way—in this aggressive surrounding the mussels get lost. The Scampi alla Ligure is an above-average shrimp appetizer. The shrimp themselves are crunchy and not the least tough; they are bathed in oil, livened with garlic and freshened with lemon—sparkling food. If you are restraining yourself in preparation for heavier things, the Stracciatella alla Romana is a thin broth loaded with fresh spinach, a miniature egg stirred in—invalid's food.

Rigatoni d'Oro alla Cipullo is a solid dish of two-inch lengths of heavy tubular pasta in a creamy sauce in which the principal weight is ground hot sausage—the cream is rich, the sausage loud, and the few mushrooms almost a leavening in this very satisfying and heavy number. The same form of pasta is also offered as Rigatoni all'Arrabbiata, which is given, helpfully, as "raging rigatoni." And truly, this is a fiery sauce of tomatoes and anchovies that is thick with long cooking. In both instances the rigatoni is firm yet tender. Excellent Fettuccine all'Uovo, in which the seemingly fresh egg noodles are moistened with little more than butter. One of those rice dishes goes by the name of Risotto Milanese al Tartufo. The rice is hot and oily, gently saffroned (saffron goes for $150 per pound these days) and crowned with grilled slivers of white truffle—crisp and nutlike. The whole is sprinkled with fresh parsley, making a simple and elegant dish.

Dreadful Pollo alla Tino Scarpa, in which the artichokes are canned, the mushrooms jarred, the chicken frozen. Poor Mignonette Peperonata, in which the filet mignon is second-rate beef, the sautéed red and green peppers in tomato more a disguise than a sauce. Not very good Saltimbocca alla Sorrentina, made with a decent enough veal, but under a layer of tasteless melted cheese and over a layer of undistinguished ham—the hefty handful of rosemary that was thrown on helps very little.

True Italian cheese cake—dry ricotta cheese, lots of candied fruit, all heavy, almost puddinglike, and pleasantly filling. The zabaglione is made to order; it is heavily wined and it is at once hot and light. You can, if you wish, have it with good strawberries. Beyond that there is an excessive Zuppa Inglese and the usual ice cream things.

Make it an evening of pasta and you will spend less and like it more—and when things are not too busy, the kitchen will prepare half-orders of pasta.

★★TORREMOLINOS

230 East 51st Street
LUNCH, MONDAY TO FRIDAY; DINNER, MONDAY TO SATURDAY. CLOSED SUNDAY.
Reservations, 755–1862.
Credit cards: AE, CB, DC, MC.
Medium-priced.

White stucco walls, bare brick, high beamed ceilings, lofty archways between rooms, old iron street lanterns, a fireplace, hanging hams and sausages and cheese and onions, shelves of crockery, a few copper pans, an old-city setting, suggesting a Spanish street café under a portico. The tables before you sound an elegant note in the earthy setting—white cloths set with brilliant-red napkins, tall red candles, long-stemmed red carnations in slender vases.

In the kitchen they start with good ingredients; they do not misuse them, sometimes they even improve them—never brilliantly, but often artfully.

If you come once, the appetizer to begin with is Gambas al Ajillo. In a little earthenware pot you get about ten little shrimps, crunchy morsels, in a thick sauce of oil, red pepper and minced fresh garlic, all very loud and lovely. You tilt the pot so that when the sauce forms a deep pool on one side, you can completely immerse each shrimp before you eat it. Since there will be a good bit of the pungent liquid left over after you have finished the shrimps, you polish that off with bread—the bread itself is terrible, but its tastelessness is utterly overwhelmed by the pepper and garlic. The Mejillones Salsa Verde are no match for the shrimps, but these mussels in a so-called green sauce are pretty good. The mussels are fresh, clear-tasting, tender; the sauce, however, is bland—not much sherry, not much parsley—and it tastes better straight than over the mussels because the mussel flavor obscures the sauce. Nevertheless, a pretty good dish. Strong black-bean soup, creamy and winy and well-flavored with pepper, thick and satisfying.

Mignonette de Ternera Riojana is veal sautéed with Rioja wine. The veal is thick, pale, tender, nicely browned in the sautéeing. It is bedecked with lengths of Spanish ham and garnished with white asparagus, a vegetable the canned version of which is not bad, and an artichoke heart, the canned version of which is. The good sauce is winy and herbed.

Filetes de Lenguado Granada is described on the menu as "Filets of Sole Sautéed with Banana and topped with Hollandaise Sauce." The sauce is not hollandaise, but the dish is good anyway, the fish fresh and fluffy. The mild white sauce and the sweet ripe bananas cover the fish and are browned under the broiler. The main courses are accompanied by good vegetables—crisp string beans, fresh sweet peas.

All the standard Spanish desserts, of course, but also a few others: a rich, wet chocolate cake that is liquored and covered with crisp almonds and powdered sugar —very good; and strawberries in a sweet sherry sauce—the sauce is a bit icky, but the strawberries are ripe and juicy.

As the evening wears on, the guitarist switches from his soulful flamenco repertoire to the requests he receives at the bar and at the tables. He does an unfortunate Guantanamera, but it brings in the tips. Sometimes (not often) he takes a break, because one of those trios of Spanish "students"—mandolin, guitar and tambourine—stop here on their rounds and fill the place with their healthy baritone voices in renditions of what are purported to be Spanish student songs. Are Spanish students allowed to *have* student songs? At any rate, it seems the students never return to their studies, because they are doing too well financing them with their nightly tours of New York's Spanish restaurants.

A happy place.

★★ TOSCANA

246 East 54th Street
LUNCH, MONDAY TO FRIDAY; DINNER, MONDAY TO SATURDAY. CLOSED SUNDAY.
Reservations, 371–8144.
Credit cards: AE, MC, V.
Very expensive.

Fifteen or so little tables in a pearly-white room, along one side a cognac-colored banquette, above that a mirrored wall, to add a slight feel of spaciousness to the wee place. The appointments are few and simple—brass chandelier and wall sconces, their lights softened by tiny white lampshades; fresh flowers in little bowls on the crisp, white-linened tables; through the horizontal windows high on the walls, you can see the ivy in the outdoor window boxes. There is a small handsome barroom. All is orderly, including your tuxedoed waiters, your white-tied captain—and even you, signor, for gentlemen must wear jackets and ties.

Happily, you may begin with simple perfection, Peperoni Arrostiti, red peppers and green peppers roasted in oil and garlic. The peppers are softened but retain much of their original crunch, and they are infused with the pure succulence of the oil and the warming fragrance of copious fresh garlic. For a bit more complexity there is Zuppa di Vongole (steamed clams), which in the white (no-tomato) version is served in a forthrightly garlicked, steaming broth of wine and the liquid from the clams—the littlenecks are fresh and tender, and a fistful of fresh parsley adds a sweet fragrance to the sturdy dish. The baked clams, with the usual bread crumbs and oil, are made with more dried oregano than any dish needs, but the clams themselves are again impeccably fresh.

Luckily, the house will sell you half-orders of pasta. Most basic of the half-dozen versions offered is Spaghettini al Pomodoro, perfectly cooked spaghetti in a thick tomato sauce—bits of garlic here and there, chunks of fresh tomato there and here—a splendid dish as is, and just as good, in a richer and heavier way, if you spoon on plenty of ground cheese. The Paglia e Fieno (green and white noodles) are prepared in a more elaborate but equally well balanced manner—the pale noodles are distinctly eggy, the green ones retain faintly the flavor of spinach, and the sauce, of mild cheese, much heavy cream, bits of ham and onion, and an abundance of fresh sweet peas, is at once rich and light. The pasta is sauced at a side stand, and reaches you hot.

The menus of New York's Italian restaurants sport little lamb, so you leap at Costolette di Agnello Fiorentina. You are not to blame, for there was no place to look before you leapt. These are loin chops, not rib chops; and you wanted them medium-rare, but they arrive so promptly that they must have been previously cooked, and they are past the medium-rare point. The spinach they are situated on, however, is the genuine, fresh vegetable, and the meat, overdone though it may be, is of good quality—you can, in the Tuscan way, liven the lamb with a squeeze of lemon. You may properly conclude that the main courses are a thin cut below the rest of the menu. Take, if you will, the Vitello alla Zingara, a perfectly good serving of nicely sautéed veal which is rather done in by its potent sauce of tomatoes, ham, mushrooms and peas—all very sturdy and satisfying food, you understand, but an unkindness to the veal. That meat is much more kindly handled in Scallopine Toscana, wherein the delicate flavor of the meat is distinctly discernible beneath a creamy sauce studded with artichokes, mushrooms and still more of those little peas. The Piccata di Vitello is a better treatment still—the buttery meat just lightly flavored with lemon and parsley. The striped bass is steamed with tomatoes, wine and a couple of clams and mussels—these last strengthen the steaming liquid and heighten the fish.

A few desserts, including well-chosen strawberries that you can have with lemon and sugar, or with wine, or with cream; Crêpes Normande l'Armorique—around the side stand a cluster of tuxedoes, the copper pan over the alcohol flame, the scent of caramel fills the little place as the sugar melts, then the aromas of heated citrus, citrus liqueurs and brandy—the crêpes are perhaps a bit heavy, and the sauce a trifle thick, but the dessert is good, surely festive, if lacking finesse. They make a good zabaglione.

On slow nights the help is too much with you, changing ashtrays with every flick of your cigarette, filling your water glass after every sip. And the tables are too small for these outsized wineglasses, and the wine list too simple for such pretentions.

★ TOUT VA BIEN

311 West 51st Street
LUNCH AND DINNER. CLOSED SUNDAY.
Reservations, 974–9051.
Credit cards: AE, V.
Inexpensive.

This is a seedy little shop overseen by a hustling little craggy Gallic satyr—in a padded-shoulder, double-breasted suit—and a handful of family Gorgons—molded hair and one dubious eye apiece. The waitresses attend, address and carry with commendable forthrightness, the corpulence of a couple of them severe trials to their brief, snug uniforms. All this in a room of maple-stained pine paneling, a row of tables down the middle, a parallel row along one wall, maybe fifteen in all. Running half the length of the opposite wall, the bar, at which local French sit and gossip gutturally, behind which the color TV sometimes flickers. Occasionally a long-quiet tippler emits a stream of French invective. It is as if he has been constructing it during his silent, meditative drinking, and his knowing bar mates croak and cackle appreciatively. Tout Va Bien is a family affair, wrapped in habit and shipped here from any of a thousand French back streets, complete with French café music from the ancient jukebox. On occasion one of the overseers stops, looks around at every person and object in the place, like a primitive foreman. If the comic crockery, map of France, trophies or theatrical photos are in any detail out of place, it will be noticed, as surely as would the disappearance of the phone-booth-size air-conditioning machine that stands just inside the front door. This is the tangible source of livelihood, and it is watched over like the farm ox.

You receive a glass dish of celery, olives, carrot sticks and ice cubes, all crisp, and a menu, limp. From the latter you will learn that the selection of first courses is both limited and commonplace, including a pâté that is little more than high-class liverwurst, though good for that. Of the few other appetizers only the Haricots Blancs are of interest—you receive a substantial platter of the little white beans. They are thoroughly cooked, so they are tender, but they retain their crunchiness; they are blanketed by a layer of slivered raw onions, recently sliced and still strong, and the two vegetables are bound together in a vinaigrette that is mostly mild oil and strong mustard —all very good. If neither the beans nor the pâté grabs you, share a main course as an appetizer—one of these orders of Moules Marinière will appetize as many as four. You receive a great mound of tender, steamed mussels, in their shells, piled in a deep plate, under it about a pint of primitive, briny broth, alive with chunks of garlic—this liquid may be slurped up with a spoon or soaked up with the chunks of toasted crust you will find in your basket of bread.

"Bouillabaisse" is emblazoned across the menu cover in big black letters, suggesting that it is an item in which Tout Va Bien specializes. And, in fact, their version of this dish justifies their pride, though for some reason, despite its being the best food in the house, it is served, in obedience to custom, on Fridays only. You are probably unaware that the conditions of the New York real estate market are responsible for violations of certain traditions in re the serving of bouillabaisse. New York rents are high. For adequate profits many restaurants compress numerous customers into compact spaces. To accomplish this requires that customers be seated at wee tables and, accordingly, there is insufficient room for a broad plate of bouillabaisse broth and another of fish and shellfish to be served simultaneously. You get the plate of broth first, a deep inch of steaming, vaguely orange liquid, oceanic, strong of lobster and lobster shell, spiced with saffron, hefty crusts of bread therein. You may, if you wish, intensify this broth with dabs of aïoli, for a huge glistening slab of the powerfully garlicked mayonnaise is served with the soup. When you have dispensed with that, a pot of solid food is brought and your waitress ladles onto your plate half a small lobster, mussels and shrimp, striped bass. It is not all perfect—on one occasion the shrimp are perhaps a bit overcooked, on another the mussels—but nothing is really bad, the bass is impeccably fresh, the lobster consistently tender and rich, all the ingredients well-flavored of the spicy broth. And if the first delivery doesn't take care of you, that pot holds enough for a second serving.

Tout Va Bien is relatively inexpensive. The food is not vastly less costly than at several other West Side French places, but many of the house dishes here are intrinsically cheap, among them Tête de Veau, not an item they stand in line for, because its translation is calf's head. This strong meat is rimmed with firm jelly; after a long soaking in cool water it is poached in stock, and several chunks of it are wrapped in linen and brought to you—you moisten the meat with a strong vinaigrette that has been laced with parsley, all of which makes for a rich and oily dish. It is served with some of New York's best French fries—tender, thin sticks, lightly crisped, lightly salted, nice foils for the soured fatty meat. Equally unappealing to casual visitors is the ivory-colored honeycombed substance known as tripe—stomach to you. It is served here as part of a gamy stew in which tomatoes, onions and peppers predominate—potatoes are added near the end of the cooking, which thickens the already sturdy dish. You can get a decent Steak au Poivre—not the primest meat available, but tender and accurately cooked, the coarse granules of black pepper embedded deeply and dominating the dish, the sauce of brandy, butter and pan scrapings tasty but relegated to the background by the pepper.

Dreary desserts, including Italian ice cream things; pastries that may as well remain in the refrigerator; a mousse that is without air.

If you have an anniversary coming up, know that "Happy Birthday" is on the jukebox, with a two-beat pause for the name of the celebrant.

• TRATTORIA

200 Park Avenue (Pan Am Building)
LUNCH AND DINNER. CLOSED SUNDAY.
Reservations, MO 1–3090.
Credit cards: AE, CB, DC, MC, V.
Medium-priced.

The Trattoria is a great big flashy place—a drinking bar at the west end, near the entrance from the Pan Am Building (it gets some of the overflow from Charlie Brown's); a great, circular serving counter where food is displayed with pride that is only occasionally justified; rows of handsome leather-upholstered booths; tables with garish but pleasing orange-and-chrome chairs; a wall of black-and-white photo posters of the swinging world we're lucky enough to live in; gleaming candy-striped hanging lamps; deep-blue walls; red pillars; shiny floors—contrast, glare, action! The service, on the other hand, is sluggish; the food, save for the pizza, an occasional pasta and the desserts, is very ordinary, and some of the waiters are simply dumb:

"We'll have one baked clams and one Pizza Trattoria, and after that one spaghetti with oil and garlic, and a Veal Francese."

"The clams take fifteen minutes."

"Then bring the pizza first."

"The pizza takes fifteen minutes too."

The clams are not bad (they come in about two minutes)—whole cherrystones, a bit overcooked sometimes, but with a nice, simple breading moistened with oil and flavored with garlic. Your individual eight-inch Pizza Trattoria is of the thin bread type, easy on the cheese and tomato sauce, with sautéed fresh mushrooms, strong fennel-flavored sausages and green peppers—very tasty. But the pasta dishes here are utterly unpredictable, though sometimes you can get one that is wonderful. On one day a fettuccine is not only *al dente* but brittle; another day you order spaghetti with oil and garlic, and the simple sauce is just perfect, with its slightly browned garlic and about half a fistful of fresh green parsley to a portion, but the pasta itself is limp and glutinous; another time your Spaghetti al Pesto is so devoid of sauce that to have any taste at all it must be rescued with three heaping spoons of the good grated Parmesan cheese served here.

Nevertheless, on balance, those are the kinds of dishes to have here—hot appetizers, pizzas, pastas, sandwiches, omelettes. The main courses of meat or chicken are simply lifeless, like photographs of food—ordorless and tasteless, but perfectly prepared. The green salad is of crisp romaine lettuce, with oregano and a strong wine-vinegar dressing.

The desserts are incredible. This place serves the most intensely chocolate-flavored ice cream in creation, and then they have the splendid audacity not merely to bury it in fresh whipped cream but to roll the thing in thick shavings of pure, black chocolate —this is called Tartufo. Something called Nugatina is a scoop of vanilla and a scoop of chocolate, covered with whipped cream and pine nuts, over which chocolate sauce has been poured—all topped with a hazelnut meringue. Of course if mere heavenly sweets bore you, there is a Zuppa Inglese here that is, it is true, sweet, but also soaked in rum, studded with candied fruit and with lumps of chocolate the size of golf balls, all covered with a lightly browned, soft and moist meringue.

• "21" CLUB

21 West 52nd Street
LUNCH AND DINNER. CLOSED SUNDAY.
Reservations, JU 2–7200.
Credit cards: AE, CB, DC, MC.
Very expensive.

Jack and Charlie's, as the cognoscenti like to call it, is probably the most successful culinary sleight-of-hand ever carried out. It has been going on since Prohibition, and the flow of customers is inexhaustible. Yet anyone who attends this place once, and then voluntarily does it again, has got to have been fooled by the reputation, the glittering clientele or the intensely masculine interior, because the food, frantically tended flames at the serving tables notwithstanding, is nothing but Stouffer's at three times the price, from the Pâté of Chicken Livers "21" (an airless mousse much like peanut butter) through the Terrapin Maryland (turtle à la king) to the Kersen Aardbeien en ys Van Urk (berries, including white strawberries, with pineapple and raspberry sherbet, in tutti-frutti sauce).

To the credit of the place, the ingredients are of decent quality, but the preparation of the food is so uniformly lackluster, and its service so pedestrian, that the only thing to be admired here, in fact to be wondered at in awe, is the list, lengthy and starry, of gourmets, epicures, columnists, dining-out authorities, travel books and restaurant guides that not only take "21" seriously but treat it with a respect usually reserved for the central figures in the world's religions.

Everyone "knows" that it's very difficult to get into "21." In fact, there is nothing to it: make a reservation and show up. It's true that the man at the desk will greet you coolly if he doesn't know you; that the coat-room attendant, if she sizes you up for a dodo, will give you your ticket and say "Don't lose it"; that you may be ignored for a while before you are transferred to one of the host's underlings; that the latter may be hard to follow as he leads you, without looking back, to a table through a thick crowd of black-jacketed captains (from whom he is impossible to distinguish); and that your captain will take your order willingly enough, but may well answer your questions, if any, with a degree of impatience that is only partly the result of his ignorance of the menu; but all that must be weighed against the security that comes of the certain knowledge that the food at "21," though tasteless, is harmless. This is a clean place.

It's best to pass up the more ambitious dishes for simpler food, though this is no guarantee of results. There is no faulting the clams or oysters, but the ratatouille appetizer, for example, is little more than a dish of poached vegetables, whereas, on the other hand, the clam-juice cocktail ($1.75) is certain not to disappoint. The Blue Lake Bean Salad tastes like cold overcooked beans, but the Bismarck herring is firm and tart. At $3.25 you can actually get unripe avocado. There is much Caesar salad eaten here as an appetizer. To call it Caesar salad is to take a liberty; to serve it at all is to take license—decent greens in an eggless, overly sour dressing. The cold Sénégalaise soup is served here in a bloodless version (imagine a few grains of curry powder combined with sour cream and minced chicken) that would be a big hit at Patricia Murphy's.

You can get good roast beef here; and the sautéed brook trout with capers is fresh and flaky, if not inspired. But "21" is supposed to be a big deal for game. If you order partridge, pheasant and quail, you can be certain that they will be given an all-American roasting to the point of stringy dryness of flesh within, limp dejection of skin without. The pitchers of currant jelly (Ann Page?) and white sauce (Wondra and milk) are actually welcome.

There is a "21" Burger listed as a *Spécialité*. (Your waiter may allow as how it is the most popular dish in the place.) This is the final triumph—the world's most ordinary dish, a hamburger, prepared without any imagination, served with a sheaf of hangdog string beans and peddled as a specialty of one of the most expensive restaurants on earth, for which board chairmen, pols, celebrities of stage, screen and tube point the noses of their liveried chauffeurs toward West 52nd Street.

You are cordially warned that soufflés take an hour. So you order the Crêpes Soufflées "21," which take only thirty minutes, except that they take an hour. (How long would the soufflé take? Is the rule to double, or to add, thirty minutes?) The Crêpes Soufflées turn out to be a bit of brandied soufflé filling in pancakes (so far not bad), served with a congealed crème Anglaise that lacks utterly the sharp flavor of cooked milk but tastes, rather, like an ulcer patient's custard. The apple pancake is better— the same pancake, filled with pretty good stewed apples.

There is a low-ceilinged barroom on the main floor, with a number of tables nearby —this is the informal part of "21." Upstairs there are wood-paneled walls, red linen, red leather chairs and banquettes, silver urns and plates on shelves and on the walls, sporting prints, horsy wallpaper—the effect is of a hunting lodge in the form of a mansion. Where else can you see, at a table for six, six gray suits?

★ UKRAINIAN RESTAURANT

140 Second Avenue (near 9th Street)
LUNCH, SATURDAY AND SUNDAY; DINNER, DAILY.
Weekend reservations only, 533–6765.
No credit cards.
Inexpensive.

This establishment, occupying a back room on the ground floor in the Ukrainian National Home, has been here since the Year One, as has the Home. Recently, however, there has been a change—the place now announces itself to the public, by way of signs out front and advertisements. As the former status of Ukrainian Private Club has been changed to Place of Public Accommodation, the Ukrainian Restaurant, to repeat its eminently definitive title, is now fat for the fire. Sizzle, sizzle.

Follow your nose down the broad entrance hallway to a dining room done in Rural Motel, with plain wooden floor, knotty-pine walls and much in the way of mirrors. To the recorded tootling strains of the "Pennsylvania Polka" and other tunes suitable for accordion rendition, you escort yourself to a table of your choice. The red-and-white checkered tablecloths are protected from your carelessness by State Quiz paper place mats, in which outlines of the forty-eight continental states are printed helter-skelter on the place mat, instead of in their correct geographical relationships to each other. You are required to guess the names of the states *from their outline shapes alone.* (Each outline is numbered, and you turn the place mat upside down, if you dare, to learn the correct answers.) Obtaining the assistance of your waitress is no fairs.

Those waitresses, by the way, wear Ukrainian native blouses. And the menu lists native food, which attracts clusters of middle-aged Slavic entrepreneurs (plump men in porkpie fedoras), couples of elderly Slavs (he in his rough broadcloth going-out suit, she with a cameo at the throat of her black silken dress), younger, courting Slavs (his hair plastered down, hers plastered up), toward closing time the late-nighters (she gowned, he sharkskinned), and lone Slavs (they drag out their dinners with paperback mysteries until it is time to return to the little pad and the little TV).

Food. Like "Jelly Pigs Feet" (presumably feet from a jelly pig), which consists of a block of murky aspic, cool, gamy and salty, in which are embedded tender shreds of meat, the buckwheat cereal called kasha, chunks of carrot, and sections of the cartilege which, when boiled, produced the binder that forms the jelly from the broth. It is a cool and rather invigorating dish, but a bit off-putting to some, like one's first oyster. Like stuffed cabbage, an egg of warm, ground and flavored meat in a shell of tender cabbage leaves. Like pierogi, a mildly seasoned patty of meat and kasha enveloped in a noodle pouch. Like "Ukrainian Borscht," the nationalistic modifier suggesting, correctly, that the soup is hot; moreover, it is sour and strong, imbued with the deep flavor of long-cooked bones.

One genius orders "Lazanski," convinced it will turn out to be nothing but emigrated lasagna, and as the almost total decline of poetic justice would have it, is close. One order of this substance is ballast for a small boat, and the genius ate it all—the fact that it tastes wonderful playing only a small part in this gluttonous feat. Lazanski consists of noodles, fried onions, slivers of oiled cabbage, plenty of soft cheese, the entire production well-salted and seasoned with cinnamon. It is easy to eat also because it is slippery.

For something even earthier, there is boiled beef, served on kasha, all under a sweetish white sauce. (Suggest that the sauce be canceled.) The meat is abundant, fibrous and gamy, and the kasha, pebbly and grainy, is a fine foil to the beef. In much the same spirit, different only in the details, are the goulash, potted veal shank, roast pork, &c.

The listing is not replete with tempting desserts, nor, for that matter, with any other kind. Cherry blintzes are not strictly a dessert, and with this doughy wrapper around these insipidly sweetened fruits, do not try to reinterpret them that way. Nor, for that matter, is the "Home Made Apple Cake" much more than stewed and sugared apples between undistinguished piecrusts.

The waitresses confess that despite the ethnic character of their garb, they are neither Ukrainian nor anything neighboring it. They carry the food from the kitchen on rectangular plastic trays, which they balance on one hand as they serve you. This is hard to do, and instead of lowering your dish to the place in front of you by lowering the hand that is holding it, they do something like a curtsy, lowering everything, by bending the knee and hip joints. This is excellent exercise.

★★UNCLE TAI'S HUNAN YUAN

1059 Third Avenue (near 63rd Street)
LUNCH AND DINNER.
Reservations, TE 8–0850.
Credit cards: AE, DC.
Medium-priced.

Squab, ham, rabbit, oysters, venison, lamb, pheasant, and captains in tuxedoes are rarities in Chinese restaurants in New York; for all but the last of which a bit of gratitude to Uncle Tai may be in order. The captains here are mechanical at best, and if you are a bit of a boor yourself, they have apparently been waiting for you, for there is nothing they like better than trading discourtesies with, say, the ill-dressed. When they see someone who looks like a displaced Pell Street noodle-shop frequenter, they stiffen. They are accustomed to families taking an hour or two off from homework and TV, discussing tales of Stuyvesant High and IBM and the difficulty of getting a cab outside Bloomie's at five.

The house is in on the act. They, too, wish to deny their origins. For example, they want to pretend that this is not a Chinese restaurant. Not only do they have these floor officials dressed in formal black-and-whites, but the wallpaper on the walls looks like something in a small-town rooming house (that is, an American, not a Chinese, small town); the hanging plants are very much the healthfood restaurant trappings of this day; the spotlights mounted under the ceiling cast the flashy glow of the steak-joint-and-rock-Muzak places that are dotted around the East Seventies. Perhaps it is all an experiment, for the grotesque icicle chandeliers, which illumined this establishment before its light renovation, are still in place. They do not turn them on, but presumably they could if the nostalgia movement catches up with Sino-Grotesk.

The Fried Oysters are battered and breaded, deep-fried until deeply browned, rapidly, so the oysters are warmed without being at all toughened. But unless you start with a tasty oyster, you will not end up with one, and this is just a well-made dish that suffers from its indifferent ingredient. Begin instead with Cold Peppered Rabbit: strands of oiled meat, sturdily spiced, over thin, crisp lengths of cucumber, the dish garnished with sprigs of fragrant coriander leaves—lively food. Or with Sliced Chicken with Hot Oil: moist slivers of good pale meat in a dark-brown sauce that is hot and winy, studded with scallion greens—this sauce has saturated the chicken, making the meat at once juicy and strong.

Proceed to Sliced Hunan Vegetable Pie, a peasant's imitation of Peking Duck, in which crunchy rectangles of browned vegetable wafer are wrapped in pancakes with hoisin sauce and florets of scallions; it is held between the fingers and eaten. The wafers have the crunchy warmth of hot fried vegetables done in good oil, and the sweet sauce and strong scallions set them off perfectly. Continue on to Sautéed Sliced Pheasant, a sweet meat here mingled with fresh ginger, snow peas, scallions, each texture and flavor clear, and yet wedded to the others in this heavily peppered sauce. Move along to Sliced Venison with Garlic Sauce, another sweet meat, this one mingled with crunchy red and green peppers, water chestnuts and scallions, big floppy mushrooms, all in a moistening of dark oil that is alive with the scent and flavor of fresh garlic.

Sliced Hunan Lamb is one of the dishes that made Hunan food a hit when it first hit town at the turn of the decade. It is nowhere made as well as it was then, but it is still good food in the version served here: substantial slices of meat, the size of silver dollars, oiled and tender and pungently accented with the hot peppers that are distributed among the slices, all flavored with garlic—the crisp taste of watercress and the sharp contrast of scallions point up the richness of the meat. Missing is the careful sautéing this dish used to get, so that each sliver of meat was browned outside, pink inside.

The Frogs' Legs Hunan Style are well-prepared, tender, moist, crusted and oiled, bits of scallion clinging to the morsels of meat. But these are frozen frogs' legs, their flavor has been tamed.

Dishes that take extra time to prepare are discouraged, particularly if ordered not long before closing, or if the place is busy.

You can do your shopping here. Every rack at the midtown department stores is represented of an evening, a touch of Barney's too.

○ UNITED STATES STEAKHOUSE CO.

120 West 51st Street
LUNCH, MONDAY TO FRIDAY; DINNER, MONDAY TO SATURDAY. CLOSED SUNDAY.
Reservations, 757–8800.
Credit cards; AE, CB, DC, MC, V.
Very expensive.

Rockefeller Center's United States Steakhouse is a theme restaurant. Its themes are the American peanut, the American hero, and meat.

The peanut. There is a pause at the end of the day's occupations known as the cocktail hour, and there is a big barroom here to which lots of the guys from upstairs in the Time-Life Building repair. They stand around the huge circular counter-height oak tables that bear giant bowls of unshelled peanuts, and they light their cigarette lighters, hoist long cold ones and crack peanuts, all without looking. They drop the peanut hulls at their feet, toss the seeds between their teeth and slowly grind them with their huge molars, their jaws rippling. After a while they are ankle-deep in peanut shells, and by seven o'clock this place looks like the elephant house.

The peanut also shows up on the menu, in cream of peanut soup, which has vegetables in it, and which is every bit as execrable as you fear; and it shows up in six-nut pie, which is every bit as etc.

The hero. Photographs of famous domestic and imported Americans hang on the walls. And boy, are they funny. Each and every one of them has the same caption, in comic-strip balloons, painted in over the head of the subject! And the constant caption (this will kill you) is: "Best £?&.:* 0%!¢ steak I ever tasted!" Cute? For example, there is a picture of Marlon Brando in *The Godfather,* and instead of saying whatever it was he was saying in that particular never-to-be-forgotten scene, what he is saying is: "Best £?&.:* 0%!¢ steak I ever tasted!" And believe it or not, there is a picture of John Vliet Lindsay looking down on the bean of Abraham Beame, and *Lindsay* is saying it. And then there is this very smiling picture of Eisenhower, Dulles and MacArthur (looking as if they just castrated Truman), and *they're* saying it. Well, you walk along the walls, and it goes on and on, a laugh a frame. Leo Durocher, Bob Hope dancing with Rocky Marciano, Marilyn Monroe flashing an acre of thigh, Franklin Roosevelt, Cardinal Spellman, Superman, Muhammad Ali, Sophia Loren in bed with Marcello Mastroianni, Dean Martin. All the greats and near-greats. The animal kingdom is spared.

Meat. Meat is served in the dining room, which features hefty wood partitions around leather-upholstered booths, big tables, thick red carpeting, and waiters and waitresses who wear aprons of chain mail, no less. Some take their work seriously, but many are between jobs, leaning on your booth or table with the insouciance of members of your party who just happen to be standing.

The best part of your dinner is on the house—a basket of warm potato chips that are crisp and not too greasy. Like all good potato chips, they are habit-forming, and efforts to restrain yourself for fear of "ruining your dinner" are ill-advised.

Everything else is fee-for-service, including an appetizer of tartar steak, a golf-ball-size dollop of raw beef, dry and underseasoned, though of freshly ground meat. The clams and oysters are usually fresh but rarely sparkling; and the shrimp are soggy and icy. The cocktail sauce with which these are garnished is itself garnished, with horseradish that was grated back when. Your waiter warns you that "Today's Stuffed Vegetable" is hot. "Lemme warn you," says he, "it's hot." It's cold.

Cold steak salad, at its best, is one of the highest achievements of the lowly art of rescuing leftovers—crisp vegetables and a tangy dressing converting last night's excessive dinner into today's light lunch. Here the procedure is reversed. Steak broiled especially for the salad is made to seem week-old with strands of tired greens and bland cheese and a lengthy immersion in the vinaigrette, which makes the meat marinated, not dressed.

The broiled steaks and lamb chops are not bad (the latter served with a stainless-steel jigger of cold green jelly), but they do not approach the balance of firmness, tenderness and moisture you find in Manhattan's best steakhouses. The chopped steaks are mushy rather than ground, and by late in the evening the roast beef, bland to begin with, is no longer rare. Avoid the immense lobsters, which are dry and fibrous. What they call "Hashed Browns With Apple" are amorphous chunks of deep-fried potato to which the bits of apple are irrelevant. No civilized person would insert decent butter into this establishment's baked potatoes. The mysterious ingredient in your salad dressing is Yankee Stadium mustard.

Cakes and pies that might be tolerable to obsessively sweet teeth are served at ruinous icebox temperatures. You cannot quarrel with the listing "Fresh Strawberries," for the word "fresh" does not connote "ripe."

★★ IL VALLETTO

133 East 61st Street
LUNCH, MONDAY TO FRIDAY; DINNER, MONDAY TO SATURDAY. CLOSED SUNDAY.
Reservations, 838–3939.
Credit cards: AE, CB, DC, MC, V.
Expensive.

This is not Nanni's North, though Il Valletto is, in fact, the recent undertaking of Mr. Nanni, proprietor of the very popular Nanni's, of East 46th Street. But here (on the premises of the blessedly defunct Running Footman) Nanni has invested some of his midtown cash in uptown posh. If you dread this address for memories of the stuffy old Footman, be assured that no trace of that dreary mortuary remains. The Italian warmth has been transfused into the premises until the entire place glows pink and brown and gold. From the moment you become hooked on the mixed nuts (no peanuts) which accompany your apéritif at the massive polished bar, you grasp that Nanni is here expressing a side of himself that was never in evidence in the travel-poster-adorned little place downtown. Through the bar to the first room—small, softly lit, the walls covered with casually striped, glowing velvet, a handful of tables, a grouping of special places. Through that to the main dining room, forty pink-linened tables under chandeliers of lights in red shades hanging from a plum-colored ceiling a couple of stories over your head. There are heavy Italian murals set into the ivory walls—you need not look up at them. One thing in common with Nanni's: the place is an amplifier—a bit of conversation hits you from across the room, and a few minutes later, still bouncing around these hard walls, it hits you again. It makes everyone, even your host, cheerful, and he calls your companion *"Cara bambina,"* though she is well past weaning.

Another thing in common with Nanni's: much is made of what is not on the menu, and much of what is not on the menu is the best food in the house. As it is not on the menu, it may not have an official title, so the waiter suggests, with technical correctness, a hot antipasto which, on description, turns out to be a hot seafood salad—dozens of tiny scallops and a lesser number of shrimps, lightly floured, sautéed, with a bit of garlic, in oil and wine which have been simmered down to a smooth and oceanic broth. The little scallops are sweet and rich, the shrimps crisp, the dish just about perfect. Also not on the menu, but on display at the entrance to the large room, the cold antipasto —the principal attraction here is the *cold* seafood salad, a sparkling intermingled collection of chunks of lobster (!), tiny mussels, shrimps and onions, all in a limpid vinaigrette—the impeccable ingredients make this an extremely refreshing and stimulating appetizer. In nearby trays there are marinated artichokes and roasted peppers, good food, the artichoke leaves cured to the point where they have lost all their fibrousness, the peppers firm and sweet.

If you are granted one dish in this restaurant before you are added to the unemployed and consigned to your own kitchen, choose yet another that is not on the menu—gnocchi, with what the waiters have been trained to call "Nanni's special sauce." These plump potato dumplings are, miraculously, at once firm and ephemeral. The lightest pressure of your tongue and palate against the pale shells effects instantaneous disappearance. But the flavor of the sauce lingers, a slightly sour and yet creamy tomato sauce, with slivers of ham, tiny peas and herbs. The dish is sprinkled with cheese and very briefly put under the broiler before it is served, creating a lightly browned, gauzelike veil which adds a sharp, heady flavor to the otherwise gentle dish.

Your standard restaurant freak is, of course, frustrated by the almost universal "ordering off the menu" practiced at Il Valletto. Where is the inside-dopester appeal of ordering off the menu if everyone is doing it? Has been discovered, to fill this gaping gap, the practice of ordering *directly from the menu,* which has a return-to-innocence snob appeal, like the Mickey Mouse watch or forties musicals at 2 A.M. What you do is read the menu, select food you think you will like and instruct the waiter to bring those dishes. It's fun, and anyone can learn to do it. Start by ordering Trenette al Pesto. (Trenette is like linguine, but even more slender; pesto is a buttery green sauce of fresh basil and two or three cheeses.) This version is weighted toward cheese—crumbly nuggets and fine grains in among the fragrant green stuff—and it is served on just-cooked noodles that are tender but firm. You will require a spoon for the pool of flavored butter that remains at the bottom of your dish.

More from the menu: Zuppa di Clams—little clams, in their shells, steamed in wine and oil and garlic until they are warmed but not the least toughened, sprinkled abundantly with parsley and served mounded up over a deep plate of the briny broth they were steamed in. Sea Bass Marechiaro—a substantial length of fresh, resilient fish, lightly floured and then sautéed, to form a thin crust, moistened with a modest sauce of wine and tomatoes, with a little garlic and a bit of parsley, and garnished (nice note) with a few steamed mussels and a mound of crunchy spinach that is soaked in oil and garlic. Scaloppine alla Francese is a better than average version of this dish. The veal is pale, tender, crusted with a batter of eggs and flour, sautéed in butter and moistened with lemon—but despite the unusual sprinkling of strands of prosciutto ham, this is less than exciting. Pollo Scarpariello—chunks of chicken that are well-crisped but rendered a bit oily in the process; the dish is redeemed, however, by the flavors of fresh garlic and parsley. The chicken and the veal are served with artichoke hearts that are filled with buttered sweet peas and bits of bacon.

Il Valletto may well be the only restaurant in New York that makes available half a dozen or more imported Italian cheeses at room temperature: Gorgonzola, ivory veined with blue, smooth, creamy and sharp; Parmesan, hard and crumbly, with a strong bite and a scent that clears the head; Romano; Fontina; etc. The sweet desserts are a varying assortment of unabashedly rich cakes.

★★ VAŠATA

339 East 75th Street
LUNCH, SUNDAY; DINNER, DAILY.
Reservations, 650–1686.
Credit cards: AE, MC.
Medium-priced.

This lovely restaurant has an immaculate glow to it; it is a comfortable place for a comfortable Middle European burgher to bring his well-fed family. The ivory walls are hung with pretty Czechoslovakian pottery and modest and simply framed photographs of Prague between the unvarnished dark wooden beams. There are comfortable chairs, and the soft banquettes are upholstered in panels of amber and blue leather.

One is presented with a basket of crusty rye bread (studded with the caraway seeds that are a staple in Czechoslovakian cooking), croissant-shaped salt sticks, rolls, an amplitude of sweet butter, and a menu which is a defiant triumph of tradition. The dishes are mostly the mainstays of Central European cooking in their pristine, Platonic form—as Plato's mother made them.

The food here is so determinedly Middle European, with emphasis on the Middle, that no seafood (or, for that matter, fresh-water fish) is served, except for herring appetizers—sweet matjes herring, and a silvery, tart marinated herring. But these can be had in restaurants of many nationalities around New York, in equally good versions, and some of the other first courses here are much more typically Czechoslovakian, and much less readily available. One may start one's dinner with tlacenka, called "Head Cheese" on the menu, but just as accurately described as a sausage. A cross section of it looks like a red stone wall: fibrous, tender morsels of meat with a cement of cool, firm jelly. The famous ham of Prague is available here (unfortunately it is now virtually unobtainable in Prague). This ham is dark pink, extremely tender, slightly smoky, and surrounded by soft, white fat—it would be a crime to make a sandwich of it. Suvorov, a salad of minced meat, pickles and vegetables, in homemade mayonnaise, is the right first course for the hungry. It is especially good with the superb light Pilsner beer served here at, unfortunately, $1.30 per bottle. The pickled calf's brains on toast are wonderfully marinated, and if you are a brain freak, this simple, bald presentation will seem perfect to you—otherwise skip it. And all the first courses here are presented with elegance and taste—the ham, for instance, rolled into a long, pink cylinder; the garnishes on all the dishes, of radishes, tomatoes, or what have you, are of good color, and are fluted, petaled and arranged to make each platter a decorative, jewel-like piece.

There are good soups (brought in silver serving cups, and poured into large soup plates), but they are heavy stuff. The tripe soup is notable for the tenderness of the tripe and the intensity of flavor that comes of cooking with huge quantities of good paprika.

Vašata is deservedly famous for its schnitzels. The Wiener schnitzel is, like all the veal dishes here, made of the choicest, most tender, white veal, which easily absorbs the flavor of the lemon marinade. The breaded crust is so perfectly formed that it stands away from the veal in large domes, and is crisp and dry. The dish is so ridiculously tender that it can easily be eaten with a wooden spoon. There is a dish of fried liver sausages which seems frightening when it arrives—two giant wursts, steaming, the color of heavily tarnished silver, in crackling casings. But they are surprisingly light, the first will go down easily, and the second just as easily if assisted by a couple of bottles of good beer. The roast duckling and chicken paprika are good here, as you would expect—the former crisp and moist; the chicken not so distinctly inundated in sour cream as in the Hungarian restaurants in this neighborhood. Vašata is rather amazing in that the listed potatoes and vegetables are all usually available—among them a sauerkraut that is not acidic (lots of caraway seeds), good simple pickled beets (only slightly vinegary), fluffy dumplings (you'll get a pitcher of gravy if your main course does not provide it), home fried potatoes (brown, with crisp edges).

The blushing Czechoslovakian busboy, who is learning to be a waiter by serving desserts, explains, in a charming accent, that except for the palacinky (thin pancakes coated with apricot preserves or strong, bittersweet chocolate), the pastries are much like French pastries. But he points to a hefty tube (explaining that in his country it is known as "curls") which turns out to be an extremely light, flaky crust filled with pure, fresh whipped cream. What could be bad?

The customers are long sitters and talkers—a Pan-Slavic (and beyond) assortment of Zsa Zsas, Landowskas, Sonja Henies, Rudolf Bings and Titos, who have made of this place their home away from Europe.

★★★ LE VEAU D'OR

129 East 60th Street
LUNCH AND DINNER. CLOSED SUNDAY.
Reservations, TE 8–8133.
No credit cards.
Medium-priced.

New York offers few prizes as coveted as a table in this legendary establishment when—at the little bar near the center of the long, narrow room—there is a crowd of people who wish they, too, had one, when still others are flowing in through the small front door, when the restaurant is, in short, its teeming self. Le Veau d'Or is the extra reward of life that is its own reward, the comfort that needs no trappings of comfort, familiarity, casual excellence. If you are condemned to eat in but one restaurant in this city for the rest of your life, choose this one. You can get better meals elsewhere any day of the week, in more luxurious surroundings, but this place is a stayer. Critics point to its flaws. It has flaws. God forbid it should be perfect.

The house colors are golden wood, red leather, white linen, the black uniforms of the waiters, all aglitter. The walls are crammed with framed and unframed objects—Paris street signs, white lettering on blue (Place de la Concorde, Boulevard St. Germain, Place Pigalle), glossy black-and-whites of Paris markets, engraved mirrors, travel posters, still lifes in gaudy hues. And there is the Golden Calf himself, in oils, asleep between the sheets, with his own private pun: *Le veau dort.*

There is something Chaplinesque about this restaurant when it is most crowded. Here is a waiter with a tray of food walking through an aisle through which no one, it is obvious, even without a tray of food, can possibly walk. Still, staring straight ahead, oblivious of his equally unseeing obstructors, he walks. Here is yet another tuxedoed madman, this one carving a duck on a serving cart that is in the middle of yet another all-but-invisible aisle, just as if half a dozen people were not hipping him as they make the turn around his posterior. It is wondrous how these men go on, as if they were working in the wide open spaces of the Four Seasons on a slow day. There is something fanciful about your host's behavior as well. He is a natty and cheerful chap, he likes to shake your hand if he thinks he has seen you once or twice before, and he suggests that you wait at the bar for a few minutes, just as if there were access to that part of the room by any method other than the knife. But reservations are taken, seating is at a fair approximation of the specified time—how it all works is a mystery, and no one seems to mind, for everyone is busy being civilized and cheerful. This is where the Upper East Side eats when they are not eating where the Stuffy Upper East Side eats. And their sons and daughters eat here when they are home from school. And sometimes the generations eat together. But—very big but—Le Veau d'Or is not a secret, and it is not a society, and it is not particularly expensive, and people have been coming here for decades, from everywhere.

Rouse yourself with Maquereau au Vin Blanc, hefty filets of strong fish in a marinade that is a little sweet and a lot sour. Or soothe yourself with Nova Scotia salmon, the genuine article, though it is a crime to serve it with this loud oil. Or warm yourself with Coquille "Veau d'Or," scallops and mushrooms in a shell, in a lightly tomatoed white sauce.

The saucisson chaud is disappointing—warm fatted sausage that lacks the sparkle and spice that can redeem this kind of leaden weight. Choose, instead, the saucisson d'Arles, a pungent salami of purple meat and white fat that is so gamy and high it is almost rank—you have to like that kind of thing. The pâté is very good, finely ground, moist and heavily seasoned. And the onion soup is one of the few versions of this dish around town that is made with onions that are cooked until they are dark—that makes for a hefty brew, and the topping here, of flavorful cheese deeply browned, is just right for the strong soup. The watercress soup is hot, thick with potato, suffused with the flavor of its strong chicken-stock base—it has little of the quality of fresh watercress, but it is an excellent cup of food.

It is not invariably on the menu, but when it is, you should not pass up this establishment's tripe à la mode de Caen. The little slices of tripe are gummy and yet tender, and they are served in a spicy red sauce that gives off a heady fragrance of country brandy. There is good chicken, served as Poussin Rôti en Cocotte, "Grand'-Mère," a very moist bird that has been cooked with browned onions, cubes of sturdy bacon, abundant mushrooms, all in a roasting-pot liquid that is redolent of the fat of the bird. The Boeuf Braisé Bourgeoise is little more than a good pot roast in a deep, sweet vegetable sauce—the sauce is wonderful on the salty noodles that accompany this dish. Crusty and tender frogs' legs Provençale are served here, with an extremely concentrated purée of tomatoes, and with Pommes Anna, thin slices of potato that have been baked in clarified butter until the potatoes are tender and oily, their edges lightly browned—altogether a simple and splendid plate of food. The not-so-secret secret of rack of lamb is good meat, accurately roasted. In this place you may get it a little rarer than you asked for—they do not want to harm this great lamb, the eye of each rib the most gentle and yet flavorful of morsels. It is served only for two, but men of normal proportions have been seen dispatching an entire six-rib production. It is served with crisp green beans that are sprinkled with bits of strong garlic and polished with butter, and with firm flageolets, the thick white beans that are somehow the ideal starch with lamb.

There is almost always some good cheese in the house—goat cheese or hard and creamy Roquefort. The big-deal dessert is Fraises "Romanoff," ripe strawberries in liquored whipped cream. The pear poached in wine is firm, stained red, winy and sweet —a very good version of this very common dessert. The mousse and fruit tarts are fine.

Le Veau d'Or could long ago have raised prices, moved to larger quarters and continued to fill every table. But a bigger, better Veau d'Or is a contradiction in terms. The excellence of this place derives from its decades of respect for tradition in the face of myriad fads, by which stationary route it arrived at its current state: it is the essence of New York—and yet few restaurants in town exude its relaxed worldliness.

• VICTOR'S CAFÉ

240 Columbus Avenue (at 71st Street)
LUNCH AND DINNER.
No reservations (TR 7–7988).
Credit cards: AE, DC.
Medium-priced.

When Victor's first established itself on this out-of-the-way corner, it was immediately accepted as the best Cuban restaurant in New York, though, admittedly, the best of only a few. And for a number of years a visit to Victor's, say, semiannually, provided sufficient culinary novelty to offset the rather crass quality of the food.

But now that Cuban food is a familiar commodity in New York, an evening at Victor's can be a disappointing experience. The place is still jammed, it is still a minor thrill to get one of the favored tables in the enclosed sidewalk section, the waiters are cheerful, helpful and earnest, and the customers are having a good (often slightly boisterous) time. So what is there to complain about?

The food, for one: always devoid of finesse, some of the dishes are now rather tasteless as well. The selection, for another: e.g., roast suckling pig, which has been a Friday-Saturday-Sunday special for years, and though the restaurant is open until one-thirty in the morning, this dish, for which people may come considerable distances, is often out by eight-thirty. Management of the dining room, for a third: you look around for your waiter, you catch his eye, he takes a deep drag on his cigarette, puts it down and approaches to ask your pleasure, talking smoke.

By far the best items on Victor's menu are the fresh orange juice (to start) and the superb, strong coffee (to conclude). In between, quality is hard to find. The depressing list of appetizers includes sardines, assorted cold cuts, shellfish cocktails, etc., and should be avoided. The soups, once hearty, are now almost Germanic in their lumpen quality—the white-bean soup is oily and mealy, which is as it should be, but lacking the spice that can make a heavy dish palatable. The red-(chili) bean soup is also rather mild, but stronger than the white, and the starch is balanced with meat. Of the lot, chicken soup is the surprising best—not only is the broth strongly flavored of chicken and supporting vegetables but as if to prove the point, an eighth of a chicken, nicely poached, comes along in the bowl.

The fried pork is a heavy and succulent dish for which sliced raw onions are a very appropriate garnish. But if a day's supply of onions are sliced up at lunchtime, by dinner hour they have lost their point. The roast fresh ham, which is supposed to be rich, is dry; and the fried beef, with garlic and onions, once an outstanding item on this restaurant's menu, now doesn't even revive memories—it is tamed for the sightseers. The Shrimp Asopao is one of those dishes which provide odd moments of pleasure during an otherwise boring experience—Oh, an olive! Goody, a caper! Wow, a shrimp! (there are five).

The side dishes are more interesting. Fried plantains are available ripe or "green." If the ripe are fully ripe, the dish has a dark, honeylike quality; if less ripe, they are hardly worth eating; the green are an acquired taste, usually acquired during a Caribbean childhood. The corn tamales—a thick corn-meal pancake stuffed with pork—are another rather bland item, but the texture is interesting—slightly grainy—and the flavor of corn meal is strong and pleasing.

The desserts? It would be impossible for a blindfolded customer to distinguish the custard from the double-egg custard from the coconut custard from the bread pudding from putty.

★★ VIETNAM VILLAGE

1 Sheridan Square (at Washington Place)
DINNER. CLOSED MONDAY.
Reservations, 255–9170.
Credit cards: MC, V.
Inexpensive.

With admirable disregard for mere appearances, Vietnam Village has altered hardly a stick of what it found when it moved into these premises—the remains of a little Mexican restaurant, rough stucco molded to archways, beamed ceilings, wrought-iron chandeliers, wine bottles in baskets behind the bar. When the steam heat starts up, the entire place shakes and everybody titters. A distinctive feature—food reaches the dining room through a little semicircular hole in the side wall—a disembodied hand hangs an oak-tag tag over the dishes on the little counter, indicating which waiter the dishes are intended for. The place is usually busy. Knowing Villagers who often spend more have found this good thing, and the city's habitual ethnic samplers are represented here nightly, murmuring "Very interesting, very interesting." The waiters are Vietnamese and slight of build, casually dressed and mustached, available and polite. Their English is as good as yours, which is a rarity in New York's Oriental restaurants. And the place is tidy—the red oilcloth on the tables is wiped down, and fresh paper placemats are provided for every new party.

You begin with Cha Gio, spring rolls that the menu identifies as the "pride of Vietnam." The crisped noodle casing is filled with ground pork, mushrooms and seasonings, and you wrap the little lengths of the roll in lettuce, with the fresh coriander and parsley that is provided. Then you dip the entire production in the little dish of nuoc mam, a salty fish extract that is used as a flavoring for much Vietnamese food —these spring rolls are crunchy and lively and the dipping liquid adds a lovely piquancy. The Banh Cuon are similar lengths of noodle casing around ground meat and mushrooms, but these are steamed, soft and light—you dip these as well, and eat them with the scallion greens and bean sprouts they are garnished with.

An occasional special of the day is a Baked Fish with Black Bean Sauce, which sounds like a standard Chinese item but has no resemblance to that. Remarkably, the fish has been permeated with the flavor of black beans, even though it has been only briefly baked—the fish, a bass, is served in a black broth that is spicy-hot and studded with ginger. Do not pass up Ga Uop Sa Ot Nuong, but ask for it as broiled chicken: chunks of chicken that are browned in a spicy oil, served with bean sprouts and watercress that are fresh and lively—you squeeze on lemon, which brightens an already lively dish.

The beef birds do not have wings, they are called Bo Nuong, and come in a compartmentalized wooden dish, with spaces for the birds and mounds of herbs—including one of Vietnamese origin for which there is no English name, its flavor a strong combination of coriander and mint—and strands of bacon. The excellent beef is stuffed with cashew nuts and flavored with garlic, and you dip it into a thick black sweet substance akin to hoisin sauce. A terrific dish.

The larky translation of Chit Kho Nuoc Dua is "pork au caramel," which will serve —nuggets of coarse, fibrous, tender meat in a sweet broth. The dish is spicy without being hot, and the meat is moist without being fatty.

If you must have a vegetable, there is something given as Chinese Greens Sautéed —bok choy and cabbage in a salty dark sauce—it is weighty stuff.

This place has been here a few years now: it is successful and cheap. You seem never to get a plate of food that is in any way "off."

★ VINCENT'S CLAM BAR

119 Mott Street (at Hester Street)
LUNCH AND DINNER.
No reservations (CA 6–8133).
No credit cards.
Inexpensive.

This institution offers one of the briefest menus and some of the freshest seafood (in a couple of the simplest of preparations) in all of New York.

Vincent's is a garish two-room restaurant/saloon in which the most tasteful element is the color TV. In the front room there is a bar, at which you drink, and a clam bar, at which you eat and drink. Behind the clam bar there are mounds of fresh seafood, battered, ready for the deep-frying that much of the hot food here gets. In the back room there are rows of Formica-topped tables, each adorned with containers of paper napkins. There are brick walls, tan plaster walls, a bright-red acoustical ceiling, yellow lanterns. A blue note is provided by the police. They parade in and out, having decided that Vincent's offers the finest men's room in Little Italy, which—as this place is sometimes very mistakenly taken for *Umberto's* Clam House, a few blocks away, where Joey Gallo got, as they say, his—may provide a feeling of security. The late-night customers are casual locals on dates, guys on the way home after the four-to-midnight shift, Greenwich Villagers who have learned that the fifteen-minute walk to this spot will provide them with better food of the kind than they can find anywhere in their own district. You can tell who's who: at the Villagers' tables there are bottles of wine; the four-to-midnight men drink beer; quarts of Pepsi are the hallmark of the neighborhood youth. You are served by gravel-voiced waiters in red vests—you have the impression that not long ago they were here drinking the Pepsi.

The menu lists littlenecks and oysters. The former are big for littlenecks, and the latter are available only in the "R" months, even though the pointless prohibition against oystering between May and August has been lifted—it seems that New Yorkers simply will not order oysters in what they consider the "off" season. Whichever you get, they are perfectly fresh and freshly opened, and the juice that remains in the half shell after you have eaten the meat is at once sweet and briny.

Then there is the hot food, all of it served with one of two sauces—medium-hot and hot. These are thick and red, indistinguishable one from the other except by the intensity of their spicing, and it is a common and accepted practice to order your food with medium-hot sauce with a plate of hot on the side, so that as your palate is numbed by the extremely hot "medium-hot" sauce, you may rouse it with a dose of the searingly hot "hot" sauce.

The sauces may be applied to deep-fried calamari—firm squid, ringlets and tufts of filament, lightly battered and crisped in hot olive oil. Like all the cooked food here, it is served with a slice of hard bread that has been dipped in water to moisten and soften it. Yes, it sounds terrible, but it is the perfect accompaniment to the unrelenting sauce and the fried fish. When soft-shell clams are in season, come here for them if you want them with a red sauce. The clams are sweet and crinkly, fried to the perfect point. There are also steamed mussels (plump and tender), steamed conch (soft, slightly rubbery, and vaguely gamy in an oceanic way), deep-fried shrimp. Everything is served in small orders or large orders, so it is possible to sample most of the menu on one visit.

No desserts.

• VIVOLO

140 East 74th Street
DINNER. CLOSED SUNDAY.
Reservations, 628–4671.
Credit cards: AE.
Medium-priced.

Avoid the appendage of this restaurant that projects out onto the sidewalk. It has lace curtains, a handful of tables, and drafts. The door from the street leads directly into it, you look pityingly on the customers who thought it a rather special place to sit because of its peekaboo out onto this dreary street, and continue into the main room, where there is, in contrast, a fireplace. Clubby snugness is about all this place has to offer. These are the premises of the defunct Soerabaja, and if you recall the look of that, you know this. The room is small, oblong, dark, low of ceiling (cum beams), mahogany of wall (paneled). No more than a dozen white-linened tables (but for those out in the weather on the sidewalk), fifteen-inch tapers thereon. At the six-stool bar on one side of the room, pals of the boss jaw with him and the Mrs., fingers snap, shoulders jiggle, toes tap. These insiders are tuned to hip music the rest of us cannot hear. The boss just jumped out of *Gentleman's Quarterly*. He is young, tailored, healthy and blank. He informs you that you may take away with you the recipe of any dish that takes your fancy. He is delusional. He thinks he is the proprietor of a real restaurant. You wonder if he ever sat on one of these chairs and wondered, as everyone must, which half to rest, which half to hang over. Your hostess is also from GQ. She must have selected the chairs.

For a moment you are had. You are poured good cold mineral water from a bottle, and it is not poured over tap-water ice cubes. But that, of course is easy. A seafood salad of fresh ingredients is not, and the Frutta di Mare, of octopus, squid and mussels, is dreary, bulked up by celery and desperate for a garlicky dressing. You squeeze on the lemon. It helps a little. The hot first courses are not much better. The Mozzarella in Carozza, for example, appears to be made with American white bread and American mozzarella cheese, which are difficult to distinguish, one from the other—it helps to squeeze on the lemon and pour over the anchovy sauce, but not much. Listed under "Insalate" (they couldn't think of a category for it) is a Frittura Mista. Try it as a first course, for it is not bad—strands of crisp zucchini, slices of eggplant, a rice ball, some of that dreadful cheese, a column of mashed potatoes, all of them deep-fried in a breaded batter, and all of them pretty lively.

Very little pasta here. There are cannelloni on occasion, pillows of green noodle filled with ground spiced veal, all in a thick creamy sauce—the dish is unimpeachable and dead. Much better the Fettuccine al Filetto de Pomodoro, even though the noodles are one time underdone and almost crisp—the simple sauce of tomatoes and ham has been cooked down until it is intense, concentrated.

The fish is of the day, one time a very nice bass, poached in broth with onions and parsley—the roasted potatoes are unfortunately served on the same plate and they are undone by being immersed in the fish-cooking liquid. The Shrimp Fra Diavolo is a decent dish of good shrimp in a tomato sauce that is spicy-hot but nothing else, as if the fiery element in red pepper has been separated from the vegetable. The dish is garnished with a couple of fresh littlenecks in their shell. No extra charge, says the witty waiter. The Bistecca alla Griglia is a block of protein under a pat of herbed butter. Good butter.

The cheese cake is OK, made of ricotta cheese, heavy and wet, with a slight almond flavor—it comes cool, which is nice when cheese cake is this moist. The Cannoli alla Vivolo is gooey.

★ WINDOWS ON THE WORLD

1 World Trade Center
LUNCH AND DINNER.
Reservations essential, 938–1111.
Credit cards: AE, CB, DC, MC, V.
Very expensive.

Weeks after you make your reservation and ninety seconds after you board the nonstop elevator to the 107th floor (having cleared your ears on the trip up with three violent swallows), you disembark to a low-ceilinged bronze-and-marble sanctum, complete with the only restaurant cigar stand in New York at which you may purchase a meerschaum pipe. Such transparent tourist titillations should not necessarily steer you to the next car down, for this lofty spot sometimes transcends its own pretentiousness—which is going some.

You are early and you are invited to wait in the "Living Lounge," a somber red-and-beige chapel with four thrones and a view of New Jersey. Instead, in an effort to nurture the festive spirit that brings you to this celebratory spot, you elect to pass your waiting time in the bar—it looks over Brooklyn and beyond, and unlike the view of Jersey—gigantic neon signs and sequined apartment houses—the vista to the east is of a trillion fallen gems, swatches of translucent light cutting through massive blocks of stone, lengthy pearl-strung bridges repeated in bottomless black water. This barroom is like a bottle-lined womb, the bar itself under a canopy of mirrors. You confidently toss a $5 bill on the counter and call for a couple of highballs. Hefty drinks and all that, in handsome crystal, but the fin will not cover two ordinary Scotches. And if you prefer to sit at one of the tables—tiers of them descend from the bar toward lofty windows and the distant views—there is a cover charge of $1.50.

Your time comes, and you slip through a futuristic maze of marble tunnels—faceted with mirrors and photomurals—until you reach a clearing, whereat your imperious host, standing at a great book. He is talking very slowly on the telephone, while a circle of supplicants attends on his first free moment. In time you are led to your place.

The spacious curved room is shrewdly terraced so that one has at least a teeny view from any seat, though of course you may have to turn your head to find your favorite spire. The place is modern, but passively so, neutrally: soft brick-colored carpeting, beige banquettes, simple chairs of cane and clear wood, brass railings that accent the lines and turns of the room. Spotlights throw mottled effects on the white walls, a cascade of wine bottles provides a bit of color here, a cluster of brass-studded columns does it there. It is cool.

French bread in a silver bowl, curls of cold butter on a saucer-size china tray. You spread the latter on the former with gleaming, plated flatware, while you consider the gleaming crystal and the little open dishes of coarsely ground pepper and salt. All is well until your adenoidal captain addresses you with a manner designed to help you relax: "Good evening, I'm Jay, your captain for the evening." (To protect the innocent, no names have been changed.) Soon he brings you a bottle of the very young wine you ordered and continues his helpful ways: "I think we should let this breathe for a while." "What if it stubbornly holds its breath?" Laughter only from Jay.

There is a prix-fixe menu ($18.50, no extras) and an extensive à la carte array (with main courses from $9.50). You may begin with Terrine of Veal and Pistachios, a coarse and spicy, garlicky and well-herbed amalgam of much meat and a remoteness of nuts. It is cloaked in tender fat and adorned with cool diced jelly and a sprig of crisp watercress—simple and satisfying food. Up a step of ambition to Ragout of Duck Livers and Raisins in Brioche, a hot and sweet little sauté of white raisins and the livers in fresh warm pastry. The livers are not invariably sautéed to crispness outside, pinkness within, but the moist raisins are always to the rescue. The Tortellini of Shrimp in Cream arrives in a six-inch silver pan with a fitted lid—the crescents of pasta are stuffed with ground shrimp and moistened with cream and strong cheese. The dish is hot and heavily seasoned, and the pasta is firm, but the flavor of the shrimp is distinctly less than that of the clear fresh article, and the dish seems contrived—someone's not very clever variant of a classic. The Pike and Spinach Pâté is an excessively salted item of little finesse, in which a sauce Aurore—tomato-flavored velouté—goes far toward taming the hard-edged pâté.

If you are on the table d'hôte side of the menu, you would do well to opt for the Roast Prime Sirloin: ample slices of good meat, tender and rare, garnished with a superb purée of mushrooms that is earthy and redolent of strong stock. On the facing à la carte page there is listed Squab Tabaka, a perfectly roasted bird, cooked through, yet with none of its moisture lost, the filmy skin browned to a crackling parchment. This is a rich bird, and the fruit sauce that accompanies it—largely of prunes, thick and acidic—is lovely against the oily meat.

But the Frogs' Legs Sautéed Provençale are plastic legs in a tomato-and-garlic sauce that seems to belong on pasta—the dish just does not add up. If you must have seafood, you will do somewhat better with Marinated Bluefish with Toasted Sesame—the marination adds a bit of herb and spice to the fish, but at the expense of its natural oiliness. The fish is carefully broiled, flaky and slightly crusty, but the sesame seeds are beside the point. Of the à la carte vegetables, the Baby Eggplant Grilled with Soy Sauce and Ginger reduces this vegetable almost to its essential vapor—it is salty and earthy and memorable. The simple green salad is of good greens and a delicate vinaigrette, but the Beefsteak Tomatoes, Basil Dressing, is, surprisingly, garlicked in the manner of garlic pizza; and you leave wondering where the basil may be.

Incredibly, it is possible to be brought a tray of petrified cheese—Brie that flowed once but never will again, blue cheese that is brown from exposure, little soft-ripening cheeses in fossilized crusts. If you put up a fuss they will find something much better. There are a couple of marvelous desserts—a Golden Lemon Tart in which paper-thin slices of lemon are atop an airy lemon mousse that is studded with clumps of sweetened pastry crumbs, the whole thing on a superbly browned crust. The Cold Sabayon is flavored with a heavy dose of white port and served onto plump, ripe berries—the effect is of sugared berries in a liquor in a cloud. Lots of elaborate ice cream concoctions are available.

The place has had plenty of time, and it is not up to its claims for itself. In the course of clearing your table, rolls are dropped, water is dribbled across your sleeve, crusts of bread are left behind. Too much management in evidence, whispered disputes, dramatic pointings, running off and running on—one begins to take sides.

An extraordinary wine list of around a hundred wines. What is most extraordinary about the selection is that almost nothing is offered that is not ready to be drunk, unlike 90 percent of New York's restaurants, where they will sell anything they have, ready or not.

● W.P.A.

152 Spring Street (near Wooster Street)
LUNCH AND DINNER.
Reservations, 226–3444.
Credit cards: AE.
Very expensive.

To name a restaurant for the Work Projects Administration of the Great Depression, here in SoHo, a neighborhood of instant bourgeois respectability (albeit with a veneer of Bohemianism), is a harmless and meaningless flap in the face of history, classic camp. But it is executed with so little panache or wit that no old memory or history lesson is revived, nothing is seen in a new, outrageous light. W.P.A. is a pun without a double meaning, a gimmick without a twist, the reference to the trials of another day providing only a few irrelevant props.

Some years back, in another city, there was a club called The Recovery Room—you know, miniature bedpans for ashtrays, thermometers for swizzle sticks, wheelchairs at the tables, waiters and waitresses and bartenders in stained surgical gowns. You were handed a rising fever chart, which was your bill, when you had had too much to drink. Very poor taste, no question about that. But at least they went all the way.

Think of what they could have done here—piles of rubble in the corners, dirt floor, rough-hewn tables set up on wooden horses, a banquette of concrete steps, the help stripped to the waist, their muscular bodies oiled and gleaming, food delivered in brown paper bags, five-cent apples for dessert. Ah, well, they blew it. This is SoHo sleek all the way, the themes of the thirties sounded mutedly in a handful of odorless murals and clean uniforms of gray-striped denim.

You enter via a long dim corridor that deposits you halfway down the length of the store, at the bar, the divide between the cocktail lounge up front and the dining room at the back. You wait your turn in the lounge, where, as throughout, all is black and gray including a couple of murals—of men at work high on the girders of a skyscraper going up; and of a decades-ago night club, high-kicking white cuties, black musicians blowing on their horns. Your drinks are served on a little circular stainless-steel tables. The sole bit of warmth in the place is the honey-colored wood of the bar you pass on the way to your table in the back, where the only light is provided by the tapers on each table and the hidden illumination that plays on yet a couple more of these stolid murals—on the east wall, muscular men handling heavy crates; on the west, their spiritual cousins harvesting grain. For some reason there is a rubber tree at the center of the room, and probably for the same reason, your table is set with jet-black linen and white napkins. The place lacks space, grace, calm, and even the most relaxed don't seem comfortable here. The artists and artisans of SoHo will not make this their hangout, though the outlands may provide plenty of the curious for a long time.

As in many mediocre restaurants you can assemble the makings of a decent meal here if you avoid the ambitious dishes. So start with the Wellfleet Oysters, the genuiness of which are attested to by the menu, the freshness by their clear sweet flavor. You get seven of them and you will do them honor by doing without the spiked vinegar that comes along—there is lemon and you may call for the pepper mill. Don't go near the Veal and Pork Pâté (with a fruit-and-wine sauce), for it has a sandy texture and a flavor that is obscured by salt. Something called a Salmon Crêpe tastes and feels like kippered salmon in a cloth wrapper, and the Belgian Endive Salad is ruined by a dressing that is made with too much vinegar, bad vinegar at that.

Though the menu specifies that the Rack of Lamb may be ordered only for two, the ruling has never been enforced. The quadruple chop is coated with a mustard-flavored, herbed breading, which makes of this mild lamb a fairly hearty dish—the thick, seemingly caramelized sauce is harmless, the frozen broccoli painful. Decent Braised Roast Pork, the roast having had a core carved out, which was stuffed with prunes, nuts and apples. The half-dozen slices of pale meat you receive all have bull's-eyes of the dark, glistening mixture of fruit and nuts—good meat, the sweet at the core nice with it, the garnish of string beans crisp and tasty. But then they will go in for this fancy stuff and cause a disaster called Veal in Brioche, a kind of Veal Wellington, in which the huge nugget of good meat is coated with pâté and ground mushrooms before it is roasted to destruction in a pastry that cannot be anything but pulpy when it is prepared this way. Very popular here is the New England Sea Kettle. The title is puzzling, for you could duplicate the dish by warming seafood scraps in Campbell's tomato soup—it all looks very promising, a big iron pot with an iron lid and ladle, but ignore the looks of contentment on the faces of its many customers, for they have been sold by the down-home Down-East presentation, nothing more.

Nice apple pie, a dark crust, no syrup to cloy the slices of well-cooked apple, a good bit of cinnamon, a dollop of real, sugarless whipped cream on top. The Orange Bavarian Cream is rubbery and horrid, garnished with slices of sour orange.

In the crowded dining room if everyone would shut up, you could hear your neighbors chew. In the hatcheck room the attendant is embedded among racks of coats, two on either side of her at floor level, two more at head level. Understandably, she looks frightened.

★ XOCHITL

146 West 46th Street
LUNCH AND DINNER. CLOSED SUNDAY.
No reservations (PL 7–1325).
Credit cards: AE.
Inexpensive.

It takes an extremely refined discrimination to distinguish among New York's Mexican restaurants, for they imitate one another right down to the printed menus that explain, in tedious detail, the differences among tacos, tostadas, enchiladas and their various forms of presentation. But there is something about Xochitl that sets it apart. The food is not distinctive, the prices not especially low by Mexican-restaurant standards, the service far from brilliant or alert. The difference between Xochitl and most of its competitors is that it is a restaurant, not a hash house, not a junk-food emporium, not a novelty eatery. That is not to say that there is anything formal about the place, rather that it is self-respecting and businesslike. It is not apologizing for itself, it is not purveying the simple food of the simple peasants to the south as a novelty, the place is not hung with quasi-Mexican paraphernalia. Xochitl is a restaurant, and it relinquishes none of the dignity that goes with that name.

Follow your eyes to the brilliant green-and-red neon beacon in the front window, through the front door and past the little plastic bar, to the restaurant proper—a couple of rows of Naugahyde-upholstered booths (orange backs, green seats, tabletops of marbelized Formica), a row of tiny tables down the middle. "Our place is small," reads the menu. "If you are alone kindly sit at the small tables during rush hours." The walls are pine-paneled, the floors asphalt composition. All is neat, looks clean. But for a handful of paintings on the walls and one small inspirational mural, nothing about the place suggests Mexico—or anyplace else.

There are available the usual combination plates, with crisp tacos stuffed with tender morsels of pork and bits of lettuce and tomato; moist enchiladas wrapped around slivers of chicken and melted cheese; tostadas, the flat crisp version of the basic tortilla, mounted with a surprisingly well balanced ground sausage—sausages in Mexican restaurants often taste like disguised bad meat, but this sausage, available in any version of the Mexican tortilla, and also as the stuffing of roasted green peppers, is actually composed of spices and sound meat; best of all are the tamales—moist, steamed cornhusks stuffed with simple ground beef and redolent of fresh corn grain.

The Chile con Carne benefits from being made with little chunks of meat rather than ground meat—it is thick and spicy and can be made hot, hotter or unbearably hot by the addition of the red liquid available in little bowls on every table. The Baby Cactus Salad, on the other hand, is a dreadful mingling of canned cactus (which tastes astonishingly like canned grass), iceberg lettuce (which tastes astonishingly like canned grass) and raw onions—you can tell them to hold the cactus and the lettuce.

Xochitl enters into the making of its chicken dishes with decent chicken—it actually seems never to have been near a freezer. Then they roast the chicken until the skin is crisp, but they carefully do not dry out the meat. You can then have it as Chicken Mole, perhaps the best version of this dish in town—the dark-brown sauce of chocolate and searingly hot spices softened by the tender meat. Or you can have it as Roast Chicken, Mexican Style, which means that it is dressed with marinated onions. The heavy, chalky refried beans are fine with both these dishes—no flavor to them, to speak of, just the solidity of beans and a trace of the grease they were fried in.

The guava and mango desserts are all preserved and undistinguished. There is ice cream.

The best beverage with Mexican food is one of the good Mexican beers available here.

When things are slow the waiters hang around the bar and gossip with the bartender at levels of voice audible throughout the store, except that sometimes they are drowned out by the jukebox. No one seems to know where the waiters go when things are busy.

About the Author

SEYMOUR BRITCHKY is the regular restaurant critic for *New York* magazine.